T0134529

Wireless Networking and Mobile Data Management

R.K. Ghosh

Wireless Networking and Mobile Data Management

 Springer

R.K. Ghosh
Department of Computer Science
  and Engineering
IIT Kanpur
Kanpur, Uttar Pradesh
India

ISBN 978-981-13-5005-4   ISBN 978-981-10-3941-6   (eBook)
DOI 10.1007/978-981-10-3941-6

Printed on acid-free paper

This Springer imprint is published by Springer Nature
The registered company is Springer Nature Singapore Pte Ltd.
The registered company address is: 152 Beach Road, #21-01/04 Gateway East, Singapore 189721, Singapore

This book is dedicated to three wonderful persons.

To my teacher Professor G. P. Bhattacharjee, who believed that my achievements were not accidental but both expected and deserved. To my wife Sarbani and to my daughter Ritwika. Without their support and understanding it would not have been possible. At times Sarbani felt the book will never appear in print though my little one never expressed it in so many words, perhaps she believed her mom.

Preface

This book grew out of the class notes around which a course on mobile computing was taught to the senior undergraduate and the masters' students at IIT Kanpur. These students unknowingly became guinea pigs in the process of my understanding of the subject.

The certain topics included in this book have been produced in different forms distributed over a number of other books or collections. In that sense, the uniqueness of the current text lies in putting the contents in an understandable form woven through a single thread. Giving a different orientation to the work of others is not quite easy. Most of the times I felt that the original text of the work is perhaps the best way to communicate. However, while teaching certain material in the class, a few interesting ideas emerged out of the queries by the students. These ideas provided cues for improved presentations. Maybe a discernable reader will find that some of the topics in this book have been presented in sufficient details, while a few other topics perhaps could have been presented in a better way. Specially, I feel a reasonable understanding of smart environment would require more space than I could allocate in this book. In trying to fit it within the scope of the book, context-aware infrastructure became a dominant theme in my presentation. However, I believe that building smart environment, in itself, is an engineering problem which is understood best by practice than by learning through literature or a book.

The book is organized into two parts consisting eight chapters each. Part I deals with wireless networking, while Part II addresses mobile data management issues. The effort was to strike a balance between the two parts and provide the readers what I believe is a comprehensive treatment of the subject. The material for the mobile data management part was more or less gathered directly from the original articles, as most of the available books in the area at the time when I start writing this book were just unrelated collections of research literature. Fortunately, there are many excellent texts on wireless networking part. But, these books were written with the target audiences having background either in electrical engineering or in physics. Very few books, if at all, dealt with protocol level details in somewhat sketchy manner. However, these texts did substantially influence the material presented in first part of the book. My class notes gradually developed over the years and matured somewhat unconsciously in the form a monograph as it appears now.

Chapter 1 of the book is an introduction to mobile distributed environment and some interesting innovative applications in the area. Instead of a conventional introduction to book, this chapter provides the reader a general understanding of the issues that arise in the context building pervasive mobile applications and smart environment. The subsequent five chapters deal with the range of wireless networking technologies. It includes cellular-based wireless communication, telecommunication protocols such as GSM, GPRS, and UMTS, and short-range radio communication protocols such as WLAN, Bluetooth, IR, ZigBee, and 6LoWPAN. The remaining two chapters of the first part deal with routings in mobile ad hoc network, mobile operating systems and application-level protocols such as Mobile IP, WAP, and Mobile Shell (Mosh).

Part II of the book deals with mobile data management. This part begins with a chapter on WSN-related protocols, namely routing, interoperability, and multi-sensor integration. Though the contents of the chapter appear to lean more toward network than data, the two main reasons for clubbing it with mobile data management are as follows: (i) WSNs unlike IP-based network are data-centric networks and (ii) multisensor integrations employ sophisticated mathematical tools for fusion of data. More precisely, data is used as a communication token for routing in WSN. On the other hand, data fusion requires rich mathematical techniques that deal with detection, association, correlation, estimation, and combination of sensory data. The next chapter deals with the techniques for location management in GSM-type network for tracking personal and terminal mobilities. Here again, the decision to classify the chapter under mobile data management part is driven by the fact that the volume of location data far exceeds the size of a database that can be handled by a conventional database application. Specially, capturing location data related to personal mobility requires interesting data management and machine learning techniques. The remaining topics related to mobile distributed environment included in this part are as follows: design of algorithms, data dissemination, indexing, caching, replications, and storage management. The last chapter of the book does not directly deal with data management issues, but it talks about context-aware infrastructure for building smart environments.

The pre-requisite relationships between the contents of chapters are shown in Fig. 1. The solid lines show direct dependencies, and dotted line indicates indirect dependencies of the chapters. The book is written in a way, so that it does not require any pre-requisite other than the standard undergraduate knowledge of computer networks and algorithms. Having a bit of working knowledge about operating system (OS) could also help the reader to understand some of the practical issues described in the context of building mobile distributed applications.

The subject matter of the book has been chosen with a balanced assessment of the requirements of a target audience that would consist of senior undergraduates, masters, as well as research students. Practicing engineers perhaps may not get particularly excited about the book, as most of the content as well as the treatment

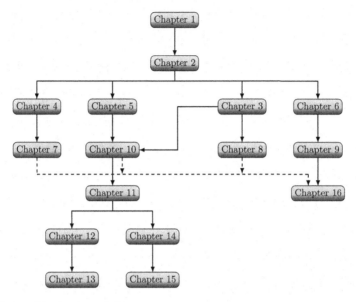

Fig. 1 Pre-requisite structure of chapters

of the contents is biased more toward theory than implementation. However, I believe that the chapter on smart environment and context-aware computing would provide a few pointers to ideas on leveraging mobile cloud computing for building smart applications.

Kanpur, India   R.K. Ghosh
December 2016

Acknowledgements

It is always a pleasure to thank all those from whom I received help, support, and encouragements directly or indirectly. Among these individuals, colleagues, and friends, one name that stands out is Hrushikesha Mohanty of University of Hyderabad. I learnt a lot about the subject with him. We jointly organized a few workshops and conferences in the general area of mobile distributed computing. Another very distinguished person who helped and always motivated me through his wisdom is R.K. Shyamasundar of IIT Bombay. It was always a pleasure to talk to him and discuss half-baked and immature ideas. I extend my sincere thanks to him. I acknowledge with thanks the support and encouragements that I received from Anup Kumar of University of Louisville. Anup is not only a great friend to have, but is always available for any help and support academic or otherwise. Several of his suggestions and comments helped me to improve the presentation of this book. I also extend my thanks to Sajal K. Das of Missouri University of Science and Technology who offered a few suggestions on initial drafts of few chapters. His suggestions were always very specific and helpful. My special thanks are reserved for all my students who silently suffered my ignorance of the subject at initial stages and made me learn the subject. Finally, working with my editor Ms. Suvira Srivastava, the project coordinator Ms. Sathya Karupaiya, and the production editor Mr. V. Praveen Kumar was fun. I thank them for their patience and perseverance.

Contents

Part I   Wireless Networking

**1   Mobile Distributed Systems: Networking and
      Data Management**   3
1.1   Introduction   3
1.2   Mobile Pervasive and Ubiquitous Computing.   4
1.3   Characterizing Mobile Distributed System   4
1.4   Mobile Cloud Computing   7
1.5   OS for Mobile Devices.   10
1.6   Mobile Applications   10
       1.6.1   mHealthcare.   11
       1.6.2   Logistic and Transport Management   12
1.7   Smart Environments   13
       1.7.1   Context Aware Computing   15
       1.7.2   Driverless Cars   15
1.8   Organization of Book   18
References.   19

2   Cellular Wireless Communication   21
2.1   Introduction   21
2.2   Frequency Planning   23
       2.2.1   Co-channel Interference.   27
       2.2.2   Cell Splitting and Sectoring.   31
2.3   Traffic Intensity.   34
2.4   Channel Assignment.   38
       2.4.1   Fixed Channel Assignment   41
       2.4.2   Dynamic Channel Assignment Policies   45
2.5   Handoff.   48

	2.5.1	Handoff Policies	50
	2.5.2	Handoff Protocols	51
	References		53

3   GSM, GPRS and UMTS 55

3.1	Introduction		55
3.2	GSM Architecture		56
	3.2.1	Mobile Station	57
	3.2.2	Base Station Subsystem	58
	3.2.3	Network Subsystem	59
	3.2.4	GSM Radio Resources	60
	3.2.5	Channel Types	60
	3.2.6	Frame Structure	63
3.3	GSM Signaling Protocols		64
3.4	Call Setup		66
	3.4.1	Mobile Terminated Calls	67
	3.4.2	Mobile Originated Calls	70
	3.4.3	Mobility Management	70
3.5	GPRS Network		73
3.6	UMTS		79
	3.6.1	UTRAN	80
	3.6.2	WCDMA	83
	3.6.3	Handoffs in UMTS	88
	3.6.4	UMTS Interface Protocol Model	90
	3.6.5	Radio Network Layer	92
	References		93

4   Wireless Local Area Network 95

4.1	Introduction		95
4.2	Mobility Support and Wireless Networks		96
4.3	WLAN Standards		98
	4.3.1	IEEE Standards	99
4.4	Network Topology		102
4.5	Physical Layer and Spread Spectrum		104
	4.5.1	Standard for PHY and MAC Layers	104
	4.5.2	Spread Spectrum	105
	4.5.3	Protocol Stack	110
4.6	MAC Sublayer		111
	4.6.1	Radio Access Technologies	111
	4.6.2	Multiple Access Protocols	112
	4.6.3	ALOHA	113
	4.6.4	CSMA/CA	115

        4.6.5   Distributed Coordination Function.   116
        4.6.6   Point Coordination Function   122
    References.   124

5   **Short Range Radio Protocols: Bluetooth and IR**   125
    5.1   Introduction   125
    5.2   Bluetooth   126
        5.2.1   Packet Format   130
        5.2.2   Protocol Stack   132
        5.2.3   Bluetooth-Enabled Applications.   135
    5.3   Infra Red   137
        5.3.1   IR Protocol Stack   138
    5.4   Comparison of Bluetooth and Infrared   143
    References.   144

6   **Low Power Communication Protocols: ZigBee,**
    6LoWPAN and ZigBee IP   147
    6.1   Introduction   147
    6.2   IEEE 802.15.4   149
    6.3   ZigBee Protocol Stack   149
    6.4   6LoWPAN   161
        6.4.1   IPV6   162
        6.4.2   IP Over IEEE 802.15.4   164
        6.4.3   Compression, Fragmentation and Reassembly   165
        6.4.4   Routing   170
        6.4.5   CoAP Protocol.   172
        6.4.6   RPL Routing Protocol   173
    6.5   ZigBee IP   175
        6.5.1   Protocol Stack   175
    References.   176

7   **Routing Protocols for Mobile Ad Hoc Network**   179
    7.1   Introduction   179
    7.2   Classification of Routing Protocols.   181
        7.2.1   Distance Vector Routing   183
    7.3   Destination-Sequenced Distance Vector Routing.   183
        7.3.1   Advertisement of Routes   184
        7.3.2   Propagation of Link Break Information   185
        7.3.3   Stability of Requirements.   185
        7.3.4   Guarantee for Loop Free Paths   186
        7.3.5   Forwarding Table and Update Propagation   187
        7.3.6   Example.   188
    7.4   Dynamic Source Routing   190
        7.4.1   Overview of the Algorithm   191
        7.4.2   Route Discovery   191

	7.4.3	Route Maintenance	192
	7.4.4	Piggybacking on Route Discovery	193
	7.4.5	Handling Route Replies	194
	7.4.6	Operating in Promiscuous Mode	195
7.5		Ad hoc On-demand Distance Vector Routing	196
	7.5.1	Design Decisions	196
	7.5.2	Route Tables	197
	7.5.3	Unicast Route Discovery and Maintenance	198
	7.5.4	Multicast Route Discovery and Maintenance	203
7.6		Zonal Routing Protocol	208
	7.6.1	Routing Zones	208
	7.6.2	Interzone Routing	209
	7.6.3	Bordercast Tree and Query Control	211
	7.6.4	Random Delay in Query Processing	213
	7.6.5	Route Caching	214
	References		214

8 Mobile OS and Application Protocols 217

8.1		Introduction	217
8.2		Mobile OS	219
	8.2.1	Smartphones	219
	8.2.2	Difficulties in Adopting Desktop OS	221
	8.2.3	Mobile OS Features	222
	8.2.4	Mobile OS Platforms	224
	8.2.5	J2ME	225
	8.2.6	Symbian OS	228
	8.2.7	Android OS	230
	8.2.8	Iphone OS (iOS)	232
	8.2.9	Comparison of iOS and Android	234
	8.2.10	Cross Platform Development Tools	235
8.3		Mobile IP	236
	8.3.1	Overview	238
	8.3.2	Agent Discovery	239
	8.3.3	Registration	240
	8.3.4	Routing and Tunneling	242
8.4		Mobile Shell (Mosh)	244
	8.4.1	Overview of Mosh	245
	8.4.2	State Synchronization Protocol	246
	8.4.3	Design Considerations of Terminal Emulator	249
	8.4.4	Evaluation of Mosh	250
8.5		Wireless Application Protocol	251
	8.5.1	Performance Bottleneck Faced by HTTP	251
	8.5.2	WAP Protocol Stack	254
	References		260

Part II Mobile Data Management

9 Data Centric Routing, Interoperability and Fusion in WSN 265
   9.1   Introduction 265
   9.2   Characteristics of WSN............................... 266
          9.2.1   WSN Versus MANET......................... 267
   9.3   Architecture of WSN 268
          9.3.1   Communication Architecture 269
          9.3.2   Network Organization 270
   9.4   Routing in Sensor Network............................ 271
          9.4.1   Classification of Routing Protocols 272
   9.5   Flat Network Based Routing........................... 273
          9.5.1   Hierarchical Routing Protocols 275
          9.5.2   Location Based Routing Protocols.............. 276
          9.5.3   Selection of Forwarding Neighbor.............. 278
   9.6   Routing Based on Protocol Operation................... 280
          9.6.1   Multipath Routing Protocols 281
          9.6.2   Query Based Routing Protocols................ 282
          9.6.3   Negotiation Based Routing Protocols. 282
   9.7   Interconnection of WSNs to the Internet................. 283
          9.7.1   NAT Based IP-WSN Interconnection 285
   9.8   Data Fusion in WSN.................................. 287
          9.8.1   Definitions................................. 288
          9.8.2   Data Collection Model....................... 289
          9.8.3   Challenges in Data Fusion.................... 291
          9.8.4   Data Fusion Algorithms...................... 291
   References... 296

10 Location Management................................... 299
   10.1   Introduction 299
          10.1.1   Registration and Paging..................... 301
   10.2   Two Tier Structure 301
          10.2.1   Drawbacks of Fixed Home Addresses 302
   10.3   Hierarchical Scheme 302
          10.3.1   Update Requirements........................ 303
          10.3.2   Lookup in Hierarchical Scheme................ 304
          10.3.3   Advantages and Drawbacks................... 304
   10.4   Caching... 305
          10.4.1   Caching in Hierarchical Scheme 307
   10.5   Forwarding Pointers 308
   10.6   Replication 309
   10.7   Personal Mobility 311
          10.7.1   Random Process, Information and Entropy 311
          10.7.2   Mobility Pattern as a Stochastic Process 315

	10.7.3	Lempel-Ziv Algorithm	320
	10.7.4	Incremental Parsing	323
	10.7.5	Probability Assignment	326
10.8	Distributed Location Management		327
	10.8.1	The Call Setup Protocol	329
	10.8.2	Update	329
	10.8.3	Data Structures and System Specification	330
	10.8.4	The Cost Model	333
References			334

11 Distributed Algorithms for Mobile Environment 337
- 11.1 Introduction 337
- 11.2 Distributed Systems and Algorithms 338
- 11.3 Mobile Systems and Algorithms 339
  - 11.3.1 Placing Computation 340
  - 11.3.2 Synchronization and Contention 340
  - 11.3.3 Messaging Cost 341
- 11.4 Structuring Distributed Algorithms 344
- 11.5 Non-coordinator Systems 344
  - 11.5.1 All Machines are Equivalent 345
  - 11.5.2 With Exception Machines 347
  - 11.5.3 Coordinator Based Systems 349
- 11.6 Exploiting Asymmetry of Two-Tier Model 351
  - 11.6.1 Search Strategy 352
  - 11.6.2 Inform Strategy 354
  - 11.6.3 Proxy Strategy 356
- 11.7 Termination Detection 361
  - 11.7.1 Two Known Approaches 362
  - 11.7.2 Approach for Mobile Distributed Systems 362
  - 11.7.3 Message Types 363
  - 11.7.4 Entities and Overview of Their Actions 365
  - 11.7.5 Mobile Process 365
  - 11.7.6 Base Stations 366
  - 11.7.7 Handoff 368
  - 11.7.8 Disconnection and Rejoining 370
  - 11.7.9 Dangling Messages 370
  - 11.7.10 Announcing Termination 372
- References 372

12 Data Dissemination and Broadcast Disks 375
- 12.1 Introduction 375
- 12.2 Data Access Issues in Mobile Environment 376
- 12.3 Pull and Push Based Data Delivery 377
- 12.4 Dissemination in Mobile Environment 379

12.5   Comparison of Pull and Push Models.   380
12.6   Classification of Data Delivery Models.   382
12.7   Broadcast Disk   384
        12.7.1   Flat Periodic Broadcast Model.   384
        12.7.2   Skewed Periodic Broadcast   385
        12.7.3   Properties of Broadcast Programs   385
        12.7.4   Advantages of Multi-Disk Program   388
        12.7.5   Algorithm for Broadcast Program   388
        12.7.6   Parameters for Tuning Disk Model   390
        12.7.7   Dynamic Broadcast Program   390
        12.7.8   Unused or Empty Slots in Broadcast Disk.   391
        12.7.9   Eliminating Unused Slot   392
12.8   Probabilistic Model of Broadcast   396
12.9   Memory Hierarchy   398
12.10   Client Cache Management   399
        12.10.1 Role of Client Side Caching   400
        12.10.2 An Abstract Formulation   400
        12.10.3 Consideration for Caching Cost.   402
        12.10.4 Cost-Based Caching Scheme: PIX and LIX.   402
        12.10.5 Pre-fetching Cost.   403
12.11   Update Dissemination.   405
        12.11.1 Advantages of Broadcast Updates   405
        12.11.2 Data Consistency Models   405
References.   406

13 Indexing in Air   409
13.1   Introduction   409
13.2   Address Matching and the Directory.   411
13.3   Preliminary Notions   412
13.4   Temporal Address Matching Technique   412
13.5   Tuning Time and Access Latency.   412
13.6   Indexing in Air.   413
        13.6.1   (1, m) Indexing Scheme.   414
13.7   Distributed Indexing Scheme   416
        13.7.1   Distributed Indexing with No Replication   418
        13.7.2   Replication Based Distributed Indexing.   419
        13.7.3   Full Path Replication Scheme   420
        13.7.4   Partial Path Replication   421
        13.7.5   Access Protocol.   425
13.8   Exponential Indexing   428
        13.8.1   Generalized Exponential Indexing   429
        13.8.2   Analysis.   432

13.9   Hash A   436
13.10   Hash B   439
References.   442

14   Caching and Data Replication in Mobile Environment   443
14.1   Introduction   443
14.2   Caching, Prefetching and Hoarding.   444
14.3   Invalidating and Refreshing Cache   446
14.4   Strategies for Caching with Stateless Servers   447
        14.4.1   TS Strategy   447
        14.4.2   AT Strategy.   448
        14.4.3   Signature Strategy   448
14.5   Requirements for Replication   452
        14.5.1   Pitfalls of Replication   455
14.6   Replication Techniques.   457
14.7   Rule Based Reconciliation Approach   458
        14.7.1   Two-Tier Replication.   458
        14.7.2   Performance Analysis   460
        14.7.3   Caching and Replication in CODA   462
14.8   Relaxed Data Consistency Models   464
        14.8.1   Requirements for Session Guarantees   467
        14.8.2   Implementation Related Issues.   471
References.   473

15   Storage Systems for Mobile Environment   475
15.1   Introduction   475
15.2   Disconnected Mode of Operation   476
15.3   Rover Toolkit   477
        15.3.1   Design of Rover Toolkit   478
15.4   Mobile Distributed File Systems.   482
15.5   CODA   482
        15.5.1   Overview of CODA.   483
        15.5.2   Scalability   486
        15.5.3   Disconnection and Failures   488
        15.5.4   Replica Control Strategy   489
        15.5.5   Visibility of Updates   492
        15.5.6   Venus and Its Operations.   493
        15.5.7   Reintegration   497
15.6   InterMezzo   498
        15.6.1   Filtering Access to Files   499
        15.6.2   Protocols   501
        15.6.3   Functions of Lento.   502
        15.6.4   Recovery and Cache Validation.   503

15.7 File System for Connected Clients 504
    15.7.1 Concurrency Control 505
    15.7.2 Conflict Detection and Resolution 505
    15.7.3 Cache Replacement 507
References... 507

16 Context-aware Infrastructures for Smart Environment 509
16.1 Introduction 509
16.2 Terminology and Historical Prospectives 510
16.3 Designing Context-aware Applications 511
    16.3.1 Representation of Contextual Data.............. 511
    16.3.2 Extraction of Contextual Data 512
    16.3.3 Adaptability................................ 514
16.4 Formal Modeling of Contexts......................... 515
    16.4.1 ConChat Model 517
16.5 System Requirements 521
    16.5.1 Inhabitants Centered Requirements 521
    16.5.2 Technology Related Issues.................... 523
16.6 Middleware Architectures 526
    16.6.1 Layered Middleware Architecture 527
    16.6.2 Service Oriented Middleware.................. 528
    16.6.3 Agent Oriented Middleware................... 530
    16.6.4 Object Oriented Middleware 532
16.7 Smart Applications 532
    16.7.1 Context-aware Applications Using Smart Phones ... 534
References... 539

Index 541

About the Author

R.K. Ghosh is a professor in the Department of Computer Science and Engineering at the Indian Institute of Technology Kanpur. Earlier, he held a professor's position in the Department of Computer Science and Engineering at the Indian Institute of Technology Guwahati. A few of the other positions he has held in the past include a UN teacher fellow at the International Institute for Software Technology (IIST) Macau, a visiting scientist at INRIA Sophia Antipolis, France, and a visiting faculty in the Department of Computer Science at the University of Texas at Arlington, USA. His primary research interests are in mobile computing, distributed systems, and wireless networks.

Dr. Ghosh has published extensively in professional journals on wireless sensor networks, mobile applications and services, parallel and distributed systems, graph theory, and the operation of large data centers. He has co-authored one book and edited several conference proceedings, as well as authored a few book chapters in the general area of mobile applications and services. Dr. Ghosh has worked on several sponsored research projects related to parallel processing, distributed software engineering, mobile computing and cloud computing. A few of these projects involved international collaborations with the researchers from the University of Trento, Italy, Airbus Industrie, France, Commonwealth Scientific and Industrial Research Organisation (CSIRO), Australia, University of Melbourne, Australia, and University of Texas at Arlington, USA. His pedagogic interests led to a collection of animation programs for teaching data structure and algorithms at the undergraduate level. A partial collection of these animation programs grouped as Ghosh's collection is available at http://algoviz.org/node/641.

Acronyms

3G	Third Generation
3GPP	Third-Generation Partnership Project
4G	Fourth Generation
5G	Fifth Generation
6LoWPAN	Low-power Network on IPv6
8-PSK	Octagonal Phase-Shift Keying
ABR	Associativity-Based Routing
ACCH	Associated Control CHannels
ACL	Asynchronous Connection Less
ACO	Augmented Channel Occupancy
AGCH	Access Grant CHannel
AMA	Active Member Address
AODV	Ad hoc On-Demand Distance Vector
AP	Access Point
API	Application Programming Interface
APL	APplication Layer
ARP	Address Resolution Protocol
ARQ	Automatic Repeat reQuest
AU	Application Unit
AuC	Authentication Center
BCCH	Broadcast Control CHannel
BCH	Broadcast CHannel
BCO	Borrowing with Channel Order
BER	Bit Error Rate
BFA	Borrow from the First Available
BFR	Borrowing From the Richest
BS	Base Station
BSA	Basic Service Area
BSC	Base Station Controller
BSS	Base Station Subsystem

BSS	Basic Service System
BSSAP	Base Station System Application Part
BSSGP	BSS GPRS application Protocol
BSSID	BSS Identifier
BTS	Base Transceiver Station
CAC	Channel Access Code
CAN	Community Area Network
CASS	Context-Aware Substructure System
CCCH	Common Control CHannels
CDMA	Code Division Multiple Access
CEPT	Conference of European Post and Telecommunication
CFP	Contention-Free Period
CGI	Common Gateway Interface
CGSR	Cluster Gateway Switch Routing
CoA	Care-of Address
CoAP	Constrained Application Protocol
CoBrA	Context Broker Architecture
CODA	COnstant Data Availability
CRC	Cyclic Redundancy Code
CS	Circuit Switching
CSCF	Control Session Control Function
CSMA/CA	CSMA with Collision Avoidance
CSMA	Carrier Sensing and Multiple Access
CTS	Clear to Transmit
DAC	Device Access Code
DAO	Destination Advertisement Object
DCA	Dynamic Channel Assignment
DCCH	Dedicated Control CHannels
DCF	Distributed Coordination Function
DDCA	Distributed Dynamic Channel Assignment
DHCP	Dynamic Host Control Protocol
DIFS	DCF Inter-Frame Spacing
DIO	DODAG Information Object
DIS	DODAG Information Solicitation
DISCUS	Distributed Source Coding Using Syndromes
DODAG	Destination-Oriented Directed Acyclic Graph
DoS	Denial of Services
DRNC	Drift RNC
DSC	Distributed Source Coding
DSDV	Destination-Sequenced Distance Vector
DSR	Dynamic Source Routing
DSSS	Direct-Sequence Spread Spectrum
DTD	Document-Type Definition
DTX	Discontinuous Transmission
EDGE	Enhanced Data rates for GSM Evolution

EIR	Equipment Identity Register
ESS	Extended Service Set
ETSI	European Telecommunication Standard Institute
ETX	Expected Transmission count
EUI	Extended Unique Identifier
FA	Foreign Agent
FAC	Final Assembly Code
FACCH	Fast Associate Control CHannel
FCA	Fixed Channel Assignment
FCCH	Frequency Correction CHannel
FCS	Frame Check Sequence
FDD	Frequency Division Duplex
FDMA	Frequency Division Multiple Access
FEC	Forward Error Correction
FFD	Full Function Device
FFH	Fast Frequency Hopping
FHSS	Frequency Hopping Spread Spectrum
FSR	Fish-eye State Routing
FTP	File Transfer Protocol
GEAR	Geographical and Energy-Aware Routing
GGSN	Gateway GPRS Support Node
GMM	GPRS Mobility Management
GMSC	Gateway MSC
GoS	Grade of Service
GPRS	General Packet Radio Service
GPS	Geographical Positioning System
GPSK	Gaussian Phase-Shift Keying
GRPH	GRouP Hello
GSM	Groupe Speciale Mobile
GSR	Global State Routing
GTP	GPRS Tunneling Protocol
HA	Home Agent
HEC	Header Error Check
HLR	Home Location Register
HRN	Handover Reference Number
HSCSD	High-Speed Circuit-Switched Data
HSS	Home Subscriber Service
HTML	Hypertext Mark-up Language
HTTP	Hypertext Transfer Protocol
IAC	Inquiry Access Code
IAM	Initial Address Message
IARP	IntrAzone Routing Protocol
IAS	Information Access Service
IBSS	Independent BSS
ICMP	Internet Control Message Protocol

IEEE	Institute of Electronics and Electrical Engineers
IERP	IntErzone Routing Protocol
IFH	Intermediate Frequency Hopping
IMEI	International Mobile Equipment Identity
IMSI	International Mobile Subscriber's Identity
IoT	Internet of Things
IP	Internet Protocol
IPv4	Internet Protocol version 4
IPv6	Internet Protocol version 6
IR	Infrared
ISDN	Integrated Service Digital Network
L2CAP	Logical Link Access Protocol
LAI	Location Area Identifier
LAN	Local Area Network
LAP	Link Access Protocol
LAPD	Link Access Protocol for ISDN D-Channel
LAR	Location-Aided Routing
LIX	LRU PIX
LLC	Link Logical Layer
LLN	Low-power Lossy Network
LM-IAS	Link Management Information Access Service
LM-MUX	Link Management MUltipleXing
LMP	Link Manager Protocol
LMR	Lightweight Mobile Routing
LODA	Locally Optimized Dynamic Assignment
LRU	Least Recently Used
LS	Location Server
LSAP	Link Service Access Point
LSAP-SEL	Link Service Access Point SELector
M2M	Machine to Machine
MAC	Medium Access Control
MAC	Medium Control Adaptation Protocol
MACT	Multicast route ACTivation
MANET	Mobile Ad hoc Network
MAP	Mobile Application Protocol
MCC	Mobile Cloud Computing
MDS	Mobile Distributed System
MGCF	Media Gateway Control Function
MGW	Media Gateway
MH	Mobile Handset
MIMO	Multiple-Input and Multiple-Output
MLME	MAC layer Management Entity
MN	Mobile Node
MOC	Mobile Originating Call
Mosh	Mobile shell

MS	Mobile Station
MSC	Mobile Switching Center
MSISDN	Mobile Station ISDN
MSRN	Mobile Station Roaming Number
MT	Mobile Terminal
MTC	Mobile Terminated Call
MTP	Message Transport Part
MTU	Maximum Transmission Unit
NAV	Network Allocation Vector
NCH	Notification CHannel
NDM	Normal Disconnected Mode
NLA	Next-Level Aggregator
NLME	Network Layer Management Entity
NRM	Normal Response Mode
NSAPI	Network Service Access Point Identifier
NSS	Network Subsystem
NWK	NetWorK layer
OBEX	OBject EXchange protocol
OBU	Onboard Unit
OCB	Office Code Book
OFDM	Orthogonal Frequency Division Multiplexing
OSI	Open System Interconnection
OVSF	Orthogonal Variable Spreading Factor
PAN	Personal Area Network
PCF	Point Coordination Function
PCH	Paging CHannel
PDA	Personal Digital Assistant
PDN	Packet Data Network
PDU	Protocol Data Unit
PHY	Physical Layer
PIFS	PCF Inter-frame Spacing
PIMSI	Packet IMSI
PIN	Personal Identity Number
PIX	Probability Inverse frequency X
PLL	Physical Link Layer
PLMN	Public Land Mobile Network
PMA	Passive Member Address
PMS	Power Management System
PS	Packet Switching
PSTN	Public Switched Telephone Network
QoS	Quality of Service
QSPK	Quadrature Phase-Shift Keying
RAB	Radio Access Bearer
RACH	Random Access CHannel Associativity-Based Routing
RAI	Routing Area Identification

RERR	Route ERRor packet
REST	REpresentational State Transfer
RETOS	Resilient, Expandable, and Threaded Operating System for Wireless Sensor Networks
RFD	Reduced Function Device
RFID	Radio Frequency IDentification
RLC	Radio Link Control
RNAAP	Radio Network Access Application Part
RNC	Radio Network Controller
RNC	Regional Network Center
RNL	Radio Network Layer
RoLL	Routing over Low-power and Lossy networks
RPL	Routing Protocol for Low-power and lossy networks
RREP	Route REPly packet
RREQ	Route REQuest packet
RRM	Radio Resource Manager
RSS	Received Signal Strength
RSSI	RSS Indicator
RSU	Road Side Unit
RTS	Request to Transmit
RTT	Round-Trip Time
SACCH	Slow Associated Control CHannel
SCCP	Signaling Connection Control Part
SCH	Synchronization CHannel
SCO	Synchronous Connection Oriented
SDDCH	Stand-alone Dedicated Control CHannel
SDP	Service Discovery Protocol
SFH	Slow Frequency Hopping
SGSN	Servicing GPRS Support Node
SIFS	Short Inter-Frame Spacing
SIM	Subscriber Identity Module
SIR	Signal-to-Interference Ratio
SLA	Site-Level Aggregator
SLP	Service Location Protocol
SMS	Short Messaging Service
SNDCP	Subnetwork Dependent Convergence Protocol
SNPDU	Subnetwork Dependent Protocol Data Unit
SNR	Signal-to-Noise Ratio
SOCAM	Service-Oriented Context Middleware
SPIN	Sensor Protocol for Information via Negotiation
SRNC	Servicing RNC
SS	Supplementary Service
SSH	Secure SHell
SSID	Service Set Identifier
SSL	Secure Socket Layer

SSP	State Synchronization Protocol
SSR	Signal Stability Routing
TAC	Type Approval Code
TCAP	Transaction Capability Application Part
TCH	Traffic CHannel
TCP	Transmission Control Protocol
TCS	Telephone Control Specification
TDD	Time-Division Duplex
TDMA	Time-Division Multiple Access
TIMSI	Temporary IMSI
TLA	Top-Level Aggregator
TLS	Transport Layer Security
TNL	Transport Network Layer
TORA	Temporarily Ordered Routing Algorithm
TRAU	Transcoder and Rate Adaptation Unit
TSN	Transient Social Networking
TTL	Time To Live
TTP	Tiny Transport Protocol
UCAM	Unified Context-Aware Application Model
UDP	User Datagram Protocol
UE	User Equipment
UMTS	Universal Mobile Telecommunication System
URL	Uniform Resource Locator
UTRAN	UMTS Terrestrial Radio Access Network
UUID	Universally Unique IDentifier
UWB	Ultra-Wideband
V2V	Vehicle to Vehicle
VHE	Virtual Home Environment
VLR	Visitor Location Register
VOC	Volatile Organic Compounds
VoIP	Voice over IP
VPN	Virtual Private Network
WAE	WAP Application Environment
WAN	Wide Area Network
WAP	Wireless Application Protocol
WCDMA	Wideband CDMA
WDP	WAP Datagram Protocol
WHART	Wireless Highway Addressable Remote Transducer
WiFi	Wireless Fidelity
WiMAX	Worldwide Interoperability for Microwave Access
WLAN	Wireless Local Area Network
WML	Wireless Markup Language
WPAN	Wireless Personal Area Network
WRP	Wireless Routing Protocol
WSN	Wireless Sensor Network

WSP	WAP Session Protocol
WTAI	Wireless Telephone Applications Interface
WTL	WAP Transport Layer
WTLS	WAP Transport Layer Security
XML	Markup Language
ZC	ZigBee Coordinator
ZDO	ZigBee Device Object
ZR	ZigBee Router
ZRP	Zonal Routing Protocol

List of Figures

Figure 1.1   WSN for patient monitoring   4
Figure 1.2   Architectural taxonomy of DS including mobility   5
Figure 1.3   Enabling technologies for MCC.   8
Figure 1.4   General architecture of MCC.   9
Figure 1.5   Mobile pervasive computing   11
Figure 1.6   System architecture for smart freight
              management [16]   13
Figure 1.7   Context aware call forwarding application [5]   14
Figure 1.8   A reference architecture for VANET [2]   17
Figure 1.9   A reference protocol architecture for VANET [2].   18
Figure 2.1   Cell packing of a coverage area.   22
Figure 2.2   Frequency reuse concept.   23
Figure 2.3   A regular hexagon inscribed in circle of radius R.   24
Figure 2.4   Cell distance using hexagonal cell geometry   25
Figure 2.5   Cluster area approximates to a regular hexagon   26
Figure 2.6   Co-channel cells   27
Figure 2.7   Interferences due to propagation of co-channel
              signals   29
Figure 2.8   Co-channel interference considering exact cell
              geometry   31
Figure 2.9   Cell splitting   32
Figure 2.10   Cell sectoring   33
Figure 2.11   Interference pattern with cell sectoring   33
Figure 2.12   Distribution of the arrival of requests
              and their servicing   34
Figure 2.13   Queuing discipline and service of call requests   36
Figure 2.14   Markov chain representing system state
              and transitions   36
Figure 2.15   Borrowing affects co-channels cells of donor cell.   42
Figure 2.16   Channel switching with borrowing   44
Figure 2.17   ACO matrix of cell i   46

Figure 2.18   Handoff scenarios at cell boundaries.   49
Figure 2.19   The generic procedure of handoff   53
Figure 3.1   GSM architecture.   56
Figure 3.2   GSM channel classes   61
Figure 3.3   Structure of a normal GSM frame or burst   63
Figure 3.4   Structures of FCCH, SCH and RACH frames
               or bursts   64
Figure 3.5   GSM network components   65
Figure 3.6   Protocol for incoming call to a mobile   67
Figure 3.7   Message flow over radio channels for mobile
               terminated call setup   69
Figure 3.8   Signaling for mobile originated call setup   69
Figure 3.9   Channel activity needed for location update   71
Figure 3.10   GSM inter BSC handover procedure   72
Figure 3.11   GPRS/GSM combined architecture.   75
Figure 3.12   GPRS protocol stacks.   77
Figure 3.13   UTRAN architecture   82
Figure 3.14   Orthogonal spreading code for different spreading
               factors   84
Figure 3.15   Elimination of near far effect.   85
Figure 3.16   Softer handoffs in WCDMA FDD mode.   89
Figure 3.17   Soft handoff in WCDMA FDD mode.   90
Figure 3.18   The UMTS protocol model   91
Figure 3.19   UMTS transport network protocols and interfaces   91
Figure 3.20   Radio network layer protocols   93
Figure 4.1   Mobility supports on LAN and WAN.   97
Figure 4.2   Channelization of 2.4 GHZ band for WLAN.   99
Figure 4.3   Lower and middle subband channelization scheme
               for 802.11a   100
Figure 4.4   Upper subband channelization scheme for 802.11a.   100
Figure 4.5   Transmit spectrum mask   101
Figure 4.6   WLAN basic topologies   103
Figure 4.7   IEEE standard architecture for PHY and MAC layers.   105
Figure 4.8   Frequency hopping spread spectrum   106
Figure 4.9   Frequency hopping spread spectrum   107
Figure 4.10   DSSS using with spreading factor 6   108
Figure 4.11   Protocol stack for 802.11   110
Figure 4.12   Contrasting different access technologies.   112
Figure 4.13   Frames generation and transmission under pure
               ALOHA   113
Figure 4.14   Hidden and exposed terminal problems.   115
Figure 4.15   Logic of DCF basic transmission mode   117
Figure 4.16   Data transmission from one station to another   117
Figure 4.17   DCF RTS/CTS mode of transmission.   119

Figure 4.18   Solutions to hidden/exposed terminal problem   119
Figure 4.19   RTS/CTS mode shortens interval of collision in DCF.   120
Figure 4.20   Receiver side solution to check LAN misbehavior   121
Figure 4.21   Effects of missing CTS.   122
Figure 4.22   Superframe structure and PCF.   123
Figure 5.1   Bluetooth network   127
Figure 5.2   Piconets and scatternet   128
Figure 5.3   Functional overview of piconet   129
Figure 5.4   Transmission slots of master and slaves   130
Figure 5.5   Single slot and multi slot Bluetooth packets   131
Figure 5.6   Frame format for Bluetooth network.   131
Figure 5.7   Bluetooth packet header   132
Figure 5.8   Bluetooth protocol stack   133
Figure 5.9   Structure of Bluetooth profiles.   136
Figure 5.10   Protocol stacks for various Bluetooth applications   136
Figure 5.11   IR for replacement of cable connection.   137
Figure 5.12   Infrared communication cone.   138
Figure 5.13   IR protocol suite   138
Figure 5.14   The IrLAP frame structure   139
Figure 5.15   Flow of IrLAP operation.   141
Figure 6.1   ZigBee protocol stack.   150
Figure 6.2   Channels in three operating frequency bands   151
Figure 6.3   ZigBee network topologies   152
Figure 6.4   ZigBee packet structure   152
Figure 6.5   IEEE 802.15.4 MAC super frame   153
Figure 6.6   Slotted CSMA-CA algorithm.   155
Figure 6.7   Unslotted CSMA-CA algorithm.   155
Figure 6.8   Beacon-enabled transmission in ZigBee   156
Figure 6.9   Illustrating address assignment (in hexadecimal)
               to ZigBee devices   158
Figure 6.10   Network formation process executed by ZC   158
Figure 6.11   The network discovery process executed
               by a child device   159
Figure 6.12   The process of joining executed by a child device   159
Figure 6.13   The process of joining executed by a parent device   160
Figure 6.14   Re-joining steps executed by orphan child
               and its parent   161
Figure 6.15   Protocol stack for an IPv6 edge router
               with 6LoWPAN support   162
Figure 6.16   Network part of IPv6 address   163
Figure 6.17   Address translation: IPv4–IPv6   164
Figure 6.18   6LoWPAN protocol stack   165
Figure 6.19   Header compression in 6LoWPAN.   166

Figure 6.20   Header compression in 6LoWPAN using stacked
               header   166
Figure 6.21   Headers for point to point short packet transmission.   167
Figure 6.22   Stateless compression of packets in 6LoWPAN   169
Figure 6.23   Fragmented packet headers   170
Figure 6.24   Header compression for mesh routing.   170
Figure 6.25   Mesh routing in 6LoWPAN network   171
Figure 6.26   Architecture of CoAP [10]   172
Figure 6.27   CoAP and HTTP stacks   173
Figure 6.28   ZigBee IP stack layering architecture   176
Figure 7.1   Ad hoc network.   180
Figure 7.2   Classifying routing algorithms   181
Figure 7.3   Count to infinity problem   183
Figure 7.4   Flooding due to fluctuations in routes.   186
Figure 7.5   An example for execution of DSDV.   188
Figure 7.6 B unicasting piggyback data (D's RREP) to S   194
Figure 7.7   Loop formation in using cached data for route reply.   195
Figure 7.8   Reflecting shorter route updates.   195
Figure 7.9   A possible loop   200
Figure 7.10   Intermediate node unicasting a RREP.   201
Figure 7.11   Route discovery.   202
Figure 7.12   Route maintenance.   203
Figure 7.13   Grafting a new branch to multicast tree   204
Figure 7.14   Pruning after a member node leave the multicast group . . .   206
Figure 7.15   Repairing link breakage in AODV   207
Figure 7.16   Two-hops routing zone of S   209
Figure 7.17   Bordercasting and operation of IERP   210
Figure 7.18   Extended routing zone of node c   212
Figure 7.19   Directing route discovery query from a source.   212
Figure 7.20   Detection of route discovery query.   213
Figure 7.21   Random delay in query processing.   214
Figure 8.1   Java 2 platforms—the big picture.   225
Figure 8.2   J2ME software stack   226
Figure 8.3   Symbian OS architecture.   229
Figure 8.4   Android software stack.   231
Figure 8.5   Life cycle of an Android application   232
Figure 8.6   iOS software stack   233
Figure 8.7   Software stack for a cross platform tool   236
Figure 8.8   DHCP operation   237
Figure 8.9   ICMP packet format for agent advertisement.   240
Figure 8.10   Registration process   241
Figure 8.11   Format of registration request message   241
Figure 8.12   Format of registration reply message   242
Figure 8.13   IP-in-IP encapsulation.   242

Figure 8.14   Tunneling and routing in mobile IP   243
Figure 8.15   Simplified view of SSH protocol [4]   246
Figure 8.16   Design of Mosh protocol [4]   247
Figure 8.17   Comparative evaluation: SSH versus Mosh [4]   251
Figure 8.18   World wide web communication model   252
Figure 8.19   WAP programming model   253
Figure 8.20   WAP protocol stack   254
Figure 8.21   Structure of a WML deck   256
Figure 8.22   Example of a WML deck   257
Figure 8.23   An equivalent WMLScript for a WML deck   258
Figure 9.1   Components of a sensor node   269
Figure 9.2   Communication architecture of sensor node   269
Figure 9.3   Layered organization of sensor node   270
Figure 9.4   Clustered organization of sensor node   271
Figure 9.5   Implosion and overlap problems   274
Figure 9.6   Funneling effect in WSN   275
Figure 9.7   Geographical forwarding in a grid deployment [22]   279
Figure 9.8   Recursive geographical forwarding [22]   280
Figure 9.9   Sequential assignment routing algorithm   283
Figure 9.10   NAT based IP/WSN integration   285
Figure 9.11   Serial forwarder for WSN to IP communication [34]   286
Figure 9.12   Downstream communication between IP
               and WSN [34]   286
Figure 9.13   Data/information fusion [35]   289
Figure 9.14   Marzullo's fusion technique with reliable sensor [52]   295
Figure 9.15   Data compression in DISCUS [35]   296
Figure 10.1   Location space of all objects   300
Figure 10.2   Move in two-tier scheme   302
Figure 10.3   Tree-based organization of location servers   303
Figure 10.4   Caching in hierarchical location scheme   307
Figure 10.5   Forwarding pointers in hierarchical scheme   309
Figure 10.6   GSM type location area map (Source [3])   315
Figure 10.7   One step state transition diagram for personal mobility   318
Figure 10.8   Trie built by classical Lempel-Ziv algorithm   323
Figure 10.9   Enhanced trie   325
Figure 10.10   The model   328
Figure 11.1   Search cost   342
Figure 11.2   Mobile to mobile communication   343
Figure 11.3   Summary of cost model   343
Figure 11.4   Atomic broadcast using fixed/moving coordinator   350
Figure 11.5   Conceptual model of a moving coordinator system   351
Figure 11.6   Illustration of handoff process   368
Figure 12.1   Client and server initiated data delivery mechanisms   378
Figure 12.2   Data delivery models   378

Figure 12.3   Taxonomy of data transfer 384
Figure 12.4   A flat broadcast disk 385
Figure 12.5   Broadcast programs [1]. 386
Figure 12.6   Formulation of maximum waiting time 386
Figure 12.7   Bandwidth allocation by broadcast algorithm. 389
Figure 12.8   Many unused slots may be generated by
               broadcast program 392
Figure 12.9   Eliminating unused slots 394
Figure 12.10   Memory hierarchy of broadcast disks [1] 398
Figure 12.11   A view of client side cache 401
Figure 12.12   Cost of prefetching 402
Figure 12.13   Illustrating pre-fetch cost 404
Figure 13.1   Illustrating timing parameters 413
Figure 13.2   Distributed indexing 417
Figure 13.3   A three level index tree [1] 418
Figure 13.4   Distributed indexing with no replication 419
Figure 13.5   Distributed indexing with full path replication 420
Figure 13.6   Partial path replication 422
Figure 13.7   Control index 423
Figure 13.8   Number of index nodes for the replicated part 426
Figure 13.9   Exponential indexing 428
Figure 13.10   Exponential indexing using data segment grouping 432
Figure 13.11   Retrieving data bucket with record key 15 438
Figure 13.12   Scenarios depicting data miss and index miss 438
Figure 13.13   Access time using modified hashing function 440
Figure 13.14   Comparison of displacements [6] 441
Figure 14.1   A transaction performs N times as much job
               with N replicas [9]. 456
Figure 14.2   Client centric consistency models. 465
Figure 14.3   RYW guarantee. 468
Figure 14.4   MR guarantee 468
Figure 14.5   WFR guarantee 469
Figure 14.6   MW guarantee. 470
Figure 15.1   Interaction of application and the components
               of Rover toolkit. 479
Figure 15.2   CODA name space in clients. 483
Figure 15.3   Remote access of shared files system 484
Figure 15.4   Fetching file in CODA. 485
Figure 15.5   Interaction of CODA components 485
Figure 15.6   Side effect of CODA's RPC2 486
Figure 15.7   Invalidation notification using RPC and RPC2. 487
Figure 15.8   Transition between cache and replication at client 490
Figure 15.9   Venus state transitions 494
Figure 15.10   InterMezzo system [11] 500

Figure 15.11 Upcall and network request handling by Lento [11] 503
Figure 16.1   Processing of sensory data to contextual
              information [2] 513
Figure 16.2   Levels of adaptability 514
Figure 16.3   Global characteristics of adaptable applications 515
Figure 16.4   Interactions of ConChat application units 520
Figure 16.5   Infrastructural framework of smart environment [1] 523
Figure 16.6   Architecture for context management 526
Figure 16.7   Generic architecture for context management [36] 528
Figure 16.8   Architecture of SOCAM [17] 529
Figure 16.9   Processing sensor data to context [29] 531
Figure 16.10 Data flow in context toolkit [12] 532
Figure 16.11 Schematic representation of a contextor [32] 533
Figure 16.12 Adaptivity scenario using smart phone sensors 534
Figure 16.13 Flow of displacement data from wheel to smart phone 535
Figure 16.14 Orientation axes of smart phone 536
Figure 16.15 Integrated health monitoring system 537
Figure 16.16 Formation of a TSN for handling a distress situation 538

List of Tables

Table 4.1   Summary of wireless communication technologies   98
Table 4.2   Physical properties of IEEE standards for WLAN 102
Table 5.1   Comparison of physical characteristics of Bluetooth
            and Infrared 144
Table 6.1   Summary of ZigBee, Bluetooth and Infrared 148
Table 6.2   Forming an EUI address from a MAC address 163
Table 6.3   Header compression 167
Table 6.4   Dispatch header 167
Table 6.5   Encoding header 168
Table 6.6   Explanation HC1 bit patterns for NH values. 168
Table 7.1   Forwarding table of MH_4 189
Table 7.2   Advertised route table for node MH_4 189
Table 7.3   Change in forwarding table of node MH_4 190
Table 7.4   Change in forwarding table of node MH_4 190
Table 9.1   Ad hoc network versus sensor network 268
Table 10.1 An encoding scheme with prefix property 312
Table 10.2 An example for LAI crossing by a mobile 316
Table 10.3 Sequence of cells representing movement history 316
Table 10.4 Frequencies of symbols corresponding to three contexts. 318
Table 10.5 Encoding of different phrases 321
Table 10.6 Decoding of phrases 322
Table 10.7 Conditional probabilities of movement prediction 327
Table 10.8 Notations used for cost analysis 333
Table 12.1 Asymmetry in link capacities of wireless networks 381
Table 12.2 Expected delays for arrival of items on channel 387
Table 12.3 Expected delays for arrival of items on channel 387
Table 13.1 Tuples corresponding to non-replicated roots 422
Table 13.2 Notations for analysis of exponential indexing 433
Table 14.1 Summary of replica update strategies. 456
Table 14.2 Notations used in description of consistency models 467
Table 14.3 Summary of operations for consistency guarantees 472

List of Algorithms

Algorithm 1   DSR algorithm 192
Algorithm 2   Actions of WAP gateway 254
Algorithm 3   Lempel-Ziv encoder 321
Algorithm 4   Decoder for LeZi update 322
Algorithm 5   Enhanced decoder for LeZi update 324
Algorithm 6   Method get_LSId(MH_id) 330
Algorithm 7   Method localUpdate(MH_id, MSC_{old}, MSC_{new}) 331
Algorithm 8   Method update(MSC, MH_id) 331
Algorithm 9   Method remoteDelete(region_Id, MH_id) 331
Algorithm 10 Method lookup(MH_id, MSC) 332
Algorithm 11 Method localLookup(MSC, MH_Id) 332
Algorithm 12 Method remoteLookup(MH_id) 333
Algorithm 13 Lamport's bakery algorithm 345
Algorithm 14 Search strategy: actions of BS 353
Algorithm 15 Search strategy: actions of MH 353
Algorithm 16 Inform strategy: actions of BS 355
Algorithm 17 Inform strategy: actions of MH 356
Algorithm 18 Proxy strategy: actions of proxy 357
Algorithm 19 Proxy strategy: actions of MH 358
Algorithm 20 Actions of a mobile process P_j^m 366
Algorithm 21 Actions of a BS process P_i 367
Algorithm 22 Handoff protocol 369
Algorithm 23 Disconnection protocol 370
Algorithm 24 Rejoining protocol 371
Algorithm 25 Handling dangling messages 372
Algorithm 26 Generation of broadcast program 389
Algorithm 27 Using empty slots 395
Algorithm 28 Generating broadcast program 397
Algorithm 29 Access algorithm for (1, 1) indexing 414
Algorithm 30 Access protocol for fetching record with key K 425
Algorithm 31 Downloading data 425

Algorithm 32   Initial probe 430
Algorithm 33   Index search 431
Algorithm 34   Global index search 431
Algorithm 35   Retrieval of data 431
Algorithm 36   Access protocol using hashing 437
Algorithm 37   TS strategy for caching 449
Algorithm 38   AT strategy for caching 450
Algorithm 39   Cache invalidation 452
Algorithm 40   Creating and opening a directory 501
Algorithm 41   Conflict detection & resolution 506

Part I
Wireless Networking

Part I of the book consists of eight chapters including Chap. 1. Chapter 1 provides a gentle introduction to the environment of a Mobile Distributed System (MDS). It begins with terminology used for describing computing in MDS environments, and then provides a characterization of MDS. Following this, enabling technologies and a few interesting mobile applications have been discussed. Chapter 2 deals with the general concepts behind cellular wireless communication system that forms the foundations of every wireless communication system. This is followed up in Chap. 3 where cellular based telecommunication protocols such as GSM, GPRS and UMTS protocols have been discussed. Additionally, it focuses on some interesting physical layer encoding issues related to management of GSM radio resources. The next two chapters deal with WLAN and WPAN, both of which are based on short range radio transmissions. However, the domains of applications of these two networking systems are different. WLAN is meant for networking of computers. On the other hand, WPAN is meant for person centric networking based on Bluetooth and Infrared. Chapter 4 deals with WLAN while Bluetooth and Infrared protocols have been discussed in Chap. 5. Wireless Sensor Network (WSN) communication works in MAC layer. A number of new standards based on IPv6 have been developed to intergrate WSNs with IP based networks. As mentioned in Chap. 1 building smart mobile applications and services rely on contextual information gathered by WSNs. WSNs are low power lossy data centric networks which need energy efficient communication protocols. Chapter 6 is devoted to ZigBee and 6LoWPAN and other related protocols which rely on IEEE 802.15.4 physical layer standards. ZigBee IP is a newer standard released for implementation in 2013. It has been developed as a super specification on existing ZigBee standards with a view to support legacy deployments. For energy efficient operations, routing is based on RoLL while CoAP provides an energy efficient implementation of REST protocol. Mobile Ad hoc NETworks (MANETs) belong to another special type of self organizing networks which play important role in the context of providing mobile services to the end users. MANETs nodes implement IP layer, but used for communication without any infrastructural support. The routing in MANETs offer interesting theoretical challenges in terms of finding shortest path in a network where node topology is highly dynamic and local processing power at nodes is low. Some interesting and classical MANET routing algorithms have been discussed in Chap. 7. The topic of Chap. 8 is mobile application framework. It provides a comprehensive review of mobile OSes currently in vogue. It also describes three generic application protocols, viz., Mobile IP, Wireless Application Protocol (WAP) and a Mobile Shell (Mosh). The goal of these protocols is to maintain internet connectivity. Our idea of including these protocols is to make the reader aware of the special design issues that come up in creating applications due to mobility of end hosts and low data rates of wireless networks.

Chapter 1
Mobile Distributed Systems: Networking and Data Management

1.1 Introduction

Convergence of wireless networking, Internet, embedded processing, and cloud computing led to a multi dimensional shift in computing paradigms. Foundations were laid through advancements in wireless networking, miniaturization, and low power embedded processing. Wireless networking itself triggered a revolution in communication landscape. It became possible to move without wire while maintaining connectivity with the network and the Internet. Miniaturization reduced the form factor of the devices. The advances in battery technology coupled with low power embedded processing capabilities made the devices light weight (such as phones, laptops, PDA), portable and powerful. With cloud computing, it was possible to implement "pay per service" model of payment as well as accessibility of personalized services any where, at any time.

Besides personal communication devices, embedded technology led to emergence of self organizing low cost Wireless Sensor and Network (WSN). Low power wireless standards such as ZigBee, 6LoWPAN, RPL, and COAP implementing IPv6 made it possible to integrate WSN with the Internet. Through WSNs, it became possible to build unattended distributed data centric networks for global information dissemination. The information gathered by WSNs could be disseminated to mediating systems for the detection of important events and to trigger appropriate responses from corresponding actuation systems. Figure 1.1 illustrates a generic diagram of a WSN based patient monitoring. In this book, our goal is to deal with two important areas namely, wireless networking protocols and mobile data management. Our aim is to focus on the foundations of enabling technologies rather than the applications. Enabling technologies provide necessary capabilities for designing and implementing innovative mobile pervasive applications. The book has been conceived and written in this context. The book consists of 16 chapters including the current one. In this chapter our aim is to examine the issues that commonly arise in building mobile distributed applications and services instead of trying to provide chapter wise summarization of the contents.

© Springer Nature Singapore Pte Ltd. 2017
R.K. Ghosh, *Wireless Networking and Mobile Data Management*,
DOI 10.1007/978-981-10-3941-6_1

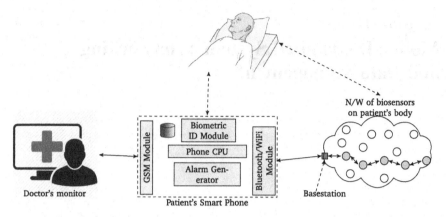

Fig. 1.1 WSN for patient monitoring

1.2   Mobile Pervasive and Ubiquitous Computing

Pervasive computing and *ubiquitous computing* are often used interchangeably in connection with the applications developed using mobile distributed systems. But there are subtle differences. Pervasiveness implies "anything whose presence is diffused". Ubiquitous, on the other hand, means "anything which is omnipresent". Pervasive computing tends to lean more towards mobile computing while ubiquitous computing is more close to embedded processing, intelligence and richness in interface experience. In some sense, ubiquitous computing subsumes a number of overlapping ideas from pervasive computing. It extends the idea of computers and networking being closely interwoven with our environment which do not require any human attention. Persons or inhabitants of the environment are important central theme of pervasive computing. In contrast, community and environment are dominant themes of ubiquitous computing where person centric computing is indirectly subsumed. Weiser [26] visualized the convergence between communication and computing in terms of availability of an omnipresent, and omniscient infrastructure servicing information. However, the ultimate goal of both computing paradigms is to bring comfort to human lives.

1.3   Characterizing Mobile Distributed System

A mobile system by definition consists of portable devices which run on batteries and have wireless communication interface for networking. Using mobile portable devices, the users can remain connected while moving from one place to the other. This introduces following two new elements in a distributed system: (i) dynamicity in networking, and (ii) asymmetry in the capabilities of the nodes. An architectural

Fig. 1.2 Architectural taxonomy of DS including mobility

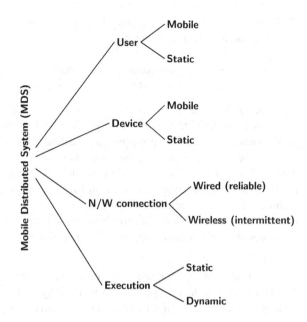

taxonomy of Distributed Systems including mobility is shown in Fig. 1.2. To understand the implications of the mobility, first we need to study the characteristics of a Distributed System (DS), and then examine how mobility complicates the computing scenario in a DS.

In defining a distributed system, one is reminded of Leslie Lamport's celebrated definition of a distributed system [14]:

Definition 1.1 (*Lamport* [14]) A distributed system is the one in which your computer becomes unusable due to failure of a computer you did not know existed.

The definition embodies the concept that a distributed system presents a single coherent system though it may typically consists of a number of geographically separated autonomous but stationary computers connected by high bandwidth network links. Some of the basic characteristics of such a computing model are:

1. An application is typically partitioned into a number of smaller tasks, and the responsibility of executing these tasks is evenly shared on by a set of participating computers.
2. Every computer is assumed to have enough resources to complete a task assigned to it in the expected duration of time.
3. Communication among computers is carried over high bandwidth wired links and mostly hidden from the users.
4. The users interact with a distributed application through a single console regardless of the location of the remote computer where interaction actually takes place.
5. Scaling is inherent, and a distributed system is extensible.
6. Partial failures can be masked.

7. Computer systems can be replaced, repaired without user being aware of occurrences of such problems during the time a distributed application is being executed.
8. Network connection is assumed to be robust.
9. The computers are assumed to be connected to main power supply.

Decoupling the location of computing [9] from the method of computing, a unified framework can be defined for a distributed system which supports mobility of all kinds. Mobility can be supported at different levels of distributed computing such as: the users, the devices, the access network, the backbone network, and the data/application nodes. Basically, it means that the location of computing is conceptually defined by realizing that every bit of information and every operation has a well-defined location at the scale of geographical experience [9]. The user's location, the location of data in the hard drive or the memory, the location of computing resources, the link location, etc., are all well-defined. The important set of locations include [9]:

1. The location of the user, where the result have to finally be intimated.
2. The location of the user's computer which may be a fixed location such as on the user's office desk, or it may be co-located and changes with the location of the user.
3. The location of network used to transmit information to or from the user's computer.
4. The location, where the information gets processed according to the user's request.
5. The location, where the necessary data is stored.
6. The location, where the input data is provided to the network or the storage locations.
7. The location, where the data get interpreted, processed, compiled or otherwise prepared for storage.
8. The location, where the data are measured.
9. The location, that are representable, the special case of geographic data.

The last pair of locations, stated above, pertain to the geographic data as these locations are always defined in the sense there is no dynamicity.

The computing in a uniprocessor system is the one in which every location except the last are the same. The only possibility of changing location is offline storing of data. The offline transfer of data to the location of computing incurs considerable cost. In the case of wired distributed systems, the locations can be widely separated and the cost for going from one location to other is low due to availability of high bandwidth (wired) network links. In the case of MDS, the cost of location change may be considerable. The cost increases across all the locations stated above, specially if a mobile user changes his/her location too frequently. In a MDS, the mobility and the portability nature of the devices together with the dynamicity of the network topology affect the cost across all the top seven locations listed above.

User's mobility and terminal mobility:
It relates to the top two locations in the list. At different stages of a computation, tracking a user's location itself may become quite expensive. Terminal mobility is normally decoupled from the user's mobility. Because a user may use a PDA, or a mobile phone, or a laptop or even a static workstation at different times. In Chap. 10 of the book, we specifically address the problem of tracking terminal mobility.

Another aspect of personal and terminal mobility is the possibilities of newer and more innovative person centric applications. We discuss a few of these applications. Important generic ideas in the context of these applications are presented in Chaps. 13–16.

Wireless and wired network:
Due to user's mobility and terminal mobility, the location of network links change very frequently. Specially, when wireless links are used, the cost shipping data increases tremendously. The mobile nodes are resource poor. Therefore, the execution cost of any computation on a mobile portable device more compared to the execution cost of the same computation on a desktop or a workstation. The inherent asymmetry in computing capabilities of fixed and mobile nodes calls for relocation of computation for minimizing computation cost. The asymmetry of costs in the fixed part versus the dynamic part of the network, necessitates a paradigm shift in the design of algorithm for mobile distributed environment. Chapter 11 of the book deals with the algorithm design issues in MDS environment in extensive details.

Both cost and interoperability are important issues in MDS due to heterogeneity of wireless network standards. A sound understanding network protocols is a foundational requirement in this respect. Therefore, Chaps. 2–9 of this book focus on various protocols and standards of wireless networks.

1.4 Mobile Cloud Computing

This book is not about cloud technology. However, as stated in the previous section, the running mobile applications and services exclusively on mobile devices is not possible, as they face severe resource constraints in terms of energy, memory, and computing power. Offloading complex computations to the fixed part of the network enables the mobile devices to conserve energy significantly and operate longer. Such an approach cuts down the response time.

Cloud computing has been recognized widely as new generation of computing infrastructure that offer utility driven software services [6] under distributed settings. The integration of mobile distributed system and cloud computing, therefore, offer a "best of both" approach in building mobile application and services. The cloud service providers such as Google, Amazon, Yahoo, offer cloud services at low cost. Resources can be rapidly provisioned on-demand, and released elastically. The management functions for cloud services are provided through publicly accessible APIs.

Through these APIs, the application developers can easily integrate cloud services into their softwares.

According to MCC forum [6]:

Definition 1.2 (*MCC Fourum*) Mobile Cloud Computing at its simplest, refers to an infrastructure where both the data storage and the data processing happen outside the mobile device. Mobile cloud applications move the computing power and data storage away from mobile phones and into the cloud, bringing applications and mobile computing to not just smartphone users but a much broader range of mobile subscribers.

An alternative view of MCC is: it combines mobile web with cloud computing to enable the users to access applications and services on the Internet [4, 15]. The infrastructure supported part of a Mobile Distributed System (MDS) has been viewed in terms of cloud immediately after the cloud computing technology was launched in 2007 [6].

It is possible to offer mobile services and run mobile applications on smartphones due to several supporting technologies in both hardware and software. These include, miniturization of computing devices, sensor network, phone OS, Wireless networking, and cloud infrastructure as illustrated in Fig. 1.3. Portable hand held devices (e.g., Android, Windows Mobile, iOS) are terminals where users access mobile services.

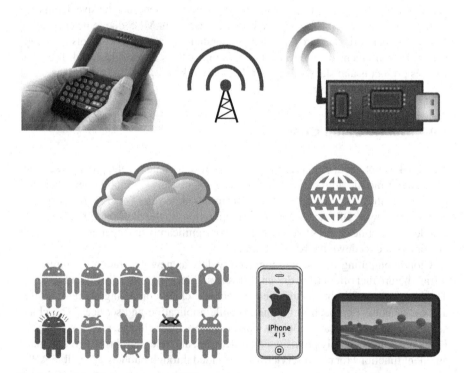

Fig. 1.3 Enabling technologies for MCC

Sensor networks are specialized low power devices for gathering contextual data that can be used for many innovative and personalized mobile services and applications. Specially, sensors are important elements for healthcare, smart home type of applications. Wireless communication is made possible through infrastructures such as GSM, WiFi, WiMAX. Taking advantage of multiple communication interfaces will need a number of supporting system softwares including mobile operating system. By integrating cloud computing with mobile distributed system through the Internet, application developers can create and deploy mobile services widely and offer mobile services anytime, anywhere and to any person. The overall architectural framework of MCC based on enabling technologies is shown in Fig. 1.4. In the general architecture of MCC, we implicitly assume that mobile devices obtain services from a remotely placed central data center. Although, functionalities of a data center are distributed over a highly parallel architecture, a mobile device has to access it through a Wide Area Network (WAN) and may at times suffer from moderate to long latency. To get around this problem, cloudlets are also deployed close to service locations. The underlying idea is to move clouds close to the mobile users by deploying cloudlets near the access points. Cloudlets can be formed dynamically on any device having resource in the LAN [24]. In the MCC architecture in Fig. 1.4, possible points where cloudlets can be placed are near AP on the LAN, near BS and close to RNC.

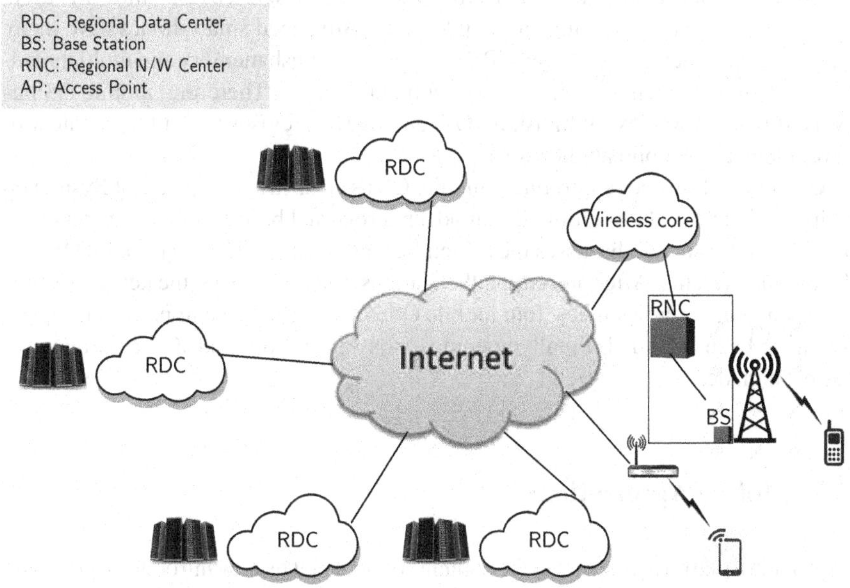

RDC: Regional Data Center
BS: Base Station
RNC: Regional N/W Center
AP: Access Point

Fig. 1.4 General architecture of MCC

1.5   OS for Mobile Devices

As explained above, a critical element of MDS is Operating System (OS) support at the end devices. An OS is a set system softwares that define abstractions for optimized access of hardware capabilities of a device. In other words, OS is an interface between system architecture and the application developers or users.

Mobile OS does not include operating systems for laptops. A laptop is seen more as convenient computing device that can be carried in a bag, weighs about 2–3 kg, having a hard disk and sufficient RAM. Laptops typically run on general purpose OSes designed for desktops or workstations. However, the same may not hold strictly for a ultra thin hybrid laptop that can function both as a PC and a tablet. Though hybrid laptops are not as big as conventional laptop, the hardware design leaves a feeling of being cramped as a laptop and too bulky as tablet or PDA. These laptops have a small size keyboard with limited functionality, limited flash memory, and small display. Such a laptop switches between two OSes to provide the required functionality of the one system or the other.

A mobile communication device is equipped with multiple wireless communication interfaces such as IR, Bluetooth, WiFi, GSM-GPRS, NFC, and GPS. It runs a set of important services such as voice calls, short messaging service, camera functionality, touch screen functionality, GPS based location service. Therefore, a mobile device needs a OS that can enable it to run these services and allow the users to access the in-built communication interfaces. Advanced smartphones have many added features such as high speed CPUs, GPUs, large flash memory and multi threading capabilities which are found in conventional laptops. Therefore, mobile OS has evolved into a complex multitasking OS, and merits a closer look in the context of development of mobile applications.

Chapter 8 of this book introduces mobile OS as an abstraction layer for System on Chip (SoC) and explains rationale behind a microkernel based approach to design of mobile OS. Further, it discusses the difficulties involved in adopting desktop OSes to the mobile systems. After presenting the features of a mobile OS, the kernel features are discussed. As case studies, four mobile OSes, viz., J2ME, Symbian, Android and iOS have been included. Finally, a comparison of Android and iOS environments has been made.

1.6   Mobile Applications

To provide a platform relevant to the contents of book, let us now introduce some basic type services one expects from a mobile distributed system. Figure 1.5 illustrates a few of these application. We investigate two of these applications a little deeper in order to provide the reader with an idea about the potentials that exist. In fact, a number of venture capitalists are ready to commit large amount of investments

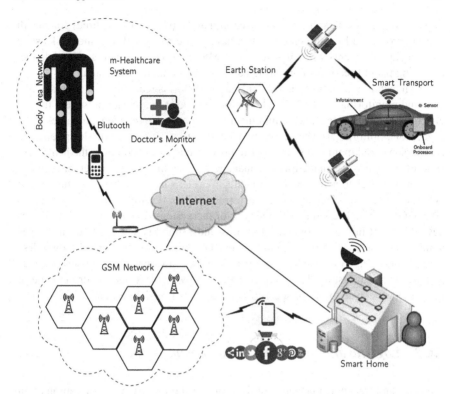

Fig. 1.5 Mobile pervasive computing

even in start up companies that come up with business plans to provide personalized services over mobile distributed systems.

1.6.1 mHealthcare

One of the very important mobile applications is round the clock health care and monitoring system for the patients with chronic diseases, and the senior citizens. Darrel West [28] cites Cisco Visual Networking Index [12] to predict that global mobile traffic may to increase by 18-folds between 2011 and 2016, and about 10 billion mobile devices could be in use world wide. According to WHO [18], the use of mobile health care is expected increase substantially in three areas:

1. Assisting the management of chronic diseases,
2. Assisting the elderly people staying alone, and
3. Assisting the pregnant mothers staying alone.

The use of mobile health apps are predominantly (over 35% of time) for health queries processed by call centers, mhealth apps are also used for other tasks such as fixing appointments with physicians by SMS, treatment reminders, telemedicine, accessing patient records, monitoring patients, physician decision support.

From technological prospectives, mHealth support is realizable for sophisticated care and monitoring [3, 10, 23]. The vision of mobile healthcare presented in [23] covers both applications and requirements of such a system. It encompasses three aspects of monitoring: (i) short term (home monitoring), (ii) long term (hospitals) and (iii) personalized monitoring. In order to provide end to end solution, the healthcare support must involve detection and management of incidences, emergency intervention, hospital transfers and treatments. Wireless network based solutions use WLAN, ad hoc wireless network, infrastructure-based wireless networks such as GSM/3G/4G/5G. The general framework of the system appears in Fig. 1.1. Varshney [23] identified that context awareness and reliability are specific challenges which have not been properly addressed in a comprehensive framework of wireless health monitoring system. The major part of context awareness can be derived from patient's medical history. But there could be also variations due to current state of the patient, the availability of specific experts and the medicines, and so on.

1.6.2   Logistic and Transport Management

Logistics and transport management form one of the important area of automation due to the inherent complexity of involved operations. Big logistics firms such as DHL, having operations over 200 countries around the globe, offer integrated logistic solution for entire supply chain from the manufacturers/suppliers to the retailers to the consumers. These companies use RFID, WSN and internet technologies to automate their supply chain management operations.

The last mile connectivity for logistic supply chain management is provided by transport vehicles. Intel offers a solution blueprint for an intelligent transport system with IoT [16]. It outlines monitoring of vehicle dynamics, intelligent navigation, fleet management along with a series of value added services. According to this solution, each vehicle is to be fitted with multiple sensing units, and an on-board terminal. The terminal will consist of data storage, GPS module, vehicle condition collection module, real-time clock, wireless communication module and a data communication interface.

Once vehicles are made to speak for themselves, linking these with customer data center applications is technologically straightforward through cloud infrastructure. An overall architecture as illustrated in Fig. 1.6 has been proposed in [16].

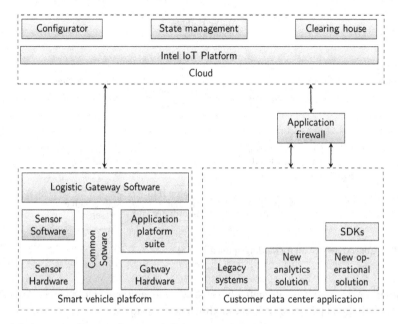

Fig. 1.6 System architecture for smart freight management [16]

1.7 Smart Environments

Smart environment is a term sometime ill-used and sometimes abused. However, in absence of proper terminology, it has been used to describe an environment where inhabitants are offered sophisticated technology based services. Weiser et al. [27] defined ubiquitous computing as:

Definition 1.3 (*Ubiquitous computing* [27]) A physical world that is richly and invisibly interwoven with sensors, actuators, displays and computational elements embedded seamlessly in everyday objects of our lives and connected through a continuous network.

We feel that the above definition succinctly captures the generic nature of any smart environment. The definition of smart environment given subsequently by Youngblood et al. [29] tries to amplify the comfort of the inhabitants over the supporting technologies describing ubiquitous computing framework.

Definition 1.4 (*Smart environment* [29]) A smart environment defined as the one that is able to acquire and apply knowledge about the environment and its inhabitants in order to improve their experience in that environment.

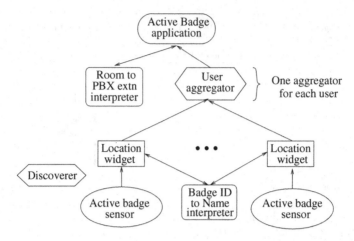

Fig. 1.7 Context aware call forwarding application [5]

Smart environment is alternatively referred to as ambient intelligence. Augusto and McCullagh [1] defined ambient intelligence as follows:

Definition 1.5 (*Ambient intelligence* [1]) A digital environment that proactively, but sensibly, supports people in their daily lives.

Definitions 1.4 and 1.5 imply that the smartness of environment is dependent on the abilities to provide added comfort to the inhabitants rather than the degree of technological sophistication. So, probably it is more appropriate to the use term *smart environment* for emphasizing physical infrastructure of sensors, actuators and network [17].

The requirements of each inhabitant vary from the other and also vary from one environment to the other. However, there is a set of common attributes which improve experience of inhabitants in a smart environment. More specifically, a smart environment

1. Optimizes productivity of inhabitants,
2. Improves ease of working,
3. Minimizes operational cost, and
4. Ensures security of inhabitants.

To this end, the environment must acquire knowledge of events and apply the same to respond to the occurrence of an event. For execution of a response, the environment should actuate actions from devices and objects in the environment which largely automate task possibly requiring minimal unobtrusive assistance from human inhabitants. It should adapt to the changes in the environment and its inhabitants. Above all privacy and security of inhabitants should be preserved. The set of generic requirements appear like a wishlist unless requirements these are seen in the context of specific environment. So, to motivate the reader we first introduce the concept of context aware computing and then follow it up with a concrete description of a smart environment.

1.7.1 Context Aware Computing

A typical application using context for its services is provided by Xerox PARC's active badge system [25, 26]. The active badge system was developed for personal emergency related communication with the wearer who is engaged in work in high security installation. Normally, considering security risks, the phone numbers are not revealed for contacting persons working in high security installations. So, establishing contact with such persons is a problem. However, by use of context awareness, the problem can be solved neatly. The entire system is explained in Fig. 1.7. The system consists of a number of infrared based sensor distributed over the installation. These sensors can detect Active Badges worn by people working inside the installation. Sensor detecting a badge then links the location of the wearer from a location widget corresponding to it. The collected information about the tag ID and its location are sent to the user's aggregator. There is a user aggregator for each user. The aggregator collects location information from each location widget for their corresponding users and shares the same to the discoverer. Every component of the application must register with the discoverer to be able to locate the users. The application then uses the discoverer to locate the user aggregator and the room to phone extension interpreter. After getting the related information, the application forwards the telephone calls. So the users can talk to each other, and in the case of emergency a person can be located and the call can be forwarded.

Dey and Abowd [5] have reported about Context Toolkit which they developed as a distributed infrastructure which provides abstractions such as widgets, interpreter, aggregators, services and discovers for building the context aware applications. The distributed infrastructure supports reliable cross platform communication between distributed objects. Simple object communication mechanisms HTTP and XML are used for encoding messages. This means TCP/IP is one of the requirement for the communication to happen. We will discuss more details about context abstractions in Chap. 16.

1.7.2 Driverless Cars

It is now common place to see people using navigation system to find routes to reach unknown addresses. The navigational applications mainly uses GPS and satellite route maps to guide people for this purpose. These software may provide some additional assistance information for safe driving. These include speed limits for the various highways and roads, weather conditions, terrain features, etc. The primary purpose is still limited to finding route from a source to a destination. However, building driverless car requires complex interplay of GPS navigation system, car cruise control and other vehicles on the road. It represents a sufficiently *smart environment* for a small number of inhabitants, i.e., the passengers of the car.

Though a number of technological challenges still remains unresolved, Google has successfully executed test runs of driverless cars on local streets [13]. It is expected by 2020, high way driving can be completely handed over to automated cruise control. Major auto makers such as Mercedes-Benz, Nissan, Volvo, BMW and Audi have already built their test models [13].

The successful realization of a driverless car is heavily dependent on integration of diverse technologies. First of all, it needs a very advanced hardware as far as car control is concerned. Two different directions of cruise controls, namely, longitudinal (break and speed), and lateral (steering and trajectory) are needed. The reaction time depends on speed of car and the colliding objects. The anticipation of colliding object's trajectory, speed assessment, etc., are important inputs to estimate how the car should apply optimum control to avoid collision or damage to self. The objects may be of different types such as a random pedestrians, or a cyclist or a speeding car or even animals. It requires a 360° view of surroundings. Inputs from multiple sensing units such as laser sensors, cameras, and radars will be needed for the purpose. Exact deployments of different sensing units needs careful simulations with normal traffic conditions on road system. The problem is to find accurate placement of sensing units so that the data collected by sensors should be able to provide enough real time data as the car is being driven. Some sensors may have to be roof mounted, others placed on the front or rear bumpers, many other underneath the car and the on different side fenders, etc. Google mapped entire California road system (172,000 miles) for a simulation purpose. It indicated that the sensors would be sending high volume and high velocity data (about 1 GB per second) [13]. It will require sophisticated big data analytics to process data and provide inputs to the autonomous driver.

Vehicle to vehicle (V2V) communication is conceptualized as peer to peer ad hoc network which can alleviate the problems by sharing information about traffic situation among vehicles in a sections of roads. V2V communication architecture consists of vehicles mounted with on board units/application units (OBU/AU), smart signals, road side units (RSU), smart street signs, and other artefacts on the street with wireless interfaces. A reference architecture is shown in Fig. 1.8. In a V2V network four communication types are possible:

1. In-vehicle communication
2. Vehicle to vehicle communication
3. Vehicle to broadband communication
4. Vehicle to RSU communication.

In-vehicle communication is for the domain inside vehicle. It typically raises alert messages related problems that is specific to a vehicle. For example, hitting low fuel, air pressure variation on wheels, driver is feeling drowsy and, so on. Vehicle to vehicle communication is used for inter vehicles domain. It may send out information related traffic situation, constructions on roads, diversion to be taken, or some vehicle needs help, and so on. Vehicle to broadband communication is related cloud processing requirements as well as infotainments. Vehicle to RSU communication enables vehicle to learn real-time updates and re-routing plans, etc.

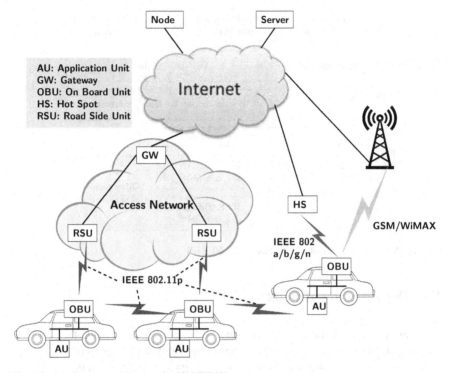

Fig. 1.8 A reference architecture for VANET [2]

The protocol architecture of V2V communication should be able to distinguish among three types of wireless communication technologies: IEEE 802.11p, conventional WLAN IEEE 802.11a/b/g/n and GPRS/UMTS. On the top these physical layer specific network layer technologies should coordinate with the transport layers. The basic reference architecture for protocols will be as shown in Fig. 1.9. However, in implementation some MAC layer could be merged into one single layer. Typically, the wireless standards for V2V network specifies a range up to 300 m. So about 5–10 hops network could disseminate information of about 1.5 km from a vehicle. Another supporting technology is cloud-based information processing. The cloud communication could be through 4G/5G with vehicle terminals.

In summary some of the research themes centered around driverless car connected to the contents of this book are:

- Modeling of wireless networks and new protocols with QoS support.
- Vehicle to vehicle ad hoc networks.
- Localization and location based services.
- Multi sensor data fusion and processing.
- Context aware computing.
- Cloud processing support with new data analytics.

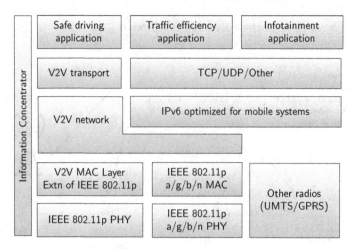

Fig. 1.9 A reference protocol architecture for VANET [2]

1.8   Organization of Book

The main purpose of the material covered in this book is to provide the reader a deeper understanding of wireless communication and data management.

The first part of the book consists of seven chapters (Chaps. 2–8), deal with different wireless networks standards, protocols, routings and applications. There are many excellent text books [8, 19, 21, 22] which cover physical layers of wireless communication system that includes mathematical theories behind characteristics and propagation of radio waves. In this book our focus is in the realm of standards, protocols, routings and applications.

A number of books addressing many aspects of mobile data management have been published in the past [7, 11, 20]. However, there are not many well known books where mobile data management appears as a central theme of the text in an organized manner. The second part of the book, consisting of eight chapters (Chaps. 9–16) dealing with mobile data management, is an attempt in this direction. We created an organization with a view that senior undergraduate students and research scholars may find it helpful to develop interests in the area.

There was a slight dilemma in deciding whether the contents of Chap. 9 can be strictly classified as under mobile data management issues. Apart from sensor fusion, it deals with two network related issues in WSNs namely, routing and integration with IP. We justify our decision to classify Chap. 9 under mobile data management on the basis of following facts:

- Sensor nodes unlike IP based nodes are data centric, and WSN routing is data centric.
- Many existing deployments of WSNs interoperate with IP network through specialized sensor gateways which implement middlewares for IP integration.

- Sensor fusion techniques included in this chapter strictly represent data management issues.

References

1. J.C. Augusto, P. McCullagh, Ambient intelligence: concepts and applications. Int. J. Comput. Sci. Inf. Syst. **4**(1), 1–28 (2007)
2. R. Baldessari, The author team. C2C and CC system (2007). http://elib.dlr.de/48380/1/C2C-CC_manifesto_v1.1.pdf
3. A. Boukerche, Y. Ren, A secure mobile healthcare system using trust-based multicast scheme. IEEE J. Sel. Areas Commun. **27**(4), 387–399 (2009)
4. J.H. Christensen, Using RESTful Web-Services and Cloud Computing to Create Next Generation Mobile Applications, *The 24th ACM SIGPLAN Conference Companion on Object Oriented Programming Systems Languages and Applications (OOPSLA)*, Oct 2009, pp. 627–634
5. A.K. Dey, G.D. Abowd, A conceptual framework and a toolkit for supporting rapid prototyping of context-aware applications. Human-Comput. Inter. (HCI) J. **16**(2-4):97–166 (2001)
6. H.T. Dinh, C. Lee, D. Niyato, P.A. Wang, Survey of mobile cloud computing: architecture, applications, and approaches. Wireless Commun. Mobile Comput. **13**(18), 1587–1611 (2013)
7. B. Reza (ed.), *Mobile Computing Principles: Designing and Developing Mobile Applications with UML and XML* (Cambridge University Press, New York, USA, 2004)
8. V.K. Garg, *Wireless Networks Evolution: 2G to 3G* (Morgan Kaufman, 2010)
9. M.F. Goodchild, D.M. Johnston, D.J. Maguire, V.T. Noronha, Distributed and Mobile Computing, *A Research Agenda for Geographic Information, Science* (2004), pp. 257–286
10. A.V. Halteren, R. Bults, K. Wack, D. Kontantas, I. Widya, N. Dokovsky, G. Koprinkov, V. Jone, R. Herzog, Mobile patient monitoring: the mobile health system. J. Inf. Technol. Healthc. **2**(5), 365–373 (2004)
11. T. Imielinski, H.F. Korth (eds.), *Mobile Computing* (Kluwer Academic Publishers, Norwell, MA, USA, 1996)
12. Cisco Visual Networking Index, Global Mobile Data Traffic Forecast Update, 2011–2016, February 14 2012
13. T. Jiang, S. Petrovic, U. Ayyer, S. Husain, Self-driving cars: disruptive or incremental. Appl. Innov. Rev. **1**, 3–22 (2015)
14. L. Lamport, Distribution. Technical report, Microsoft, 1987
15. L. Liu, R. Moulic, D. Shea, Cloud service portal for mobile device management, *The 7th IEEE International Conference on E-Business Engineering (ICEBE)*, Nov 2010, pp. 474–478
16. G. Moakley, Smart freight technology powered by internet of things. http://www.intel.com/content/www/us/en/internet-of-things/solution-briefs/smart-freight-technology-brief.html, Jan 2014
17. H. Nakashima, H. Aghajan, J.C. Augusto, *Handbook of Ambient Intelligence and Smart Environments* (Springer, 2009)
18. World Health Organization, mhealth: new horizons for health through mobile technologies. Second Global Survey on eHealth 3 (2011)
19. K. Pahlavan, P. Krishnamurthy, *Principles of Wireless Networks: A Unified Approach*, 1st edn. (Prentice Hall PTR, Upper Saddle River, NJ, USA, 2001)
20. E. Pitoura, G. Samaras, *Data Management in Mobile Computing* (Springer, 2012)
21. T.S. Rappaport, *Wireless Communications: Principles and Practice*, 2nd edn. (Prentice Hall PTR, 2002)
22. J.H. Schiller, *Mobile Communications* (Addison-Wesley, 2003)
23. U. Varshney, Pervasive healthcare and wireless health monitoring. Mobile Netw. Appl. **12**, 113–127 (2007)

24. T. Verbelen, P. Simoens, F.D. Turck, B. Dhoedt, The Third ACM Workshop on Mobile Cloud Computing and Services (MCS '12), *Cloudlets: Bringing the Cloud to the Mobile User* (ACM, New York, NY, USA, 2012), pp. 29–36
25. R. Want, A. Hopper, V. Falcao, J. Gibbons, The active badge location system. ACM Trans. Inf. Syst. **10**(1), 91–102 (1992)
26. M. Weiser, Some computer science issues in ubiquitous computing. Commun. ACM **36**(7), 75–84 (1993)
27. M. Weiser, R. Gold, J.S. Brown, The origins of ubiquitous computing research at PARC in the late 1980s. IBM Syst. J. **38**(4), 693–696 (1999)
28. D. West, How mobile devices are transforming healthcare. Issues Technol. Innov. **18**(1), 1–11 (2012). May
29. G.M. Youngblood, D.J. Cook, L.B. Holder, E.O. Heierman, Automation intelligence for the smart environment, *The International Joint Conference on Artificial Intelligence*, pp. 1513–1514 (2005)

Chapter 2
Cellular Wireless Communication

2.1 Introduction

Originally, the focus of mobile radio systems design was towards increasing the coverage of a single transceiver. A single powerful base station was employed to provide connectivity to all mobile devices in a service area. Since spectrum length allocated for private communication is limited, it led to spectral congestion in the service area when large number of mobile clients became concurrently active. Typically, in radio communication system, a user requires about 30 kHz for voice communication. Therefore, if a high power antenna is mounted on a large tower to cover an entire town, it can support just about 25 MHz/30 kHz = 833 users, assuming that 25 MHz spectral band is available for private communication. An obvious way to get around the technical limitations and increase both the capacity and coverage is to reuse allocated frequencies without interferences. The idea was driven by a simple counter thought to the use of high powered transceiver. When a limited range transceiver is used then the wireless connectivity can be provided only in a small finite area of few hundred square meters. However, the frequency of an already deployed transceivers can now be reused by deploying another similar transceiver at a distance where the new transceiver does not interfere with the transceivers which were deployed earlier. In other words, spectral congestion can be eliminated by developing an architecture that would allow spatial multiplexing.

The concept of cellular architecture [3, 5, 6, 9] became the turning point in wireless communication technologies based on frequency reuse. The success of spatial multiplexing depends not only on elimination of interferences but also to provide continuous uninterrupted coverage. To provide continuous coverage, the uncovered gaps in coverage area should be serviced by the transceivers operating with frequencies different from the previously deployed transceivers. The proposed deployment of transceivers is equivalent to partitioning of a large coverage area using certain small finite continuous area which may be appropriately called as a cell and serviced by a single transceiver.

© Springer Nature Singapore Pte Ltd. 2017
R.K. Ghosh, *Wireless Networking and Mobile Data Management*,
DOI 10.1007/978-981-10-3941-6_2

The frequency reuse problem can be viewed in terms of map coloring. In a map, regions are typically demarcated by different colors. If two adjacent regions are colored by same color then it is difficult to distinguish one from the other. Since, multi-colored printing is expensive, as few colors as possible should be used for coloring of a map. It is well known that map coloring can be accomplished by use of four colors [11]. In a way, frequency reuse can be seen as similar to reuse of colors in coloring of a map. There are, however, many differences. Frequency reuse requires a minimum separation between cells which is dependent on the strength of signal interferences between the cells. However, one single color can be used for coloring two regions in a map provided a separation of one region exists in between the two. The problems like co-channel and adjacent channel interferences which are encountered in planning of frequency reuse have no parallels in the map coloring.

Under ideal scenario, wireless signals may be assumed to propagate equally in all directions. Therefore, a cell representing the coverage area of an antenna can be considered as a circle. To provide continuous coverage, we need to find a packing of the desired area using circles, each having an area equal to that of a cell. The packing has to be done in a way such that there are no uncovered gaps in the service area. This is possible in the way as illustrated by Fig. 2.1 where the circles overlap minimally. The common chords of a circle with adjacent overlapping circles define a hexagonal area within that circle as indicated by the hexagon in the figure. The collection of hexagons like the one shown in the figure, packs the service area without leaving gaps. From here on, we will consider a cell to be a regular hexagon as explained. In reality, however, this is not the case. Radio waves like light waves are affected by reflection, refraction, diffraction, absorption, polarization and scattering. In reality terrain structures could be very different from one coverage area to another. There may be tall buildings, hillocks and tall trees which come in the way of signal

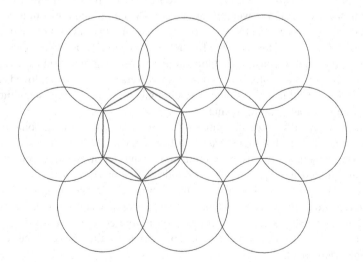

Fig. 2.1 Cell packing of a coverage area

transmission. The actual shape of a cell is typically determined by field measurements radio signal propagation. But for convenience in presentation of basic ideas, assuming the cell to have a hexagonal boundary would suffice.

2.2 Frequency Planning

Figure 2.2 illustrates the frequency reuse concept. The set of cells in same shade, use the same frequency. Typically, an antenna is designed to work over the entire frequency spectrum. But it is possible to block most part of the spectrum and leave only a small group of selected channels on an antenna. So, a cell can be assigned a selected group of channels for communication inside it. The group of channels allocated to one cell will thus be different from the groups of channels assigned to the antennas of its geographically adjacent cells. The process of allocating channel groups to cells in a coverage area is called frequency reuse or frequency planning.

If a system has C duplex channels then each cell x can be allocated a set of C_x channels, where $C_x < C$. Assuming that C channels are equally divided among a group of N cells where each cell gets C_x number of channels, $C = N \times C_x$. The group of N cells which collectively share C channels is called a cluster. If there are R_c replicated clusters, the capacity K of the system is $K = R_c \times N \times C_x = R_c \times C$. This means that the capacity of a cellular system is directly proportional to the number of clusters. Since a cluster defines a full reuse of the set of allocated frequencies, the

Fig. 2.2 Frequency reuse concept

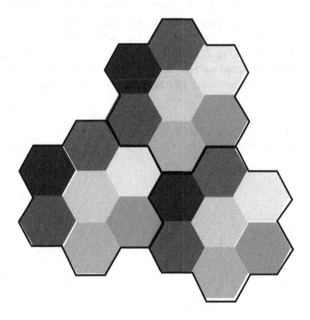

size of a cluster is the determining factor for capacity of a cellular based wireless communication system.

The cells which use same frequencies for communication are referred to as co-channel cells. Co-channel interferences can be minimized by increasing the reuse distance. So, if the cell radius is not changed, the cluster size N should be increased in order to increase the co-channel distance. But if N becomes large then a given service area can be covered by only a few number of clusters. So, the capacity of the service area, which depends on the replication of clusters, cannot be increased substantially. If the value of N is decreased then more clusters will be needed to cover the service area, so the capacity will increase. When cluster size becomes small, the distance between co-channel cells will become small. Though it allows reuse of the same frequency more frequently, the co-channel interferences increase. Thus, in order to maximize the capacity over a coverage area while it is desirable to keep N low, care should be taken so that co-channel interferences do not begin to affect the quality of communication.

The effect of frequency reuse can be best understood through a simple example. Suppose, initially a single high power transceiver was operating with a private spectrum of 25 MHz. This transceiver was replaced by 28 low power transceivers. Let the cluster size be 7. Then the effective spectrum allocation increases by four fold to 25 MHz $\times$ 4 = 100 MHz after replacing the high power transceiver. Each cell gets an allocation of 25 MHz/7 = 3.57 MHz of spectrum under the new system. Assuming voice communication to require 30 KHz, each cell can support up to 3.57 MHz/30 kHz = 119 users. The number of users in each cluster remains at 119 $\times$ 7 = 833. However, due to replications of clusters, the total number of users that can be supported under the new system increases by four fold to 833 $\times$ 4 = 3332.

With underlying assumption of a hexagonal layout of cells, it is possible to derive the formula for reuse distance. Let us first examine the geometry of a hexagonal cell. As shown in Fig. 2.3, the length of a side of a regular hexagon inscribed in a circle of radius R is also equal to R. Each side of this regular hexagon is at a distance $R\sqrt{3}/2$ units from the center of hexagon. The area of such a hexagon is $6(\sqrt{3}/4)R^2$ unit^2.

Fig. 2.3 A regular hexagon
inscribed in circle of radius R

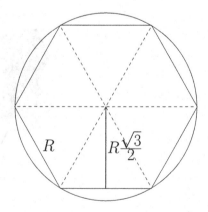

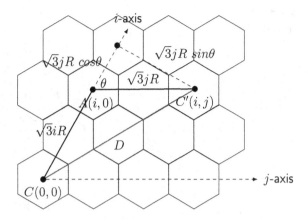

Fig. 2.4 Cell distance using hexagonal cell geometry

Now let us see how the reuse distance can be calculated. But, before that the unit for measurement of distance should be abstracted out from consideration. To realize it, we assume the centers of cells to be at integer coordinates. The arrangement of the cell centers according to hexagonal layout, thus, form a grid system whose axes are at an angle of $\pi/3$. Using the above fact and some simple properties of regular hexagon, the following lemma provides the relationship between the distance of a co-channel cell from a cell.

Lemma 2.1 *Let the coordinate of a cell C be (0, 0) and that of its co-channel cell C′ be (i, j). Then co-channel distance $D = CC′$ is equal to $R\sqrt{3(i^2 + ij + j^2)}$, where R denotes the length of a side of the regular hexagon representing a cell.*

Proof Consider the Fig. 2.4. Since, the coordinates of the cell centers are given by a pair of integers, and the axes of the coordinate system between them form an angle of $\theta = \pi/3$, $C′$ can be reached from C by traversing i cells in one axial direction then turning $\pi/3$ in clockwise and then hopping j cells in the other axial direction. From the above figure, distance $AB = \sqrt{3}jR\cos \pi/3$, $BC′ = \sqrt{3}jR\sin \pi/3$. So

$$
\begin{aligned}
D^2 &= (\sqrt{3}iR + \sqrt{3}jR\cos \pi/3)^2 + (\sqrt{3}jR\sin \pi/3)^2 \\
&= R^2(3i^2 + 6ij\cos \pi/3 + 3j^2\cos^2 \pi/3 + 3j^2\sin^2 \pi/3) \\
&= R^2(3i^2 + 3ij + 3j^2) \\
&= 3R^2(i^2 + ij + j^2)
\end{aligned}
$$

Each cell in a cluster is assumed to have identical wireless range, and equal number of channels. So, the number of cells, N, per cluster can be obtained by determining the area of the cluster and then dividing it by the area of a cell. The area of a cluster can be found easily from the simple analysis of hexagonal geometry.

Fig. 2.5 Cluster area
approximates to a regular
hexagon

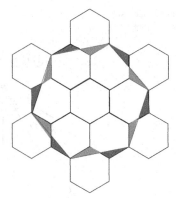

(a) Cluster hexagon.

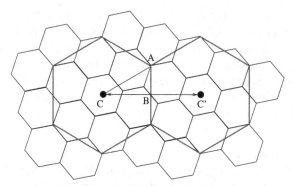

(b) Area of cluster hexagon.

Lemma 2.2 *The cluster size* $N = i^2 + ij + j^2$.

Proof Consider the diagram in Fig. 2.5a. Let the large regular hexagon enclosing a cluster be referred to as cluster hexagon for brevity. Consider the shaded tiny triangles in the figure. A pair of adjacent shaded triangles one inside and the other outside the cluster hexagon are congruent. So the area of the cluster of cells is equal to the cluster hexagon indicted in Fig. 2.5a.

Now consider Fig. 2.5b. The distance between the centers C and C' of two adjacent cluster is D. The angle CAB is equal to $\pi/3$. So, the length $CA = (D/2)/\sin \pi/3 = D/\sqrt{3}$ which is equal to the radius of the cluster hexagon.

As explained earlier, the area of a single hexagonal cell of side R is $6R^2\sqrt{3}/4$. Since, a cluster is also a regular hexagon of side $D/\sqrt{3}$, its area is given by $Cluster_{area} = 6\frac{D^2}{4\sqrt{3}}$. Since the area of cluster divided by the area of one cell should be equal to N, we have

Fig. 2.6 Co-channel cells

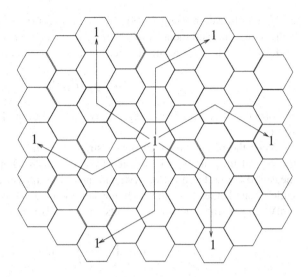

$$N = \left(\frac{D^2}{4\sqrt{3}}\right) \bigg/ \left(\frac{R^2\sqrt{3}}{4}\right) = \frac{D^2}{3R^2} = \frac{3R^2(i^2 + ij + j^2)}{3R^2}$$
$$= i^2 + ij + j^2$$

Figure 2.6 depicts co-channel cells of a cell which use the same frequency. Here $i = 2$ and $j = 2$, and cluster size is $N = 2^2 + 2.2 + 2^2 = 12$. The ratio $D/R = \sqrt{3N}$ denoted by Q represents co-channel reuse ratio. A small value of Q means N is small. This leads to large capacity. However, when Q is large, it leads to low interference; hence better transmission quality. A trade off has to be made between capacity and transmission quality.

2.2.1 Co-channel Interference

Co-channel interference is one of the major problem faced by service providers in setting up wireless communication service. For a good understanding of how interference could affect communication, it is important to examine radio signal measurement and propagation.

DeciBel is the unit used for the measurement of relative strengths of radio signals from two different radios. Ten deciBels (dB) equals one Bel (B) which represents the power ratio of 1:10. A power ratio of 1:100 equals 2 B or 20 dB. Similarly, the power ratio 1:1000 is measured as 3 B or 30 dB. Use of log scale in measurement of relative power strengths simplifies the calculation. The log scale expression $\log_{10}(P_2/P_1)$, gives the measurement of relative power strength due to amplification in Bels. For example, if an amplifier outputs 100 W with an input of 100 mW, then the power gain due to amplification is $\log_{10}(100/0.1) = \log_{10} 1000 = 3$ B or 30 dB. In the case of radio signal measurements, power ratios are usually very small. So, deciBels is the preferred unit for expressing smaller power ratios. Accordingly, the formula

$$10 \log_{10} (P_2/P_1),$$

is normally used for measuring relative power strengths between the two radio sources.

When the measurement of power strength is made with reference to 1 W then the unit of measurement is denoted by dB or dBW. Sometimes power strength is measured with reference to 1 mW, and the unit of measurement is denoted by dBm. Unless stated otherwise, the unit of measurement here will be dBm. Zero dBm equals 1 mW. In general, a power of P watts equals x dBm, where

$$x = 10 \log_{10} \left(\frac{P}{10^{-3}} \right) = 30 + 10 \log_{10} P$$

A negative gain indicates a signal decay or attenuation, which is represented by a power ratio less than 1.

Let us consider an example to understand the significance of log scale in computation. Suppose, a micro-wave system uses a 10 W transmitter. This transmitter is connected by a cable with 0.7 dBm loss to a 13 dBm antenna. Let the atmospheric loss be 137 dB on transmission. The receiver antenna with 11 dBm gain connected by a cable with 1.3 dBm loss to a receiver. Then the power at the receiver can be calculated as follows:

Transmitter output: 10 W = 10000 mW.
Amplification gain at transmitter: $10 \log_{10}(10000/1) = 40$ dBm.

Then the relative strength of power at the receiver equals $(40 - 0.7 + 13 - 137)$ dBm $= -84.7$ dBm including the amplification gain, atmospheric loss and loss due to cable connecting the amplifier to its antenna. On the receiver side, the antenna and the connecting cable together lead to $(11-1.3)$ dBm gain. So the net power received by the receiver is $(-84.7 + 9.7)$ dBm $= -75$ dBm.

The co-channel interferences experienced by a cell is due to the use of same group of channels in the nearby cells. The quality of the signals received from the current base station is affected by co-channel interferences. As Fig. 2.7 depicts, the wireless signals from the base stations in co-channel cells around a cell ripple out much like waves in water when a stone is thrown into the center of a pond. The ratio of the signal strength from the current cell and the strength of co-channel interferences, provides a measure for the quality of communication. The Signal to Interference Ratio (SIR) should be monitored by individual mobile terminals. If the strength of interference increases compared to the strength of signal, then the quality of communication deteriorates. A Mobile Terminal (MT) experiencing low SIR should try to switch to a neighboring cell which may provide better SIR. The SIR is given

Fig. 2.7 Interferences due to
propagation of co-channel
signals

$$S/I = S/\left(\sum_{i=1}^{i_0} I_i\right),$$

where I_i is the interfering signal received from co-channel i, and i_0 is the number of adjacent co-channel cells.

In free space, the average signal strength known to decay according a power law involving the distance between the transmitter and the receiver. Let d be the distance between the transmitter and the receiver, and P_0 be the power received at a near-by reference point in the far-field region (with a distance of 2λ) of the transmitter antenna. Then the average received power P_r at receiver from the transmitting antenna is given by:

$$P_r = P_0\left(\frac{d}{d_0}\right)^{-n}.$$

In reality P_r is proportional to the expression in the right hand side of the equation. Here, the constant of proportionality is assumed to be 1. However, its actual value will depend on antenna gain, path loss exponent and carrier wavelength. The above equation for power received, when expressed in terms of dBm, becomes

$$P_r(\text{dBm}) = P_0(\text{dBm}) - 10n\log_{10}\left(\frac{d}{d_0}\right).$$

Now let us examine the topological configuration of cells, and study how a MT may arrive at a better approximation of SIR. Suppose, the MT is at a distance D_i from i-th co-channel cell. The distance is measured from the cell center where the corresponding base station is located. So, the signal attenuation from ith co-channel cell is proportional to D_i^{-n}. The signal strength beamed from the current base station to the mobile terminal is proportional to R^{-n}, where R is the radio range of the base station. Assuming all interfering co-channel base stations to be at equal distance from the MT, the SIR (in dB) is equal to

$$S/I = \left(R^{-n} / \left(\sum_{i=1}^{i_0} D_i^{-n} \right) \right)$$
$$= \frac{(D/R)^n}{i_0} \tag{2.1}$$
$$= \left(\sqrt{3N} \right)^n / i_0.$$

Let the minimum value of SIR for good voice quality be 18 dBm. In order to check whether a cluster size of $N = 7$ in a cellular based wireless system with the path loss exponent $n = 4$ would meet the requirement of voice quality, let us compute SIR value received by a MT which is located at center of its current cell. Using Eq. 2.1:

$$10 \log_{10}(S/I) = 10 \log_{10} \left(\left(\sqrt{3N} \right)^4 / i_0 \right)$$
$$= 10 \log_{10} \left(\left(\sqrt{21} \right)^4 / 6 \right)$$
$$= 10 \log_{10} 73.5$$
$$= 10 \times 1.865$$
$$= 18.65$$

As the SIR value is above the required threshold of 18 dBm, a cluster size of 7 is alright when path loss exponent is 4.

When cell sectorization is used with 120° sectors, the number of co-channel cells which is reduced from 6 to 2 for $N = 7$. Therefore,

$$S/I = \frac{1}{2} \left(\sqrt{3N} \right)^n$$

Thus the increase in SIR with sectorization is 3 times more than that without sectorization.

The scenario that a MT will be located at the center of the current cell, occurs very rarely. So, topological configuration of the current cell, its co-channel cells and the position of MT should be taken into account for computing SIR. Figure 2.8 [10] depicts a realistic topological configuration. It is assumed that MT is located at the

Fig. 2.8 Co-channel interference considering exact cell geometry

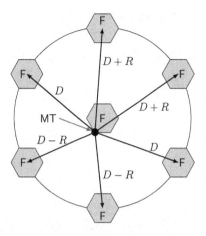

boundary of its current cell. The signal strength received by MT at this position from is at the lowest possible level. With cluster size of 7, there will be two co-channel cells at a distance $D - R$ from MT, two at a distance D and two others at a distance $D + R$ as indicated in Fig. 2.8. So the ratio of power strengths of the current base station and the other interfering base stations, with path loss factor $n = 4$, is

$$S/I = \frac{R^{-4}}{2(D - R)^{-4} + 2D^{-4} + 2(D + R)^{-4}}$$
$$= \frac{1}{2(\sqrt{21} - 1)^{-4} + 2(\sqrt{21})^{-4} + 2(\sqrt{21} + 1)^{-4}}$$

The above expression is equal to 49.56. In terms of deciBels the value of SIR will thus be $10 \log_{10} 49.56 = 17$ dBm. Since the value of SIR is lower than acceptable threshold the voice quality will not be good.

2.2.2 Cell Splitting and Sectoring

As observed earlier, frequency reuse can be increased using smaller cells. But smaller cells will lead to shorter co-channel distance; and therefore, an increase in co-channel interferences. The challenge is to keep interference low and increase the capacity. After a cellular service area has been planned and the infrastructure is in place, any incremental change like adding channels to a cell for handling the increase in traffic load is expensive and difficult to execute. However, two simple ideas, namely,

1. Cell splitting
2. Cell sectoring

are found to be quite effective for handling the increase in traffic load.

Fig. 2.9 Cell splitting

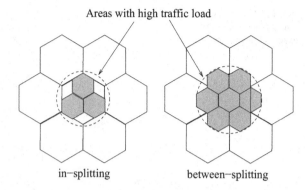

Cell splitting allows creation of smaller cells out of a standard cell. The advantage of cell splitting is that it uses the same idea of spatial multiplexing with smaller cells called microcells. The antennas can be placed on the top of buildings, hills and even on the lamp posts. Smaller cells are placed in or between large cells. Figure 2.9 illustrates the two possible splittings where radius of every microcell is half the radius of a standard cell. Splitting increases the number channels because the number of channels per unit area increases. But the trade off is in terms of increase in co-channel interference. As Eq. 2.1 in Sect. 2.2.1 indicates, co-channel interference can be controlled by keeping the ratio D/R unchanged. If D is decreased, R must also be decreased to keep the ratio at same value. Thus, the transmission power of newly introduced microcells must be reduced to avoid the co-channel interference.

Let P_s be the output power of the transceiver of a standard cell, and P_m be the output power of the transceiver of a microcell. Then the received power P_r at cell boundaries of the two cells are:

$$P_r[\text{original cell}] \propto P_s R^{-n}$$
$$P_r[\text{micro-cell}] \propto P_m (R/2)^{-n}$$

It means that the ratio of transmit powers of a microcell versus a normal cell is 1:16 when path loss exponent is 4. It is not necessary to split all the cells. Sometimes it becomes difficult to exactly identify the coverage area that would require cell splitting. So in practice different cell sizes may co-exist. This calls for careful fine-tuning of power outputs by transceivers so that a safe distance is maintained among the co-channel cells and the co-channel interference is kept at a minimum level. But it makes the channel assignment quite complicated. As we observed, two different transmit powers will be needed to support cell splitting. The channels in a normal cell needs to be divided into two groups: (i) the one corresponding to normal transmit power, and (ii) the other corresponding to a reduced transmit power. The splitting determines the sizes of two channel groups. Initially, only a few channels belong to the reduced transmit power group. But as traffic grows, more and more channels will be required, causing the group of channels with reduced transmit power to grow in size. The splitting continues until the channels used in an area are all of low transmit power. However, the presence of dual cell size calls for better channel switching with mobility of the users. The movements within microcells will lead to more frequent channel switching compared to the movements within normal cells.

Cell sectoring is also used to address the problem of capacity increase. With this approach transmit power of channel is concentrated into a finite sector of the cell. The omni-directional antenna of the cell is replaced by several directional antennas. The sectoring causes receipt of co-channel interference and transmission only within a specified region of the cell. So, it leads to greater reuse of frequencies. Normally a cell is partitioned into three sectors of 120° or six sectors of 60° each as in Fig. 2.10. When sectoring is used the channels of a cell are partitioned into sectored groups, and the channels of a group is used only in one sector. As may be observed from Fig. 2.11, with cluster size of 7, the cells labeled F are co-channel cells. Each cell can

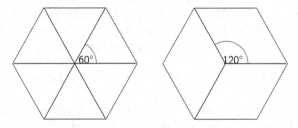

Fig. 2.10 Cell sectoring

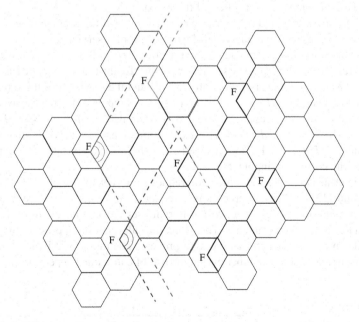

Fig. 2.11 Interference pattern with cell sectoring

receive signals only from two co-channel cells to its left. So, the cells at the center, which is within the signal propagation cones of its two co-channel cells on the left, may receive signals only from these two cells. The signal propagation cone of the co-channel cell vertically up to the left does not include the center cell, so the latter is not affected by co-channel interference due to the former cell.

2.3   Traffic Intensity

An important measurement related to capacity is traffic intensity. In a Telecom system, this measurement is an estimation of traffic pattern, pick load, and channel requirements. The traffic intensity varies over the day. The probability of securing a connection in busy hours is directly related to traffic intensity. The unit of measurement is *Erlang* [2]. One Erlang is equal to the total traffic generated by the voice calls amounting to 60 min. For example, if there are 40 calls in 1 h with each call having an average duration of 5 min, then the traffic in Erlang is:

$$\text{Traffic in hour } = (40 \times 5)/60 = 3.33 \text{ Erlangs.}$$

Formally, in a lossy system, Grade of Service (GoS) determines the probability of call blocking, which is computed by *Erlang B* traffic model. Erlang B traffic model is used by Telecom companies to determine the number of lines required to run a service based on anticipated traffic and future expansion.

Let λ be arrival rate and μ be service rate. Then $1/\lambda$ is the average time between arrival of two consecutive requests and $1/\mu$ is the average service time. For example, if the average duration of a connection is 3 min, then $1/\mu = 0.05$ (hour), equivalently, in an average $\mu = 20$ calls can be serviced per hour. To illustrate a concrete case, refer to Fig. 2.12 depicting the arrival of call requests and the servicing of these requests for 5 users. The intervals $I_i = a_{i+1} - a_i$, for $1 \leq i \leq 4$ represent the inter-arrival time. The duration of call services are represented by intervals $S_1 = d_1 - a_1, S_2 = d_2 - d_1$, $S_3 = d_3 - d_2, S_4 = d_4 - d_3, S_5 = d_4 - d_5$. The arrival and service rates are given by expressions $1/E(I_i)$ and $1/E(S_i)$ respectively, where $E(.)$ represents the expected values of the corresponding intervals.

The inter-arrival times for connection requests are typically modeled by Poisson distribution [13]. A Poisson process is a sequence of events which are randomly spaced in time. In a wireless network different users seek connections at different times independent of one another. Therefore, the call requests (representing events) in a cell can be represented by a Poisson process. The rate λ of a Poisson process is the average number of number events (arrival of call requests) per unit time over

Fig. 2.12 Distribution of the arrival of requests and their servicing

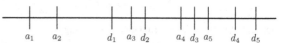

a long period. The probability of n call requests arriving during an interval of time $[0, \delta)$ under Poisson process is,

$$Pr[n_{t+\delta} - n_t = n] = \frac{(\lambda\delta)^n}{n!}e^{-\lambda\delta}, \text{ for } n = 0, 1, \ldots,$$

where n_t denotes the number of arrivals since the time $t = 0$, and δ is the call inter-arrival time. For example, if we observe a system from some arbitrary time $t \geq 0$ during a small interval of time $\delta \geq 0$, the probabilities of arrival of number of call requests are:

$$Pr[n_{t+\delta} - n_t = 0] = 1 - \lambda\delta + O(\delta^2)$$
$$Pr[n_{t+\delta} - n_t = 1] = \lambda\delta + O(\delta^2)$$
$$Pr[n_{t+\delta} - n_t \geq 2] = O(\delta^2),$$

where $O(\delta^2)$ represents the probability of more than 1 call request arriving in time δ. Since, δ is small, no more than 1 call request can arrive at the system during this interval. Therefore, the event of two or more calls arriving in the system within an interval of δ can be considered as impossible. In other words, terms of $O(\delta^2)$ can be safely ignored.

Assume that the number of channels is C. It means C connection requests can be serviced concurrently. Therefore, we have $M/M/C$ kind of queuing system [2] with following parameters:

- The arrival process is Poisson with arrival rate λ.
- The service time is exponential with servicing rate μ.
- The number of servers or the channels for serving the connection requests is C.
- The capacity or number clients which can be in the queue is also C.

The service scenario is best understood as a system with a limited number service lines connecting a large number of input lines (one for each call request) as shown in Fig. 2.13a. Figure 2.13b illustrates the same, but depicts how some of the service requests are met and others are dropped with probability of dropping a request being P_b.

Initially, 0 channels are used by system. Over a small interval the system may continue in state 0 with a probability of $1 - \lambda\delta$. The system will change to state 1 from state 0 with a probability $\lambda\delta$. But if one channel is already in use (i.e., system in state 1) then transition to state 0 will take place with a probability of $\mu\delta$. This implies that the systems continues in state 1 with a probability of $1 - \lambda\delta - \mu\delta$. So the system states and transitions is depicted by Fig. 2.14. Over a long period of time, the system reaches steady state. In a steady system if n channels remain occupied then, writing global balance equation for the steady state, we get

$$\lambda\delta P_{n-1} = n\mu\delta P_n, n \leq C,$$
$$\lambda P_{n-1} = n\mu P_n,$$
$$P_1 = (\lambda P_0)/\mu.$$

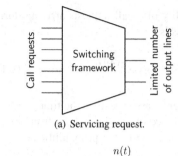

(a) Servicing request.

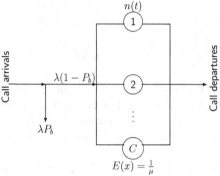

(b) Queueing discipline.

Fig. 2.13 Queuing discipline and service of call requests

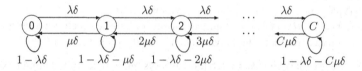

Fig. 2.14 Markov chain representing system state and transitions

The equation expresses the fact that transition from P_{n-1} to P_n is same as the transition from P_n to P_{n-1}. Solving the recurrence in balance equation,

$$P_n = P_0 \left(\frac{\lambda}{\mu} \right)^n \frac{1}{n!}.$$

Note that the sum of probabilities of the system being any of the states $n = 0, 1, 2, \ldots$, is 1. So, we have $\sum_0^C P_n = 1$. Now substituting for P_n in summation in terms of P_0,

$$\sum_0^C P_0 \left(\frac{\lambda}{\mu} \right)^n \frac{1}{n!} = 1$$

Therefore,

$$P_0 = \frac{1}{\sum_{n=0}^{C} \left(\frac{\lambda}{\mu}\right)^n \frac{1}{n!}}.$$

We already know that $P_C = P_0 \left(\frac{\lambda}{\mu}\right)^C \frac{1}{C!}$. This leads us to the expression for P_C as follows:

$$P_C = \frac{\left(\frac{\lambda}{\mu}\right)^C \frac{1}{C!}}{\sum_{n=0}^{C} \left(\frac{\lambda}{\mu}\right)^n \frac{1}{n!}}$$

The traffic intensity is determined by the ratio of arrival and departure rates. This ratio should not be allowed to exceed 1, otherwise request queue will build up. So, traffic intensity is actually a measure of congestion in the system. Let the traffic intensity be represented by $A = \lambda/\mu$. Now substituting A for traffic intensity Erlang B formula becomes:

$$P_C = \frac{A^C \frac{1}{C!}}{\sum_{n=0}^{C} A^n \frac{1}{n!}}.$$

The above formula is known as *blocked call cleared* formula as it determines the GoS for traffic system without a queue for blocked calls. Using Erlang B formula, the probability that a client's call request will not be serviced in a blocked call cleared system is:

$$Pr[\text{call blocking}] = \frac{A^C/C!}{\sum_{n=0}^{C} A^n/n!}.$$

To make computation of probability simple, the right hand side of the above equation can be rewritten as follows:

$$\frac{A^C/C!}{\sum_{k=0}^{C} A^n/n!} = \frac{1}{1 + \sum_{1}^{C} \left(\frac{C}{A}\right)\left(\frac{C-1}{A}\right)\ldots\left(\frac{C-n+1}{A}\right)}$$

The expression under summation in the numerator can be unrolled and recast using Horner's rule as follows:

$$\frac{C}{A} + \frac{C}{A}\cdot\frac{C-1}{A} + \ldots + \frac{C}{A}\cdot\frac{C-1}{A}\ldots\frac{1}{A} = \frac{C}{A}\left(\ldots\left(1 + \frac{2}{A}\left(1 + \frac{1}{A}\right)\right)\ldots\right).$$

The use of above expression restricts round-off and truncation errors in computation.

For an illustration of Erlang B formula, consider the following example. Suppose there are 240 connection requests per hour in peak time. So, the arrival rate is $\lambda = 240$. Let the average call duration be 3 min, or 0.05 h, then the service rate $\mu = 20$. It gives $A = 240/20 = 12$. Note that average number of request per hour $1/\lambda$, and the average call duration is $1/\mu$. Hence, the ratio $A = \lambda/\mu$ being equal to the product of the average number of requests and the average duration of the calls, is called the *busy hour traffic* (BHT). If there are 25 channels then the probability of call being blocked due to non-availability of a channel is given by

$$P_b = \frac{12^{25}\frac{1}{25!}}{\sum_{n=0}^{25} 12^n \frac{1}{n!}} = 3.78 \times 10^{-4}.$$

For a fixed value of A, we can indeed prove that the call blocking probability for busy hour traffic decreases with increase in C. When the number of channels increased by 1, the number of channels become $C + 1$. In steady state, balance equation tells us that $(C + 1)\mu P_{C+1} = \lambda P_C$. Applying a sequence of simplifications we get:

$$\begin{aligned}
P_{C+1} &= \frac{\lambda}{\mu} \frac{P_C}{C+1} = \frac{A}{C+1} \cdot \frac{A^C/C!}{1 + \sum_1^{C+1} A^k/k!} \\
&< \frac{A^C/C!}{\frac{C+1}{A} \sum_1^{C+1} A^n/n!} \\
&= \frac{A^C/C!}{\frac{C+1}{A} \sum_0^C A^{n+1}/(n+1)!} \\
&= \frac{A^C/C!}{\sum_0^C ((C+1)/(n+1))(A^n/n!)} \\
&< \frac{A^C/C!}{\sum_0^C A^n/n!} = P_C.
\end{aligned}$$

The boundary values for the above probability distribution function are $Pr[C = 0]$ = 1, and $Pr[C = \infty] = 0$. Since the function is monotonic, with a given value of A, and a given value of call blocking probability p, there is a smallest integer C, such that the inequality $Pr[C] < p$ holds. This implies that the method of bisection can be applied to obtain the value of C.

2.4 Channel Assignment

Frequency planning consistent with the twin objective of increasing the capacity and guaranteeing the minimum co-channel interference is very important for efficient communication over wireless interfaces. The objective of frequency reuse can be met by employing different techniques such as partitioning the spectrum along frequency, time, or code. Frequency division scheme partitions spectrum allocating distinct frequency bands. A small guard band is placed between two adjacent bands to separate the frequencies. Time division achieves channel separation by disjoint time intervals called slots, while code division ensures channel separation by using different modulation codes. It is possible to combine different channel separation schemes. For example, time division and frequency division can be combined to divide each frequency band (obtained from frequency division) into time slots. The bottom line of the division principles is to maximize the separation of a channel with desired quality and also to maximize the channel utilization.

Broadly speaking channel assignments can be classified either as fixed or dynamic. The choice of specific channel assignment policy affects the performance. The impacts are felt in terms of quality of services as a connected mobile device moves from one cell to another. For example, an active communication may get terminated if mobile terminal moves from one cell to another which has no free channel. Thus channel assignment is one of the critical element of mobile communication.

Each cell is allocated a fixed number of channels in a fixed channel assignment scheme. A new connection in a cell can be activated only if there is a free channel. If all the channels are occupied then the request for a connection cannot be accommodated. It means an active communication will get terminated if a connected mobile terminal moves from a cell to another having no free channel. Many variations to fixed channel assignment scheme exists in order to eliminate the unpleasant interruptions during an ongoing communication. The process by which an active connection can be maintained as a mobile terminal moves from one cell to another is called *handoff*. Handoff provides the basic capability of mobility with an active connection in a cellular based wireless communication system, a detailed discussion on handoff can be found in Sect. 2.1.

In dynamic channel allocation schemes, no channel is permanently allocated to any cell. Each time a base station requires a channel to be allocated for a call, it requests the mobile switching center (MSC) for the allocation of a channel. The switch then allocates a channel using some sophisticated algorithms that can take care of the future call blockings, the volume of inter-cell and intra-cell handoffs, and co-channel interferences among other things. The effectiveness of dynamic channel allocation depends on MSC's ability to collect real-time data on channel occupancy, traffic distribution and received signal strength indication (RSSI) of all channels on a continuous basis. So, dynamic channel allocation increases both storage and computational load on the MSCs.

Channel assignment schemes can be implemented either in centralized or in decentralized fashion. In a centralized assignment, a central controller assigns the channels. In a decentralized assignment, many possibilities exists. The channels may be assigned by the local cell, or by the cell where the call originated, or even selected by mobile devices.

A general approach for the solution of the channel assignment problem is to use graph abstraction for representing cellular system, and transform the problem into a graph coloring problem. Then, the existing solutions for graph coloring can be applied for solving channel assignment problem.

Interference graph plays an important role in planning channel assignment. Such a graph is defined as follows:

- Every vertex represents a cell or a base station.
- Each edge (u, v) is associated with a weight $W(u, v)$ which is proportional to the maximum strength of signal interference between cells represented by u and v.
- There is also a system wide value W representing the minimum separation (maximum permissible signal interference) between any pair of channels allocated to the same cell.
- Each vertex v is also associated with a non-negative integer which indicates the channel requirements for the cell represented by v.

In theory, such a graph is a complete graph with lot of edges having 0 weights. In order to avoid interference, two channels a and b can be allocated to different cells u and v provided $|a - b| \leq W(u, v)$. This means frequency band representing channel a and that representing channel b cannot have mutual interference exceeding the prescribed weight $W(u, v)$. The value W is used to ensure minimum channel separation for channels allocated to a single cell. That is, if channels a and b are used in the same cell, then $|a - b| \leq W$.

The graph theoretic formulation given above is not quite concrete. From the point of view of a service provider, the important formulations are those that can handle both resource allocation and traffic constraints in different cells. Let us, therefore, discuss about such formulations. Suppose the number of cells be N_{cell}, and T_i is projected traffic requirement in cell C_i, $i = 1, 2, N_{cells}$. Then along with the constraints as stated earlier, new constraints concerning traffic requirements should be added. Therefore, the formulation of channel assignment is as follows:

Problem formulation *Given a number of cells C_i, $1 \leq i \leq N_{cells}$, the requested traffic T_i per cell C_i, the interference graph with weights W_{ij} and local interference constraint W, assign channels to cells so that*

1. *All frequency constraints are met.*
2. *Cell C_i gets T_i channels chn_{ij}, $1 \leq i \leq N_{cells}$, $1 \leq j \leq T_i$.*
3. *The quantity*

$$N_{channels} = \max\{chn_{ij}\}$$

is minimized.

The above formulation implies that each cell gets channel allocation according to its traffic requirements, and the overall system requirements for the channels is as small as possible.

In most general setting, the channel assignment can be posed as constraint satisfaction problem. An $n \times n$ symmetric matrix $C = \{c_{ij}\}$, known as compatibility matrix is defined, where c_{ij} represents the minimum frequency separation required between cells i and j, and n represents the number of cells. The minimum separation between the frequencies used by two cells ensures that the communication in each cell is free from the interference due to the communication in the other. Since the frequency bands are the evenly spaced, they can be identified by integers. The number of channels required for each cell is represented by a requirement vector $M = \{m_i\}$,

$i = 1, \ldots, n$. The frequency assignment vector $F = \{F_i\}$ is such that F_i is a finite subset of the positive integers which defines the frequencies assigned to cell i. F is admissible provided it satisfies the following constraints:

$$|F_i| = m_i, \text{ for } i = 1, \ldots n$$
$$|f - f'| \geq c_{ij}, \text{ where } f \in F_i \text{ and } f' \in F_j$$

The first constraint is needed to satisfy the channel requirement and the second constraint is needed to satisfy the interference free compatibility between each pair of cells. The largest integer belonging to F is known as the span of the frequency assignment. Note that the largest integer represents the minimum number of channels required for the frequency assignment. So, F with the minimum span constitutes the solution to the problem channel assignment. The problem is known to be NP hard [3].

2.4.1 Fixed Channel Assignment

In fixed channel assignment (FCA) scheme, a fixed number of channels is assigned to each cell. The set of available channels is partitioned into N disjoint sets, where N is the cluster size. As we already know $N = D^2/3R^2$ is related to reuse distance D, and cell radius R.

In a FCA scheme, each of the N cells in a cluster are assigned the same number of channels. If the distribution of traffic load is uniform, then the uniform channel distribution works fine. The overall average call blocking (connection not materializing due to non-availability of a channel) probability will be same as call blocking probability in a cell. But, hardly such an ideal situation ever occurs. There may be both temporal and spatial fluctuations in traffic across the cellular service area. Due to short term variations in traffic, most of the times a FCA scheme is not able to maintain the quality of service and network capacity that may be attainable even with static traffic demand.

2.4.1.1 Borrowing

To remedy this, when a request for a connection is placed in a cell that has no nominal free channels, a common sense driven approach is to borrow a free channel from one of its neighboring cells. The cell which borrows is referred to as the *acceptor* while cell which lends is known as the *donor*. The selection of a free channel from a donor cell should be such that it does not adversely affect the donor cell's ability to satisfy a subsequent request for a connection, and at the same time the borrowed channel does not introduce added interferences on the existing connections in the acceptor cell. In other words, the selection of both the donor cell and the channel to be borrowed should minimize:

1. The probability of donor cell not being able to service a connection request due to non availability of a nominal channel, and
2. The interference due to communication over the borrowed channel on the active communications in the acceptor cell.

The first condition can be met by selecting the donor from one of the neighboring cells (of the acceptor cell) that has the largest number of free channels. The strategy of Borrowing From the Richest (BFR) will also most likely meet the second condition. Because with the availability of more channels, the probability of the borrowed channel interfering with the other active channels in the acceptor's cell will be expectedly low. Once the borrowed channel has been identified, it is locked in the co-channel cells of the donor cell which are at a distance smaller than channel reuse distance from the acceptor cell. Furthermore, the channel that is allocated should be the one that locked in most cells.

To understand the above constraints let us consider an example as shown in Fig. 2.15. Let $C1$ be richest neighboring of C which requires a channel. C will then borrow a channel from $C1$. The borrowed channel should be locked in cells C_1, C_2 and C_6 as the distances of these cells from C are smaller than the prescribed reuse distance. Therefore, borrowing of a channel affects several channels. However, if borrowing is planned carefully then the same channel may concurrently serve as a borrowed channel in different acceptor cells. For example, if cell X now needs to borrow a channel from its neighboring cell $C5$, then $C5$ can loan out the channel that C has borrowed from $C1$. This is because, C and X are at a distance more than the required reuse distance from each other. Therefore, using the same borrowed channel at C and X will not create any additional interference in communication.

Any sophisticated borrowing method will incur penalties for complex searchings. So, a simpler option could be to Borrow from the First Available (BFA) channel from a neighboring cell. However, for implementing BFA, the initial channels assignment is bit different than direct assignment of channels to cells as is done in other FCA schemes. The set of channels is first divided into groups and each group is assigned to cells at a reuse distance D. The channels in a group are numbered in sequence. A group of channels assigned to a cell is subdivided further into two subgroups A and B. The channels belonging to A are used exclusively for calls originating from

Fig. 2.15 Borrowing affects co-channels cells of donor cell

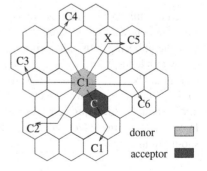

a cell. A cell C can lend channels to another neighboring cells C' only when one is available in subgroup B of C. On arrival of a call request, the nominal channels in the cell are scanned in order and the first available channel is assigned for the call. If no nominal channel is found, then (acceptor) cell C' searches for a free channel in an adjacent cell C having the largest number of channels in group B. As explained earlier, a channel is considered available for borrowing if it is also free in two other co-channel cells (using directional locking strategy) of that chosen neighboring cell. The first free channel encountered in this order is borrowed. This method is known as Borrowing with Channel Order (BCO). Interestingly, BCO compares favorably with the system that performs exhaustive complex searches to identify the channel to be borrowed from a neighboring cell. Furthermore, it has an advantage over other methods by being computationally less expensive.

After the communication over the borrowed channel is complete, that the borrowed channel should be returned to the donor cell. Since borrowing is done due to non-availability of a nominal free channel, the question which naturally arises is whether the borrowed channel should be returned as soon as one of the nominal channels of the acceptor cell becomes free. Interestingly, the decision whether or not to free a borrowed channel could influence systems performance.

Channel reallocation concept is used in conjunction with directional lockings to improve the performance of the system and minimize connections on the borrowed channels. The rules for the channel reallocation are as follows.

1. When a nominal channel becomes free and there is an active connection on a higher order nominal channel in the same cell then this connection is transferred to the lower order nominal channel.
2. When a nominal channel in local cell becomes free and there is an active connection on a borrowed channel from a neighboring cell, then the borrowed channel is returned to neighboring by transferring the connection to a newly freed nominal channel.
3. When borrowed channel becomes free due to termination of a connection in neighboring cell, and there is another active connection on a lower order borrowed channel in the same cell, then communication on lower order channel is transferred to the higher order channel. This requires a channel switching neighboring cell.
4. A nominal channel in a cell may be blocked due to lending by a co-channel cell to a different cell. If such a channel becomes is completely unlocked (in all directions), then any active connection on either on a borrowed channel or on a higher order channel is immediately switched to the unlocked channel. It leads to a channel switching in local cell.

The reallocation rules are illustrated by Fig. 2.16. Figure 2.16a shows a channel switching within the same cell. It happens because there is ongoing communication on a lower order nominal channel, i.e., channel no. 7 when a higher order nominal channel, i.e., channel number 4 becomes free. Figure 2.16b shows a channel switching that takes place between two cell. The acceptor cell on the top has borrowed channel no. 19 from the donor cell at the bottom. Once nominal channel 7 becomes

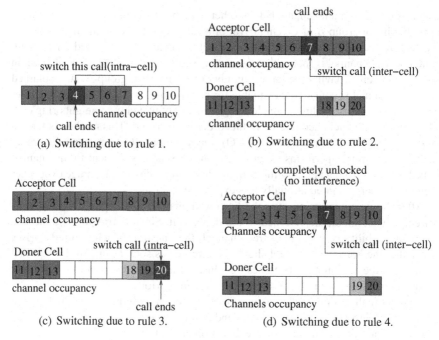

Fig. 2.16 Channel switching with borrowing

free in the acceptor cell then channel 19 is returned back to the donor cell. An inter-cell handoff is executed to realize such a channel switching. Figure 2.16c illustrates the switching, where the borrowed channel of the donor is switched to a lower order channel if such a channel becomes free in the donor cell. Finally, Fig. 2.16d illustrates the switching when a locked nominal cell become unlocked in the acceptor cell. Note this case refers to situation where borrowing is implemented with directional locking, and channel 7 is also be locked in other directions due to borrowing by another adjacent cell.

The channel borrowing strategies, outlined above, result in lower blocking than fixed allocation under light and moderate traffic conditions [15]. Under heavy traffic condition, channel borrowing could create domino effect due to blocking of borrowed channels in respective co-channel cells. These cells being deprived of their nominal channels would in turn have to resort to borrowing and, thus, creating the domino effect that would require a comprehensive channel reallocation strategy as in [15]. So fixed channel allocation sometimes may provide better performance than schemes relying on channel borrowing.

2.4.2 Dynamic Channel Assignment Policies

Due to temporal bursts in traffic, FCA schemes are found to be inadequate for handling traffic and lead to inefficient channel utilizations. DCA schemes have been proposed as remedies, where no channel is allocated permanently to any cell. Channels are allocated to cells on need basis. After a connection terminates, the channel is returned back to the central pool. So, the key idea behind DCA scheme is to evolve a procedure for the evaluation of cost in using each candidate channel for a connection request. The cost function should take into account: (i) radio signal strength measurements at the end devices, (ii) the acceptable average call blocking, (iii) the number of future call blocking, (iv) the distribution of channel occupancy under the current traffic conditions, (v) co-channel/adjacent channel interferences, and (vi) the QoS related requirements by the clients. So, DCA strategies can be designed to adaptively adjust to the traffic conditions as well as assurance of desired GoS and QoS. The design of a perfect cost function is understandably difficult as it needs to balance complex trade offs in optimization involving several attributes as indicated above. These difficulties in design of cost function made DCA an area of intensive research [5].

DCA algorithms are of two types based on the type of control, viz., centralized and distributed. In centralized DCA, a central controller determines the channel allocation for each connection request. There is no fundamental difference between different centralized DCA schemes except for the difference in cost function used in the selection of a channel. Some of the known approaches under this category are:

- First available (FA): it assigns the first available channel by ensuring that the channel reuse constraints are not violated. The search for the candidate channel is fast, and the scheme is simple. FA is found to perform better than most of the FCA schemes by 20% in low to moderate traffic conditions.
- Locally optimized dynamic assignment (LODA): it assigns the channel in response to a request from a cell by minimizing the future call blocking possibilities in the nearby cells.
- Channel reuse optimization: it tries to optimize reuse distance while allocating a channel for a new request. The fundamental idea behind this approach is to maximize spatial multiplexing. The shorter is the reuse distance, the greater is the channel reuse over the service area. Therefore, with this scheme network capacity also increases.
- Maximum use in reuse ring: it selects the channel for allocation by finding the one that is used in most cells in co-channel set. Note that co-channel cell form a reuse ring as explained earlier in Figs. 2.6 and 2.7.
- Mean square: it selects the channel that minimizes the mean square of the distances among cells using same channel.
- Nearest neighbor: it selects the available channel occupied in the nearest cell in distance $\geq D$.

Most of the channel reuse optimization schemes [5] as described above try to employ local optimizations. The 1-clique [7] scheme, however, employs a global

Fig. 2.17 ACO matrix of cell i

Cell Number	1	2	3	4	5	6	7	8	...	M	Free Channels
i		x					x		...		0
i_1	x			x			x		...		0
i_2			x						...		2
i_3	x				x	x			...		0
i_4			x			x			...	x	4
⋮	⋮	⋮	⋮	⋮	⋮	⋮	⋮	⋮	⋮	⋮	⋮
i_{k_i}			x		x				...		3

optimization scheme. It builds a graph for every channel, where each vertex represents a cell, and two vertices in this graph are connected by an edge if and only if the cells corresponding to the end vertices do not have co-channel interference. So, each graph reflects channel allocations possibilities. An actual channel assignment is done from several possibilities so that as many vertices as possible, still remain available for allocation. The scheme works fine for small number of channels and a small service area (with few cells). But for a coverage area with large number of cells and large number of channels the computation time becomes prohibitive.

Distributed DCA (DDCA) schemes depend either on local information about availability of free channels in the neighborhood of the requesting cell or rely on signal measurements [12]. The focus of the most of the work in DDCA schemes has been on channel reuse [1] sometimes even at the cost of interference.

The cell based DDCA schemes rely on local information. Each cell keeps track of free channels by storing the information in an augmented channel occupancy (ACO) matrix along with sufficient additional information that enables a base station to determine if a channel can be assigned. ACO matrix at cell i is an $(M + 1) \times (k_i + 1)$ matrix, where M is the number of channels in the system and k_i is the number of neighboring cells within the co-channel interference distance from cell i. Figure 2.17 shows ACO matrix for some cell i. When the column corresponding to a channel has no entry, it means that channel is free and can be assigned to cell i. Each entry in the last column gives the number of assignable channels available in the cell represented by the entry. Note that this number would be equal to the number of empty columns in ACO matrix of the corresponding cell. For example, $ACO[i, M + 1] = 0$ represents the fact that the cell i does not have any assignable free channel. Therefore, the ACO matrix for cell i has no empty column. Similarly, $ACO[i_2, M + 1] = 2$ indicates that there are 2 free channels in cell i_2. Equivalently, ACO matrix of cell i_2 has 2 empty columns.

Since no free channels are available in a cell as in i, when cell i needs an additional channel, it searches for channel that corresponds to an empty column in the first row of the ACO matrix. However, assigning any such channel may lead to a number of reassignments of other channels. The reassignment cost should also be minimized. Therefore, the candidate channel should be one that has no entry in the first row and also has minimum number of total entries. For example, column 6 of the ACO matrix has no entry in first row, and has only one entry for row i_4. It indicates that channel 6 is currently occupied by only cell i_4. Since, $ACO[i_4, M + 1] = 5$, cell i_4 has 5 assignable free channels. Therefore, the ongoing call in cell i_4 on channel 6 can be shifted to one of the free channels. If the shifting is successful then channel 6 becomes assignable in cell i. The contents of ACO matrix is updated by collecting channel occupancy information from the interfering cells. The cell corresponding to each entry of the chosen column is requested to shift its ongoing call from the current channel to a free channel. After each of the requested cells reports completion of call shifting, the chosen channel is declared free and assignable in the requester cell. However, requests to multiple cells for shifting could cause unpredictable delays and lead to higher probabilities of failures. So, from implementation prospectives, processing only one channel shifting request appears practical.

In addition to co-channel interference, adjacent channel interference (ACI) caused by use of close frequency channels results in premature handoffs, call drops, and cross connectivity. The effects of ACI can be minimized by use of sophisticated channel filters, but cannot be eliminated altogether. DCA methods discussed so far have focused only on co-channel interference. But it is possible to address the issue of ACI by adding extra restriction on the channel selection from the ACO matrix in DDCA algorithm described above. Assume ACI effects to be negligible with channel separation of N_{adj}. Then for every column which have an entry in the first row of the ACO matrix for a cell, $N_{adj} - 1$ adjacent columns either to the left or the right cannot have an entry in the first row. It means if a channel k has been allocated to a cell i then all channels corresponding to adjacent columns $k - j$, and also those corresponding to adjacent columns $k + j$, for $j = 1, \ldots, N_{adj} - 1$, cannot be allocated by the cell i.

At the time of assigning a new channel c to cell i, the algorithm should ensure that the channels corresponding to $N_{adj} - 1$ adjacent columns to the left or to the right of column c for the row i in ACO matrix do not have a entry in the first row of ACO matrix for cell i. It means those group of channels should not have been allocated earlier to cell i.

The channel allocation algorithm based on the above strategy works as follows. When cell i receives a connection request, it searches the first row of the ACO matrix for a consecutive group of $2N_{adj} - 1$ empty entries such that column corresponding to the column at the center of the group is empty. If the search is successful, the cell i assigns the channel represented by the central column. If no group of $2N_{adj} - 1$ empty columns can be found, then cell i looks for a group of consecutive $2N_{adj} - 1$ empty columns in the first row where center column c has a single entry and the related cell (let it be j) has an assignable free channel as indicated by a non-zero entry in $ACO[j, M + 1]$. After the column j has been identified, cell i requests cell j to shift the ongoing call on the channel c to one of its free channels. Once the shifting is over, and j reports the completion, cell i can assign channel c to new call request.

As an example, suppose $N_{adj} = 2$. To satisfy a request for assigning a new channel, a search is initiated for a group of 3 consecutive columns having no entries in first row of the ACO matrix provided in Table 2.17. Any such group can only be identified between columns 3–7. However, no group of 3 empty columns can be found between columns 3–7. So, we try to find a group of 3 columns such that center column has just one entry and that the cell related to the entry has assignable free channels.

The columns 5–7 provide such a group, with only cell i_4 occupying the channel 6. Since i_4 has 4 assignable free channels it can be requested to shift the ongoing communication from channel 6 to some free channel satisfying the adjacent channel interference restrictions. After cell i_4 vacates channel 6, cell i can allocate the same to the new request.

Some DDCA techniques considers the channel allocation as a resource sharing problems [4]. The underlying idea is that channel is a resource which must be shared among neighboring cells in a mutual exclusive manner. There are two important differences in classical mutual exclusion (ME) and channel sharing among neighboring cells.

- Firstly, in classical ME two competing processes are not allowed to share a resource, but a channel sharing among cells are permitted as long as they satisfy the constraint of reuse distance.
- Secondly, in channel allocation, not a single but a collection of resources should be handled.

Many DCA schemes exists for the channel assignment. An interested reader may look at some excellent references [5] for more details on the topic.

2.5   Handoff

Mobility is the key feature of a cellular based wireless communication system. However, in a bid to increase the capacity, increasingly smaller cell size are used. Maintaining continuity of service poses a challenge with use of reduced cell size. Normally on cell crossings, a mobile user experiences deterioration in the quality of ongoing communication. The deterioration of service is attributed to one of the following two reasons:

1. **Signal quality deterioration**. The quality of a signal is determined by a set of parameters such as, RSS, Signal to Noise Ratio (SNR), and bit error rate (BER). RSS attenuates with distance from the serving base station, slow fading (shadow fading or lognormal fading) and fast fading (Rayleigh fading) [10].
2. **Traffic load**. When the capacity of the current cell has either reached or is about to reach its maximum capacity.

With smaller cells, the frequency of cell crossing by a mobile user is expected increase. Under this circumstance, the continuity of an active connection for a mobile user can only be maintained by handoffs (or handovers) through a sequence of intermediaries (intermediate cells).

The RSS from the base station of the cell from which a mobile user is moving away decays gradually. As opposed to this, the RSS from the cell, into which the mobile is moving, increases gradually. If the link to the new base station is formed either before or almost immediately around the time when the link to old base station goes down, then it is possible to keep connection active. Thus, a handoff is the transition of signal transmission from one base station to another geographically adjacent base station. By executing a handoff *in-session* mobility to a user can be supported. As explained in Sect. 2.4, a frequency switching may sometimes be needed when a mobile terminal is moving within a cell. Such a switching is called an intra-cell handoff. Our attentions here, however, is limited to only inter cell handoffs.

Cells overlap, so a mobile terminal or the device could be within the range of multiple base stations around the boundary of a cell. It facilitates maintenance of an active connection while the user migrates from one cell to a geographically adjacent cell. The network decides—with or without the assistance of user's mobile handset (MH)—which base station will handle the transmission of signals from and to the MH. Handoff should be transparent to the user. In other words, it should provide assurance that the communication will neither be lost nor be terminated unless user's hardware is out of the range of all base stations.

The important first step of a handoff process is the early detection of the handoff condition. The handoff can then be initiated before the current connection is broken. Once an active connection is completely severed there is no way to restore it. A particular threshold of signal is needed for acceptable level of ongoing communication. In the case of voice communication it could be between -90 and $-100\,\text{dBm}$. A slightly stronger signal level is used as the threshold for initiation of handoff process. The margin between the threshold signal for handoff and the minimum usable signal level is known as the handoff *hysteresis* Δ. Formally, hysteresis can be defined as

$$\Delta = S_{handoff} - S_{min},$$

where $S_{handoff}$ represents the threshold for performing handoff, and S_{min} denotes the minimum level of signal strength needed for the voice communication. The value of Δ can neither be too large nor be too small for the handoff to work smoothly.

Figure 2.18 depicts the different handoff situations when a mobile terminal travels from station BS_1 to BS_2 along a straight line. At time t_0 the mobile host receives signal only from BS_1. At time t_1 received signal strengths from both base stations become

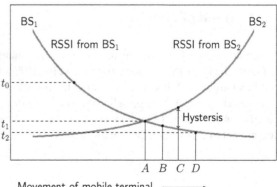

Fig. 2.18 Handoff scenarios at cell boundaries

comparable. But as the mobile user reaches point B, the signal strength received from BS_2 dominates, even though the signal from BS_1 is still above the acceptable level. The handoff must begin after mobile terminal reaches point A and completed before it reaches point C. If handoff latency is δt then, the handoff must be performed δt time before reaching the threshold C. Therefore, handoff should start when strength of signal from BS_1 is little higher and should be completed on or before reaching C. If handoff is not complete before the mobile reaches point C then the signal from BS_1 deteriorates fast. So, when the mobile reaches point D, the call gets terminated.

It has already been indicated that handoff should be performed when the received signal strength is below a certain threshold. However, the signal measurement mechanism for handoff should not be considered as a simple one-off instantaneous measurement. The reason is due to multipath fading, instantaneous measurement of signal may not provide a correct estimation of distance between the mobile and its current base station. So, the signal strength should be measured over a certain time interval, and the average of such measurements should be the basis for the decision to perform a handoff.

The window of time for performing handoff is provided by length of hysteresis. To reduce the overhead of handoffs, the attempt should to optimize Δ. The value of Δ depends on several factors such as:

- Environment.
- Speed of direction of mobile's movement.
- Time required to perform handoff.

The use of hystersis is aimed at reducing the ping-pong effect. However, the delay is also not without cost. It increases interference, reduces the quality of service. The delay could as well lead to a call dropping. A velocity adaptive handoff algorithm could enforce more frequent measurement of signal strengths by adjusting length of averaging window in which RSSs from neighboring BSes are averaged. The direction parameter assigns more weightage to execution of handoff in favor of BSes towards which the mobile is moving [8].

2.5.1 Handoff Policies

A simple approach would be to prioritize the channel assignments for handoff requests ahead of the requests for new calls. It results in a tolerable increase in call blocking probability while reducing the probability of dropped calls.

Another approach is to pre-allocate a certain number of handoff channels called guard channels. Only these channels should be used for handoffs. If the guard channels are not available then the handoff will be serviced by other channels.However, if all guard channels are occupied then, a handoff call should compete with new call for allocation of the channels outside the guard band of channels. This strategy keeps the probability of a call blocking under an acceptable level, but increases the probability of a dropped call. There is also a possibility that guard channels are under utilized, while new call requests cannot be met due to non-availability of free channels. Such a situation leads to an inefficient spectrum utilization. The concept of reserved channels would be appropriate for dynamic channel assignment scheme. Because the guard channels can be allocated from a central pool. So the non-availability of a free channel for new call requests does not become a local problem.

Typically, when no channel is available, new call requests are made to wait in a queue with the hope that handoff calls or some of the ongoing connections may release their respective channels. Once a channel becomes free, one of the queued new call request can be serviced. The strategy works well because, a user any way has to wait for an interval of time before expecting establishment of a connection against his/her request. In the case of a handoff too, there is a certain finite time interval during which the existing call connection is retained, and a new channel is assigned for the handoff. Therefore, it is also possible to enqueue a handoff request albeit for a small interval of time. The position of handoff request in the queue depends on how close the mobile is to the boundary of the cell. Higher priorities can be assigned to the mobiles that are close to a cell boundary or moving very fast while lower priorities can be assigned to the mobiles still inside a cell boundary, or are moving slowly.

Whichever entity (the network or the mobile terminal) that makes the handoff decision uses some metrics. It applies the relevant algorithms on the basis of those metrics, and assures required performance guarantees. The most critical metric for a handoff decision is the measurements of signal strengths received at the mobile from the current base station and the neighboring base stations which are probable candidates to handle the frequency switching. The measurement process should be able to avoid unnecessary handoffs. For example effecting handoff during a temporary fading may result in *ping pong* effect and put pressure on network due to unnecessary handoffs. On the other hand, if a distance dependent fading (caused by mobile user moving away from current base station) is not properly detected it could result in termination of the connection before handoff can be initiated.

2.5.2 Handoff Protocols

Three types of entities are involved in a handoff:

1. User's mobile handset (MH),
2. Base station (BS) to which MH is currently connected and BSes in the neighborhood of MH's movements, and
3. MSCs controlling the above group of BSes.

So, both network entities (BSes and MSCs) as well as user's MH may initiate and control a handoff process. Based on the nature of controlling entity or the entities, the handoff protocols can be classified into three basic types.

- Network controlled.
- Mobile assisted.
- Mobile controlled.

In network controlled protocol, the decision for handoff is based on measurements of RSSs of mobile terminal at a number of adjoining base stations. The entire handoff process which includes measurements, channel switching and network switching, etc., takes approximately around 100–200 ms. As opposed to this, in mobile assisted handoff process MH measures the RSSs it receives from BSes in its neighborhood and the decision for handoff is made by the network entities. Mobile assisted handoff may take upto 1 s. In mobile controlled handoff user's MH takes decision to execute handoff. This type of handoff requires a short reaction time, just about the order of 0.1 s. MH measures RSS of neighboring BSes and interference levels of all channels. Then it initiates handoff if the signal strength from the serving BS is lower than another neighboring BS by a pre-determined threshold. Mobile controlled handoff being a completely decentralized process, relieves the network from a high overhead specially in a high density micro-cellular system.

Several different mechanisms exist for realizing handoff. However, the common goals which every handoff mechanism should try to achieve are:

1. Handoffs should be performed quickly.
2. Interruption in connection due to a handoff should be imperceptible to users.
3. Handoffs should be performed infrequently.
4. Handoffs should be performed successfully.

Figure 2.19 illustrates the generic procedure for execution of handoff. The mobile terminal reports about the signal measurements to serving base station. If the serving base station decides about the handoff, it informs the Mobile Switching Center (MSC) that a handoff is required. The MSC then send a handoff request to the new base station. The new base station allocates the required resources for the handoff and sends handoff request accept to the MSC. Then the MSC issues handoff command to the old base station which informs the same to the mobile terminal. The mobile terminal requests for a link establishment with the new base station. After link has been established, handoff completion command is issued by the new base station to the MSC. Following this, the MSC instructs the old base station to flush the resources for the mobile terminal being used for communication. The old base station flushes the resources and the handoff is complete. The basic handoff procedure described above may be augmented by other participating components such as one or more base station controllers (BSC) and one or more MSCs depending on the structure of the network. There are many resources to be managed in wireless cellular communication system. These include channel assignment, signal to interference ratio (SIR), transmit power control, etc. All these may influence handoff decisions in some way or the

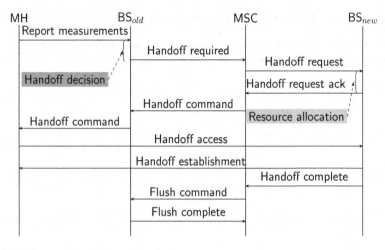

Fig. 2.19 The generic procedure of handoff

other. So, for a better overall performance, adaptive handoff protocols have been designed by integrating such resource optimization with handoff decisions [14].

References

1. F.A. Cruz-Pérez, D. Lara-Rodfiguez, Distributed dynamic channel assignment with violation to the reuse pattern for microcellular networks. IEEE Trans. Veh. Technol. **51**(6), 1375–1385 (2002)
2. D. Gross, C.M. Harris, *Fundamentals of Queueing Theory*. Wiley Series in Probability and Statistics, 4th edn. (Wiley, New York, USA, 2008)
3. W.K. Hale, Frequency assignment: theory and applications. Proc. IEEE **68**, 1497–1514 (1980)
4. J. Jiang, T.H. Lai, N. Soundarajan, On distributed dynamic channel allocation in mobile cellular networks. IEEE Trans. Parallel Distrib. Syst. **13**(10), 1024–1037 (2002)
5. I. Katzela, M. Naghshineh, Channel assignment schemes for cellular mobile telecommunication systems: a comprehensive survey. IEEE Pers. Commun. **3**, 10–31 (1996)
6. V.H. MacDonald, AMPS: the cellular concept. Bell Syst. Tech. J. **58**, 15–41 (1979)
7. K. Okada, F. Kubota, On dynamic channel assignment strategies in cellular mobile radio systems. IEICE Trans. Fundam. Electron Commun. Comput. Sci. E75-A:1634–1641 (1992)
8. T. Onel, C. Ersoy, E. Cayirci, G. Parr, A multicriteria handoff decision scheme for the next generation tactical communications systems. Comput. Netw. **46**, 695–708 (2004)
9. G.P. Pollini, Trends in handover design. IEEE Commun. Magaz. 82–90 (1996)
10. T.S. Rappaport, *Wireless Communications: Principles and Practice*, 2nd edn. (Prentice Hall PTR, 2002)
11. N. Robertson, D. Sanders, P. Seymour, R. Thomas, The four-colour theorem. J. Comb. Theor. **70**, 2–44 (1997)
12. M. Serizawa, D.J. Goodman, Instability and deadlock of distributed dynamic channel allocation, *43rd IEEE VTC*, 1993, pp. 528–531
13. D. Stirzaker, G. Grimmett, *Probability and Random Processes* (Oxford Science Publication, Oxford University Press, 1992)

14. N.D. Tripathy, J.H. Reed, H.F. VanLandingham, Handoff in cellular systems. IEEE Pers. Commun. **5**, 26–37 (1998)
15. M. Zhang, T.P. Yum, Comparisons of channel-assignment strategies in cellular mobile telephone systems. IEEE Trans. Veh. Technol. **38**(4), 211–215 (1989)

Chapter 3
GSM, GPRS and UMTS

3.1 Introduction

Groupe Spéciale Mobile (GSM) was established by an initiative from Conference of European Post and Telecommunication (CEPT). The group had several committees with representatives from all major European telecom operators and manufacturers. The aim of these committees was to develop standards for pan-European digital land-mobile telecommunication service targeting mobile users by replacing incompatible analog system. The responsibilities of developing the standards now rests with European Telecommunication Standard Institute (ETSI). ETSI re-defined the abbreviation GSM as Global System for Mobile. The aim is to formulate a set of common specifications for European wide public mobile telephone system with following criteria:

- Good speech quality.
- Efficient spectral usage.
- Low terminal and service cost.
- Mobile hand-held terminal support.
- International roaming support.
- ISDN capabilities.

The first GSM standard was released in 1990. The commercial GSM service started in 1991. By 1993, GSM technology spread outside Europe and became de facto world standard for mobile telephone service. GSM allows terminal mobility via a Subscriber Identity Module (SIM) which carries a personal number issued to the mobile user. SIM contains many subscriber related information including a personal identity number (PIN), and PIN unblocking code as a safeguard against any unauthorized use. Undoubtedly, GSM is most widely deployed and the fastest growing cellular based mobile telephone technology in the world today. It is still undergoing a continuous process of evolution. High Speed Circuit Switched Data (HSCSD) [1], Enhanced Data rates for GSM Evolution (EDGE) [2] and General Packet Radio Service (GPRS) [3] were added to GSM network to provide enhanced features, new

© Springer Nature Singapore Pte Ltd. 2017   55
R.K. Ghosh, *Wireless Networking and Mobile Data Management*,
DOI 10.1007/978-981-10-3941-6_3

functionalities and increased data rates. GPRS standards were released in 1997 by
ETSI. It eliminates the annoying requirement for repetitive dial-ups to establish connections. Furthermore, it provides throughput in excess of 40 Kbps. Advanced competing technology like UMTS has entered into the commercial market for providing
data rates better than GPRS. However, in reality UMTS is not radically different
from GSM. It redefines base station technology, but requires GSM as base support
technology. In this chapter our discussion is mainly centered around the base GSM
technology. We take a look on GPRS and also examine how UMTS has been positioned up the ladder of mobile communication technology by re-jigging GSM.

3.2 GSM Architecture

GSM network was developed over the generic cellular architecture discussed in the
previous chapter. It employs mainly three basic equipment and modules for implementing the functionalities of mobile telephone network over the cellular architecture. These are:

- Mobile Station (MS) or the subscriber's equipment and the modules.
- Base Station Subsystem (BSS).
- Network Subsystem (NSS).

Figure 3.1 outlines GSM architecture. A MS or a Mobile Station consists of a subscriber equipment or a handset with a SIM card. The five main components of the
Network Switching SubSystem (NSS) are: AuC, HLR, VLR, MSC and EIR. The Base

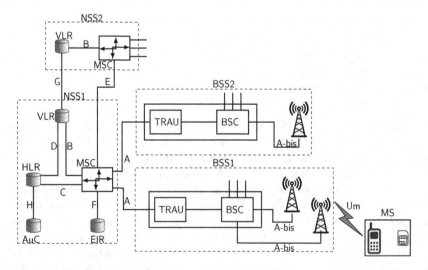

Fig. 3.1 GSM architecture

Station Subsystem (BSS) has two major components, namely, a Base Station controller (BSC) and a number of Base Transceiver Stations (BTSes). Let us now examine various subsystems of the GSM architecture in more details.

3.2.1 Mobile Station

A subscriber's equipment and its associated module consist of a hand-held equipment known as a Mobile Station (MS) (also known as Mobile Handset (MH)) and a Subscriber Identity Module (SIM).

Mobile Handset (MH):
The equipment or the MH is essentially a combined unit for transmission and reception of voice and data having circuits responsible for:

- Time and frequency synchronizations,
- Measuring and reporting signal strengths from BTSes,
- Encoding speech and messages,
- Error correction codes for transmission over the air, and
- Compressing and decompressing data and speech.

Each mobile terminal has a unique identity known as International Mobile Equipment Identity (IMEI). IMEI number is usually inscribed on the battery compartment of an MS. This number can be retrieved from a mobile phone by keying-in "*#06#". An IMEI number maps a valid device to a user, and works as a safeguard against stolen device. IMEI number is a 15 digit number which carries:

- Six digit Type Approval Code (TAC),
- Two digit Final Assembly Code (FAC),
- Six digit Serial Number (SN),
- One checksum digit (C).

FAC is a manufacture specific number. FAC has been discontinued since April 1, 2004, and TAC has been expanded to eight digits. The first two digits of the expanded TAC represents the country code. The remaining six digit are for the manufacturer's identity. The checksum is calculated using Luhn's (or "modulus 10") algorithm [4] by involving all digits. The check digit is neither transmitted over radio nor stored in Equipment Identity Register (EIR).

On a user's request the service provider can blacklist an IMEI, preventing unauthorized use of a stolen device. However, IMEI number have no relationship with the personal data concerning a user or a subscriber.

Subscriber Identity Module (SIM):
A subscriber needs to insert a SIM into his/her mobile equipment to be able to make voice call or access data services. A SIM is a portable smart card having a small memory. It carries following important information related to a user:

1. International Mobile Subscriber's Identity (IMSI)
2. Authentication Key K_i,
3. Cipher Key K_c,
4. Three important confidentiality algorithms known as A3, A5 and A8.

SIM also stores some permanent as well as temporary data related to the user. These include access control, location area identity, forbidden Public Land Mobile Network (PLMN), additional GSM services and the subscriber specific information.

IMSI and PIMSI (Packet IMSI) belong to the class of permanent data stored in a SIM. IMSI is a 64-bit field. It is sent to the GSM network when a user requests a connection. The network uses IMSI to retrieve information related to the subscriber's credentials and subscription. However, most of the time when an MS, is roaming TIMSI (a randomly generated data from IMSI) is sent in place of IMSI. TIMSI is assigned by the locally responsible VLR. Therefore, it is not possible to determine the presence of a mobile in a cell just by listening to radio channels.

The authentication key K_i is a 128-bit value also stored on database of GSM network known as Authentication Center (AuC). K_i can not be retrieved by SIM interface. SIM provides an algorithm referred to as $A3$ to pass K_i to AuC. K_i is required for the purpose of authentication.

Algorithm $A5$ is used for encryption and decryption of data between MS and BS. For encryption, SIM uses a cipher key K_c which is a 64-bit value generated using a random number through key generator algorithm $A8$.

3.2.2   Base Station Subsystem

The BSS consists of three components: (i) Base Transceiver Station (BTS), (ii) Base Station Controller (BSC) and (iii) Transcoder and Rate Adaptation Unit (TRAU). A BTS usually referred to as a Base Station (BS). No confusion should arise, if we use these terms interchangeably in the text. A base station provides the last mile connectivity to an MS. It is the key communication equipment in a cell service area. It is responsible for communication with MS. Its functions include antenna, modem and signal processing.

A Base Station Controller (BSC) manages radio resources of one or more BSes. It handles channel setup, frequency hopping, handoffs and also acts as an interface between a Mobile Switch Center (MSC) and its BSes. A BSC receives measurements from the MSs and controls handoffs for the MSs. A BSC can manage upto 40 BSes. However, an MSC which controls several BSCs would typically provide a few lines to a BSC. Therefore, one of the important task of BSC is to act as a concentrator. Many low capacity BS connections to BSC are concentrated into a relatively small number of connections from an MSC.

Mobile to mobile transmission path involves BSS to NSS and then NSS to BSS transitions. The bit rate supported by GSM radio interface is 13 Kbps for full rate and 5.6 Kbps for half rate. An MSC is basically a PSTN/ISDN switch which supports a data rate of 64 Kbps. The compression and formats of two sides are different which necessitates transcoding and rate conversion. Rate adaptation adapts the transmission rate of digital voice or data traffic on radio links (which is about 16 Kbps) to the standard data rate of 64 Kbps achievable from an MSC through the conventional networks. Transcoding involves conversion of formats as well a compression. The voice and data traffic originating from mobile stations through BSes are compressed and converted into 64 Kbps data format. The method consists of multiplexing a few of the low speed speech or data streams and convert them into standard 64 Kbps format. Using compression TRAU could bring reduction in the transmission cost by as much as 75%. TRAU is placed close to MSC and between MSC and BSC. TRAU is also responsible for generating comfort noise for discontinuous transmission (DTX). DTX is used to increase power efficiency in operation of transmitter. It takes advantage of the fact that in a normal conversation, only about 40% of an active connection time is used. The transmitter can be turned off during the silence period for power efficiency. Therefore, the biggest challenge here is to detect voice activity. The detection process must distinguish between noise and voice. If voice is misinterpreted as noise and transmitter is turned off annoying clipping will be heard at the receiver end. On the other hand, if noise is misinterpreted as voice then efficiency of DTX goes down. So, TRAU generates comfort noise, matching the background noise, which indicates the receiver end that the transmitter is not dead.

3.2.3 Network Subsystem

An MSC is the key component of a GSM network subsystem. It provides the functionalities needed to handle mobile subscriber's handset such as registration, authentication, location updates, handoffs, connection routing, and mobility. It needs to keep track of the updated status and the location of an MS. The location database is partitioned into Home Location Register (HLR) and Visitors Location Register (VLR). Location databases may be stored in separate location servers, but VLR is usually co-located with MSC. The other elements of GSM network include:

1. Gateway MSC (GMSC), which is connected to PSTN and ISDN network,
2. Equipment Identity Registers (EIR), and
3. AUthentication Center (AUC).

EIR store MS's IMEI while AUC is an important database used to authenticate the mobile user.

Guaranteeing transmission of voice or data of a given quality over the radio link is an important function of GSM network. There is another set of equally important functions which a GSM network should perform. Supporting user's mobility is one of these. The network should be able to detect movements of individual mobile users and switch active connections to the channels under new cells to which the respective users may have migrated. The task of preserving an active connection is realized by implementing handoff (also known as handover) mechanism on GSM network. Handoff ensures that existing communication remains active across many transient movements of the users. The other important function of GSM network is to facilitate both national and international roaming support for the mobile subscribers. Allowing migration from one administrative network domain to another involve credential checks like identity, and authenticity. After establishing user's credentials the network should be able to reroute connection and keep track of each user's locations as the user moves. The GSM network provides a number of functions for efficient handling of roaming. These functions are handled through signaling protocols between the different components of the GSM networks mentioned above.

3.2.4   GSM Radio Resources

Before, discussing GSM protocols it is important to understand the radio resources and management of these resources. GSM uses a mix of FDMA and TDMA and combines this with frequency hopping schemes for allocating radio resources. FDMA allocates a dedicated frequency to each user for the duration of his/her use. For a FDMA system, a large frequency bands is needed to handle communication among large number of users. Since, only a limited radio frequency band is available, FDMA system is not scalable. TDMA allows several users to share a channel by time-sharing the usage. TDMA is normally used in conjunction with FDMA. A frequency channel is partitioned into fixed number of time-slots, and a selected time-slot is allocated to a user for the duration of his/her communication.

3.2.5   Channel Types

The operating bands in GSM are 900 MHz, 1800 MHz and 1900 MHz. Each of the above frequency band is divided into uplink and downlink. For example, GSM 900 MHz split into: (i) 890–915 MHz for uplink (mobile to BS), and (ii) 935–960 MHz for downlink (BS to mobile). Each of these 25 MHz band is partitioned into 124 carriers of 200 KHz each leaving 200 KHz guard band from the left edge of the band. Similarly, the uplink and downlink bands for other two GSM operating bands are:

- 1800 MHz: 1710–1785 MHz for uplink, and 1805–1880 MHz downlink,
- 1900 MHz: 1850–1910 MHz for uplink, 1930–1990 MHz for downlink.

The 1800 MHz band provides 374 pair of carriers whereas the 1900 MHz band provides 299 pairs of carriers.

Each carrier is segmented using TDMA into 8 time-slots of duration 0.577 ms per-slot. So, each carrier lasts for 8 slots 0–7 called a frame or a burst. A frame/burst time is 0.577 ms × 8 = 4.165 ms. The recurrent pattern of a particular time slot in

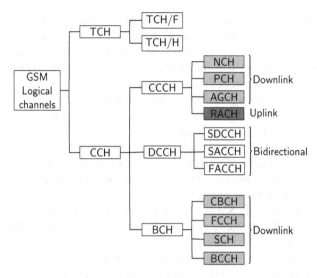

Fig. 3.2 GSM channel classes

each frame constitutes a single logical channel. The repetition of a particular time slot occurs every 4.615 ms which is the time interval for one frame.

GSM logical channels are built on the top of physical channels. Logical channels address the issues related to information exchanges between MS and BSS. As Fig. 3.2 indicates, GSM distinguishes between traffic channels (for user data) and control channels (for network control messages). Some of the channels are unidirectional while others are bidirectional. The unidirectional downlink channels are for communication from BS to MS. Same TDMA structuring of channels is used for both down and up links. However, the numbering of the slots for Traffic CHannels (TCH) is staggered by 3 time slots to prevent a mobile from transmitting and receiving at the same time. Traffic channels are defined using multiframe structures consisting of 26 TDMA frames with a recurrent interval of 120 ms (=4.615 ms × 26). Out of 26 TDMA frames 24 are used for traffic, 1 frame is used for Slow Associated Channel and 1 frame is left unused. Control channels are defined in a multiframe structure consisting of 51 (=4.615ms × 51) TDMA frames having recurrent interval of 235.4 ms.

GSM control or signaling channels can be divided into four classes, namely,

1. Broadcast CHannels (BCH),
2. Common Control CHannels (CCCH),
3. Dedicated Control CHannels (DCCH), and
4. Associate Control CHannels (ACCH).

The broadcast control channels are used by BS to provide synchronization information to MS. Depending on information flow, we can distinguish the broadcast channels further into four different subtypes, namely, (i) Broadcast Control CHannel (BCCH),

(ii) Synchronization CHannel (SCH) and (iii) Frequency Correction CHannel (FCCH), and (iv) Cell Broadcast CHannel (CBCH). BCCH is used by a base station to provide network parameters to an MS. SCH is used to inform training symbol sequence for demodulating transmitted information by a BS. FCCH is reserved for providing frequency reference of the system for synchronization of an MS. CBCH is used for transmitting messages to be broadcast to all mobile stations within coverage of a cell. For example, it can be used as an option for emergency warning systems for broadcast of an emergency situation.

The common control channels support establishing links between mobile stations and network. The important CCCH are: (i) Random Access CHannel (RACH), (ii) Access Grant CHannel (AGCH), (iii) Paging CHannel (PCH) and (iv) Notification CHannel (NCH). RACH is a purely uplink channel used by the mobiles to access of services such as voice call, SMS, responding to paging and sending registration. It employs the principles of slotted ALOHA (see Sect. 4.6.3) for competitive multiple access by different mobile stations. The remaining three control channels are downlink channels. PCH is used for searching or paging a mobile device by its IMSI or TIMSI. AGCH is used to grant accesses when a mobile has either been successfully paged on PCH or it has initiated a request through RACH. It sets up signaling by assigning a stand-alone dedicated control channel (SDCCH) or a TCH to a mobile station. NCH is used to notify a group of mobiles about voice broadcast service. CCCH channels occupy slot 0 in a frame and repeat back every 51 frame times. When more capacity is required slots 2, 4, or 6 can be used.

Dedicated Control CHannels (DCCH) are for bidirectional information flow between mobile stations and base stations. Two main DCCHs are: (i) Stand-alone Dedicated Control CHannel (SDCCH), and (ii) Slow Associated Control CHannel (SACCH). A SDCCH channel is maintained between a mobile station (MS) and a BS for exchange of message relating to call establishment, authentication, location update, SMS, etc. An associate channel does not exist by itself. Slow Associated Control CHannel (SACCH) is always associated with a TCH or SDCCH. It is used to inform MS about frequencies of neighboring cells, time synchronization and power control on the downlink. The uplink is used for sending signal measurements and other parameters from MS that aids in arriving at handover decisions. It can be used to transmit SMS when associated with a TCH. This is the reason why an SMS can be delivered when the user is busy with a call.

A Fast Associated Control CHannel (FACCH) is not a control channel in true sense. It is a TCH that turns momentarily into a control channel thereby stealing some time slots from associated TCH for urgent information such as handoff, call disconnect, call connect, etc. After the use of FACCH is over, the channel turns back into the traffic channel.

3.2.6 Frame Structure

There are four types frame or burst structures, namely,

1. Normal frame, used to carry voice or data,
2. Frequency correction frame, used on FCCH,
3. Synchronization frame, used on SCH,
4. Random access, used on RACH.

Each of these frames has a length of 156.25 bits and a slot duration of 0.577 ms, but have different structures. The first three frames carry 142 bits of information, while the information contents in the last frame is 77 bits. The structure of a normal frame is shown in Fig. 3.3. The tail bits form a group of 3 bits placed at both at the beginning and the end of a frame to allow the mobile to adjust to the required power levels (which increase and decrease sharply on transitions between active and inactive states). The data bits are coded in two groups of 57 bits each separated by 26 bits of training sequence. The training sequence is used for synchronization of the receiver to eliminate or mask multipath propagation effects. A guard period equivalent to 8.25 bits length is used to avoid any possible overlap of two mobiles during power build up time. There is 1 bit stealing flag after each group of Data bits. Stealing bit indicates whether the data bits pertains to signal or user data. An associated control channel would set stealing bit when it temporarily uses the channel to send signals. The Channel quality depends on propagation effects or multipath fading. To ensure average channel quality, a slow frequency hopping is employed. It changes frequency every frame time. Frequency hopping additionally helps to reduce co-channel interference.

The structure of the remaining three frames are shown in Fig. 3.4. Traffic channel frames are transmitted in groups of 26 known as *26-multiframe*. Since, transmit time of each TDMA frame (8 slots) is 4.615 ms, the transmit time for a 26-multiframe is 4.615 ms × 26 = 120 ms. Control frames, on the other hand, are transmitted in groups

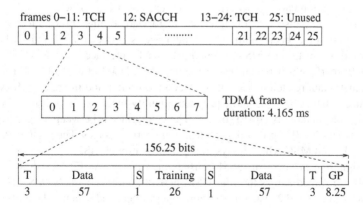

Fig. 3.3 Structure of a normal GSM frame or burst

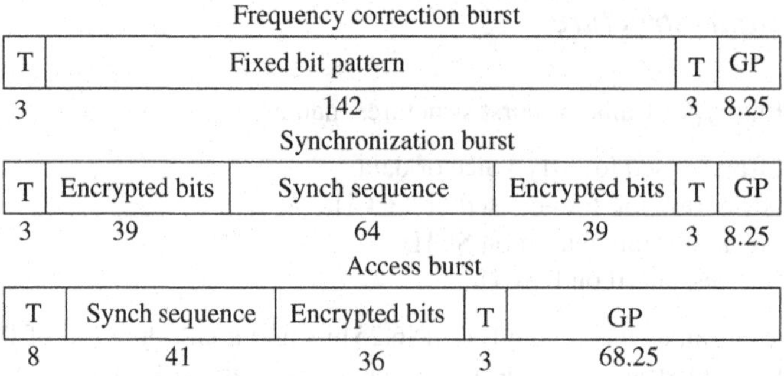

Frequency correction burst

T	Fixed bit pattern	T	GP
3	142	3	8.25

Synchronization burst

T	Encrypted bits	Synch sequence	Encrypted bits	T	GP
3	39	64	39	3	8.25

Access burst

T	Synch sequence	Encrypted bits	T	GP
8	41	36	3	68.25

Fig. 3.4 Structures of FCCH, SCH and RACH frames or bursts

of 51, known as *51-multiframe*. A superframe consists of either 51 of 26-multiframes or 26 of 51-multiframes. A hiperframe consists of 2048 superframes. Thus, a hiperframe consists of $2048 \times 26 \times 51$ frames, and has a transmit time 1566 ms.

3.3   GSM Signaling Protocols

The GSM has two different types of interfaces: Um and Abis. Um refers to air interface, and used for communicating between MS and BSS. Abis collectively consists of 9 interfaces from A to I. The interface A is between BSS and MSC. It manages allocation of radio resources for mobility of MS and its management. The interfaces B to H are internal to MSC functions. Location database may be maintained at some location servers different from MSC. So, B, C, D are wire interfaces for accessing HLRs and VLRs. Most MSCs store VLR database locally. So interface B may be internal to MSC. C interface is between HLR and Gateway MSC (GMSC). The calls originating from outside GSM go through a GMSC to extract routing information. Mobile Application Part protocol (MAP/C) is used over C interface to get this information. MSC may also use this interface to forward billing information to HLR after connection has been setup. The D interface is between VLR and HLR. The data related to location of MS is exchanged over D interface using MAP/D protocol. The E interface is between two different MSCs. Handoff uses MAP/E protocol for exchange data related to handoff between the anchor and the relay MSCs. The F interface is between MSC and equipment identity register (EIR). It uses MAP/F protocol to check identity (IMEI) of MS. The G interface is between MSC and SMS gateway, it uses MAP/G protocol for transfer of short messages. The I is the interface between MS and MSC which relays transparently through BSS.

The signaling protocol of GSM consists of 3 layers. As Fig. 3.5 shows, GSM protocols are spread across the four GSM network entities, namely, MS, BS, BSC and MSC. Layer 1 and 2 respectively represent physical and data link layer. Layer 3, unlike in OSI model, does not exactly represent the network layer. Its protocols are

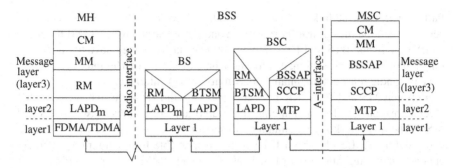

Fig. 3.5 GSM network components

used for communication of network resources, mobility, code format and call related messages between network entities. So, it is more appropriate to refer layer 3 as the message layer rather than network layer.

Layer 2 protocol is provided by $LAPD_m$ which is a modified version of Link Access Protocol for ISDN D-channel (LAPD) of ISDN stack to work within the constraints of radio paths. $LAPD_m$ does not use any flag. Consequently, bit stuffing type of mechanism cannot be employed for the purpose of frame delimitation. Frame delimitation is handled at the physical layer. The two main modifications affected in LAPD are for:

1. Handling the requirements for tight synchronization of TDMA.
2. Distinguishing the padding and the information part in transmission frames.

The information part in a transmission frame is indicated by inclusion of a length field which replaces LAPD flags while FEC flag is removed altogether.

Layer 3 consists of three sublayers, namely,

1. Resource management (RM) is implemented over the link between MS and BSS. This sublayer oversees the establishment and the maintenance of stable uninterrupted communication links spanning both radio and wired links between MS and MSC. A part of RM's responsibility is also to manage handoffs. MS and BSS control most of the functions in RM, though some are also performed by MSC.
2. Mobility management (MM) sublayer handles mobility management and maintains the location information of MS apart from performing authentication and the related crypto controlled procedures.
3. Connection management (CM) sublayer sets up connection at the user's request. Its functions are divided among three distinct tasks, viz., connection control, SMS and supplementary services. Connection control is related to circuit oriented services. SMS provides for point to point short message service. Supplementary services allows modification and checking of supplementary services.

Layer 3 implements Message Transport Part (MTP) of SS7 which is used for communication in wired part of PSTN. It also handles the Signaling Connection Control

Part (SCCP) over the link between MSC and BSS. MM and CM sublayers provide certain functionalities of transport, session and presentation layers of OSI model.

BSS elements, BTS and BSC implement dual stacks as they have to handle not only radio resource allocation, deallocation, handover, etc., on Um interface but also have to handle relay and maintain connectivity over A interface.

Between MS and BTS, RR protocols are for radio resource management. RR layer is responsible for maintaining both radio and fixed links between MS and MSC. The major task is to maintain radio session which is the time when MS is in dedicated mode. Besides this RR layer also responsible for configuration of radio channels including allocation of dedicated channels. MM layer protocols are for keeping track of mobility of MS so that the when calls are made they can be routed to MS. MM protocols are also responsible for authentication and security of MS. CM layer is responsible for maintaining circuit connectivity, supplementary services and SMS.

BSC protocols are made up of layers communicating over Abis interface. The RR sublayer of BTS stack is changed to BTS Management (BTSM). BTSM's task is to oversee link relay function between BTS and BSC. Some radio resource management functions are also performed at BSC. The services to be managed include paging of MS, handover calls, power control and call termination. Accordingly, RR protocols are responsible for use, allocation, reallocation and release of GSM channels. The part of dual stack at BSC which communicates with MSC over A interface has to supervise the relay using MTP of SS7. For communication between MSC and BSC, BSS Mobile Application Part (BSSMAP) and Direct Application Part (DTAP) of SS7 protocol are used.

Besides having corresponding protocols to communicate with BSC, MSC stack includes RR and CM sublayers. The protocols of these sublayers are required for mobility management of MS and resources related radio communication. Each user has a HLR that stores a user's location and the list of services which the user has subscribed to. A user location is tracked by using VLR. When a user roams, it notifies a new VLR about its new location. The said VLR then uses SS7 [5] based signal to relay the location information to the corresponding HLR.

3.4 Call Setup

In GSM there is a distinction between the calls originating from a mobile (outgoing) and the calls terminating at a mobile (incoming). In case of an incoming call, the process will be same irrespective of the fact whether the call originates from a mobile or a PSTN landline. So, we examine the issues of call terminating at mobile separately from call originating at mobile.

3.4.1 Mobile Terminated Calls

An incoming call to a mobile is known as a Mobile Terminated Call (MTC). An incoming call is initiated when a subscriber dials a mobile ISDN number. Though mobile stations MS keep GSM network informed about their locations, it is not sufficient for setting up a call to a mobile station. After a calling party dials the number, PSTN first identifies the network to which the called MS belongs, and locates the GMSC for that network. Figure 3.6 illustrates the steps involved in processing of a MTC incoming call. As indicated by the figure, the process of call setup can be broken down into three basic tasks, namely, (i) finding route to the MSC responsible for the MS, (ii) paging the correct mobile and obtaining response from it, (iii) assigning a traffic channel for the call. Steps 1–4 are for discovering the route to the correct MSC, while the actual routing of call to the target MSC is done in step 5. Steps 6–8 are responsible for paging related task. Authentication, and security related checks are performed in steps 9–12. We provide a stepwise description of these activities below.

Step 1: The identity of network is extracted from MSISDN itself. PSTN sends initial address message (IAM) to the GMSC.

Step 2: GMSC forwards the MSISDN to HLR and requests for the routing information.

Step 3: HLR extracts the IMSI and SS7 address for the MSC/VLR which is currently servicing the MS. It then contacts the concerned MSC/VLR and requests it to assign an MSRN to the call. MSRN or mobile station roaming number is allocated by MSC/VLR from a set of available roaming numbers.

Step 4: MSC/VLR forwards the MSRN to HLR. HLR forwards both MSRN and routing information to GMSC. MSRN is used by GMSC for routing telephone call to target MSC.

Step 5: GMSC then sends an IAM with MSRN to the servicing MSC/VLR for routing the call.

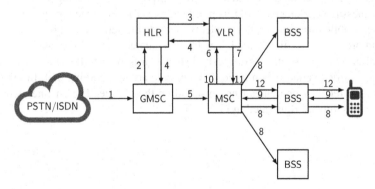

Fig. 3.6 Protocol for incoming call to a mobile

Step 6–7:   After MSC/VLR receives the MSRN it releases the same and proceeds with call set up related activities. It gets Location Area Identity (LAI) from VLR. The released MSRN can now be reused.

Step 8:   MSC sends a paging request for locating the BS under which the called MS is active.

Step 9:   Since IMSI and TIMSI are included in the paging message, the called MS recognizes that the paging request and responds.

Step 10–12:   After getting paging response, the next task that network does is to establish the authenticity of the MS. Once authenticity check becomes successful, the mobile is requested to turn into cipher mode. Then the setup message for incoming call is also sent by the base station.

Finally, the call is complete when the caller disconnects. The process discussed above gives a top level description of call setup procedure. It does not deal with the critical issues related to management of radio resources during call setup. Let us, therefore, examine how radio resources are allocated for establishing a successful call.

Initially the called mobile is in idle state. During this state a mobile handset keeps getting system parameters over broadcast control channel BCCH (step 0). As explained earlier, GMSC first obtains MSRN and contacts MSC for paging the called mobile on PCH channel (step 1). The mobile responds to the paging message over the uplink channel RACH (step 2) with intention to connect but does not respond to paging until it gets SDDCH assigned to it. The message flow over different radio channels for successful materialization of paging and subsequent authentication of mobile are shown in Fig. 3.7a. BSS responds to the mobile's request for call setup on AGCH (step 3) by sending an immediate assignment message informing MS about the SDDCH. The network does not yet know the identity of the paged MS, until it sends a paging response over SDCCH (step 4). BSS then sends a random number for MS to generate cipher key and also sends challenge to MS (step 5) for the purpose of authentication. MS responds to this message by sending signaling response and generation of the cipher key K_c (step 6). In the next step (step 7), BSS requests MS to transmit in cipher mode to which MS respond by an acknowledgement (step 8). All the message exchanges until this point (steps 3–8) takes place over SDDCH.

After mobile turns into cipher mode, BSS sends the setup message for incoming call and provides a traffic channel. The traffic channel is initially treated as control channel and once connection is fully established it turns into a traffic channel. So, BSS allocates traffic channel when it alerts the mobile about incoming call. In response to alert, the receiver generates ringing sound on the mobile. The channel activities for the call setup are illustrated in Fig. 3.7b.

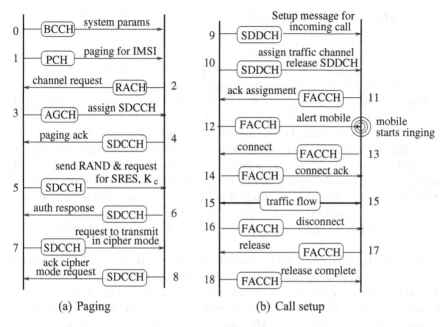

Fig. 3.7 Message flow over radio channels for mobile terminated call setup

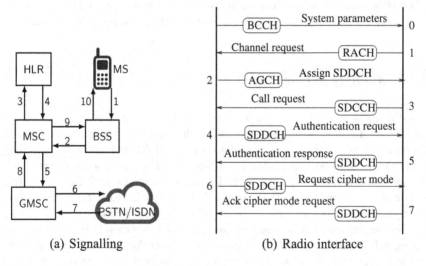

Fig. 3.8 Signaling for mobile originated call setup

3.4.2   Mobile Originated Calls

A mobile originated call may terminate at a mobile or a PSTN number. The signaling requirements for mobile orginated call is shown in Fig. 3.8. When a call request is made from a mobile device, network first seeks authenticity of subscriber (steps 1–2 in Fig. 3.8a. Once authenticity has been established, security checks are performed (steps 3–4). Check on resource availability (steps 5–8) is performed after security checks becomes successful. Finally the call is established (steps 9–10).

Earlier in the previous section, we saw that the availability radio resources is critical for a connection to materialize in mobile terminated call. Likewise, a call originating from mobile requires radio interface before establishment of a connection. A mobile originated call may terminated at mobile or a landline. We have already examined the channel activity at radio interface for a mobile terminated call. So, it suffices to just focus on the exchanges that occur on the radio channels at the caller's side.

Initially, when a mobile wishes to make a call, it sends a request on RACH channel for the allocation of a stand-alone dedicated control channel (SDCCH). BSS uses AGCH to inform mobile about the access grant by allocating a SDCCH. Following the allocation of a SDDCH, the information relating to mobile's authentication and security checks are carried out. After this a traffic channel (TCH) is assigned to MS, and the voice transfer occurs. The details of signaling mechanism for acquiring SDCCH for a mobile terminated call has been illustrated in Fig. 3.7a. The channel activity which occur on radio interface at caller's side is illustrated in Fig. 3.8b.

3.4.3   Mobility Management

Mobility management is the key issue in GSM network. The issue of mobility management for an active connection (handoff) with respect to generic cellular network has been discussed earlier in the previous chapter. In GSM implementation, a group of cells constitutes what is known as *paging area*. The whole service area is partitioned into a number of paging areas. For the purpose of establishing a call to a mobile, its paging area should be searched. If the mobile is active then it responds to paging message. However, it can do so only if the message is correctly directed to the mobile's paging area. Furthermore, paging area should not be very large. Otherwise, paging will generate unnecessary message flows over the network. To handle this problem, each mobile updates its location area identity (LAI) every time there is a change in paging area. MS gets notification about LAI from its base station. SIM stores current LAI and TIMSI whenever a change occurs. If the LAI stored in SIM is not the same as the LAI being broadcast by BS, then a change is noted and the LAI update is performed by MS. MS needs radio resources to register the change in HLR. The channel activities for the same is explained in Fig. 3.9.

Fig. 3.9 Channel activity
needed for location update

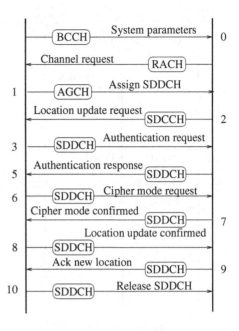

Location update handles mobility when a mobile moves from one paging area to another. However, a more challenging problem in handling mobility occurs when a mobile is holding an active connection. In this case, the major requirement is for channel switching. We have discussed mobility management of active mobile in cellular network in the context of handoff. The way channel switching or the handoffs are managed in GSM network, is not very different from what we discussed in a cellular network. So, our focus here is on the handoff procedure specific to GSM. Handoff involves three basic steps, namely,

1. Signal measurement,
2. Handoff decision, and
3. Handoff execution.

Signal measurement report is transmitted periodically by MS. MS gather measurement values of 16 neighboring BSes and sends a report containing six strongest measurements over one of the 4 interleaved SACCHs. The handover decision and selection of target cell are made either by BSC or MSC. BSC makes a decision if the cell to which MS should be handed over is under its control. Otherwise BSC sends its global cell ID and a BSSMAP message for *handover request* to MSC. MSC then sends a BSSMAP message for *handover request* to new BSC. The message includes channel type, and whether queueing is permissible or not.

The new BSC on receiving the request sends a BTSM channel activation message to its BS. It includes Handover Reference Number (HRN), handover type, channel number and type. Once the BS's acknowledgement is received the new BSC sends acknowledgement to the MSC's handover request message with HRN or handover

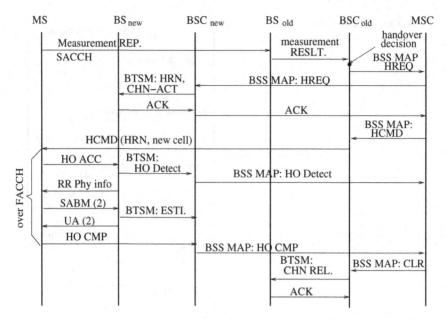

Fig. 3.10 GSM inter BSC handover procedure

reference number. The MSC now responds to the old BSC with handover command. The old BSC in turn sends handover command to the MS over FACCH. The MS sends a handover access message to the new BS over FACCH. The new BS on the receipt of this message sends a BTSM handover detected message to the new BSC. The new BSC then sends BSSMAP handover detection message to the MSC. After this the BS sends physical information message providing the physical channels to be used for transmission by the MS. The MS responds by Set Asynchronous Balance Message (SABM) to the new BS. The new BS then sends two messages one to the new BSC indicating link establishment and the other to the MS which is a unnumbered answer layer-2 message.

The MS finally sends a handover complete message to the new BSC. The new BSC forwards the handover complete message to the MSC. At this point handover is complete. So, the MSC sends a BSSMAP message asking the old BSC to clear radio resource used for MS. The old BSC sends a BTSM channel release message to the old BS. Once the old BS acknowledges the same, handover is complete. The entire process is illustrated by Fig. 3.10.

In GSM, a intra-BSS handoffs due to channel switching within same cell or between cells under the coverage of same BSS may be handled independently by the BSS itself. But after performing an intra-BSS handoff, the BSS informs the MSC about the completion of the process. Intra BSC handover follows a process similar to inter BSC handover. Furthermore, channel switching may occur within same cell, between different cells under the coverage of a single BSS, or between cells under the coverage of different BSSs, and even different MSCs.

3.5 GPRS Network

GSM is a circuit switched network that allows low speed data services. The transfer of data is allowed only during the time, the user occupies channel. Since data exchanges tend to be bursty, the circuit switched networks are unsuitable for large volume data transmission. A user has to pay for the entire duration of connection regardless of actual percentage of time the channel is engaged in transfer of data. General Packet Radio Service (GPRS) leverages GSM network to build a packet based mobile cellular network. It is architectured as an overlay network on GSM through a core IP based network consisting of two new nodes, some enhancements to BSS, certain software upgrades for HLR/VLR, and some new network interfaces. The important nodes in the GPRS core network are Serving GPRS Support Node (SGSN) and Gateway GPRS Support Node (GGSN). The upgrades for existing GSM nodes MSC, BTS, BSC, HLR and VLR are required to make them handle packetized data transfers. The BSC is connected to SGSN through frame relay link [6].

The two fundamental advantages of exchanging data on GPRS over that on GSM are:

1. Flow of data involving many users can be multiplexed and routed through multiple routes by packetizing data, and
2. Long latency for reconnection is eliminated by providing an *always on* connection.

Furthermore, due to packetized data transfers, GPRS supports a data rate that is 3 times more than what can be supported by GSM network. The billing is done according to the number of packets transmitted by an individual user rather than the duration of connection time. By multiplexing data transfers for several users, the service providers can also increase the capacity of data services offered by them.

The data rate supported by GPRS is in the range 9.6–171 Kbps depending on the radio conditions. Under good radio conditions, it can reach speed upto 50 Kbps downstream and upto 20 Kbps upstream as opposed to GSM's maximum rate of 14.6 Kbps with HSCSD (High Speed Circuit Switched Data) service. On the top of this, GPRS also provides robust connectivity. By using increased redundancies in data encodings, it provides resistances to radio losses during data transfers. GPRS uses 4 different coding schemes CS1–CS4 [7] depending on radio conditions. CS1 has highest level of error correction, while CS4 has the least error correction support. CS2 is equivalent to GSM Circuit Switched Data (CSD) bearer service [8]. A data rate of 9.05 Kbps with 1 slot is attainable by using CS1. Whereas the highest data rate 171.4 Kbps is reached with 8 slots using CS4. Though theoretical data rate achievable is 171.4 Kbps, normal allocation includes:

- 1 slot for a control packet,
- at least 2 slots to be set aside for voice traffic, and
- the remaining slots may possibly allocated to packet traffic.

In all 29 combinations of downlink and uplink slots can be defined. The maximum data rate one user can expect consists of 4 slots downlink and 1 slot for uplink. The 4 slots downlink provides a data rate of 4×13.4 Kpbs $= 53.6$ Kbps, and 1 slot uplink gives 13.4 Kbps.

Retransmission ensures data reach BSS before it gets forwarded on to GPRS core network. Since GPRS is packet based, all IP applications like email, web access, instant messaging, file transfers, ssh, etc., can run on GPRS. It can also provide end-to-end VPN accesses to private campus networks, e.g., a university LAN.

The mobile subscribers need specialized GPRS enabled mobile devices to connect to GPRS network. GPRS mobile stations (MSs) are backward compatible with GSM for voice calls, but GSM MSs cannot handle packetized data or the enhanced radio interfaces. Since GPRS packetizes the traffic, multiple users can share the radio resources. The specific upgrades required over GSM network elements for building GPRS overlay are as follows:

- BSS augmented with an additional hardware module called Packet Control Unit (PCU) manages the packet transfers between an MS and GPRS core network apart from supporting data frame retransmission and other GPRS functions. PCU can be a separate unit associated with a BSS.
- HLR and VLR databases need software upgrades to handle packet data for GPRS traffic, GPRS related subscriber's data, and the mobility management. Since, the location information can only be accessed via the SS7, GPRS network nodes also have to interact with the SS7 network.
- A set of new network interfaces are needed for interaction between network elements for handling GPRS connections. The need for defining these interfaces have been necessitated by the fact that in pure GPRS units signaling is transported on IP backbone, whereas GSM elements use SS7 for transport of signals. So, interfaces are needed for interoperability between two signaling methods.

The core GPRS network consists of IP network with two additional new nodes GGSN and SGSN. SGSN is directly connected to BSS. For GPRS services SGSN performs a role similar to what MSC/VLR do in GSM. It controls the link between network and MS by providing session management and GPRS Mobility Management (GMM) functions such as handover, paging, attach, detach, etc. SGSN has to access GSM databases for performing mobility management functions and fetching the individual GPRS subscriber's profile. The other important task of SGSN is to keep the count of packets exchange involving individual MSs for the purpose of billing. The flow of data between GGSN and SGSN is tunneled by use of GPRS Tunneling Protocol (GTP).

GGSN is the GPRS gateway to the external network or public Packet Data Network (PDN). Its role in GPRS network is similar to that of GMSC in GSM network. GGSN is responsible for

- Handling roaming of MS by rerouting incoming traffic to the appropriate SGSN where the MS may be available.
- Authenticating access requests between GPRS and PDN.

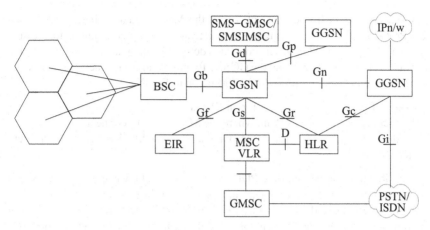

Fig. 3.11 GPRS/GSM combined architecture

- Connecting to HLR through new Gc interface.
- Providing firewall function on Gi interface to PDN.
- Providing tunneled accesses from GPRS network to Virtual Private Networks (VPNs),
- Providing Quality of Service,

The most important job of GGSN is to route incoming packet to appropriate SGSN so that it can reach the destination MS. GGSN converts GPRS packets from SGSN to format of packet data protocol for the external network. It also converts the destination IP address of incoming packets to GSM address of the destination MS, and forwards those packet to responsible SGSN.

The GSM and GPRS combined network architecture is illustrated by Fig. 3.11 [6].

A user's mobile station must attach with GPRS support node SGSN to avail GPRS services. It is a GMM process. It is transparent to BSS and executed by SGSN. The execution of attach is initiated by an MS which supplies mobile's IMSI (International Mobile Subscriber's Identity) or P-TMSI (Packet Temporary Mobile Subscriber's Identity) to SGSN. The IMSI is same as in GSM. P-TMSI has similar role as Temporary Mobile Subscribed Identity (TMSI) assigned by MSC/VLR. TMSI is used in GSM for identity confidentiality of the MS used by the user. P-TMSI is assigned if the user wants only GPRS service as specified by the attach type. The type of attach specifies whether an MS wants only GPRS or both GPRS and GSM services. To initiate an attach, the MS also supplies a number of other attributes which includes the type of attach requested, Routing Area Identification (RAI), and Ciphering Key Sequence Number, etc. The SGSN executes attach and informs HLR if RAI has changed. If the attach type is both GSM and GPRS then SGSN also performs location update with VLR if Gs interface exists. A detach simply disconnects the user from GPRS network.

A successful attach does not yet permit the MS for data exchanges. A Packet Data Protocol (PDP) context is required to activate a packet communication session between a MS and the SGSN. The context is defined by the mapping and the routing information between the MS and the GGSN. To initiate an context activation process, the MS has to provide the following information to SGSN.

- A static IP address, or a request for an IP address.
- The identity of the Access Point where the MS wishes to connect.
- The desired Quality of Service (QoS) and a Network Service Access Point Identifier (NSAPI).

It is possible to establish multiple PDP context sessions between an MS and SGSN for different concurrently running of applications. For instance, the applications for mail, and Internet could run concurrently. The NSAPI discriminates the packets of different applications from one another identifying them. After SGSN has obtained information needed for context activation, it determines the GGSN connected to the access network and forwards the request to that GGSN. The GGSN then connects the MS to the desired AP. The GGSN also assigns transaction identifiers for the communication of data to the specific MS between the GGSN and SGSN. The SGSN's request includes information on a negotiated QoS, based on the subscription information of the user and the availability of the services. When the communication and activation at GGSN become successful, the appropriate information is forwarded to the mobile.

Three operation modes of a GPRS enabled MS are:

1. Class A mode: where the MS is allowed simultaneous GSM and GPRS services being attached to both services.
2. Class B mode: where the MS is attached to both services but can operate only one service at a time.
3. Class C mode: where the MS is attached only to GPRS service.

For optimized use of radio resources, mobility management and attach procedures are combined for class A and class B mode. Since GPRS is an always-on network, the state of MS with respect to this network is important for location update and routing purposes. In GPRS network a mobile can be one of three states, viz., *idle*, *standby*, and *ready*. In the idle state the mobile is unreachable. When it performs a GPRS attach the mobile moves to the ready state. It remains in the ready state till its ready timer expires. On performing a detach from the ready state a mobile goes back to the idle state, and all PDP contexts get deleted. The standby state is reached when the mobile has not sent or received any data for a long time, this causes the ready timer to expire.

Figure 3.12 [6] shows GPRS protocol stacks. The protocols can be viewed from two planes,

- Signaling plane: consist of protocols providing control and support functions for the protocols in transmission plane.

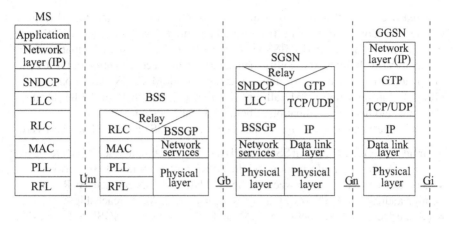

Fig. 3.12 GPRS protocol stacks

- Transmission plane: consists of protocols for transmission of users' data and associated signaling. The protocols of this plane can be divided into three classes, namely,

1. Between MS and SGSN,
2. Between SGSNs and between SGSNs and GGSNs, and
3. Interfacing with SS7.

Some of the functions of the protocols belonging to signaling plane are discussed earlier. GMM and Session Management (SM) form the signaling protocols between MS and SGSN. GMM provides functions for mobility and location update of MS. SM supports activation, modification, and deactivation of PDP contexts. Between two GGSNs, the important signaling protocols are GTP, TCP, and UDP. GTP (GPRS Tunneling Protocol) is responsible for tunneling signal messages between SGSNs and between SGSNs and GGSN in the core GPS network. For reliable transfer of PDUs, TCP (Transmission Control Protocol) can be used across the Gn interface between SGSN and GGSN if they belong to same PLMN. However, Gp interface is to be used between SGSN and GGSN if they belong to different PLMNs. In fact, many-to-many relationship exists between SGSNs and GGSNs [7]. One GGSN routes data form one PDN to many SGSNs, while one SGSN may route data to many GGSNs interfacing with different PDNs. User Datagram Protocol (UDP) carries PDUs across the same Gn interface when reliability is not important. IP (Internet Protocol) is used to route user data and signaling information across the Gn interface.

The protocols facilitating interoperability of GPRS and SS7 on signaling plane are MAP, SCCP, TCAP and MTP. MTP (message transfer part) allows exchange of signaling messages in SS7 network. MAP (mobile application part) is essentially a mobile specific extension of SS7. It allows mobility related signals like location updates, users' profiles, handoffs, etc., to be transported within different nodes of GSM-GPRS network across SS7 network. The exchange of MAP messages are realized over TCAP (transaction capabilities application part) and SCCP (Signal Connection Control Part). The Base Station System Application Part (BSSAP+) includes functions of GSM's BSSAP. It helps to transfer signal information from SGSN to VLR. It involves mobility management when a coordination of GPRS and GSM nodes is needed. For example, a combined GSM-GPRS attach, paging via GPRS for an incoming GSM call, or a combined GPRS and non-GPRS location update would need a coordination of both GPRS and GSM nodes.

There interfaces used for signal exchanges between SS7 and GPRS networks are:

- Gr interface: exists between SSGN and HLR. Through Gr interface SSGN retrieves or updates location information and the GPRS profile for mobile subscriber.
- Gc interface: is defined between GGSN and HLR. GGSN contacts HLR to determine address of SGSN to which MS is located and if MS is reachable.
- Gf interface: is defined between SGSN and EIR. It is used by SGSN to fetch IMEI of the mobile station from EIR.
- Gs interface: connects databases of SSGN and MSC/VLR. It allows coordination of circuit switched and packet switched pagings in the SGSN as well as location information of any MS attached to both packet switched and circuit switched services. BSS Application Part (BSSP) allows mobility functionality to be managed in Gs interface.
- Gd interface: defined between an SGSN and gateway for short message service. The progress of a SMS for delivery to an MS in circuit or packet mode requires a gateway function between mobile network and the network that provides access to SMS center. An SMS delivered to an MS is routed from the gateway of SMS towards SGSN on Gd interface when SMS is delivered on GPRS.

The transmission plane protocols and their functions are described below:

- Subnetwork Dependent Convergence Protocol (SNDCP): is used for transfer of packets between the mobile and the SGSN. It converts network layer Packet Data Units (PDUs) into suitable format (called SNPDUs) for the underlying subnetwork architecture and also compresses the SNPDUs for efficient data transmission. SNDCP manages transfer of PDUs for multiple PDP contexts.
- Data link layer: it consists of two sublayers, LLC (between MS and SGSN) and RLC/MAC (between MS and BSS). LLC establishes a reliable logical link between an MS and its SGSN. It ensures data confidentiality by using ciphering functions. RLC/MAC stands for Radio Link Control and MAC. RLC's task is to establish a reliable radio link between MS and BSS. It performs MAC functions like segmentation of LLC frames into RLC blocks as well as reassembly of RLC blocks into LLC frames. The MAC controls the accesses radio channels by several MSs. The primary responsibility of MAC is thus contention management and collision avoidance. RLC/MAC layer can support both ack and non-ack modes of operation.
- Physical layer: it is split into two sublayers, Physical Link Layer (PLL) and physical Radio Frequency Layer (RFL). PLL oversees data transfer over physical channel between MS and BSS. Its responsibilities include data unit framing, data coding, detection and correction of transmission errors over the physical medium. PLL

uses RFL services whose basic responsibility is for modulation and demodulation of physical wave forms and checking conformity with GSM specification.

• BSS GPRS application Protocol (BSSGP) is concerned with delivery of routing and QoS information between BSS and SGSN.

GPRS support both IPv4 and IPv6. Gi interface is for interoperability of IP network with external or public data network. From outside GPRS appears like any other IP subnetwork with GGSN acting as a gateway to that IP network. A user wanting to exchange data with an IP network gets an IP address from the set of IP address space of the GPRS operator. For mobile users, it is necessary to have a dynamic IP assigned. So, a DHCP server is installed in GPRS network. Address resolution between GSM and IP addresses is performed by GGSN using appropriate PDP context. Tunneling between GPRS private IP and external IP network prevents any unauthorized accesses to PLMN. Thus, the configuration of GPRS network is designed with an aim to make it appear as a wide area wireless extension to the Internet for the mobile devices.

3.6 UMTS

The architectural enhancements to radio based wide area wireless networks introduced in the form of 2G networks [9]. Higher data rates supported by 2G networks redefined the way mobile networks were used. Still 2G networks suffer from a number of limitations. The important among these are low transfer rates, low efficiency of circuit-switching data transfers, proliferation in number of standards. So, the efforts to enhance 2G networks were focused around removing these limitations. It resulted in High Speed Circuit-Switched Data (HSCSD) [1], GPRS standards [3], and Enhanced Data Rates for Global Evolution (EDGE) [2]. The common objective of all these initiatives was to find solutions that would yield higher transfer rates without requiring any major architectural changes in the existing network. The reason for avoiding major architectural change was mainly dictated by the fact that the substantial investments were made for setting up 2G networks. Any large scale change will not only require huge investments but old investments also have to be written off as non performing assessts.

HSCSD approach gets around the problem of low data rate simply by bundling multiple time slots together instead of using single slot for transfer of data. GPRS supports packetized data transfers by introducing only minimal changes in core GSM network. The migration from circuit-switching domain to packet-switching domain is considered to be the major advantage of GPRS networks. It is possible to offer data rates upto 115 Kbps in GPRS. EDGE employed better modulation techniques to increase data rates of GSM and GPRS up to 3 times. It used Octagonal Phase Shift Keying (8-PSK) in place of Gaussian Minimum Phase Shift Keying (GPSK). So EGPRS (GPRS enhancement with EDGE) is able to support data rates up to 384 Kbps. But these enhancements of existing standards are considered inadequate in terms of bandwidth and the capabilities needed to support 3G services. The air interface is found to be the main bottleneck in providing greater bandwidth.

In 1998, the 3rd Generation Partnership Project (3GPP) [10] was launched in cooperation with six partners led by European Telecommunication Standard Institute (ETSI). The objective of 3GPP was to develop third generation mobile system with the core network based on GSM. After a year, another 3G Partnership Project for wide area cellular wireless networks called 3GPP2 was launched by American National Standard Institute (ANSI). Their objective was to keep ANSI-41 network as the core for 3G networks.

International Mobile Telecommunication-2000 (IMT-2000) group formed under the International Telecommunication Union to define interfaces between the two parallely developing 3G networks, one evolving out of GSM and the other out of ANSI-41. The key motivation for the defining interfaces is to offer seamless roaming services between 3GPP and 3GPP2 networks. Realizing the importance of this universal roaming characteristic, 3GPP adopted the name Universal Mobile Telecommunication Service (UMTS) for 3G mobile systems. The process of evolution from 2G to 3G can thus be seen to happen along three planes, viz., technical, network and services.

In technical plane, the evolution is centered around an all IP cellular based wide area wireless network unlike GSM/GPRS which are predominantly based on switch centric networks. The first version of UMTS specification, known as 3GPP release 99 [10], while retaining majority of the core GPRS/GSM network functionalities introduced a new wireless access technology known as Wide band Code Division Multiple Access (WCDMA) [11]. With WCDMA technology, it was possible to increase capacity of 2G networks to support higher data rates. The new 3GPP release 4 [12] optimizes air interface even further. Though most modifications are directed towards the core GSM/GPRS network elements, backward compatibility is retained for supporting 2G services.

3.6.1   UTRAN

UMTS Terrestrial Radio Access Network (UTRAN) [13] constitutes the main extension to GSM Core Network (CN) for providing and maintaining connectivity with User Equipment (UE). UTRAN sits between Uu and Iu interfaces.

In the network plane, the UMTS is organized under three functional groups of network elements:

1. Radio Access Network, known as UTRAN, responsible for both Radio Resource Management (RRM), and Mobility Management (MM).
2. Core Network (CN) responsible for communication management. It involves all switchings and routings of calls and data connections to the external networks, besides managing sessions, and mobility related information.

3. User equipment (UE) represents the end device. With UE the user roams about in the service area, and accesses 3G services.

The evolution along the service plane is evaluated on the basis of classes of data carrier services supported by 3G networks as against those supported by 2G or 2.5G networks. The services provided to the end users are the yard-stick for measuring the benefits of using 3G over 2G/2.5G. The question is: what killer applications can be supported by these networks? The throughput of 2.5G networks provide bandwidth sufficient for web browsing, large email messages, maps for real-time navigation and basic multimedia services. But killer applications like video conferencing, voice over IP, full motion video, online 3D gaming and streaming music require enhanced data rates which can only be provided by 3G networks. The *always on* characteristic of 3G network offers some additional advantages. For example, in applications like road navigation, it will be preferable to have real-time traffic and other navigation related information. There are four QoS classes of service in 3G for different types of traffic.

- *Conversation class* consisting of voice, video, telephony and video gaming.
- *Streaming class* representing multimedia video on demand and webcast.
- *Interactive class* such as web browsing, network games, data base access.
- *Background class* which includes email, SMS and downloading.

In addition to the above, UMTS supports Virtual Home Environment (VHE). VHE presents the portability of personal service environment to the users across network boundaries. A user can consistently retain the same personalized features even with world wide roaming capabilities. VHE has capabilities to adapt to both network and the UE. It automatically converts the messages to formats suitable for the UE.

UMTS is developed as a layered architecture independent of the underlying network. This is possible by defining standard interfaces between the network layer and the application layer. The network layer comprises of network elements under the control of service provider. The application layer or the service layer may be controlled by service logic and algorithms running over third party servers. So, the problem of proliferation of standards can be short-circuited by defining open standards for the interfaces.

Figure 3.13 illustrates the organization of UTRAN architecture and its interfaces with rest of the CN. The main task of UTRAN is to create and maintain Radio Access Bearers (RAB) for communication between the user equipment (UE) and the core network (CN). RAB offers an illusion to the CN about the existence of a fixed communication path to UE. This relieves CN from the burden of maintaining radio connectivity with UE. The two open interfaces Uu and Iu link UTRAN to UE and CN respectively.

UTRAN consists of two new nodes, namely, Node B and Radio Network Controller (RNC). A set of Node Bs are controlled by one RNC. A RNC and its set of Node Bs together define Radio Network Subsystem (RNS). The role of a RNC may be viewed as similar to that of a Base Station Controller (BSC) in a GSM network. Likewise, a Node B is functionally is similar to a Base Station in a GSM network.

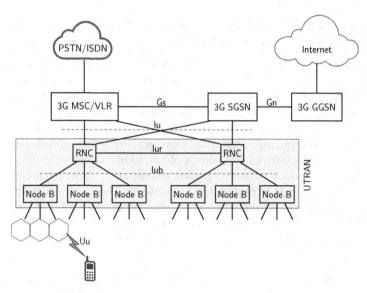

Fig. 3.13 UTRAN architecture

The rest of the GSM and GPRS network entities like MSC, SGSN, HLR, etc., are extended to adapt to UMTS requirements. So, all three service, GSM, GPRS and UMTS are integrated into overall network having interfaces A, Gb, Abis and the new interface Iub and Iur. Where Iub and Iur respectively represent the interfaces between a RNC and a Node B and between two RNCs. These two interfaces are open. So, RNC and Node B may be brought from different vendors and can be connected via Iub interface.

UTRAN communicates with CN via Iu interface which has two components, namely, Iu-CS and Iu-PS. Iu-CS supports circuit switching services whereas Iu-PS supports packet switching services. Iu-CS connects RNC to MSC in a similar way as GSM-A interface does. Iu-PS connects RNC to SGSN as the interface Gb does in GPRS. The interface, Iur, between two different RNCs has no equivalent in GSM network. RNC enables autonomous Radio Resource Management (RRM). It handles the exchanges of control messages across Iu, Iur and Iub interfaces besides being responsible for the operation and maintenance of RNS elements. The user's packetized data coming from Iu-PS, and the circuit switched data coming from Iu-CS are multiplexed together for multimedia transmission via Iur, Iub and Uu interface to and from the user's equipment. The last two interfaces, Iu and Uu are also open interface. Thus, UMTS has four new open interfaces, viz., Iub, Iur, Iu and Uu.

The functionalities of a RNC can be grouped into two, RRM, and control function. It uses Iur interface to autonomously handle RRM relieving CN from the burden of RRM. RRM consists of a set of algorithms which determines a stable radio path and also assures QoS through efficient sharing and managing of the radio resources. The control functions comprise of certain support functions for RRM, setup, maintenance and release of the radio bearers. All serving control functions such as call admission, handoffs, congestion, etc., are managed by a single RNC. This RNC is called Serving RNC (SRNC). Thus SRNC terminates Iu link for both UE and Radio Network Access Application Part (RNAAP) signaling to and from CN. The RNCs which control the cells used by an UE are known as Drift RNCs (DRNCs). When a handoff occurs, one of the DRNCs becomes the SRNC. So, a DRNC is involved in inter-RNC soft handoff. A soft handoff is characterized by *make before break*. This means the UE remains connected with the DRNC while connection is being established with SRNC. So, at intervening time between connection establishment and completion of handoff UE is actively connected to two RNCs.

Node B is the network entity which provides physical radio connection to UE in a cell. It can be co-located with a GSM base station. Node B connects to UE via WCDMA Uu radio interface and connects via Iub interface to RNC. The main task of Node B is to convert data from Uu interface. It includes forward error correction, rate adaptation, WCDMA spreading and despreading, and also quadrature phase shifting key (QSPK) modulation on air interface. It also performs the measurement of the quality of connection, determines the frame error rate, and communicates these measurements to RNC for soft handoffs. Additionally, Node B assists in helping UE for power adjustments on both on downlink and uplink.

The UMTS UE is equivalent to MS in GSM. It has a UMTS SIM (USIM) card. The Mobile Equipment (ME) is enabled to receive UMTS service when it has a USIM. UE has three classes of functions as counterparts for functions of Node B, RNC and CN respectively. For example, Node B and UE participate for power control, radio measurements, signal spreading/despreading, modulation and demodulation of signals. Similarly, RNC and UE counterparts interwork for radio resource control, ciphering and deciphering, handoff management. UE and CN counterparts collaborate for MM, authenticity check, session management and QoS negotiation.

3.6.2 WCDMA

UTRAN air interface uses Wide Band CDMA (WCDMA). WCDMA is a DSSS based CDMA where user's data is spread over a wide band. A certain amount of power is needed for transfer of information. Let this power be denoted by P_i. If P_i is spread over a wide band then effective power requirement for information transmission over a carrier frequency (small point in the band) is very low. Let it be denoted by P_e.

$$P_i = \int_{entireband} P_e$$

A small increase in P_e increases total power by a significant amount; and hence the amount of information transmitted. Furthermore, the transmitted information, being spread over a wide band by a pseudo random code, cannot be distinguished from

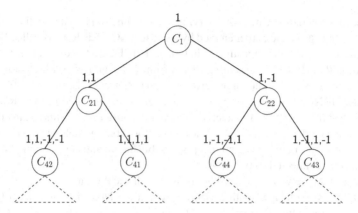

Fig. 3.14 Orthogonal spreading code for different spreading factors

noise. So, direct sequence spread spectrum (DSSS) is ideal for coded information exchanges.

WCDMA uses a wider band than CDMA for spreading data signals. The data is encoded twice before it is sent over air interface. The first encoding involves multiplication with channelization code. The channelization codes belong to Orthogonal Variable Spreading Factor (OVSF) code family [14]. The orthogonality of OVSF codes enables separation of different coded channels transmitted over the same air interface. In the uplink direction this code is necessary to separate data and control information from the same UE. In the downlink direction this encoding separates different users in the same cell. With OVSF codes it is possible not only to maintain orthogonality of codes with different spreading factors (different lengths), but also to support different user data rates. The orthogonal spreading code of different spreading factors can be constructed from a binary tree form as shown in Fig. 3.14.

The recursive formula for generating this code can is as follows:

$$
c_{2n} = \begin{pmatrix} c_{2n,1} \\ c_{2n,2} \\ \vdots \\ c_{2n,2n} \end{pmatrix} = \left(\begin{pmatrix} c_{n,1} & c_{n,1} \\ c_{n,1} & -c_{n,1} \\ c_{n,n} & c_{n,n} \\ c_{n,n} & -c_{n,n} \end{pmatrix} \right)
$$

The second encoding step is a scrambling process. It does not expand the required bandwidth, but it just rearranges the bit order. In uplink direction, scrambling helps to distinguish between UEs, and in downlink it becomes necessary to distinguish between different cells of same base station. The scrambling codes belong to Gold family [15]. Each code has a length of 10 ms resulting in a code of length 38400 chips if a 3.84 Mcps chip rate is used.

Fig. 3.15 Elimination of
near far effect

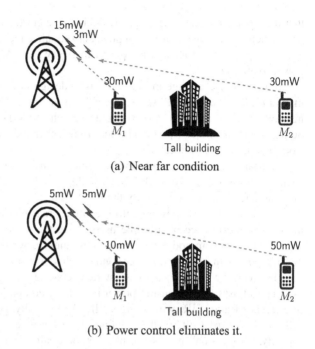

(a) Near far condition

(b) Power control eliminates it.

WCDMA incorporates functions for control of multiple radio accesses and their users. The four main functions among these are power control, soft and softer hand-offs, admission control and congestion control.

The biggest disadvantage of DSSS is the near-far effect. All stations may be transmitting at the same time. Since, every station has a different code, simultaneous transmission is possible. However, a receiver may be unable to detect weaker signals due to the presence of a stronger signal. Figure 3.15a depicts the condition for near far effect. It shows two transmitters (mobile stations M_1 and M_2) are transmitting at the same time to a base station (BS). As signal strength decays according to inverse square law. Therefore, even if M_1 and M_2 transmit their respective signals at the same strength, the received signal strength from M_1 is much lower than the received signal strength from M_2. It happens due to the fact that M_2's distance is more than M_1's distance from BS. Furthermore, M_2's signal experiences blocking due to tall objects like office buildings as depicted in the figure. The near far effect can be eliminated by power control. The idea is to equalize the received signal strengths from various transmitters. For example, suppose initially

1. M_1 transmits its signals at 30 mW, and the received signal strength at BS is 15 mW, and
2. M_2 transmits its signals at 30 mW and the received signal strength at BS is 3 mW.

M_1's signal strength is cut to half when it is received at BS. On the other hand, M_2's signal strength is reduced by a factor 10 when it reaches BS. Suppose BS determines that the received signal strength of 5 mW is sufficient for it. BS should asks M_1 to adjust their respective transmission powers to equalize the received signal strengths. So, M_1 decreases its transmission power to 10 mW, and M_2 increases transmission power to 50 mW.

So, the major challenge in WCDMA is to design power control algorithms that maintain all signals having same power level at the receiver. Figure 3.15b shows near-effect can be nullified by power control mechanism. The idea is to reduce power output from transmitter C_1 which is close to BS, so that the received signal strengths from both C_1 and C_2 are equal.

The shared downlink in WCDMA resource consists of transmission power and channelization codes in Node B (UMTS analogue of BS in GSM), while in the uplink the shared radio resource basically the involves management of user interference at BS. As indicated above, power control regulates transmission power of terminal and minimizes interference of multiple users using the same carrier frequency. More users could be accommodated in the same frequency, by proper adjustment of transmission power. In summary, power control helps to establish good quality link over time between the user and the base station regardless of the distance between the two. The adjustment of transmit power is done by comparing the current Signal-to-Interference Ratio (SIR) with a target SIR. Additionally, power control can help in cell breathing [16]. Cell breathing defines the balance between the coverage and the capacity. With a small number of users, good quality can be achieved over a long distance. So the cell size can be large. As the number of users becomes large, the users must come closer to base station to get a good quality link, or equivalently the cell size should be small.

WCDMA does not place a hard limit on network capacity. So, the entry of a new user is welcome as long as a code is available for that user. But entry of a new user will cause interference level to go up. Thus the capacity is physically bounded by the rise in noise level due to increased load on the system. So, the cell breathing gets reduced. The admission control is a mechanism which reduces overloading of the system [11] and avoids reduction in cell breathing. It permits or denies the new connection on the basis of admissible load of the network. The admission control is employed in both uplink and downlink because of the system's capability for serving different services with different requirements related to capacity and quality.

Hdandoff as explained in Sect. 3.6.3 is an important part of a cellular communication system which provides the basic mobility support to a user with an active connectivity. Soft and softer handoff types are supported when WCDMA uses frequency division duplex (FDD) mode. WCDMA uses two duplexing methods, time division duplexing (TDD) and FDD. FDD needs paired frequency bands for downlink and uplink, whereas TDD needs unpaired frequency bands. TDD does not allow large propagation delay between transmission and reception as it could cause collision between transmit and receive time slots. So, TDD can be suitable for environments with low propagation delays, and for small cells [11]. One advantage of TDD mode is that a large asymmetry is possible between uplink and downlink rates. With careful network planning, TDD mode can be used for applications that derive advantage out of asymmetry between downlink and uplink, web browsing is an example of such an application. Handoff strategy in WCDMA depends on the duplexing mode. Since, UMTS combines with GSM-GPRS network, handoff type will depend on the interface being used.

The basic idea in executing a soft or a softer handoff is to choose a data stream that will provide the best connection quality. The final signal in WCDMA is constructed by summing up the signals from different sources. Two combining operations viz., micro diversity and macro diversity are employed for the same. In WCDMA, the Node B receiver uses a rake receiver. A rake receiver is a system of multiple small receivers, called fingers, designed to counter multipath fading. A signal on radio path is reflected from trees, buildings, ground and even water. At the receiving end many copies of the same signal reach with a different phase and time. Each finger of a rake receiver decodes a different multipath component. Then contributions of all fingers are combined to make best use of different transmissions in each of the transmission path. This combining process is known as micro-diversity. So, Node B functions as a micro diversity point and summed up signal is used. A UE may get signals from different cells. These cells constitute its active set. So, an UE may also use cells belonging to different Node Bs. Therefore, macro diversity also exists at RNC level. But RNC does not have a rake receiver. So combining signal at RNC should use some other approach like quality of data. Thus the two combining techniques micro diversity at Node B and macro diversity at RNC level help to counter multi path fading effects and help to determine which data stream will provide the best quality.

At times, even with admission control, the system may get overloaded. This can happen due to excessive movements of UEs. When the system load exceeds a threshold, congestion control measures are activated. It consists of following techniques.

1. Reducing bit rate of services that are insensitive to increase in delays.
2. Inter-frequency handoffs.
3. Handoffs for moving the users to GSM.
3. Dropping connections.

All the above mentioned measures attempt to prevent degradation of the quality of the user's experience in an overloaded cell untill congestion problem is solved. If the first action fails to work, the next action is to move some of the users to less loaded alternative frequencies. If inter-frequency handoff does not help, then third action is to move some users to GSM. The final and drastic action is to drop some of the connections, so that the quality on the remaining connections does not degrade.

The UMTS CN is responsible for handling all communication services. It includes switching of circuit-switched calls and routing of data packets. CN offers functionalities in two domains, Circuit-Switching (CS) domain and Packet-Switching (PS) domain. The entities specific to CS domain in CN are MSC, Media Gateway (MGW), and GMSC. The functions of these entities have been discussed earlier in connection with GSM network.

CN offers PS type connection in PS domain. A PS type connection transports user's information by dividing it into equal sized blocks of concatenated bits or packets. These packets are reassembled at the receiver end to provide the actual information. The two basic entities of CN in PS-domain are derived from GPRS core network nodes SGSN and GGSN. The functions of these entities have been discussed under GPRS. UMTS CN supports four QoS classes of communication as explained earlier.

The IP Multimedia Subsystem (IMS) represents the entities of CN that provision for multimedia services in UMTS. The task of provisioning includes the collection of signalling and the bearer related network multimedia services. These services are based on IETF defined session control capabilities [17]. IMS consists of three main logical functions, namely, Call Session Control Functions (CSCF), Media Gateway Control Function (MGCF) and the Media Gateway (MGW). A Home Subscriber Server (HSS) is also introduced to keep the profile of the user function in a similar way as the HLR does in GPRS.

3.6.3   Handoffs in UMTS

The possible handoff types in UMTS are:

- FDD soft/softer handoff
- FDD inter-frequency hard handoff
- FDD/TDD handoff (change of cell)
- TDD/FDD handoff (change of cell)
- TDD/TDD handoff
- Handoff to UMTS (from GSM)
- Handoff to GSM

In FDD mode, WCDMA supports two types of handoffs, viz., soft and softer. The user equipment (UE) is allowed to use two air interfaces in overlapping areas of two adjacent cells. In soft handoff the user's equipment is simultaneously connected to two or more cells on the same frequency with two or more base stations.

Normally a soft intra-frequency handoff takes place in softer handoff. It occurs between different carrier frequencies in a high capacity area. Handoffs enable the User's Equipment (UE) to maintain a good quality active connection while moving between cells. In reality softer handoff is not a handoff. For softer handoff, the UE combines more than one radio link to improve the quality of signal. Node B combines the data from more than one cell to obtain good quality data from the UE. A UE can simultaneously support up to eight radio links, though actual number of links depends on the number of fingers in the rake receiver. Typically four links are simultaneously accessible to a UE. A radio connection initially established in one cell. The network then initiates intra-frequency measurements to determine if the UE can connect to another cell for improving the quality of data exchanges between itself and the RNC. On finding a suitable cell, active set update procedure is executed. It adds and deletes one or more radio links to active set of the UE. The process of update is such that at least one common link is always present. Figure 3.16 depicts the softer handoff scenario.

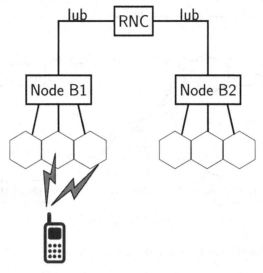

(a) Involving one Node B.

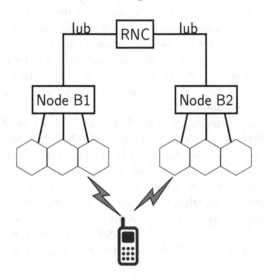

(b) Involving different Node B.

Fig. 3.16 Softer handoffs in WCDMA FDD mode

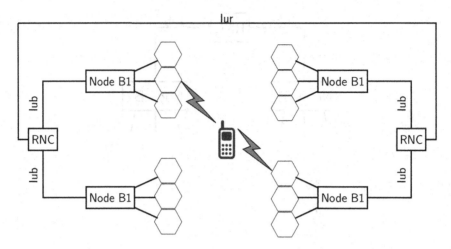

Fig. 3.17 Soft handoff in WCDMA FDD mode

Soft handoff is same as softer handoff except that cells involved belong to more than one Node B. In this case combining of link measurements is done by RNC. Softer handoff becomes a bit complicated when it involves between cells under different RNCs. In this case, an Iur connection is established by Drift RNC (DRNC) (from where the UE moved) and data is transferred to Serving RNC (SRNC). Since handoffs are initiated by RNC, the core network is not burdened to handle them. Figure 3.17 illustrates the soft handoff scenario.

Hard handoff is characterized by break before make. It means the current connection is snapped before new connection is established. It exhibits a temporary interruption in connectivity. Intra-frequency hard handoff occurs in TDD mode. In this case channelizing code and scrambling code for the UE would change, but the frequency is unchanged. Inter-frequency hard handoff requires that the UE should be capable of supporting more than one frequency. Handoff process can be initiated either by the network or by the UE. Normally network initiates it through radio bearer control messages. The UE initiated handoff occurs when the UE performs a cell update and sends this to the RNC on a different frequency from the one it is connected.

3.6.4 UMTS Interface Protocol Model

The generic UMTS protocol model is structured as a set of horizontal and vertical layers as shown in Fig. 3.18. The horizontal layering separates the generic transport related issues from the UMTS specific issues related to air interface. The bottom most layer is called Transport Network Layer (TNL). It is responsible for general purpose transport services to all UMTS network entities across the interfaces. The remaining layers, namely, Radio Network Layer (RNL) and System Network Layer (SNL) are responsible for UMTS specific functions among the network elements. Usually the control data and the user data are also distinguished by creating vertical separations across all three horizontal layers. The functions related to transfer of control data are referred to as control plane functions and those related to transfer of user data are known as user plane functions.

The TNL functions handle transport and routing of both control and user data across all network interfaces. The TNL protocols can be further divided into two layers: physical layer and data link layer. The physical layer of UMTS radio interface is based on WCDMA technology, whereas the physical layer of the UMTS terrestrial interfaces can be based on a different transmission technology such as ATM. The transport layer protocols and its interworking across both radio and terrestrial interfaces are shown in Fig. 3.19.

In UTRAN, the data generated at the higher layers are carried over the air interface by different physical channels. The transport channels are unidirectional which can be either shared by multiple users or dedicated to a few selected users. SRNC is responsible for the radio interface activities of the UE on the WCDMA transport channel. The nodes labeled B only maintain the WCDMA physical channels.

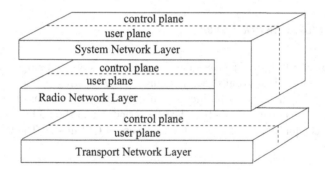

Fig. 3.18 The UMTS protocol model

Fig. 3.19 UMTS transport network protocols and interfaces

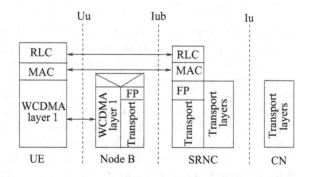

The data link layer over the Uu interface is defined by two link layer protocols, namely,

1. Medium Access Control (MAC), and
2. Radio Link Control (RLC).

The responsibility of MAC protocol is to map logical channels onto the appropriate transport channels depending on the type of data to be transported. RLC is responsible for segmentation and reassembly of variable-length higher layer Protocol Data Units (PDUs) into a number of RLC-PDUs. It also provides for packet retransmission to handle transmission errors. On the control plane, the RLC services known as signalling Radio Bearers, are used by the RRC network layer. On the user plane, RLC services are used by the service-specific protocol layers such as Packet Data Convergence Protocol (PDCP) on the PS domain.

The terrestrial part of TNL use existing protocols from ATM and TCP/UDP/IP family of protocols. These non UMTS protocols are included on the stack along with some adaptation protocols such as GPRS Tunneling for IP or AAL(n) for ATM. IP based transport is applied only for PS domain user plane traffic in backbone network and at the Iu interface. But ATM transport protocol dominates in UTRAN side.

3.6.5 Radio Network Layer

The fundamental task of UTRAN radio interface protocols is multiplexing traffic flows of different kinds from different sources. The layering applied to RNL is dictated by the distinct responsibilities assigned to the layers in terms of OSI model. However, the layers named simply as layer 1, 2 and 3, and should by no means be considered as equivalent to the three lowest layers of OSI model. The three layers are:

1. Radio physical layer
2. Radio link layer
3. Radio network layer

The physical layer provides services as a set of WCDMA transport channels. So, the physical layer performs initial multiplexing task, i.e., mapping flows between transport channels to WCDMA physical channels in both forward and reverse directions.

The overall layering architecture of the RNL protocols is depicted in Fig. 3.20 The radio link layer is another multiplexing layer. However, it does not make any significant contribution to dynamic sharing of the capacity in WCDMA radio interface. Its job is to provide a kind of wrapper service, so that upper layer gets a unified view of existence of a set of radio bearers on which different types of traffic can be carried over the radio. The medium access control (MAC) sublayer controls the use of the transport block by ensuring that the allocation decisions (done on UTRAN side) are enforced on both ends of the radio interface. The Radio Link Control (RLC)

Fig. 3.20 Radio network
layer protocols

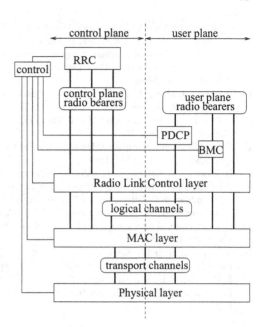

sublayer provides link layer functionality to the logical channels provided by MAC sublayer. RLC includes some adaptations in usual link layer functions to cater to the special characteristics of radio transmission. Network layer protocols operating on the top of RNL create communication service for the UEs over the communication paths maintained by RNL. The control plane protocols which control communication between UEs and CN comprise of two sublayers. The lower sublayer is responsible for Mobility Management (MM). The top sublayer operating on the top of MM consists of a number of service specific communication management protocols such as Session Management, Short Messaging Service, Supplementary Service (SS).

References

1. G.T.G.S.M. Specifications, 02.34. High speed circuit switched data (HSCSD), Stage 1. Version **5**(2) (1997)
2. A. Furuskär, S. Mazur, F. Müller, H. Olofsson, EDGE: Enhanced data rates for GSM and TDMA/136 evolution. IEEE Pers. Commun. Mag. **6**(3), 56–66 (1999)
3. J. Cai, D. Goodman, General packet radio service in GSM. IEEE Commun. Mag. **35**(10), 122–131 (1997)
4. H.P. Luhn, Computer for verifying numbers, US patent US2950048 A, August 2005
5. T. Russell, *Signaling System #7*, 4th edn. (McGraw-Hill, New York, 2002)
6. B. Gharibi, L. Logrippo, Understanding GPRS: The GSM packet radio service. Comput. Netw. **34**, 763–779 (2000)
7. C. Bettsetter, Mobility modeling in wireless network categorization, smooth movement, and border effects. ACM SIGMOBILE: Mob. Comput. Commun. Rev. **5**(3), 55–66 (2001)

8. J. Eberspächer and H.J.Vögel, *GSM Switching, Service and Protocols* (John Wiley, 2001)

9. V. Perira, T. Sousa, P. Mendes, and E. Monteiro, Evolution of mobile communications: from voice calls to ubiquitous multimedia group communication. In *The 2nd International Working Conference on Performance Modelling and Evolution of Hetergeneous Networks (HT-NET'04)* (Yorkshire, UK, 2004)

10. A. Scrase, J. Meredith, and E. Group, Overview of 3GPP release 99: Summary of all releases 99 features, Version 05/03/04 (2004)

11. E. Dahlman, S. Parkvall, and J. Sköld, *4G LTE/LTE-Advanced for Mobile Broad Band* (Academic Press, Elsevier, 2011)

12. ETSI. 3GPP a global initiative: The mobile broadband standard. (2001), http://www.3gpp.org/specifications/releases/76-release-4

13. H. Kaarnen, A. Ahtianinen, L. Laitinen, S. Naghian, V. Niemi, *UMTS Networks: Architecture* (Mobility and Services, Wiley Online Library, 2001)

14. B.D. Andreev, E.L. Titlebaum, and E.G. Friedman, Orthogonal code generator for 3g wireless transceiver. In *GLSVLSI' 03* (Washington DC, USA, April 2003) pp. 28–29

15. R. Gold, Optimal binary sequence for spread spectrum multiplexing. IEEE Trans. Inf. Theor. **13**(4), 619–621 (1967)

16. V. V. Veeravalli and A. Sendonaris, The coverage capacity tradeoff in cellular CDMA system. *IEEE Transaction on Vehicular Technology* (1999) pp. 1443–1451

17. J. Rosenberg, H. Schulzrinne, G. Camarillo, J.P. Johnston, R. Sparks, M. Handley, and E. Schooler, SIP: Session initiation protocol. RFC-3261 (2002), http://www.ietf.org/rfc/rfc3261.txt

Chapter 4
Wireless Local Area Network

4.1 Introduction

All radio communication technologies are developed on cellular architecture. However, the major technological hurdle in use of radio communication is the ability to build seamless convergent solutions for mobile users. Availing services across heterogeneous networks is still a problem for mobile users. The numerous challenges encountered in this respect are mainly due to the following reasons.

1. Multiple access technologies, and administrative domains.
2. Multiple types of services such as voice, data, video, etc.
3. Availability of services every where and all the time.
4. Efficient delivery of traffic.

From the stand point of application development and convenience of usages, innovations in building convergent solutions are more important than the discovery of new networking technologies. Still availability of new networking technology would eventually lead to easy and efficient implementation of convergent communication solutions in overcoming heterogeneity of networks. Thus, a sound understanding of wireless network is an important starting point for developing exciting new applications for mobile computing systems.

In general, wireless data networks can be divided broadly into four different categories based on their intended use.

1. *Wide area networks* (WANs) are created and maintained by cellular carriers. WANs can be viewed as connectionless extensions to circuit switched networks, created in order to facilitate communication between persons and groups belonging to geographically dispersed locations spread over large areas, such as across cities or across countries. The main utility of WANs lies in connecting different LANs and MANs, so that computers and users of one domain can communicate with computers at different domains located far apart.
2. *Metropolitan area networks* (MANs) are created and maintained as a backbone network technology for interconnecting a number of local area networks or LANs.

© Springer Nature Singapore Pte Ltd. 2017
R.K. Ghosh, *Wireless Networking and Mobile Data Management*,
DOI 10.1007/978-981-10-3941-6_4

Its coverage spans a large geographical area such as a city or a block of buildings spread over a sufficiently large physical area or a campus.

3. *Local area networks* (LANs) are created and maintained by small institutions or organizations for close communication related to professional interactions, collaboration between persons and groups belonging to an institution or an organization.

4. *Personal area networks* (PANs) are created by individuals, usually self-organize, self-maintained. PANs are exclusively for person centric communication with interfaces to local neighborhood and the rest of the world.

Though both WLAN and PAN are based on short range radio transmission technologies, the two have distinct domains of applications. PAN applications typically require low volume, more secure transmission compared to WLANs. Therefore, low range radio transmission technologies such as Bluetooth or ZigBee, are ideally suited for person centric data services as needed by PANs.

In contrast, GSM is the core radio based transmission technology for the applications that require data service over WANs. GSM offers very low speed data service, because mobility management in wide area network is the main focus in GSM. GPRS, EDGE, HSCSD standards which were developed around GSM provided enhanced data rates over WANs by creating packet based network extensions to conventional circuit switched connection of the GSM network.

GSM, GPRS and UMTS have been discussed in the previous chapter. We plan to study PAN separately in Chap. 5 while limiting the focus of the current chapter to the principles and the theories on which wireless LANs are established and used. In order to organize this chapter as a precursor to subsequent discussion on wireless networks, we also take closer looks at: (i) how mobility affects the data rates, and (ii) the details of standards for different wireless networks.

4.2 Mobility Support and Wireless Networks

Figure 4.1 gives a brief introduction on the relationship of achievable data rates with mobility support. WLAN supports only slow mobility while WAN (GSM/wideband cellular) supports range of mobilities starting from discrete and slow to continuous fast (vehicular) mobility. For example, PAN, implemented over Bluetooth, supports slow mobility in an enclosed room, and lies somewhere between fixed and slow mobility (no more than the speed of walking). The mobility in Bluetooth is neither fully controlled nor discrete like in wired LAN. Though wired LAN is fixed, with DHCP, it can provide very limited discrete and slow mobility. A user can access network resources by moving to different locations within a single network administrative domain by changing the terminal's point of attachment with the wired network through DHCP.

Wide area network data services are typically based on telephone carriers, and built over the new generation voice plus data networks. It offers continuous fast mobility

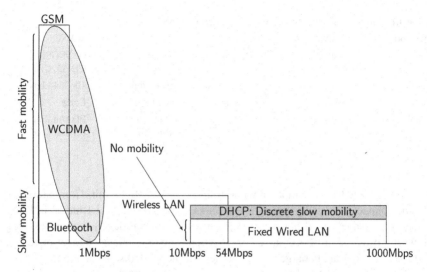

Fig. 4.1 Mobility supports on LAN and WAN

at a vehicular speed. So, GSM and wideband cellular data services has become as ubiquitous as voice calls over the cell phones. Over WANs, the reachability of the data is more important than the quality of the data. The cost of infrastructure supporting WAN services is very high. So, data services over WANs are more expensive compared to those offered through WLAN or Bluetooth.

Wireless MAN (WMAN) is used mainly as a back haul network connecting different wireless LANs. It is ideal for a broadband wireless point to point and point to multipoint connectivity. So, WMAN serves as alternative to cable and DSL modem for last mile broadband access. It can support a few other interesting applications such as IPTv and VoIP. WMAN is based on industry standards known as WiMAX [9] (Worldwide Interoperability for Microwave Access) as it works on Microwave band. There are two variants of WiMAX, one operating in unlicensed frequency band 2–11 GHz while the other operating on licensed band 10–66 GHz. WMAN offers a range up to 50 km and data rate up to 80 Mbps.

Wireless LAN is supported usually by wired infrastructure and provide one-hop wireless connectivities to the clients within a small distance. The typical coverage area could be a university, small enterprise, hospital, airport, etc. Considering the requirements of the clients, wireless LAN should support high data transfer rates as opposed to WANs. WLANs operate on the unlicensed part of the wireless communication spectrum. Its range may spill over to the streets and exposed to vulnerability if the placement of access points are not planned carefully.

In contrast, Bluetooth allows wireless accessibility in enclosed rooms and offers some sort of a physically supervised access. For example, the room access may be through passkey/card, and the devices could either block visibilities through software or demand pass keys for allowing access. Accessories like keyboard, mouse, etc.,

Table 4.1 Summary of wireless communication technologies

Networks	PAN	LAN	MAN	WAN
Standards	Bluetooth	802.11a/g/b	802.16	GSM/GPRS, CDPD, CDMA
Speed	<1 Mbps	1–54 Mbps	22+ Mbps	10–384 kbps
Range	Short	Medium	Medium-long	Long
Applications	P-to-P	Enterprise network	P-to-P and P-to-MP	PDA/mobile cellular access

can be connected to a computer without cables using Bluetooth. Computers can also be connected to cell phones, or cell phones to head sets over Bluetooth. PANs sometimes termed as ad hoc networks, since they do not depend on pre-existing network infrastructure for connectivity. The participating nodes connect in ad hoc fashion when they are in range of one another. The network disappear as participating nodes move away. PANs like WLAN also support one hop communication and can be seen more as value addition to WLANs. They should not be confused with wireless ad hoc network which are multi-hop network and their usability is independent of WLANs.

The usage of different wireless communication technologies characterized by speed, range and applications are summarized in Table 4.1.

4.3 WLAN Standards

Wireless local area network or WLAN extends a wired infrastructure network by attaching devices known as wireless Access Points (APs). An AP provides network connectivity for a short distance, up to 500 m in the clear air. Multiple number of clients can connect through one access point. WLAN may, therefore, be viewed as a point to multi-point communication technology much like a community radio network. The architecture of WLAN is not just for replacement of cable, it also provides untethered broadband internet connectivity. It is a solution for coverage of *hot spots* like airports, university campus, hospitals, convention centers, government/corporate offices, plants, etc. CISCO, Intel, IBM, Apple are among the companies which manufacture equipment and accessories to setup WLANs. WLAN can support significantly lower data transfer rates between 11 and 54 Mbps. The latest WLAN standard IEEE 802.11n [7] could offer speed up to 300 Mbps. As opposed to WLANs, Wired LANs can support data rates between 100 and 1000 Mbps. Most high performance computing platforms rely on wired LANs that can reach peak transfer rates up to 40 Gbps over point-to-point connections.

4.3.1 IEEE Standards

WLANs mostly use wireless Ethernet technology based on IEEE 802.11 standards [6]. There are three well known operational standards for WLANs, namely, IEEE 802.11a, IEEE 802.11b and IEEE 802.11g. IEEE 802.11 standard was first proposed in 1997. After two years in 1999, IEEE 802.11b [13], known popularly as WiFi, was released. It uses 2.4 GHz unlicensed spectrum, and supports the transfer rates in the range of 5–11 Mbps. IEEE 802.11a was also released around the same time. The industry name for the implementation of IEEE 802.11a is WiFi5 because it uses the frequency spectrum in 5 GHz band. It uses more efficient transmission method called Orthogonal Frequency Division Multiplexing (OFDM) in its physical layer for better performance. In 2003, IEEE announced 802.11g standard in 2.4 GHz band using OFDM. It supports a raw data rate of 54 Mbps as against 11 Mbps by 802.11b. As both 802.11g and 802.11b operate in same 2.4 GHz band, they are compatible to each other. Total of 14 overlapping channels exists at a spacing of 5 MHz from the left outer band edge as shown in Fig. 4.2. Since each channel width is 22 MHz, and the center frequency f_c of channel 1 is 2.412 GHz, the upper frequency f_u of channel 1 must be 2.423 GHz. This means any channel whose lower frequency f_l is higher than 2.423 GHz would be non-overlapping with channel 1. Since, channel 6's $f_l = 2.426$ GHz, channel 6 is non-overlapping with channel 1. Similarly $f_u = 2.448$ GHz for channel 6, and f_l of channel 11 is 2.451. So channel 11 is non-overlapping with 6. Therefore, in IEEE 802.11b supports just three non-overlapping channels, namely 1, 6 and 11, and uses transmit spectrum mask to limit power leakage to the adjacent channels. It causes the energy outside ± 11 MHz around the center frequency f_c to drop down by 30 dB relative to the peak energy at f_c. Similarly, the signal must attenuate by at least 50 dB outside ± 22 MHz around f_c relative to peak energy at f_c. Note that this may still cause some amount of interference in adjacent channel.

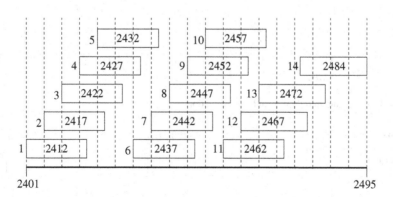

Fig. 4.2 Channelization of 2.4 GHZ band for WLAN

IEEE 802.11a is particularly well suited for multiple users running applications that require high data rates. It supports a maximum raw data transfer rate of 54 Mbps. 802.11a is designed originally for three distinct subbands 5.15–5.25, 5.25–5.35 and 5.725–5.825 GHz. This implies that every 40 MHz channel spans over 4 channel numbers. The lower and middle subbands have total of eight carriers of width 40 MHz at 20 MHz spacing. The upper subband has four carriers also at 20 MHz spacing. The outermost channels in lower and middle subbands are at 30 MHz spacing from the band edges. Figure 4.3 illustrates the channelization scheme. However, the outermost channels in the upper subband are at 20 MHz spacing from the band edges. Channelization for the upper subband is illustrated by Fig. 4.4. A spectral mask is used in 802.11a to limit the power leakage into the adjacent channels. The power output drops down sharply after a spacing of 9 MHz on both the sides of central frequency. After 11 MHz spacing from the central frequency, the power output goes down steadily and becomes as low as −40 dB at ±30 MHz from the central frequency f_c as shown in Fig. 4.5. In Europe the lower and the middle segments are free, so a total of eight non-overlapping channels are offered. Each channel is of width 20 MHz centered at 20 MHz intervals. Since, 802.11a uses OFDM, it can employ multiple carriers. OFDM is based on the inverse idea of code division multiple access (CDMA). CDMA maps multiple transmissions to a single carrier whereas OFDM encodes a single transmission into multiple sub-carriers. OFDM is able to use overlapping sub-carriers because one can be distinguished from the other due to orthogonality. However, 802.11a was not as popular as 802.11b. Due to higher frequency, the range of 802.11a network is short compared to that of 802.11b. It covers just about one fourth of the area covered by 802.11b. Furthermore, 802.11a signals cannot penetrate walls and other obstructions due to shorter range. The use of 802.11a, thus, never really caught on.

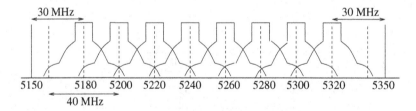

Fig. 4.3 Lower and middle subband channelization scheme for 802.11a

Fig. 4.4 Upper subband channelization scheme for 802.11a

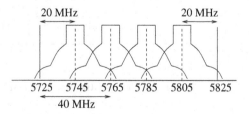

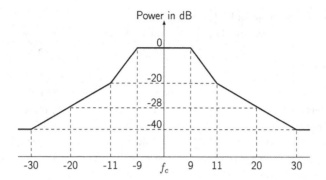

Fig. 4.5 Transmit spectrum mask

The IEEE 802.11b standard, using DSSS as physical layer, sets aside 14 channels for WLAN usage. But the governmental restrictions in different countries may not allow the use of certain channels. USA and Canada allow channels 1–11, most of Europe except Spain and France allow 1–13 channels. Where Japan allows all 14 channels for WLAN usage. France allows four (10–13) and Spain allows only two (10–11) channels for WLAN. The channels are overlapping. For avoiding adjacent channels rejection at the receiver end, there should be a gap of 30 MHz between neighboring channels. The center frequencies (the actual channel frequency used for communication between a receiver and transmitter) are located at 5 MHz intervals. According to the adjacent channel rejection demand, there should be five channels in-between to avoid interference caused by the neighboring access points. So, out of fourteen channels, at most three are non-overlapping. In other words, at most three access points can be placed adjacent to one another.

IEEE 802.11n is a relatively new standard, finalized in 2009 [7]. It could achieve higher transfer rate by relying on multiple input and multiple output (MIMO) antennas [15]. It operates on both 2.4 and 5 GHz bands. IEEE 802.11n allows up to four transmit and four receive antennas. The number of simultaneous data streams is restricted by the minimum number of antennas used on both ends of a connection. The notation $n_1 \times n_2 : n_3$, where $n_3 \leq \max\{n_1, n_2\}$, is used to describe a MIMO antenna's capabilities. The first parameter n_1 gives the maximum number of transmit antennas, the second parameter n_2 specifies the maximum number of receive antennas that can be used by the radio. The third parameter n_3 restricts number of spatial data streams that can be used by the radio. That is the number n_3 indicates that the device can only send or receive on n_3 antennas. Therefore, on a $2 \times 2 : 2$ radio a device have two receive and two transmit antenna, however, only two simultaneous data streams can be supported.

A summary of physical properties of different IEEE standards for wireless local area network appears in Table 4.2.

Table 4.2 Physical properties of IEEE standards for WLAN

Standard	IEEE 802.11a	IEEE 802.11b	IEEE 802.11g
Bandwidth (Mbps)/Chanl. width (MHz)	300/20	83.5/22	83.5/22
Basic N/W size[a]	254	254	254
Maximum packet size	104 B	341 B	2048 B
Inter-node range	10m	1–10m	1 m
Protocol stack size	4–32 kB	>250 kB	≈425 kB
Number of channels[b]	12/8	11/3	11/3
Maximum raw data rate Mbps	54	11	54
Modulation	OFDM	DSSS/CCK	DSSS/PBCC
Topology	BSS	BSS	BSS
Architecture			
Protocol	CSMA/CA	CSMA/CA	CSMA/CA
Traffic type	Text	Text, audio, compressed video	File, and object transfers
Battery life	Years	Days	Months
Success matrics	Reliability, low power, low cost	Low cost, low latency, convenience	Reliability, secured, privacy, low cost
Application	Sensor network	Consumer electronics, cell phones	Remote control

[a]0 and 255 are special addresses
[b]Total and number of non-overlapping channels

4.4 Network Topology

IEEE 802.11 supports two basic topologies for wireless networks: (i) independent networks, and (ii) infrastructured networks.

A single access point and all stations associated with this access point together define a Basic Service Set (BSS). A BSS is different from the coverage area of an access point which is referred to as a Basic Service Area (BSA). A Basic Service Set IDentifier (BSSID) uniquely identifies each BSS. So, a BSSID can be seen as analogous to a work group in Microsoft .NET environment. The MAC address of the access point for a BSS serves as the BSSID for that BSS. Though MAC address is machine friendly, a user will find it difficult to remember. It is, therefore, unfair to expect that a user would provide BSSID to connect to a BSS. A user friendly name known as Service Set IDentifier (SSID) is used to identify a BSS. An SSID is referred to as a name of a WLAN or the network. Typically, a client can receive the SSID of a WLAN from its access point. However, for security reasons, some wireless access points may disable automatic SSID broadcast. In that case client has to set the SSID manually for connecting itself to the network. An Independent BSS (IBSS) is an ad hoc network that does not have an access point. In an IBSS every station should be

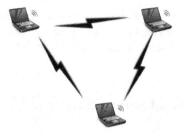

(a) Independent network topology.

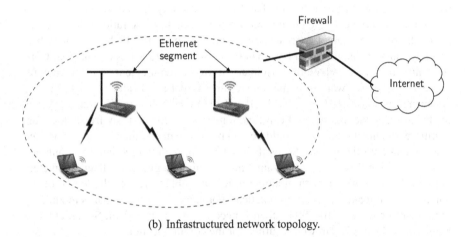

(b) Infrastructured network topology.

Fig. 4.6 WLAN basic topologies

in range of each other. The first station which starts the network chooses the SSID for IBSS. Each station in an IBSS broadcasts SSID by turn which is performed in a pseudo random order.

Figure 4.6 depicts the two basic topologies described above. Independent network services are available to the stations for communication within a small geographical coverage area called a Basic Service Area (BSA) much like a cell in a cellular architecture. In the case of infrastructured network, the communication among nodes is controlled by a distributed coordination function which will be discussed later in Sect. 4.6. There are specialized nodes called access points (APs) through which wireless stations communicate. The communication can span over at most two wireless hops. One from the sender to its AP, and the other from the AP of the receiver to itself when both the sender and the receiver are wireless enabled. Both the receiver and the sender may be linked to same AP or two different APs. APs essentially act as relay points and vital to the WLAN architecture. The placement of the APs should be planned in advance to provide coverage to the wireless stations. The planning should consider issues such as maximizing coverage, minimizing interferences, restricting blind spots (the areas with no wireless coverage), minimizing unwanted signal spillovers, and maximizing opportunities for implementing the Extend Service Set (ESS). ESS facilitates Internet connectivity for mobile nodes.

4.5 Physical Layer and Spread Spectrum

The purpose of a communication system is to transfer information. But transmission in baseband suffers from many problems. Firstly, baseband signals, being limited to few kHz, cannot fully utilize the bandwidth. Secondly, the noise due to external interferences and electronic circuits reduce the signal to noise ratio at the receiver. Thus, the receiver cannot receive the transmission properly. If the wire length is shorter than wavelength (as in base band), the wire would act as an antenna. Consequently, the biggest challenge originates from the requirement of infrastructure. For example, if we want to communicate in a signal bandwidth of 3000 Hz, the wavelength $\lambda = c/3.10^3 = 3.10^8/3.10^3 = 100$ km. The theory of antenna [5] tells us that any conducting material can function as an antenna on any frequency. Furthermore, the height antenna should be about one quarter of the wavelength in free space on smooth flat terrain. So, with $\lambda = 100$ km, the required height of antenna would be 25 km. Erecting vertical antennas reaching heights more than few meters is impractical. However, with modulation it is possible to reduce the length of the antenna which makes its erection practical. For example, if the signal is modulated with a carrier wave at 100 MHz, then λ becomes $c/10^8$ m = 3 m. So, an antenna height of (3/4) m = 75 cm would suffice for the communication.

4.5.1 Standard for PHY and MAC Layers

IEEE standards focus on the bottom two layers, physical (PHY) and medium access control (MAC) of the OSI model [14]. The Logical Link Layer specification is available in IEEE 802.2 standard. The architecture is designed to provide a transparent interface to the higher level layers for the clients. The client terminals may roam about in WLAN yet appear stationary to 802.2 LLC layer and above. So existing TCP/IP remains unaffected and need not be retooled for wireless networks. Figure 4.7 shows the different IEEE standards for MAC and PHY layers.

IEEE standards specify use of two different physical media for connectivity in wireless networks, namely, optical and radio. Infrared (IR) supports wireless optical communication. Frequency Hopping Spread Spectrum (FHSS) and Direct Sequence Spread Spectrum (DSSS) are meant for radio based connectivity. Both IR and FHSS operate in 2.4 GHz band, while DSSS operates in 5 GHz band.

IR operates only in baseband, and is restricted to the Line Of Sight (LOS) operations. In order to minimize damages to human eye, IR transmission is restricted to about 25 m. The LOS requirement restricts mobility. But diffused IR signal [11]

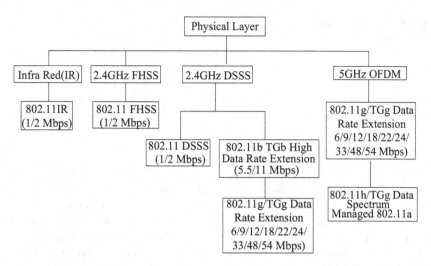

Fig. 4.7 IEEE standard architecture for PHY and MAC layers

can fill enclosed area like ordinary light, so it offers a better option for operating in baseband. For diffused IR, the adapters can be fixed on ceiling or at an angle, so that signals can bounce off the walls, and consequently changing the location of the receiver will not disrupt the signal.

4.5.2 Spread Spectrum

Spread spectrum uses radio frequency transmission as physical layer medium. Two spread spectrum strategies are Frequency Hopping Spread Spectrum (FHSS) and Direct Sequence Spread Spectrum (DSSS). FHSS is an intra building communication technology whereas DSSS is for inter building communication. Spread spectrum essentially spreads a signal, so that it can be transmitted over a wider frequency band than the minimum bandwidth required by the signal. The transmitter spreads the energy initially concentrated on a narrow band across a number of frequency band channels using a pseudo-random sequence known to both the transmitter and the receiver. It results in increased privacy, lower interference, and increased capacity. The generic technique of spread spectrum transmission is as follows:

1. Input is fed into channel encoder, it produces analog signal with narrow bandwidth.
2. Signal is then modulated using spreading code or spreading sequence. The spreading code is generated by pseudo-noise whereas spreading sequence is obtained by pseudo-random number generator.

The modulation increases the bandwidth of the signal to be transmitted.

Fig. 4.8 Frequency hopping
spread spectrum

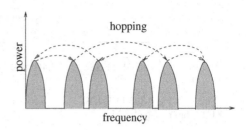

Figure 4.8 illustrates the transmission pattern of a FHSS radio. FHSS changes transmission frequency periodically. The hopping pattern of frequency is determined by a pseudo-random sequence as indicated by the figure. FHSS partitions the 2.4 GHz band into 79 channels, each of 1 MHz wide, ranging from 2.402 to 2.480 GHz. It allocates a different frequency hopping patterns for every data exchange. The signal dwell time cannot exceed 400 ms in a particular frequency. A maximum length packet takes about 30 ms. Thus, a small amount of data is sent on each channel for a designated time period before FHSS radio hops to a different frequency. After hopping, the transmitter resynchronizes with the receiver to be able to resume the transmission. The pseudo-random sequence of hopping pattern minimizes probability of interference. The radio spends only a small amount of time in any single carrier frequency. So, it would experience interference, if at all, only for that duration. The chance of experiencing interference in every carrier frequency is low. It is virtually impossible to design any jammer for FHSS radios. FHSS comes in three variants, namely, slow frequency hopping (SFH), intermediate (rate) frequency hopping (IFH) and fast frequency hopping (FFH).

Let T_h be the hop period and T_b be the bit period. A SFH transmitter uses a frequency for several bit periods. Equivalently, T_b is smaller than T_h in a SFH, i.e., $T_b = T_h/k$, for $k = 1, 2, 3, \ldots$. Thus, in a SFH the base band message rate $R_b = 1/T_b \geq R_h$. As shown in Fig. 4.9, the transmitter $Tx1$ uses frequency $f3$ for $2T_b$ periods. The period for which a transmitter uses the same frequency is referred to as *dwell time* T_d. For slow hopping, $T_d \geq T_b$. Figure 4.9 also shows hopping pattern for transmitter $Tx2$. It dwells in a particular frequency for half the T_b period. In general, for FHF $T_d < T_b$, and $T_b = kT_h$ for $k = 1, 2, 3, \ldots$. The number of frequency hopping for $Tx2$ is twice the number for $Tx1$. Bluetooth system uses frequency hopping spread spectrum.

FHSS uses only a small portion of bandwidth at any time. As opposed to FHSS, DSSS uses a fixed carrier frequency for the transmission. But instead of using a narrow band, it spreads the data over a wide frequency band using a specific encoding scheme called PN (pseudo-noise) code. The justification of spread spectrum is provided by Shannon-Hartley channel capacity equation [12]

$$C = B \times \log_2(1 + S/N).$$

Fig. 4.9 Frequency hopping spread spectrum

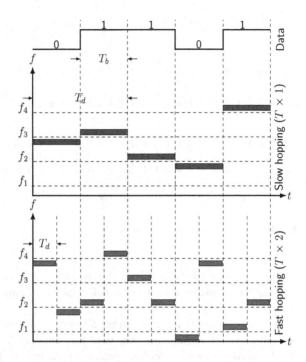

In the above equation, C represents the capacity in bits per second which is the maximum data rate for a theoretical bit error rate (BER). B is the bandwidth and S/N is signal to noise ratio. Since, S/N represents environmental condition, and the frequency is limited, the equation essentially means that B is the cost to be paid if the performance, C, is to be increased. Another way to look at the equation is that even in difficult environmental condition, i.e., when S/N is low, it is possible to increase performance (C) by injecting more bandwidth. Now let us try to eliminate $\log_2$ term from the above equation. Converting the log term in base 2, and assuming $S/N \ll 1$,

$$
\begin{aligned}
C/B &= (1/\ln 2) \times \ln(1 + S/N) \\
&= 1.443 \times ((S/N) - (1/2) \times (S/N)^2 + (1/3) \times (S/N)^3 - \ldots \\
&= 1.443 \times (S/N), \text{ neglecting higher order terms.} \\
&\approx S/N
\end{aligned}
$$

The above simplified equation implies that for a given noise to signal ratio, error free transmission can be ensured by spreading which is equivalent to increasing bandwidth. As along as, the PN codes are orthogonal, data of users can be distinguished from one another on the basis their respective PN codes even if these data occupy the same spectrum all the times. The pseudo-noise code is more popularly referred to as chipping sequence. To transmit each bit of actual data, a redundant bit pattern of bits or *chips* is generated. For example, as shown in Fig. 4.10 a single bit of data

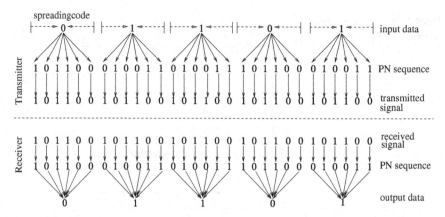

Fig. 4.10 DSSS using with spreading factor 6

is represented by six chips. This implies that each user's bit has a duration T_b, while the chipping sequence consists of smaller pulses or "chips" such that each chip has a duration of T_c ($\leq T_b$).

Instead of using 0 and 1 for chips, a bipolar notation where -1 replaces 0 and $+1$ replaces 1, is more commonly used for denoting the chip sequence. The ratio T_b/T_c is called *spreading factor*, which represents the number of chips used for one bit of actual data. Longer the spreading ratio, more resistent is the transmitted data to interference. Equivalently, the probability of recovering the actual data is high. In most applications involving private/public communication, a spreading factor between 10 and 100 is used. As opposed to that, the applications related to military and security may use spreading factors upto 10,000. IEEE 802.11, for example, employs Barker code [2] sequence 10110111000, which has a spreading factor of 11. Barkar code is short, have a good balance (difference between 1s and 0s is small) and exponentially decreasing number of run lengths ($1/2^k$ of the runs have length 2^k, $k = 0, 1, \ldots$). and exhibit good correlation properties. Since adjacent bit correlation is very low, Barkar codes are ideal for CDMA [10]. Also Shanon-Hartley's equation tells us that lower the spreading factor, higher is the bandwidth available to the user.

It may be noted that the chipping code is related to a user, and independent of data or signal. If a sequence such as 101100 is used for encoding 0 then the 1's complement of the sequence, 010011 is used for encoding 1 as depicted in Fig. 4.10. The product (bitwise XOR) of the spreaded data is transmitted. Since the radio transmission is analog, the spreaded data should be modulated with a radio carrier before transmitter can actually send it. For example, if a user's signal requires a bandwidth of 1 MHz, employing 11-chip Barker code would result in a signal of 11 MHz bandwidth. After converting the digital data to analog signal, the radio carrier has to shift this resulting signal to the carrier frequency, i.e., 2.4 GHz band.

For recovering data at the receiver end, the two step modulations of transmitted data is reversed using the same carrier as the transmitter. It results in the signal which is of the same bandwidth as the original spreaded signal. Some additional filters may be used to generate this signal. The receiver must use the same chipping sequence as employed by the transmitter's end in order to recover the spreaded data by one XOR operation. The receiver should be synchronized precisely with the transmitter in order to know this chipping sequence and bit period. During a bit period, an integrator adds all these products. The process of computing products of chips and signals, and the adding of the products in an integrator is known as the *correlation*. The device executing the process is called a *correlator*. After the sum of products are made available by the integrator, a decision unit samples these sums for each period and decides if a sum represents a 0 or an 1.

For the output at the receiver end to be identical to actual data, the following equation must hold:

$$s_i(t).c_i(t).c_i(t) = s_i(t),$$

where $s_i(t)$ is signal, $c_i(t)$ is the spreading code for ith mobile. In other words, the spreading code must be such that $c_i(t).c_i(t) = 1$. After recovering the spreaded data, it is multiplied (bitwise XOR) with the chip sequence corresponding to transmitter and integrated. To illustrate this, let us take a small example with 11-bit Barker code 10110111000. Let the actual data be 011. Barker code spread binary 0 to 10110111000 and binary 1 to 01001000111. So the spreaded code for actual data 011 is equal to:

[10110111000 **01001000111 01001000111**]

The XOR operation of spreaded data with Barker chipping sequence followed by the integrator's sum at the end of each bit-stream interval will be shown below.

| spreaded data: [10110111000 **01001000111 01001000111**] |
| chip sequence: [10110111000 **10110111000 10110111000**] |
| XOR: [00000000000 **11111111111 11111111111**] |
| sums over $T_b, 2T_b, 3T_b$: $(0)_{10}$ $(11)_{10}$ $(11)_{10}$ |

The sum over a chip interval would map either to binary 0 or 1. In the above example, sum $(0)_{10}$ maps to 0, whereas sum $(11)_{10}$ maps to 1. So, the data received is 011. In general, integration does not result in a clear distinction between 0 and 1 as shown above. This necessitates use of a threshold comparator to take care of the worst case scenario with maximum number of channels in the system. With the above technique, even if one or more chips are flipped in transmission due to noise, it would be possible to get the correct information. As an example, suppose we use 11 bit Barkar code and the information received is such that

• two of the bits were flipped in the first and the third blocks, and
• one of the bits was flipped in the second block,

as shown below:

$$\text{spreaded data: } [10110111000 \ \mathbf{01001000111} \ \mathbf{01001000111}]$$
$$\text{received: } [00100001000 \ \mathbf{11110111111} \ \mathbf{11011110111}]$$

$$\text{sums over } T_b, 2T_b, 3T_b: \qquad (2)_{10} \qquad\qquad (9)_{10} \qquad\qquad (11)_{10}$$

Then the threshold comparator can still map the information received to 011.

DSSS uses more bandwidth than FHSS, yet considered to be more reliable and rejects interference. The processing gain G is provided by the ratio of spreading bandwidth against the information rate R, i.e., $G = B/R$. Note that the information rate R is the inverse of bit stream interval T_b. Consequently, the signal to noise ratios for input and output are related by the processing gain as follows.

$$(S/N)_{out} = G \times (S/N)_{in}.$$

Similarly, the bandwidth requirement is $1/T_c$, where T_c is chip interval. So, processing gain G can be alternatively expressed as the ratio T_c/T_b.

Since, distinct orthogonal scrambling codes are used, the user data can be distinguished from the data mix at the receiver end. Spreading introduces redundancy in data, so even if some bits are damaged in transmission user data can be recovered without the need for the retransmission of signal.

4.5.3   Protocol Stack

The physical layer corresponds more or less to the OSI physical layer. Physical layer has a variety of implementation options, namely, IR, Bluetooth or FHSS, 802.11a OFDM, 802.11b DSSS, 802.11g OFDM, etc. Each one will also have a MAC sublayer. Together with logical link layer, MAC sublayer constitutes the Data Link Layer as indicated in Fig. 4.11.

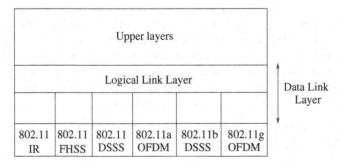

Fig. 4.11 Protocol stack for 802.11

4.6 MAC Sublayer

The responsibility of medium access control (MAC) layer is to ensure that radio systems of different nodes share the wireless channels in a controlled manner, i.e., with mutual fairness and without collisions. The two resources of a radio system are (i) frequency, and (ii) time. So, the radio access methods of wireless channels can be classified either in frequency domain or in time domain. In frequency domain, sharing is ensured by using non-overlapping frequency bands within the allocated communication spectrum. On the other hand, sharing in time domain is made possible by allowing entire bandwidth to each node for a short period of time called *slot.* Since, data transmission can be carried out in bursts, sharing is possible among multiple nodes in both frequency and time domains. In this type of sharing scheme, each user can use a certain frequency on certain time slots. The idea of two dimensional sharing is extended to a third dimension where multiple senders use orthogonal code sequences to send data at the same time in full bandwidth. Orthogonal codes ensures that concurrent communications can be separated at the receiving ends using the respective orthogonal codes employed by the transmitters. The sharing of wireless channels in this way can be referred to as sharing in code domain.

4.6.1 Radio Access Technologies

Thus, in summary the different access technologies used by the radio systems are:

1. FDMA: assigns channels using distinct frequencies in frequency domain.
2. CDMA: assigns orthogonal code sequences in code domain.
3. TDMA: assigns time slots for transmission in time domain.
4. CSMA: assigns transmission opportunities on statistical basis on time domain.

In FDMA, a frequency is allocated to a transmission on demand. It will remain engaged until the transmission is over. A frequency can be reallocated for another transmission only when the ongoing transmission on that band is complete. But, a channel sits idle when not in use. Normal channel bandwidth is 30 kHz with guard band of 30 kHz. FDMA is best suited for analog transmission. Since transmission is continuous, it does not require any framing or synchronization. But tight filtering is required to reduce interferences.

TDMA supports multiple transmissions by allocating frequency for a specified time slot to each transmission. Once the slot time is over, the same frequency may be assigned to another transmission. TDMA allocates further time slots to an unfinished transmission in future to complete the communication. It may, thus, be viewed as enhancements over FDMA achieved by dividing spectrum into channels by time domain. Only one user is allowed in a time slot either to receive or to transmit. Slots are assigned cyclically.

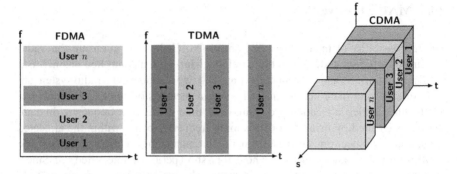

Fig. 4.12 Contrasting different access technologies

CDMA utilizes entire spectrum for each transmission. Each transmission is uniquely coded using a randomly generated code sequence which are known before hand to both sender and the receiver (they synchronize). Then the data is encoded using random code sequence before transmission. Since code sequences are orthogonal, transmitted data can be recovered at receiver end even if the receiver gets a combination of different transmissions by different senders in the same time span. Figure 4.12 shows hows multiple transmissions are carried out using different access technologies.

CSMA (Carrier Sensing and Multiple Access) is a statistical based technique for allowing opportunity of radio access for transmission to competing station. The idea is derived from human way of carrying out conversation. Listening to channel before initiating a transmission could save unnecessary efforts in retransmissions by avoiding probable collisions. Before initiating a transmission, a station senses the channel, and if a signal is detected then the initiating station defers its transmission.

4.6.2 Multiple Access Protocols

Each mobile station has a wireless interface consists of transmitter unit and receiver unit. These units communicate via a channel shared among other different mobile stations. Transmission from any node is received by all nodes. This creates the problems of contentions. If more than one station transmit at the same time on the same channel to a single node then the collisions occur. Thus, a protocol must be in place for the nodes to determine whether it can transmit on a specific channel. Such a protocol is referred to as a multiple access protocol. Multiple access protocols are of two different types, namely,

1. Contention protocols: these protocols function optimistically, and try to resolve contention by executing a collision resolution protocols after each collision.
2. Conflict-free protocols: these protocols operate by preventing any occurrence of a collision.

4.6.3 ALOHA

ALOHA is a simple minded contention type MAC protocol developed at the University of Howaii [1, 3]. There is no explicit allocation of a shared channel for communication under the pure ALOHA scheme. The transmitting stations start sending whenever they have data. Under this scenario, collisions do occur and the received frames are often damaged. Since wireless transmissions are broadcast based, the sending stations can determine the collisions by listening to the channel. When a collision is detected the sending station backs off for a random time before attempting a retransmission. In absence of possibility of listening, acknowledgements are needed to determine if the sent data were received correctly.

A possible scenario of transmission of frames in pure ALOHA involving three transmitting stations is depicted in Fig. 4.13. There is just one receiver and many senders. Each sender may send new frames and also retransmit the frames which were damaged due to collisions. It implies there may be attempts to transmit several frames per frame time, taking into account both new and old (due to retransmissions) frames. The question one would ask is why this simple scheme may work at all? This can be answered best by analyzing its performance.

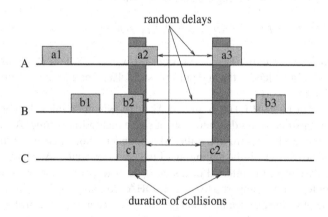

Fig. 4.13 Frames generation and transmission under pure ALOHA

For the convenience of analysis, following assumptions are used:

1. Total number of stations is N.
2. Frames are of equal length, i.e., frame time is t.
3. All user transmits with a probability p during time t.

According to the above assumptions, the average number of frames in a pure ALOHA system is Np. The stations are assumed to operate independently. So, the frame transmissions are independent events which can be modeled by Poisson distribution

$$P(k) = \frac{\lambda^k e^{-\lambda}}{k!},$$

where $\lambda = Np$ is the frame transmission rate, and $P(k)$ is the probability of k transmission occurring in a frame time t.

Let the time be divided into slots of frame time t. So, frame transmission started by a station at time $t_0 + t$ suffers a collision if some other station generates a frame in time intervals $(t_0, t_0 + t)$ and $(t_0 + t, t_0 + 2t)$. It implies that the period of vulnerability of a frame in transmission is $2t$. In other words, a generated frame always gets successfully transmitted provided there is no other frame available for transmission during its vulnerable period of $2t$. The probability $P_0[2t]$ for no traffic being generated during time $2t$ is obtained from the Poisson distribution with rate $\lambda' = 2Np$:

$$P_0[2t] = \frac{(2Np)^0 e^{-2Np}}{0!} = e^{-2Np},$$

Throughput is obtained by multiplying $P_0[2t]$ and the mean number of frames available for transmission during a frame time, which is:

$$P[success] = Np.P_0[2t] = Np.e^{-2Np}.$$

The maximum value of $P[success]$ occurs at $Np = 1/2$, i.e., $P_{max}[success] = 1/2e = 0.184$. Equivalently, throughput is just 18.4%. Though the performance is bad, ALOHA does work.

A variation of pure ALOHA is slotted ALOHA which doubles the capacity. In this protocol, the time is divided into slots of size equal to frame time. A station has to agree to align each transmission with a slot boundary. So, whenever a station has a packet to send, it wait till the beginning of the next slot boundary. So the collision can occur only during the interval of a slot. It leads to cutting down the period of vulnerability to half as compared to pure ALOHA. So, the probability that no other frame is generated during a frame time $P_0[t] = e^{-Np}$. Therefore, the probability that a frame will not suffer a collision during its transmission is $P[success] = Np.e^{-Np}$. This implies that the maximum throughput achievable in slotted ALOHA is $1/e$, i.e., 36.8%.

4.6.4 CSMA/CA

As explained in Sect. 4.6.1, CSMA is a probability based multiple access scheme for radio resources for WLAN. IEEE standard specifies two ways to resolve contention in medium access through CSMA when multiple nodes attempt to transmit simultaneously. It supports two transmission modes, viz., asynchronous and synchronous:

1. Distributed Coordination Function (DCF) is a mechanism for resolving contention without a central arbiter when access attempts were made independently by a multiple number of stations. The protocol resolves contention by employing virtual carrier sensing.
2. Point Coordination Function (PCF) is a mechanism for restricted resolution of contention within infrastructure BSS. It does so with help of a coordinator residing in access point itself.

DCF supports asynchronous mode while synchronous mode is supported by PCF. Since PCF supports synchronized mode, it provides a connection oriented mode. Implementation of DCF is mandatory in all 802.11 equipment, but PCF's implementation is optional. Furthermore, implementation of PCF relies on DCF. It cannot operate in ad hoc mode, while DCF can operate in both independent and infrastructure modes.

Since, PCF depends on DCF, let us examine DCF first. DCF supports asynchronous mode of transmission. The major problem in design of DCF is in handling hidden and exposed terminals. The hidden terminal problem, as shown in Fig. 4.14a, occurs if the transmitting station accesses the medium even when another station is actually using the medium. Using carrier sensing, station A is not able to detect presence of carrier as A is not in the range of C. So, it accesses medium for transmitting to B when C is actually transmitting data to B. A and C are hidden from each other. The crux of the problem is that the absence carrier does not necessarily mean idle medium.

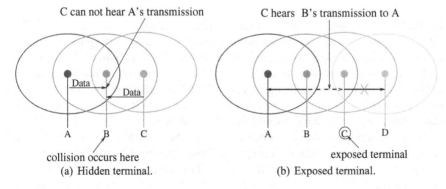

(a) Hidden terminal.   (b) Exposed terminal.

Fig. 4.14 Hidden and exposed terminal problems

The exposed terminal case, as indicated by Fig. 4.14b, occurs when stations *A* and *B* are already talking, and station *C*, which is within *B*'s range, wrongly concludes the carrier to be busy overhearing the ongoing transmission between *A* and *B*, and refrains from initiating exchanges with *D*. Stations *C* and *D* are exposed terminals. So, in the context of exposed terminals, the problem is other way round, i.e., the presence of carrier does not necessarily mean busy medium.

4.6.5 Distributed Coordination Function

DCF solves both hidden and exposed terminals problems by getting rid of carrier sensing. The protocol CSMA/CD is modified as CSMA/CA. That is, collision detection (CD) is replaced with the mechanism of collision avoidance (CA). In CSMA/CA, a transmitting station first checks to ensure that channel is free for a fixed duration of time. Each station then chooses to wait for a randomly chosen period of time. From among the contending stations, the station whose waiting time expires first gains access to the channel. The randomly chosen waiting time for a station is known as its backoff timer. As soon as the channel is occupied by a station, the countdown of back timer in each unsuccessful station is suspended until the channel becomes free again.

To understand the role of backoff timer and collision avoidance, a more detailed examination of DCF protocol is needed. DCF consists of a basic mode and an optional RTS/CTS access mode. In the basic mode, sending station senses channel before transmitting. If the medium is free for a DIFS interval it is assumed to be free. The sender then waits for backoff period and starts sending. The backoff period is set from an interval $[0, W - 1]$, where W is set to a pre-specified value, and is known as contention window.

4.6.5.1 DCF Basic Mode

For the basic DCF mode, the MAC frame transmission logic is provided in Fig. 4.15.

When a station wishes to transmit multiple number of packets, the protocol forces every subsequent packet except the first one to have a minimum of one random backoff even if the channel is free. Therefore, the generation of a random backoff is enforced after the transmission of the first packet. If by chance backoff timer is set to 0 every time the attempt to transmit a new packet is made then the sender could cause other contending stations to wait for indefinite time.

Once a station gains the access of the medium, the countdown of backoff timers of all other contending stations is suspended. The countdown is resumed when the medium becomes idle again for DIFS period. The use of backoff timers has three important uses:

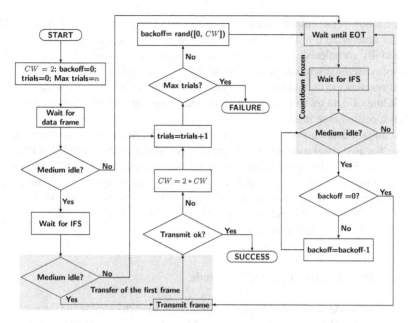

Fig. 4.15 Logic of DCF basic transmission mode

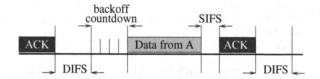

Fig. 4.16 Data transmission from one station to another

1. *Collision avoidance*: avoid collision among contending stations,
2. *No starvation*: no waiting station will be blocked from gaining access of medium indefinitely,
3. *Bounded wait*: the stations waiting for a longer time gain priority over other waiting stations.

The process of transmitting data from a station A to another station B is illustrated in Fig. 4.16.

A collision may still occur in the case when backoff timers of two or more contending stations simultaneously reach zero countdown. In this case, each sending station must choose a random backoff value to avoid repeated collision. The value of the random backoff is:

$$backoff = \lceil rand() \times slotTime \rceil,$$

where i is number of consecutive failures, $rand()$ is chosen from interval $[0, W - 1]$, and slot time is 20 µs. The contention window is set dynamically, when a station successfully completes a data transfer it restores the window value W to W_{min}. The value of contention window is doubled, each time a station fails to transmit a frame, until it reaches the maximum value W_{max}. It implies the value $W \in [W_{min}, W_{max}]$. The failure of data transmission is determined by non-receipt of acknowledgement within specified time interval.

For unicast data transfer, the receiver sends an ACK. An ACK packet has a higher priority because if a station is made aware of successful transfer, it would not retransmit the data. This helps to cut down the pressure on the available bandwidth. To ensure that transmission of ACK is not cut in the race among the contending stations trying to access of the medium, the receiving station (which wishes to send ACK) waits only for   a Short InterFrame Spacing (SIFS). The typical value of SIFS is 10 µs, whereas DIFS = 2 × $slotTime$ + SIFS = 50 µs.

4.6.5.2   DCF Advanced (RTS/CTS) Mode

In RTS/CTS mode, at first a dialogue is initiated between the sender and the receiver. The sender sends RTS (request to send) which is a short message. RTS contains NAV (network allocation vector) that includes times for

1. Sending CTS (clear to send),
2. Sending actual data, and
3. Three SIFS intervals.

A CTS is sent by a receiver to a sender in order to signal the latter to access the medium. CTS is considered as a short high priority packet much like ACK. So, before gaining access to medium, for sending CTS, the receiver waits for SIFS time. After the CTS is received by the sender, it just waits for SIFS time before accessing the medium, and following which the sender starts to send data. Finally, when the data have been received, the receiver waits for a SIFS time before sending the ACK. This explain why 3 SIFS are needed along with the time for sending CTS and data. CTS also includes NAV, so that other station trying to gain access to medium would know the duration for which the medium will remain busy between the sender and the receiver. But NAV of CTS does not include CTS itself unlike NAV of RTS. The RTS/CTS mode of DCF is illustrated in Fig. 4.17. As indicated in the figure, once A has been cleared by B for sending, C has to wait till

$$DIFS + NAV(RTS) + contention\ interval$$

before it can try to gain access to the medium.

By including NAVs, the stations involved in exchange of RTS and CTS inform other stations in their respective neighborhood about the duration of time the conversation would continue. In other words, these stations receive carrier busy information in advance.

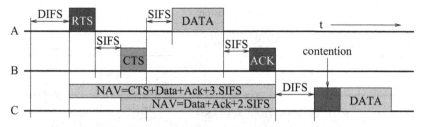

Note: NAV(RTS) does not include RTS, but carried by RTS
NAV(CTS) does not include CTS, but carried by CTS

Fig. 4.17 DCF RTS/CTS mode of transmission

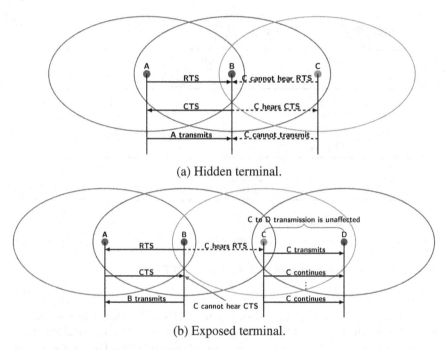

(a) Hidden terminal.

(b) Exposed terminal.

Fig. 4.18 Solutions to hidden/exposed terminal problem

DCF with RTS/CTS mode solve both hidden and exposed terminal problems. The solution to hidden and exposed terminal problem is illustrated by Fig. 4.18. In hidden terminal problem (see Fig. 4.18a) station C becomes aware of medium being busy when it hears the CTS from B in response to RTS request from A. So, C defers its attempt to access the medium until NAV set in CTS from B expires. To understand how RTS/CTS mode solves exposed terminal problem refer to Fig. 4.18b. The RTS sent by station B to station A is heard by station C. However, C being not in range of A, does not hear the CTS from A. Therefore, C would conclude that the carrier is free, and may initiate a RTS/CTS dialogue with D.

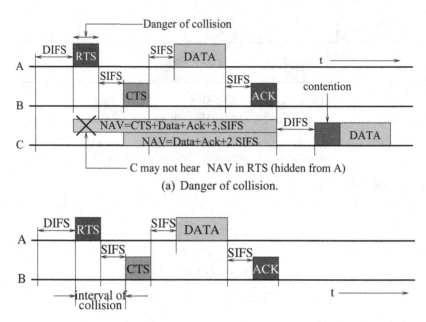

(a) Danger of collision.

(b) Collision interval.

Fig. 4.19 RTS/CTS mode shortens interval of collision in DCF

Still there is a possibility of a collision even in RTS/CTS mode. This is exhibited by Fig. 4.19a, where a station C, not being in the range of station A, is unable to hear RTS sent to station B. However, the interval of collision in RTS/CTS mode is limited to RTS plus the SIFS interval as indicated by Fig. 4.19b. The figure also provides a comparison of the intervals of collision in two modes of DCF. In DCF basic mode, the interval of collision is equal to the duration of data transmission plus the SIFS interval which may at times be unpredictably long.

4.6.5.3   Monitoring of Misbehaving Stations

There may be a smart station which uses a number of tricks to increase its chance of accessing the medium in order to increase its throughput. If traffic is known to be bursty, then a misbehaving station could send burst of packets ignoring MAC rules and minimize its average delay. Some of these tricks could be [4, 8]:

- Node may choose backoff timer from a smaller range of values than the contention window range $[0, W - 1]$.
- Contention window is not doubled after a collision.
- DIFS, SIFS and PIFS are not used properly. For example, a node may delay CTS and ACK; or instead of waiting for DIFS time, the node may transmit when it senses the channel to be idle.
- When exchanging RTS-CTS, NAV can be set to a value much larger than actually needed.

By using the first trick, a station gets an unfair advantage in accessing the medium ahead of other contending stations, since countdown of backoff timer of the misbehaving station reaches 0 faster than that of others. With the second trick, a misbehaving station can always outsmart other well-behaved stations when a collision occurs.

We need some solutions to block the unfair advantages that a misbehaving station might gain by resorting to trick mentioned above. Some possible approaches could be

1. Monitor throughput of each sender.
2. Monitor the distribution of per packet backoff for each sender.
3. Receiver side detection mechanisms.

Monitoring requires a delay. Because the relevant meta data must be logged for a while before an analysis can be done. Furthermore, sending station can choose a random backoff but send burst of traffic in a bursty traffic environment to ward off monitoring mechanism. The receiver side solution looks better. The access point can monitor each of the sender's behavior. The receiver side monitoring process is explained in Fig. 4.20. The receiver side solution is summarized as follows.

1. The receiver assigns a backoff b to the sender. So, the receiver can control the backoff behavior and the monitoring becomes simple.
2. The receiver then verifies whether the sender has actually backed off for an interval exceeding assigned backoff.
3. If observed backoff is less than assigned backoff then the receiver adds extra penalty to new backoff.

The use of RTS-CTS handshake was proposed mainly for solving hidden and exposed terminal problem through virtual carrier sensing mechanism. It also improves throughput by reducing the probability of collisions by limiting the period of collision to a short interval (bounded by RTS+SIFS). However, the stations involved in RTS collision fail to get CTS, and prevented from sending data. The network also incurs

Fig. 4.20 Receiver side solution to check LAN misbehavior

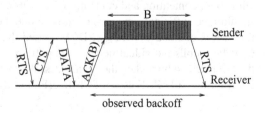

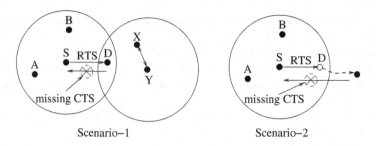

Fig. 4.21 Effects of missing CTS

an overhead due to increase in number of RTS-CTS control packets. As the number of RTS-CTS packets increases, the probability of RTS collision also increases. Though an analysis of overhead is difficult due to complexity and unpredictability of wireless environments, there is a possibility of under-utilization of channel capacity due to implementation of virtual carrier sensing mechanism. It may occur due to non-receipt of a CTS. Two scenarios involving missing CTSs and their effects have been illustrated in Fig. 4.21. In the first case, there is an ongoing communication between stations X and Y. On overhearing the above exchange, station D concludes that carrier is busy and would not send CTS to S's RTS. The problem may get aggravated further, as stations A and B which are in range of S on hearing RTS set their NAVs. So, A and B would be prevented from communicating until their NAVs expire. In the second case, the destination node D simply has moved to a new location and unable to respond to RTS from S. However, A and B set their NAVs on hearing RTS from S. The CTS never materializes from D, but the NAVs set by A and B prevent both from engaging into a conversation.

It may be noted that IEEE 802.11 standard specifies use of the same MAC layer for different physical layer implementations like IR, FHSS and DSSS. However, the numerical values of MAC parameters such as slot time, SIFS, DIFS, frame size, etc., are different for different physical layer implementations.

4.6.6   Point Coordination Function

The Access Point (AP) works as the coordinator for PCF. The time is divided into superframes each consisting of a Contention Allowed Period (CAP) and a Contention Free Period (CFP). The maximum duration of a superframe should be bounded to allow both contention and contention free traffic to co-exist. The contention period should give sufficient time to send at least one data frame. The maximum duration for CFP is denoted by CFP_{max}. DCF is used during CAP and PCF is used during CFP. PCF polls individual nodes in its polling list, which is arranged according to the priorities, to find when they can access the medium. To block DCF stations from interrupting CFP, PCF uses a PCF InterFrame Spacing (PIFS) between PCF data

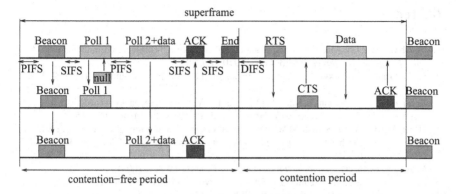

Fig. 4.22 Superframe structure and PCF

frames which is shorter than DCF InterFrame Spacing (DIFS). In order to prevent starvation during CFP, there should be space for at least one maximum length frame to be sent during CFP. It ensures that every station is allowed to send at least one frame.

The access point which acts as the coordinator, polls the stations in the round robin fashion. The polled station must always respond. If there is no data to be sent then a polled station must respond with a null frame. If all stations cannot be polled during a CFP, then the polling is resumed at the next station during next CFP. If a polled station is unsuccessful in sending data then it may retransmit data during subsequent CFP when polled.

Figure 4.22 provides the structure of the superframe. At the beginning of every contention free period, the AP sends beacon frame to all station in basic service area (BSA) after it finds the medium to be idle for PIFS interval. The beacon frame contains CFP_{max}, beacon interval, and the BSS identifier. All stations in the BSS set their network allocation vector (NAV) appropriately, and do not attempt to initiate CAP communication during CFP after a CFP-begin beacon has been received.

AP polls each station in its polling list by sending a data and CF-poll frame. When a station receives Data and a CF-poll frame, it responds after waiting for SIFS period. The response would consist of Data and CF-ACK frame or only CF-ACK frame (with no payload). AP after receiving frames from the station may again send Data, CF-ACK, a CF-poll frame or just Data and a CF-poll frame. Notice that if CF-ACK not received from AP then it indicates that data has not been received. Once again the receiving station responds to AP with Data or null frame as explained above. AP continues the polling of each station until it reaches CFP_{max} time. When time bound is reached the AP terminates contention free period by sending a CF-end frame.

References

1. N. Abramson, The ALOHA system—another alternative for computer communications, *Fall Joint Computer Conference* (AFIP Press, 1970), pp. 281–285
2. R.H. Barker, Group synchronizing of binary digital sequences. Commun. Theor. 273–287 (1953)
3. R. Binder, N. Abramson, F. Kuo, A. Okinaka, D. Wax, ALOHA packet broadcasting—a retrospect, *1975 National Computer Conference* (AFIPS Press, 1975), pp. 203–215
4. H. Li, M. Xu, Y. Li, Selfish MAC layer misbehavior detection model for the IEEE 802.11-based wireless mesh networks, *The 7th International Symposium, APPT 2007*, vol. LNCS-4847 (2007), pp. 381–391
5. Y. Huang, K. Boyle, *Antennas: From Theory to Practice* (Wiley, 2008)
6. S. Kerry and The Author Team IEEE-SA, Part 11: wireless LAN medium access control (MAC) and physical layer (PHY) specifications (2007)
7. B.P. Kraemer and The Author Team IEEE-SA, Part 11: wireless LAN medium access control (MAC) and physical layer (PHY) specifications (2009)
8. P. Kyasanur, N.H. Vaidya, Selfish MAC layer misbehavior in wireless networks. IEEE Trans. Mobile Comput. 4(5), 502–518 (2005)
9. B.G. Lee, S. Choi, *Broadband Wireless Access and Local Networks: Mobile WiMAX and WiFi* (Artech House, 2008)
10. A. Mitra, On pseudo-random and orthogonal binary spreading sequences. Int. J. Inf. Commun. Eng. 4(6), 447–454 (2008)
11. E.L. Oschmann, J.P. Welch, Wireless diffuse infrared LAN system (1994)
12. C.E. Shannon, The mathematical theory of communication. Bell Syst. Techn. J. 27, 379–423 (1948)
13. IEEE-SA standard board, Part 11: Wireless LAN medium access control (mac) and physical layer (phy) specifications: higher-speed physical layer extension in the 2.4 Ghz band (1999)
14. A.S. Tanenbaum, *Computer Networks*, 6th edn. (Prentice Hall, 2015)
15. The Author Team-IEEE-SA, IEEE 802.11n-2009-amendment 5: enhancements for higher throughput (2009)

Chapter 5
Short Range Radio Protocols: Bluetooth and IR

5.1 Introduction

A personal communication model is defined in terms of a person's interactions in three spaces [10], namely,

1. Personal space,
2. Immediate neighborhood, and
3. The rest of the world

A *personal space* is centered around a person, or in close vicinity of the person. An *immediate neighborhood* is the community where a person lives in. The *rest of the world* is the space outside the community of a person. The description of personal communication model (given above) though generic, looks imprecise. The space boundaries are loosely defined. So, there is a need to concretize the space modeling through practical examples. The Book of Visions 2000 [10] describes three typical scenarios, namely, (i) a smart healthy home, (ii) a professional environment, and (iii) a futuristic multimedia traveler. Customized extensions of these scenarios can be found in military environment too [4].

An example oriented modeling creates more confusion instead of eliminating the ambiguities. It is, therefore, important to abstract out the definitions of the spaces via use-case semantics. For example, the person centric communication space originates from a user's interaction requirements around the close proximity. A person's close proximity is defined through the wearable and the portable devices on the person's body. A person's apparels, and PDAs or laptops form a Personal Area Network (PAN) [5]. The reach of a PAN is only a few meters centered around a person. But it offers capabilities to communicate with the person's community as well as with the rest of the world via wired or wireless backbones. The communication among the members in a community is facilitated by Community Area Network (CAN) [11], while communication outside CAN is handled through Wide Area Network (WAN). A PAN may be wired or wireless. A wired PAN uses a USB or an IEEE 1394 interface (serial bus) for the network connectivity. Wireless PANs are formed using

© Springer Nature Singapore Pte Ltd. 2017   125
R.K. Ghosh, *Wireless Networking and Mobile Data Management*,
DOI 10.1007/978-981-10-3941-6_5

wireless network technologies like Infra Red, Bluetooth, Ultra-wideband (UWB) [9], HomeRF [8], Z-wave [13], or ZigBee [2].

The purpose of this chapter is to discuss about two popular wireless personal area communication technologies, namely, Infra Red, Bluetooth. ZigBee, on the other hand, is a PAN communication technology that is more relevant to machine two machine communication. ZigBee protocol is, therefore, discussed separately in the following chapter.

Bluetooth is originally conceived as a wireless technology for replacing cables connecting portable and fixed devices located within a short distance from one another. The main focus of development in Bluetooth is the interoperability of the devices manufactured by different vendors. So, Bluetooth cannot just be considered as a wireless communication interface, but it should allow devices to discover, explore and utilize services offered by one another.

Infra Red (IR) is not based on radio communication. It provides optical wireless communication in unregulated space. IR network adapters can offer virtually unlimited bandwidth. It is easy to confine IR signals by opaque barriers in the line of sight (LOS). Therefore, IR provides low cost secure communication which is ideal for WPAN.

5.2 Bluetooth

Bluetooth specification [6] defines a radio based short range, low power wireless communication technology. Bluetooth was initially conceived and developed by Ericson as a cable replacement technology for connecting peripherals and accessories such as headphone, keyboards to devices like laptops, desktops, mobile phones, tablets, etc. Since then it has evolved as an industry standard for short range radio based wireless communication technology for Personal Area Network (PAN). It is, therefore, appropriate to view Bluetooth as wireless communication technology for PAN of all the devices tied to the *personal operating space* of an individual. Bluetooth network operates like a seamless peer-to-peer, self configurable, one hop network. It is different from WLAN. Bluetooth needs a host for its existence, whereas WLAN is a network component and independent of a host. IEEE 802.15.1 [5] standard (released in 2002) reviewed Bluetooth technology and provided additional resources for implementing Bluetooth on devices.

A Bluetooth radio works in 2.4 GHz unlicensed Radio Frequency (RF) band. It forms an 1-hop ad hoc network using frequency hopping spread spectrum, which hops 1600 times per second between 79 frequencies in the frequency band from 2.402 to 2.48 GHz. Each frequency channel is of 1 MHz wide. Frequency switching time is 220 μs. Bluetooth supports a maximum data rate of 710 kbps with a maximum packet size exceeding 300 bytes.

Depending on transmit power requirements, Bluetooth devices can be classified into three classes:

Fig. 5.1 Bluetooth network

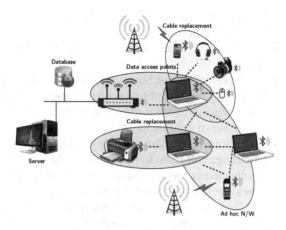

1. Class 1: up to 100 mW, but the devices dynamically adjust their requirements to avoid interferences with other devices.
2. Class 2: up to 2.4 mW, and
3. Class 3: up to 1 mW.

Three principal usage models for Bluetooth network have been described by Fig. 5.1. These include:

1. Cable replacement,
2. Data access, and
3. Peer to peer ad hoc connection.

The primary use of Bluetooth is a person centric communication technology is rooted at connecting laptops with cell phones, mouse, headphones and other accessories without wires. The second most important use of Bluetooth is for LAN and Internet connectivity. A cell phone can be turned into a wireless hot spot to which devices can hook up to the Internet via Bluetooth connectivity. Likewise, GPRS or CDMA based public pay phones at the airports can be upgraded to work as Bluetooth modems and allow Internet access to the travelers. Of course, this has to be made possible by the assistance of higher-level protocols such as PPP on the top of serial port. The other main use of Bluetooth is to create an ad hoc peer to peer network of devices for person centric services.

The usage models dictate some of the engineering challenges in the operations of a Bluetooth network.

- *Flexible application topology*: Bluetooth devices should have capabilities to choose and connect to the peers in its neighborhood.
- *Self configurable*: Even with the constraints of selective connectivity requirements, Bluetooth should still be self configurable.The users will find it too complicated

to use, unless a Bluetooth device figures out by itself whom should it or should it not talk, and how.

- *QoS for voice*: Bluetooth must be able to provide QoS support for voice communication.
- *Low power operation*: Since, Bluetooth is primarily positioned as a communication technology for PAN, the power requirement to support its capability must be very low. If there is a need for frequent recharging of battery then the users would find it irritating to use Bluetooth.
- *Small form factor*: The portability requirements for the PAN devices enforce the requirement for a small form factor for these devices. Adding Bluetooth capabilities should not cause an increase in size of the devices.
- *Low cost*: Though it will be convenient to have Bluetooth replace cables, the cost factor cannot be ignored. So, Bluetooth enabled devices should not be more expensive than their wired counterparts.

A set of Bluetooth nodes, sharing a common channel, consists of at most 8 nodes organized in the form of a star topology. One of these (center of star) is called the *master*, and the remaining nodes are known as *slaves*. This basic star topology is referred to as a *piconet* [3]. It is possible to extend a piconet by merging two or more piconets to form a what is known as a *scatternet*. When a device is present in more than one piconets, it should time-share and synchronize with the masters of the respective piconets to avoid interference. As shown in Fig. 5.2, a node common to two piconet, known as a bridge and may be a slave in both piconets. The bridge node may also act as a master in one piconet and slave in the other. The master node controls transmission schedule of all devices in piconet.

Bluetooth devices waiting to be connected to a piconet are in *standby* or listening mode. In this mode, the radios of the devices waiting to be discovered by other radios of other devices or for a request to be connected to the piconet. The process of discovery is triggered by an *inquiry* command by a Bluetooth device. The listening radios respond with their FHS (Frequency Hopping Sequence) packets. It provides the inquiring node a list of all the Bluetooth devices in the range with their respective Global ID (GID). To establish a connection, the master node pages a responding slave with its own GID. The paged radio then responds giving its GID. Following

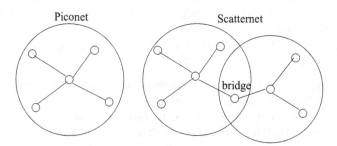

Fig. 5.2 Piconets and scatternet

Fig. 5.3 Functional
overview of piconet

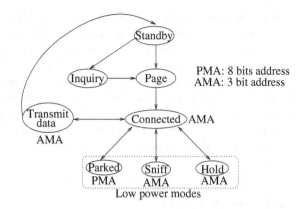

PMA: 8 bits address
AMA: 3 bit address

Low power modes

this the master node's radio sends an FHS packet to the slave. The paged slave then loads master's GID, adjusts its own clock offset to synchronize with the master's clock, and this completes the establishment of a connection.

When a Bluetooth device joins a piconet, it gets a 3-bit Active Member Address (AMA). After a piconet has 8 members (including the master), the master can take subsequent slave devices and put them on *park* mode in the piconet. The radios of parked devices are synchronized with the master's clock, but are assigned 8-bit Passive Member Addresses (PMA) instead of 3-bit AMAs. AMA and PMA combination allow up to 256 radios to reside in a piconet. However, only eight of these can be active at any time. The parked radios listen at a beacon interval to get any data addressed to them.

Figure 5.3 gives a functional overview of forming and maintaining a piconet. Apart from the park mode, a Bluetooth device can be in two other low power modes: (i) *sniff*, and (ii) *hold* as shown in above figure. In the sniff state, a device can be told to transmit data on specific intervals. For example, the keyboard of desktop can be asked to send data after 25 slots. However, in the hold state no data transmission can take place. The park state differs from the two low power states mentioned above. In the parked state, a Bluetooth device keeps its radio synchronized with the master device, and a PMA, instead of an AMA, is assigned to it. A parked device can become active on receiving a wakeup call from the master. On each beacon interval, it looks for a wakeup call from the master and finds out (i) if the device has been asked to become active, or (ii) wishes to become active, or (iii) have been sent any broadcast data.

Bluetooth supports two types of physical links:

1. Synchronous Connection Oriented (SCO), and
2. Asynchronous Connection Less (ACL).

A SCO link is a point to point link between a master and a slave. Typically, SOC links carry voice transmissions, and use only reserved time slots. A master can support upto 3 SCO links to one or multiple slaves. A slave can also support upto 3 links to the same master, but can support only two SCO links to different masters. The master transmits to a slave in its own reserved time slot (even numbered) while the slave responds in the following slave-to-master time slot (odd numbered). SCO packets are just single slot packets, and none of them carries a CRC. Since Bluetooth uses Forward Error Correction (FEC) code and a slot time is very small, the degradation of voice transmission is not noticeable even in a noisy environment. Therefore, SCO packets are never retransmitted. ACL links are used for data transmission. There can be just one ACL link per piconet. Only the addressed slave can respond to data transmission by the master. Though ACL can also use FEC in payload, automatic repeat request (ARQ) can also be applied causing packets to be retransmitted.

5.2.1 Packet Format

Time division multiplexing is used to share channel across multiple slaves. Each channel is divided into slots. The master node determines the slot time in which a slave sould transmit. The slaves can sleep during inactive slots. A slot time is 625 μs. The slots are numbered from 0 to $2^{27} - 1$ using master node's clock time with cycle of length 2^{27}. A 28 bit counter is used for the clock which wraps around after $2^{28} - 1$. The length of one clock tick is 312.5 μs. So, a slot consists of 2 clock ticks, and a Bluetooth clock ticks at the rate of 3.2 kHz. The repetition interval for the clock is approximately 23 h.

The transmission of packets between a master and a slave is illustrated in Fig. 5.4. A Bluetooth packet or frame may be of 1, 3 or 5 slots long. With single slot packets a maximum data rate of 172 kbps can be reached. However, with multislot packets, higher data rates due to reduction in the packet header overhead and better turn around time. A single slot packet can hop at the rate of $1/(625 \times 10^{-6}) = 1600$ hops per second.

A 5-slot packet has a payload of 341 bytes or 2728 bits. The total time for a 5-slot transmission should also include 1 extra slot for transmission of acknowledgement (ACK) from the master. Since a slot is 2 ticks long, in 12 clock ticks 2728 bits are transmitted. The time required for the same is 6×625 μs = 3.75 ms, giving a maximum bandwidth = (2728/0.00375) bits per second, or 710 kbps. A comparison

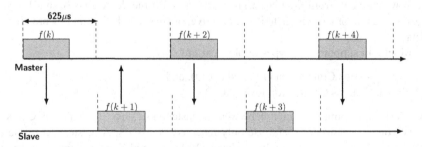

Fig. 5.4 Transmission slots of master and slaves

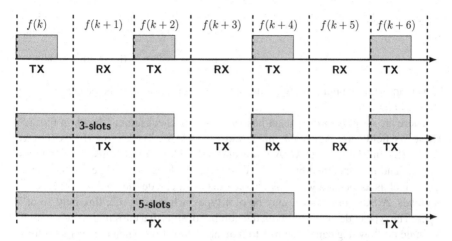

Fig. 5.5   Single slot and multi slot Bluetooth packets

Fig. 5.6 Frame format for
Bluetooth network

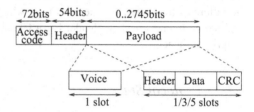

of single slot and multi-slots packet is shown in Fig. 5.5. The figure also identifies
the transmission slots TX and RX.

The structure of a Bluetooth frame is shown in Fig. 5.6. Each Bluetooth frame
starts with a 72-68 bits long access code. It consists of a preamble, a sync word, and
a trailer. A fixed zero-one pattern of 4 symbols defines a preamble. It is used to signal
the arrival of a packet at a receiver. Sync word is used for timing synchronization
with the receiver. A 4 bit trailer gets appended to the sync word if packet header
follows immediately thereafter. So, the length of access code is dependent on the
presence of the packet header. If the packet header is present then the length access
code is 72 bits, otherwise it is 68 bits.

Access codes are of three types:

1. Channel Access Code (CAC): identifies a piconet with the master's ID. All
   packets sent over same piconet channel will have same channel access code.
2. Device Access Code (DAC): used for special signaling requirements such as
   paging and response to paging.
3. Inquiry Access Code (IAC): has two subtypes, namely, General IAC (GIAC)
   and Dedicated group IAC (DIAC). GIAC is used to inquire about any Bluetooth
   device while DIAC is used to inquire about group of devices that share a common
   characteristic.

The packet header, if present, consists of 18 bits. To avoid retransmission, rate
1/3rd FEC is used. In this FEC scheme, each bit is transmitted 3 times and a triplet of

Fig. 5.7 Bluetooth packet
header

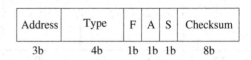

Address	Type	F	A	S	Checksum
3b	4b	1b	1b	1b	8b

bit is mapped to the majority bit in the same. So, total length of the header becomes
$18 \times 3 = 54$ bits.

There are 6 fields in the packet header besides a checksum as shown in Fig. 5.7.
These six fields are: Active Member Address (AMA), Type, Flow (F), ARQ (A),
SEQN (S) and HEC. The AMA represents the address of an active member in a
piconet, and it is specified by 3 bits. A 4-bit type field is used to specify the packet
type which is associated with link characteristics. It can define 16 different types of
payloads. A SCO link packet may be of 4 types, whereas a ACL link may be of 7
types. The type code also tells about the number of slots that current packet occupies.
A single bit flow flag can be set to 1 to indicate "stop" flow when receiver's buffer is
full. It is only applicable for ACL links. SCO packets can flow in even if stop bit is
set. The next bit is for Automatic Repeat reQuest (ARQ). It indicates the success or
the failure of transmission. The 1 bit field which follows ARQ is SEQN. SEQN is
inverted with a new packet. Header Error Check (HEC) is a 8-bit field for checking
integrity of header.

5.2.2 Protocol Stack

Bluetooth stack consists of four set of layers:

1. Bluetooth core protocol,
2. Cable replacement protocol
3. Telephone control protocol, and
4. Adopted protocol.

The core protocol layer is present in every Bluetooth devices. It provides four important set of protocols on the top of Bluetooth RF layer. These core protocols are:
Baseband, Link Manager Protocol (LMP), Logical Link Control Adaptation Protocol (L2CAP), and Service Discovery Protocol (SDP). The protocols of other layers
are used on need basis. The cable replacement protocol RFCOMM provides RF-
oriented emulation of the serial cable line settings and the status. It emulates full
9-pin RS 232 serial port over an L2CAP channel. Telephone Control Specification
Binary (TCS Binary) provides three functionality, namely, call control, group management and connectionless TCS. Call control deals with signalling for establishing
and releasing voice and data connection between Bluetooth devices. Group management handles signalling for management of groups within Bluetooth devices.
Connectionless TCS deals with exchange of signalling information not related to an
ongoing call. The adopted set of protocols are defined by specification of standards

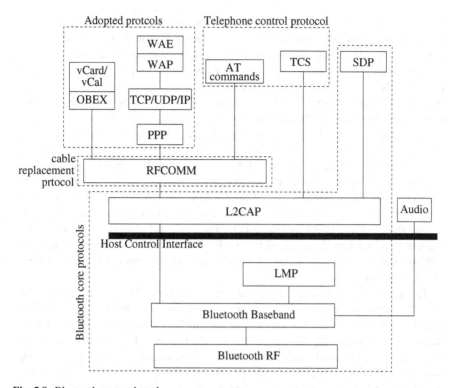

Fig. 5.8 Bluetooth protocol stack

by other organizations and integrated with overall Bluetooth protocol. The idea is that the protocols from other existing standard should not be reinvented and would be incorporated with Bluetooth on need basis.

Apart from the protocol layers, there is also a Host Control Interface (HCI). HCI specifies the implementation of commands for Bluetooth hardware through uniform interface for accessing baseband commands, link manager commands, hardware status registers and event registers.

The architecture of Bluetooth protocol suite is as shown in Fig. 5.8. Besides exhibiting functional dependencies among the four layers of Bluetooth stack, it also illustrates how the various Bluetooth protocols interact.

The combination of RFCOMM, TCS-Binary and adopted protocol layer essentially provides application oriented transport protocols for allowing applications to run over Bluetooth core layer. Since Bluetooth specifications are open, additional protocols like HTTP, FTP, etc., can be integrated in an interoperable fashion on the top of Bluetooth transport framework or on the top of application oriented protocols that leverage Bluetooth specific transport service.

Bluetooth devices form a piconet via physical RF links, established through Baseband and Link Control layer. Inquiry and paging mechanisms are used by the layer to synchronize frequency hopping sequence and clocks of different Bluetooth devices. Baseband provides both SCO links and ACL and multiplexes the packets on the same

RF link. ACL packets are used for data while packets meant for SCO link may contain audio or a combination of audio and data. The audio data is transferred between devices by opening an audio link. It does not have to go through L2CAP.

Link Manager Protocol (LMP) is responsible for setting up the link between Bluetooth devices. It is concerned with authentication, security and encryption. Apart from negotiating Baseband packet sizes. Additionally, it is also responsible for power control and duty cycle of Bluetooth units in a piconet.

Logical Link Control Adaptation Protocol (L2CAP) may be viewed as the data plane for the Bluetooth link layer. The size of Baseband packets are too small for transportation to higher layer protocol. So L2CAP provides a thin layer for exporting big size packets to higher layers. This task, obviously, can be realized through a generic segmentation and reassembly protocol. But L2CAP is highly optimized for the job together with the Baseband layer. For example, since the Baseband packets are already CRC protected, there is no need to check data integrity. Likewise, the Baseband packets are assumed to be reliably delivered in proper sequence. So, L2CAP could just concentrate on the simple logic for segmentation and reassembly of Baseband packets.

The higher layer protocols can be multiplexed and demultiplexed by using channels. A channel should be viewed a logical instance of connection between two L2CAP end points serving a single application. It is possible to create multiple instances of a channel between any two L2CAP end points. Each data stream is carried in a different channel. Each packet sent over the channel carries a tag identifying the channel. The receiver can uniquely identify both the source and the protocol being transported over the channel by examining the channel identifier tag. L2CAP specification also has a provision for a connectionless channel in order to support broadcast and multicast group communication. However, this is still under development [6].

In order to be able to exchange data over a Bluetooth link, the end devices must support compatible sets of protocols. So, prior to starting of an application, sometimes it may be necessary to configure protocol and set the stack parameters. Bluetooth's Service Discovery Protocol (SDP) standardizes the procedure for a device to query and discover the types of services supported by another device. SDP operates in client-server mechanism. The server provides a list of service description records about the characteristics of the services. A client can issue SDP queries to browse through all available service description records, and retrieve the required attribute values of a service from the corresponding records.

A universally unique identifier (UUID) is assigned at the time of defining the service. The uniqueness of identifier provides the ability to distinguish between two independently created services. This is similar to placing a UDDI registry record as in the case of web services. If the UUID of the service is already known to a client, then the specific service attributes can be queried easily. The alternative search procedure, as indicated earlier, is to browse and select one out of the list of available services. Thus, Bluetooth SDP is not as powerful as other generic service discovery protocols like SLP (Service Location Protocol) and Jini. But SDP is optimized to run over L2CAP. The limited search capabilities can also lead to efficient and small foot print for implementation on small devices.

To establish a L2CAP channel, the link manager is expected to perform certain Baseband-specific control checks. The important among these are creation of piconet, assignments of master-slave role, and link configuration. These control functions are part of the Bluetooth link layer, and depend on the link manager to exchange link manager packets. Depending on the operating environment, the link manager must adjust certain piconets as well as link-specific parameters. A few of these adjustable parameters are for: adjusting power level, increasing the packet size, and changing the QoS demand on an ACL.

The primary objective of the Bluetooth specifications is interoperability. The interoperability requirements originates from the following incompatibilities:

1. Applications may run on different devices.
2. A device may use a protocol stack from one vendor and a Bluetooth chip from a different vendor.

Interoperability between the applications can only be achieved if the implementations conform to the same core and profile specifications. All Bluetooth chips implement the Baseband and LMP specifications. So, at the lowest layer, this uniformity ensures interoperability over the air. However, part of Bluetooth stack consisting of L2CAP, SDP, and RFCOMM layers may be implemented either in firmware or in software. At the lowest layer, a Bluetooth stack interfaces with a Bluetooth chip through the standard Host Control Interface (HCI). This seems to suggest that porting a Bluetooth stack from one platform to another may not be difficult. However, the task of porting is not as easy due to absence of a standardized API for accessing the control functions. An application should use the API provided by the stack implementor to initiate a Bluetooth inquiry for discovering other devices in its neighborhood. It forces the application developers to know API specific to the stack implemented by a vendor.

5.2.3 Bluetooth-Enabled Applications

Applications are implemented using Bluetooth profiles. Bluetooth profiles specify wireless communication interface between a pair of Bluetooth enabled devices. There is a wide range of profiles which describe different types of applications. Three key information in a Bluetooth profile are: (i) the format of user interface, (ii) the dependence on the other profiles, (iii) the part of Bluetooth protocol stack needed by the profile. A Bluetooth device must be compatible with the subset of Bluetooth Profiles in order to provide services such as file transfer, cable free connectivity, wireless modem connectivity, personal area network, etc. These profiles sit on the top of Bluetooth core protocols and may require some additional protocols. The structure of the general Bluetooth access profile with protocol requirement is shown in Fig. 5.9. The generic access profile consists of service discovery profile, telephone control specification profile, and serial port profile. Serial port profile requires the communication and generic object exchange profiles. Apart from the core Bluetooth protocols, the requirements of other protocols for implementation of a Bluetooth application will depend on the specific profile and its dependence on other profiles. The protocol requirements of some of the applications are given in Fig. 5.10.

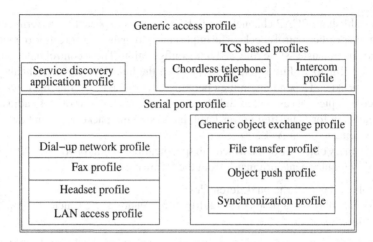

Fig. 5.9 Structure of Bluetooth profiles

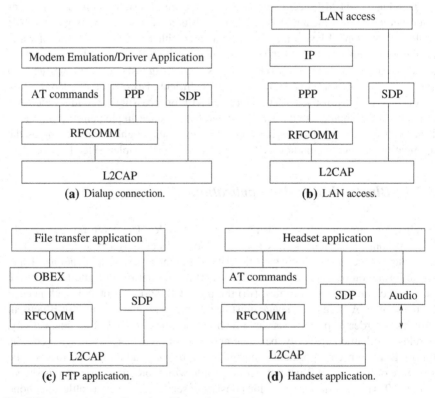

Fig. 5.10 Protocol stacks for various Bluetooth applications

5.3 Infra Red

IrDA (Infrared Data Association) standard [7] provides the specification for short-range free space optical communication based on Infra Red (IR) light which have a wavelength in the range of 859–900 nm. The approximate communication distance supported by IR is 1 m with a maximum data rate of up to 4 Mbps. A low power IR standard is also defined, whose range can be as low as 20 cm. Lower range prolongs the life of batteries.

There are many advantages in using IR connectivity. First of all, no prior regulatory approval is required for optical communication. Unlike radio frequencies, IR is free from interferences. Therefore, it provides robust connectivity leading to safe use in environments such as avionics, medical instruments, or military equipment. IR-enabled wireless connectivity facilitates easy mobility in personal space. Finally, the cost of IR connection is as low as wire connection. So, replacement of wired connection using IR is advantageous on many counts.

IR is predominantly used for replacing wire connection (RS 232 port) in short range communication. A normal wired connection to a host is illustrated in Fig. 5.11. The connection is through a host controller. The host controller has a RS 232 line driver and provides RS 232 port as the connection interface to outside world. RS 232 port is attached to a DB-9 connector and then a serial cable. DB-9 is a common 9 pin connector for serial cable. For the replacement of cable, MCP21xx protocol handler substitutes RS 232 line driver and DB-9 connector is replaced by optical transceiver. The emittance of light performs the functions of cable connection.

IR based communication is restricted within a range of a circular cone having 30° half angle with respect to the axis of communication. The receiver can receive the signal within a circular cone having a half angle of 15°. As illustrated in Fig. 5.12 transmission from the source S_1 would be able to reach receiver R_1, but it cannot reach receiver R_2 as it falls outside the stipulated *communication cone*.

Communication in IR system resembles client/server programming model TCP and WinSock APIs. Transmission is half duplex, i.e., simultaneous transmission and reception are not possible. The receiver is blinded by the light of its own transmitter when the transmission is on. However, two way communication is possible by alternately switching between transmission and reception modes. The client application connects to a server application by providing the server device address on that server. Applications on different devices can open multiple reliable connection between themselves for sending and receiving data.

Fig. 5.11 IR for
replacement of cable
connection

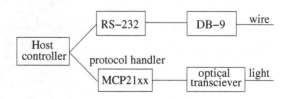

Fig. 5.12 Infrared
communication cone

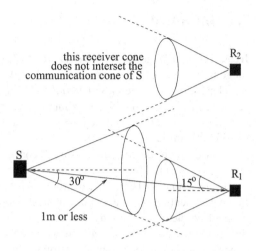

this receiver cone
does not interset the
communication cone of S

A base IR equipment, consists of a pair of devices, the one is primary and the other is secondary. A primary device is responsible for selecting a secondary device in its visual space. Initially, a primary device enters the *discovery* phase, and examines every device visible within its communication cone. A secondary device responds to the primary device's discovery, then two devices negotiate their capabilities, and jump to highest common transmission speed. So, notwithstanding the existing differences in respective capabilities, the connection can be optimized to match each other's capabilities. The primary device controls the timing of the link for two way communication. But both primary and secondary devices are bound by some hard constraints and communicate fast by turning around the link.

5.3.1 IR Protocol Stack

IR protocol stack consists of two groups of layers, viz., mandatory and optional as shown in Fig. 5.13. The mandatory set of protocols (shaded dark) consists of:

Fig. 5.13 IR protocol suite

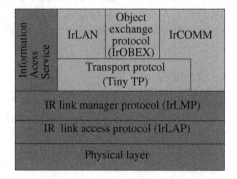

- *Physical Layer*: which is responsible for signal management or the optical portion of the transmission.
- *Link Access Protocol* (IrLAP): it establishes the basic reliable connection.
- *Link Management Protocol* (IrLMP): its role is to multiplex services and application on the link access protocol.
- *Information Access Service* (IAS): it provides directory (yellow page) services on a device.

The set of optional protocols (lightly shaded) usually found in an IrDA implementation are:

- *Tiny Transport Protocol* (TinyTP): it adds per-channel flow control to keep data transmission smooth.
- *OBject EXchange protocol* (IrOBEX): it assists in easy transfer of files and data objects. Usually be needed by many applications.
- *Parallel, and serial port emulation protocol* (IrCOMM): it enables existing applications using parallel or serial communication to work with IR communication without any problem.
- *Local Area Network access protocol* (IrLAN): it enables LAN access for laptops and other devices with slow pedestrian mobility.

The communication begins at a normal data rate of 9600 bits per second, then settles at a speed compatible with the receiver device. The possible data rates could be 2400, 9600, 19200, 38400, 57600, 115200, 4000000 bps. Apart from optical transmission, the other major responsibility of physical layer is framing. The framer is a software layer which accepts incoming frames from hardware and presents it to IrLAP. The framer also adjusts the speed of the hardware as desired by IrLAP. The format of IrLAP frame [1] is depicted in Fig. 5.14. The Beginning of a Frame (BoF) and End of a Frame (EoF) are specified by a unique identifier. The Frame Check Sequence (FCS) is, a 8-bit value, calculated from contents of IrLAP packet. BoF, EoF and FCS are implemented by the framer (in the physical layer). The 7 bits of the address field represent the address of the secondary device, and the remaining 1 bit indicates whether the frame is a command or a response. The control field contains sequence numbers (not relevant for the unnumbered frames), frame type identifiers (supervisory/information), and command codes. The information field contains the actual data and can have a maximum size of 2048 bytes. Interested reader can refer to [1] for more details on frame format.

IrLAP, which sits on the top of the framer, corresponds to the data link layer of OSI model. It is based on high level and synchronous data link control. For reliable data transfer, IrLAP supports retransmission, low level flow control, and error detection. However, it is advisable to use Tiny TP in place of low level flow control. Data delivery

Fig. 5.14 The IrLAP frame structure

BOF	Address	Control	Data	FCS	EOF
8b	8b	8b	16384b	16b	8b

may fail if the path of infrared beam is blocked. The environmental characteristics influencing the development of IrLAP are:

- *Point-to-point connections*: such as the connection between digital camera and desktop/laptop. The distance range is usually 1 m or less.
- *Half-duplex transmission*: as explained earlier, only half duplex communication is possible. But link can be switched around frequently for bi-directional communication.
- *Narrow cone of communication*: as illustrated by Fig. 5.12, the communication is possible if the receiver's communication cone is within the transmitter's communication cone.
- *Hidden nodes*: the nodes not in current communication cone of an IR device, cannot immediately receive the transmission. They must wait to find if the link turns around before they can enter into a communication.
- *Interference*: IrLAP of a device must overcome the interference from other IR devices, ambience light of room including the sun light and the moon beams.
- *Absence of collision detection*: any collision should be handled at software level, hardware design does not include protection against collisions.

The operations in IrLAP are divided between a master and a slave with each having distinct responsibilities. In each connection, one device plays the role of a primary device. A primary device shall not normally suffer from resource problem. Typically, a desktop or a laptop would take up the role of a primary station. The three main responsibilities of primary station are:

1. Sending control frames to initiate a connection,
2. Controlling data flow, and
3. Dealing with unrecoverable data link errors.

The slave or the secondary station sends only response frames. The typical IR secondary devices are printer, camera and other resource constrained or less complex devices. IrLAP has three operational modes, viz., link initialization, normal (disconnected), and connected. During initialization IrLAP chooses a random 32-bit address for the device. It is possible for IrLAP to choose the same device address for multiple devices. But there are mechanisms to detect and resolve conflicts arising out of choice of same address. After a link has been initialized IrLAP enters normal disconnected mode (NDM). In NDM mode, the device must listen to find if a communication is ongoing (medium is busy). The absence of activity for more than 500 ms implies that the medium is free, and a connection can be established. The other mode of operation is known as normal response mode (NRM). A device in connected state operates in this mode. Figure 5.15 explains the state transitions in IrLAP's operation.

The responsibility of device discovery procedure is to detect other IrDA devices within communication range of the host. If some of the participating devices have duplicate addresses, then address resolution procedure is initiated by one of the conflicting devices. The initiator asks the other device to choose another address.

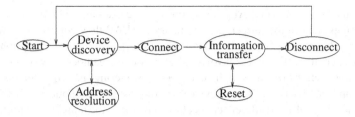

Fig. 5.15 Flow of IrLAP operation

A specific slot marker is also given to the conflicting device to respond with a new address. If the conflict still exist, the process of address resolution is repeated. After resolution process is completed, the application layer may be able to decide about connecting to one of the discovered devices. The connection is established when the application layer requests for a connection. The connection request is serviced by IrLAP by generating a Set Normal Response command Mode (SNRM) frame with poll bit on. The poll bit mandates a response from the remote device. It basically tells that the source (requester) wishes to initiate a connection. If the remote device wishes to accept the connection request, then it responds by an Unnumbered Ack (UA) frame with final bit set. After that the requester becomes the primary and the connection accepting remote node becomes the secondary.

The IrLMP is the third layer of IrDA specification. It provides support for two main functions, viz., (i) Link Management MUltipleXing (LM-MUX), and (ii) Link Management Information Access Service (LM-IAS). LM-MUX, which sits on top of IrLAP layer, provides link multiplexing support for application level. LM-IAS provides directory service through which applications can discover devices and access the information base in a remote device. LM-MUX used for addressing individual connection among those multiplexed. It adds an overhead of 2 bytes to address fields of each IrLAP frame. These address fields uniquely identify the Link Service Access Points (LSAPs) in both source and destination. Each LSAP is addressed by 7-bit selector (LSAP-SEL). LSAP-SELs within range (0x)01 to (0x)6F can be used by application. LSAP-SELs (0x)00 and (0x)70 respectively are for IAS server and connectionless data service. The remaining LSAP-SEL values from (0x)71 to (0x)7F are currently unused. LM-IAS works like a service registry. It maintains information about the services provided by a host device. Remote devices may discover the services available on host, and learn about the configuration information for accessing the services through LM-IAS. For example, IAS provides LSAP-SEL value which is the most important piece of information for locating a service.

With several IrLMP connections operating together, the data flow among the peers becomes complicated. IrLMP shares the link provided by IrLAP between primary and secondary devices. IrLAP's flow control mechanism is not equipped to handle such problems. The simple reason is that once the IrLAP flow control is turned on one side, the flow of data on LAP connection (which carries all the LMP connections) ceases completely in that direction. So, unless the LAP flow control is turned off, the other side cannot get any data. However, this causes serious disruption in its function, specially if timers are involved. Furthermore, deadlock may occur or flow in some connections could as well be uneven considering the requirements of the applications. For example, while a device is waiting for its peer application's response before releasing buffer, a different connection may use up the remaining buffer space. This would cause IrLAP to flow control the link until buffer space becomes available. Now, if both connection wait for responses from remote devices before releasing the respective buffer spaces then a deadlock situation can occur.

Tiny TP (TTP) [12] is IrDA's transport protocol. It lies on the top of IrLMP layer. TTP is responsible for maintaining per-channel flow control, and oversees the overall smooth communication. Maintaining multiple IrLMP connections on a single IrLAP connection is complex. TTP maintains flow per-LMP connection basis. TTP applies a credit based mechanism to control per-LMP connection. One credit point is assigned for the permission to send one LMP packet. The receiver sends credits to the transmitter. The number of credits can vary between 1 and 127. Periodically, the receiver would issue more credits. If the sender has no credit it cannot send data. So, the senders using up credits at faster pace are likely to suffer. Note that the role of the sender, and the receiver are not fixed, both sides of a LMP connection can send as well as receive. So, both sides will issue credits and use credits issued by each other. Credit bytes are sent as part of a LMP data packet. So there is no need to use extra packets as long as there is data to send and credit to issue. The design of a good credit policy requires careful planning. The other function of TTP is segmentation and reassembly. TTP breaks large data into pieces called service data units (SDU). The maximum size of SDU is negotiated at the time of TTP/LMP connection. The broken pieces should be re-assembled at the receiving end.

IrOBEX stands for infrared object exchange. The protocol's responsibility is for transfer of files and other data objects. It functions like a mini HTTP for IrDA. However, it does not have resources like HTTP, and its target devices have different usage models than web. Furthermore, HTTP is more a pull based object exchange architecture, while IrOBEX is evenly balanced supporting both pull and push. IrOBEX design is quite comprehensive, which simplifies the development of communication based applications. It has following components:

- Session protocol: it specifies the rules for operations like Get and Put related to exchange of object during a connection. It allows termination of an object transfer without closing the connection, and also a graceful closing of the connection.
- Object model: it basically specifies a flexible and extensible representation for describing objects.
- Use and extension rules: it allows defining new session operations and new object types.
- IAS entry: for a default OBEX server and the description of its capability.

The infrared communication protocol (IrCOMM) provides for serial and parallel port emulation. It enables the legacy applications that use serial and parallel communication to use infrared without change. Basically, IrCOMM aids in replacement of cables by virtual wires for connecting computers with its peripherals like keyboard, mouse, printer, etc. It enables direct synchronization of such devices by selecting a virtual COM port of the computer.

IrLAN Provides LAN access for laptops and other devices. It offers following capabilities:

- A computer can attach to a LAN via an Access Point Device, an IR LAN Adapter.
- Two computers can communicate as though they are attached to a LAN with access to the other machines' directories and other LAN capabilities. So, a computer can be attached to a LAN through a second computer if the latter is already attached to the LAN.

The description on IrDA protocol in this section touches all mandatory and a few important optional IrDA protocols. Yet, it remains incomplete without a discussion on how an arbitrary data object is exchanged from one device to another. Object exchange protocol IrOBEX or OBEX is the most basic and desirable feature of IrDA stack. A wide range of objects can be exchanged through IrOBEX which functions much like HTTP protocol. Both are designed as request-response type of protocol for exchanging arbitrary data between the devices. Both support GET and POST commands make it possible to transfer binary data between the devices. Both have headers which describe the content and the body. In fact, it will not be an over statement to call OBEX as IrDA HTTP protocol. Yet there are many dissimilarities between the two. The design of HTTP is more pull oriented compared to OBEX which is evenly balanced for both pull and push. OBEX is designed specially for resource constrained devices and works only on single hop distance between the source and the destination devices. OBEX is stateful unlike HTTP which is fundamentally stateless but uses cookies to maintain state.

OBEX consists of two important components, namely, (i) representation model for objects, and (ii) a session protocol which puts a structure around the conversation between two devices. The session protocol resides on the top of TinyTP, which is a reliable transport protocol. No additional protocol is needed except for the upper layer APIs which allow communications through TinyTP. The protocol layering remains as indicated in Fig. 5.13.

5.4 Comparison of Bluetooth and Infrared

A comparison of the physical characteristics of Bluetooth and Infrared is provided in Table 5.1. Bluetooth works over radio communication, whereas Infrared is an optical communication framework. So it can avoid detection. Therefore, it can find use in

Table 5.1 Comparison of physical characteristics of Bluetooth and Infrared

	Bluetooth	Infrared
Standard	802.15.1	IrDA
Focus	Cable replacement	Remote control
Basic N/W size	8	Limited by LOS
Maximum packet size	341 B	2048 B
Inter-node range	1–10 m	1 m
Protocol stack size	>250 kB	≈425 kB
Number of channels	79	30° cone
Baseband (kb/s)	710	115–4000
Spreading	FHSS	Optical, 860 nm
Topology	Ad hoc	Client/server
Architecture	Star, Tree, Cluster	Peer-to-Peer
Protocol	Pt to Multi Pt	Pt to Pt
Traffic type	Text, Audio, Compressed Video	File, and object transfers
Battery life	Days	Months
Success matrics	Low cost, low latency, convenience	Reliability, secured, privacy, low cost
Application	Consumer electronics, cell phones	Remote control

short range communication between computers aboard naval warships, planes and armoured vehicles. Yet, the requirement of line of sight for optical communication is a major handicap for IR based communication.

References

1. P. Barker, A.C. Boucouvalas, Performance modeling of the IRDA protocol for infrared wireless communications. IEEE Commun. Mag. 113–117 (1998)
2. P. Baronti, P. Pillai, V. Chook, S. Chessa, A. Gotta, Y.F. Hu, Wireless sensor networks: a survey on the state of the art and the 802.15.4 and zigbee standards. Comput. Commun. **30**(7), 1655–1695 (2007)
3. F. Bennett, D. Clarke, J.B. Evans, A. Hopper, A. Jones, D. Leask, Piconet: embedded mobile networking. IEEE Pers. Commun. **4**(5), 8–15 (1997)
4. L. Boucher, M. Churavy, T. Plesse, D. Marquart, G. Stassinopoulos, S. Kyriazakos, N. Papaoulakis, D. Nikitopoulos, T. Maseng, *Wireless personal area networks (WPANs)*. Technical report, NATO Research and Technology Organization (2005)
5. I. Gifford, C. Bisdikian, T. Siep, IEEE 802.15 WPAN task group 1 (TG1) (2002), www.ieee802. org/15/pub/TG1.html
6. Bluetooth Special Interest Group, Bluetooth core specification, https://www.bluetooth.com/specifications/bluetooth-core-specification. Accessed 30 June 2010
7. C.D. Knutson, J.M. Brown, *IrDA Principles and Protocols* (MCL Press, 2004)

8. K.J. Negus, A.P. Stephens, J. Lansford, Homerf: Wireless networking for the connected home. IEEE Pers. Commun. **7**(1), 20–27 (2000)
9. D. Porcino, W. Hirt, Ultra-wideband radio technology: potential and challenges ahead. IEEE Commun. Magaz. **41**(7), 66–74 (2003)
10. Wirelss Strategic Initiative-IST Project, *The Book of Visions 2000: Wireless World Version 1.0* (Wireless World Research Forum, 2000)
11. C.A. Szabo, I. Chlamtac, E. Bedo, Design considerations for broadband community area networks, *The 37th Hawaii International Conference on System Sciences* (2004)
12. S. Williams, D. Suvak, P. McClellan, F. Novak, *A Flow-Control Mechanism for Use with irlmp* (Tiny tp, 1996)
13. Z-wave, Z-wave protocol overview, May 2007. v.4

Chapter 6
Low Power Communication Protocols: ZigBee, 6LoWPAN and ZigBee IP

6.1 Introduction

IEEE 802.15.1 wireless standard, using Bluetooth for marketing and compliance, targeted the segment of consumer communication applications. It supports medium to high data rates for text, audio, voice, and video. But, IEEE 802.15.1 is not suitable for the unique needs of sensor and control devices. IEEE 802.15.4 [1] standard adopted a generic approach to meet the challenges of wireless sensor networks. The motivation behind this approach was to address the control and monitoring requirements of smart homes and hospitals, industrial automation, ship navigation, weather prediction, crop and habitat monitoring, and security and surveillance management. ZigBee [2] alliance, of more than 100 companies, was set up for marketing and compliance of IEEE 802.15.4. ZigBee provides supports low range wireless personal area network. The power consumption of a ZigBee chip is very low. In fact, at this level of consumption, a AAA battery can last for a year.

ZigBee devices spend most of time in snoozing, and thus have very low duty-cycles. It uses a simple protocol stack compared to Bluetooth. Its implementation also requires a smaller software code compared to Bluetooth. Therefore, ZigBee should not be treated as a competing but a complementary technology to Bluetooth. ZigBee is oriented more towards monitoring and controlling applications than actual data transfers. It supports two way communication between multiple devices over simple networks, using very little power. The low power consumption is the unique selling point of ZigBee and positions it ideally for WPAN as well as for number of applications involving smart/pervasive environments. Some of the potential ZigBee applications could be:

- Sensors monitored automation control for industrial and commercial applications.
- Sensor monitored control and alert system for critical in-patients at hospitals.
- Security surveillance, lighting, and ambience control application for smart homes.
- Remote controlled toys and games.
- PC and peripheral (mouse, key board, joystick, etc.) networking without cables.

© Springer Nature Singapore Pte Ltd. 2017
R.K. Ghosh, *Wireless Networking and Mobile Data Management*,
DOI 10.1007/978-981-10-3941-6_6

Table 6.1 Summary of ZigBee, Bluetooth and Infrared

	ZigBee	Bluetooth	Infrared
Standard	802.15.4	802.15.1	IrDA
Focus	Control and monitoring	Cable replacement	Remote control
Basic N/W size	255/65535	8	Limited by LOS
Maximum packet size	104 B	341 B	2048 B
Inter-node range	10 m	1–10 m	1 m
Protocol stack size	4–32 kB	>250 kB	≈425 kB
Number of channels	27	79	30° cone
Baseband (kb/s)	20–250	710	115–4000
Spreading	DSSS	FHSS	Optical 860nm
Topology	Ad hoc	Ad hoc	Client/Server
Architecture	Star	Star, Tree, Cluster	Peer-to-Peer
Protocol	CSMA/CA	Pt to Multi Pt	Pt to Pt
Traffic type	Text	Text, Audio, Compressed Video	File, and object transfers
Battery life	Years	Days	Months
Success matrics	Reliability, low power, low cost	Low cost, low latency, convenience	Reliability, secured, privacy, low cost
Application	Sensor network	Consumer electronics, cell phones	Remote control

- Various consumer electronic applications like remote program controlling of TV, home theatre, etc.

Table 6.1 provides a comparative summary of the Bluetooth and IR with ZigBee protocol.

The major problem with ZigBee network is that it lacks seamless integration with IP based networks. ZigBee network provide interoperability through a complex application level gateway node which implement a serial forwarder to handle two way communications.

The communication is based on multicast address. Therefore, seamless integration of ZigBee and IP based network is a subject of intense research. 6LoWPAN, developed initially with a focus to optimize the use of IEEE 802.15.4 stack, has emerged as a competing network technology. It provides interoperability through a simple bridging device. 6LoWPAN is based on IPv6 addressing scheme. So individual nodes in 6LoWPAN network are addressed using IPv6 addresses. However, 6LoWPAN has lagged behind ZigBee in acceptability. Though on the acceptability and the popularity parameters ZigBee out-rivals 6LoWPAN, there are many compelling reasons for the use of IP based networks. The most important among these reasons is the emergence of intelligent embedded systems. Through the logic of embedded processing one device on its own can initiate communication with other devices over the Internet. This paradigm of Machine to Machine (M2M) communication over the Internet has made it possible to realize the concept of Internet of Things (IoTs).

In the context of M2M communication, some of the important requirements are as follows:

- Uniform addressing, naming, discovery and lookup.
- Interoperability of all IP networks irrespective of underlying network technology such as GPRS, WiFi, Ethernet.
- Uniform routing mechanism.
- Availability of network management tools, ping, traceroute, etc.
- End to end reliability and hop by hop reliability.

Recognizing the importance of M2M communication specially for implementing Smart Energy Meters, ZigBee IP was developed as super specification on ZigBee in 2008 [3]. It was then released in 2013 for vendor implementation [4]. In this chapter, we address these issues in course of discussion centered around ZigBee, 6LoWPAN and ZigBee IP protocol stacks.

6.2 IEEE 802.15.4

IEEE 802.15.4 is the standard for 2.4 GHz low power, low date rate wireless embedded communication system. The standard was proposed initially in 2003 and then revised in 2006 [1]. Some of the features of this standard are:

- Supports data transfer rates between 20–250 kbps.
- Supports 128-bit AES encryption.
- Uses CSMA for channel sharing, and has provisions for MAC level acknowledgements for reliability.
- Supports both long (64-bit) and short (16-bit) addressing modes with unicast and broadcast capabilities.
- Supports maximum payload of 127 bytes in physical layer.
- Only 72–116 bytes available for payload after MAC layer framing.

IEEE 802.15.4 standard only defines MAC and PHY layers. ZigBee, 6LoWPAN, Wireless HART, ISA100.11a are defined on the top of IEEE 802.15.4. It supports two types of devices: Full Function Device (FFD) and Reduced Function Device (RFD).

6.3 ZigBee Protocol Stack

The full ZigBee protocol stack is a combination of IEEE 802.15.4 PHY, MAC along with network, security and application protocols made available through ZigBee alliance. In other words, ZigBee leverages IEEE 802.15.4 [1] specification for WPAN

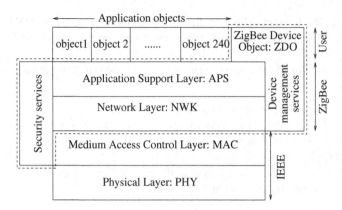

Fig. 6.1 ZigBee protocol stack

at the two lowest layers, viz., PHY and MAC. Network (NWK), and Application (APL) layers are defined by ZigBee standards as shown in Fig. 6.1. Though the responsibility for application development rests on the user, ZigBee alliance developed specification for some application profiles in areas such as smart energy, home automation, telecom applications, plant monitoring, commercial building automation, and health care. An application profile specify the type of messages to be transmitted over the air for the application. The devices having same application profiles can interoperate. The actual application code is supplied by equipment designer.

Besides transmitting and receiving packets across the physical medium, the physical layer (PHY) is responsible for the activation and the deactivation of radio transceiver, energy detection, link quality indication, channel selection, clear channel assessment. PHY is based on Direct Sequence Spread Spectrum, operating on two frequency bands, namely, 2.4GHz, and 868–915MHz. The data rates offered at these bands are 250Kbps for 2.4 GHz and 40Kbps at 915 MHz and 20Kbps at 868MHz. Low data rates at low frequency provide lower propagation losses and longer range. On the other hand, higher rate leads to better throughput, lower latency and lower duty cycle. In physical layer IEEE 802.15.4 specifies channel access through CSMA-CA or slotted CSMA-CA protocol. A total of 27 channels are available over three unlicensed bands: (i) 16 in 2.4 GHz band, (ii) 1 in 868.3MHz, and (iii) 10 in 902–928MHz. Figure 6.2 illustrates the channels availability in the three operating frequency bands. The sensitivity of receivers for 2.4 GHz band is −85dBm, while that for 868/915MHz is −92dBM. The advantage of 6–8dBm in lower frequency band comes from the low data rate. The device range depends on the receiver sensitivity and the transmit power.

MAC layer employs 64-bit IEEE and 8-bit short addressing. Short addressing is used for ad hoc network IDs. Theoretically, ultimate network size could be as large as 2^{64} with long addressing; and in most case this is more than what may be needed for building a smart environment. Even with 8-bit local addresses, the network size can be of 255 nodes, which is also more than the requirements involving a personal area networking in most cases. Three classes of devices are supported, namely,

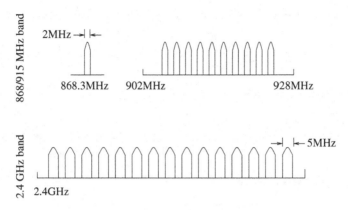

Fig. 6.2 Channels in three operating frequency bands

1. Reduced Function Device (RFD),
2. Full Function Device (FFD), and
3. Network Coordinator.

Each ZigBee device is mapped to one of three classes RFD, FFD and N/W coordinator. RFDs operate in snooze mode, and wake up infrequently for sending data, then go back to sleep. ZigBee supports three different network topologies: mesh, tree and star. Each network has at least one FFD and a combination of FFDs plus RFDs. One of the FFDs functions as the coordinator while others function as routers for WPAN. RFDs are end devices. The routers are intermediate nodes which allow exchange of data from the end devices to the coordinator and extend network beyond the radio range of the coordinator. Since a router acts as local coordinator for end devices, it must implement most of the coordinator's capabilities. Normally FFDs (coordinator and routers) are powered by the main power supply, and their radios are on all the time. In contrast, the end devices are designed to function in a very low-duty cycle, allowing them to extend their battery life as much as possible by long period of snoozing. A star network is a 1-hop network, where all devices are connected to the coordinator FFD. In a mesh network, a RFD node is connected to a FFD which routes data to and from the coordinator. Figure 6.3 shows instances of star, mesh and tree topologies. As indicated by the figure, the end devices (RFDs) are linked to FFDs or routers. A cluster of one FFD with its associated RFDs forms a star topology. For a tree topology the coordinator is at the root and end devices may communicate with the coordinator either directly or through a router. There are several alternative routes from an end device to the coordinator through different routers in the mesh topology. The existence of alternative routes provides reliability in transmission, but is transparent to the end devices.

A simple frame structure is used for messaging. The frame structure combined with message acknowledgement provides reliable transmission. For improving latency, nodes rely on beacon structures described below. ZigBee packets are smaller compared to Bluetooth packets. But unlike Bluetooth which allows up to 8 nodes

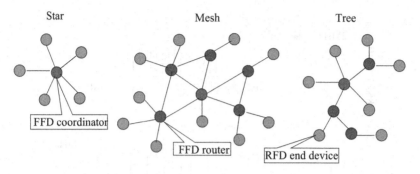

Fig. 6.3 ZigBee network topologies

FC	FSN	Address Field	Payload	FCS
2B	1B	0–20B	<=127B	2B

Fig. 6.4 ZigBee packet structure

in a piconet, ZigBee allows formation of a large wireless mesh network which may consist of up to 254 nodes. A ZigBee MAC frame consists of 5 fields including the payload. The first field is 2-byte long frame control, which indicates the type of the MAC frame being transmitted. The next 1-byte field denotes the frame sequence number. The third field represents address field. It specifies the format of the address field and controls the acknowledgement. The size of the address field varies from 0 to 20 bytes. The payload size cannot exceed 127 bytes. The last field is 2-byte frame check sequence which is used for CRC. The packet format is shown in Fig. 6.4.

IEEE 802.15.4 MAC defines four separate frames:

1. *Beacon frame*: which is used by the coordinator to transmit beacons.
2. *Data frame*: which is used for data transfers.
3. *Acknowledgement frame*: which is used for confirming the successful reception of a frame.
4. *MAC command frame*: which is used for all MAC peer-to-peer entity control transfers.

There are two different channel access mechanisms: (i) beacon-enabled, and (ii) beaconless. In the beaconless mode, devices rely on acknowledgement feature for reliable transmission. Since, power management is an area of concern, the use of beacon-enabled channel access is recommended for improved latency and longer snoozing periods. In beacon-enabled networks, ZigBee routers transmit periodic beacons to advertise their presence in the network. The beacon frames sent by the coordinator act like a clock. It supports a slotted transmission scheme. The beacon interval may vary between 15 ms and 252 s. The nodes may sleep between beacon intervals, and thus, lower their duty-cycles. It not only helps in improved latency, but also to extend battery life. The end devices (RFD nodes) synchronize their duty-cycle to wakeup only when a beacon is about to be broadcast. The beacons, therefore, are important for mesh and tree networks. The RFDs can save battery energy and increase their life expectancies by planning their sleep and wakeup cycles with beacon broadcasts.

The channel access is split into:

1. Contention Free Period (CFP), and
2. Contention Access Period (CAP).

A CFP consists of Guaranteed Time Slots (GTS) assigned by the coordinator to the devices, no CSMA-CA is needed for channel access during this time. There may be up to 7 GTS, and the duration of a GTS may be more than 1 slot period. The minimum duration of a CAP is 60 symbols. During a CAP, the nodes use CSMA-CA to access channel.

The values of `macBeaconOrder`, BO, and `macSuperFrameOrder`, SO, determine the duration of different portions of the super frame. BO specifies the interval at which the coordinator should transmit its beacon frames. The beacon interval BI and BO are related by the formula

$$BI = \texttt{aBaseSuperFrameDuration} \times 2^{BO}, 0 \leq BO \leq 14.$$

The super frame is ignored if $BO = 15$. SO determines the length of the active portion of the super frame. The super frame duration, SD, and SO are related by the formula

$$SD = \texttt{aBaseSuperFrameDuration} \times 2^{SO}, 0 \leq SO \leq 14.$$

If $SO = 15$ then the super frame should not remain active after the beacon.

The active portion of each super frame is partitioned into equally spaced slots of duration $2^{SO} \times \texttt{aBaseSlotDuration}$, and consists of three parts, namely, (i) beacon, (ii) a CAP and (iii) a CFP. The beacon is transmitted at the beginning of slot 0 without using CSMA-CA. CAP follows immediately after beacon. The CAP duration should be minimum of `aMinCAPLength` unless more time is required. CFP may or may not be present. But when present, it should always follow CAP at the beginning of a slot boundary. The length of CFP is equal to total length of all GTSs. Figure 6.5 shows a beacon bounded super frame structure with GTS, CAP, CFP and inactive period.

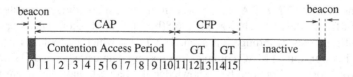

Fig. 6.5 IEEE 802.15.4 MAC super frame

For transmissions within a CAP, two variations of CSMA-CA algorithm are used: (i) slotted CSMA-CA, and (ii) unslotted CSMA-CA. In the slotted CSMA-CA algorithm, the backoff period boundaries of every device in a ZigBee network is aligned with a superframe slot boundaries of the coordinator. Each time a device wants to transmit a data frame during contention period, it synchronizes to the boundary next to the backoff period. In unslotted case, no such synchronization is required.

For execution of CSMA-CA algorithm, 3 important variables are maintained by each device:

1. NB: the number of times the algorithm backs-off while attempting a new transmission, it is initialized to 0 for a new transmission.
2. CW: contention window which is initialized to 2 before a new transmission attempt and reset to 2 each time the medium is found busy.
3. BE: Backoff exponent which gives the number of backoff periods that a device must wait before attempting to access the medium.

The unit of time is a slot time (aUnitBackoffPeriod) that has a default value of 20 symbols. In slotted CSMA-CA, all three values are initialized, and the next backoff period is located. In unslotted CSMA-CA, NB and BE are initialized and the transmission attempt is delayed by random backoff periods in the range $[0, 2^{BE} - 1]$, then the physical layer is requested to perform a Clear Channel Assessment (CCA), and the subsequent steps of MAC algorithm are executed if possible. But if the medium is not idle, then BE is incremented ensuring that $BE \leq$ maxBE. In the slotted case CW is also reset to 2. If the value of $NB <$ maxCSMAbackoffs, then the sender returns back to a fresh attempt for channel access. Otherwise the sending attempt fails and CSMA-CA terminates. In slotted CSMA-CA, the MAC layer checks to ensure that contention window has expired before transmission. CW is first decremented, if $CW = 0$, then transmission is allowed on the boundary of next backoff period. Otherwise, it asks once again for a channel clear assessment by physical layer. In unslotted case the transmission begins immediately if channel is idle. The slotted and the unslotted CSMA-CA algorithms are provided in Figs. 6.6 and 6.7 respectively.

ZigBee allows three different types of data transfers. The type of transfer is dependent on transfer end-points, viz., from a coordinator to a device, from a device to a coordinator, and between two peer devices. Figure 6.8 illustrates the control and data exchanges for two-way transmission between a device and the coordinator in beacon-enabled mode. A device must first listen to the beacon from the coordinator before it attempts to transfer. As shown in Fig. 6.8(a), when a beacon is found, the device synchronizes to superframe structure and sends the data to the coordinator at the correct time using slotted CSMA-CA. In the beacon mode, the coordinator transfers data on request from a device as shown in Fig. 6.8(b). The coordinator indicates pending message from a device through a beacon. The device which periodically listens to beacon, first transmits a MAC command requesting data using slotted CSMA-CA. The coordinator could optionally acknowledge the request, and subsequently send the requested data. Finally, device may also optionally send an acknowledgement.

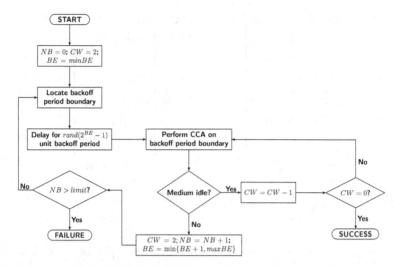

Fig. 6.6 Slotted CSMA-CA algorithm

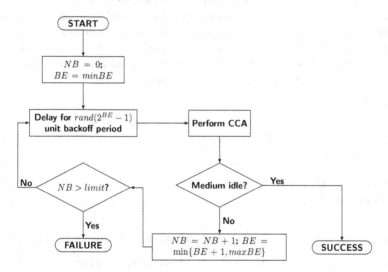

Fig. 6.7 Unslotted CSMA-CA algorithm

In the beaconless mode, IEEE 802.15.4 uses a slightly modified CSMA-CA. It does not involve RTS-CTS exchange. So, it does encounter hidden terminal problem in a multihop settings. After successful transmission of a data frame, a SIFS interval is reserved. A SIFS interval should be longer than ACK message but shorter than ACK window duration. Each device listens before it attempts to transmit. This strategy reduces the probability of occurrence of a collision. The waiting period is chosen randomly from an contention window duration which is defined at the network start

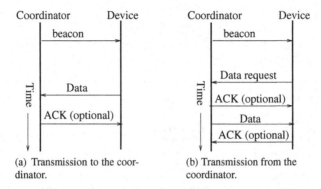

(a) Transmission to the coordinator.

(b) Transmission from the coordinator.

Fig. 6.8 Beacon-enabled transmission in ZigBee

up. A device tries to transmit its packet only after the expiry of contention time. When a collision is detected then the transmitting node backs off by doubling its previous waiting time. After five transmission retries are made the waiting interval is set to its maximum value. The modification in back off algorithm is considered justified because the traffic loads in ZigBee network are not expected to be high. In a situation with low traffic load, the modified back off algorithm will eventually allow a device to transmit its packet. The network layer of ZigBee performs several critical responsibilities for topology management and routing such as:

- *Starting a network*
- *Joining and leaving a network*
- *Configuring a new device*
- *Generating NPDU*
- *Addressing*
- *Topology specific routing*
- *Neighbor discovery*
- *Route discovery*

These responsibilities are shared by three components of network layer namely,

1. Network Layer Data Entity (NLDE): is responsible for generation of Network level PDU (NPDU) and topology specific routings.
2. Network Layer Management Entity (NLME): is responsible for configuring a new device forming a network, joining and leaving a network, addressing, neighbor discovery, route discovery and reception control.
3. Network Information Base (NIB): maintains current settings of the network layer. This includes information on the number of retries, PANId or network address of a particular node. Such information may be set through management commands.

From a functional view point, as explained earlier, ZigBee network consists of end devices, routers and a coordinate. A ZigBee coordinator is an FFD which manages the whole network. A coordinator is capable of initiating and forming a network.

All ZigBee devices must provide at least two simple topology control capabilities, namely, (i) joining a network, and (ii) leaving a network. The coordinator has additional responsibilities such as (i) assignment of logical network addresses, and (ii) maintaining a list of neighboring devices, (iii) accepting a join request. A coordinator assigns a 16-bit short network addresses to its children by using a mathematical function. Further, it specifies certain parameters for any router node to assign logical addresses to its children. These parameters are:

- The maximum number of children C_m any device may have,
- The maximum number of children R_m out of C_m ($C_m \geq R_m$) that may have router capability.
- The maximum depth D_m of a Zigbee End Device (ZED).

The nodes having no routing capabilities are known as ZED. The depth, associated with each device, determines the number of hops to reach the coordinator following child-parent links. The depth of coordinator is 0, each of its children has a depth 1, and so on. A device uses the parameters C_m, R_m, D_m and its depth d to determine its capabilities to accept children. It computes a value $Cskip$ as follows:

$$Cskip(d) = \begin{cases} 1 + C_m(D_m - d - 1), & \text{if } R_m = 1 \\ \dfrac{1 + C_m - R_m - C_m R_m^{D_m - d - 1}}{1 - R_m}, & \text{otherwise} \end{cases}$$

If $Cskip(d) = 0$, then the device is a ZED. The value of $Cskip(d) \neq 0$ for a non ZED. Essentially $Cskip$ pre-allocates a sub-block of addresses to a device for assignment of short addresses to children under it.

A parent device, with a non-zero $Cskip$, assigns an address one greater than its own address to its first associated child router device. The other child routers get addresses separated by $Cskip(d)$ of parent according to the following formula.

$$A_{child} = \begin{cases} A_{parent} + (n - 1) \times Cskip(d) + 1, & \text{for } n = 1 \\ A_{parent} + (n - 1) \times Cskip(d), & \text{for } n > 1, \end{cases}$$

where A_{parent}, A_{child} are the addresses of the parent and the child respectively, and $1 \leq n \leq (C_m - R_m)$ is the number of children having router capabilities.

The address of a child end device (without router capabilities) is calculated according to the following formula.

$$A_{child} = A_{parent} + R_m \times Cskip(d) + n$$

Figure 6.9 provides an example illustrating the address allocation according to rules discussed above. The values used are: $C_m = 5$, $R_m = 3$, $D_m = 3$. For the particular example shown in Fig. 6.9, the PAN coordinator reserves address blocks: 1–21, 22–42, 43–63 for the three permitted children devices with router capabilities. The addresses 64 and 65 are reserved for the two permitted child end devices.

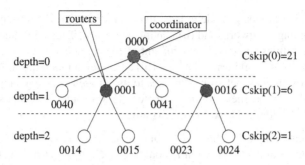

Fig. 6.9   Illustrating address assignment (in hexadecimal) to ZigBee devices

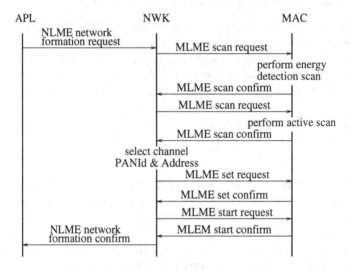

Fig. 6.10   Network formation process executed by ZC

A FFD may wish to become a ZigBee Coordinator (ZC) by scanning all channels to locate one suitable channel. After channel selection, ZC broadcasts a beacon containing PAN identifier to initialize a PAN. A ZigBee Router (ZR) or a ZigBee Device Object (ZDO) which hears a beacon from an existing network may join this network by invoking association process. If multiple beacons are available to a device, then it chooses the beacon sender with smallest hop count as the coordinator. It is up to the beacon sender whether to accept the join request or not on the basis of its current capacity and the permitted duration of association. If the association becomes successful, the coordinator's response will be a short address assignment to the requesting device. A device encounters the orphan problem when all its neighbors have run out of their respective capacities and unable to accept any additional join request.

The procedure for network formation by a ZC is explained in Fig. 6.10. The application layer (APL) in the coordinator node starts with network formation request to its

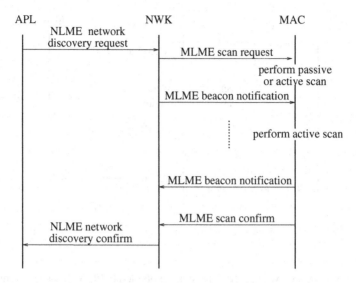

Fig. 6.11 The network discovery process executed by a child device

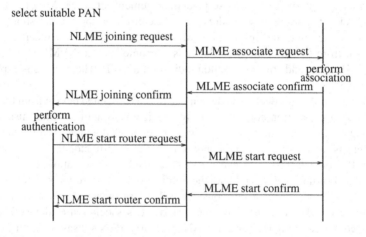

Fig. 6.12 The process of joining executed by a child device

Network Layer Management Entity (NLME). The NLME request triggers sequence of message exchanges between network layer and MAC layer. The MAC Layer Management Entity (MLME) performs scans to assist NLME to select a channel. The subsequent exchanges finally leads MLME to confirm formation of the network which is passed on to APL and the formation completes.

Joining a network is governed by a similar process executed by the child devices. The child device may be a ZR or ZDO. The request can be accepted only by a ZC. The first step of join is to go for a network discovery. The discovery process is explained in Fig. 6.11. After the discovery has been done the child performs the

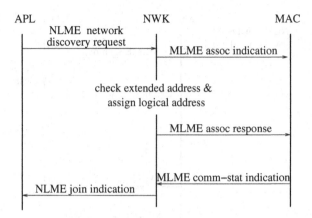

Fig. 6.13 The process of joining executed by a parent device

actual joining process by executing the steps explained in Fig. 6.12. The parent of the node requesting join must execute corresponding association process. On receiving association indication from the MAC layer management entity (MLME), the network layer checks its sub-block of addresses and determines appropriate short logical address for the child and responds to MAC Layer's request. On receiving status indication from its child, the MLME sends the same back to NLME at the parent. The NLME then sends this association indication to APL. The process is explained in Fig. 6.13.

When a coordinator decides to detach one of the associated device from the PAN, it sends a disassociation notification to the device using indirect transmission. On receiving the notification, the device sends an acknowledgement. But the acknowledgement is not a necessary pre-condition for the coordinator to disassociate the device. If a device wishes to leave a PAN, it sends disassociation notification to its current coordinator. On receiving the notification, the coordinator would send an acknowledgement. Device would consider itself as disassociated even if the acknowledgement from the coordinator does not arrive. Disassociation of device becomes completed by removing reference to PAN. Similarly, PAN's disassociation from the device is complete when the coordinator removes all references to the departing device.

A device may lose its association due to reception problem or when the coordinator switches its communication channel. When it happens the device is said to be orphaned. An orphaned device may attempt to rejoin a coordinator by performing an orphan channel scan. The coordinator on receiving orphan notification, checks to determine if the device was associated with it previously. If so, then the coordinator sends a command for re-association. The orphan rejoining procedure executed by child and parent devices are explained in Fig. 6.14.

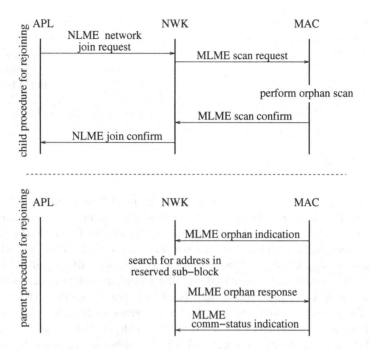

Fig. 6.14 Re-joining steps executed by orphan child and its parent

6.4 6LoWPAN

The motivation behind 6LoWPAN proposal is to define IP over IEEE 802.15.4 stack. The idea is to leverage the IP networking while taking advantage of low energy operations of MAC and PHY layers of IEEE 802.15.4 standards. It enriched the application space from all small, handheld battery powered devices to embedded control and monitoring devices including sensor nodes. It created the space for what is widely known as "Internet of Things" (IoT). 6LoWPAN uses IPv6 address space to overcome the problem of scaling in device addressing. Therefore, it is more appropriate to define 6LoWPAN as IPv6 over Low-Power wireless networks. It is defined mainly by IETF standards RFC 4919 [5] and 4944 [6]. Interoperability between IPv6 and LoWPAN network is due to edge routers with 6LoWPAN support. Within 6LoWPAN network, the routers or the hosts need not work with full IPv6 or UPD header formats. The protocol stack at edge router must have support for both conventional IPv6 as well as LoWPAN adaptability as shown in Fig. 6.15.

Fig. 6.15 Protocol stack for
an IPv6 edge router with
6LoWPAN support

IPv6 (Network Layer)	
Ethernet MAC	6LoWPAN adaptation
	IEEE 802.15.4 MAC
Ethernet PHY	IEEE 802.15.4 PHY

6.4.1   IPV6

Let us first understand how IPv6 is important for defining IoT space. IPv6 is defined in RFC 2460. IPv6 is not merely an extension of IPv4, but a complete reformulation IP addressing scheme. The host identity is decoupled from network address. IPv6 allow for auto configuration when routers are not present. So, both routing and address management become simple. Though majority of network traffic is still IPv4, this address space is completely exhausted. So, all machines, as well as routers now provide for IPv6 addressing support. Most organizations are now on the IPv6 transition phase. The growth of IPv6 traffic over the last few years has been phenomenal.

An IPv4 address consists of 4 octets or a 32-bit address. IPv6, on the other hand, uses 128 bit address space consisting of 3.4×10^{38} possible addresses which provides roughly about 15 million addresses per square inch of the Earth's surface. IPv6 eliminates the need for NATing and simplifies the routing. There is no need for ARP or DHCP even Mobile IP for supporting unrestricted mobility of nodes. IPv6 address is computed from layer 2 or MAC address. Each address has a life time and three scopes, namely, (i) link-local, (ii) site-local, and (iii) global. The total length of 3 ID fields in an IPv6 address is 128 bits. The lengths of individual IDs are as follows:

1. Global ID is 48 bits,
2. Subnet ID is 16 bits, and
3. Interface ID is 64 bits.

The interface ID is constructed from 48-bit MAC ID by expanding it to 64-bit Extended Unique Identifier (EUI). The six octets of 48-bit MAC address is partitioned into 3 higher and 3 lower octets. Then leading octet's second bit from the right is flipped. A pair of octets FE:FE is inserted in between these two parts to form an 8-octet address. The process of forming EUI from a MAC address is illustrated in Table 6.2. This way every LAN segment gets a 64 bit address. Thus, up to 2^{64} interface IDs are possible. As shown in Fig. 6.16, the network part of the address also has 64 bits. It is partitioned into 16-bit subnet address and 48-bit global address. A single global network address, i.e., one single site can have up to $2^{16} = 65536$ subnets. The subnet address is also referred to as Site Level Aggregator (SLA). The remaining 48 higher address bits defining the global network ID has three fields:

1. The first 3 bits define address types.
2. The next 13 bits define Top Level Aggregator (TLA)
3. The remaining 32 bits are for Next Level Aggregator (NLA)

Table 6.2 Forming an EUI address from a MAC address

MAC address: 00:0E:81:2E:B6:D1	
Flip the second LSB of the leading octet	02:0E:81:2E:B6:D1
Split the address into two halves	02:0E:81 and 2E:B6:D1
Insert FE:FE between two halves and contenate	02:0E:81:FE:FE:2E:B6:D1

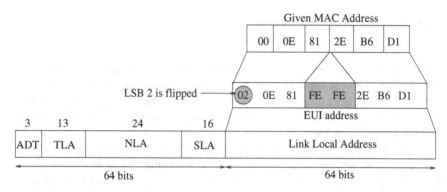

Fig. 6.16 Network part of IPv6 address

Possible address types are: (i) unicast link-local, (ii) anycast, and (iii) multicast.

A unicast address is defined as the address for a single interface. But, a unicast address also has a scope. So, one interface ID could be associated with three different unicast addresses. The possible scopes can be unique global, unique local and link-local. All link-local addresses are identified by the prefix FE80::/10. A link-local address is used for communication between source and destination in a single LAN, and not forwarded off the router. Each interface ID has an associated link-local address. Unique local address is recognized by the prefix FC00::/7. However, it requires 8th bit to be set 1 for locally assigned local address, and if 8th bit is unset then the address is not used (reserved for future use). So, in reality the prefix is for the unique local unicast address FD00::/8. A unique local address is reachable outside a particular link but not routable across the Internet. It has limited meaning inside a particular domain. For a global address, 40 bits are reserved. Global addresses are reachable across the Internet. There are different prefixes for global unicast addresses that identify the unique regional registry to which the address belongs. For example, prefix 2400:0000::/12, 2600:0000::/12, 2800:0000::/12, 2A00:0000::/12, 2C00:0000::/12, refer respectively to APNIC, ARNIC, LACNIC, RIPE NCC, and AfriNIC registries.

A multicast address represents a set interfaces belonging to many nodes. Multicast addresses also have assigned scopes. Link-local multicast addresses are meant for nodes within a link and not meant for forwarding off that link. Organizational multicast addresses are recognizable within a limited scope of one particular domain and

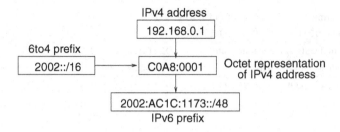

Fig. 6.17 Address translation: IPv4–IPv6

not meant to be valid across Internet. Global multicast addresses are usable across the Internet. Some of the known prefixes for multicast addresses are: FF02::1, FF02::2 and FF02:0:0:0:0:1:FFXX:XXXX which respectively represent link-local for all node addresses, link-local for all routers, and link-local for all nodes with matching interface IDs.

Anycast packets get delivered to any one of the host interfaces configured for anycast address, which usually is the nearest one according to distance measurements by routing protocol. A multicast packet is delivered to all members of a multicast group.

To give an idea about the basic features of IPv6 addressing scheme, let us begin with an example where two IPv6 networks are connected over an IPv4 router. The network prefix 2002::/16 is reserved for IPv6-to-IPv4 traffic. The next 32 bits of network prefix is reserved for IPv6-to-IPv4 router. Let the IPv4 address of router be 192.168.0.1. The octet representation of the IPv4 address is C0A8:0001. Therefore, IPv6 prefix of the router will be 2002:C0A8:0001::/48 as shown in Fig. 6.17. When a IPv6-to-IPv4 router gets a packet with prefix 2002::/16, it knows that next 32 bits represents IPv4 address, and tunnels the packet to the correct IPv4 address.

6.4.2 IP Over IEEE 802.15.4

6LoWPAN defines IPv6 over energy constrained wireless area network [5, 6]. The implementation of 6LoWPAN requires low memory and overall code size is small. On the top of this, it facilitates direct end-to-end integration with the Internet. A 6LoWPAN node can be programmed using standard socket API. There are many factors which influence the architecture of IP over IEEE 802.15.4. Some of the keys issues are:

1. *Design of header.* In standard IP network, an IP packet header is 40 bytes while IEEE 802.15.4 supports a MTU of 127 bytes. Usually, the payload is in form of parameter value pair which is not more than 8 bytes.
2. *Packet fragmentation.* The interoperability requirement implies that incoming packet length from IP network can often be very large. IPv6 links can support up to 1280 bytes [7].

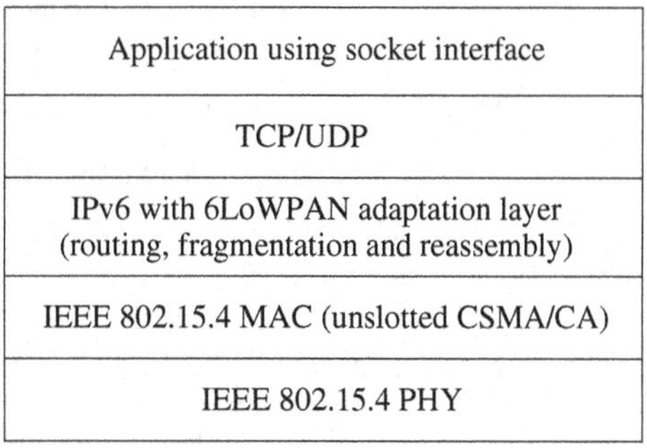

Fig. 6.18 6LoWPAN
protocol stack

Application using socket interface
TCP/UDP
IPv6 with 6LoWPAN adaptation layer (routing, fragmentation and reassembly)
IEEE 802.15.4 MAC (unslotted CSMA/CA)
IEEE 802.15.4 PHY

3. *Link layer routing.* A single IEEE 802.15.4 node may have multiple radios. Either the origin or the destination or both may use short 16 bit addresses or long 64 bit EUI addresses.
4. *IP layer routing.* IEEE 802.15.4 supports multiple radios, so it can utilize any of the available radios over a single hop. IP layer on top of this should also be able to handle routing over a mesh of 802.15.4 nodes.
5. *6LoWPAN impact on energy.* Implementing IP over IEEE 802.15.4 puts certain inherent overheads. Optimizing the overhead will be a challenge.

The protocol stack is illustrated by Fig. 6.18. The transport layer of 6LoWPAN does not provide for TCP connection while network layer uses IPv6. In some sense, 6LoWPAN can be viewed as an adaptation layer for handling routing, fragmentation and reassembly over IEEE 802.15.4 MAC layer. Three major functions of adaptation layer are:

1. TCP/IP header compression,
2. Packet fragmentation and reassembly, and
3. Routing.

6.4.3 Compression, Fragmentation and Reassembly

The header length of an IPv6 packet is 40 bytes. Apart from IPv6 header, UDP and ICMP headers consume additional 4 bytes each. The length of TCP header is 20 bytes. Since, the size of an IEEE 802.15.4 frame is just 128 bytes, without compression, it leaves just a few bytes for payload. Without the header compression, as Fig. 6.19 indicates the maximum payload size of a IPv6 UPD packet is only 53 bytes. Apart from MAC, UDP and IPv6 headers, there is also a 2B 6LoWPAN header marked L. Without compression 64 bit addressing is used. However, when header compression is applied, 16 bit addressing can be used. When compression is applied on both IPv6 and UDP headers, only 6B is needed. This implies that the maximum size of payload

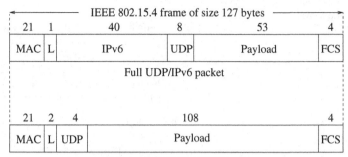

Fig. 6.19 Header compression in 6LoWPAN

802.15.4 header	IPv6 compressed header	IPv6 payload

802.15.4 header	Fragment header	IPv6 compressed header	IPv6 payload

802.15.4 header	Mesh routing header	Fragment header	IPv6 compressed header	IPv6 payload

Fig. 6.20 Header compression in 6LoWPAN using stacked header

can be stretched to 108 bytes. The format of compression is defined in RFC 4944 [6].

Low power wireless technology supports link layer addressing. So, there is a need for mapping between link layer addressing and IPv6 addressing, which is achieved through compression. The nodes are assumed to be part of one IPv6 subnet with unique MAC addresses. Global prefix is assumed to be known to all nodes in the network, while link-local prefix is indicated by header compression format. So, only compressed header for local prefix can be used. Multicast addresses are also compressed. As Fig. 6.20 shows, the compression scheme is based on the concept of stacked headers. The compressed header being encapsulated within the payload of 802.15.4 MAC frame. Three examples of using stacked combination of header layouts are:

1. Point to point short packet transmission,
2. Fragmented IP packet transmission, and
3. Mesh transmitted packets.

Every 6LoWPAN packet header carries a single byte dispatch value which identifies the packet and the applicable compression type. The first two bits of dispatch header indicate type of the packet. Five defined types are as illustrated in Table 6.3.

Table 6.3 Header compression

00	Not a Low PAN packet
01	Normal dispatch
10	Mesh header
11	Fragmentation header

6.4.3.1 Stateless Compression of IPv6 Packets

The payload of a short packet can be accommodated within a single 802.15.4 MAC frame. Leaving aside the 2 bits dispatch header, the remaining six bits for point to point transmission of short packets are set according to the type of header compression that is expected to follow. Out of 64 possible dispatch header patterns, only five have been defined so far. One extension byte may be used for dispatch header to allow up to 256 header types. The extension byte is indicated when all six pattern bits are set to 1 in the first byte. A layout of dispatch header for 6LoWPAN frames is shown in Table 6.4. The full layout of packet header for point to point transmission of short packets is shown in Fig. 6.21. The use of HC1 scheme is based on the fact that interface ID part of IPv6 is created from MAC address of the host. Therefore, both can be elided. However, compression of network part of IPv6 address poses difficulty. It can only be compressed if the network address is a link-local address, i.e., FE80::/64. HC1 allows for independent compression of each half of both source and destination addresses by appropriately setting the respective groups bits in HC1, namely, SA (Source Address) and DA (Destination Address). SA and DA occupy 2 bits each. This encoding is depicted in Table 6.5. The remaining part of HC1 header represent following components of an IPv6 header:

Table 6.4 Dispatch header

Identifier	Header compression
000001	IPv6 header is uncompressed
000010	HC1 compression encoding used for IPv6 header
111111	Additional byte for dispatch header

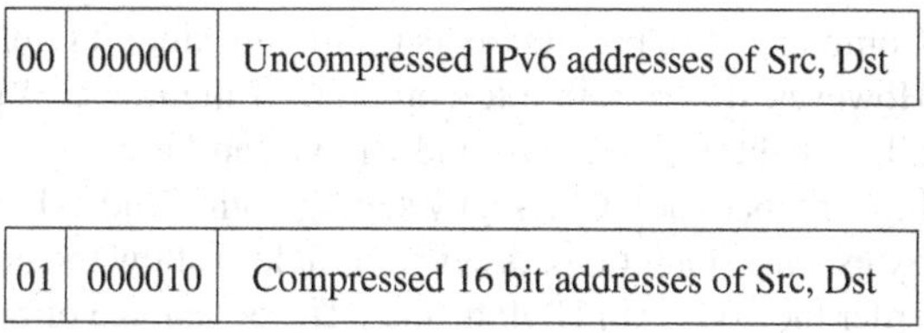

Fig. 6.21 Headers for point to point short packet transmission

00	000001	Uncompressed IPv6 addresses of Src, Dst

01	000010	Compressed 16 bit addresses of Src, Dst

Table 6.5 Encoding header

SA/DA	Prefix	Interface ID
00	Sent in-line	Sent in-line
01	Sent in-line	Derived from L2 or mesh address
10	Assumed to be link-local (FE80::/64)	Sent in-line
11	Assumed to be link-local (FE80::/64)	Derived from L2 or mesh address

Table 6.6 Explanation HC1 bit patterns for NH values

Pattern	Description
00	Next header is sent in-line
01	Next header = 17 (for UDP packet)
10	Next header = 1 (for ICMP packet)
11	Next header = 6 (for TCP packet)

1. Version number which is alway 6, and not sent.
2. Two fields indicating traffic and flow class, and are usually set to 0 in IPv6. C bit is set if these fields are 0. If C bit is clear then these bits are included in non-compressed header.
3. Payload length can be extracted from remaining part of length of a 6LoWPAN packet. So, this field is not sent.
4. The size of the next header (NH) is 1 byte. It contains a number of values that are found more normally than others.
5. Hop limit is not compressed and sent in-line with non-compressed fields.

HC1 bits are set as shown in Table 6.6 for interpretation of NH values. Non-compressed fields follow HC1 and HC2 headers with hop limit being the first field. The non-compressed fields occur in the same order as they do in HC1 header.

Besides, HC1 compression scheme, 6LoWPAN also allows for UDP header compression through HC2 scheme. However, as stated earlier, if HC2 were to be present then the NH value should be inferred as 17 from HC1. The first three bits of HC2 indicate compression of source port, destination port and the length. Length compression is easy, as it can be computed from number of bytes remaining in 6LoWPAN frame. Compression of port numbers is difficult, since it implies that ports are known apriori. However, it is possible to compress if the range of ports are known. For example, all ports between 61616 and 61631 can be compressed to lower 4 bits, assuming higher bits to be F0B. So, by setting both S and D bits in HC2 it is possible to save 3 bytes. Any non-compressed UDP fields follow the non-compressed fields of HC1 in order they occur in UDP header. The advantage of both HC1 and HC2 compression schemes is that they work without any input concerning state. Stateless compression

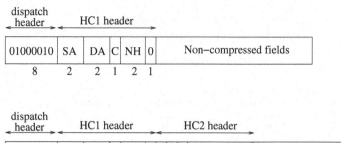

Fig. 6.22 Stateless compression of packets in 6LoWPAN

scheme need no synchronization and require simple algorithms. Figure 6.22 illustrates the stateless header compression as explained above for HC1 (without HC2) and also for both HC1 and HC2.

6.4.3.2 Header Format for Fragmented Packets

If the payload fits into a single IEEE 802.15.4 frame, then it is unfragmented and 6LoWPAN encapsulation should not contain a fragment header. However, if the datagram cannot be accommodated within a single frame then the datagram is fragmented, and the corresponding frames would contain appropriate headers for the fragmented frames.

The dispatch header for fragmented packet transmissions of large packets requires 5 bits. The initial two bits are set to 11. The next 3 bits are set to 000 for the first fragment of a large packet. The bit pattern 100 is used for the remaining fragments of the large packet transmission. Notice that 3 bits are left out from the original 8-bit dispatch header. These bits are now included to define an expanded 11 bit fragment size. Except for the first fragment, all subsequent fragments also require an offset to calculate the correct address of the first byte of payload carried by the current frame. The header layout for fragmented packet transmission is shown in Fig. 6.23. The fragmented packets also carry a tag of size 2 bytes. It represents the sequence number of the packet carrying the current fragment.

6.4.3.3 Compression of Mesh Header

The dispatch header for mesh under routing is represented by bit pattern 10 which requires just 2 bits. The next two bits indicate the addressing used for source (S) and destination (D). These bits are set as indicated below:

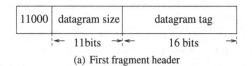

11000	datagram size	datagram tag

← 11bits →←   16 bits   →

(a) First fragment header

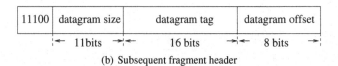

11100	datagram size	datagram tag	datagram offset

← 11bits →←   16 bits   →← 8 bits →

(b) Subsequent fragment header

Fig. 6.23 Fragmented packet headers

Fig. 6.24 Header compression for mesh routing

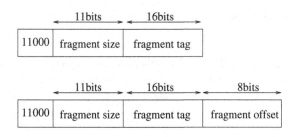

$$S/D = \begin{cases} 0, \text{ source/destination address is 64 bit EUI} \\ 1, \text{ source/destination address is 16 bit short address} \end{cases}$$

The next 4 bits represent hops left, which allows up to a maximum 16 hops in mesh under routing. This limitation is not restrictive, as normally 6LoWPAN networks have a small diameter. Hops left is followed by source and destination addresses, and require either 16 or 64 bits depending on whether short or long addressing is used. So, for mesh under routing header compression reduces the packet header to 5 bytes as indicated in Fig. 6.24.

The second major function of adaptation layer is to handle fragmentation and reassembly of packets. This is necessitated by the fact that IPv6 layer supports an MTU of 1280 bytes. Therefore, for two way communication between IP network and 6LoWPAN nodes fragmentation and reassembly are important basic steps.

6.4.4 Routing

The problem of routing requires attention in two different spaces, namely,

1. Mesh routing in PAN space, involving only 6LoWPAN nodes.
2. Routing packets between IPv6 domain and PAN domain.

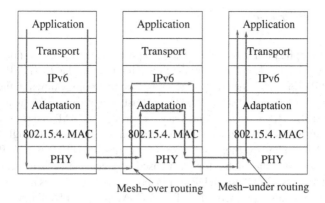

Fig. 6.25 Mesh routing in 6LoWPAN network

Mesh routing in 6LoWPAN can occur either in link layer, or in network layer. Link layer mesh routing is known as mesh-under and transparent to IP. IP or network layer routing is known as route-over. Figure 6.25 illustrates these routing.

Mesh-under routing is performed at the adaptation layer, the network layer is not involved. Routing and forwarding is performed by the link layer using 6LoWPAN header. In order to send packet to the destination either the EUI 64-bit or 16-bit short address is used. As indicated in Fig. 6.25, multiple mesh under routings may be needed to send packets close to the destination, located at a single IP hop from the source. As both link layer originator's address and the address of the final destination are included in header, mesh routing for any protocol is possible in adaptation layer. IP packets are fragmented at the adaptation layer and different fragments are sent to the next hop by mesh routing. These fragments may follow different paths to reach the destination. When all fragments are received successfully, reassembly is performed by the adaptation layer at the destination before delivering these to the upper layer.

As shown in Fig. 6.25, routings decisions in mesh-over routing are made in network layer. Each link layer hop is also an IP hop. The network layer uses encapsulated IP header, available as payload of MAC frame, to take decision on routing. The job of adaptation layer is to map MAC frame and IP headers. A fragments of a fragmented IP packet are sent to next hop as stored by routing table. When all fragments arrive successfully, adaptation layer creates an IP packet by reassembling the fragments and sends to the network layer. If the packet is for the receiving node, then the IP packet is delivered to the upper layer. Otherwise, the network layer forwards the packet to the next hop closer to the destination.

6.4.5 CoAP Protocol

Constrained Application Protocol (CoAP) [11] provides a request response type of interaction model for M2M communication which is similar to HTTP. The idea behind CoAP proposal is meant for extending web technology down to the requirements of small constrained devices [11] as illustrated by Fig. 6.26. It is basically an efficient REST (REpresental State Transfer) protocol. CoAP is designed to meet several requirements that originates from a constrained network. Though similar to HTTP, CoAP has a low overhead and allows for multicast. HTTP uses TCP as transport service which is unsuitable for push based services. HTTP is too complex for constrained devices. CoAP uses UDP as transport service, so it does not require complex congestion control protocol of TCP. But CoAP provides UDP bindings for the reliability and multicast support. CoAP uses REST methods GET, POST, PUT and URI like HTTP. To cope up with the unreliability of UDP, CoAP employs a retransmission mechanism. Therefore, CoAP is not just a compression of HTTP protocol, it is designed as a clean efficient REST protocol. However, it is not a replacement for HTTP. The variations in HTTP and CoAP stacks are depicted in Fig. 6.27. Transaction layer of CoAP handles single message exchange between the end points. It supports four different type of messages:

1. Confirmable: requires an acknowledgement.
2. Non-confirmable: does not require any acknowledgement.
3. Acknowledgement: acknowledges a message.
4. Reset: indicates a confirmable message has been received but the context is missing.

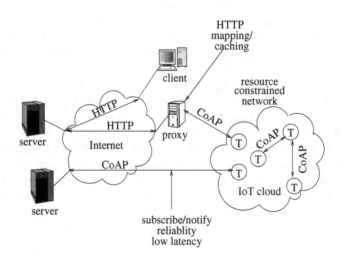

Fig. 6.26 Architecture of CoAP [10]

Fig. 6.27 CoAP and HTTP
stacks

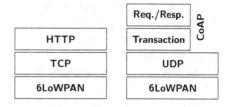

The request/response layer is responsible for the transmission of requests to the devices and getting the corresponding responses. The REST request are piggybacked on confirmable/non-confirmable messages, and the responses are piggybacked on the corresponding acknowledgement messages. A confirmable message is retransmitted after a default timeout and an exponential backoff is used between timeouts until the recipient sends an acknowledgement. If a CoAP server is unable to handle a request immediately, it sends an acknowledgement for the received message. The response is sent afterwards. Tokens are used for matching the responses with the corresponding requests. For more details on CoAP the reader is referred to the original IETF draft on CoAP [11].

6.4.6 RPL Routing Protocol

Link state routing algorithms maintain routes by scoped flooding while distance vector based routing algorithms use periodic updates to propagate routing updates. Both approaches are unsuitable for low bandwidth lossy networks. RPL is a distance vector based algorithm with the design objectives spelt out in a series of RFCs [12–15]. The protocol is designed for Low power, Lossy Network (LLN) that uses IPv6. RPL uses two important techniques to reduce control traffic for topology maintenance, namely,

1. Polite gossip, and
2. Parent switching.

The routing updates are propagated using Trickle Algorithm [12]. It uses polite gossip to react quickly to the updates, but as the same update gets circulated in the network, the algorithm quickly ceases its activity. The technique is as follows:

- An update is broadcast locally by a node, if its own data is not consistent with what it hears from others.
- But if a node hears the same update then it becomes silent, i.e., transmission is suppressed.
- On hearing an old update, a node broadcasts the most recent update.

In other words, on hearing a new update, a node broadcasts the same in order to trigger other nodes to broadcast. On hearing an old update, node understands that there is at least one node (from which it received the old data) which has not received the new update.

The other important technique that RPL uses is switching parent to achieve reliability. Since LLN is an unstable network, the nodes tend to lose connectivity frequently. To take care of such instability, each node maintain multiple potential parents and switches quickly away from the routes that are no longer available. It keeps track of the variability in link state by estimating ETX, i.e., estimated number of transmissions. As a result, it does not have to initiate route repair as often as other existing routing algorithms do.

6.4.6.1   DODAG Construction

The most important idea behind the routing scheme is the construction of a Destination Oriented Directed Acyclic Graph (DODAG). A DODAG is built for a single destination or sink. The sink node is also referred to as the root of the DODAG. A DODAG is built by using a single Objective Function (OF) that determines how the routing metric is computed. The use of different OFs define different DODAGs to co-exist over the same physical network. For example, on the same physical network one OF may be used to define a DODAG on the basis of expected transmission and another OF may be used to define a DODAG based on residual battery power of the nodes.

Each node n computes its rank, where the rank gives its relative position with respect to the root. So, rank of n increases or decreases depending on whether it moves away or moves towards the root. The rank can be based on simple hop count or defined by a function which depends on certain constraints. It requires four types of control messages:

1. DIO (DODAG Information Object): Stores routing control information. It includes for example, the rank of a node in current instance of RPL, IPv6 address of the root node.
2. DAO (Destination Advertisement Object): Its main purpose is to propagate destination information upstream along the DODAG. This information is used for downstream routing.
3. DIS (DODAG Information Solicitation): It enables a node to acquire DIO message from a reachable neighbor.
4. DAO-ACK: It is an acknowledgement sent by the recipient of a DAO message.

These four types of control messages are defined as ICMPv6 information messages [16].

As explained above, for topology maintenance, it extends trickle algorithm [12] for controlled sending of DIO messages over the network. For a stable network, DIO messages are sent infrequently, but in an unstable network, DIO messages are sent frequently. From a DIO message, the recipient gets the RPL instance and knows which DODAG it is a part of. Hence it can compute its own rank. The rank computation would depend on the rank of the parent and OF carried by the DIO message. If a node is moving closer to the root, then it can apply "make before break" approach to poision the existing route after it activates the new route. Because this can never lead to a loop.

Most of the time, the local repair can reconnect a node to its DODAG, if current parent becomes unresponsive. Most of the time, the local repair increases the rank of the node, and needed when an inconsistency is detected. The need for global repair arises when the root wants to reconfigure the network. Each node recomputes its rank and selects a new parent set.

For supporting source routing to various nodes, each node sends out DAO message which carries information about parent set on DODAG until it reaches the root. The root gathers DAO information for each node in order to construct downstream route for the node. For more details on DODAG construction and routing, the readers are referred to [17].

6.5 ZigBee IP

One of the major problems in interoperability of ZigBee with IP based networks is security. To connect a ZigBee node to the Internet, two different sets of security associations are needed:

1. One to handle the connection between a ZigBee node to ZigBee Gateway, and
2. Another to handle the Gateway to IP node connectivity.

Therefore, vulnerability to the attacks increases manifold. In contrast, 6LoWPAN uses IPv6, and does not require any additional security mechanism for end-to-end communication. Additionally, it also leaves more room for payload [8]. So, a relook was necessary on ZigBee stack to incorporate support for IP.

6.5.1 Protocol Stack

ZigBee IP is a super specification for IPv6 stack and developed initially for Smart Energy Meter application. The approach in developing super specification is dictated by the following two important reasons:

1. Implementing a full stack from scratch would have created problem interoperability with legacy ZigBee networks already deployed in the field.
2. The cost of interoperability should not increase the complexity and the size of the code for ZigBee stack too much.

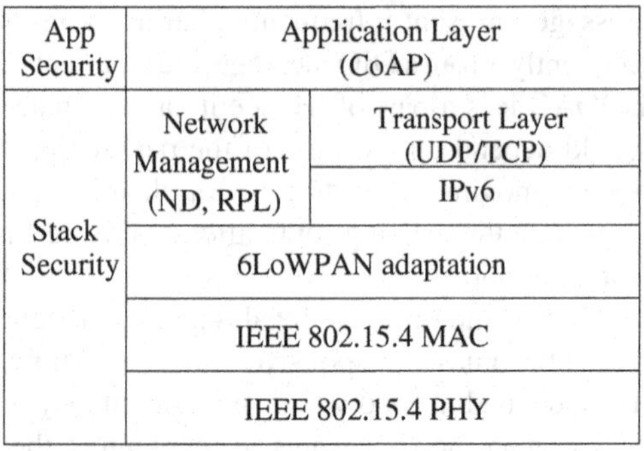

Fig. 6.28 ZigBee IP stack
layering architecture

App Security	Application Layer (CoAP)	
Stack Security	Network Management (ND, RPL)	Transport Layer (UDP/TCP)
		IPv6
	6LoWPAN adaptation	
	IEEE 802.15.4 MAC	
	IEEE 802.15.4 PHY	

ZigBee IP draws much of the concepts from 6LoWPAN, especially the header compression and the fragmentation ideas. It uses Routing Protocol for Low-power and Lossy Networks (RPL) for routing. The downstream routing is managed without IP tables. The network nodes route their data to a central device which uses source routing to route data back to devices. It also supports both transport protocols: UDP and TCP. Figure 6.28 shows the layering architecture of the stack. Besides 6LoWPAN adaption layer for header compression and fragmentation, the network management incorporates IPv6 Neighbor Discovery (ND) [9] to find IP addresses of directly reachable neighbors. Neighbor discovery works for networks where the router is always on [9]. The basic problem in transmission between an IP node and a ZigBee node arises due to mismatch in sizes of MTUs in the two networks. MTU size is 1280 octets in IPv6 and that in IEEE 802.15.4 consists of 127 octets. For downstream transmission, an incoming IPv6 datagram is broken down into small pieces called fraglets. The size of a fraglet is 127 octets including the payload and the compressed header. Each fraglet of an IP packet is sent as a separate downstream packet. For upstream transmission fraglets are recombined into a single datagram and then handed over to upper IP layer.

References

1. P. Kinney, P. Jamieson, J. Gutierrez, IEEE 802.15 WPAN task group 4 (TG4) (2004), www.ieee802.org/15/pub/TG4.html
2. P. Baronti, P. Pillai, V. Chook, S. Chessa, A. Gotta, Y.F. Hu, Wireless sensor networks: a survey on the state of the art and the 802.15.4 and zigbee standards. Comput. Commun. **30**(7), 1655–1695 (2007)
3. ZigBee Standard Organization. Zigbee smart energy profile specification, Dec 2008. Document 075356r15
4. ZigBee Alliance. ZigBee IP: The first open standard for IPv6-based wireless mesh networks, Mar 2013
5. N. Kushalnagar, G. Montenegro, C. Shumacher, IPv6 over low-power wireless personal area network (6LoWPAN): overview, assumptions, problem statement, and goals, http://www.rfc-editor.org/info/rfc4919. Aug 2007. RFC-4919

6. G. Montenegro, N. Kushalnagar, J. Hui, D. Culler, Transmission of IPv6 packets over IEEE 802.15.4 networks, https://tools.ietf.org/html/rfc4944. Sept 2007. RFC-4944
7. S. Deering, R. Hinden, Internet protocol, version 6 (IPv6) specification, https://tools.ietf.org/html/rfc2460. Dec 1998. RFC-2460
8. E. Toscano, L. Lo Bello, Comparative assessments of IEEE 802.15. 4/ZigBee and 6LoWPAN for low-power industrial WSNs in realistic scenarios, in *The 9th IEEE International Workshop on Factory Communication Systems (WFCS)*, 115–124, 2012
9. T. Narten and The Author Team for RFC-4861. Neighbor discovery for ip version 6 (IPv6), https://tools.ietf.org/html/rfc4861. Sept 2007. RFC 4861
10. Z. Shelby, Coap: The web of things protocol, https://www.youtube.com/. May 2014
11. Z. Shelby, K. Hartke, C. Bormann, The constrained application protocol (coap), https://tools.ietf.org/html/rfc7252. June 2014. RFC-7252
12. A. Brandt, J. Buron, G. Porcu, Home automation routing requirements in low-power and lossy networks, 2010. RFC 5826
13. The Author Team for RFC-5548. Routing requirements for urban low-power and lossy networks, https://tools.ietf.org/html/rfc5548. May 2009. RFC-5548
14. J. Martocci and The Author Team for RFC5867. Building automation routing requirements in low-power and lossy networks, https://tools.ietf.org/html/rfc5867. June 2010. RFC-5867
15. K. Pister and The Author Team for RFC-5673. Industrial routing requirements in low-power and lossy networks, https://tools.ietf.org/html/rfc5673. Oct 2009. RFC-5673
16. A. Conta, S. Deering, M. Gupta, Internet control message protocol (ICMPv6) for the internet protocol version 6 (IPv6) specification, https://tools.ietf.org/html/rfc4443. Mar 2006. RFC-4443
17. T. Winter and The Author Team for RFC-6550. Rpl: Ipv6 routing protocol for low-power and lossy networks, https://tools.ietf.org/html/rfc6550. Mar 2012. RFC-6550

Chapter 7
Routing Protocols for Mobile Ad Hoc Network

7.1 Introduction

A Mobile Ad hoc NETwork (MANET) is a multihop wireless network consisting of a number of mobile devices forming a temporary network. No established wired infrastructure or centralized network administration exists to support communication in a MANET. A MANET differs from a wired network in many ways. Some of these are attributable to general characteristics of wireless networks, while the others are due to the characteristics specific to MANETs [4]. Some of the typical characteristics a MANET are:

- The users in a MANET may neither wish nor be in a position to perform any administrative services needed to set up or to maintain a network.
- The topology of a MANET changes dynamically due to mobility of the nodes.
- Each node in a MANET is completely autonomous and acts both an ordinary node and a router.
- A node in a MANET has relatively less resources compared to a node in wired network.
- All nodes have similar capabilities and identically responsible for communication in a MANET.
- Any mobile node may either join, or leave MANET at any point of time.

The problems associated with wireless connectivity combined with the limitations of MANET create a number of difficulties in designing routing protocols. In particular, these protocols are expected to address and resolve the following important issues.

1. Communication in a MANET is broadcast based. Unless carefully designed, routing protocols may generate high volume of unnecessary traffic in the network leading to flooding and congestion.
2. In order to participate in discovery and maintenance of the routes, the nodes in a MANET should be in active mode. However, no node should be forced to wake up when it is operating in low energy mode to save its battery power.

© Springer Nature Singapore Pte Ltd. 2017
R.K. Ghosh, *Wireless Networking and Mobile Data Management*,
DOI 10.1007/978-981-10-3941-6_7

Fig. 7.1 Ad hoc network

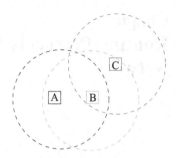

3. The processing load due to discovery and maintenance of routes should be distributed as much evenly as possible among the nodes in a MANET.
4. Many redundant paths have to be maintained between every pair of source and destination. This may causes unnecessary increase in the size of routing updates that must be sent over the network.

Each node in a MANET has a fixed wireless range. Any mobile host which appears inside the range of a transmitting host can listen/capture the messages being transmitted. In a MANET, every active node is expected to participate in forwarding a message towards the destination node. If a destination host is not directly reachable from a source then all hosts which receive the transmission from the source, forward the same to their respective neighbors. The neighbors, in turn, repeat the same until the message finally reaches the destination. For example, consider Fig. 7.1 where A, B and C represent three mobile hosts. The wireless ranges of these hosts are indicated by the respective circles having centers at A, B and C. The figure indicates that A and B are within the wireless range of each other, so are B and C. But C cannot receive any transmission directly from A, as it is not in the range of A. If A were to send a message to C then B must cooperate to forward the same to C. Thus, the design of an efficient routing protocol in MANET poses a number of difficulties depending on the degree of severities of the constraints mentioned above. This explains why the area offers a rich source of problems for research.

A number of routing schemes have been proposed [1, 8, 9, 11, 12, 14–16] for mobile ad hoc networks. Most of these algorithms based on existing Internet routing algorithms. The performance evaluations of the routing algorithms can be based on a set of common parameters, namely,

- Distributiveness in execution.
- Ability to find loop-free paths between a source and a destination.
- Ability to find cheaper routes between a source and a destination.
- Ability to restrict flooding the network with broadcast transmission during route discovery.
- Ability to quickly establish a route between a source and a destination.
- Ability to avoid congestion at nodes by providing alternative routes between a source and a destination.

- Ability to maintain or repair a route between a source and a destination quickly, by localizing the route maintenance, when the network topology undergoes a change.
- Ability to provide quality of service (QoS).

An exhaustive study of the routing algorithms could be a book by itself. An interested reader may refer to an excellent collection of selected articles on ad hoc network [13]. Only a few important and widely cited routing schemes are the subject of our discussion here.

7.2 Classification of Routing Protocols

Routing in any network can be viewed abstractly as finding and maintaining the shortest-path between two communicating nodes in a weighted graph. Each node maintains a preferred neighbor, which is the next hop on the path to reach a destination. Each data packet should have the address of the destination in its header. An intermediate node forwards a data packet to the next hop closer to destination by consulting the locally maintained table known as route table. The routing protocols differ in the manner in which the routing tables are constructed and maintained. Based on characteristics of the routing protocols, Royer and Toh [17] have suggested a classification scheme. As shown in Fig. 7.2, the routing schemes can be classified into two broad classes, namely,

- Table driven or proactive, and
- Source initiated on-demand or reactive

Examples of distance vector based table driven protocols are Destination Sequenced Distance Vector (DSDV) [14], Wireless Routing Protocol (WRP) [10] and Cluster Gateway Switch Routing (CGSR) [2]. DSDV is a distributed version of Bellman-Ford shortest path algorithm which relies on destination sequence numbering scheme to avoid loops. CGSR protocol is a logical descendant DSDV protocol. But, it uses

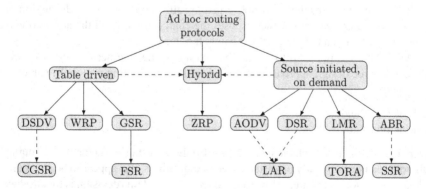

Fig. 7.2 Classifying routing algorithms

a clustered multihop organization scheme for network instead of a flat structure. WRP [10] does not use sequence number, but uses second-to-last hop information for each destination. It forces each node to check consistency of its predecessor's information to avoid count-to-infinity problem. Fisheye State Routing (FSR) [12] protocol is a direct descendant of Global State Routing (GSR) [1] protocol. GSR is a link state routing algorithm it exchanges vector of link states among the neighbors during route discovery.

Examples of source initiated reactive protocols are Ad hoc On-demand Distance Vector (AODV) [15], Dynamic Source Routing (DSR) [8], Lightweight Mobile Routing (LMR) [7] and Associativity-Based Routing (ABR) [18]. AODV [15] is inspired by DSDV protocol. Instead of proactively maintaining routes, AODV reactively discovers routes when needed. Like DSDV, it uses destination sequence number to avoid formation of loops. In DSR [8], each source provides the complete path to a chosen destination for routing a packet. Each node maintains a route cache for the routes to other nodes that it is aware of. The route cache of a node is updated as the node learns about new routes to more destinations. Location Aided Routing (LAR) [9] uses location information to reduce flooding during route discovery. The major problem in LAR is that it requires nodes to be aware of their location information. Route discovery and establishment is similar to AODV and DSR.

LMR [7] is a link reversal based routing scheme based on Gafni-Bertsekas [6] algorithm. The objective of LMR is not to find shortest path but to find any path between a source and destination pair. Temporarily Ordered Routing Algorithm (TORA) [11] is a direct descendant of LMR. The key feature of TORA is localization of control messages in the neighborhood where the topology changes occurs in the network. In order to accomplish it, the nodes maintain routing information about immediate neighbors. ABR [18] obtains stable route by selecting routes on the basis of degree of association stability among mobile nodes. Every node sends out periodic beacons to notify its existence which is used to update the respective associativity ticks of the current node with the beacon dispatch nodes. Association stability of one node with another is defined by connectivity over time and space. Signal Stability Routing (SSR) [5] is a logical descendant of ABR. It chooses route based on signal strength and location stability.

In this chapter our attempt is not to give a full review, but focus discussion on a few interesting protocols which exposes the characteristics and the abstraction of routing problem in a network with dynamic topology.

All MANET routing protocols are based on existing Internet routing protocols. Primarily three design approaches are used for Internet routing protocols, namely,

- Distance vector,
- Link state, and
- Link reversal.

Our discussion in this chapter is restricted only to distance vector based routing algorithms. Focusing only on distance vector algorithms may appear to be an incomplete exploration of the area. However, the reasonbehind this decision is to introduce

Fig. 7.3 Count to infinity
problem

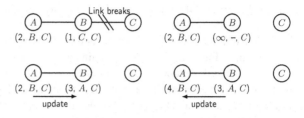

the problem domain to the reader rather than just throwing up research challenges. Furthermore, we believe that ad hoc networks are mostly low diameter and small sized networks. Therefore, the research efforts made in design of multihop, scalable routing algorithms have only theoretical value with no practical utility.

7.2.1   Distance Vector Routing

The abstract model of an underlying ad hoc network is a graph. Every node v maintains the table of distances d_{vw}^x for each destination node x, where $w \in L_v$ (adjacency list of v). In order to send a message from a source v to a destination x the next hop is selected among the neighbours of v which returns the minimum value of the metric d_{vw}^x. At an intermediate hop, the same rule is applied to forward the message to the next hop. The process is repeated till the destination is reached. The message is, thus, forwarded from a source to a destination by a sequence of hops via the shortest possible path between the two nodes.

A major problem that may arise in formation of a route using a distance vector routing scheme is referred to as *count-to-infinity*. Figure 7.3 provides an illustration of the problem. Initially, A knows distance to C via B to be 2 units. Suppose the link B to C breaks (e.g., timer expires). But before B can advertise its own routing table, it receives update from A indicating there is a path of 3 units to C available through A. B updates the distance to C as 3 not knowing the fact that route via A includes itself. B then sends the update to A. After receiving the update from B, A updates distance to C as 4. The cycle of update exchanges keep continuing resulting in count-to-infinity problem.

7.3   Destination-Sequenced Distance Vector Routing

Destination Sequenced Distance Vector (DSDV) is a distance vector based routing protocol. It is essentially a distributed version of the classical Bellman-Ford [3] shortest path algorithm modified for dynamically changing network topology. The fundamental problem in employing the distance vector routing algorithm in a mobile environment is formation of loops. Since, the nodes are mobile, the change in network topology occurs rapidly. Consequently, the information maintained at each node quickly becomes stale. It may, therefore, not only introduce loop but may also exhibit *count to infinity* problem.

DSDV maintains routing tables at each node for routing packets from a source to a destination. Each routing table contains a list of destinations with the number of hops to reach a destination. Each entry of a routing table is tagged with a sequence number assigned by the corresponding destinations. The source node consults its routing table for the destination and sends the data packet to the next hop in the path to the desired destination. The next hop repeats the actions and forwards to the node which is the next nearest hop to the destination and so on, until the destination is reached. The major issue in DSDV is the maintenance of the routing tables.

7.3.1 Advertisement of Routes

All nodes periodically transmit the route updates, or as soon as any new information about the change in topology is available. However, there is no fixed time interval for the propagation of updates. This follows from the fact that the mobile hosts are not expected to maintain any kind of time synchronization in movements.

Each mobile node advertises its own routing table to its current neighbors. Since the routes may change frequently due to movement of mobile nodes, the advertisement of routing table is carried out on a regular basis. The regular advertisement of routes allows the mobile hosts to continue in *doze* mode and resume as they wish. So, even if a node (not in active mode) misses out the current route advertisements, it receives a route advertisement on turning to active mode.

Forwarding a message from a source to a destination requires support from other mobile hosts. However, the nodes operating in doze mode should not be forced to participate in forwarding of a message. A route advertisement packet broadcast by a node consists of the following important information.

1. The recent most destination sequence number of the route to a destination as known to the source.
2. The address of the destination.
3. The number of hops required to reach the destination.

A node on receiving a new route information should broadcast the same to its neighbors. Apart from adding a new broadcast sequence number, the transmitting node increments the number of hops by one to indicate that the new route to destination includes itself as a hop. The broadcast sequence number is different from the destination sequence number. A broadcast sequence number helps to eliminate repeated forwarding of the same route advertisement. Unless stated otherwise, a sequence number always means a destination sequence number.

For the purpose of forwarding a data packet, the route with most recent sequence number is used though the same is not typically used for route re-advertisement. The route re-advertisement is held back to allow some settling time for a new route information.

Two different route updates are advertised: (i) incremental update, and (ii) full update. The incremental updates are small and advertised more frequently than the full updates. An incremental update typically needs less than a single NPDU (Network Protocol Data Unit). As number of updates grows, due to increased mobility of nodes with time, just sending incremental updates do not work. The number of entries in the forwarding table becomes large to fit into a single NPDU. In this situation it is preferable to go for a full dump. Full dumps are transmitted relatively infrequently and may require a number of NPDUs. The interval of time between two full dumps will depend on the frequency of movements of the mobile hosts.

7.3.2 Propagation of Link Break Information

When a node N detects a broken link to a neighbor M, then N generates a fresh sequence number and modifies the distance of each destination to ∞ for which M was an intermediate hop. This is the *only instance* in DSDV where a sequence number for a route table entry is generated by nodes other than the destinations. The sequence numbers for real (finite) routes are always *even numbers*. The sequence numbers of the routes with broken links (with route metric ∞) are always *odd numbers*. A broken link is, thus, easily identified as the one tagged with an odd sequence number.

7.3.3 Stability of Requirements

DSDV requires a stability time for propagation of route information. It helps to absorb fluctuations in the route tables during the period of quick changes of network topology. It also eliminates the need to rebroadcast the route updates that arrive with the same sequence number. The new information about topology received at a node is allowed to settle for a while, before being advertised by the node.

It is possible that during the interval of route settling time, the network experiences further changes in topology after the arrival of the *latest* route update. The reason behind this can be attributed to continuity of node movements. If a node has just began to move then it is expected to continue move for some time before it pauses at a place for a while. By employing a delay in route advertisement, the problem re-advertisement of the routes in quick successions (which may lead to a *broadcast storm*) is controlled. If the stability delay is not employed, flooding can occur even when a destination does not move. Such a scenario can be constructed as follows as depicted in Fig. 7.4 adopted from the example from the original DSDV paper [14]. The route update for the destination node $M8$ reaches a node say $M6$ from both $M5$ and $M7$. The collection of nodes in the network is such that paths reaching $M6$ from $M8$ can be grouped into two classes. One set of these paths is such that every path in it passes through $M5$ and do not intersect any of the paths from the second set each of which passes through $M7$. Suppose $M6$ receives the route update from

Fig. 7.4 Flooding due to
fluctuations in routes

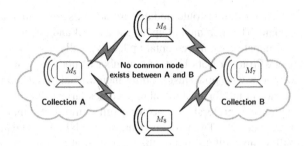

$M7$ eight seconds earlier than that from a path via $M5$. Also let the number of hops in a path via $M5$ is 20 and that in a path through $M7$ is 19. Suppose this happens every time a new sequence is issued by $M8$. Then the path information for $M8$ at $M6$ fluctuates back and forth every time a new sequence number is issued at $M8$. If any new route information gets propagated without stability delay, the receiving node propagates the routes with new metrics in quick succession to its neighborhood. It causes flooding in the network.

7.3.4 Guarantee for Loop Free Paths

Assume that system is in steady state. All tables of all nodes have converged to actual shortest paths. Then the collection of next hops for any destination D is logically an inverted rooted tree with the root at D.

Consider an inverted tree for one destination, say x, and examine the changes that occur due to movements of the nodes. Let $G(x)$ be the directed graph of x defined by the edges of the form $(i, n_i(x))$, where $n_i(x)$ is the next hop for destination x at node i.

Lemma 7.1 *The operation of DSDV ensures at every instant $G(x)$ is loop-free.*

Proof Potentially a loop may be introduced if $n_i(x)$ changes. If $n_i(x)$ is set to *nil*, it implies a link break. Therefore, a loop cannot be formed.

Assume that $n_i(x)$ is changed to a non-null next hop. There are two ways in which $n_i(x)$ at i can change when i receives an update about a new route to x from a neighbor, say k with sequence number $s_k(x)$, namely

1. $s_k(x) > s_i(x)$, where $s_i(x)$ is the sequence number for destination x in the route table at i.
2. $s_k(x) = s_i(x)$, but metric $d_k(x) < d_i(x)$.

In the first case i cannot introduce a loop. Because i propagates the sequence number $s_i(x)$ to its downstream neighbors only after receiving it from any of its current neighbors. Therefore, the sequence number stored at any of the neighbors of i is always greater or equal to that stored at the node i. In fact, the set of sequence numbers stored at intermediate nodes upstream from any node i to the destination x forms a non-decreasing series. If indeed, k were to introduce a loop, then it would mean $s_k(x) \leq s_i(x)$ which contradicts the assumption $s_k(x) > s_i(x)$.

The loop-free property in the second case follows from the fact that in the presence of static or decreasing link weights, the algorithm always maintains loop-free paths.

7.3.5 Forwarding Table and Update Propagation

A forwarding (routing) table stored at each node is used to forward packets from the node to the next hop along a route to a destination. A basic routing table entry consists of the following fields:

- *Destination*: the address of the destination node.
- *Next hop*: the next node along the path from the current node to destination.
- *Metric*: the number of hops required to reach the destination.
- *Sequence number*: the sequence number assigned by the destination to the current table entry.
- *Install time*: the time when the current entry was made. It helps to determine when the stale routes are to be deleted.
- *Stable data*: is a pointer to a structure holding information of a new route which is likely to supersede the current route after sometime.

If all links on a route to a destination are live then the corresponding sequence number for that destination must be even. Install time is used to detect if any route has become *stale* (expired). However, install time is not very critical for working of DSDV algorithm, because detection of a link breakage is propagated through the ad hoc network immediately.

The stable data is a pointer to a structure that stores the information about the stability of routes to a destination. The stability information is used to dampen fluctuations routes. The fluctuations may happen due to continuity of the node movements that has not yet settled. The stable data records the last and the average settling time for every route. Therefore, when a node, say N, receives a new route R, N does not immediately advertise R unless it is a route to a previously unreachable destination.

A new route to an existing destination is advertised only after 2*(*average settling time*). Essentially, DSDV keeps two routing tables. One table is used for forwarding the packets, and the other one is used for advertising of the route updates. The advertised route table of a node is constructed from its stable data, and has the following structure:

```
destination
metric
sequence_number
```

For advertising routes, a node places the route to itself as the first entry. Then all the nodes which have experienced significant change in topology, since the previous advertisement, are placed. A change in route metric is considered as a significant change. The rest of the advertised route table is used to include all nodes whose route sequence numbers have changed. If too many updated sequence numbers are advertised then a update cannot be included in a single packet. To get around this problem, a fair selection policy may be used to transmit the updates in round-robin fashion by several incremental update intervals.

7.3.6 Example

Consider the snap shot of the routes in an ad hoc network shown in Fig. 7.5. This figure is adopted from the original paper [14]. Prior to the movement of a mobile host MH_1 to a new position as indicated in the figure, the forwarding table [14] for a node, say MH_4, could be as shown in Table 7.1. The above table does not include

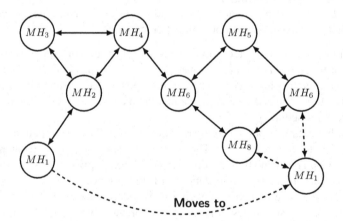

Fig. 7.5 An example for execution of DSDV

Table 7.1   Forwarding table of MH_4

Destination	Next hop	Metric	Flag	Sequence number	Install time
MH_1	MH_2	2		S180_MH_1	T001_MH4
MH_2	MH_2	1		S384_MH_2	T001_MH4
MH_3	MH_2	2		S444_MH_3	T001_MH4
MH_4	MH_4	0		S236_MH_4	T001_MH4
MH_5	MH_6	2		S352_MH_5	T002_MH4
MH_6	MH_6	1		S278_MH_6	T001_MH4
MH_7	MH_6	2		S232_MH_7	T002_MH4
MH_8	MH_6	3		S190_MH_8	T002_MH4

Table 7.2   Advertised route table for node MH_4

Destination	Metric	Sequence number
MH_4	0	S236_MH_4
MH_1	2	S180_MH_1
MH_2	1	S384_MH_2
MH_3	2	S444_MH_3
MH_5	2	S352_MH_5
MH_6	1	S278_MH_6
MH_7	2	S232_MH_7
MH_8	3	S190_MH_8

information concerning stable data. However, the advertised route table for the node MH_4 may be as the one shown in Table 7.2. Suppose now MH_1 moves to a new position as shown in Fig. 7.5 by a dashed line; the direction of movement is indicated by the arrow head. The new position is within the neighborhood of nodes MH_7 and MH_8. The old link between MH_1 and MH_2 gets snapped. The new route to destination MH_1 is advertised and a new metric is finally received by node MH_4 after sometime. The internal forwarding table at node MH_4 changes as indicated by Table 7.3. Notice that the flag for MH_1 has been set to M indicating that the route entry has changed. The install time of the entry also has changed. The advertised route table also changes at MH_4. This table has new information as illustrated by Table 7.4. Except for the node MH_1 the metrics for all other nodes remain unchanged.

Table 7.3 Change in forwarding table of node MH_4

Destination	Next hop	Metric	Flag	Sequence number	Time instal
MH_1	MH_6	3	M	S580_MH_1	T500_MH4
MH_2	MH_2	1		S486_MH_2	T001_MH4
MH_3	MH_2	2		S634_MH_3	T001_MH4
MH_4	MH_4	0		S856_MH_4	T001_MH4
MH_5	MH_6	2		S502_MH_5	T002_MH4
MH_6	MH_6	1		S378_MH_6	T002_MH4
MH_7	MH_6	2		S358_MH_7	T002_MH4
MH_8	MH_6	3		S390_MH_8	T002_MH4

Table 7.4 Change in forwarding table of node MH_4

Destination	Metric	Sequence number
MH_4	0	S856_MH_4
MH_1	3	S580_MH_1
MH_2	1	S486_MH_2
MH_3	2	S634_MH_3
MH_5	2	S502_MH_5
MH_6	1	S378_MH_6
MH_7	2	S358_MH_7
MH_8	3	S390_MH_8

7.4   Dynamic Source Routing

Dynamic source routing [8] is a reactive protocol. DSR uses source routing to route the messages. In other words, the entire sequence of hops from a source to a destination is embedded with message packets that gets exchanged between the two nodes. This is in contrast with the other reactive routing protocols such as TORA [11], or AODV [15], where the sender just has to know the next hop to the destination. The advantages of keeping the route information with the source are as follows.

- The requirement for periodic route advertisement is eliminated.
- In a less dynamic environment DSR provides valid routes more often than not.
- DSR finds a route also when links are unidirectional.
- DSR initiates a route discovery in the case when route becomes invalid.

Periodic route advertisement not only consumes bandwidth, but also requires the nodes to be in connected state in order to receive the route advertisements. So, DSR by eliminating periodic route advertisements enables wireless devices to conserve battery power when no significant node movements take place, i.e., network topology remains mostly static. If the routes between source and destination pairs are known, DSR can almost always provide valid routes. In the wireless environments, the quality of message transmission between hosts may not exactly be the same in both directions. DSR may initiate a route discovery in order to send a route reply. More specifically, DSR approach to routing does not require the network links to be bidirectional.

The basic assumptions for DSR to work properly are as follows.

- The hosts can move without notice, but they do so with a moderate speed with respect to packet transmission latency.
- The speed of movement of nodes is also moderate with respect to the wireless transmission latency of the underlying network hardware in use.
- The hosts can turn into *promiscuous* mode to listen to the activities within their respective wireless range to learn about new routes.

7.4.1 Overview of the Algorithm

Each node in the network maintains a route cache. The routes learned by a node are stored in its route cache. In order to send a packet, a node first checks the route cache for a valid route to the desired destination. If no route can be found, then a route discovery is initiated to discover a route to the destination. The normal processing at the node continues, pending the route discovery. The packets meant for the desired destination may be buffered at the sending node till such time when a route to the destination has been determined. Alternatively, the packet may be discarded and retransmitted after the path to the destination has been discovered. This eliminates the need to buffer the packet. Each entry in route cache is associated with an expiry time, after which the route entry is purged from the cache. It is possible that a route may become invalid due to any node (the source, the destination or an intermediate node) on the path moving out of wireless transmission range, failing or being switched off. Monitoring the validity of the route is called route maintenance. When route maintenance detects a problem of the kind mentioned above, route discovery may be called again to discover a fresh route to the destination.

7.4.2 Route Discovery

The route discovery scheme works by flooding a *Route REQuest* (RREQ) packet. An RREQ packet contains *source ID*, *destination ID*, *route record* and a unique *request ID*, set by the source. The request ID allows intermediate nodes to discard the duplicate RREQ and to prevent network flooding.

The RREQ processing is quite straightforward. When an intermediate node N receives a RREQ, it should first ensure that either the same RREQ or a RREQ for

---

Algorithm 1: DSR algorithm.

begin
    if *source ID and request ID matches with any recent RREQ packets* **then**
        | discard the packet // `Duplicate RREQ.`
    end
    else
        if *address of target ID matches with any recently seen RREQs* **then**
            | discard the packet // `RREQ for same target from a different`
                `source.`
        end
        else
            if *target ID matches with the ID of the processing node* **then**
                | extract the route record from the request packet; // `Accumulated in`
                    `the route record of RREQ packet`
                | Unicast a reply back to source by using the extracted route;
            end
            else
                | // `Processing node is an intermediate node.`
                | append address of self with the route record of RREQ packet;
                | re-broadcast RREQ;
            end
        end
    end
end

---

the same destination has not been forwarded by it earlier. In both these cases N is awaiting a route reply to arrive from the destination. So, it need not forward another copy of the RREQ. The processing of RREQ has been described in Algorithm 1. There is also a slight anomaly in sending a unicast reply. When a route reply has to be sent to the initiator of the route discovery, the possible alternatives are:

- If the destination has an entry for the source in its own route cache, this route may be used to send the reply packet.
- Otherwise, it is possible to use the reverse of route record extracted from the request packet. In this case we consider that the route is bidirectional (with symmetric links).
- The third possibility is to let the reply packet ride piggyback to source on a RREQ packet initiated by the destination for the discovery of a route to source.

7.4.3 Route Maintenance

Since, DSR is a source initiated routing scheme, route maintenance is basically limited to monitoring link breaks along a route at the time of message transmission. There are three ways of monitoring the error in route.

1. Hop-by-hop acknowledgement.
2. Passive acknowledgement.
3. End-to-end acknowledgement.

In hop-by-hop acknowledgement, at each hop, the node transmitting the packet can determine which link of the route is not functioning, and sends an error packet to the source. But the hop-by-hop acknowledgement would require a low level (data link layer) support. If the underlying network does not support such a low level acknowledgement mechanism, passive acknowledgement can be utilized to discover the route in error. The passive acknowledgement works as follows. After sending a packet to next hop a node promiscuously listens to the transmission of the packet by the next hop to the subsequent hop. If no transmission could be detected then the it may be assumed that there is a break in link between next hop and the hop following it. The other straightforward technique could be to seek explicit end-to-end acknowledgement by setting a bit in forwarding message packet itself, which indicates an acknowledgement should be sent to the source. The problem of sending explicit acknowledgement back to the source is quite similar to the problem of sending a corresponding route reply packet back to the original sender of a route request. If the wireless transmission between two hosts works equally well in both directions the acknowledgement can be sent in the reverse direction using the same route as the one used by the original message. Otherwise, the host detecting a broken link, sends the error packet back to the source if the former has an entry for the latter in its route cache. When there is no unicast route to the source, the error packet can be sent by the detecting host by piggybacking the error on a RREQ packet for the original sender.

7.4.4 Piggybacking on Route Discovery

When the links are unidirectional, the concept of piggybacking of data along with the route discovery can be used to amortize the message delivery time with route discovery delay. If a RREQ is propagated all the way upto a destination, piggybacking has no problem except that the size of piggybacked data must be small. However, the piggybacked data is lost if some intermediate node on the route that has a cached route to the destination sends a route reply from the cached data and discards the RREQ packet.

Without the loss of generality, let us examine the problem for the case that a route discovery from source to destination is over and a route reply should now be sent from the destination back to the source. As shown in Fig. 7.6, a route $S \rightarrow G \rightarrow H \rightarrow D$ has been detected after a route discovery was initiated by S for D. Now a route reply (RREP) should be unicast to S by D. But suppose no such unicast route from D to S is known. Then D must now initiate a route discovery for the target S, but it sends RREP as piggyback data on RREQ for S. Suppose (an intermediate) node B on the route from D to S has a route, say $B \rightarrow A \rightarrow S$, in its route cache. So B can unicasts

Fig. 7.6 *B* unicasting
piggyback data (*D*'s RREP)
to *S*

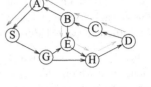

> RREP for S to D route from D
> RREQ with piggyback RREP
> RREP for D to S route from B

RREQ for the route from *D* to *S*, via *B* → *E* → *H* → *D*. But piggybacked data (RREP) from *D* to *S* will be lost unless *B* unicasts to *S* the RREP being piggybacked by *D* with its RREQ to *S*. The blue arrows represent unicasting of RREP from *D* for *S* to *D* path by the intermediate node *B*. The green arrows represent unicasting of RREP from *B* for *D* to *S* route. The red arrows indicate the RREQ from *D* for destination *S* which carries piggyback RREP from *D* for the *S* to *D* path.

7.4.5 Handling Route Replies

Problems may arise when several mobile hosts receiving RREQ from an initiator send RREPs from their respective local route caches. Two noticeable problems arise due to asynchronous and autonomous operations of mobile hosts.

1. A number of hosts may send replies creating a flooding problem.
2. It is possible that the reply reaches the initiator from a host which is at a longer distance slightly ahead of time than that from a host at a shorter distance from the destination.

In order to avoid the problem of simultaneous replies and to eliminate replies indicating longer routes, following simple mechanism may be employed. Every node with a cached route to the destination delays the sending of RREP. The delay is set as $d = H * (h - 1 + r)$, where, H is a suitably chosen small constant, $0 < r < 1$ a randomly generated number, and h is the number of hops to reach the destination from the node sending the route reply. The delay d in sending route replies takes care of the situation where a reply with a poor route metric being sent earlier to the initiator than a reply with a better route metric. By operating in promiscuous mode a host may listen to all route replies reaching at any of its neighbours during the delay period. The host will not transmit the RREP packet if it listens to any RREP for the same target (the destination address for the RREQ packet) of a route request.

   The more serious problem in using route cache for route reply is formation of a loop. Though the cached data for route entries themselves may not include loops, a loop may appear when a route gets established during the route discovery phase. For example, consider Fig. 7.7 where *A* has a cached route to destination *D* when

Fig. 7.7 Loop formation in
using cached data for route
reply

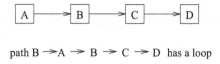

path B $\to$ A $\to$ B $\to$ C $\to$ D has a loop

node B initiates a route discovery for D. Node A sends the route to D from its cached
data to B, which is $A \to B \to C \to D$. So the source route from B to D will become
$B \to A \to B \to C \to D$. This route contains a loop, any message from B to D has
to traverse $A \to B$ path once in backward direction and once in forward direction.
To avoid such a loop formation, a possible approach could be as follows. If a route
reply from cached data also includes the initiator, then this route is spliced into two
parts. The first part is from the host that sent reply to the initiator and the second part
is from the initiator to the target. The latter part is cached locally at the initiator. So,
the entire path $B \to A \to B \to C \to D$ is spliced at A and the part $B \to C \to D$
is sent to B in route reply. However, DSR prohibits any node from sending a RREP
for the route where the node itself does not appear. There are two reasons why this
is not allowed.

1. Firstly, if a node N is a part of the route it returns, the probability of route's
   validity increases. This is due to the fact, that N will get a RERR if the route
   were invalid.
2. Secondly, if and when a route becomes invalid then N, which originally sent the
   RREP, also gets the RERR when the route is invalidate. This ensures that stale
   data is removed from N's route cache in a timely manner.

7.4.6 Operating in Promiscuous Mode

As discussed earlier in the previous subsection, the problem of receiving several
route replies and the routes longer than the shortest route to the destination can be
eliminated by turning into promiscuous receive mode. Operating in promiscuous
receive mode is found to be advantageous in reflecting shorter route updates, specially in mobile environment. Consider the situation as depicted in Fig. 7.8. Node
N1 transmits a packet to some destination through the nodes N2 and N3 with N2
being the next hop and N3 being the second hop on the route. Since nodes operate
in promiscuous receive mode, N3 receives the packet being sent from N1 to N2, and
infers that the actual route can be shortened by eliminating the hop N2. This situation

Fig. 7.8 Reflecting shorter
route updates

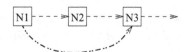

can occur when N1 moves closer to N3. In this case N3 sends an *unsolicited* RREP to N1 which can then update the local route cache. But the major problem in operating in promiscuous receive mode is that the nodes must be power-on most of the time.

7.5   Ad hoc On-demand Distance Vector Routing

Ad hoc On-demand Distance Vector (AODV) [15] routing is an adaptation of the classical distance vector routing algorithm to the mobile case. It is a distributed routing algorithm, and like DSDV algorithm employs a sequence number for each entry in the routing table maintained by a node. The sequence number is created either by the destination or by the leader of the group in a multicast group. A node always uses the route with the highest sequence number from among the available alternatives routes to a destination.

AODV uses three basic types of messages:

1. Route REQuest (RREQ),
2. Route REPly (RREP) and
3. Multicast route ACTivation (MACT).

The first two types of messages have obvious meanings. MACT message is used along with RREQ and RREP to maintain multicast route trees. The significance of MACT message will be clear when multicast routing is discussed.

Each node along a route from a source to a destination maintains only the next hop entry in AODV. Therefore, the size of route table at each node is small. AODV reduces the need for system wide broadcasts by localizing the propagation of changes in the network topology. For example, if a link status does not affect the ongoing communication or the maintenance of a multicast tree then no broadcast occurs. A global effect is observed only when a distant source attempts to use a broken link. One or more nodes that are using a link are informed when it breaks.

AODV also maintains a multicast tree for group communication. Hence multicast, broadcast and unicast all are integrated into a single protocol. The route tables also create or update the reverse route as a RREQ is being pushed progressively from the source towards the destination. So any node, on a path along which RREQ has been forwarded, can reach the source node by using the reverse pointers.

7.5.1   Design Decisions

Some of the design decisions in AODV are as follows.

- The routes not used are expired and discarded.
- After the primary route has expired, an alternative route is used, if one is available

- If available, an alternative route can be used to bypass a broken link on the primary route.

By expiring the unused routes, maintenance of stale routes can be avoided. However, managing simultaneous aging process of multiple routes between a source and a destination is not easy. Although in theory, the use of alternative routes is possible, the same may also become invalid by the time primary route expires. Furthermore, bypassing broken link may not always be possible if all alternative routes use the same broken link.

7.5.2   Route Tables

AODV does not attempt to maintain routes. The routes are discovered as and when needed, and maintained as long as they are used. AODV uses sequence number to eliminate loops. Every node maintains its own sequence number. The sequence number of a multicast group is maintained by the leader of the group. A route table and a multicast route tables are maintained at each node.

The four important parts of a route table entry are: `next hop`, `destination sequence number`, `hop count`, and `life time`. A typical entry in a route table consists of the following fields:

```
Source and destination IP addresses
Destination sequence number
Hop count
Next hop
Expiry time
Routing flags
Last hop count
List of precursors
```

Each intermediate node N along a route maintains a list of active nodes which use N as the next hop to forward data packets to a given destination D. All such nodes are called precursors of N. A node is considered active if it originates or forwards at least one packet for the chosen destination within `active_timeout` period. The `active_timeout` period is typically 3000 ms. The precursor list is required for route maintenance when a link breaks. The routes to a destination from all the precursors of a node N become invalid if and when the route from N to the destination becomes invalid.

The entries in a multicast route table are similar to route table except for the following additional information:

- More than one next hops are stored.
- Each hop associated with activated flag and a direction.
- A route can be used only after activated flag has been set.

• Direction is either upstream or downstream relative to the group leader.

The requirement for maintaining these extra fields will become clear when the discovery and the maintenance of multicast routes are discussed.

7.5.3   Unicast Route Discovery and Maintenance

A node which needs a route to a destination broadcasts a RREQ. Any intermediate node with a current route destination can unicast a RREP to the source. The information obtained by RREQ and RREP messages help to build routing tables. The sequence numbers are used to eliminate the expired routes.

7.5.3.1   Creating a RREQ

A node wishing to send a packet to some destination, first searches the local routing table for a matching entry. If the source has a route then it forwards the packet to the preferred next hop. Otherwise a route discovery is initiated by creating a RREQ. The required fields for a RREQ are:

```
Src_ID
Dest_ID
Src_seqNo
Dest_seqNo
Broadcast_ID
```

The Src_seqNo number is used to refresh the reverse routes to a source. The Broadcast_ID and Src_ID pair uniquely identify a RREQ. After forwarding a RREQ, a node stores the same in a RREQ cache for sometime. It helps to restrict flooding. For example, if an old RREQ arrives again at a node possibly through an alternative path, then the node by examining RREQ cache can determine it, and discard the RREQ. It prevents an RREQ from looping around.

Since AODV assumes bidirectional links, a RREQ is also used for constructing a reverse path to a source. By storing the reverse next hop, an intermediate node can unicast a received RREP to the source. The source broadcasts the RREQ and sets a time out for the reply. Timeout for the reply ensures that a node does not wait indefinitely for receiving a RREP. Dest_seqNo is the sequence number of the last known path to the destination.

7.5.3.2 Processing a RREQ

On receiving a RREQ, a node first checks its RREQ cache to determine if the current RREQ was an old RREQ already seen by the node. If the source ID and the broadcast ID match a RREQ present in the cache, the recipient node discards the RREQ. Otherwise it sets up a reverse route entry for the source node in the route table. The reverse route entry consists of `<src_ID, src_seqNo, hop_cnt, nbr_ID>`, where `nbr_ID` is the ID of the neighbor from which the RREQ was received. Thus, for the reverse path `nbr_ID` becomes the `next_hop`. As and when a RREP is received for the RREQ, the current node can forward the RREP to the source through the downstream neighbor on the reverse route towards the source. An intermediate node, receiving a RREQ, can also unicasts a RREP back to the source if it has an unexpired entry for the destination, and the sequence number of this entry is greater than or equal to the destination sequence number (the last known sequence number) carried by the RREQ packet. Note that the unexpired path means that the path is active.

AODV provides a loop free route from a source to destination by employing sequence numbers like DSDV. A formal proof for the fact that AODV avoids formation of a loop is provided in Lemma 7.2.

Lemma 7.2 *AODV provides a loop free paths between source and destination pairs.*

Proof The key idea behind the proof is that a route from a source to a destination imposes a logical ordering of the nodes along the path, based on the destination sequence numbers and hop count. The proof is based on the following two key assumptions:

- A higher sequence number has precedence over hop count, and
- For the same sequence number, lower hop count has the precedence.

AODV forces discovery of loop-free route from a source to destination by imposing the above conditions on the sequence numbers. According these, a node v can select w as its next hop on the path to a destination D provided

- The destination sequence number at v is less than the destination sequence number at w, or
- The destination sequence numbers are same but $DIST(v, D) < DIST(w, D)$

We can rephrase the sequence number conditions using the notion of downstream and upstream nodes on a path. If on a path from v to D, w is closer to D than v, then w is considered as downstream to v with respect to D. The loop freedom is guaranteed because AODV never finds a path to a destination from a downstream node (w) via an upstream node (v). Let us assume that a loop exists as shown in the Fig. 7.9. The table shows the sequence number and the next hop for the route to destination D corresponding to the intermediate nodes I_1, I_2 and I_3. The loop is represented by the links $I_1 \rightarrow I_2$, $I_2 \rightarrow I_3$ and $I_3 \rightarrow I_1$. According to the sequence number condition:

$$T_1 \leq T_2, T_2 \leq T_3, \text{ and } T_3 \leq T_2 \text{ so, } T_1 = T_2 = T_3 \qquad (7.1)$$

Fig. 7.9 A possible loop

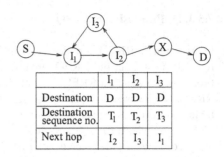

	I_1	I_2	I_3
Destination	D	D	D
Destination sequence no.	T_1	T_2	T_3
Next hop	I_2	I_3	I_1

Let H_i the number of hops from $I_i \rightarrow I_{i+1 \ mod \ 3}$. Now applying the sequence number condition with relations 7.1 we must have $H_i = H_{i+1} + 1$. But for our example, $H_1 = 1$, $H_2 = 1$ and $H_3 = 1$. So $H_3 \neq H_1 + 1$, which is a contradiction. Therefore, a loop cannot exist.

7.5.3.3 Expanding Ring Search

By localizing the search area for route discovery, it is possible to restrict flooding. For localizing the search, the trick is to use an expanding ring search by setting a TTL (time to live) value. The TTL specifies the diameter of the subsection of N/W in which RREQ must be flooded. If a route to the target not found in that subsection of the N/W, a new RREQ with an increased TTL is launched. The TTL value is recorded in the route table. For subsequent route discovery to the same destination, the starting TTL is set to the value in the route table. This approach progressively enlarges the section of the network in which route request packet is to be flooded. It localizes the route request to a portion of the network where the destination is most likely to be found.

RREP processing
An RREP packet has five fields:

```
Src_ID
Dest_ID
Dest_seqNo
Hop_cnt
Lifetime
```

When any node receives a RREQ, it can generate and send RREP for the RREQ provided that:

Fig. 7.10 Intermediate node
unicasting a RREP

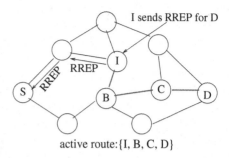

active route:{I, B, C, D}

1. The node has an active route to the destination, and
2. The destination sequence number of the route currently being used by the node equal to or greater than the destination sequence number carried in the RREQ packet.

If an intermediate node generates an RREP, then it should include hop count to the destination, lifetime for the expiry of the current route, and the destination sequence according to the information available in its own routing table.

The scenario where an intermediate node can send RREP is illustrated in Fig. 7.10. Node *I* sets the hop count to 3 as it is 3 hops away from the destination node *D*. When no intermediate node along the path from source to destination has any active path, the RREQ eventually will reach the destination. On receiving RREQ, the destination node will generate and send a RREP.

An intermediate node sets up the forward path to destination when it receives a RREP. At first, it creates a local route entry for the forward path as follows.

- Takes the node ID from RREP to define the next hop to destination.
- Takes the ID of destination for indexing the route table.
- Adds 1 to hop count and stores the same in the entry.
- Takes the lifetime from RREP and places it in the entry.

After a route table entry has been created, the hop count carried by RREP is incremented by one. This ensures that if the route to destination were to pass through the current intermediate node, then the hop count would also include the current node. Finally, the RREP is forwarded towards the source by using the next back hop or the next hop of the reverse route entry. Finally the RREP reaches the source and a route entry corresponding to destination is created. Clearly, RREP is a targeted unicast packet, because it is forwarded by using the next hop entries available in the routing tables of the nodes upstream towards the source.

Each time a route is used, its life time is updated. The route discovery process is explained in Fig. 7.11. The flooding of RREQ is shown by solid lines, the arrows denote the direction of flooding. The dashed lines with arrows indicate the direction in which RREP traverses. The time outs received by the source, from the nodes not having routes to the destination are also indicated in the figure.

Fig. 7.11 Route discovery

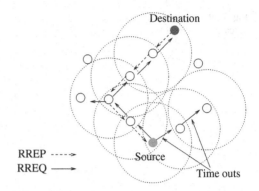

7.5.3.4 Route Maintenance

A route is maintained as long as it is needed. The movements of the nodes affecting active paths are only considered. The route maintenance is responsible primarily for:

1. Detecting link breaks on active paths, and
2. Building alternative paths when node movements occur.

Routes may become invalid due to movement of nodes. For example, if the source node moves, a route discovery should be re-initiated if the path to destination is still needed. Every node must maintain its neighborhood information to detect any movement as soon as it happens.

Neighborhood information
Typically, the neighborhood information at a node is maintained by periodic broadcast of hello messages from its neighbors. If a node N has not sent anything (either a message or a hello message) within the last `hello_interval`, N sends a `hello` packet to inform the neighbors that it is still in the vicinity. Hello packet is in reality an unsolicited RREP. Hello packet is not rebroadcast, as it carries a TTL = 1. A change in neighborhood of a node N is indicated if N fails to receive consecutive `allowed_hello_loss` of packets from another node, which was previously in the neighborhood of N. The typical value of `allowed_hello_loss` = 2. On receiving a hello message from a neighbor, a node updates the lifetime of that neighbor. If an entry for the neighbor does not exist, then the node creates one.

Link breaks
A link break on a route from a source to a destination is detected when the downstream neighbors of that link on the route fails to receive consecutive `allowed_hello_loss` hello packets in the usual hello interval. Link break is propagated upstream by sending a RERR packet. The RERR packet originates from the upstream end node detecting the break. As explained earlier, every node maintains a list of precursors for each destination. A precursor is an upstream neighbor of the node that uses the current node as the next hop for a valid route to a chosen destination. For each broken link, the upstream end node (the end node closer to the source)

Fig. 7.12 Route
maintenance

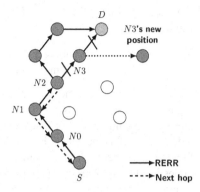

sends RERR to all the nodes in its list of precursors. These precursors are exactly those nodes which use the upstream end node as the next hop for a valid route to the destination.

A source re-initiate route discovery when it receives a RERR packet from each of its downstream neighbors has next hop entry for an active route to the destination. Figure 7.12 shows an active path from source *S* to destination *D* passes through four intermediate nodes *N*0, *N*1, *N*2, *N*3. After a while node *N*3 moves away to a new position. Due to breakage of links (*N*1, *N*2) and (*N*2, *N*3), the route from *S* to *D* is no longer valid. The route has to be invalidated by sending a route error packet (RERR) from *N*2 which is the farthest upstream intermediate node on the route. The dashed arrows indicate the path that RERR traverses using precursors on the route from *N*2 to *S*.

7.5.4   Multicast Route Discovery and Maintenance

A multicast route discovery is essentially an extension of unicast route discovery. A node *N* initiates a multicast route discovery if

- Either *N* wants to send data to a group, or
- *N* wants to join a multicast group.

N initiates a multicast route discovery by creating a RREQ with destination IP address of the group. If *N* knows about the group leader *G* and has a valid path to *G* then it can unicast the RREQ by including the IP address of *G*, the last known sequence number of the group, and a `join` flag if *N* is interested to join the group.

If RREQ is marked `join` then only members of group can respond. Otherwise, any node with fresh enough path to group can respond. A RREQ with `join` is processed by a node *N* as follows:

- If *N* is not a member of the multicast group, it creates a reverse entry for the source and rebroadcasts the RREQ.
- If *N* is a group member then it responds to RREQ by adding an *unactivated* entry for the source in its multicast table.

If N receives a RREQ (without `join` flag) for a group then RREQ is processed as follows:

- If N is not a member of the group and does not have a route to the group it creates a reverse entry to the source and rebroadcasts RREQ.

The source waits for a time out to receive a reply. It can rebroadcast RREQ incrementing the broadcast ID by one. The source continues rebroadcast RREQ till it receives a reply or the number of broadcast becomes equal to `rreq_retries` after which it declare itself as the leader. Figure 7.13a illustrates how RREQ with `join` flag gets flooded in the network and a new tree branch is grafted into the multicast tree. The nodes labeled by R are not members of the multicast group, but are routers for the group. The new node N which wants to join the multicast group sends RREQ with `join` flag on. After RREQ has spread through the network RREPs originate from two router nodes and two group members. Then RREPs spread in the network as

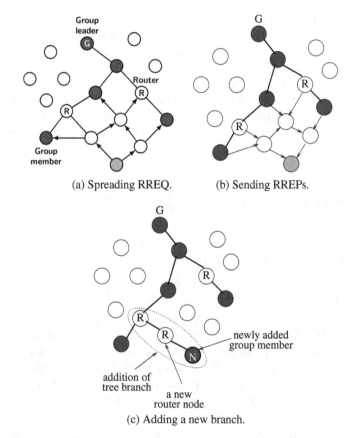

(a) Spreading RREQ.   (b) Sending RREPs.

(c) Adding a new branch.

Fig. 7.13 Grafting a new branch to multicast tree

illustrated by Fig. 7.13b. Finally, Fig. 7.13c shows that the new tree branch consisting of a new router node and N are added into the tree.

After a tree branch is added to the multicast tree, the nodes in the newly grafted branch should be activated by sending an explicit *activation* message on the branch. The reasons for requirement of an explicit activation are:

- RREPs for join request should trace out the path to the source so that one of the potential tree branches can be grafted into multicast tree.
- Besides forwarding of the RREP with join request, the RREPs for non-join requests may also be forwarded in order to set up paths to multicast tree. Grafting a tree branch for non-join request is not warranted.
- Multicast data packets are sent as broadcast traffic. So, all the nodes which forwarded the RREPs to the source node have fresh routes to multicast tree. If explicit activation were not needed, potentially, all these nodes which sent RREPs for a branch can forward data packets to multicast group.

The last point is particularly important, as it may lead to inefficient use of bandwidth when all nodes involved may potentially create large amount of network traffic. Therefore, only one of possible branches should be allowed to forward data to multicast group.

The source waits for the length of the interval for route discovery before it can use the path. At first, the source unicasts a MACT message to the node from which it received the RREP. The upstream neighbour sets active flag against the source in its own route table before forwarding the same to the next hop upstream towards the originator. Each node on the route sets active flag for hop, and forwards MACT to the next upstream neighbor until it reaches the originator of RREP.

MACT message is used also for deactivating an existing path if it is not needed any more. The deactivation proceeds as follows. If a leaf node (of the multicast group) wishes to leave the group, then the node may just prunes itself from the multicast tree. The next upstream hop deletes the entry corresponding to the deserter. But if a non-leaf node wishes to leave the group, it *cannot* detach itself from the tree. Such nodes must continue to serve as a router for the multicast group. On receiving a MACT with prune flag, a node N deletes the entry corresponding to the source of the current MACT. If N is a router and the deletion of the previous hop turns into N a leaf node, then N would initiate its pruning by sending a MACT with prune flag. But if the N is a group member, then it may not want to revoke its group membership. The deletion of branch using MACT is shown in Fig. 7.14.

7.5.4.1 Maintenance of Multicast Routes

A unicast route is maintained only as long as it is required. However, in the case of musticast routes, a multicast tree should be maintained for the entire lifetime of the existence of the group. Every link requires maintenance so that each group member can access the multicast group. A link is assumed to have a lifetime which is equal to

hello_lifetime = (1 + allowed_hello_losses) × hello_interval).

Fig. 7.14 Pruning after a
member node leave the
multicast group

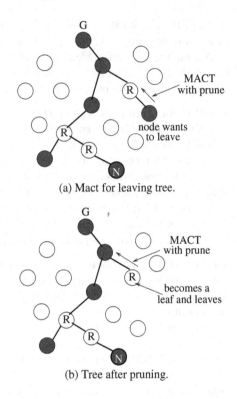

(a) Mact for leaving tree.

(b) Tree after pruning.

If no data packet is sent within a fixed interval called `hello-interval`, each node
must receive a broadcast from its next hop neighbor in multicast tree. The broadcast
may either be a RREQ, or a group hello or a hello packet. The hello packet, as stated
earlier, is a RREP with TTL value 1.

If a link $M \rightarrow N$ breaks, then the downstream node N of the broken link initiates
a route discovery for the multicast group. The upstream node of the broken link M
may just be a router for the multicast tree. If M becomes a leaf node after link break,
it tries to detach itself. It does so, by sending a MACT with prune flag to its upstream
node in the tree. However, MACT is sent only after `prune_timeout`. The idea
behind allowing a timeout is that M may still be available nearby N. If N initiates
a route discovery to multicast tree, it may get connected to the multicast tree by an
alternative path through M. For repairing the route, N sends a RREQ packet with a
small TTL value, which includes also its distance of N from the group leader. The
reason for a small TTL is that M may still be available nearby. Any node X, having
an active route to multicast group, can respond to RREQ provided X is as close to
the group leader as N. The above restriction prevents any node in the same side of
break as N from responding. If this check is not enforced then a loop can occur if
route replies were received from the nodes on both side of the link break. Figure 7.15
illustrates the route repair process. After N is able to add its subtree to multicast

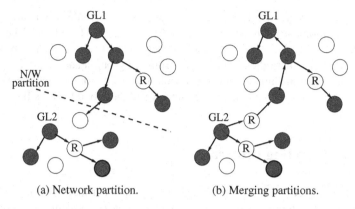

(a) Network partition.   (b) Merging partitions.

Fig. 7.15 Repairing link breakage in AODV

tree, it sends a MACT message to its next hop for activating the link. N also sends a MACT with update flag to its downstream neighbors. This message includes the new depth of N from the group leader. The downstream descendants in N's subtree update their respective depths from the group leader when they receive the MACT with update flag.

If node initiating repair does not receive any RREP after `rreq_retries`, then it is assumed that network is partitioned. Under this scenario, the partitioned nodes must also declare a new group leader. If N is a member of the multicast group then it can declare itself as the group leader. It sends then MACT message with update flag to its downstream neighbors. If N is not a group member and becomes a leaf node after link break, then it can decide to prune itself by sending a prune message to next hop downstream. This action is also repeated at the downstream successor if N has only one neighbor. However, if N has more than 1 downstream successors then it selects one of the successors and sends a MACT with the group leader flag indicating the next node which is a member of the group receiving the MACT should become the new group leader. After the group leader is selected the multicast group has more than 1 group leaders due to partition.

Topological changes over time may reconnect the two network partitions. The nodes in a tree partition learn about connectivity status when a GRouP Hello (GRPH) message is received from another partition. The ID of the group leader they receive will be different from known ID of the group leader. If a group leader receives GRPH message for the group for which it is the leader, then the leader with lower IP address $GL1$ initiate a reconnection by unicasting a RREQ with repair flag to the other group leader $GL2$ using the node from which it received GRPH. The RREQ also includes $GL1$'s multicast group sequence number. Every node in $GL2$'s tree which receives this RREQ forwards it towards $GL2$. When RREQ reaches $GL2$, it updates the group sequence number by taking the maximum of two and adding 1 to it. Then a RREP is sent back to $GL1$. This RREP also should have repair flag. As the RREP traverses back on the path from $GL2$ to $GL1$ every link along the path is oriented towards $GL1$, the nodes update their routing tables, activate the link. The tree partitions are connected when RREP reaches $GL1$ with $GL2$ becoming the leader. Every node is updated about the new group leader's identity by GRPH message. GRPH is periodically broadcast from the group leader as an unsolicited RREP with TTL value larger than the diameter of the network. It reaches every node in the tree which update their sequence number and the group leader's ID.

7.6 Zonal Routing Protocol

Zonal Routing Protocol (ZRP), proposed by Haas and Perlman [16], is a dynamic zone based hybrid routing scheme. The scope of proactive scheme is restricted to a local neighborhood of each node called its *zone*. A route to a distant node is determined by querying a subset of nodes in the network. The protocol relies on the following important observation.

- Routing can be efficient if the topology changes in network can be quickly disseminated in the local neighborhood.

The above basic idea of restricting the propagation of changes in network topology only to the local neighborhood where the changes take place is also used by fishey state routing (FSR) [12]. However, the granularity of propagation in FSR is controlled only by varying the periodicity of update propagation according to distance. FSR distributes information about topology changes over the whole network at some regular though larger time interval compared to DSDV.

ZRP combines the characteristic of creating a route on-demand as in reactive routing schemes with the property of fast convergence that is typical to proactive routing algorithms. It restricts the propagation of topology changes to the local neighborhoods of the involved nodes, and creates a route between a pair distant nodes on-demand. Only active routes between distant nodes are maintained as the topology changes. Topology changes are not propagated over the entire network.

7.6.1 Routing Zones

A node maintains routes to all destinations within its local neighborhood called its *routing zone*. In other words, a node's routing zone consists of all nodes which may be reached from it by a fixed number of hops, say 1 to 2. This fixed number, denoted by ρ, defines the routing zone is called *zone radius*. For example, in Fig. 7.16 the routing zone for s consists of nodes $\{a, b, c, e, h, i, j, k\}$ which are within two hops from s. The nodes $\{e, f, g, h, i, k\}$ are peripheral nodes of the routing zone of s. The radius ρ of a routing zone is adjustable, and usually a small constant. Since it is not possible to control or predict the presence of the number of mobile nodes in an area, the number of nodes in a routing zone may potentially be very large if ρ is not small.

Fig. 7.16 Two-hops routing
zone of S

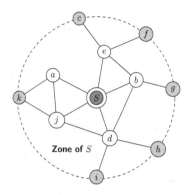

A large routing zone would generate a large amount of update traffic. This apart, the diameter of an ad hoc network usually does not exceed 5 or 6. Consequently, the very purpose of ZRP is defeated if a large zone radius is selected. In other words, with large zone radius, ZRP no longer remains a hybrid protocol.

Each node proactively maintains information about the routes to all other nodes within its routing zone. Therefore, the updates are propagated locally. Periodic routing updates do not flood the entire network, and full dumps for routing updates are not needed. The nodes use a proactive protocol called *IntrAzone Routing Protocol* (IARP) to maintain the routing information in its routing zone. It is interesting to observe that nothing prevents a node from using a different proactive schemes from other nodes. However, the problem in this approach is that different control packets of varying length and structures will be needed to maintain intrazone routes. Usually DSDV [14] is used for IARP.

7.6.2 Interzone Routing

An *IntErzone Routing Protocol* (IERP) is used for discovery of route on-demand to the destinations beyond a source's own routing zone. Theoretically, IERP can be based on any reactive protocol. It does not matter which reactive protocol is chosen for IERP as long as that protocol is able to exploit the information about local routing zone topology maintained by IARP to guide the query for route discovery. This is achieved by delivering the route request queries from a receiving node to the peripheral nodes in its routing zone. The delivery service is called *bordercasting*. The bordercasting is illustrated by Fig. 7.17. The source labeled S has a zone radius $\rho = 2$. The nodes $\{a, b, c, d, e, h, i\}$ belong to its routing zone. If S were to send a datagram to D and does not have a valid route to D then a route discovery is initiated by S. Since, D does not belong to routing zone of S, S bordercasts a route request to the peripheral nodes $\{e, f, g, h, i\}$ of its routing zone. Each node receiving bordercast checks for availability of the destination in their respective zones before a

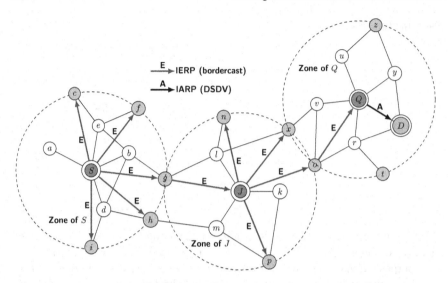

Fig. 7.17 Bordercasting and operation of IERP

repeat bordercast of the query in their own zones. So g bordercasts the request to J. Since, D does not belong to J's routing zone, J again bordercasts route discovery to n, x, o and p. Node o's bordercast finally reaches Q. Since, D belongs to routing zone of Q, the route discovery is over. The bordercasts collectively construct a tree. The branches of the tree are indicated in Fig. 7.17 by solid links labeled T. The forwarding path $S \rightarrow g \rightarrow J \rightarrow Q$, thus, gets created. The discovery process is complete when a route reply is sent back to the source. The procedure for route discovery by a source S to a destination D is summarized below:

- S first checks its own routing zone to find D. If D is found, then S sends the packet to D using local routing table of S.
- Otherwise (D does not belong to routing zone of S), S bordercast (unicasts to border nodes) RREQ to peripheral nodes of its zone.
- If any of the peripheral nodes finds D in its zone, then it responds by sending RREP to S. If a peripheral node does not have a path to D then it re-bordercasts the RREQ.

In Fig. 7.17, the dotted circles represent the routing zones of the respective nodes S, J and Q. Routing zones of g, o, and other involved nodes have not been shown as these zones are not relevant to the route. Node Q finds D in its routing zone, so it sends RREP to S. The routing zones of other nodes involved in route discovery procedure are not explicitly shown as it will clutter the figure. However, the reader can imagine how a bordercast is carried out.

7.6.3 Bordercast Tree and Query Control

A bordercast tree is defined by a root node r and the peripheral nodes of r's routing zone. The root of the tree appends complete forwarding path map in a RREQ packet. For example, node S include the path map as shown below.

Query message	
Border node	Relay node
e	c
f	c
g	b
h	d
i	d

The overhead of including forwarding path in RREQ grows linearly with the size of routing zone. Therefore, the number of hops defining a routing zone should be a small constant ρ. Bordercast effectively introduces an exponential path multiplying scheme into route discovery procedure. Therefore, though the route discovery is expected to be fast, control of flooding remains an issue.

ZRP supports a distributed construction of bordercast tree. This allows an interior node of a routing zone to participate in construction of bordercast tree. Each node proactively tracks topology of a region extending beyond its own routing zone. An interior node x of a bordercast tree constructs an entire tree ρ hop tree from the root node by proactively tracking a topology of the region consisting of $\rho + \rho - 1 = 2\rho - 1$ hops away from it. Figure 7.18 depicts extended routing zone for relay interior node c of S's routing zone. Maintaining an extended routing zone adds overhead to IARP, because router re-advertisements should include information about extended zone. However, it helps interior nodes to save on query traffic overhead in the reactive route discovery (IERP). So there is a trade-off between overhead of maintaining an extended routing zone and saving in RREQ traffic.

The main motivation of query control mechanism is to ensure that search for destination is guided from the source in all outward directions. It serves to reduce flooding, and also to guide the query reaching the destination quickly. The implementation framework is to prevent a query from re-entering a covered zone. Figure 7.19 illustrates how the query should be dispersed from a source node in all directions [16] so that it reaches targeted destination and prevented from re-entering already covered regions.

Two types of advance query detection techniques QD1 and QD2 are used for early termination of route discovery queries [16]. QD1 is concerned with direct relay of bordercast messages. When an interior node relays a bordercast message, it prevents messages flowing over downstream branches leading to peripheral nodes inside the covered region of the network. As Fig. 7.18 demonstrates, node c has full knowledge of S's routing zone. Therefore, c can terminate re-bordercast of S's query back to its routing zone from a node belonging to the uncovered region in c's extended

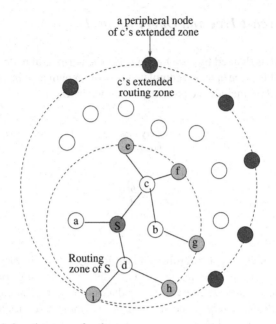

Fig. 7.18 Extended routing zone of node *c*

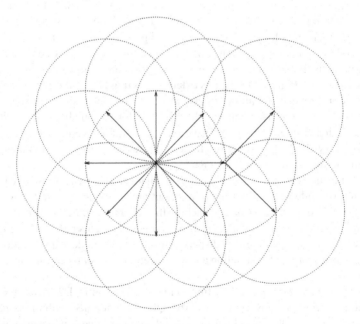

Fig. 7.19 Directing route discovery query from a source

Fig. 7.20 Detection of route discovery query

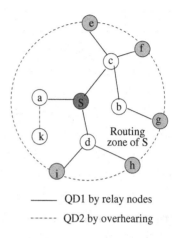

QD1 by relay nodes

QD2 by overhearing

zone. The query detection technique QD2 is used by the nodes of a routing zone which have overheard a route discovery query. These nodes can terminate the query if a re-bordercast is received directly from any node in the uncovered region. In a single channel transmission, QD2 can be detected by any node in transmission range of a relaying node. The capability for QD2 can be implemented through IP and MAC layer broadcasts. For example, as illustrated in Fig. 7.20 node k in S's routing zone overhears query from a, and participates in preventing the same query from re-entering S's region. The other nodes in S use QD1 as all of these node participate in forwarding the query.

7.6.4 Random Delay in Query Processing

Random query processing delay introduces asynchronicity in forwarding queries. The idea behind the approach is to ensure that the same query does not reach a node simultaneously by different paths. Each node waits for a random time before it constructs the bordercast tree. As the nodes waits to send the query, it could also detect queries from other bordercasting nodes and prune the overlapping branches in the bordercast tree. For example, as shown in Fig. 7.21 nodes a and b both receive query at the same time. If they both rebroadcast the query simultaneously, they will later come to know that both were spreading the same query in overlapping regions and wasting bandwidth. But using the random delay approach, b withholds the query, while a schedules its query much in advance. Furthermore, a uses QD1 to know about the same query from b when it launches its own query. Therefore, a can prune its downstream branches belonging to b's zone.

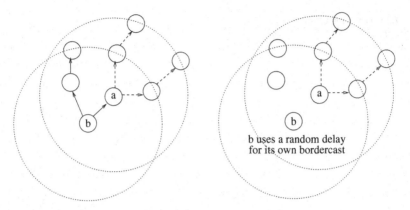

b uses a random delay
for its own bordercast

Fig. 7.21 Random delay in query processing

7.6.5 *Route Caching*

Active routes are cached at intermediate nodes. The route cache can be used to reduce frequency of route discovery. When the nodes on an active route move, that route becames invalid. If the link breaks occur upstream towards the destination then instead of initiating a fresh discovery of route, it will be less expensive to repair the existing route locally with the help of route cache. A local repair works by patching the invalid route to the destination from the nearest upstream node from the first link break. Thus the local repair constructs a bypass to avoid the first broken link on the existing path. In theory a route may be patched up many times. But in practice, the route may deviate appreciably from a shortest route after one or two such patchings. Therefore, after a few local repairs, the source may decide to initiate a fresh route discovery. This scheme follows the approach similar to that we found in use of forward pointer for location update schemes described earlier.

References

1. T.W. Chen, M. Gerla, Global state routing: a new routing scheme for ad-hoc wireless networks, *1998 IEEE International Conference on Communication* (1998), pp. 171–175
2. C.-C. Chiang, W. Hsiao-Kuang, W. Liu, M. Gerla, Routing in clustered multihop, mobile wireless networks with fading channel. IEEE SICON **97**, 197–211 (1997)
3. T. Corman, C. Leiserson, R. Rivest, C. Stein, *Introduction to Algorithms* (MIT Press, Cambridge MA, USA, 2001)
4. S. Corson, J. Macker, Mobile ad hoc networking (MANET): routing protocol performance issues and evaluation considerations, http://www.ietf.org/rfc2501. January 1999. RFC-2501
5. R. Dube, C. Rais, W. Kuang-Yeh, S. Tripathi, Signal stability-based adaptive routing (SSA) for ad hoc mobile networks. IEEE Pers. Commun. **4**(1), 36–45 (1997)
6. E. Gafni, D. Bertsekas, Distributed algorithms for generating loop-free routes in networks with frequently changing topology. IEEE Trans. Commun. **29**(1), 11–18 (1981)

7. L. Ji, M. Corson, A lightweight adaptive multicast algorithm, *Globecom'98* (1998), pp. 1036–1042

8. D.B. Johnson, D.A. Maltz, DSR the dynamic source routing protocol for multihop wireless ad hoc networks, ed. by C.E. Perkins. *Ad Hoc Networking*, Chap. 5 (Addison-Wesley, 2001), pp. 139–172

9. Y.B. Ko, N.H. Vaidya, Location-aided routing (LAR) in mobile ad hoc networks. Wireless Netw. **6**(4), 307–321 (2000)

10. S. Murthy, J.J. Garcia-Luna-Aceves, An efficient routing protocol for wireless networks. ACM Mobile New. Appl. J. 183–197 (1996)

11. V.D. Park, M.S. Corson, A highly adaptive distributed routing algorithm for mobile wireless networks, *IEEE INFOCOM'97* (1997)

12. G. Pei, M. Gerla, T.W. Chen, Fisheye state routing in mobile ad hoc networks, *ICDCS Workshop on Wireless Networks and Mobile, Computing* (2000), pp. D71–D78

13. C.E. Perkins (ed.), *Ad Hoc Networking* (Addison-Wesley, 2001)

14. C.E. Perkins, P. Bhagawat, Highly dynamic destination-sequenced distance-vector (DSDV) algorithm for mobile computers. Comput. Commun. Rev. 234–244 (1994)

15. C.E. Perkins, E.M. Royer, Ad-hoc on-demand distance vector routing, *The 2nd IEEE Workshop on Mobile Computing Systems and Applications* (1994), pp. 90–100

16. M.R. Perlman, Z.J. Haas, Determining the optimal configuration of the zone routing protocol. IEEE J. Sel. Areas Commun. **17**(8), 61–81 (1999)

17. E.M. Royer, C.K. Toh, A review of current routing protocols for ad-hoc mobile wireless networks. IEEE Mag. Pers. Commun. **17**(8), 46–55 (1999)

18. C.K. Toh, Associativity-based routing for ad-hoc mobile networks. Wireless Pers. Commun. **4**, 103–139 (1997)

Chapter 8
Mobile OS and Application Protocols

8.1 Introduction

Protocol level details on how a mobile network such GSM/GPRS, WLAN or WPAN functions is of no concern to most of the users of mobile technology. An ordinary user is interested for ubiquitous access of information over mobile devices. In other words, the users would expect these mobile access protocols to work seamlessly giving a feeling that the access is as easy as it is on wired networks. For instance, a mobile user will be interested to access information and interact with services provided over the Internet. Some of the popular form of interactions include Web browsing, messaging service, SSH, etc.

Mobile devices maintain connectivity to the rest of the world through various cellular based wireless networks such as GSM, GPRS, 3G, LTE, Bluetooth and IEEE 802.11x. The network connectivity is intermittent due to inadequate coverage, signal interferences, and low bandwidth. So mobile OS are designed to manage service interruption and ad hoc reconnection attempts. When reconnecting back to network, a device may use a new wireless channel. From the prospective of use case scenarios, many of the utility services accessed by the mobile users are location dependent. Therefore, Mobile OS should be able to opportunistically combine location service from different networks, GPS and compass for the benefit of applications. Normally, a user is careful about losing mobile devices, yet small devices are prone to accidental mishandling as well as misplacement. Though a mobile OS cannot provide a complete security solution, it should at least incorporate provisions by which services can be stopped from unauthorized accesses. Increasingly, mobile devices are getting more powerful and resource rich. Research on mobile grids have explored way to harness aggregated computational capabilities of mobile devices. However, this research still in infancy and remains within confines of academic and research labs. Considering OS issues are just too many, the discussion on mobile OS in this chapter is organized around the basic features, focusing on the minimality and the essential components.

In addition to mobile OS, our aim is to cover three protocols, namely, Mobile IP, Mosh and WAP. Mobile IP [1] is a modification of wire line IP at the Internet level

© Springer Nature Singapore Pte Ltd. 2017
R.K. Ghosh, *Wireless Networking and Mobile Data Management*,
DOI 10.1007/978-981-10-3941-6_8

which allows a user to receive messages irrespective of his/her home registration area. A wire line IP assumes a fixed unique attachment point for a node. Messages can be delivered over the Internet by tagging them with corresponding IP addresses of the nodes. An IP address with a port number identifies a unique connection from among several concurrent services that may be running on a node. A route from node S to a destination node D may not be the same as the route in the reverse direction. Between two communicating end points, TCP [2] distinguishes one internal session from another by using IP addresses of the respective endpoints along with the demultiplexing selector for each session. IP address allows to identify a route to a destination. The only other thing that may influence routing of packets is network congestion due to excessive traffic.

SSH [3] command is quite familiar in the context of accessing remote computers from any where. SSH works beautifully when network delays, and packet losses are within tolerable limits. However, SSH does not support IP roaming. It works on a terminal emulator which processes one character at a time. This implies SSH traffic from a server consists of a lot of packets having very small payloads. All the echos or in-line editing are performed by a remote computer known as the server. Therefore, it becomes completely useless when packet losses occur. In other words, SSH cannot handle intermittent network connections or networks experiencing long delays. Wireless networks, on which mobile services are based, often experience long delays and intermittent connectivity. On such an environment SSH becomes ineffective and useless. Mosh [4] or mobile shell is a remote terminal application which not only can handle IP roaming, but also supports client side predictive echoing and line editing. It does not require any change in the server side software for running applications. Mosh is essentially a shell application that can work without requiring a connection to be maintained over flaky links to support a user's movements. Since SSH uses TCP, preserving terminal session becomes an issue for supporting IP address roaming as the user moves about. Mosh on the other hand uses UDP.

Wireless Application Protocol (WAP) [5] is a framework for accessing many value added services over Internet and enterprise intranets using mobile devices. Apart from known hurdles in information access over wireless interfaces, small form factor of mobile devices calls for a whole new approach to the presentation of information. WAP framework was formulated as an industry wide global standard to bring development of all applications over mobile wireless networks. The targeted applications include microbrowsers, scripting, email, chat, instant messaging service among others. So, WAP is not just a single protocol but a protocol suite. Accessing Internet resources on hand held wireless devices becomes efficient through WAP.

It is expected that the discussion in the chapter will provide enough pointers to create applications which can interoperate irrespective of communication technologies and a whole range of hand held devices with different capabilities as well as form factors.

8.2 Mobile OS

A Mobile Operating System (MOS) is designed for mobile devices such as PDAs, tablets, and smartphones. Although laptop computers are also portable mobile devices, they do not belong to the category of devices which can be classified as mobile phones. Usually, laptops run on desktop OSes. Unlike smartphone, laptops are neither equipped with modems nor possess a variety of sensors. However, some variety of ultra thin hybrid laptops have touch screen support, foldable display, front/back cameras, detachable or sliding keyboards, pen support, and a few sensors such as accelerometer, ambient light sensor, gyroscope, GPS and compass. When equipped with modems, these devices can also function as tablets.

Mobile OSes have been implemented taking various resource constraints of mobile devices into account. These include limited energy and limited computing capabilities, small form factors and non conventional input/devices. It forces implementation to be oriented more towards gestures, touch and voice based interactions. Mobile devices maintain connectivity to the rest of the world through various cellular based wireless networks such as GSM, GPRS, 3G, LTE, Bluetooth and IEEE 802.11x. The network connectivity is intermittent due to inadequate coverage, signal interferences, and low bandwidth. So mobile OSes are designed to manage service interruption and ad hoc reconnection attempts. When reconnecting back to network, a device may use a new wireless channel. From the prospective of use case scenarios, many of the utility services accessed by the mobile users are location dependent. Therefore, Mobile OS should be able to opportunistically combine location service from different networks, GPS and compass for the benefit of applications.

8.2.1 Smartphones

Among various mobile devices, smartphones dominate mobile device market. Most people, specially those in age group of 18–35 years, tend to access mobile services through smartphones. So, the discussion on mobile OS remains incomplete without a reference to smartphones.

Smartphones have brought in a sea of changes and convenience in daily lives world over. An estimate [6] projects that the smartphone users base will reach 2.87 billion by 2020. As of 2016, there are about 2.1 billion users of smartphones. The rate of growth is more in emerging economy than in rich economy. The reason is attributable to the fact that smartphones serve endpoints for maintaining both connectivity and control over contents and services even if the conventional communication infrastructure is not very good. Therefore, people belonging to low and middle income group depend heavily on smartphones for their livelihood.

8.2.1.1 OS as an Abstraction Layer for SoC

Battery life is a critical aspect in determining the user's experience on a smartphone. Due to portability reasons, the phone battery should be slim, light weight and a long lasting power pack. As opposed to an ordinary cell phone, the design goals of a smartphone are: thinner device, slimmer battery, bigger screen, faster CPU, and larger memory size. Some of the design goals are mutually conflicting. To achieve these goals, smartphones use SoC (System on Chip) [7] processors. SoC defines an integrated design that includes CPU, GPUs, a number of co-processors, and memory. Roughly speaking, SoC is equivalent to the mother board of a desktop computer.

Our focus in this chapter is not smartphone architecture. However, the performance and the speed of execution of applications depend on the architectural parameters of a computer. A user's experience is not only determined by the applications that run on a smartphone but also how fast the applications can run.

An operating system leverages hardware and provides software abstractions that can be exploited by the developers to provide rich user's experience. In abstraction, a SoC design can be viewed as a collection of network of modules. Each module provides a specific service. The connection between services is supported by bus or network. The OS requirements as follows [8].

- In order to take take full advantages of modularity of SoC architecture, OS design must be modular. To provide the best performance, it should be possible for a developer to abstract out the application design according to the knowledge whether a particular OS functionality is implemented in hardware or software.
- Modular approach in the SoC design means, the hardware designers may also regroup SoC components even during the development process. Smartphone OS design should be able to adapt to these changes without requiring a redefinition of hardware abstractions presented to the application layer.
- If a specific hardware functionality is defined by overly generic abstractions, then it might prevent an application from exploiting the advantages of that the hardware component through the specific OS abstraction.
- OS should also provide for the protection and the concurrency control. It implies different parts of the OS and the application (e.g., interrupt handlers, drivers, application code, etc.) cannot (expect to) interfere with each other.
- Due to the application specific nature of SoC, it will be necessary to port the OS to many different platforms. The OS and application code should, therefore, be highly portable. There should not be any cross dependency involving different functions of the OS. In other words, each OS function must be well encapsulated.
- Since, most SoC systems have real-time and dependability requirements, it is desirable that OS abstractions are amenable to verification of correctness and temporal analysis.

In view of the above, a micro kernel based approach to the design of OS appear to be ideal for (reconfigurable) SoC based devices.

8.2.1.2 OS as a Interface Layer for Applications

At the highest level, the design and the implementation of an OS is dependent on type of the system and the hardware. At a level lower than hardware abstraction layer, OS must be designed meet the requirements of both the users and the system. The user requirements stem from the convenience in use, reliability, security and speed. In contrast, the system goals are guided by ease of implementation, maintenance, flexibility, performance and efficiency as explained in Sect. 8.2.1.1.

A number of studies have made been made to explore of the diversity in the use of smartphones [9]. These studies primarily indicate two different aspects in the use of a smartphone, viz., (i) convenience, and (ii) innovation. In an average, about 22 Apps are installed by an Android user while about 37 Apps are installed by Iphone user [10]. The voice based communication over a smartphone is not substantially different from the level it is found with a ordinary cell phone. In an average, the number of voice calls per phone is around 5.7 calls per day [11]. The use of a smartphone is found to be oriented predominantly for non-voice based applications [12]. All the user sessions concerning applications or computation except for voice calls, are referred to as non-voiced. Texting forms a major part of the non-voice usages. According to one study, each user in an average access SMS or instant messaging app 11.2 times per day [11]. Still there is substantial diversity in the use of non-voice Apps. The types of usages can be classified as follows [11]:

- Recreational
- Instant messaging
- Communication and Internet
- Transport and travel
- Banking and m-commerce
- Knowledge and work

A few knowledge user (those having background in CS) may use a smartphone for App development, but this type of users are only a few. Considering the usage patterns and the diversity of use, two the major concerns in wide spread use smartphones are: (i) energy drainage, (ii) resource scarcity. Some of the resource limitations include low CPU capabilities, display, memory, user interfaces, etc.

8.2.2 Difficulties in Adopting Desktop OS

From the point of view of OS kernel, the difference between desktop OS and Mobile OS is little. About 250 patches (amounting to 3MB of code) were defined for the Linux kernel to tailor it for Android [13]. These patches are primarily aimed at fulfilling the requirements of certain basic functionalities, and overall conservation of resources. Mobile devices should enforce tight power management features, support non-conventional I/O devices. For example, the inputs may be gesture based or through keypad, touch screen, camera, and audio. For portability reasons, a mobile device has a small form factor, and depends on the battery for its operation. So, the conservation of resources is extremely important. Some of the enhancements includes incorporating of new drivers [14]. For example, in Android, a Alarm driver manages timer, which wakes up the device from sleep. Ashmem drivers manages sharing of memory at kernel level. Mobile devices normally support only a small flash memory. So, sharing data and services is important when a device runs multiple applications. Binder driver is needed for interprocess communication. Interprocess communication is supported through the use of shared memory. A service which registers as a IPC service does not have to keep track of different threads in execution. The binder monitors, handles and manages all the threads, and facilitates communication between the processes through shared memory. The binder also takes care of synchronization between the processes.

Mobile OS generally does not kill an application. All other applications opened by a user continue to run in the device even after the user switches to a new application. A running application is killed only when the device runs out of memory. Even then, the state of the application is saved to enable quick launch. The desktop version of Linux distribution comes with a huge GNU C library. It provides library routines as per ISO standard C specification for programming. This library is far too large for mobile phones. For example, glibc also provides Native POSIX Thread Library (NPTL). NPTL offers high performance, but only suitable for the computers having adequate resources as they require large disk foot prints. For a device with limited resources, NPTL is not suitable. Only a few threads may run concurrently in a mobile device. So, many of the features like mutex conditional variables are considered as unnecessary [14].

8.2.3 Mobile OS Features

Three major responsibilities of an OS are memory management, process management and inter process communication. The implementation of virtual memory is a major requirement of memory management for a desktop computer. In a mobile device, implementation of virtual memory is not needed. In the event of a device hitting a low memory level, the running applications are simply killed in increasing order of their priorities. Therefore, many complications including swapping which are necessary for the implementation virtual memory could be eliminated. However, a mobile OS should implement highly secure memory protection schemes to ensure applications do not access each others data or address space.

Normally, for memory protection, desktop computer employ Address Space Layout Randomization (ASLR) technique [15]. It randomizes base point of the stack, the heap, the shared libraries and the base executables. So, it becomes difficult to guess the foot prints of a code residing in the memory. As a result, network based control hijacking attack become difficult. Mobile OS spends time to minimize the boot time, the power consumption, the memory foot prints and the application launch time. Typically, the libraries are pre-linked for this purpose. Sometimes even library addresses are hard-coded. Furthermore, due to security reasons the file system on device is mounted in the read only mode. So, it is not possible for a binary editor to modify the image of a device memory. In [16] a modified randomization scheme is proposed for the pre-linked code in a mobile devices.

Generally, mobile OS employs user initiated event driven interactions. Therefore, the client-server session based IPC is an ideal choice for the communication mechanism among user space components.

8.2.3.1 Kernel

Mobile OS typically employ micro kernel approach for provisioning OS services. The approach does not just mean that the kernel is of small size, rather it provides a set of essential OS services which are used by a different set of other processes that team up together to provide high level OS services to the applications. The system level services such as file system, network interface and TCP/IP are implemented as user libraries, and do not need privileged executions. Access to these services are coordinated by the kernel through a client-server mechanism. The kernel is directly responsible for the management and the protection of memory for both the user applications and the applications providing the OS services. The kernel also provides few other core system services such as process management, scheduler service, and driver modules. Since, high level OS services are implemented as non-privileged processes, it is possible to extend the OS services using APIs in the user written applications.

8.2.3.2 Execute in Place (XIP)

Diskless devices support execute In Place (XIP). XIP is used in smartphones in order to execute programs directly from storage without copying them into the RAM. Mobile OS leverage XIP to optimize the use of memory during the execution of an application. XIP not only speeds up execution, but also indirectly extends the amount of shared memory. Therefore, the total memory requirement is also reduced.

8.2.3.3 Application Framework

Mobile users have options to avail the services offered via a plethora of mobile Apps. Many of the Apps are designed for the convenience in transactions related to banking, travel and electronic commerce. A rich set of Apps also exists for social networking, gaming, fitness, healthcare, and multi-media entertainment. There is a huge scope for abusing the Apps route with malicious intent to harm the users of the mobile devices. Therefore, mobile security poses big challenge. Sandboxing is a simple idea to isolate the Apps and prevent any malicious app from monitoring the activities or the execution of another App. Sandboxing works as follows. A user ID

(UID) different from the invoking user is assigned to an application at the time of installation. The access control for each application's UID are statically assigned at the time of installation. Mobile OS enforces the discretionary access control regime according to the UID of each application when it executes.

Although Apps run in a sandbox environment, the application specific data are often stored in shared resources. Therefore, it may be possible for one App to access the data of another App. By collecting footprints of various data items, it may also be possible to make intelligent guesses about the transactions through data mining and other learning techniques. Therefore, data caging is used in conjunction with sandboxing to isolated application data.

8.2.3.4   Security Issues

One of the simple techniques is filtering out unverified Apps and controlling the release of third party Apps. Employing the process of App vetting before the release of an App could be a practical solution in this respect. For Android system, Google developed Bouncer testing mechanism [17]. It is a well known way of app vetting. However, malicious App developer may use evasive techniques to dodge the App vetting process. One simple way is to employ obfuscation techniques whereby, a malicious App uses the finger prints of dynamic analysis of the vetting system and avoids the detection of malicious code. So, when the same App subsequently runs in a actual device the malicious code get triggered.

Antivirus is another complementary method of used to ensure security. However, antivirus softwares have limitations [18]. An antivirus program typically scans the code and package information in an App, but cannot understand the runtime behaviors. Monitoring of runtime behavior is necessary for better detection method. One possible idea could be to instrument Apps for monitoring their runtime behaviors. So, Apps need to be repackaged. However, application repackaging is not supported by most systems. Another approach could be to identify all sensitive calls that an application makes to Java API, and replace them by special functions that monitors the behaviors. However, this approach is possible only for the Apps written in Java. Any other approach will require changes in different layers of OS stack.

8.2.4   Mobile OS Platforms

A variety of Mobile OS platforms exists and used. Notable among these are:

- J2ME
- Palm OS
- Symbian
- BlackBerry OS
- Android

- Windows Mobile OS
- iOS

Any attempt to provide a comprehensive review of the internals of mobile OSes is beyond the scope of this book. Therefore, our focus in this chapter is restricted to review of four widely used mobile OSes, namely, J2ME, Symbian, Android and iOS. The choice has been dictated by the historical aspects of the development of mobile OSes as well their popularities among the users.

8.2.5 J2ME

Sun Microsystems released three different editions of Java 2 platform to meet the entire range of computing requirements from enterprise servers to small personal devices. Java 2 Enterprise Edition (J2EE) provides the server based solutions for the computing needs of enterprises. Java 2 Standard Edition (J2SE) is cut out for the software solutions on desktops and workstations. Finally, Java 2 Micro Edition (J2ME) addresses the computing requirements of Java enabled hand held portable devices such pagers, personal organizers, PDAs and phones. The Java big picture is illustrated by Fig. 8.1.

A set of specifications defines a J2ME platform for programming of small personal devices. It consists of three building blocks, namely, Configuration, Profiles, and Optional packages. Optional packages define a set of APIs for supporting some additional behaviors and common features. Bluetooth and JDBC may be present as a part of optional packages. Configuration and Profile are two important building blocks of the J2ME architecture. Each specification set is referred to as a profile.

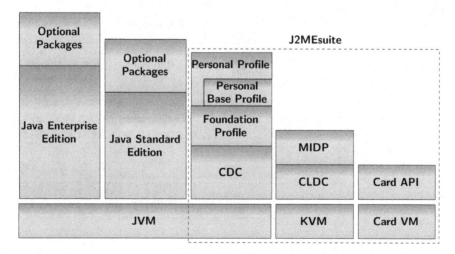

Fig. 8.1 Java 2 platforms—the big picture

Each J2ME profile is built by extensions of the basic capabilities of the configuration layer in J2ME stack. The configuration and the profiles for a device are developed on the basis of the hardware features of the device and the targeted for the use of the device.

8.2.5.1   Configuration

Configuration layer defines the abstractions for generic mobile devices having similar capabilities. Configuration layer is implemented over the host JVM that relies on the host OS as shown in Fig. 8.2. Configuration layer is closely inter-woven with JVM in order to capture the essential capabilities of each family of devices. The members of a family of devices are distinguished by the specifications defined by the profile layer. A profile specification is implemented by a set Java class libraries. To meet the requirements of a new device type, either a set of new class libraries should be added or the existing libraries should be modified and extended suitably.

There are two different types of configurations, CDC (Connected Device Configuration) and CLDC (Connected, Limited Device Configuration). CDC configuration is meant for virtual machines hosted on a desktop or on a laptop. CDC consumes higher memory resources compared to CLDC. CLDC requirements are supported through a small virtual machine called KVM defined on the top of JVM. KVM is designed for Java programs that require a total memory of only few kBs. KVM can be viewed as a restriction or contraction mapping of JVM functionalities. It support as much JVM capabilities as possible for nontrivial Java programming on resource constrained devices. Basic KVM features and its responsibilities can be outlined as follows:

Fig. 8.2 J2ME software stack

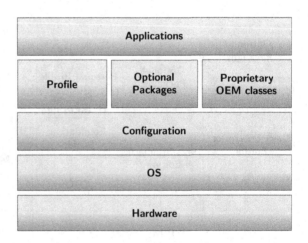

- The design goal of KVM is to create the smallest possible complete JVM for running Java programs in an environment limited by a total memory size of few kilo bytes. In other words, KVM is a light weight JVM for hand held devices.
- The static memory foot print of KVM should be under 100 kB.
- KVM should allow programming on the small devices retaining all the important features of Java programming.
- KVM should be portable to any device without requiring retrofitting. However, KVM should be modular, and customizable on the installed devices.
- KVM is written in C. So, it can be compiled and used on both Window and Unix based platforms.

CLDC ensures security in following way. Firstly, all the downloaded Java class files are subjected to a verification step by the virtual machine. Secondly, the applications are executed in isolation under a sandbox environment. Overriding of classes in protected system packages are disallowed.

CLDC also provides a set of APIs for new I/O types and known as Generic Configuration Framework (GCF). GCF is a part of `javax.microedition.io` package. It specifies interfaces for the different types of inputs and outputs. CDC being a superset of CLDC includes GCF. CDC requires GCF for file and datagram support. CDC based profiles requires resource rich devices and does not work on low end devices.

8.2.5.2 Profiles

Several generic profiles are available. Some of these are:

1. Foundation Profile (FP)
2. Personal Basis Profile (PBP)
3. Personal Profile (PP)
4. Personal Digital Assistant Profile (PDAP)
5. Mobile Information Device Profile (MIDP)

Foundation Profile is the Base Profile on which all other profiles are created. FP only targets for the device with network connectivity but without GUI. Personal Basis Profile adds basic user interface to FP profile. The devices which can support complex user interfaces typically use Personal Profile. PDAP defines profile for personal digital assistants. Functionally, PDAP is similar to MIDP. MIDP is responsible for three important tasks: (i) display, (ii) storing of simple database tables in non-volatile memory, and (iii) HTTP based connectivity using CLDC-GFC. MIDP works in an environment where the device is characterized by certain minimum capabilities:

- At least 96×56 pixel display on device,
- At least about 170 kB of non-volatile memory, out of which

1. At least 128 kB should be set aside for running Mobile Information Device (MID),
2. At least 8 kB should be available for storage of MIDlets data, and
3. At least 32 kB should be reserved for JVM operations,

- A keypad, or a keyboard, or a touch screen is available on the device for user's input, and
- The device has bi-directional wireless connectivity.

Apart from hardware capabilities, MIDP also requires following assistance from native OS of the device.

- To be able to run JVM, it is absolutely essential for the host OS to implement exception handling and process interrupts.
- The host OS should provided for the scheduler capabilities.
- Though file system is not a requirement, OS should provide support for basic read and write operations on the persistent storage.

MIDP applications are known as MIDlets in keeping with the well known Java terminology of referring executable program as a (*) lets. MIDlet applications are subclasses of `javax.javamicroedition.midlet.MIDlet` defined in MIDP profile. MIDlets can be viewed as applets on Java enabled mobile phones.

A MIDlet life cycle has three states, namely, (i) start, (ii) pause, and (iii) destroy. In the start state, a MIDlet acquires resources and starts execution. In a pause state, the resources are released and MIDlet remains in the wait state. From the pause state, a MIDlet may either resume in the active state, or enter the destroy state. On entering the latter state, the MIDlet releases all the resources and kills itself by halting the execution of the associated threads. A MIDlets suite is packaged as a JAR file. All MIDlets in a single JAR can access the database of one another. Since, the focus here is Mobile OS, we do not to go into the details of MIDlet programming. An interested reader may refer to other resource including complete reference to J2ME for the same.

8.2.6 Symbian OS

SIBO [19] was an early incarnations of Symbian OS introduced in 1988. It is, essentially, a 16-bit organizer coded in C. SIBO's Unique Selling Point (USP) was power management. It could be ported easily to a variety of devices including PCs. By mid 1990s 32-bit devices started appearing, and SIBO was junked in the favor of a 32-bit system known as EPOC [19]. EPOC was developed with an object oriented approach right from the beginning and was written in C++. Communication capabilities were added, so that hand held devices could access various system services as well as coordinate the accesses to the peripheral devices. It also opened up possibility of expanding communication to provide multimedia services.

Symbian was developed as an open OS support for the devices manufactured by different companies. Nokia, Ericsson, Sony Ericsson together contributed for 75%

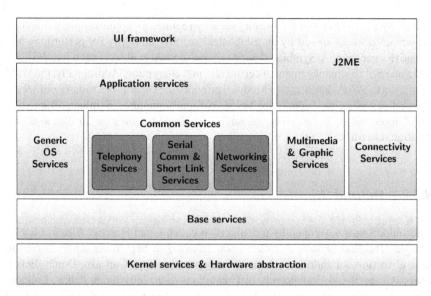

Fig. 8.3 Symbian OS architecture

of the stakes in Symbian. Symbian based phones were immensely successful until Android and iPhone based smartphones started to appear in the market.

Symbian OS ran only on ARM processors. Symbian architecture is described in Fig. 8.3. It separates the user interface from the OS engine. It is a micro kernel based architecture that supports preemptive multitasking and multithreading execution with memory protection. Micro kernel approach reduces kernel size to a minimum by provisioning only essential services. This is appropriate for the resource poor devices. Symbian micro kernel contains a scheduler, provides services for both memory and device management. An important concept for memory protection is data caging. Using data caging an application protects its own data in a private partition which cannot be accessed by other applications. For example, data caging is ideal for the applications which carry out financial transactions.

Accesses to various system services are designed along the lines of the client-server access model. The client can access the services through the APIs exposed by the base service layer. Network, telephony and file system support are accessible through a set of libraries which form the OS base service layer. Networking stacks include TCP/IP (dual mode IPv4/IPv6), WAP, IrDA, Bluetooth, and USB. Most Symbian devices have pre-built telephony supports for circuit switched voice and data (CSD and EDGE ECSD) and packet switched data (GPRS and EDGE EGPRS), CDMA circuit switched voice and data and packet switched data. Furthermore, it is possible to implement newer standards using extensible APIs of the telephony subsystem.

Symbian provides abstraction to the hardware and supports device independent Hardware Abstraction Layer (HAL) which is located below the OS base service layer. Real-time guarantees to both kernel and user threads are provided through kernel. Symbian OS employs a strong security regime. An application is required to present credentials signed by an established security authority for performing any sensitive operation. A Symbian device rely on secured protocols such like HTTPS, TSL, and SSL for management of certificates and encryption. Additionally, the WIM Framework (WAP Identification Module) provides the capabilities to carry out secure transactions using non-repudiation based on digital signatures. Symbian offers a rich set of applications for browsing, messaging, multimedia, over the air data synchronization, file transfers, etc.

8.2.7   Android OS

Android OS was developed by a consortium called Open Handset Alliance led by Google. The first version of android was released in September 2008. There are several versions of android each has a fancy name such as Cupcake, Donut, Eclair, Froyo, GingerBread Honeycomb, IceCreamSandwich, Jelly Bean, Kitkat, Lolipop, Marshallmallow, and Nougat [20]. Nougat is the latest stable release of Android system.

Android OS stack consists of four layers as shown in Fig. 8.4. The bottom-most layer is basically the Linux kernel. This layer should be viewed as the hardware abstraction layer. It performs four important tasks, namely, memory management, interprocess communication, driver support and power management. Driver support is available for a number of drivers including display, camera, keypad, WiFi, flash memory, binder, audio, etc. Through driver support, Android can be ported to new devices. Power management is extremely important for any mobile phone. So, kernel abstractions are useful for enforcing power management polices. Binder driver handles interprocess communication.

The next layer from the bottom consists of a set of libraries including the runtime system for Android. The runtime system consists of a set of core library routines and Dalvik VM. Dalvik VM is essentially an optimized implementation of Java runtime system and provides for a Java like programming framework. Application framework is the next higher layer of the software stack. All the user applications are implemented on the top of this layer.

The life cycle of an Android application is shown in Fig. 8.5. There are three main states in the life cycle of an application, namely, *active*, *pause*, and *destroy*. From the start state, an application migrates to the active state. In active state, the application is in execution. From the active state, an application can transit to the pause state in order to allow execution of another application. An application in the pause state, may either resume its activities or migrate to the destroy state where all its activities are shutdown. An application in the pause state may also be killed, if enough free memory is not available for another application activated by the user. The killed application is reactivated when the user navigates back to the killed application. From the pause state, the application may also be stopped and destroyed or shutdown.

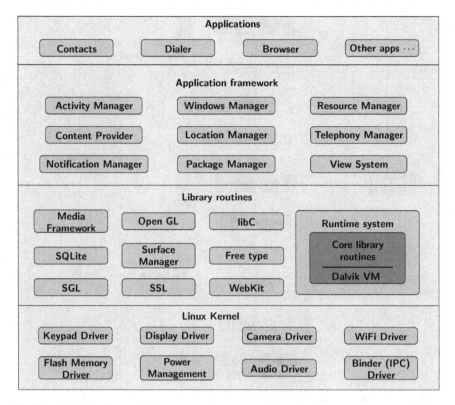

Fig. 8.4 Android software stack

The interesting part of Android memory management is in enforcement of the life cycle model for an application in preference over the usual virtual memory implementation with swapping. At a high level, the application swapping employed by Android and the swapping employed by OS are the same. The aim is to free memory for another active application. Life cycle model avoids the complications associated with the implementation of virtual memory. An important reason for avoiding swapping is to minimize the number of writes on the flash memory. A flash memory has limited longevity as far as the number of writes is concerned. Whereas, repeated writes have little impact on the longevity of a normal hard disk.

Android uses two different types of memory killers to free memory. Out Of Memory Killer (OOMK) is a kill all kind of killer which kills minimum number of applications to free enough memory for a new application. This kill method does not distinguish between applications. So, it may remove important applications from the memory to create free space for a foreground application. On the other hand, Low Memory Killer (LMK) distinguishes the applications in decreasing order of priorities into six different classes, namely,

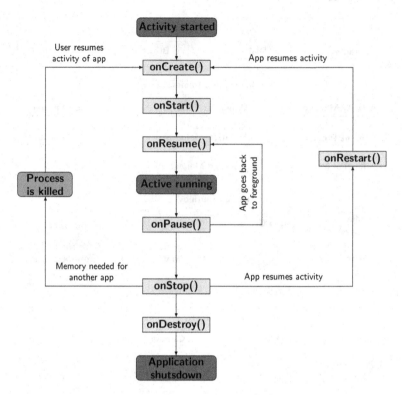

Fig. 8.5 Life cycle of an Android application

- *Foreground_App*: a process which is currently running in the foreground.
- *Visible_App*: a process only hosting the activities that are visible to the user.
- *Secondary_Service*: a process holding a secondary server.
- *Hidden_App*: is a process only hosting the activities that are not visible.
- *Content_Provider*: a process with a content provider.
- *Empty_App*: a process without anything currently running in it.

LMK starts killing applications in increasing order of the priorities until sufficient free space is created in the memory for the foreground application.

8.2.8   *Iphone OS (iOS)*

Iphone operating system (iOS) like Mac OS X is based on Mach kernel. Mach kernel was developed at CMU in a bootstrapped manner from Free 4.2BSD. It requires about half a GB of storage in the device. Ordinarily, no third party application is allowed. However, jailbreaking can be used to run third party applications in an Apple phone or IPad. The software stack consists of five layers as indicated in Fig. 8.6. Core OS

Fig. 8.6 iOS software stack

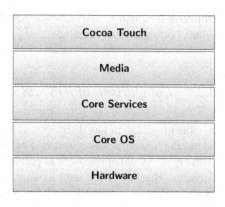

layer essentially represents the OS kernel. Apple developers performed an evolution of Mach OS X micro kernel (Darwin) make it ready for ARMv5 chipset which was used in iPhones and IPads. Besides kernel, the Core OS layer is made up of drivers and basic OS interfaces. Kernel is responsible for the memory management while drivers provide interface to the hardware. Libraries are used by Apps to access low level features of device hardware. Core service layer basically consists of core foundation network (CFN). CFN presents a set of C based interfaces for the data management and the fundamental software services that are useful to the application environments and the applications. CFN defines abstractions for common data types, and supports internationalization with Unicode string storage. It also provides utilities such as plug-in support, XML property lists, URL resource access, and preferences. The second layer from top is referred to as media layer. Media layer defines a software framework for the application developers to make use of audio, graphics and various multimedia capabilities of an iOS based device in the user Apps. The top layer of the software stack is known as Cocoa Touch Layer (CTL). App developers make use UIKit framework of CTL for look and feel of their Apps. UIkit framework provides support for key apple technologies like multi touch events and control, push notifications, multitasking among others. It provides interfaces to accelerometer, localization and camera. App developers rely heavily on gesture based inputs such as tapping, pinching and swiping which form a part of CTL's touch based technology.

iOS SDK bundles tools necessary for designing, creating, debugging, testing and optimizing softwares. It also includes native and web applications, and dynamic libraries but excludes device drivers. SDK has built-in framework, shared libraries, Xcode tool, iOS simulator and iOS developer's library. Like Eclipse platform, Xcode is used for managing application projects, editing, compiling, running, and debugging code. There is also an Interface Builder tool for assembling the UI. Similarly, an instruments tool is available for performing runtime analysis and debugging. iOS Simulator can be used for testing iOS applications by simulating the iOS technology stack on a Mach OS X. It makes testing faster, since a developer does not need to upload the application to a mobile device. The iOS Developer Library is the source for documentation helpingapplication development. iOS applications are written in

Objective C which is derived from ANSI C and augmented by objective oriented syntax borrowed from Smalltalk.

8.2.9 Comparison of iOS and Android

Symbian foundation has disintegrated completely. The last Symbian based smartphone Purview 808 was introduced by Nokia in February 2012 [21]. From 2012, virtually no Symbian release was publicly announced, as Nokia moved it to closed licensing. Blackberry till date remains a closed platform, and has failed to reach masses. Window mobile has not been quite popular among the general users. Nokia, after abandoning Symbian, has migrated to windows mobile system. According to a statistics [22] Android OS commands 87%, while iPhone commands just about 11% of the market share of mobile phone OS market world wide for the second quarter of 2016. This implies only 2% of the smartphones have other OSes. Therefore, Android and iOS are the two main competitors in mobile OS segments. Our focus in this section is on comparison of these two systems.

Being an open system, Android has several advantages over iOS. Android application can be crowd sourced. The users can get their hands on Android system and customize applications according to their likes and dislikes. However, downloading applications from the sources outside Google play store may introduce viruses or worms in the device. Only Googly play store has a serious vetting process with antivirus features. iOS does not allow Apps to be downloaded from any sources other than the official App store. Apple enforces a code signing process whereby an application developer must sign the code using the Apple issued certificate before uploading the same to the App store. Unsigned codes cannot be uploaded. It ensures that codes do not possess any malwares or viruses. It does not mean apple devices are completely immune to hacking, malware, spyware or viruses. However, the chances of these happening to an iOS device is much less compared to an Android device.

Both iOS and Android implement memory randomization or Address Space Layout Randomization (ASLR) for memory protection. iOS had employed address randomization right from beginning. In Android, ASLR was added since the Jelly Bean release. Memory randomization makes it difficult for the viruses or the malwares to guess the exact locations for attacking the application code.

Encryption mechanism is used in both iOS and Android. But device encryption was not available for Android release lower than 3.0. Encryption API for Android was release first time in Ice Cream Sandwich 4.0. Device encryption in iOS was introduced in iPhone 3GS.

8.2.10   Cross Platform Development Tools

For the application developers, it becomes a productivity linked difficulty if every application needs to be retooled for one or the other OS. Consequently, cross platform development tools have become an important development framework [23] for applications. There are many cross platform tools such as: Rhomobile [24], Titanium [25] and PhoneGap [26]. These tools allow UI development using web technologies like HTML, CSS and Java. However, the UIs developed over native development framework are always rated better than the corresponding UIs developed over cross platform tools.

Some of the important requirements of a cross platform development tool are as follows [23]

- *Multiple OS support*: The platform must support application developments for multiple mobile OSes particularly Android and iOS.
- *Rich UI set*: It should provide support for a rich set of UIs, and possibly include support for customizable parameters based UI programming. Multimedia I/O, 2D and 3D animations enhances the user's experience. So, it should be possible to develop such interfaces on the cross platform tools.
- *Backend connection support*: Many mobile Apps for information, entertainment, navigation, social media interactions need backend connectivity. Therefore, the tools should also provide smooth support for backend connectivity protocols and platform independent data format.
- *Optimization for power consumption*: Energy drainage is a common issue affecting all portable devices, irrespective of native OS support. The generated Apps should be optimized for power consumption.
- *Security and privacy*: Security are privacy are two important area of concerns in use of mobile applications. Typically, mobile phones store highly sensitive and private data concerning personal identity. Therefore, the developers would always be apprehensive about the security support provided by cross platform tools.
- *Installed app extension support*: A extension to old installed Apps should be possible through updates or patches.

A generic layered architecture of a cross platform development tool is provided in Fig. 8.7.

The application developers use web technologies to implement the functionalities of applications. Cross platform tools enable implementation of interface, access of storage facility, and device specific features (e.g., sensors, camera, contacts) which interact with a JavaScript API. The Javascript API interacts with the native API of the mobile platform. Finally, executables for different platforms are generated by building the application.

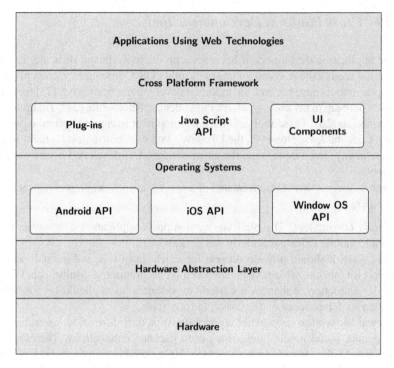

Fig. 8.7 Software stack for a cross platform tool

8.3   Mobile IP

Mobile IP [1] is a modification of wire line IP at the level of Internet enabling mobile users receive messages independent of the point of attachment. A wire line IP address refers to a unique fixed point of attachment for a node. Messages can be delivered by tagging them with IP address and port number pairs. This means an IP address allows to identify a node from millions of available nodes in the Internet. By having a stable IP address assigned to a computer, IP packets from other computers in the Internet can always be delivered at the same computer. In a wired network, the nodes are mostly static with a fixed point of attachment to the Internet. Dynamic Host Control Protocol (DHCP) [27] provides discrete slow mobility to static nodes in a wired LAN. It combines IP address assignment protocol with mobility. Using DHCP, a node can change its point of attachment with limited functionality. Figure 8.8 illustrates how DHCP service operates. For assignment of an IP address, a newly booted machine broadcasts a DHCP DISCOVER packet. A DHCP relay agent is needed for each LAN, as limited broadcast may not reach DHCP server if the server does not belong to the same LAN. DHCP relay agent has the IP address of DHCP server. It intercepts all DHCP packets including DISCOVER packet and send DHCP DISCOVERY packet as a unicast packet to the DHCP server which may be located in a distant network.

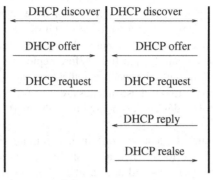

(a) DHCP discovery.

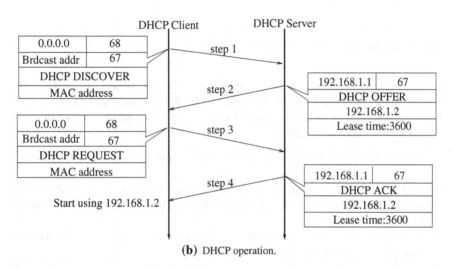

(b) DHCP operation.

Fig. 8.8 DHCP operation

DHCP leases out a new IP address to a requesting node for a limited period. The lease period is renewed before expiry as long as the node remains connected and keeps sending renewal requests. When a node changes its attachment to the Internet its IP changes, and as a result all IP clients on the node will stop working. The node needs to restarts its Internet subsystems. Typically, users do not selectively restart the Internet services, but reboot the system. So, the DHCP mechanism, at best, can provide mobility to the extent that the point of attachment of a terminal in the network can be changed. It essentially implies that the requirement of a stable IP address is in direct conflict with node's ability to become mobile.

The portability of nodes enabled through DHCP is also fairly complex. Most application use Fully Qualified Domain Name (FQDN) which should be mapped to an IP address. In order to find mapping of FQDN to an IP address, an application typically seeks assistance from a DNS service. However, when IP addresses are allocated dynamically, the DNS will be unable to resolve the mapping unless mapping updates are provided to DNS for each and every FQDNs. Since DNS is the most important administrative component of a network, any application designed to alter data must have to be tested and trusted fully before deployment. The updates have to be applied to DNS at frequent intervals. So, there is a possibility that the entire network service may go for toss if these updates are incorrect. Specially, in network having large number mobile devices, even providing DNS portability would be fairly complex task.

In view of the technical complications in maintaining IP connectivity of a portable and mobile device to Internet, a simple and easily scalable approach is needed. Notably, the approach should neither affect the protocol stack nor require re-engineering of the applications.

8.3.1   Overview

Mobile IP protocol provides a simple mechanism to deliver packets to a mobile node when it moves out from its home network. Mobile IP has been designed to avoid all the complications of DHCP mentioned above. It supports mobility of nodes through cooperation of three subsystems:

1. A *mobility discovery* mechanism which allows a mobile node to detect its movements in the Internet,
2. An *IP registration* mechanism which allows the mobile node to register its IP address with an agent of the home network after the node obtains an IP address from the new network.
3. A *packet delivery* mechanism which delivers packets to a mobile nodes when it is away from the home network.

The interactions between three subsystems are accomplished through the following three functions:

1. **Agent discovery**. There are routers which advertise their availability to offer service on a wireless link to mobile nodes appearing in the neighbourhood.
2. **Registration**. After a node successfully obtains an IP address (called its care-of address) in a foreign network, registration process enables the node to inform the newly acquired IP address to an agent belonging to home network.
3. **Tunneling**. It is a process by which the home agent encapsulates the datagram meant for a mobile node to be delivered to the care-of address (foreign agent) of the mobile node.

Sometimes an additional function called *reverse tunnel* may also be needed. Reverse tunneling is a process through which the foreign agent encapsulates datagram meant for a correspondent node from a mobile host to be delivered at the home agent. Home agent decapsulates the packet before directing the same to the correspondent node.

In a foreign network, a mobile node effectively uses two IP addresses at a time: (i) a *home address* (HA) and (ii) a *care-of address* (CoA). The HA is static. It is used to identify a mobile node's TCP connections, if any. A CoA is dynamic, which changes as often as the mobile node changes its point of attachment to the Internet while roaming. Therefore, CoA can be viewed as a topologically significant address of a mobile node. CoA specifies the network number that identifies the point of current attachment of a mobile node with respect to the network topology. HA insulates other communicating nodes from the complications of following the mobility a mobile node. Therefore, other nodes on the Internet are oblivious to roaming of a mobile node, and transmit packets to the latter by using its HA.

Mobile IP requires the existence of a topologically static network node or a router called the *home agent*. A mobile node (MN) registers IP of its new point of attachment (i.e., CoA) with a home agent when it is away from home network. The home agent intercepts all the packets having MN as destination, and delivers these packets to MN's current point of attachment in the *foreign network*. So, it is important for the home agent to know a mobile node MN's new attachment point as it moves. MN should register its new *care-of address* (CoA) with the home agent every time its CoA changes. It is the responsibility of the home agent to deliver packets from the home network to CoA of MN. In other words, when a MN is away from home network, HA acts as a proxy for the MN.

All the packets with the MN as destination are intercepted by HA. HA then creates a new packet corresponding to each packet it receives on behalf of MN. It constructs a new IP header with CoA of MN as the destination address. The corresponding old packet forms the payload of a newly created packet. Each newly created packet uses a higher level protocol number indicating that the next protocol header is also an IP header. Then each such a newly created packet is transmitted by the home agent. The packet modification as explained above is essentially a redirection process called *tunneling*. The mobile node's home address is prevented from influencing the routing of the encapsulated packet till it reaches at CoA of the node. The packet from a sender S for a mobile node MN, located topologically in a foreign network, is encapsulated by creating a IP header. The packet is tunneled to foreign agent which decapsulates the packet and redirects it to correct destination (or the mobile node MN).

8.3.2 Agent Discovery

Agent discovery is similar to the one that is used by the nodes in Internet for discovery of routers running ICMP (Internet Control Message Protocol) router discovery protocol [28]. It involves the routers to broadcast router advertisements periodically. The agent advertisement is the most critical component of Mobile IP functions. The structure of the ICMP packet for agent discovery in Mobile IP is illustrated in Fig. 8.9. The packet has following fields:

Fig. 8.9 ICMP packet format for agent advertisement

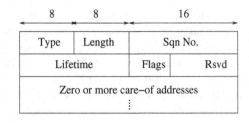

1. *Type*: It distinguishes among various extensions to ICMP router advertisements which may be used by a mobility agent. Provision exists for many extensions, the most important being extension the type 3 which is for the advertisement of mobility agent.
2. *Length*: Specifies the length of a single extension. For example, the length of type 3 extension depends on many care-of address that may be defined. Typically, one care-of address is defined.
3. *Sequence number*: It essentially represents freshness of the router advertisement. Sequence number is incremented by 1 for each successive advertisement.
4. *Lifetime*: Specifies the expiry time of the current advertisement.
5. *Flags*: There are seven flags representing various features supported by mobility agents. We will discuss more about the flags, later in the text.
6. *Care-of address*: IP addresses to be used by mobile nodes.

A home agent need not necessarily offer a care-of address service. But it still needs to broadcast mobility agent advertisement in order to allow a mobile node to detect that it has returned back to home network. A mobility agent need not provide the default router address as it would be found in other ICMP router advertisement.

The flags H and F respectively represent home and foreign agent. A mobility agent may offer both services, so both H and F may be set. The flag B set to indicate that the foreign agent is busy. However, B cannot be set unless F is also set. The flag R denotes registration required, and is meaningful for care-of address co-located with the mobility agent. Encapsulation protocol preferred by the foreign network is known by three flags: G, M, and V. M is used when minimal encapsulation [29] is preferred.

8.3.3   Registration

The process of registration involves a MN registering its CoA with the designated HA in its home network. Figure 8.10 illustrates the sequence diagram of the registration process. As one may notice, it is similar to the process of acquiring IP address from DHCP. Initially, MN sends a registration request to foreign agent. Foreign agent forwards the request to home agent on behalf of MN. Home agent sends a registration reply back to foreign agent which completes the registration process. The format of the registration request appears in Fig. 8.11. Flag G or M indicates a

Fig. 8.10 Registration
process

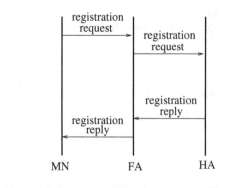

Fig. 8.11 Format of
registration request message

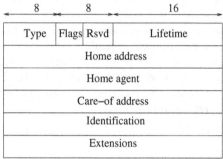

home agent whether IP-in-IP or minimal encapsulation is preferred by the foreign agent. Setting V bit, in request message, tells the foreign agent that Von Jacobson header [30] compression is desired. Registration message is sent using UDP protocol.

The structure of a registration reply is shown in Fig. 8.12. It consists of type, code, and lifetime field. Lifetime field informs a mobile node about the duration of time for which the registration of the care-of address will be honored by a home agent. When a registration request is rejected, code field tells the mobile node what went wrong. In the case, a registration request is accepted, the code field contains a 0. Request may be rejected either by foreign agent or by home agent. An interesting scenario occurs when the registration request sent by mobile node contains a directed broadcast address for finding a home agent. The registration request is rejected by every home agent. However, the reject replies received by the mobile node contains addresses of the available home agents. So, the mobile node can try again with a valid home agent address for a fresh registration, and it will succeed.

Registration request procedure has been designed to resist two types of attacks: (i) masquerade attack, and (ii) replay attack. In first type of attack, a node impersonates as a foreign agent and diverts all traffic meant for a mobile node to itself by sending a fake registration message. In the second case, a malicious agent replays an old registration message and effectively isolates a mobile node from the network.

In order to guard against malicious users registration, the registration request is protected by inclusion of a non-reproducible value with the identification field of

Fig. 8.12 Format of registration reply message

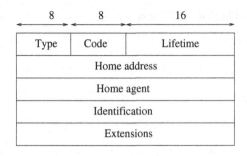

the request. The value changes with each new request. The value may either be a timestamp or a *nonce*. The home agent and the mobile node should agree, before hand, on the unforgeable values that could accompany the registration request.

Three different authentication extensions are defined for use in mobile IP. These are: (i) mobile to home, (ii) mobile to foreign and (iii) foreign to home. Each uses a different security parameter index (SPI). SPI defines the security context to be used to compute authenticator. The context consists of authentication algorithm, and the secret (keys) to be used.

8.3.4   Routing and Tunneling

After the CoA registration for a mobile node becomes successful, the home agent intercepts all datagrams meant for the mobile node. The home agent then tunnels (encapsulates) all these packets to the same to care-of address provided by the mobile node. Although there may be many ways to encapsulate, the simplest one is IP-in-IP [31] encapsulation [32]. Figure 8.13 illustrates the encapsulation technique. The care-of address becomes destination address in the tunnel header. By including IP protocol value of 4, the encapsulated packet indicates that payload carried by it is again an IP packet. The inner packet is not modified except for decrementing TTL value by 1. Compared to IP-in-IP encapsulation minimal encapsulation has less overhead. But it can be used, if all the entities, namely, mobile node, home agent and the foreign agent agree to do so. Minimal encapsulation uses protocol value 55 against 4 of IP-in-IP encapsulation. The length of minimal encapsulation header is 12 or 8 depending on whether or not the original source IP address is present. It allows the original datagram to be fragmented at home agent. However, this encapsulation cannot be used if the original datagram is already fragmented, because there is no room to insert fragmentation information.

Fig. 8.13 IP-in-IP encapsulation

outer IP header	tunnel header	inner IP header	Data

If the delivery of a tunneled datagram to care-of address fails, then ICMP error message is received by the home agent. But an ICMP error message can incorporate only 8 bytes of datagram in error. So, when an ICMP error message is returned, it may not contain original source of the tunneled packet. Under this scenario, how would a home agent notify about the error to the original source of the datagram? If a home agent keeps track of a care-of address including the sequence number of the tunneled packet then the returned ICMP error message may be matched against the stored information, and a notification can be relayed back to original source. However, there is a small problem in forwarding the notification. The correspondent node must not be aware of the existence of a tunnel. So, a home agent needs to modify ICMP error message from *network unreachable* to *host unreachable*. A home agent also keeps track of many other tunnel parameters such as maximum transmission unit (MTU), TTL for the encapsulated datagrams. The collection of tunnel parameters can be found in [32].

Mobile IP allows a mobile node to send data packets to a host directly using standard IP routing scheme. So, the packet flow in both directions constitute a triangle routing pattern. Inward flow is routed through home agent to care-of address of mobile node, while outward flow from mobile node to a correspondent does not require any rerouting and follows standard IP routing. However, due to security reasons, ingress filtering used at a network may discard packets originating from any foreign node (belonging a different network). This implies that mobile node cannot transmit packets directly to a node outside the network it is visiting. The solution to this problem is to apply a tunneling also in the reverse direction [33]. All datagrams from mobile node in a foreign network can then be routed through the home agent. The tunneling and the reverse tunneling are illustrated pictorially in Fig. 8.14. As it is clear from the figure, with reverse tunneling the overhead of routing data packets between a mobile node and a correspondent node (CN) increases considerably specially when

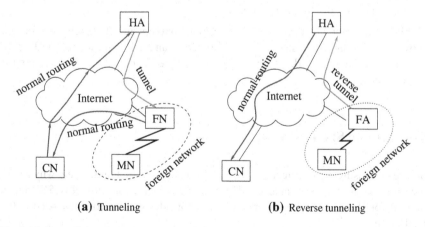

(a) Tunneling   (b) Reverse tunneling

Fig. 8.14 Tunneling and routing in mobile IP

CN, in turn, belongs to a foreign network. In this case, the two-way traffic between CN and MN has to pass through double-tunneling.

Mobile IP has been designed to operate together with normal IP routing. The network may have both types of nodes: those which implement mobile IP and those which do not. It should be possible for an normal correspondent node, not implementing mobile IP, to communicate with a mobile node. The normal node would use normal IP routing. It sends an ARP (address resolution protocol) request to home network for resolving the address of mobile node before sending any message. This works fine as long as mobile node is actually present in home network. The nodes in the home network may also cache the address of the mobile node for use. However when the mobile nodes moves away to a foreign network, ARP would be unable to resolve any request. Also the nodes that have cached mobile node's address, and attempts to use stale information while trying to communicate with the mobile node. In either case, any attempt to communicate with the mobile node fails.

Mobile IP is expected to handle both the situations stated above. It deals with these situations in the following way. The home agent broadcasts gratuitous ARPs to all nodes. The objective of broadcasting gratituitous ARPs to ensure that all nodes which have cached the MAC address of the mobile node should update the corresponding cache entry. The details of handling ARP request for a roaming mobile node, are as follows:

1. Home agent supplies its own MAC address and continues gratuitous broadcasts for sometime to ensure that every node in the network has received the ARP broadcast and updated their respective cached entry.
2. During the time a mobile node MN is away from its home network, the home agent intercepts any ARP request meant for MN and supplies its own link-layer address
3. As soon as the mobile node MN comes back to home network, the home agent sends another series of gratuitous ARPs to assist other nodes to evict stale cache entries concerning the mobile node.

Mobile IP does not, however, specify a mechanism to update ARP cache in a foreign network. So, mobile nodes should never broadcast an ARP request or an ARP reply packet in a visited network. Otherwise it will be hard to contact mobile node after it moves away.

8.4 Mobile Shell (Mosh)

Before discussing the architectural design of Mosh, let us first understand why a new shell program is necessary at all? SSH [3] has been in use since mid 90s. SSH lacks support for IP mobility. To understand why, consider the environment needed for SSH to run.

1. Firstly, SSH runs on TCP [2]. A TCP connection is represented by a connection tuple: (`src_IP, src_port, dest_IP, dest_port`). A TCP connection breaks if any of the four fields of its connection tuple is modified.

2. Secondly, in SSH every character is echoed and in-line editing is performed at a server or a remote computer.
3. More importantly, in a cellular mobile environment, the performance of a TCP connection is severely affected by micro mobility protocols (handoff) which introduce packet losses and duplications, delays, jitters and break before make, etc. [34].

In summary, the basic assumptions for SSH to operate is an efficient, non-lossy high bandwidth network. It does not understand what to send. Therefore, it sends out everything that an application puts out. The size of data can be in megabytes. To support rendering of SSH output at the client terminal, the round trip time should be typically in few milliseconds. In contrast, in a relatively unloaded 3G network, the round trip latency may exceed several hundreds of milliseconds. The delay may cause the buffers to overflow due to concurrent bulk transfers. A delay of several orders in magnitude of the tolerable range of milliseconds, renders SSH useless for any interactive operations on mobile devices.

8.4.1 Overview of Mosh

Having understood the reasons behind the obvious inadequacies of SSH in dealing with IP mobility, Winstein and Balakrishnan [4] set the design goals of Mobile Shell (Mosh) which offers solutions to the problems mentioned above. Mosh supports IP roaming. It can operate on intermittent and inherently lossy low bandwidth network connection. One of the smart approach employed in Mosh is predictive client-side echoing and line editing. So, Mosh gives the user a feeling that the remote computers are local. This becomes possible because Mosh uses a different approach in local echoing. It runs the terminal emulator at the server-side. The client and the server maintain images of the terminal states synchronized. In contrast, SSH sends an octet stream over the network and hands it over to the terminal emulator on the client side for its display. In summary the two major techniques which makes Mosh advantageous compared to SSH are:

1. *State Synchronization Protocol* (SSP). This is a secure object synching protocol which runs on the top of UDP [2]. SSP synchronizes abstract objects with IP roaming on intermittent and low bandwidth lossy network.
2. *Speculative Display Rendering*. Display is rendered immediately when the client is able to guess with confidence. It is also possible to repair the display even if prediction is not 100% correct.

8.4.2 State Synchronization Protocol

SSH protocol is simple. As illustrated by Fig. 8.15, it consists of two basic elements, namely, a *pseudo terminal* and a *terminal emulator*. SSH client runs the terminal emulator on the top of the pseudo terminal. The server side application conveys the output octet stream over encrypted TCP connection that exists between the client and the server. The pseudo terminal on the SSH client uses the terminal emulator for rendering the display on screen.

The technical contribution from Mosh research [4] was to synchronize abstract objects instead of octet stream. The goal was to build a low latency object synchronization protocol and to combine this with a local user interface that replaces SSH. The protocol does not need to know the inner details of an object, but it can distinguish between two states of an object. An object also has to provide a *patch vector* that can be applied to its previous state for synchronization of the two states. It is the object implementation that determines the synchronization. In other words, if the object implementation is incorrect, then SSP may lead to wrong synchronization.

In the specific case of mobile terminal emulation, the recent most state of the screen is sent to a client by the server using a frame rate that adjusts to the network conditions. So, the network buffers do not experience overflow conditions. The server side can buffer the generated keystrokes and optimize the transfer of the resulting octet stream. However, this luxury is not possible on the client side which must send each and every keystroke. SSP runs in both directions, client and server. At the client side, the objects represent the history of the user's input while at the server side the objects represent the responses in terminal window.

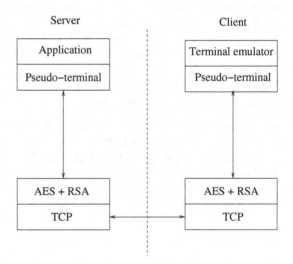

Fig. 8.15 Simplified view of SSH protocol [4]

The design goals of SSP are as follows:

1. It should ensure authentication and login through existing infrastructure, namely, SSH.
2. It should not use any privileged code.
3. It should update the remote host to the sender's current state as fast as possible.
4. It should allow a roaming client to change its IP, and the change should be transparent to the client.
5. It should recover from the errors due to dropped or reordered packets.
6. It should ensure authenticity and confidentiality.

Since SSP does not have any privileged code, the key exchanges take place outside the main SSP activities. The bootstrapping of the terminal session performed by running a script under a privileged server. Login to a remote host is performed through established means of a connection like SSH. The server program listens on a higher order UDP port and provides a random shared encryption key. After this the SSH connection is no longer needed, and can be stripped down. This approach represents a smart way of leveraging existing infrastructure for a reliable and secure authentication. After login becomes successful, and SSH connection has been teared down, the client talks directly on the established UDP port.

As shown in Fig. 8.16, SSP basically works on object layers and runs on UDP. The server side exports an object called screen. This object has the contents of the terminal display from application running at the server. The client side, on the other hand, exports the object called key strokes which is a verbatim transcript of the key strokes made by the user of the client.

Datagram layer maintains roaming connectivity. The payload received from the transport layer is appended with an incrementing sequence number, and then encrypted by the datagram layer before being sent it as a UPD datagram. The

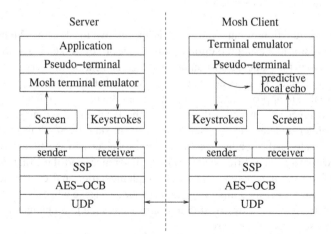

Fig. 8.16 Design of Mosh protocol [4]

datagram layer is also responsible for maintaining the round trip time estimate of the link and the user's public IP address.

8.4.2.1 Authentication and Privacy

Mosh encryption mechanism is designed on the top of AES-128 [35] in Offset Code Book (OCB) mode [36]. OCB integrates message authentication with block cipher encryption. Therefore, it provides both privacy and authenticity through only a single key. Repeated and reordered packets are handled by diff operator. Every datagram represents a diff between a numbered source state and a numbered target state. No replay cache or history state needs to be maintained.

8.4.2.2 Mobility

The server comes to know about client's roaming by naming connection independent of network. The connection which is traditionally known by IP and port numbers, now mapped to a sequence number protected by encryption. When the server receives an authenticated packet from the client with a higher sequence number, it stores client's IP and UDP port numbers from the received datagram. So knowing about client's roaming becomes simple and automatically maintained. The approach appears bit of a reversal of SSH where application writes into a TCP socket and oblivious to network conditions. However, SSP forces the application to be aware of the network conditions and the alerts. SSP is responsible for the rest of the synchronization for maintaining the connection.

8.4.2.3 Speculative Local Echo

Another major function of datagram layer is speculative local echo. The client side terminal emulator makes a prediction on the effect of keystrokes made by the user and later verifies the same against authorative screen sent by the server. The user's keystrokes in most of the Unix applications are echoed at the current cursor location. So, it is possible to approximate the response from the remote application.

Transport layer synchronizes the states of the local and the remote hosts. The transport sender updates the receiver to the current state by sending three things, namely, the state of the sender, the state of the receiver and the binary difference between two states. The difference is logical difference, and the exact details are computed from the object type and object implementation and do not depend on SSP. For instance, the user's input depend on every keystroke whereas the difference in screen states is defined by creating a minimal message that changes the client's screen to the server's current screen.

8.4.2.4 Update Frame Rate

As SSP does not need to send every octet it receives from the remote host, the frame rate can be controlled to suite the conditions of the network. The minimal interval between frames is set to half the RTT estimate. So, just one instruction will ever be in transit from the client to the remote host. The maximum frame rate is fixed at 50 Hz which roughly matches the limit of human perception. This frame rate also saves unnecessary traffic on low-latency links.

The transport sender uses delayed acks to reduce the volume of the packets. A delay of 100 ms was found to be sufficient to piggyback a delayed ack on the host data. The server also takes a pause since the time its object is modified before sending off an instruction. This is a clever way of avoiding sending of partial updates in quick successions. A collection interval of 8 ms was recommended as optimal on the basis of some application traces.

SSP also sends heartbeats, so that the server gets fast updates on the change in client's IP. Additionally, it helps the client terminal to warn the user when there was no recent response from the server. An interval of 3 s was used for sending a heartbeat. It reduces unnecessary traffic due to heartbeats but at the same time found to be sufficient for handling IP roaming.

8.4.3 Design Considerations of Terminal Emulator

Terminal emulator has to be redesigned suitably in order to comply with the requirements of the SSP's object interface. The client's keystrokes are sent to the server and applied on the server side emulator. The authoritative state is maintained by the server side terminal and SSP synchronizes this back to the client. The client speculates the effects of keystrokes, and in most cases applies them immediately. The client learns about the success of its predictions when receives the authoritative state from the server. This observation allows it to raise its confidence level in deciding whether to display the predictions on the client terminal. In case of high latency connection, the predictions are underlined to ensure that user is not misled about the result. As and when the server's responses arrive the underlined text disappears gradually. If there are mistakes in predictions, they are removed within one RTT time. This approach of predictive display works because most Unix applications either echo the user's keystroke at the current cursor location or wait for the response from the application. In fact, the choice is between display of keystrokes or to wait for the octet streams to arrive from the server. In high latency networks, clearly the choice for speculative echo boosts interactiveness and distinguishes it from one with packet losses. The predictions are not made immediately, the strategy used is to predict when the user hits a key but not to display it immediately. The predictions are grouped together in form of an *epoch*, and displayed together. So either all predictions for an epoch are correct or incorrect. The predictions are made in the background. If one prediction is confirmed by the server then all predictions for the epoch are displayed immediately to the user.

The prediction of echo and its display needs assistance from the server side. In order the display to function correctly, the Mosh client should be able to get a confirmation on its prediction from the server. The initial attempt was to determine whether the predicted echo was displayed on the screen by the time Mosh server has acknowledged the keystroke. This strategy was not satisfactory, because some applications could take a long time to respond after the input was presented to them. So, the server's acknowledgement for a keystroke may arrive before echo is present in the screen state. This leads the client to conclude that the prediction is wrong even if the response from application was correctly predicted. It produces flickers on the screen as the echo is initially displayed, then removed, and when the response arrives from the server, it is displayed again.

One solution to remove flickers was to use a timeout on the client side. A prediction can be considered as correct until a certain timeout occurs or the server's response arrives. However, due to network jitters the acknowledgement from the server may arrive well after the timeout. Using a long timeout interval does not make sense as there is a possibility that the incorrect prediction would stay on for a long time.

The solution that works out well is to implement a server side timeout. This timeout is fixed at 50 ms. This value is arrived at on the consideration that the timeout interval should be fast enough to detect a mis-prediction and at the same time should be sufficiently long for a response to arrive from a reasonably loaded server. So, the client is associated with a terminal object. It contains an echo ack field that represents the latest keystroke given as input to the application for at least 50 ms, and the effect of the keystroke should appear on the current screen. This ensures that client does not timeout on its own. So network jitters cannot affect the client ability to predict echos correctly. The down side is that the server keeps sending an extra packet every 50 ms to send an echo ack after a keystroke.

8.4.4   Evaluation of Mosh

As the paper indicates [4], the Mosh was evaluated by using traces from 40 h of real-world usage by six users who contributed about 10,000 keystrokes together. The plot reproduced from original paper shown in Fig. 8.17 indicates that 70% of the time Mosh was confident in prediction and the responses were almost instantaneous. A major portion of the remaining 30% keystrokes where Mosh predictions failed were for navigations such as north, south east or west of an application screen such as the mail client. So latency distribution in these cases are as comparable as SSH. When Mosh prediction was erroneous, it was able to correct the keystrokes within RTT time for 0.9% of keystrokes. The errors were found to occur due to word wrap, i.e., for the characters which were printed near the end of a line moved to the next line at an unpredictable time. Overall Mosh response latency was less than 5 ms compared to 503 ms for SSH. Mosh is available for download from http://www.mit.edu. Elaborate

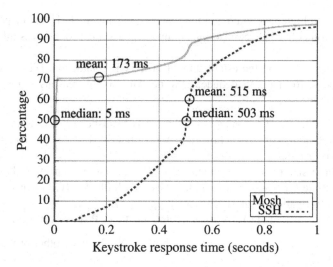

Fig. 8.17 Comparative evaluation: SSH versus Mosh [4]

installation instructions for all flavors of Linux environments, Android app for client terminal and also Chrome add-on are available for Mosh terminal.

8.5 Wireless Application Protocol

Wireless Application Protocol (WAP) [37] defines a set of standards for developing mobile services over wireless networks. The necessity of defining protocol standards for mobile services arose due to the facts that

1. Internet protocols are neither designed to operate efficiently over mobile networks nor optimized for low resources, and
2. Small factor of mobile devices. For example, it is not possible to fully display desktop versions of web sites.

At first we need to understand why a new protocol such as WAP is necessary at all when HTTP (Hyper Text Transfer Protocol) together with HTML have been used so successfully for web services over wired networks.

8.5.1 Performance Bottleneck Faced by HTTP

HTTP defines the information exchange standards over world wide web [38]. It supports information flow between a web browser (HTTP client) and a web server (HTTP server). It is a stateless, request-response type of protocol designed for networks with high bandwidth and long latencies. Though HTTP is independent of transport protocol, a TCP connection is implicitly assumed for lossless information exchange.

Being dependent on the establishment of a TCP connection, HTTP suffers all TCP related performance inadequacies. Some of the notable reasons for performance degradation due to TCP are:

- For establishing a TCP connection a three way handshake is necessary.
- The lower bound of transaction time for a client's HTTP request to reach the webserver is at least two RTTs.
- The default size of a TCP segment is 536B for remote connection though TCP can negotiate for a maximum segment size of 1460B. So TCP breaks the output stream into smaller chunks before sending.
- The performance of HTTP is also affected due to TCP slow start mechanism.

Apart from the TCP related performance bottleneck, there are other problems with HTTP such as:

- It uses long protocol headers, transmits the contents in uncompressed form, and employs primitive caching mechanism.
- It expects two communicating ends to speak HTML [39] language.
- Though multiple HTTP requests can be made over a single TCP connection, each object request has to be a separate transaction. This implies that every request has to make a separate trip.

HTML is basically a description language for passing the data through HTTP. HTML assumes high resolution, high color displays, existence of mouse and hard disk. Typically, the web page designers ignore capabilities of end system, they only focus on optimizing the design of the webpage. In summary, HTTP is designed for networks with high bandwidth and long latencies.

The overall picture of Internet communication model over HTTP is illustrated by Fig. 8.18.

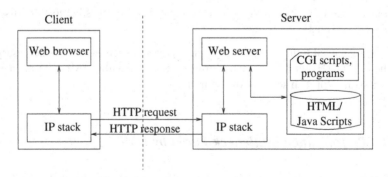

Fig. 8.18 World wide web communication model

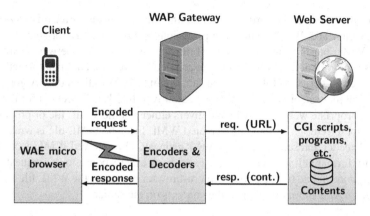

Fig. 8.19 WAP programming model

Cellular service providers anticipated enormous scope for business reach that could lead to effective globalization by having real time interactive services related to travel, banking, finance, weather, stock trading, etc. However, cellular service providers quickly realized that in view of the limitations of HTTP/HTML mentioned above, the existing web infrastructure has to be re-engineered for defining a new communication standard over cellular network. This led to Ericsson, Motorola, Nokia and others to form a consortium for working on a standard which will enable mobile application developers to build interactive applications with enhanced interactive value added services that provide near real-time responses.

As shown in Fig. 8.19, WAP programming model consists of three main components: the client, the WAP gateway and the web server. The important elements of WAP programming model are:

1. *WAP device*: It is basically a wireless enabled, portable client device such as a smart phone, or a PDA.
2. *WAP client*: An entity which receives the web contents from the WAP gateway.
3. *WAP content/application server*: An entity where information or web/WAP application resides.
4. *WAP gateway*: Also known as WAP proxy. It acts both as a client and a server and performs translation of WAP protocol stack to WWW protocol stack. It also has content encoder/decoder.

The client's micro-browser uses web server contents accessible over the network. In a wired network, a HTTP GET request is made by the client to the web server. The content of the URL in the form of a HTML page sent as a HTTP response to the client. However, services created through HTML page are not only excessively resource intensive but also too heavy for mobile devices, considering display limitation of small screens. Compute-intensive services carrying redundant information should be optimized for their accessibility on mobile devices. WML (Wireless Markup Language) standards [40] were developed precisely for this. Typically WML pages are encoded in binary in order to reduce the amount of data transmission over a wireless interface. WAP architecture provisions a WAP gateway for such encoding of the WML pages. The gateway machine acts as a mediator between wired and wireless network domains by helping in protocol conversion and data formatting. A WAP gateway performs following four important tasks as indicated by Algorithm 2. The HTTP request, created by the WAP gateway at line 1, is processed for the URL by an appropriate web server which delivers either a static WML file or processes a CGI script to return a dynamically created WML file. The WML file is wrapped by a HTTP header and sent back to the WAP gateway. The received WML is compiled in binary format at line 5, before being sent back as a response to the request of the mobile phone at line 6. The phone's micro-browser processes the WML file received from the WAP gateway to display the contents on the screen.

Algorithm 2: Actions of WAP gateway

begin

    // Request is binary encoded

1   receive a WAP-request from a mobile device;

2   translates WAP-request into a HTTP form for URL;

3   sends HTTP-request;

4   await for a WML response from an web server;

5   compile and encode received-WML in binary format;

6   send encoded WML response back to mobile;

end

8.5.2 WAP Protocol Stack

The protocol stack for WAP is shown in Fig. 8.20. It consists of several components which include wireless application environment (WAE), session (WSP) and trans-

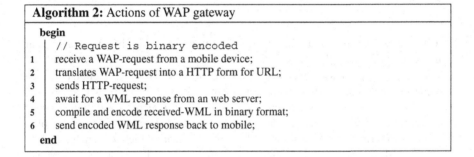

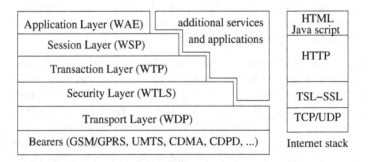

Fig. 8.20 WAP protocol stack

action support (WTP), security (WTL) and data (WDP). At the bottom of the WAP stack, WDP sits on a number of wireless service bearers such as GSM, SMS, CDMA, HSCD, CDPD, HSCD, etc. With respect to OSI reference model, WAE is analogous to Application Layer. WSP, WTP, WTL, and WDP have responsibilities comparable to corresponding layers of OSI reference model as illustrated by Fig. 8.20.

8.5.2.1 Wireless Application Environment

WAE provides environment for a mobile client to interact with web applications through a micro-browser. So the basic elements of WAE are as follows:

- Specification for a micro-browser that controls the user's interface and is able to interpret both WML and WML script.
- Content generators applications, written in WML script, which produces the content formats in response to a specific micro-browser requests.
- Content encoders, such as wireless bitmap, which allow the micro-browser to support color, images, audio, video, phone book, animation, etc.
- Wireless telephony application (WTAI) is basically a collection of extensions for call and feature control mechanisms.

Micro-browser acts as the user agent, and initiates the requests for contents. Apart from the requested contents, additional contents can be generated depending on the capabilities of the mobile device. The device capabilities are inferred from the user agent based on standard negotiation mechanism. This negotiation is performed through WSP mechanism. Three important characteristics exchanged during the negotiation are: versions of WML, WML-script supported, support for image format, and floating-point.

Wirelss Markup Language:

WML is an XML based markup language, designed specifically for wireless handheld devices, optimized for small screens and limited memory capacity. A WML document is called a *deck* and a WML page is called a *card* which is a separate viewable entity and the basic unit of navigation like an HTML page. Sometimes, people try to compare WML entities to HTML entities. But there are a few difference. Each viewable HTML page is represented by a separate HTML file. But a WML deck is represented by a URL address like an HTML page. WML files are stored as static text files on a web server. These files are encoded in binary format by the WAP gateway for onward transmission to a browser by the wireless connection. HTML page undergo no such transformation when transmitted to client. WML browser reads an entire deck of cards at a time. So, while navigating between the cards, the browser does not need any interaction with the web server. This structure is organized by keeping in mind that typically phone users quickly flip through cards before viewing a specific card of their interest. While creating code for a card, WML developer should be aware of the screen boundaries of a phone display. One of the important problem that one has to worry about is that there are many WAP devices of varying screen

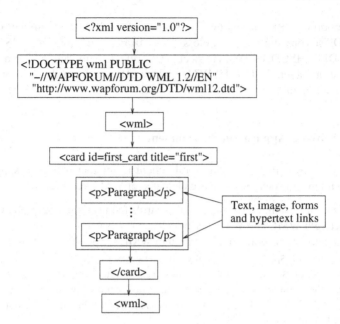

Fig. 8.21 Structure of a WML deck

sizes. Therefore, WML card size needs to be tested at least on a set of few important phones. On the other hand, an HTML developer does not have to worry about screen boundaries, as static devices have sufficiently large screens.

The structure of a WML document or deck is shown in Fig. 8.21. First two lines declare that the document is an XML document and its document type definition (DTD) [41] with its URL. The first line specifies the version number of XML being used. A deck can have many cards, the figure shows only one card. The structure of other cards will be similar. The card may have links to other WML documents, images, and media files. Figure 8.22 illustrates an example of a WML document. Figure 8.22(a) gives the WML file for the page which is displayed in Fig. 8.22(b).

WMLScript:

As explained earlier, WML was created to provide web service accessibility similar to HTML on mobile devices in a resource optimized manner. Dynamic code cannot be written using WML. WMLScript, developed precisely for this purpose, is based on ECMAScript which is a standardized version of JavaScript [42]. However, WMLScripts are not embedded within WML pages, WML pages contains URL links for WMLScripts. So, the WMLScript code is placed in a file separate from WML. The scripts are compiled at the server into byte code before being sent back to clients. They serve the following important functions:

1. Validation of the user's inputs.
2. Accessing functionalities of a user agent.
3. Generation of messages and dialog boxes for alerts, errors.

```
<?xml version="1.0"?>
<!DOCTYPE wml PUBLIC "-//WAPFORUM//DTD WML 1.2//EN"
"http://www.wapforum.org/DTD/wml12.dtd">

<wml>

<card title="Card Example">
<p align="center">
Wirless Networking &amp; Mobile Data Management <br /> Author:  R. K. Ghosh.
</p>
</card>

</wml>
```

(**a**) Source WML document.

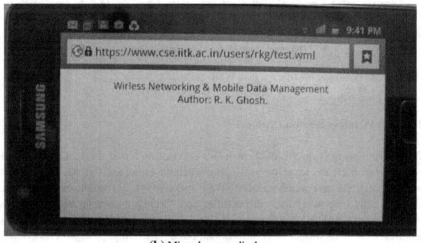

(**b**) Micro-browser display.

Fig. 8.22 Example of a WML deck

4. Seeking confirmation from the user for execution of certain actions. It basically saves a round trip time and bandwidth for giving a response.
5. Extension of WAP devices for accessing device or vendor specific APIs.
6. Addition of conditional logic by downloading procedural logic as required.

Many useful functions are available in standard WMLScript library. The details about using WMLScript library is beyond the scope of this book. However, for the sake of completeness, we just include a small example in Fig. 8.23.

```
<?xml version="1.0"?>
<!DOCTYPE wml PUBLIC "-//WAPFORUM//DTD WML 1.3//EN" "http://www.wapforum.org
/DTD/wml13.dtd">

<wml>
  <card id="card1" title="Using WMLScript">
    <p>
      <a href="bookScript.wmls#bookTitle()">Run WMLScript</a><br/>
      $(message)
    </p>
  </card>
</wml>
```

(a) Source WML document.

```
extern function bookTitle()
{
  WMLBrowser.setVar("message", "Wireless Networking &amp; Mobile Data Management<br>
R. K. Ghosh")
  WMLBrowser.refresh();
}
```

(b) WML script for the deck in Figure 8.22(a).

Fig. 8.23 An equivalent WMLScript for a WML deck

8.5.2.2   Wireless Session Protocol

WSP (Wireless Session Protocol) provides connection based services to the application layer. It creates an active session between the client and the WAP gateway in order to facilitate the content transfers. WSP also enables thin mobile clients to operate efficiently over low bandwidth cellular and wireless communication networks. WSP browsing application is based on HTTP 1.1 standards [38] with some additional features such as mobility of client terminal, binary encoding, push data functionality, service parameter negotiation, session suspend and resume. WSP supports both WDP and WTP. WDP (Wire Datagram Protocol) is a connectionless datagram service, whereas WTP (Wireless Transaction Protocol) is a connection oriented service defined on the top WDP.

8.5.2.3   Wireless Transaction Protocol

WTP operates on the top of unreliable datagram service. Therefore, WTP is built as a transaction or request-response model well suited for the requests for web contents. WTP cannot handle streams. So, TCP based streaming applications such as telnet or SSH cannot be carried over WTP. However, WTP provides reliability on the top of unreliable WDP.

8.5.2.4 Wireless Transport Layer Security

The most important security weakness in WAP can be attributed to use of the WAP gateway. WAP Transport Layer Security (WTLS) used between the WAP gateway and the device. WAP does not specify any security infrastructure for exchanges between a WAP gateway and a web server. After information has been delivered at the WAP gateway, it flows in *clear text* unless a SSL session is established between the WAP gateway and the web server. Even if SSL/TSL is used, the WAP gateway has access to unencrypted data for a brief period of time before it flows out to the web server. So it is the responsibility of the gateway vendors to ensure that no unencrypted data gets stored into the disk, and the memory used by decryption and encryption processes are cleared before the same is handed over to the OS of the machine. WAP gateway should prevent OS from swapping in or swapping out member pages. WAP standards have no explicit specification for the trust that is expected to exist between the mobile device user and the WAP gateway. So, for any sensitive data such as electronic banking transactions, a bank should not rely on a client's default WAP gateway [43].

WTLS security protocol operates above transport layer and is based on TLS. TLS, built over Secure Socket Layer (SSL) which is a widely used security protocol for the Internet applications such as email, online payment systems, etc. WTLS's responsibilities are to ensures data integrity, data confidentiality, authentication and protection against DoS (Denial of Services) attacks. However, the responsibility of WTLS ceases once the communication reaches WAP gateway where wireless network terminates. In a wired environment, a web client and a web server communicate directly. Therefore, end-to-end security could be ensured by SSL session. Over wireless when transaction is made on a mobile phone (client), WTLS first establishes a session between a WAP gateway (server). The security parameters such as encryption protocols, public keys, and other associated long term security associations are negotiated during this handshaking phase. There is also a lightweight handshaking phase where security parameters are not negotiated but these are borrowed from another session. After the session has been established, all communication between client and server are encrypted accordingly. It is possible for a session to last for few days. However, allowing a session to continue for long increases probabilities of attack. So, WTLS allows keys to be also renegotiated during a session. Though WTLS allows use of certificates, it demands storage at mobile nodes and incurs cost for transmission over the wireless interface.

WAP also provisions for a tamper-proof device called Wireless Identity Module (WIM). WIM is an WAP equivalent of SIM in GSM. It provides private and public keys to perform digital signature and verification of security certificates.

8.5.2.5 Wireless Datagram Protocol

WDP (Wireless Datagram Protocol) is the basic elements of the WAP transport layer. It specifies how the existing data transport services should be used to deliver data to the upper layers. WDP is an adaptive datagram service, and supports different bearer services. For example, if IP bearer is used then WDP protocol adapts UDP, while for SMS bearer it specifies mandatory use of source and destination port numbers. All the details are hidden from the upper layer which see WDP as the only consistent vehicle for data transport. Therefore, WTLS can operate in a consistent manner over WDP.

References

1. C.E. Perkins, in *Mobile IP Design Principles and Practice* (Pearson Education, 1998)
2. J. Postel, Transmission control protocol, https://tools.ietf.org/html/rfc793. September 1981 (RFC 793)
3. T. Ylonen, C. Lonvick, The secure shell (SSH) connection protocol, https://tools.ietf.org/html/ rfc4254. January 2006 (RFC-4254)
4. K. Winstein, H. Balakrishnan, Mosh: an interactive remote shell for mobile clients, in *2012 USENIX Annual Technical Conference* (Sunny Boston, Mass., USA) pp. 171–182, 13–15 June 2012
5. O.M. Alliance, Wireless application protocol architecture specification, http://technical. openmobilealliance.org/affiliates/wap/wap-210-waparch-20010712-a.pdf. 12 July 2001
6. The Statista Portal. Number of smartphone users worldwide from 2014 to 2020 (in billions), https://www.statista.com/statistics/330695/number-of-smartphone-users-worldwide/. Accessed 27 Dec 2016
7. G. Martin, H. Chang, System-on-chip design, in *ASICON 2001, 4th International Conference on ASIC Proceedings* (2001), pp. 12–17
8. F. Engel, I. Kuz, S.M. Petters, S. Ruocco, Operating systems on SOCS: a good idea? in *25th IEEE International Real-Time Systems Symposium (RTSS 2004)*, pp. 5–8
9. H. Falaki, R. Mahajan, S. Kandula, D. Lymberopoulos, R. Govindan, D. Estrin, Diversity in smartphone usage, in *Proceedings of the 8th International Conference on Mobile Systems, Applications, and Services* (ACM, 2010), pp. 179–194
10. C. Shin, J.-H. Hong, A.K. Dey, Understanding and prediction of mobile application usage for smart phones. in *Proceedings of the 2012 ACM Conference on Ubiquitous Computing* (ACM, 2012), pp. 173–182
11. T.M.T. Do, J. Blom, D. Gatica-Perez, Smartphone usage in the wild: a large-scale analysis of applications and context, in *Proceedings of the 13th International Conference on Multimodal Interfaces* (ACM, 2011), pp. 353–360
12. A. Rahmati, L. Zhong, Studying smartphone usage: lessons from a four-month field study. IEEE Trans. Mob. Comput. **12**(7), 1417–1427 (2013)
13. The eLinux Community Portal. Android kernel features (2015), http://elinux.org/Android_ Kernel_Features. Accessed 28 Dec 2016
14. F. Maker, Y.-H. Chan, A survey on android vs. linux. Technical report, University of California, 2009
15. H. Shacham, M. Page, B. Pfaff, E.-J. Goh, N. Modadugu, D. Boneh, On the effectiveness of address-space randomization, in *Proceedings of the 11th ACM Conference on Computer and Communications Security* (ACM, 2004), pp. 298–307
16. H. Bojinov, D. Boneh, R. Cannings, I. Malchev, Address space randomization for mobile devices, in *Proceedings of the Fourth ACM Conference on Wireless Network Security* (ACM, 2011), WiSec'11, pp. 127–138
17. H. Lockheimer, Android and security, google mobile blog (2012), http://googlemobile. blogspot.fr/2012/02/android-and-security.html. Accessed 27 Dec 2016
18. Neal Leavitt, Mobile phones: the next frontier for hackers? IEEE Comput. **38**(4), 20–23 (2005)

19. B. Morris, in *The Symbian OS Architecture Sourcebook: Design and Solution of a Mobile Phone OS* (John Wiley & Sons, 2007)

20. Community Editors, Android version history (2016), https://en.wikipedia.org/wiki/Android_version_history. Accessed 28 Dec 2016

21. I. Lunden, Nokia confirms the pureview was officially the last symbian phone, https://techcrunch.com/2013/01/24/nokia-confirms-the-pure-view-was-officially-the-last-symbian-phone/. January 2013. Accessed 27 Dec 2016

22. The Statista Portal. Global mobile OS market share in sales to end users from 1st quarter 2009 to 1st quarter 2016 (2016), https://www.statista.com/statistics/266136/global-market-share-held-by-smartphone-operating-systems/. Accessed 27 Dec 2016

23. I. Dalmasso, S.K. Datta, C. Bonnet, N. Nikaein, Survey, comparison and evaluation of cross platform mobile application development tools, in *9th International Wireless Communications and Mobile Computing Conference (IWCMC)* (IEEE, 2013), pp. 323–328

24. The Rohmobile Community Portal. Rohmobile suite documentation, http://docs.rhomobile.com/en/5.4/home. Accessed 28 Dec 2016

25. The Wikipedia Community Portal. Appcelerator titanium, https://en.wikipedia.org/wiki/Appcelerator_Titanium. Accessed 28 Dec 2016

26. The Wikipedia Community Portal. Apache cordova, https://en.wikipedia.org/wiki/Apache_Cordova. Accessed 28 Dec 2016

27. R. Droms. Dynamic host configuration protocol (1997), https://tools.ietf.org/html/rfc2131 (RFC 2131)

28. S. Deering (ed.), The author team of RFC-1256. ICMP router discovery messages, http://www.ietf.org/rfc/rfc1256.txt. September 1991 (RFC-1256)

29. C. Perkins, Minimal encapsulation within IP, http://tools.ietf.org/html/rfc2004. October 1996 (RFC-2004)

30. V. Jacobson. Compressing TCP/IP headers for low-speed serial links, https://tools.ietf.org/html/rfc1144. February 1990 (RFC-1144)

31. W. Simpson, IP in IP tunneling (1995), https://tools.ietf.org/html/rfc1853 (RFC 1853)

32. C. Perkins, IP encapsulation within IP (1996), http://tools.ietf.org/html/rfc2003 (RFC-2003)

33. G.E. Montenegro, Reverse tunneling for mobile IP, revised (2001), https://tools.ietf.org/html/rfc3024 (RFC 3024)

34. G. Bhaskara, A. Helmy, TCP over micro mobility protocols: a systematic ripple effect analysis, in *IEEE 60th Vehicular Technology Conference, VTC2004-Fall*, vol. 5 (IEEE, 2004), pp. 3095–3099

35. T. Krovetz, P. Rogaway, The software performance of authenticated-encryption modes, in *The 18th International Conference on Fast Software Encryption, 2011 (FSE 2011)*, pp. 306–327

36. Ted Krovetz and Phillip Rogaway. The OCB authenticated-encryption algorithm (2014), https://tools.ietf.org/html/rfc7253

37. O.M. Alliance, Technical_wap2_0_20021106 (2002), http://technical.openmobilealliance.org/Technical/technical-information/material-from-affiliates/wap-forum#previous

38. R. Fielding, J. Gettys, J. Mogul, H. Frystyk, L. Masinter, P. Leach, T. Berners-Lee, Hypertext transfer protocol-HTTP/1.1, https://www.ietf.org/rfc/rfc2616.txt. June 1999 (RFC-2616)

39. Tim Berners-Lee and Team of Contributors of HTML. Html living standard (2016), https://whatwg.org/pdf

40. Wireless Application Protocol Forum. Wireless application protocol wireless markup language specification (2000), http://technical.openmobilealliance.org/tech/affiliates/wap/wap-238-wml-20010911-a.pdf (Version 1.3)

41. World Wide Web Consortium et al., Html 4.01 specification (1999)

42. A. Rauschmayer, in *Speaking JavaScript: An In-depth Guide for Progammers* (O'Reilly, 2014)

43. D. Singelée, B. Preneel, The wireless application protocol (WAP). Cosic Internet Report (2003)

Part II
Mobile Data Management

Part II of the book deals with Mobile Data Management. It consists of eight chapters. There was a slight dilemma in deciding whether the contents of Chap. 9 can be strictly classified as under mobile data management issues. Apart from sensor fusion, Chap. 9 deals with two network related issues in WSNs namely, routing and integration with IP. We justify the decision to classify this chapter under mobile data management due to following reasons:

- Sensor nodes unlike IP based nodes are data centric.
- Many existing deployments of WSNs interoperate with IP network through specialized sensor gateways which require middlewares for IP integration.
- Sensor fusion techniques fall strictly in realm of data management issues.

Chapter 10 deals with location management issues. It addresses both terminal and personal mobilities. Tracking personal mobility is modeled through a random process quantifiable in terms of infromation entropy. Tracking terminal mobility requires support of a location database. The focus here is primarily on how location database should be organized to optimize tracking. In Chap. 11 of the book, the issues related to design of algorithms in mobile distributed environment have been discussed. We examine some generic issues like relocation of computation, synchronization and coordination in the context of general strategies for design of algorithms for MDS environment specially with a view to optimize messages over wireless channels. In Chap. 12, our focus is on data dissemination in a mobile distributed environment. The basic idea discussed here is to treat the medium of air as a storage medium. By provisioning for caching at both client and server sides, a multi level memory hierarchy is defined for push based data delivery systems. Chapter 13 is concerned with mixing of index information with broadcast data. It explains clever mapping of conventional indexing into strictly a sequential medium. Through partial replication of indexing information with data it is possible to perform random access on a sequential medium like air. Chapter 14 is concerned with caching and replication issues in mobile environments. It considers mobility of end nodes and new application semantics in use of caching and replication strategies in mobile environment. Chapter 15 deals with mechansims for sharing of data in mobile distributed systems. Three different mechansims, namely, distribute objects, replicated storage system, and file system have been described. But the main focus of the chapter is on CODA file systems, as it addresses a range of network outages typically experienced by a mobile node due to intermittent network connectivity. Chapter 16 deals with the role context aware computing in building smart environments. We do not confine ourselves specifically to any smart environment. Our idea is to make the reader aware of the issues around building smart environment.

Chapter 9
Data Centric Routing, Interoperability and Fusion in WSN

9.1 Introduction

Wireless sensor networks (WSNs) are mostly used for sensing and gathering data from environment on a continuous basis. The gathered data may pertain to various events related to monitoring and controlling applications such as:

- Environmental conditions,
- Vital parameters of patients,
- Movement and migration of habitats.
- Pest attacks on crops,
- Radiation levels in nuclear plant,
- Deep sea navigation,
- Seismic activities,
- Electronic surveillance, etc.

Accurate detection of specific events and monitoring of the events for the intervals of occurrences could be critical to implementation of certain functionalities of smart devices (smart phone, house hold appliances, or IoTs [1]). Furthermore, in response to these events, the behaviors of "things" or the devices must change in expected ways. The actuation of a specific behavior in a device is made possible through two important preparatory stages related to gathering of actuation data:

1. Dissemination of queries to sensors.
2. Collection of observed data from sensor nodes.

There are also passive monitoring applications, where the query dissemination is unimportant. Data collected through passive monitoring generally are collated by human experts and the actuation process is set in motion on the basis of a decision support system used by the human experts. So, it makes sense to consider the above two activities as parts of overall data gathering process using WSNs. Many sensors may report similar observations when they are in close proximity. The flow of redundant data generates unnecessary network traffic and affects performance. A smart

© Springer Nature Singapore Pte Ltd. 2017 265
R.K. Ghosh, *Wireless Networking and Mobile Data Management*,
DOI 10.1007/978-981-10-3941-6_9

approach would be to fuse the data in some way to reduce the network traffic, and yet not lose any significant observation. As far as query dissemination is concerned, one idea could be to spread a query from the data sinks assuming bi-directional links. However, random spreading of queries may lead to congestion in WSN network due to redundant traffic. On the other hand, unicasting queries to the targeted nodes is not possible due to absence of node addressing mechanism for WSNs.

In Chap. 6, the focus was on ZigBee, 6LoWPAN and ZigBee IP protocols for low power wireless communication. These network protocols define IPv6 based standards for internetworking large number of sensors and connecting them to the Internet. Yet most of the existing WSN deployments, do not support any addressing mechanism for individual nodes. Any discussion on WSNs and their importance in realization of IoTs and smart environments remains incomplete without an understanding of the operational details concerning data gathering by WSNs. Therefore, in this chapter the focus of our discussion will be on the following four interrelated issues concerning data collection by WSNs:

1. Architecture of WSN.
2. Routing in WSN.
3. Integrating IP and WSN.
4. Data fusion in WSN.

9.2 Characteristics of WSN

Two of the most important technical limitations that distinguish the operations of WSNs from other network of computing devices as explained earlier are:

1. Lack of IP based addressing mechanism.
2. Resource scarcity at nodes, particularly the stored energy.

A WSN is a data centric network unlike Mobile Ad hoc NETwork (MANET). It is not possible to send a query to a specific sensor node. However, a query can be disseminated to sensor nodes for reporting values of a attribute or a class of attributes of the observed data. It is also possible to restrict dissemination of queries to a selected bunch of sensor nodes in close proximity to a location, or a region. Energy is a major resource bottleneck for continuous operation of WSN. Generally, it is assumed that the power consumption is mainly due to the operations of the radio interface [2–4]. Therefore, excessive attention has been placed in developing energy aware communication protocols.

Power consumption due to sensing module of a sensor node is generally ignored. However, emissions of toxic gases are measured in units of voltage levels. For accuracy in measurements, voltage levels are allowed to settle down for a while. Consequently, the sensing modules may consume comparatively more energy than the radio interfaces depending on the type of sensors being deployed. For example, NO_2, or VOC (Volatile Organic Compounds) sensors may at times can account for about

2/3rd of total energy consumption [5]. The application developers, therefore, have to understand the specification of a sensor in order to develop efficient code for sensor specific power control mechanisms. Kim et al. [5] developed an automated Power Management System (PMS) on the top of RETOS [6] operating system for sensor nodes . Following similar approaches, it may be possible to build PMS for many other types of sensor nodes. However, the utility of PMS may become obsolete with newer approaches based on the concept of energy packetization generally used in smart grid [7, 8]. The approach combines the transfer of power units with the communication from one source to another. So, the communication can still be carried out even when the intermediate nodes are about to die out. Novel energy aware routing schemes based on energy distribution through packetization can be developed in future for transmission of sensory data.

In summary, the following are some of the important characteristics of WSN which we need to keep in mind while dealing with WSNs:

1. Highly distributed architecture of WSNs.
2. Nodes in a WSN operate autonomously with very little local coordination.
3. Nodes in a WSN do not have any global addressing mechanism like IP, the communication is carried out in data centric mode.
4. Energy consumption is a major design consideration in operation of sensor nodes. So, communication and data processing must be performed in energy efficient manner.
5. Scalability of WSN depends on the density of the nodes per unit area.

9.2.1 WSN Versus MANET

An ad hoc network like a WSN is also a self organized wireless network of autonomous nodes which depend on battery. But the similarity between the two ends there. Sensor nodes are mostly static while the nodes in an ad hoc network are mobile. An ad hoc network is address centric and each node has a global IP address. Ad hoc nodes are represented by PDAs and handheld devices carried by the users who happen to be human. In contrast, sensor nodes are not carried by people. These nodes mostly are deployed in different environments some of which could be inaccessible. The number of nodes in a sensor network is several orders higher in magnitude than the number of nodes in a mobile ad hoc network. The sensors collect data objects of all kinds, related to both animate and inanimate things belonging to an environment. A node in ad hoc network in more powerful has more resources compared any sensor node. The routing protocols for mobile ad hoc network function

Table 9.1 Ad hoc network versus sensor network

Property	Ad hoc network	Sensor network
Hardware	Ad hoc nodes use the state of the art processors, and have reasonably better resources	Sensor nodes are cheap and have lower computing and communication capabilities
Deployment	Deployment is sparse. Depends on the number of active users in the area	Dense unattended deployment with large number of nodes. Typically many orders higher in magnitude than ad hoc network
Topology	Highly dynamic	May vary due to the variation in wireless signals but mostly static
Mobility	Ad hoc nodes are mobile	Sensor nodes are usually static unless mounted on vehicles, or worn by living beings
Routing	Address centric, each node has an IP address. Operate at IP layer	Data centric, operate at MAC layer
Energy	Uses stored battery power, but battery can be changed or recharged	Nodes operate in tighter power budget. Being deployed in unattended inaccessible places, battery change or charging is usually impossible
QoS	QoS is driven by the requirements to minimize network traffic	QoS is driven by the requirements to minimize energy
Applications	Distributed computing	Monitoring and data gathering

at network layer and require significant amount of resources whereas the routing in WSN typically function at MAC layer. Table 9.1 summarizes the differences.

9.3 Architecture of WSN

Building of tiny devices such as a sensor node was possible due to advances in Micro Electro-Mechanical Systems (MEMS) [9]. By inter-networking hundreds or thousands of sensors, a WSN is created. To give a background, let us begin with architecture of a sensor node.

At a very basic level, a sensor node as shown by the block diagram in Fig. 9.1 consists of three components:

1. A battery or power source,
2. A processor board with CPU, memory and sensing hardware,
3. A radio board with transceiver, which is connected by an antenna.

Fig. 9.1 Components of a
sensor node

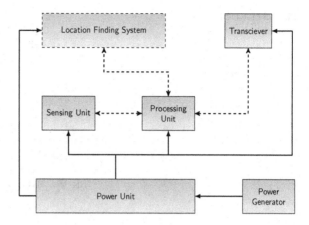

As the figure illustrates, the processor board connects CPU with sensing h/w and
a small flash memory. There is a wireless transceiver which implements the physical
and MAC layers, and connected to a radio antenna. Sensor nodes runs one of the
many variants of OSes [10]. Among these, Tiny OS [11] and Contiki [12] are popular
among the implementers.

9.3.1 Communication Architecture

The protocol level details and the communication architecture of sensor node were
discussed earlier in Chap. 6 in context of ZigBee and 6LoWPAN. For the sake of completeness in discussion, we provide a logical view of communication architecture in
Fig. 9.2. The network layer located in sensor board is responsible for routing, topology control, in-network data processing, data dissemination, storage and caching.

Fig. 9.2 Communication
architecture of sensor node

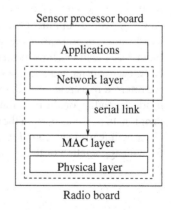

Fig. 9.3 Layered
organization of sensor node

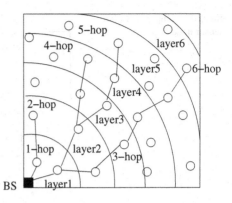

The MAC layer and the PHY layer are located on the radio board. The responsibilities of PHY layer include radio communication, access to sensing hardware, controlling actuation circuit, and signal processing hardware. The MAC layer is primarily responsible for sleep and wake up scheduling, and channel access schemes.

9.3.2   Network Organization

WSN use two basic type of organizations for data communication.

1. Layering,
2. Clustering.

Mostly the nodes are homogeneous and assumed to have a fixed communication range. Assume that sensor nodes are distributed in a rectangular region as shown in Fig. 9.3 with the base station (BS) being located at the left bottom corner of rectangle. In layering organization, the nodes 1-hop away from BS form layer-1, the nodes 2-hop away form layer-2 and so on as indicated in the diagram. The problem of funneling is quite common in a layered organization. It happens due to the fact that the nodes closer to BS die out must faster compared to the nodes at the periphery of network.

Clustered organization was proposed primarily to eliminate funneling problem. Figure 9.4 illustrates how clustered organization communicate data to the BS. Basically, each cluster head act as an intermediate data sink for the nearby nodes which are referred to as regular nodes. A network may have about 5–10% nodes as cluster heads depending on the requirements. Cluster heads may in turn form a layered organization. In practice, most of the cluster network topologies are two tiered, though it is also possible to create complex hierarchical topologies. Cluster heads are responsible for data aggregation of their respective clusters before data gets routed to BS.

Fig. 9.4 Clustered
organization of sensor node

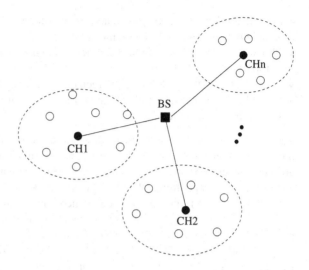

9.4 Routing in Sensor Network

Let us first examine some of the basic characteristics of sensor networks which influence design of routing protocols. One of the important difference from IP networks is addressing of the sensor nodes. Typically, hundreds and thousands of sensor nodes form a WSN. The nodes have to establish connectivity irrespective of distribution of nodes in the network. Most applications do not care about the node IDs from which data is received but are interested only in observed data from certain locations.

Mostly the sensor nodes are static. As opposed to this in conventional IP networks, the nodes may have slow discrete movements. In most cases, a sensor network is deployed to serve only one specific application. Knowing geographic positions (latitude, longitude) of a node is advantageous in some applications as the observed data can be meaningfully associated with a specific geographical area. However, using GPS hardware in a node is infeasible due to following reasons:

- GPS does not work indoors, it may not even work in dense jungle, construction sites or deep canyons.
- GPS operation requires some power. Energy drain out occurs comparatively faster when GPS hardware is integrated with a sensor node.
- Integrating GPS with sensor node also increases the cost of sensor nodes.

Therefore, localization (determining position) of nodes is performed through various geometric and approximate method based on the idea of trilateration [13]. Trilateration methods are not only compute-intensive but also error prone. Observed data exhibit certain amount of locality. So, there may be a fair amount of redundancy in data flowing into base station. Eliminating redundancy in data flow could extend the life of the network. Considering the inherent characteristics of WSNs in mind, the design of routing protocols

- Should not depend on any global addressing schemes like IP.
- Should balance energy levels of the nodes.
- Should be able to handle sudden failures of the nodes, and unpredictable changes in topology.
- Should work without GPS or any precision positioning system.
- Should be power aware and minimize redundant information flow by applying various data fusion techniques.

Lack of global addressing mechanism is not a big problem, as a WSN is more a data centric than a node centric network. The information is requested based on the attribute values. For example, suppose we have a deployment of sensors to measure environmental temperature. Then the query may be of the form: "Is temperature is above $50\,^{\circ}$C?" Then, only those nodes which have measured value $v > 50$ should report their measurements. The discovery and maintenance of routes in a WSN are nontrivial problems. This is due to the fact that WSNs have to operate with low energy budgets. Some nodes may die out quickly if network traffic is not uniformly shared by all the nodes. Even without GPS, locations can be prestored in the nodes before deployment, or locations can be estimated after the deployment by using trilateration techniques. So, the position information of the nodes can be used to route the data to the desired region rather than flooding into the whole network.

9.4.1   Classification of Routing Protocols

One of the excellent surveys on the routing protocols in sensor networks is made by Al-Karaki and Kamal [14]. There are several ways to classify the routing protocols. One classification scheme based on the network structure classifies the protocols into three classes, namely,

1. Flat-network based routing.
2. Hierarchic-network based routing.
3. Location-based routing.

In a flat network structure, every node is equal in status, and perform the same set of operations. In hierarchical network structure, the nodes have an implicit difference in roles and perform operations according to their assigned roles. In location based routing, the nodes exploit positional advantage to guide data to flow in and out of the selected region in the network. Some routing protocols can adapt to the changing network conditions such as topology change, change in energy level of nodes, etc.

Another way to classify routing protocols is based on the operation of protocols. It defines five different types of protocols, namely,

1. Negotiation based routing.
2. Mutilate based routing.
3. Query based routing.
4. QoS based routing.

5. Coherent based routing.

To give a flavor of various routing protocols, we plan to discuss only a few well known protocols. The readers who are interested to explore more, may refer to the original survey paper by Al-Karaki and Kamal [14].

9.5 Flat Network Based Routing

In this class of routing algorithm, every node has the same role, and they cooperate together to distribute data over the entire network. Typically, in such networks, the base station sends out queries for data either from a selected region or on the basis of certain attributes and waits for the same to arrive. Each sensor having data matching to a query responds. To facilitate the responses, each query should contain an accurate description of the needed data. A number of data centric routing protocols exist in literature. It is neither possible nor the focus of this book to discuss all the routing protocols. A short summary of SPIN [15] is provided as it is one of the earliest work in the area which focuses on energy saving issues.

SPIN (Sensor Protocol for Information via Negotiation) was proposed by Heinzelman et al. [15]. It belongs to a family of adaptive routing protocols. SPIN treats each node as a potential base station or data sink. So, any node may be queried to obtain all information about gathered data. Basically, the approach is to eliminate three common problems noticed in most sensor routing protocols:

- *Implosion*: The nodes in classical routing algorithms work by flooding, i.e., sending data to all the neighbors. It leads to the same data being received by a node multiple number of times as shown in Fig. 9.5(a). Node E receives data item d multiple number of times.
- *Overlap*: The data from the same overlap region arrives via different paths which results in increases in network traffic and leads to the wastage of bandwidth, and the energy. This problem is illustrated by Fig. 9.5(b). Node C receives overlapping data $d1$ and $d2$ multiple number of times.
- *Resource blindness*: No node cuts down its activities, even if the energy level is low. Since the nodes operate with pre-stored power resources, cutting down activities of the nodes with low energy level helps to extend the overall network lifetime.

SPIN is based on two main ideas, namely

1. Negotiation, and
2. Resource-adaptation.

SPIN uses negotiation before sending data. It uses principle of locality to control data dissemination. The underlying idea is that the nodes in same neighborhood most likely have similar data. So, each node should only distribute those data which other nodes do not have. A node on receiving new data broadcasts the meta data in the form of advertisements (ADV messages) to the neighborhood in the first stage. Meta

Fig. 9.5 Implosion and
overlap problems

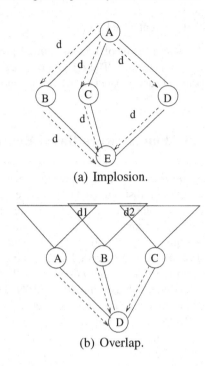

(a) Implosion.

(b) Overlap.

data is a short synopsis of data which the node possesses. SPIN does not specify the format of the meta data, the format is decided by the application developers. However, the guiding principles for the creation of meta data are:

1. The meta data descriptors of distinguishable data are also distinguishable.
2. Likewise the meta data descriptors of the non-distinguishable data are also non-distinguishable.

The nodes which receive ADV messages (meta data) check whether they have the corresponding data. If not, then they send out request (REQ messages) for the advertised data. On receiving REQ message, the advertising node sends DATA to the requesting node. The same three stage process {ADV, REQ and DATA} of data dissemination repeated at a new node. This way the data propagates throughout the whole network. Each node also has a resource manager to monitor its current level of resources. Before processing or transmitting data, the application needs to check resource level by querying the resource manager. Depending on energy threshold, the node may reduce its participation in the protocol. A node may participate if it can be sure of completing the three stage distribution process.

Fig. 9.6 Funneling effect in WSN

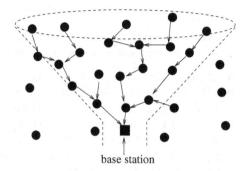

base station

9.5.1 Hierarchical Routing Protocols

Hierarchical routing protocols defines two separate roles for the sensor nodes, viz., cluster heads and regular nodes. The idea of having certain nodes to perform the roles of cluster heads is mainly to eliminate funneling effect on nodes near the base station (BS). Figure 9.6 illustrates funneling effect. It occurs due to the fact that in multihop routings, energy drains out faster from the nodes near the BS than the nodes at the periphery. Since, the drain out of energy is not evenly distributed among the nodes, some of the nodes end up with shorter lifetime than the others. To mitigate the funneling effect the concept of 2-tier routing was proposed [16]. The role of cluster heads is assigned to nodes with higher energy levels. The nodes having lower energy levels, perform sensing and send the observations to a cluster head in proximity. A cluster head, typically, performs data aggregation/fusion. It reduces the number of messages needed to transmit the data pertaining to observations made by a set of sensors deployed in a region. Apart from mitigating funneling effect, the 2-tier routing protocols also contribute to the overall efficiency, the scalability and extending the lifetime of a network [14].

Low Energy Adaptive Cluster Hierarchy (LEACH) [16] is an example of two-tier routing algorithm. It uses a randomized rotation approach to assign the roles of cluster heads to the sensor nodes so that the battery of no particular sensor node drains out faster than the others. LEACH also applies compression of data by fusion technique to optimize the volume of data transmission from the cluster heads to the base station.

The cluster heads are elected from among the regular nodes. The number of cluster heads is determined in advance. It depends on a number of network parameters such as topology, relative costs of computation versus communications [16]. A node n chooses a random value v, where $0 < v < 1$. If $v < T(n)$, then the node becomes cluster head for the current round r. The threshold $T(n)$ is defined as follows:

$$T(n) = \begin{cases} \dfrac{P}{1 - P * (r \mod \frac{1}{P})}, & \text{if } n \in G \\ 0, & \text{otherwise} \end{cases}$$

where,

P is the desired percentage of cluster heads in the network, and
G is the set of nodes that have not been cluster heads in the last $\frac{1}{P}$ rounds.

For example, if 5% nodes are to be assigned the role of cluster heads then $P = 0.05$. Initially, $r = 0$, and each node has the probability P to become a cluster head. Once a node becomes a cluster head then it cannot become a cluster head for subsequent $\frac{1}{P} = 20$ rounds. The nodes which were cluster heads for round number r, become eligible for cluster head role in $r + \frac{1}{20}$ round.

The cluster heads broadcast an advertisement offering data aggregation service to the rest of the other nodes. The cluster heads use CSMA MAC protocol for the advertisement using the same transmit energy. The regular nodes should be in listen mode during this phase of the algorithm. Once the first phase is over, the regular nodes will know which cluster they belong to. This decision will be based on the RSSI of advertisement messages from the various cluster heads. The nodes then send their leader acceptance message to their respective cluster heads. Again CSMA MAC protocol is used for this transmission. During this phase the cluster heads must keep their receivers on.

Based on the received acceptance messages, each cluster head creates a TDMA schedule for receiving transmission from its cluster members. This schedule is broadcast back to the members. After the transmission schedule has been decided, transmission begins. Each node sends it data during its allocated transmission schedule. To receive the transmission the cluster head must keep its receiver on. After all transmissions are received, each cluster head applies compression and fusion techniques to create a consolidated message for the data received from the region under it. In the last phase of a round, a cluster head sends the report about the data pertaining to its region to the base station. Since the base station may be located far away from a cluster head, this is high energy transmission phase. The important conclusions from LEACH experimentation are as follows [16]:

1. LEACH cuts down the requirement for communication energy by a factor of 8 compared to direct transmission protocol.
2. The first death in network occurs 8× times later.
3. The last death in network occurs 3× times later.

9.5.2   Location Based Routing Protocols

Location of a node is the fundamental element of information used by this class of routing algorithms. The relative positions of the source and the destination provides a sense of direction in which the data should flow thereby restricting the flooding. The localization or the estimation of the positions of nodes is a one time task as the sensor nodes are mostly static. There are many GPS less localization algorithms that can estimate locations of the nodes by exchanging information between neighbors [13,

17–19]. Most of the algorithms in this category apart from restricting flooding also prescribe a sleep and wake up schedule for the nodes in order to save energy [20, 21]. Some of the location-based algorithms were developed for mobile ad hoc networks [20, 21], but are also applicable to sensor networks.

As an example, we discuss Geographical and Energy Aware Routing (GEAR) [22], which is motivated by the fact that most of the time the queries for data are location (region) related. In other words, a query packet is routed to a set of nodes (forming a region or a neighborhood) instead of a single node. It assumes every node is aware of its current location.

GEAR relies on recursive dissemination of a query, and considers energy level in nodes while selecting neighbor for forwarding the queries. There are two phases in the process to disseminate a query to a targeted region of a network, namely,

Phase 1: It uses energy aware neighbor selection to push the query to the target region.

Phase 2: Inside the target region, it uses two different rules to forward the query to the destination.

In the first phase while packets are pushed towards the target region, the residual levels of energy is considered.

- If there is a node closer to the target region than the query forwarding node, then the query is forwarded to all such nodes.
- Otherwise, the distance is also used in combination with the energy to get around an energy hole.

In the second phase, the query gets disseminated inside the target region. Either a recursive geographic forwarding, or a restrictive flooding is used. The recursive geographic forwarding works as follows. A node N_i receiving the query creates four sub regions. Then it creates four copies of the query and sends one copy to each of these four sub regions. The recursive query dissemination is carried out until the farthest point of the region is within the direct range of the forwarder but none of the neighbors are within the region. However, the recursive splitting may be expensive when the density of sensors is low. Additionally also it may create routing loops. So in this case pure geographical distance metric is used for efficiency.

The most important idea that can be termed as the main operating logic of the protocol is computation of the energy aware neighbor. The centroid of the target zone R is considered as the logical destination location D. On receiving a packet, a node N sends the packet progressively towards the target region while balancing the energy consumption across all the neighbors.

Each node N maintains a cost $lc(N, R)$, known as learned cost, from zone R. N infrequently updates $lc(N, R)$ to its neighbors. If a node does not have $lc(N_i, R)$ for a neighbor N_i, then it estimates a cost $ec(N_i, R)$, given below, as a default value for $lc(N_i, R)$.

$$ec(N_i, R) = \alpha d(N_i, R) + (1 - \alpha)e(N_i)$$

where,

1. α is an adjustable value in range (0, 1),
2. $d(N_i, R)$ is distance of N_i from centroid D of region R, and
3. $e(N_i)$ is the consumed energy at node N_i normalized by the maximum energy consumed across all the neighbors.

Once a node N has selected a neighbor N_s, it updates its own energy status as follows:

$$lc(N, R) = lc(N_s, R) + C(N, N_s),$$

where $C(N, N_s)$ is the energy consumed for sending a packet on link (N, N_s). $C(N, N_s)$ is a function of residual energy levels at N_s and N and the distance between N and N_s.

A discerning reader will notice that ec is a weighted sum of distance of a neighbor from the target region, and the normalized consumed energy at the neighbors. The estimated function, ec, is basically derived from an obvious considerations of the energy drain out principle. It is borne out from following two significant observations:

- In circumstance where all the neighbors have same level of residual energy, the value of ec depends on distance from the target region. Consequently, it amounts to selection of the neighbor using a greedy approach, where the node closer to the target region becomes the automatic choice.
- If, on the other hand, all the neighbors are at the same distance from the target region, the choice is dependent on the local minimization, which is essentially a load balancing strategy.

9.5.3   Selection of Forwarding Neighbor

Having understood the cost functions, let us find how selection of forwarding neighbor is carried out. Two possible scenarios that need to be examined are:

1. Each packet P carries ID of the target region R. If there are neighbors close to R, then a neighbor having minimum $lc(N_i, R)$ value will be picked up for forwarding. So, P will be routed progressively closer to R while balancing energy usage.
2. If all neighbors are far away from N itself, then N is said to be in a hole. When there is no hole the learned cost $lc(N_i, R)$ and the estimated cost $ec(N_i, R)$ are the same. If there is a hole, then the learned cost and the update rule help to avoid the holes in the path to destination.

To see how it works, we consider the example quoted in the original paper [22]. Figure 9.7 illustrates a grid deployment where three nodes marked G, H and I have no residual energy to participate in forwarding. The target node is T and packet originated from S. Assume that grid nodes are placed at equal distance from its east,

Fig. 9.7 Geographical forwarding in a grid deployment [22]

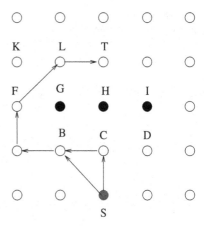

west, north and south neighbors. Without loss of generality, we may assume these distances to be one unit each. The grid layout imply each node has 8 neighbors: east, north-east, north, north-west, west, south-west, south, south-east.

Initially, at time 0, learned costs and estimated cost will be same.

$$lc(S, T) = 3, lc(B, T) = ec(B, T) = \sqrt{5}$$
$$lc(C, T) = ec(C, T) = 2, \quad lc(D, T) = ec(D, T) = \sqrt{5}$$

On receiving a packet P, S forwards it to the lowest cost neighbor, i.e., C. But C finds itself in a hole as all of its neighbors are a larger distance than itself. So, C forwards it to the neighbor N with minimum $lc(N, T)$. If ties occur, then they are broken by node ID. This implies among the neighbors C will pick B, and update its learned cost

$$lc(C, T) = lc(B, T) + C(C, B) = \sqrt{5} + 1$$

At time 2, when node S receives another packet P' for same region T, the values of learned cost for B, C and D are as follows:

$$lc(B, T) = \sqrt{5}, lc(C, T) = \sqrt{5} + 1, \text{ and } lc(D, T) = \sqrt{5}$$

So, S has a choice to forward P' to B or D, but B's ID is lower than D. Therefore, S will forward P' to B instead of C. In actual execution of the algorithm, packet forwarding from S will oscillate between C and B. Once a packet is delivered to T, the learned cost (LC) value will be propagated 1 hop back, and every time a packet is successfully delivered LC-value will be propagated 1 hop back, and finally it will converge after delivery of n packets if distance from S to T is n hops. Intuitively, LC-value together with update rule assist the scheme to avoid holes. For further details in this regard, the readers may refer to [22].

Fig. 9.8 Recursive
geographical forwarding [22]

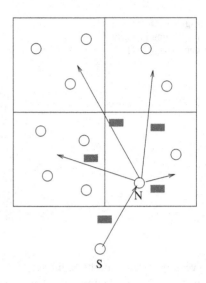

After a packet *P* reaches the target region *R* it can use simple flooding with duplicate suppression method to guide the packet to actual destination. A recursive forwarding method has been proposed in LEACH to control flood. Since, packets are forwarded to the centroid of target region *R*, the bounding box of *R* can be split into one subregions as illustrated in Fig. 9.8, and one copy of packet *P* is sent to the centroid of each of the subregion recursively. The recursive forwarding is continued until the stopping condition is met. The stopping criterion is met when either a region has no other node in its subregion. To determine the stopping condition we check if the farthest point of the region is within the range of the node but none of its neighbors are inside the region.

9.6   Routing Based on Protocol Operation

The set of routing protocols we will discuss in this section are based on characteristics of operation of protocols. A protocol may be of three types:

1. Multipath based routing.
2. Query based routing.
3. Negotiation based routing.

Multipath routing uses multiple paths to a destination. This category of routing protocols enhance the network performance and are resilience to failure of the links. In query based routing, source nodes propagate the query for fetching the data. The nodes having matching data send replies back to the node that initiated the query. In negotiation based protocols, the routes are obtained through negotiation based on the QoS metrics such as delay, energy or bandwidth, etc. The main advantage of a negotiation based routing protocols is that it eliminates redundant transmissions of data which is specially important for a resource poor networks. Let us have a closer look at some instances of these three classes of routing protocols.

9.6.1 Multipath Routing Protocols

Since, multiple paths to a destination are used, these routing protocols have overhead in terms of generating higher network traffic compared to those which use single path. Alternative paths are maintained by sending control packets from time to time. These protocols, therefore, assure increased reliability in data delivery and resilience to failures. The resilience can be measured by the number of paths available between the source and the destination. Many instances of multipath routing protocols are available in literature [23–28].

Most of the protocols in this category, focus on the energy issues and choose to activate one of the available paths on the basis of either the residual energy on the path or pro-actively route data to maintain a balance of energy at different nodes. The idea is to extend the network lifetime as well as reliability. In [24], the focus is particularly on enhancing the reliability. It introduces a function for analyzing the trade-off between the degree of multipath and the failing probabilities of the available paths. It partitions a packet into subpackets with an added redundancy and sends each subpacket through one of the available paths. Due to availability of redundant information, the reconstruction of the original packet is possible even if some subpackets are lost.

The other interesting idea in class of multipath routing algorithms is presented by directed diffusion [26]. It uses the idea of publish and subscribe approach to send data of interest to the inquirers. An inquirer expresses an interest I. The sources that can service the interest I send the data to the inquirer. The inquirer effectively turns into a data sink and floods the interest. A forwarder typically maintains a local cache of the interests and stores an incoming interest if it is not already present in the cache. Initially an interest is diffused at a low data rate. Bidirectional gradient is established on all the links during the flooding. The sensor system samples data at the highest rate of all the gradients. The data is sent out using unicast as the reverse links are formed while the gradient is established. The initial low rate is known as exploratory. Once a sensor is able to report data, the reinforcement of the gradient occurs. Positive reinforcement is triggered by the data sink resending the interest with shorter intervals. The neighbor node witnessing the higher rate positively reinforce at least one neighbor that uses its data cache. It usually selects an empirically low latency path.

9.6.2 Query Based Routing Protocols

Directed diffusion [26] also represents a query based routing algorithm as interest diffusion essentially amounts to sending queries. Another instance of query based algorithm is presented by rumour routing protocol [29]. It essentially works in two stages. Initially, long-lived agents are used to create paths to the events when they occur. When a query related to the event is generated, it gets routed along that path.

The basic idea is as follows. The agents are basically long-lived messages circulating in the network. Each node maintains a list of its neighbors and a table of events with forwarding information to all events. The events may have an expiration time to restrict size of the event table. When a node generates an event, it probabilistically creates an agent with route length 0. The probability is used, because other nodes noticing the event, may also create agents. It may be too much of overhead if each node noticing the event creates a separate agent. The agent then travels in the network with a TTL (time to live) value in terms of the number of hops. When an agent travels, it combines the event table of the originating node with the visited nodes. It also updates the event table when a shorter path is found at a visited node. A node generates a query unless it learns a path to a required event. If no route is available, the node transmits the query to a random direction. If the response is not received after a finite wait time, the node then floods the network with the query. Clearly, the routing protocol has a significant overhead due to agent circulation, random query initiation, etc.

9.6.3 Negotiation Based Routing Protocols

Negotiation based routing are typically the choice for QoS requirements. However, as explained in SPIN protocol [15] earlier in the text, negotiation can be used for suppressing unnecessary transmissions. In fact, even in QoS requirement based routing, the path which cannot provide required QoS, will also not receive unnecessary network traffic. There are many other examples of routing protocols [30, 31] where negotiation is the main basis for routing.

In general, QoS metrics could be specified by

1. Application,
2. Protocol's overall goal,
3. Protocol's strategy to route data.

For example, at the application level QoS may refer to the frequency of data, and the quality of data. At protocol level, the strategy could be the shortest path, on occurrences of events, etc. The overall goal of a routing protocol could be extending lifetime, minimizing energy, etc. Most QoS based algorithm will require frequent recomputation of the routes as existing ones may no longer promise QoS after extended periods of use.

Fig. 9.9 Sequential
assignment routing algorithm

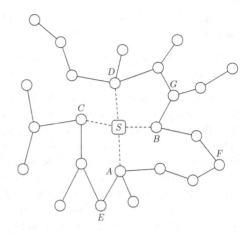

Sequential Assignment Routing (SAR) [31] is stated to be one of the earliest routing algorithm that utilized negotiation [14] involving factors such as energy, QoS on path and the priority levels of the packets. SAR creates multiple trees with root of the tree and the data sink being within each others ranges. Each tree grows outward from the sink avoiding the nodes with low throughput or high delay. It can provide multiple paths for the data to be transmitted from each node to the data sink. So, the higher priority data packets can be transmitted via low delay paths, at the same time the lower priority packets from the same node can take a higher delay but a higher residual energy path. An example is provided in Fig. 9.9. As the figure shows, nodes E, F, G have alternative paths to sink. E can be reach S via A or C with paths of length 2 and 3 respectively. Similarly, F can reach S through paths of lengths 4 and 3 respectively from A and B. G can reach data sink S either through B or through D with respective path lengths of 3 and 2. Depending on which path provides better value for chosen QoS metric, the data to sink can take one of the possible alternative paths.

9.7 Interconnection of WSNs to the Internet

Initially, the objective of WSN research was on data gathering connected with specialized systems for automation, control and monitoring. Instead of standardized protocols, highly specialized protocols using one or more gateways were considered as adequate for accessing WSN data over the Internet. However, WSNs without IP integration offered an inflexible framework for the development of newer applications. It required retooling of network protocols within WSNs [32].

New IPv6 based standards such as 6LoWPAN and ZigBee IP were proposed for WSN in order to introduce flexibility and easy interoperability with computer networks. The problems in integration of IP with WSN may be seen from two different aspects:

1. Differences in the communication pattern and capabilities WSN and IP, and
2. Expected operational capabilities of WSNs after integration.

The problems arising out of the differences in communication pattern are due to practical usage scenarios involving WSN deployments. The flow pattern of data in TCP/IP network is between the two ends of a connection. In contrast, the data flow patterns in WSN are either many to one, or one to many. For example, a query may be broadcast from a sink node to all sensors for reporting their individual measured values. Similarly, all sensors having values above the threshold placed by a query should report their respective measurements to the sink node.

The problem arising out of the difference in communication capabilities are due to the variations in standards defining the two protocol stacks: WSN and TCP/IP. Firstly, any non trivial deployment of WSN would consist of hundreds and thousands of nodes. So building and maintaining a global addressing scheme for even a mid sized WSN deployment is not quite easy. It requires prohibitive administrative overheads. Secondly, the ad hoc nature of deploying sensor requires WSNs to be self-configurable. Thirdly, in an IP based network bandwidth requirement for data transfer is high (images, video, sound, etc. can be transferred). This implies IPv4 is not feasible for WSNs. IP header itself too large compared to IEEE 802.15.4 PPDU which is the defined standard for physical layer of sensor nodes. Fourthly, a number of existing WSN deployments do not implement IP stack. The only way to communicate with sensor nodes belonging to such a WSN is possible through specialized gateways. Therefore, the integration IP networks with WSNs not implementing either 6LoWPAN or ZigBee IP is a real concern for interoperability.

WSN protocols work at link layer not at IP layer. MAC protocols for WSN are specially designed for periodic listen and sleep schedule. If the schedules of listen and sleep can be properly planned then it helps to reduce energy wastage and enhance lifetime of WSN. The main sources of energy waste can be attributed to following [33]:

1. Collisions: it not only increases latency but retransmissions also contribute substantially in energy drain out.
2. Overhearing: a node unnecessarily picks up a piece of data not destined for itself.
3. Control packets: using large number of control packets is another source of energy waste.
4. Idle listening: the major source of wastage is wait and listen for packets that may not come. In fact, at least half the time is lost in idle listening, and it may consume energy in excess of 50%.

Considering the energy wastage issue, MAC layer scheduling makes sense.

9.7.1 NAT Based IP-WSN Interconnection

Non IP based solutions to integration of IP with WSN are motivated by two favorable aspects of the whole problem. Firstly, in WSN, each node gather data from environment and reports its observation to a single data sink either directly or may be via multiple hops. So, a WSN effectively operates like an inverted directed tree with base station or the data sink as the root. Secondly, the nodes in WSN are accessible only through base station which acts as a gateway or a proxy. So, a WSN appears like a private network with an independent gateway. Therefore, the most common approach, to integration of WSN and IP, is motivated by NAT semantics for accessing the Internet from private networks.

A WSN operates with IP network through a proxy or gateway. The proxy needs to implement both the protocol stacks: IP and WSN. The scenario of integration is illustrated by Fig. 9.10. Proxy becomes a gateway for communicating with sensor node from IP network. Sending data upstream from sensors to a IP node is not a big problem. Placing a serial forwarder between base station and IP node would serve this purpose [34] as illustrated in Fig. 9.11.

The downstream communication is problematic. Frame structure of two networks are different. A server module can be created specially for providing a NAT like semantic for IP to sensor communication. The problem of sensor not having IP address is solved by treating the sensor network as private network and providing NAT services to address a specific sensor node. A one to one mapping sensor nodeIDs and portIDs is created. The server assigns a portID to each nodeID. For downstream routing, reverse mapping is necessary. So, server module stores the reverse mapping of portIDs to nodeIDs. One of the problem with this solution is that the mapping is not static due to variation in propagation pattern of radio signals. Therefore, provision should be made to ensure change in mapping specially regarding change of parents in the tree. The sensor nodes send control packets from time to time to make the server aware of modification in tree structure. Accordingly, the server modifies its information and maintains the WSN tree.

Initially, IP nodes desiring to access data service from a specific WSN are required to register with the respective servers. A server offers this registration service on a

Fig. 9.10 NAT based
IP/WSN integration

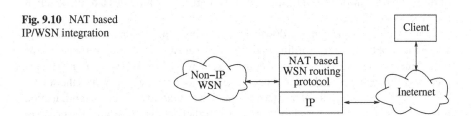

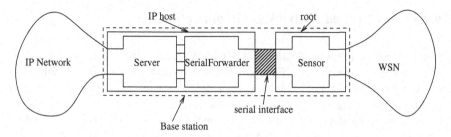

Fig. 9.11 Serial forwarder for WSN to IP communication [34]

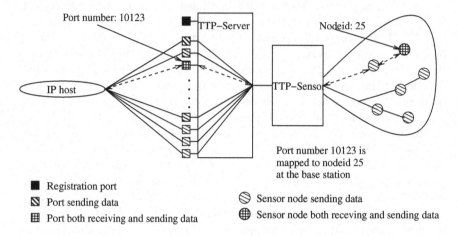

Fig. 9.12 Downstream communication between IP and WSN [34]

known universal port. When data is received from sensor nodes, the same is disseminated to all registered IP hosts as UDP packets. The payload of WSN data packet is sent as payload of UDP packet at a universal port for availing services of downstream communication. The server node stores a mapping of sensor nodes to port numbers. When a registered IP node wants to communicate with a specific sensor node, the node sends the packet addressed to specific port ID. The server module takes care of disseminating information to specific node. Figure 9.12 provides a brief sketch of the process involved.

Source routing is needed for downstream routing. The reason for this is it needs very little support from forwarding node. MAC level ACK is used for retransmission requirements, if any. The server module takes care of packet formation when it receives a downstream packet for a specific sensor node. The server creates the source routing packet with the help of the tree information available to it. The communication is then staged through the serial forwarder. For further details concerning the protocol the reader is referred to [34].

9.8 Data Fusion in WSN

In a data centric network, the communication paradigm is driven by flow of data. Communication is mostly point to multipoint, i.e., either multicast or any cast. The data and its context defines the destination of a data flow. The shift in communication paradigm from address centric to data centric introduces the problem of organizing *data as communication token*. In particular, when network has comparatively large, the number of data generation sources, like in a WSN, the volume of data is unmanageably high. Only meaningful data with assured quality should participate in communication. This implies (i) the accuracy of data, and (ii) the elimination of unwanted data should be included among the important parameters for the definition of the quality of data. Data fusion in WSN primarily achieve the aforesaid objectives. Before going deeper into data fusion techniques, let us examine the question: why data fusion is important in the context of WSNs?

Sensors measure raw data, for example, temperature, pressure, humidity, luminosity, radiation levels, air pollutants, etc. There may be errors in these measurements due to various reasons including the sensors being erroneous. Furthermore, these raw data make little sense unless they are processed and interpreted. So, the key to use of WSN is the interpretation of the sensed raw data. Typically the sensed data received from multiple data sources are combined to improve the quality and the efficacy of interpretation. Apart from eliminating errors, combining data from multiple sources also helps to eliminate sensor failures, temporal and spatial coverage problems. Sensor fusion is particularly important for supporting applications for smart environments. For example, in smart health care system the vital parameters of a critical patient are monitored on continuous basis, and alarms should be raised when these parameters exhibit abnormalities. If the measurements are not accurate, then the patient's life could be endangered. Similarly, if the radiation levels in operations of a nuclear power plant are not correctly monitored it can lead to disastrous consequences. In summary, the sensor equipped monitoring systems lead to the detection of events which sets in motions actuation processes to enhance the ability of a system to respond smartly. Data fusion can be seen as the process of combining data collected from multiple sources to enhance the quality of data in a cheaper way and raises its significance.

Simple aggregation techniques like summing, finding minimum or finding maximum have been used to reduce the volume of data in order to minimize the traffic or data flow. Other sophisticated fusion techniques are used for enhancing quality of data. There is some amount of confusion as well as disagreements in understanding the terminology of data fusion [35]. The problem comes from the fact that the terminology has been developed out of various systems, architectures, applications, methods, theories about data fusion [35]. There is no unified terminology for description of data fusion. Nakamura et al. [35] mention many different ways to describe general term of data and information fusion.

9.8.1   Definitions

Let us discuss a few of these definitions just to understand why lot of confusions surround the concept of data diffusion. The first definition is from the lexicon of US Department of Defense [36]. It says:

Definition 9.1 Data fusion is a multi-level and multifaceted process dealing with automated detection, association, correlation, estimation and combination of data and information from multiple sources.

The above definition does not restrict itself to sensory data alone. Data can be sourced from a variety of other sources such as satellites, remote sensing equipments, robotics, etc. The objective of the second definition proposed in [37] is to capture the improved accuracy of data. According to this definition:

Definition 9.2 Data fusion is combination of data from multiple sensors, and related information provided by associated databases, to achieve improved accuracy and more specific inferences than could be achieved by the use of a single sensor alone.

The third definition is developed with an objective of describing enhanced quality of data [38] in the context of application or applications it is intended to serve. It defines:

Definition 9.3 Data fusion is a formal framework in which are expressed means and tools for the alliance of data originating from different sources. It aims at obtaining information of greater quality; the exact definition of *greater quality* will depend upon the application.

The fourth one is a verbose definition used in the context of data fusion in robotics and vision. It tries to capture both the use of fusion data, and its interaction with the environment. It prefers the term multisensor integration over data fusion. According to this definition multisensor integration [39] is:

Definition 9.4 The synergistic use of information provided by multiple sensory devices to assist in the accomplishment of a task by a system; and multisensor fusion deals with the combination of different sources of sensory information into one representational format during any stage in the integration process.

However, among the community of WSN researchers, fusion is typically seen as an aggregation of data [40–42]. In some sense, the definition of data aggregation appears to refer to composition of raw data into piece of information that can be used for filtering unwanted information and also to summarize the contents. Accordingly, data aggregation [40] is defined as follows.

Definition 9.5 Data aggregation comprises the collection of raw data from pervasive data sources, the flexible, programmable composition of the raw data into less voluminous refined data, and the timely delivery of the refined data to data consumers.

Fig. 9.13 Data/information
fusion [35]

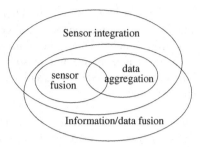

Figure 9.13 [35] illustrates the subtle differences that exist among multisensor integration, data aggregation, sensor fusion and information/data fusion. Information essentially refers to processed or organized data. However, certain data may already be organized in some way before it gets accessed by destinations. So, two terms at times refer to the same concept and can be used interchangeably. In a coarse granularity, sensor fusion and data aggregation encompassed within the both sensor integration and data/information fusion. Multisensor integration relates to fusion of data only from sensors. So, it is restrictive in general context of data fusion. Though sensor fusion can be just aggregation of data from sensors, it can include more elaborate form of data processing. Similarly, the generic meaning of data aggregation does not just relate to aggregation of data collected from sensors alone.

9.8.2 Data Collection Model

The key design issues in sensor data diffusion are:

1. How do the interests to acquire sensor data get disseminated?
2. How do the sensor nodes keep track of different interests?
3. How do the nodes propagate data when subscribed events occur?
4. How do the nodes apply data processing (aggregation/fusion) as the data get propagated towards the sink?

The interests are expressed on the basis of the attributes. For example, if the sensors are deployed to monitor forest fire, then an interest can be expressed as follows:

$$\{Type = Fire, Subtype = Amber, Interval = 2\,m,$$
$$Time = 1\,h, Region = [-20, 20, 300, 200]\}$$

The interest gets disseminated to all sensors belonging to region specified by the bounding box $[-20, 20, 300, 200]$. The sensors are supposed to monitor the fire. The fire can be of different Subtypes, e.g., subtype *Amber* could mean that a forest fire breakout is predicted. Other subtypes could be *Red*, or *Black* meaning that fire is now on, and may have disastrous consequences. The time parameters instructs the sensor to send observations for the next 1 h in intervals of 2 m. The interests are flooded into the network. All the sensor nodes with matching data commence reporting to data sink from which the interest originated.

Now, let us examine how a sensor node reports when an event occurs? For example, suppose a sensor node sensed a high temperature in its vicinity, it could create a tuple of the form:

$$\{Type = Heat, Subtype = VeryHot, Temperature = 200,$$
$$Location = [101, 205], Timestamp = 14 : 50 : 05, Confidence = 0.7\}$$

It includes three key items of information, namely, location of the source, timestamp and confidence value apart from the attribute values. So, the data sink can analyze the occurrences of the events.

The diffusion starts with initial expression of interests for data by the sink. The interest may be viewed as a subscription for the events in a broader framework of a publish subscribe model. The interest and the arrival of data are combined cleverly to set up a gradient for the data to flow. The process is described as follows:

- The initial interest is essentially an exploration phase. During this phase, the data sink sets a larger interval for the data sampling by the sensor nodes.
- The second phase is concerned with the creation of gradient and its reinforcement. After receiving the first few data items related to interest, the sink refreshes the interest by using the reverse path. In the refreshed interests, the sink lowers the sampling interval for the sensor nodes.

In exploration phase, the interests are sent with larger interval primarily to reduce flooding. The interest get disseminated by flooding.

The processing of interest dissemination works as follows

1. Each node creates an interest cache.
2. When a node receives an interest, it checks if the interest has an entry in the local interest cache.
3. If no entry exists, then the node caches the interest and also creates a reverse gradient by listing the neighbor who sent the interest.
4. It then forwards the interest to its other neighbors excluding the neighbor from which it received the interest.

Many routes may be created in the reverse direction (from sources to sink) for the flow of data. If the flow of data is allowed with high frequency from the sources, it could lead to huge network traffic even before the best path can be determined. Unnecessary network traffic should be minimized.

The flow of data requires time to settle for the best route as it starts flowing. For settling on the best route, there is no need to use any extra control packets. By making use of flow of data and refreshing interest, the best route can be settled. A gradient is formed when data starts arriving at the sink from the targeted sensors. The data sink tries to reinforce the reverse path through which first few items of data arrived. So, it sends refreshed interests by lowering the monitoring interval. This way the route settles down with an appropriate gradient and flooding can be restricted.

As far as reporting is concerned, the interval of reporting is the key consideration. There are three possibilities here. The system may depend on a periodic reporting. For example, in the application that requires monitoring of some kind, the sensed data is sent periodically for analysis. In other applications, reporting may be based on the queries. In yet another set of applications event-triggered reporting could be important.

9.8.3 Challenges in Data Fusion

Data fusion addresses four qualitative aspects of the data [43], namely

1. Imperfection,
2. Correlation,
3. Inconsistency, and
4. Disparateness.

Imperfection covers uncertainty, imprecision and granularity. Uncertainty raises doubts about the value of data, while imprecision originates from the measurement related errors. It includes vagueness, ambiguity and incompleteness in the measurement. The degree of data granularity represents its ability to expose level of details.

Correlation exhibit dependencies in data. Fusion of correlated data may create problems unless dependencies are handled carefully. Inconsistencies mean that the same data from different sources do not match. Integrity of data becomes an issue if data is not consistent. Finally, disparateness means data presented from different sources in different format. Some data may be raw, some may be semi-processed and others may be processed. Fusion of such data could be challenging.

Imperfection in data mostly handled by methods having origins in statistical methods. Some of this methods are based on probability theory [44], rough set theory [45], fuzzy set [46], Dempster-Shafer theory [47]. Probability theory is used to handle uncertainty. Fuzzy set used to remove vagueness. Evidential and belief theory (Dempster-Shafer) is used to eliminate both uncertainty and ambiguity in data. Rough sets are used for granularity problem.

9.8.4 Data Fusion Algorithms

There are many ways data fusion can be performed. Classification of fusion techniques can be made on the basis of various criteria such as (i) data abstraction level (ii) purpose, (iii) parameters (iii) types of data, and (iv) mathematical foundations. Nakamura et al. [35] have presented an excellent comprehensive review on the topic. The contents, presented here, have been drawn largely from the above paper. But our focus is limited to only a few algorithms designed on the basis of interesting mathematical framework.

According to [35], the purpose of applying a fusion algorithm can be the following:

1. To derive an inference that can assist in making a decision.
2. To estimate certain value or a vector of values from the sensor observations.
3. To determine the features representing aspects of an environment from the raw sensory data.
4. To compute reliable abstract sensors which can be used for time synchronization so that the sensors can maintain upper and lower bounds on the current time.
5. To aggregate sensor data for the purpose of overcoming the problem of implosion and overlap of data (explained earlier in 9.4.1).
6. To compress similar data by exploiting spatial correlation among sensor data.

Apart from the classes of algorithms mentioned above, there has been some attempts to tackle data fusion problem based on information theory [48]. The purpose is to increase the reliability by fusion of data from multiple sensors. For example, it may be possible to correlate observations from multiple sensing capabilities such as acoustic, magnetic, luminosity, etc. It increases reliability as well confidence in sensor observations. This class of algorithms are still in infancy. They need to overcome the difficulties such as uncertainties in measurements of entropies of source nodes, and efficient conversion of observations to entropies.

9.8.4.1 Bayesian Inference and Dempster-Shafer Belief Model

Let us examine two inference models which have been used extensively in data fusion area [35]. The first one is the Bayesian inferencing model, where the uncertainty is represented by conditional probabilities describing the belief. It is based on the well known and classical Bayes' rule [49]:

$$Pr(Y|X) = \frac{Pr(X|Y)Pr(Y)}{Pr(X)},$$

where the probability $Pr(Y|X)$ represents the belief of hypothesis Y with known information X. It essentially states that the probability of Y given X is obtained by multiplying $Pr(Y)$ with the probability $Pr(X|Y)$ of X given Y is true, with $Pr(X)$ being a normalizing constant. The problem with Bayesian rule is it requires either the exact or near approximate guess of probabilities $Pr(X)$ and $Pr(X|Y)$. In WSN, Bayesian inference rules have been used mostly for localization problem based on fusing information from the mobile beacons [50].

Dempster-Shafer theory [47] is a mathematical tool for combining independent evidence components in order to arrive at a decision. It determines the degrees of belief for one question from the subjective probabilities of a related question. This theory is extensively applied in the expert system [51]. The main features of this theory are:

- Each fact has a degree of support belonging to interval [0, 1], where

  - 0 represents no support,
  - 1 represent full support.

- A set of possible conclusions is represented by

$$\Theta = \{\theta_1, \theta_2, \ldots, \theta_n\}$$

where:

  - Each θ_i is mutually exclusive, i.e., only one can hold.
  - Θ is exhaustive, i.e., at least one θ_i must hold.

Dempster-Shafer theory is concerned with the evidences that support subsets of outcomes in Θ. The power set of Θ is defined as the *frame discernment* which represents all possible outcomes. For example, if $\Theta = \{a, b, c\}$ then the frame of discernment is given by:

$$\phi, \{a\}, \{b\}, \{c\}, \{a, b\}, \{b, c\}, \{c, a\}, \{a, b, c\}$$

The empty set ϕ has probability 0. Also $\{a, b, c\}$ has probability 0, because by assumption only one of the outcomes would hold, not all.

Furthermore, it defines four different measurable functions:

- Mass function: For a $A \subseteq P(\Theta)$ mass function $m(A)$ is simply the proportion of all the evidences that support A. The mass expresses all the relevant evidences that supports the claim that actual state belongs to A and not to any particular subset of A.
- Belief function: The belief in $A \subseteq P(\Theta)$ is defined as the sum of masses of an element which are subsets of A including itself. For example, if $A = \{a, b, c\}$, then

$$bel(A) = m(a) + m(b) + m(c) + m(a, b) + m(b, c) + m(c, a) + m(a, b, c)$$

- Plausibility function: Plausibility of A, $pl(A)$ is the sum of all the mass of the sets that intersect with A.
- Disbelief function. Disbelief or doubt in A is simple $bel(\neg A)$. It is calculated by summing all mass values of elements that do not intersect A.

Dempster-Shafer theory associates a certainty with a given subset A by defining a belief interval which is $[bel(A), pl(A)]$. The belief interval of a set A defines the bounds within which probability of outcome A lies. Dempster-Shafer theory also defines a composition rule for combining effects of two basic probability masses:

$$m_1 \oplus m_2(\phi) = 0$$
$$m_1 \oplus m_2(A) = \frac{\sum_{X \cap Y = A} m_1(X) m_2(Y)}{1 - \sum_{X \cap Y} m_1(X) m_2(Y)}$$

Dempster-Shafer theory has been used in sensor data fusion because it is considered to be more flexible than Bayesian inference rule. It allows each source to contribute different levels of details to information gathering [35]. For example, to quote an example from [35], suppose there are two different sensors S_1 and S_2. Suppose S_1 can recognize the roar of a male feline, while S_2 can recognize the roar of a female feline. Now a third sensor, S_3 is also there that can distinguish between the roars of a Cheetah and a Lion. Dempster-Shafer theory allows us to combine the data from three sensors to conclude whether the recorded roar is that of a male/female Cheetah. Dempster-Shafer theory does not assign a priori probabilities to unknown events unlike Bayesian model. The probabilities are assigned only when supporting facts are available.

9.8.4.2 Reliable Abstract Sensors

Marzullo [52] proposed the idea of a reliable abstract sensor for arriving at an interval that will always contain the actual value of a desired physical state variable. It has been used in the context of time synchronization, wherein the sensors can perform external synchronization by maintaining the upper and lower bound on the current time.

The term reliable abstract sensor has been used to define one of the three sensors: concrete sensor, abstract sensor and reliable abstract sensor. A concrete sensor is a physical sensor, an abstract sensor is an interval of value representing the measurement of a state variable provided by a concrete sensor. A reliable abstract sensor is the interval that assuredly always contain the real value of the physical variable. So, abstract sensors are mathematical entities representing the concrete sensors.

Marzullo [53] proposes a fault tolerant averaging algorithm for agreement in distributed system. This algorithm is the basis for NTP [54]. Subsequently Marzullo [52] adopted the same algorithm for reliable abstract sensors. It assumes that at most f out of $n \geq 2f + 1$ sensors can be faulty. Let $\mathscr{I} = \{I_1, I_2, \ldots, I_n\}$ be the set of intervals produced by abstract sensors. The idea is to compute $M_n^f = [low, high]$ by fault tolerant averaging, i.e.,

1. low is the smallest value belonging to at least $n - f$ intervals,
2. $high$ is the largest value belonging to at least $n - f$ intervals.

The algorithm computes the fault tolerant averaging in $O(n \log n)$. Clearly, M_I^f cannot give more accurate value than the most accurate sensor when $n = 2f + 1$. Also any minor changes in input could produce a very different output. In other words, the result is unstable. To appreciate the implication of fault tolerant averaging consider an example illustrated by Fig. 9.14. It represents intervals I_1, I_2, I_3 and I_4 reported by four sensors S_1, S_2, S_3 and S_4, respectively. Let one of these four sensors be faulty. Since, I_2 and I_3 do not intersect, one of S_2 and S_3 must be faulty. Marzullo's interval overlapping method produces the intervals M_I^f as shown in Fig. 9.14. It produces unstable output, as can be checked by shifting the interval I_3 to right.

Fig. 9.14 Marzullo's fusion technique with reliable sensor [52]

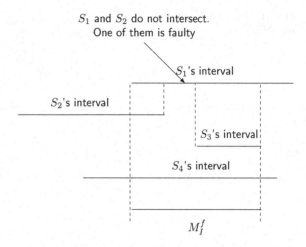

9.8.4.3 **Compression**

Distributed Source Coding (DSC) is a compression technique for correlated data from multiple sources [55]. The sources are distributed and do not communicate for coding. The compressed data is sent to a central sink node for decoding. Kusuma [56] and Pradhan et al. [57] proposed Distributed Source Coding Using Syndromes (DISCUS) framework for data compression.

To understand the coding, let us consider an example. Suppose the observations from sensors are coded in a 3-bit word. So, the possible observations are {000, 001, 010, 011, 100, 101, 110, 111}. These observations are grouped into 4 cosets whose elements have hamming distance of three, i.e.,

1. Coset 1: {000, 111} with index 00
2. Coset 2: {001, 110} with index 01
3. Coset 3: {010, 101} with index 10
4. Coset 4: {011, 100} with index 11.

A node sends its observation by sending only the corresponding index. A node S_2 can decode S_1's observation by the fact that hamming distance between its own observation and the observation of S_1 is 1. For example, if S_1's observation is 101, it sends 10 to S_2. Let S_2's observation be 101, then S_2 and can decode S_1's observation from the index 10 and the fact that hamming distance between two observations is 1. The overall framework of data compression by DISCUS framework is illustrated by Fig. 9.15.

The data fusion is not just limited to sensor fusion or multisensor integration. It refers to the larger context of fusion of data from various source as in robotics, remote sensing, etc. So, the data fusion techniques have their origin even before wireless sensor were deployed. But interestingly, it was possible to adopt many of the techniques of fusion to multisensor integration. In this chapter, the scope of

Fig. 9.15 Data compression in DISCUS [35]

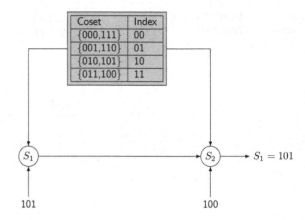

Coset	Index
{000,111}	00
{001,110}	01
{010,101}	10
{011,100}	11

S_1

S_2 → $S_1 = 101$

101   100

discussion is limited to the extent of exposing mathematical richness of a few of these techniques to the reader. However, sufficient pointers to extensive literature have been provided for an interested reader to follow up further readings.

References

1. S. Distefano, G. Merlion, A. Puliafito. Sensing and actuation as a service: a new development for clouds, in *The 11th IEEE Internation Symposium on Network Computing and Applications* (2012), pp. 272–275
2. G. Anastasi, M. Conti, M. Di Francesco, A. Passarella, Energy conservation in wireless sensor networks: a survey. Ad hoc Netw. **7**(3), 537–568 (2009)
3. K.C. Barr, K. Asanović, Energy-aware lossless data compression. ACM Trans. Comput. Syst. (TOCS) **24**(3), 250–291 (2006)
4. G.J. Pottie, W.J. Kaiser, Wireless integrated network sensors. Commun. ACM **43**(5), 51–58 (2000)
5. S. Choi, N. Kim, H. Cha, Automated sensor-specific power management for wireless sensor networks, in *5th IEEE International Conference on Mobile Ad Hoc and Sensor Systems* (IEEE Computer Society, Atlanta, GA, USA. Atlanta, GA, USA, 2008), pp. 305–314
6. H. Kim, H. Cha, Towards a resilient operating system for wireless sensor networks, in *USENIX Annual Technical Conference, General Track* (2006), pp. 103–108
7. X. Fang, S. Misra, G. Xue, D. Yang, Smart gridthe new and improved power grid: a survey. IEEE Commun. Surv. Tutor. **14**(4), 944–980 (2012)
8. T. Hikihara, Power router and packetization project for home electric energy management, in *Santa Barbara Summit on Energy Efficiency* (2010), pp. 12–13
9. J.M. Kahn, R.H. Katz, K.S.J. Pister. Next century challenges: mobile networking for "smart dust", in *Mobicom'99* (Seattle, Washington, USA, 1999), pp. 271–278
10. M.O. Farooq, T. Kunz, Operating systems for wireless sensor networks: a survey. *Sensors***11**(6), 59005930 (2011) (Basel, Switzerland)
11. P. Levis, S. Madden, J. Polastre, R. Szewczyk, K. Whitehouse, A. Woo, D. Gay, J. Hill, M. Welsh, E. Brewer, D. Culler, TinyOS: an operating system for sensor network, in *Ambient intelligence* (Springer, Berlin Heidelberg, 2005), pp. 115–148
12. A. Dunkels, B. Gronvall, T. Voigt, Contiki-a lightweight and flexible operating system for tiny networked sensors, in *29th Annual IEEE International Conference on Local Computer Networks* (IEEE, 2004), pp. 455–462

13. J. Wang, R.K. Ghosh, S.K. Das, A survey on sensor localization. J. Control Theory Appl. **8**(1), 2–11 (2010)
14. J.N. Al-Karaki, A.E. Kamal, Routing techniques in wireless sensor networks: a survey. IEEE Wirel. Commun. **11**(6), 6–28 (2004)
15. W. Heinzelman, J. Kulik, H. Balakrishnan, Adaptive protocols for information dissemination in wireless sensor networks, in *The 5th ACM/IEEE Mobicom Conference (MobiCom 99)* (Seattle, WA, 1999), pp. 174–85
16. W. Heinzelman, A. Chandrakasan, H. Balakrishnan, Energy-efficient communication protocol for wireless microsensor networks, in *The 33rd Hawaii International Conference on System Sciences (HICSS 00)*, January 2000
17. N. Bulusu, J. Heidemann, D. Estrin, GPS-less low cost outdoor localization for very small devices. Technical report, University of Southern California, April 2000. Technical report 00-729
18. S. Capkun, M. Hamdi, J. Hubaux, GPS-free positioning in mobile ad-hoc networks, in *The 34th Annual Hawaii International Conference on System Sciences (HICSS'01)* (2001), pp. 3481–3490
19. A. Savvides, C.C. Han, M. Srivastava, Dynamic fine-grained localization in ad-hoc networks of sensors, in *The Seventh ACM Annual International Conference on Mobile Computing and Networking (MobiCom)*, pp. 166–179, July 2001
20. B. Chen, K. Jamieson, H. Balakrishnan, R. Morris, SPAN: an energy-efficient coordination algorithm for topology maintenance in ad hoc wireless networks. Wirel. Netw. **8**(5), 481–494 (2002)
21. Y. Xu, J. Heidemann, D. Estrin, Geography-informed energy conservation for ad-hoc routing, in *The Seventh Annual ACM/IEEE International Conference on Mobile Computing and Networking* (2001), pp. 70–84
22. Y. Yu, D. Estrin, R. Govindan, Geographical and energy-aware routing: a recursive data dissemination protocol for wireless sensor networks. Technical report, University of California at Los Angeles, May 2001
23. J.H. Chang, L. Tassiulas, Maximum lifetime routing in wireless sensor networks, in *Advanced Telecommunications and Information Distribution Research Program (ATIRP), College Park* (MD, USA, March, 2000), p. 2000
24. S. Dulman, T. Nieberg, J. Wu, P. Havinga, *Trade-off between Traffic Overhead and Reliability in Multipath Routing for Wireless Sensor Networks* (In WCNC Workshop, New Orleans, Louisiana, USA, 2003)
25. D. Ganesan, R. Govindan, S. Shenker, D. Estrin, Highly-resilient, energy-efficient multipath routing in wireless sensor networks. ACM SIGMOBILE Mob. Comput. Commun. Rev. **5**(4), 1125 (2001)
26. C. Intanagonwiwat, R. Govindan, D. Estrin, Directed diffusion: a scalable and robust communication paradigm for sensor networks, in *ACM MobiCom 00* (Boston, MA, 2000), pp. 56–67
27. Q. Li, J. Aslam, D. Rus. Hierarchical power-aware routing in sensor networks, in *The DIMACS Workshop on Pervasive Networking*, May 2001
28. C. Rahul, J. Rabaey, Energy aware routing for low energy ad hoc sensor networks, in *IEEE Wireless Communications and Networking Conference (WCNC)*, vol 1 (Orlando, FL, USA), pp. 350–355. 17–21 March 2002
29. D. Braginsky, D. Estrin, Rumor routing algorithm for sensor networks. In *International Conference on Distributed Computing Systems (ICDCS'01)*, November 2001
30. J. Kulik, W.R. Heinzelman, H. Balakrishnan, Negotiation-based protocols for disseminating information in wireless sensor networks. Wirel. Netw. **8**, 169–185 (2002)
31. K. Sohrabi, J. Pottie, Protocols for self-organization of a wireless sensor network. IEEE Person. Commun. **7**(5), 16–27 (2000)
32. A.P. Castellani, N. Bui, P. Casari, M. Rossi, Z. Shelby, M. Zorzi, Architecture and protocols for the internet of things: a case study, in *8th IEEE International Conference on Pervasive Computing and Communications (PERCOM Workshops)* (IEEE, 2010), pp. 678–683

33. W. Ye, J. Heidemann, D. Estrin, An energy-efficient MAC protocol for wireless sensor networks, in *The 21st International Annual Joint Conference of the IEEE Computer and Communications Societies (INFOCOM), New York* (USA, June, NY, 2002), p. 2002
34. S. Shekhar, R. Mishra, R.K. Ghosh, R.K. Shyamasundar, Post-order based routing and transport protocol for wireless sensor networks. Pervasive Mob. Comput. **11**, 229–243 (2014)
35. E.F. Nakamura, A.A. Loureiro, A.C. Frery, Information fusion for wireless sensor networks: methods, models, and classifications. ACM Comput. Surv. **39**(3) (2007)
36. F.E. White, Data fusion lexicon. Technical report, U.S. Department of Defense, *Code 4202* (NOSC, San Diego, CA, 1991)
37. D.L. Hall, J. Llinas, An introduction to multi-sensor data fusion. Proceedings of IEEE **85**(1), 6–23 (1997)
38. L. Wald, Some terms of reference in data fusion. IEEE Trans. Geosci. Remote Sens. **13**(3), 1190–1193 (1999)
39. R.C. Luo, M.G. Kay (eds.), *Multisensor Integration and Fusion for Intelligent Machines and Systems* (Ablex Publishing, New Jersey, USA, 1995)
40. N.H. Cohen, A. Purakayastha, J. Turek, L. Wong, D. Yeh. Challenges in flexible aggregation of pervasive data. Technical report, IBM Research Division, Yorktown Heights, NY, USA, January 2001. IBM Research Report RC 21942 (98646)
41. K. Kalpakis, K. Dasgupta, P. Namjoshi, Efficient algorithms for maximum lifetime data gathering and aggregation in wireless sensor networks. Comput. Netw. **42**(6), 697–716 (2003)
42. R. Van Renesse, The importance of aggregation, in *Future Directions in Distributed Computing: Research and Position Papers*, ed. by A. Schiper, A.A. Shvartsman, H. Weatherspoon, B.Y. Zhao, vol NCS 2584 (Springer, Bologna, Italy, 2003), pp. 87–92
43. B. Khaleghi, A. Khamis, O. Karray, Multisensor data fusion: a review of the state-of-the-art. em. Inf. Fus. **14**(1), 28–44 (2013)
44. H.F. Durrant-Whyte, T.C. Henderson, Multisensor data fusion, in *Handbook of Robotics*, ed. by B. Siciliano, O. Khatib (Springer, 2008), pp. 585–610
45. Z. Pawlak, *Rough Sets: Theoretical Aspects of Reasoning about Data* (Kluwer Academic Publishers, Norwell, MA, USA, 1992)
46. A. Zadeh, Fuzzy sets. Inf. Control **8**(3), 338–353 (1965)
47. G. Shafer, *A Mathematical Theory of Evidence*. Princeton University Press, 1976
48. P.K. Varshney, *Distributed Detection and Data Fusion* (Springer, New York, USA, 1967)
49. T.R. Bayes, An essay towards solving a problem in the doctrine of chances. Philosop. Trans. R. Soc. **53**, 370–418 (1763)
50. M.L. Sichitiu, V. Ramadurai, Localization of wireless sensor networks with a mobile beacon, in *The 1st IEEE International Conference on Mobile Ad Hoc and Sensor Systems (MASS 2004)* (IEEE, Fort Lauderdale, FL, USA, 2004), pp. 174–183
51. P.P. Shenoy, Using dempster-shafer's belief-function theory in expert systems, in *Advances in the Dempster-Shafer Theory of Evidence*, ed. by R.R. Yager, J. Kacprzyk, M. Fedrizzi (John Wiley & Sons, Inc., New York, NY, USA, 1994), pp. 395–414
52. K. Marzullo, Tolerating failures of continuous-valued sensors. ACM Trans. Comput. Syst. (TOCS) **8**(4), 284–304 (1990)
53. K. Marzullo, Maintaining the time in a distributed system: an example of a loosely-coupled distributed service. PhD thesis, Stanford University, Department of Electrical Engineering, Stanford, CA, 1984
54. D.L. Mills, *Computer Network Time Synchronization: The Network Time Protocol* (Taylor & Francis, 2011)
55. Z. Xiong, A.D. Liveris, S. Cheng, Distributed source coding for sensor networks. IEEE Signal Process. Mag. **21**(5), 80–94 (2004)
56. J. Kusuma, L. Doherty, K. Ramchandran, Distributed compression for sensor networks, in *The 2001 International Conference on Image Processing (ICIP-01)*, vol 1 (IEEE, Thessaloniki, Greece, 2001), pp. 82–85
57. S.S. Pradhan, K. Ramchandran, Distributed source coding using syndromes (DISCUS): design and construction. IEEE Trans Inf Theory **49**(3), 626–643 (2003)

Chapter 10
Location Management

10.1 Introduction

The most important problem arising out mobility support is tracking of mobile objects. A mobile object may represent an automobile, a cellular phone, a PDA, a laptop or even a piece of software. The location management is concerned with the ability to track or locate a moving object with an intention to communicate.

At an abstract level, a location management scheme involves two operations:

- Look up or search which locates a mobile object.
- Update which records the new location, each time a mobile object makes a move.

The search and update operations are also basic to a conventional database system. But there are three significant differences in operation of a database and a location management scheme:

- A database records only precise data, whereas a location management scheme has to deal with imprecisions of various kind in location data.
- The update requirements in a database is directly linked with data consistency problem. An update must be applied to a database as soon as it is received. The update requirements in maintaining location data, depends on the ability of a location management scheme to tolerate the degree of imprecision in location data.
- The number of updates handled by a location management scheme is several times more than the updates any moderate sized database can handle.

The reason behind large number of updates that any location management is expected to handle can be explained as follows. There is absolutely no control in proliferation of mobile devices. In a cell size of about half a kilometer radius, roughly about 1000 mobile devices may be active at any point of time. Assuming every such mobile object makes just about five moves in a day (in 12-h period), the total number of updates exceeds 10,000 calculated at the rate of one insertion and one deletion per move

© Springer Nature Singapore Pte Ltd. 2017
R.K. Ghosh, *Wireless Networking and Mobile Data Management*,
DOI 10.1007/978-981-10-3941-6_10

Fig. 10.1 Location space of
all objects

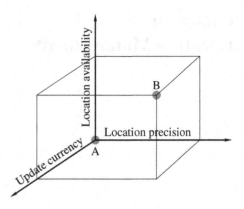

per mobile object. Suppose a small city has a cellular coverage area of 1000 cells
of the above kind. The active mobile devices operating in this city may potentially
generate up to a minimum of a million location updates in 12-h period. Clearly, no
conventional database can match the scale of updates expected to be handled by a
location management scheme.

The three dimension of the approaches to the management of location information
and its use can thus be identified as

- *Availability*: Represents the availability of location information at all the network
  sites or at a few selected places in the network.
- *Imprecision*: Represents the exactness of the location information.
- *Currency*: Represents the regularity of the location updates.

An abstract view of the space of location management problem is depicted in
Fig. 10.1. The position *B* in the location space refers to the situation when exact
information is maintained for each and every network sites. The location updates is
required for every move and should be disseminated to all the sites. Under this scenario look up becomes immediate. The other extreme case represented by position
A. It refers to the situation where no information about the location of any object
is maintained anywhere in the network. The search for a mobile object under this
situation becomes an exhaustive search of all the network sites. In between the above
two extremities, several combination of approaches regarding location updates and
look ups are possible.

We implicitly assume that location management is supported by a cellular network
architecture acting as the backbone. Furthermore, location management is handled
either in the data link or the network layer. Though cellular architecture is not the only
possibility, it is a good candidate to understand the issues that arise in the location
management. In absence of a infrastructures backbone architecture, an alternative
approach such as global positioning system has to be used to locate mobile objects.

10.1.1 Registration and Paging

There are two distinct mobility types involving mobile devices [2].

1. *Terminal mobility*: Allows a terminal identified by an identity independent of its point of attachment in the network. It allows a terminal to be attached to different points of a fixed network at different time. Therefore, allows mobility with respect to the point of attachment with the fixed network.
2. *Personal mobility*: It is associated with a user. A user gets a distinct identity independent of terminal s/he uses. Personal mobility allows the users to receive or make calls any where through any terminals.

In practice there is no distinction between terminal and personal mobilities in a mobile network. Since, terminals are portable and carried by the users, a personal mobility always accompanied by a movement of the terminal carried by the user. In other words, personal and terminal mobilities occur concurrently.

In order to facilitate location tracking, a mobile user has to explicitly register, and notify about the location of the terminal to one or more location servers belonging to the fixed network [2]. The granularity of location data may vary from a single cell to a group of cells. The paging process is a system initiated polling by sending signals to the likely locations to track the users. When the exact location of a user is known, a single paging operation suffice. By changing the size of registration area, flexibility in combination of paging and registration can be attained.

10.2 Two Tier Structure

In two tier scheme [13], there are two location registers per mobile hosts:

1. *home location register* (HLR), and
2. *visitors location register* (VLR).

Every mobile user is associated with a HLR which is located at a network location prespecified for each user. It is essentially a database for the home location of a user. Home location is a group of cells in which a user is normally expected to move around. Initially, a user registers his/her mobile handset in home location to avail the cellular service. A HLR maintains the current location of an user. The HLR entry corresponding to a user gets updated every time the user makes a move.

Each zone also maintains a VLR database, each entry in VLR is associated with a user currently active in that zone. In HLR-VLR scheme, the call setup is quite straightforward. When a user A in a location area LAI_i wants to communicate with another user B in a cell belonging to LAI_j, then the VLR in LAI_i is searched first. If there is no entry for B, the search is then directed to the HLR maintained at LAI_b which is the home location area of B. Thus, the location update process for tracking movement of an user is as follows:

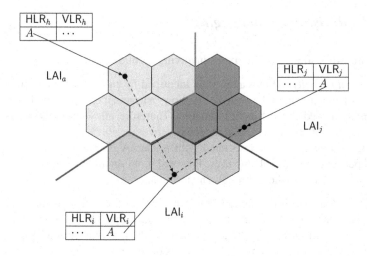

Fig. 10.2   Move in two-tier scheme

- When a user moves from a cell in LAI_i to a cell under LAI_j then the HLR of the user in its home location area gets updated.
- The VLR entry for the user is deleted from VLR database for area LAI_i, and an entry for the user is created in VLR database maintained for area LAI_j,

Figure 10.2 illustrates the movement of user A from a cell under LAI_i to a cell under LAI_j. LAI_a denotes the home location of A.

10.2.1   Drawbacks of Fixed Home Addresses

The home location is permanent. Thus long-lived mobile objects cannot change their homes. In other words, porting a mobile phone from one neighborhood to a different neighbourhood is not possible without explicit intervention by the service operators. The two-tier approach does not scale up too well as a highly distributed system would. Often the distant home locations may have to be contacted for look up even in the case of moderately mobile objects. In other words, the locality of the moves is not captured very well in a two-tier system.

10.3   Hierarchical Scheme

Hierarchical schemes [1, 8] are designed to take advantage of locality of movements. The location database at an internal node contains location information of users in the set of zones under the subtree rooted at the node. The information stored may simply

Fig. 10.3 Tree-based organization of location servers

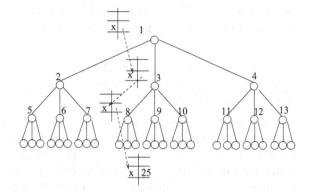

be a pointer to the lower-level location server or the current location. A leaf node serves a single zone. The organization of location servers in a tree-based hierarchical scheme is illustrated in Fig. 10.3. A zone can be considered as a location area or a single cell served by a mobile support station.

The performance of any location management scheme is clearly dependent on two factors [5, 6], namely,

1. The frequency of the moves made by the users.
2. The frequency of the calls received by each user.

Based on these factors we can define two performance metrics:

(i) *local call to mobility ratio*, and
(ii) *global call to mobility ratio*.

Let C_i be the expected number of calls received, and let U_i be the number of location area crossings made by a mobile user over a duration of time T. The fraction C_i/U_i is the global call to mobility ratio for time T. If C_{ij} represents expected number of calls from location LAI_j to the user in time T, then the local call to mobility ratio (LCMR) is the ratio C_{ij}/U_i. Local call to mobility ratio $LCMR_{ij}$ at any internal node j of tree hierarchy can be computed as $\sum_k LCMR_{ik}$, where k is a child of j.

10.3.1 Update Requirements

Typically, location information at internal nodes of in the hierarchy are stored as pointers. As an MH A moves from a cell in LAI_i under location server LS_i to a new location, say to the cell LAI_j under location server LS_j, the tree paths:

- from $LCA(LS_i, LS_j)$ down to LS_i and
- from $LCA(LS_i, LS_j)$ down to LS_j

should be updated. For example in the Fig. 10.3 each node represents a location server. Each leaf server store location information of mobile users in one location area. When a mobile user A moves from a cell in the location area under the server 25 to a cell in location area under the server 26, then updates will be needed at the nodes 3, 8, 9, 25, 26.

- At 8, 25 entries for A should be deleted.
- At 3, the entry for A should be updated.
- At 9, 26 new entries should be created for A.

If actual information on cell ID is stored at each node from the root to a leaf, then path from the root to $LCA(LS_i, LS_j)$ also has to be updated. However, typically pointers are stored. For example, if A is in a cell under 25, nodes 1, 3, 8 should have pointers leading to node 25 which indicates that A is in a cell under 25, and the cell ID information for A would be available in node 25. After a time t, suppose A moves to cell under 26, then all the nodes 1, 3, 9, 26 must be updated to indicate that A is now in a cell under 26. The information about location of A from node 25 should also be deleted.

10.3.2   Lookup in Hierarchical Scheme

The look up operation in hierarchical scheme can start with search for a mobile object A getting initiated at the neighbourhood, i.e., bottom up in the tree hierarchy. If A is not found in the current level of the hierarchy then the search process is just pushed one level up the hierarchy. Since the root maintains information about all the objects, the look up is bound to succeed at a higher level of the hierarchy. For example, suppose a search is initiated at a cell under LAI_i for the mobile object O_m which is currently located in a cell under LAI_j. The look up for O_m begins at location server LS_i, until it reaches $LCA(LS_i, LS_j)$ where an entry for O_m will be found. After that following the pointers to O_m, the search traverses down the hierarchy along the path from $LCA(LS_i, LS_j)$ to LS_j.

10.3.3   Advantages and Drawbacks

The tree-based hierarchical scheme does not require HLR and VLR type databases to be maintained. It supports locality of call setup process. However, it requires updates to be done at a number of location servers on different levels of hierarchy. The location information for each mobile object has to be replicated at each node on the tree path from the root to the leaf node corresponding to the location area in which the mobile object is located. The load for updates increases monotonically at the internal nodes higher up the hierarchy. The storage requirement also increases at higher levels.

10.4 Caching

Caching of locations [1, 6] is used primarily to reduce the lookup cost. It also helps to reduce the delay in establishing links. The idea has its root on the conventional use of caching.

In the two-tier architecture, when a large number of calls originate from the coverage area under a specific MSC to a particular mobile belonging to a different MSC, then the ID of the mobile and the address of its serving VLR can be stored at the calling MSC. This helps not only to reduce the signaling cost but also to reduce the delay in establishing the connection. Each time a call setup is attempted, the overhead associated with caching is as follows:

- First, the cached information of VLR is checked at calling MSC. If a cache hit occurs, the VLR of the callee is contacted directly.
- When the called mobile moves out of cached VLR, a cache miss occurs. Then the HLR of the called mobile is contacted to establish the call.

Checking cache at calling MSC adds little to overhead. On the other hand, if cache hit occurs, then the saving on signaling cost and the call setup latency improves. However, when called mobile crosses over to a new location area, old cache entry becomes invalid. So a cache revalidation is made by updating the old entry.

From the point of view of pure location update (no cache), new VLR address should be registered with HLR [9], and old VLR address should be purged from HLR. So, a location update cost is:

$$\text{update}_{nocache} = \text{cost}(\text{VLR}_{new} \leftrightarrow \text{HLR}) + \text{cost}(\text{VLR}_{old} \leftrightarrow \text{HLR})$$

For establishing a call in absence of a cache, HLR of the called mobile should be queried to obtain the address of VLR of the new region where the mobile is active. So, the cost of a lookup in a system without cache is:

$$\text{search}_{nocache} = \text{cost}(\text{VLR}_{caller} \leftrightarrow \text{HLR}) + \text{cost}(\text{HLR} \leftrightarrow \text{VLR}_{callee})$$

If the expected number of calls from a particular MSC to a particular mobile is ρ, then the cost for establishing calls will be

$$\text{update}_{nocache} + \rho \times \text{search}_{nocache}$$

Estimation of ρ requires an analysis of the call traces. A study [11] reveals that a user typically receives 90% of calls from his/her top 5 callers. A location area can be ranked according to the number of calls a user receives from that area.

Computation of local call to mobility ratio (LCMR) allows us to obtain a theoretical estimate of cache placement policy. Let us first model the calls received by a mobile and its mobility. Calls to a mobile and its movements are unrelated. Let the call arrival time at a mobile in a service area is exponentially distributed with mean arrival rate λ. Then probability distribution function is:

$$\lambda e^{-\lambda t}.$$

Similarly, let the residence time of a mobile in a location area be exponentially distributed with mean residence time $1/\mu$, i.e., the probability distribution function for the residence time is:

$$\mu e^{-\mu t}.$$

Let p_{cache} represent the probability that the cached information for a mobile at a location area is correct. In other words, p_{cache} defines the probability that mobile has not moved from its current location since it received the last call from the same location area. So,

$$p_{cache} = \text{Prob}[t < t_1] = \int_0^\infty \lambda e^{-\lambda t} \int_t^\infty \mu e^{-\mu t_1} dt_1 dt = \frac{\lambda}{\lambda + \mu}$$

In order to know if caching could beneficial, we need to find the relationship between calls received by a mobile and the number of moves it makes in between receiving calls. Let,

1. C_B represent the lookup cost of connection setup in basic scheme, i.e., if caching is not used, and
2. C_H represent the cost when caching is used.

In other words, C_H is the cost of retrieving the address of VLR associated with the MSC where the called mobile is active directly from the VLR associated with MSC from where the call originated. Estimation of C_B, on the other hand, involves two things: (i) the cost of accessing HLR entry of the called mobile from VLR of calling MSC, and (ii) the cost of retrieving VLR address of called mobile and caching the same at the caller MSC. Hence,

$$C_H = \text{cost}(VLR_{caller} \leftrightarrow VLR_{callee})$$
$$C_B = \text{cost}(VLR_{caller} \leftrightarrow HLR) + \text{cost}(HLR \leftrightarrow VLR_{callee})$$

A cost saving is possible in caching scheme, only if

$$p_{cache} C_H + (1 - p_{cache})(C_B + C_H) \le C_B,$$

where p_{cache} is the probability of a cache hit. From the above inequality, we find that $p_T = \min\{p_{cache}\} = C_H/C_B$. This implies that caching would be useful in saving cost, if

$$p_{cache} > p_T \ge C_H/C_B,$$

where p_T denotes threshold for the cache hit.

Calling MSC typically uses Local Call to Mobility Ratio (LCMR) for determining if caching could be cost effective. LCMR is equal to λ/μ. Relating LCMR to threshold for cache hit, we have

$$\text{LCMR}_T \geq p_T/(1 - p_T)$$

10.4.1 Caching in Hierarchical Scheme

In a hierarchical architecture, caching can be deployed to reduce the lookup time. Combined with *forward* and *reverse* bypass pointers, caches can be placed at a higher level of the hierarchy to service the calls originating from a group of cells rather than a single cell. The tradeoff of placing cache at a higher level is that the calls have to traverse a longer path. The idea is illustrated by Fig. 10.4. When a connection setup is requested from a mobile phone in a location area LAI_i to a mobile phone in location area LAI_j, the control message traverses up the tree from LS_i to $LCA(LS_i, LS_j)$ and then downwards to LS_j. The call setup requires an acknowledgement (ack) to be sent from LS_j back to LS_i along the same path. All the ancestors of LS_i in the hierarchy overhear this ack message, and one of them, say LS_i^a, can create a forward bypass pointer to LS_j. Likewise, a reverse bypass pointer can be created from an ancestor of LS_j to LS_i. A cache can be deployed at LS_i^a for the callees located in the cells belonging to LAI_j. Then subsequent calls from the callers active under coverage area LAI_i may be able to reach the location database LS_j via a shorter route through the forward bypass pointer at LS_i^a. Similarly, the acknowledgement messages originating

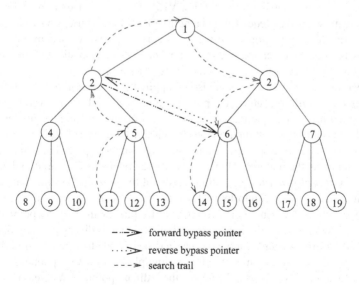

- - ·> forward bypass pointer
- · · ·> reverse bypass pointer
- - - ➤ search trail

Fig. 10.4 Caching in hierarchical location scheme

from the callees under LAI_j traverse a shorter path to LS_i using the reverse bypass pointer. If the level of LS_i^a is high then all the callers from its subtree can use the forward bypass pointers for the callees under the subtree of LS_j. But each call have to traverse a longer path up to LS_i, and may incur longer average lookup time, because the latency for locating the callee in the subtree of LS_j^a would depend on its size.

10.5   Forwarding Pointers

For a mobile user receiving relatively less calls compared to the moves, it is expensive to update all the location servers holding the location of the user on every move. It may be cheaper to leave a forwarding pointer to the new location at the previous location of the user. Then any call arriving at the old location can be re-routed to the current location by the forward pointer, and the update to the database entries holding a user's location can be made less frequently.

In two-tier architecture, if a user is frequently away from home, and the user's moves are mostly localized around the neighborhood of its current locations, then the location updates to the user's HLR would require long latencies. In order to avoid such updates requiring long latencies, forward pointers may be used. It works as follows. Whenever the user makes a move in the neighborhood of its current location, a forward pointer for the new location is placed in the VLR of the serving location. Therefore, when a call to the user reaches its home location server, the call can be diverted to the present location of the user. The call diversion is possible because HLR can access the VLR associated with the user's first location away from home. The other locations of the user can now be reached by following a chain of forward pointers starting from the first VLR. The chain of forward pointers are allowed to grow up to a predetermined length of K. When the user revisits a location, the potential loop condition in forward pointers chain is avoided by an implicit compression due to a location update in current VLR on a fresh move by the user. The approach of forwarding is applied on a per user basis.

Forwarding pointer strategy can also be applied to the hierarchical architecture. In a *simple forwarding* strategy, the pointers are placed in the leaf level. No update is performed up the tree path as a user moves from one location to another. But a forwarding pointer is left at the previous location to the current location.

In a *level forwarding* strategy, the forwarding pointer is placed at a higher level location server in the hierarchy. In this case, more updates are required to delete the database entries of lower level location servers of the previous location, and also to insert the current location into lower level ancestor location servers of the current location. Figure 10.5 illustrate the two schemes for placing the forward pointers. The dashed pointers illustrate the level forwarding while the ordinary pointers illustrate simple forwarding. Assuming mobile user *mu* to be initially located in cell 11 decides to move to a the cell 14, then simple forwarding places a forward pointer at the old leaf level location server 11 as indicated by the ordinary pointers. Whereas in the case of level forwarding, a forward pointer is placed at the ancestor location server 2 at

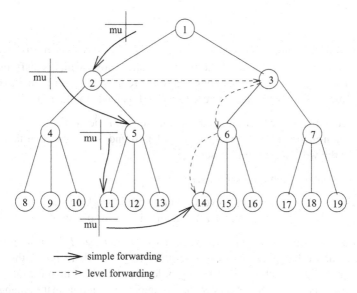

$\longrightarrow$ simple forwarding

- - - $>$ level forwarding

Fig. 10.5 Forwarding pointers in hierarchical scheme

level 3 which points to the location server 3 which is an ancestor of the new location. In this case, the updates are more than that required in simple forwarding. This is because, the entries concerning new location of *mu* should be made at nodes 3, 6, and 14 and database entries for *mu* at nodes 2, 5, and 11 are to be deleted.

10.6 Replication

Replication [5, 8] is another mechanism to reduce the cost for lookup. A high CMR (call to mobility ratio) value is the guiding principle for replication of the location of a user at selected nodes in the hierarchy.

In a two-tier architecture, replication may be employed, if the cost of replication is not more than the cost for non-replication. When many calls originate from a location area LAI_j to a mobile user, it may be cost effective to replicate the location of the user at the location server LS_j. However, if the user moves frequently then the maintenance of the replica incurs a heavy cost. A replica does not merely have location information. It also includes service information parameters such as call blocking, call forwarding, QoS requirements like the minimum channel quality and the acceptable bandwidth. Thus replicas should not be considered merely as extension of cache entries. Replicas may maintained both at the caller and the callee. If C_{ij} is the expected number of calls made from cells in LAI_j to a user over a period of time T, α is saving on replication at LS_j, β is the cost per update, and U_i is the number of updates then

$$\alpha.C_{ij} \geq \beta.U_i \tag{10.1}$$

should hold in order that the replication of the user at LS_j to be cost effective. The replicas of the user are kept at all the frequent callers areas which satisfy inequality 10.1. The set of the caller locations where the replica of a user is maintained is called a *working set* for that user. Every time a call is made to the user:

- From a member of the user's working set, no update is needed,
- From a non-member then if inequality 10.1 is found to be true then that cell is added to the working set of the user.

On the other hand, when the user makes a move:

- Inequality 10.1 is evaluated for every member of the working set,
- If it fails to hold for location area LAI_k, then it is removed from the working set.

The storage requirement for a single user's profile of size F in basic multi-tier location database having L levels is $F + ptr \times (L - 1)$, where ptr is the size of a pointer (user ID + database ID). If the profiles are replicated then the cumulative storage requirements should not exceed the storage space available in the database [7].

Apart from storage constraint, the decision to place a replica should also be based on minimization of network communication cost. In two-tier model, LCMR (local call to mobility ratio) is used for this purpose. A user i's profile is replicated a database j, only if LCMR$_{ij}$ exceeds a minimum threshold, say R_{min}. In hierarchical database, it is impossible to arrive at a single parameter for databases at different levels of the hierarchy. However, by using an additional parameter R_{max}, it is possible to arrive at a decision. The computation of $LCMR_{ij}$ for hierarchical database is done by a simple bottom up summing the $LCMR$ values of its children. Clearly, if high $LCMR$ value is the criterion for the selection of replication then when a node is selected for placing a replica, all its ancestor nodes also should be selected for replica placement. Therefore, this selection process results in excessive updates at higher levels of databases. This calls for setting a number of constraints including high (R_{max}) and low (R_{min}) marks for $LCMR$ values to determine the nodes in the hierarchy which may be selected for placing replicas. The rules for selecting replication site are as follows [7]:

1. If LCMR$_{ij} < R_{min}$, replica of i's profile is not placed at site j.
2. If LCMR$_{ij} \geq R_{max}$, then always place replica of i's profile at site j if the constraints on L and N are satisfied, where L represents hierarchy level, N is the bound on the number of maximum number of replicas for a user.
3. If $R_{min} \leq$ LCMR$_{ij} < R_{max}$, then the decision to place i's profile at site j will depend on database topology.

The other constraints are the level of location server in the hierarchy, and the maximum number of replicas to be placed. The reader is referred to [7] for details of analysis and the algorithm for placing replicas.

10.7 Personal Mobility

In the context of location management, there is a trade off between search and update. Most of the location management schemes are based on the approach to balance between search and update. To what extent the trade off can swing between the two will depend on the bound on signaling requirements. But the question is how to define a bound on signaling requirements? Furthermore, even if a bound can be defined, is it possible to reach the bound? Due to technological limitations, it is difficult to find satisfactory answers to above questions. However, analyzing problem of location management from a different track, we notice that terminal mobility and personal mobility are tightly coupled in a cellular communication network. In reality a mobile equipment is a portable device, and cannot move on its own. The movement of a mobile terminal is caused by the movements of the user carrying it. The movement of a person or the user of a mobile terminal can be considered as a path in some random process [3, 12].

10.7.1 Random Process, Information and Entropy

Let us explore a bit about the randomness of a process. If the volume of information content in a random process is high then the unpredictability is low. The probability of occurrence of an event contains the amount of information about the event. For example, if the probability of occurrence of an event A is known to be more than the probability of occurrence of another event B, then the amount of information available about A is more than that available for B. In other words, A's occurrence is more predictable than B's occurrence. This qualitative measure of information can be interpreted in terms of *surprisal*. Shannon [10] formulated surprisal as measure of information content in a system. It captures the following two important aspects:

1. The extent of randomness is determined by the size of entropy.
2. If randomness of a process is more, its unpredictability is higher.

For example, if an event E is known to happen always, then there is no surprisal in its occurrence. Equivalently, E's occurrence carries no information at all. In contrast, if E is a rare event, the fact that E has occurred is a surprise. So, the information it provides is high. The relationship between probability $p(E)$ of an event E and the size of expected information $H(E)$ of E's occurrence can be expressed as follows:

$$p(E) \rightarrow 0 \text{ implies } H(E) \rightarrow \infty$$
$$p(E) \rightarrow 1 \text{ implies } H(E) \rightarrow 0,$$

where

$p(E)$: proability of event E

$H(E)$: expected information conent in occurrence of E

In other words, the richness in information varies as the inverse of the information. The above connection between $p(E)$ and $H(E)$ is captured by Shannon as follows:

$$H(E) = p(E) \times \frac{1}{\log p(E)}$$

The reason for using logarithmic function instead of simple inverse is that it makes entropy an extensive property. In other words, if there are two systems A and B, then the total entropy should be additive. Any base greater than 1 should work. Typically, the base of logarithm is taken as 2, since $\log_2 q$ bits are needed to represent a quantity q.

The amount of information is measured in number of bits. For example, 3000 bits are needed in order to transmit the results of 1000 rollings of an unbiased hypothetical eight sided dice. If the dice is known to be biased, and the probability distribution is known, then a variable length encoding can be used. Since, the information bits are transmitted together, the encoding should be such that it is possible to disambiguate the block of bits representing the results of different rollings of the dice. This implies that the encoding must have *prefix property* which ensures that no code is a prefix of any code.

For example, let the probability distribution for a biased dice be:

$$p(i) = \begin{cases} 1/2^i, & \text{for } i \leq 7 \\ 1/2^{i-1}, & \text{for } i = 8, \end{cases}$$

Since, half the number of rollings result in 1, the shortest code should be used for 1. On the other hand, the code for the rarest event (a rolling that results in 8) could be the longest. A possible encoding scheme with the above mentioned properties would be as illustrated in Table 10.1. The above encoding satisfies the prefix property. The average number of bits needed for encoding the result of 1000 rollings is

$$\frac{1}{2} + 2 \times \frac{1}{4} + 3 \times \frac{1}{8} + \ldots + 7 \times \frac{1}{128} + 8 \times \frac{1}{128} = 1.984$$

So, with more information, the average number of bits required for transmitting the result 1000 rolling of the biased 8 sides hypothetical dice is reduced from 3000 to 1984 bits.

To reinforce our understanding, consider flipping of a biased coin. Suppose head shows up just once in 1000 flips. Let a 0 represent the fact that the result of a toss

Table 10.1 An encoding scheme with prefix property

Results of rolling	1	2	3	4	5	6	7	8
Code	0	10	110	1110	11110	111110	1111110	1111111

is a head. Similarly, let 1 represent a tail. Suppose the coin is tossed one million times. Without using any clever encoding, 1 bit will be required for the result of each toss. So, transmitting the result of one million tosses requires a million bits. Since a head shows up only once in 1000 flips of the biased coin, we may just record the sequence number of tosses that resulted in a head. The missing sequence numbers will then represent tails. Any number between 1 and 10^6 can be represented by at most $\log 10^6 = 20$ bits. Therefore, the information transfer for the result of 1000 flippings of biased coin will need just 20 bits. A total of 20000 bits will be needed for transmitting the results of one million tosses.

From the above examples, let us try to abstract out the answer to the general case of information coding for a random event. Consider a conventional dice with six faces to find an answer to the above question. If the dice is unbiased, the probability of occurrence of any value is $p = 1/6$, the number of bits required $= \log 6 = -\log(1/6) = -\log 6$. The result of one throw requires $\log 6 = 2.58$ bits. It is not immediately apparent how the result any particular throw of a dice can be encoded by less than 3 bits. However, if we group g successive throws, the results can coded by less than 6^g bits. For example, the number of possible outcomes for a group of three throws $= 6^3 = 216 < 255$, and 0–255 can be coded using 8 bits. Thus, for a biased probability distribution, the number of bits required for the optimal code is determined by

$$-\sum_x p(x) \times \log p(x).$$

The examples discussed in this section, point to the fact that a rare event (probability of occurrence is low) has a high information content. In the coin toss example, the information content in occurrence of a head is $-\log(1/1000) = \log 1000 = 9.9658$. So, 10 bits will be needed to represent the occurrence of a head. As against this information contents in appearance of a tail is $-\log(999/1000) = 0.0044$ bit. The average information content is given by:

$$(1/1000) \times 10 + (999/1000) \times 0.0044 = 0.0114 \text{ bit}.$$

Let us try to generalize the method of determining information content as outlined in the above example. Suppose, the probability of an outcome A_i of a random event A is $p(A_i)$. Then the expected value of self information in A

$$H(A) = \sum_{i=1}^{n} p(A_i) \times \log\left(\frac{1}{p(A_i)}\right)$$

$$= -\sum_{i=1}^{n} p(A_i) \times \log p(A_i)$$

According to Shannon [10], $H(A)$ represents the entropy of A.

Suppose X and Y is a pair of discrete random variables with joint probability distribution $p(x, y)$, where $x \in \mathcal{X}$, $y \in \mathcal{Y}$. The joint entropy of X and Y is:

$$H(X, Y) = - \sum_{x \in \mathcal{X}} \sum_{y \in \mathcal{Y}} p(x, y) \log p(x, y)$$

Assume that the conditional entropy $H(Y|X)$ represents the information content of a random event Y given that some event X has occurred. $H(Y|X)$ is given by the formula:

$$H(Y|X) = \sum_{x \in \mathcal{X}} p(x) H(Y|X = x) = - \sum_{x \in \mathcal{X}} p(x) \sum_{y \in \mathcal{Y}} p(y|x) \log p(y|x)$$

$$= - \sum_{x \in \mathcal{X}} \sum_{y \in \mathcal{Y}} p(x, y) \log p(y|x)$$

Joint entropy and conditional entropy are closely related. Joint entropy is the sum of entropy of the first random variable and the conditional entropy of the second random variable given the first.

$$H(X, Y) = - \sum_{x \in \mathcal{X}} \sum_{y \in \mathcal{Y}} p(x, y) \log p(x, y)$$

$$= - \sum_{x \in \mathcal{X}} \sum_{y \in \mathcal{Y}} p(x, y) \log(p(x)p(y|x))$$

$$= - \sum_{x \in \mathcal{X}} \sum_{y \in \mathcal{Y}} p(x, y) \log p(x) - \sum_{x \in \mathcal{X}} \sum_{y \in \mathcal{Y}} p(x, y) \log p(y|x)$$

$$= - \sum_{x \in \mathcal{X}} \sum_{y \in \mathcal{Y}} p(x, y) \log p(x) + H(Y|X)$$

$$= - \sum_{x \in \mathcal{X}} p(x) \log p(x) + H(Y|X)$$

$$= H(X) + H(Y|X) = H(Y) + H(X|Y).$$

The generalization of the above result, known as chain rule, says:

$$H(X_1, X_2, \ldots, X_n) = \sum_{i=1}^{n} H(X_i|X_{i-1}, \ldots, X_1).$$

If the random variables are known to be independent then according to the chain rule:

$$H(X_1, X_2, \ldots, X_n) = \sum_{i=1}^{n} H(X_i).$$

10.7.2 Mobility Pattern as a Stochastic Process

In order to capture the personal mobility, a user's movement is considered as a random process. In a cellular infrastructure, a user's mobility can be represented as a sequence of cells that the user has visited. In a GSM type network, each symbol represents a Location Area Identity (LAI) consisting of several cells. There is a possibility that certain substrings of LAIs have repeated occurrences in a string of LAIs representing a user's movement. Such repetitions essentially represent locality of a user's movements. By characterizing mobility as probabilistic sequence, mobility can be interpreted as a stochastic process.

At first we need to be clear on two issues:

1. How a user may move in a service area?
2. How the movements may be recorded?

Figure 10.6 illustrates an example for a service area consisting of eight LAIs a, b, c, d, e, f, g, h. The shapes of actual cell areas are not hexagonal, but irregular geometric contours. The cell contours are determined by actual field measurement of signal strengths. Multiple cells are grouped into an LAI. The topology of LAIs in coverage area can be abstracted in form of a graph shown along side. Each node in the graph represents an LAI. Two nodes are connected with edge if and only if the corresponding LAIs are adjacent to each other. With the graph abstraction as explained above, the mobility pattern of a user is represented as a walk in the graph. A walk is formed by the updates of the user's locations as a user moves and enters new LAIs.

The mobiles send their location updates to network subsystem. The frequency of update is controlled by one of following three possible ways.

- *Distance based updates*: In the distance based updates, mobile terminals keep track of the Euclidean distance from the time of the last update. If distance travelled from the last update crosses a threshold D, the mobile should send an update.
- *Movement based*: A mobile sends an update if it has performed n cell crossings since the last update.
- *Time based*: a mobile sends periodic update.

It is also possible to combine three update schemes in several possible ways. For example, distance based updates can be combined with movement based updates or

Fig. 10.6 GSM type location area map (Source [3])

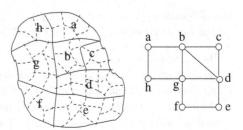

Table 10.2 An example for LAI crossing by a mobile

Crossings in morning

Time	11:04	11:32	11:57	
Crossing	$a \to b$	$b \to a$	$a \to b$	

Crossings in afternoon

Time	3:18	4:12	4:52	
Crossing	$b \to a$	$a \to b$	$b \to c$	

Crossings in evening

Time	5:13	6:11	6:33	6:54
Crossing	$c \to d$	$d \to c$	$c \to b$	$b \to a$

Table 10.3 Sequence of cells representing movement history

Update scheme	Movement history
$T = 1$ h	aaabbbbacdaaa...
$T = 1/2$ h	aaaaabbbbbbbbaabcddcaaaa...
$M = 1$	abababcdcba...
$M = 2$	aaacca...
$T = 1$ h, $M = 1$	aaababbbbbaabccddcbaaaa...

time based updates. Similarly, movement based updates can be combined with time based updates, and so on.

Let us consider an example to understand how different updates schemes would generate the updates. Suppose the service is started at 9.00 AM. An example of LAI crossings is provided in Table 10.2. With the movement history, shown earlier in Table 10.2, the LAI sequences reported by different update schemes may be as shown in Table 10.3.

In summary, the movement history of a user is represented by a string $v_1, v_2, v_3, \ldots$, where each symbol v_i, $i = 1, 2, \ldots$, denotes the LAI reported by the mobile in ith update. The symbols are drawn from an alphabet set $\mathcal{V}$ representing the set of LAIs covering the entire service area. The mobility of a user is characterized as a stationary stochastic process $\{V_i\}$, where V_i's form a sequence of random variables, and each V_i takes a value v_i from set $\mathcal{V}$.

Before proceeding further, let us define a stochastic process.

Definition 10.1 (*Stochastic process*) A stochastic process is stationary if the joint probability distribution does not change when shifted in time or space.

If observed over time, a normal mobile user is most likely to exhibit the preference for visiting known sequence of LAIs in a time invariant manner. Equivalently, the correlation between the adjacent LAIs in the string of visited locations remains unchanged over all periods of time. Consequently, personal mobility pattern can be treated as a stationary stochastic process. Thus,

$$\Pr[V_1 = v_1, V_2 = v_2, \ldots, V_n = v_n] = \Pr[V_{l+1} = v_1, V_{l+2} = v_2, \ldots, V_{l+n} = v_n].$$

The above general model could aid in learning, if a universal predictor can be constructed. Let us explore the possibility of evolving a statistical model for a universal predictor. The common models used for interpreting the movement history are:

- Ignorant Model (IM)
- Identically Independent Distribution (IID)
- Markov Model (MM)

IM disbelieves and disregards past history. So the probability of any LAI residence is the same, i.e., 1/8 for each of the 8 LAIs for the chosen example.

IID model assumes that the values random variables defining a stochastic process are Identically and Independently Distributed. It uses relative frequencies of symbols for estimating the residence probabilities of the LAIs. Assuming time and movement based scheme the probabilities for the string aaababbbbbaabccddcbaaaa, are:

$$p(a) = 10/23, p(b) = 8/23, p(c) = 3/23, p(d) = 2/23,$$
$$p(e) = p(f) = p(g) = p(h) = 0.$$

The string consists of 23 symbols. Symbols e, f, g, h do not occur at all. While the probability of occurrence of any of the remaining symbols is determined by its relative frequency.

The simplest Markov model is a Markov chain where distribution of a random variable depends only on distribution of the previous state. So, this model assumes the stochastic process to be a stationary (time-invariant) Markov chain defined by:

$$Pr[V_k = v_k | V_1 = v_1, \ldots, V_{k-1} = v_{k-1}]$$
$$= Pr[V_k = v_k | V_{k-1} = v_{k-1}]$$
$$= Pr[V_i = v_i | V_{i-1} = v_{i-1}]$$

for arbitrary choices of k and i. Notice that the LAIs e, f, g, h are not visited at all. This implies each of these four LAIs have zero residence probability or equivalently, the effective state space is $\{a, b, c, d\}$. One step transition probabilities are:

$$P_{i,j} = Pr[V_k = v_j | V_{k-1} = v_i],$$

where $v_i, v_j \in \{a, b, c, d\}$, are estimated by relative counts. So, the movement profile can be represented by the corresponding transition probability matrix:

$$P = \begin{bmatrix} 2/3 & 1/3 & 0 & 0 \\ 3/8 & 1/2 & 1/8 & 0 \\ 0 & 1/3 & 1/3 & 1/3 \\ 0 & 0 & 1/2 & 1/2 \end{bmatrix}$$

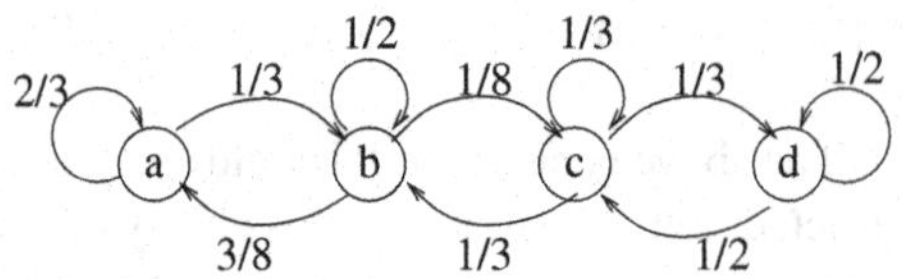

Fig. 10.7 One step state
transition diagram for
personal mobility

Table 10.4 Frequencies of symbols corresponding to three contexts

Order-0	Order-1	Order-2
a(10)|Λ	a(6)|a b(1)|c	a(3)|aa a(2)|ba a(1)|cb
b(8)|Λ	b(3)|a c(1)|c	b(2)|aa b(1)|ba d(1)|cc
c(3)|Λ	a(3)|b d(1)|c	a(1)|ab a(1)|bb d(1)|cd
d(2)|Λ	b(4)|b c(1)|d	b(1)|ab b(3)|bb b(1)|dc
	c(1)|b d(1)|d	c(1)|ab c(1)|bc c(1)|dd

Note that a occurs 6 out of 9 times in context of a and 3 times out of 8 times
in context of b. The values of other transition probabilities can be found likewise.
Thus, the state transitions with the respective probabilities can be viewed as shown
in Fig. 10.7. Let $\Pi = [p(a)\ p(b)\ p(c)\ p(d)]^T$ be in steady state probability vector.
Solving $\Pi = \Pi \times P$ with $p(a) + p(b) + p(c) + p(d) = 1$, we obtain $p(a) = 9/22$,
$p(b) = 4/11, p(c) = 3/22$ and $p(d) = 1/11$.

To summarize the above discussion, though IID is the first step toward adaptive
modeling, it can never be adaptive. The optimal paging strategy dependents on the
independent probabilities of symbols $\{a, b, c, d, e, f, g, h\}$. But, if we already know
that the user has reported the last update as d then neither a nor b should be paged.
So, IID ignore the knowledge of the previous update.

Order-1 Markov model carries information to the extent of one symbol context. For uniformity, IM is referred to as order-(-1) Markov model, and IID
as order-0 Markov model. Order-2 Markov model can be constructed by counting the frequencies of symbols appearing in order-2 contexts for the sequence
aaababbbbbaabccddcbaaaa. Table 10.4 provides frequencies of different symbols for all three contexts.

According to order-1 model the probability of taking the route a $\rightarrow$ b $\rightarrow$ c $\rightarrow$
b $\rightarrow$ c $\rightarrow$ d is:

$$=(9/22) \times (1/3) \times (1/8) \times (1/3) \times (1/8) \times (1/3)$$
$$=1/4224 = 2.37 \times 10^{-4}$$

It is unlikely that any user will ever take such a zig-zag route. Though the probability is very low; still it is not zero. However, if order-2 model is used then the
proposed route will be impossible. So, the richness of the information helps.

The question is how much of the past history should be stored so that it could lead
to a good prediction? Storing the movement history for every movement of a user
is not practical. The conditional entropy is known to be a decreasing function of the

number of symbols in a stationary process [4], implying that the advantage of higher order contexts die out after a finite value. To appreciate this fact, we need compare per symbol entropy rates $H(\mathcal{V})$ for a stochastic process $\mathcal{V} = \{V_i\}$. This quantity is defined as

Definition 10.2

$$H(\mathcal{V}) = \lim_{n \to \infty} \frac{1}{n} H(V_1, V_2, \ldots, V_n).$$

if the limit exists. The conditional entropy rate $H'(\mathcal{V})$ for the same process is defined by

$$H'(\mathcal{V}) = \lim_{n \to \infty} \frac{1}{n} H(V_n | V_1, \ldots, V_{n-1}),$$

if the limit exists.

Using the above definition, let us compute $H'(\mathcal{V})$ for the three different models for the example for personal mobility we have used in the text.

- Order-(-1) model:
  V_is are independently and uniformly distributed, so $p(v_i) = 1/8$ for all $v_i \in \{a, b, c, d, e, f, g, h\}$ in the chosen running example. Due to independence of events, $p(v_n | v_1, \ldots v_{n-1}) = p(v_n)$. Therefore,

$$H(\mathcal{V}) = H'(\mathcal{V}) = -\sum_{v_i} p(v_i) \log p(v_i)$$

$$= \sum_{i=1}^{8} (1/8) \log 8 = \log 8 = 3.$$

  The above equation implies that the per symbol entropy rate is 3 bits for order-(-1) model.
- Order-0 model:
  In this case, V_is are Independently and Identically Distributed. Due to independence $p(v_n | v_1, \ldots v_{n-1}) = p(v_n)$. Therefore,

$$H(\mathcal{V}) = H'(\mathcal{V}) = -\sum_{v_i} p(v_i) \log p(v_i)$$

$$= (10/23) \times \log(23/10) + (8/23) \times \log(23/8)$$
$$+ (3/23) \times \log(23/3) + (2/23) \times \log(23/2)$$
$$\approx 1.742.$$

Therefore, the per symbol entropy rate for order-0 model is 1.742 bits which is much better than order-(-1) model.

- Order-1 model:
  In this case, V_is form Markov chains. So $p(v_n|v_1 \ldots v_{n-1}) = p(v_n|v_{n-1}) = P_{v_{n-1},v_n}$.
  Substituting steady state probabilities $p(a) = 9/22$, $p(b) = 4/11$, $p(c) = 3/22$
  and $p(d) = 1/11$, we find

$$
\begin{aligned}
H'(\mathcal{V}) &= -\sum_{v_i} p(v_i) \left(\sum_j P_{i,j} \log P_{i,j} \right) \\
&= \frac{9}{22} \left(\frac{2}{3} \log \frac{3}{2} + \frac{1}{3} \log \frac{3}{1} \right) + \frac{4}{11} \left(\frac{3}{8} \log \frac{8}{3} + \frac{1}{2} \log \frac{2}{1} + \frac{1}{8} \log \frac{8}{1} \right) \\
&\quad + \frac{3}{22} \left(3 \times \frac{1}{3} \log \frac{3}{1} \right) + \frac{1}{11} \left(2 \times \frac{1}{2} \log \frac{2}{1} \right) \approx 1.194.
\end{aligned}
$$

Note that 3 bits are sufficient to represent any symbol from a space of eight symbols $\{a, b, c, d, e, f, g\}$. So order-(-1) model cannot resolve uncertainties in any of the three bits. But both order-0 and order-1 models exhibit richness in information and gradual decrease in entropy rates. The entropy rates $H(\mathcal{V})$ and $H'(\mathcal{V})$ are same in both order-(-1) and order-0 MM due to independence of the events related to symbols. However, when order-1 MM is used, the per symbol entropy rate is 1.194 bits. It improves the entropy rate substantially over order-(-1) and order-0 models.

A mobile terminal's location is unknown for the interval between two successive updates. The approach in LeZi update is to delay the updates, if the path traversed by mobile is familiar. The information lag does not impact paging, because system uses prefix matching to predict location with high probability.

10.7.3   Lempel-Ziv Algorithm

LeZi update is based on Lempel-Ziv's text compression algorithm [14]. The algorithm provides a universal model for variable-to-fixed length coding scheme. The algorithm consists of an encoder and decoder. The encoder incrementally parses the text into distinct phrases or words (which have not been observed so far). A dictionary is gradually built as phrases keep coming. LeZi update's encoder is identical to the encoder of Lempel-Ziv's algorithm (see Algorithm 3). It runs at mobile terminal. The encoding process can be best explained by executing it on a string of symbols. Let the example string be:

aaababbbbbaabccddcbaaaa

Table 10.5 illustrates how encoding of each phrase is realized. The first incoming phrase is a, Λ or the null phrase is its prefix. The null phrase is assumed to be a prefix of any phrase having one symbol, and the index of Λ is set to 0. So, a is coded

---

Algorithm 3: Lempel-Ziv encoder

---

begin
    `// Encoder at mobile or compressing algorithm.`
    dictionary = null;
    phrase w = null;
    while *(true)* **do**
        wait for next symbol v;
        if *($w.v$ in dictionary)* **then**
         | $w = w.v$;
        end
        else
            encode $< index(w), v >$;
            add $w.v$ to dictionary;
            w = null;
        end
    end
end

Table 10.5 Encoding of different phrases

Index	Prefix	Last symbol	Input phrase	Output
1	Λ	a	a	(0, a)
2	a	a	aa	(1, a)
3	Λ	b	b	(0, b)
4	a	b	ab	(1, b)
5	b	b	bb	(3, b)
6	bb	a	bba	(5, a)
7	ab	c	abc	(4, c)
8	Λ	c	c	(0, c)
9	Λ	d	d	(0, d)
10	d	c	dc	(9, c)
11	b	a	ba	(3, a)
12	aa	a	aaa	(2, a)

as 0a. The index of an incoming phrase is determined by the position of the phrase in the dictionary which is largest proper prefix of the current phrase. A proper prefix excludes the last symbol in a phrase. For example, let us see how the next incoming phrase aa is encoded. The largest proper prefix of aa is a. Since the position of a is 1 in the dictionary, the index of the incoming phrase is 1. Therefore, appending *a* to 1, we get the encoding of aa as 1a. Therefore using encoding algorithm the string aaababbbbbbaabccddaaaa is encoded as: 0a, 1a, 0b, 1b, 3b, 5a, 4c, 0c, 0d, 9c, 3a, 2a.

A code word consists of two parts (i) an index, and (ii) a symbol. The index represents the dictionary entry of the phrase which is the prefix of the code word. The prefix completely matches with the code word symbol-wise except for the last symbol. Therefore, the decoding consists of finding the prefix and appending the last symbol to it. The major distinction between LeZi update and Lempel-Ziv's algorithm is in the decoder part. In the case of LeZi update, the decoder executes at the network side. The decoder algorithm is provided in Algorithm 4.

Algorithm 4: Decoder for LeZi update

begin
   // Decoder at the system side. It basically decompresses the string.
   while *(true)* **do**
      wait for the next code word $< i, s >$;
      decode phrase = dictionary[i].s;
      add phrase to dictinary;
      increment frequency of every prefix of the phrase;
   end
end

To see how the decoding process works, we consider code word specified in terms of tuples <index, last_symbol> and illustrate the decoding with the help of Table 10.6. When the code word tuple is received, the index part is extracted first. For example index part in the input tuple (0, a) is 0. The index is then used to retrieve the phrase from the dictionary. Since, index of Λ is 0, the phrase retrieved is Λ. Then symbol of input codeword is concatenated with retrieved phrase, i.e. a is appended to λ. Since Λ+a = a, the decoding of (0, a) outputs the phrase a. Similarly, when the code word (5, a) is received, the phrase having index 5 is extracted from the dictionary, and the symbol a is appended to it producing the output bba. Along with

Table 10.6 Decoding of phrases

Input tuple	Prefix phrase	Last symbol	Output phrase
(0, a)	Λ	a	a
(1, a)	a	a	aa
(0, b)	Λ	b	b
(1, b)	a	b	ab
(3, b)	b	b	bb
(5, a)	bb	a	bba
(4, c)	ab	c	abc
(0, c)	Λ	c	c
(0, d)	Λ	d	d
(9, c)	d	c	dc
(3, a)	b	a	ba
(2, a)	aa	a	aaa

the decoding, frequency count of all the prefixes are incremented. For example, when phrases (0, a), (1, a), (1, b), (4, c), and (2, a) get decoded a's frequency count is incremented. So, total frequency count for a is 5. Similarly, frequency count aa is incremented during decoding of (1, a) and (2, a), and total frequency count of phrase aa is computed as 2.

The decoding process helps to build conditional probabilities of larger contexts as larger and larger phrases are inserted into the dictionary. So, dictionaries are maintained at system as well as at each mobile terminal. A mobile terminal sends the updates only in coded form. It delays sending of update until a pre-determined interval of time has elapsed. The updates are processed in chunks and sent to the network as a sequence code words of the form $C(w_1)C(w_2)C(w_3)\ldots$, where each phrase w_i, for $i = 1, 2, \ldots$, is a non-overlapping segment of symbols from the string $v_1v_2v_3 \ldots$ that represents the LAIs visited by the mobile since the time of sending the last update to the network. So, LeZi update can be seen as a path based update scheme instead of LAI based update.

10.7.4 Incremental Parsing

The coding process is closely inter-twined with the learning process. The learning process works efficiently by creating the dictionary and searching it for the existence of incoming phrases. An input string $v_1v_2\ldots v_n$ is parsed into k distinct phrases $w_1, w_2, \ldots, w_k$ such that the prefix (all symbols except the last one) of the current incoming phrase w_j is one of the previously occurring phrases w_i, $1 \le i < j$. So, the context statistics related to all prefixes can be updated during the parsing of the current phrase itself. In addition, the prefix property also allows to store the history efficiently in a trie.

Figure 10.8 depicts the trie produced by classical Lempel-Ziv algorithm for the string in the example. The numbers alongside the symbols represent the frequency

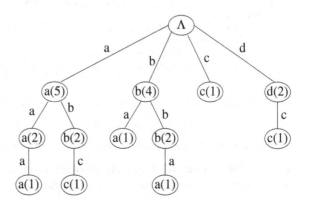

Fig. 10.8 Trie built by classical Lempel-Ziv algorithm

computed by Lempel-Ziv algorithm. The process of computing frequencies has been explained in the previous subsection.

A new dictionary entry can be created by appending one symbol to an already existing phrase in the dictionary. An existing phrase terminates at a node of the trie. An appended symbol to an existing phrase appears as a label of an edge leading from terminating node of the phrase to another. As the incremental parsing progresses, larger and larger phrases are stored in the dictionary. Consequently, conditional probabilities among the phrases starts to build up. Since there is limit to the richness of higher order Markov model, Lempel-Ziv's symbol-wise model eventually converge to a universal model.

As far as personal mobility is concerned, the location updates can be viewed as that of generating a new symbol for the sequence representing the movement history of the form $v_1 v_2 \ldots v_n$. So, the movement history can be parsed into distinct substrings and new update can be inserted into a trie which gradually builds the personal mobility pattern.

However, we cannot use Lempel-Ziv compression based model in a straightforward way. One serious problem with the above compression model is that it fails to capture conditional entropy early on due to following reasons:

- It works on one phrase at a time.
- Decoding algorithm counts only the frequencies of the prefixes of a decoded phrase.
- It is unaware about the contexts that straddle phrase boundaries.

All of the above slow down the rate of convergence. LeZi update uses an enhanced trie, where frequencies of all prefixes of all suffixes are updated. So instead of using the decoder of the previous section LeZi update uses a slightly altered decoder as provide by Algorithm 5. By doing so, it captures the straddling effect.

Algorithm 5: Enhanced decoder for LeZi update

begin
    // Works for symbols straddling phrase boundaries.
    while *(true)* **do**
        wait for the next code word $< i, s >$;
        decode phrase = dictionary[i].s;
        add phrase to dictinary;
        increment frequency of every prefix of every suffix the phrase;
    end
end

The revised frequency counting method for phrases in LeZi update is as follow:

- Find all the prefixes of all the suffixes of each incoming phrase.
- Increment the frequency each time a particular prefix is encountered starting from zero.

Fig. 10.9 Enhanced trie

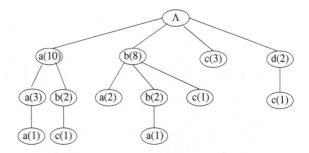

Let us examine the effect of considering all prefixes of all the suffixes in generating frequency counts for symbols in the example string. For the phrase aaa:

- Suffixes are aaa, aa and a, so the frequency counts of all prefixes of aaa, aa, and a are incremented.
- The frequency counts of aa incremented by 2.
- The frequency counts of a incremented by 3.

The total count for a can be found by considering phrases a, aa, ab, ba, abc, bba, and aaa. The enhanced trie obtained by LeZi update method is provided by Fig. 10.9.

In order to estimate the effectiveness of the new model for personal mobility against the model that is based on the classical Lempel-Ziv compression scheme, let us compute the entropies for each case. The conditional entropy without considering suffixes (see Fig. 10.8):

$$H(V_1) = \frac{5}{12} \log \frac{12}{5} + \frac{1}{3} \log 3 + \frac{1}{12} \log 12 + \frac{1}{6} \log 6$$
$$\approx 1.784. \text{ bits, and}$$

$$H(V_2|V_1) = \frac{5}{12} \left(2 \times \frac{1}{2} \log 2 \right) + \frac{4}{12} \left(\frac{1}{3} \log 3 + \frac{2}{3} \log \frac{3}{2} \right) + \frac{1}{6} \log 6$$
$$\approx 0.723 \text{ bits.}$$

Other two terms of $H(V_2|V_1)$ being 0 are not included in the expression. The estimate for $H(\mathscr{V}) = (1.784 + 0.723)/2 = 1.254$ bits. The conditional probabilities of all order-2 contexts are 0.

When all the prefixes of all the suffixes are considered, the frequency count would be as shown in trie of Fig. 10.9. With enhanced tries, we still have

$$H(V_1) = \frac{10}{23} \log \frac{23}{10} + \frac{8}{23} \log \frac{23}{8} + \frac{3}{23} \log \frac{23}{3} + \frac{2}{23} \log \frac{23}{2}$$
$$\approx 1.742. \text{ bits, and}$$

$$H(V_2|V_1) = \frac{10}{23} \left(\frac{3}{5} \log \frac{5}{3} + \frac{2}{5} \log \frac{5}{2} \right) + \frac{8}{23} \left(2 \times \frac{2}{5} \log \frac{5}{2} + \frac{1}{5} \log 5 \right)$$
$$\approx 0.952 \text{ bits.}$$

Therefore, the estimate for $H(\mathscr{V}) = (1.742 + 0.952)/2 = 1.347$ bits when all the prefixes of all the suffixes are considered, implying that the suggested enhancements carry more information. Hence, location update based on the enhancements is expected to perform better than the simple Lempel-Ziv compression method.

10.7.5   Probability Assignment

The prediction of a location for mobile terminal is guided by the probability estimates of its possible locations. The underlying principle behind the probability computation is PPM (prediction by partial matching). PPM uses the longest match between the previously seen strings and the current context. Our interest is in estimating the probability of occurrence of the next symbol (LAI) on a path segment that may be reported by the next update. A path segment is an LAI-sequence generated when traversing from the root to a leaf of the sub-tries representing the current context. The conditional probability distribution is obtained by the estimates of the conditional probabilities for all LAIs given the current context.

Suppose no LeZi type update is received after receiving aaa and we want to find the probability of predicting the next symbol as a. The contexts that can be used are all suffixes of aaa except for itself, namely, aa and a and Λ (null context). PPM tells that to determine the probabilities only the previously seen phrases should be considered. Therefore, the possible paths that can be predicted with the contexts aa, a and Λ are as shown in Table 10.7. Start from the highest order context, i.e., aa. The probability a in this context is 1/3. The probability of a null prediction in the context aa is 2/3. It leads to order 1 (with null prediction) context, where the probability of a's occurrence is $2/10 = 1/5$. Now fall back to order-0 (with null prediction), which has probability $5/10 = 1/2$. The probability of a's occurrence in order-0 is 5/23. So the blended probability of the next symbol being a is

$$\frac{1}{3} + \frac{2}{3} \left(\frac{1}{5} + \frac{1}{2} \left(\frac{5}{23} \right) \right) = 0.5319$$

To examine a variation, consider the occurrence of phrase bba after receiving aaa. The phrase bba does not occur in any of the contexts 1 or 2. The probabilities of escape from the order-1 and the order-2 contexts with null prediction are:

Table 10.7 Conditional probabilities of movement prediction

aa (Order-2)	a (Order-1)	Λ (Order-0)		
a(1)|aa Λ(2)|aa	a(2)|a aa(1)|a b(1)|a bc(1)|a Λ(5)|a	a(5)|Λ aa(2)|Λ ab(1)|Λ abc(1)|Λ b(3)|Λ	ba(2)|Λ bb(1)|Λ bba(1)|Λ bc(1)|Λ c(3)|Λ	d(1)|Λ dc(1)|Λ Λ(1)|Λ

- *Order 2 context*: (with phrase aa), the probability of null prediction is 2/3 (out of 3 occurrences of aa).
- *Order 1 context*: (with phrase a), the probability of null prediction is 1/2, because Λ occurs 5 times out of 10.

In summary, the idea of prediction works as follows. It starts with a chosen highest order of context, and then escape to the lower orders until order 0 is reached. This essentially means given a path segment we try to predict the next symbol with high probability.

Therefore, the blended probability of phrase bba is

$$0 + \frac{2}{3}\left(0 + \frac{1}{2}\left(\frac{1}{23}\right)\right) = 0.0145$$

Since a occurs once and b occurs twice in the phrase bba, the individual probabilities of symbols a and b respectively are: $(1/3) \times 0.0145 = 0.0048$, and $0.0145 \times (2/3) = 0.0097$.

10.8 Distributed Location Management

In earlier sections of this chapter, we discussed about various location management schemes. Each scheme essentially uses some form of distribution of location information across the network. The underlying ideas is that location information is organized in a way such that the cost and latency in determining the exact location of a mobile device are minimized. Yet, the effect of information distribution on the performances of lookups and updates could be limited for wide area roaming of the mobile users. This is due to the fact that the distant network messages have to be exchanged to support wide area roaming. In this section, we describe a distributed system for storing and accessing location information.

The scheme grew out of the idea of maintaining the location information of a user in a single database at a time instead of replicating in several levels of hierarchy as described in Sect. 10.3. The entire coverage area is divided into several location areas or regions and consists of three levels of hierarchy. Each region consists of a

Fig. 10.10 The model

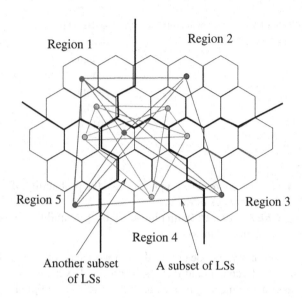

number of mobile switching centers (MSC), and the area under coverage of each MSC consists of a number of cells. Each cell is served by a base station (BS). Logically all mobile users which visit a region are partitioned into groups. There will be a Location Server (LS) in a region of coverage corresponding to each group of the mobile users. The location data of a mobile user is always stored in the LS that corresponds to its group in the region when the user visits a region. The grouping of mobile stations and the region division could be unrelated or related in some way. The matching LSs of the matching groups of mobile users in different regions are connected to each other. In other words, the model consists of

- LSs partitioned up into subsets.
- The LSs belonging to same subsets are interlinked.
- There is a LS of each subset in every region.
- Each mobile user can map to only one such subset.
- The location data of a mobile host MH visiting a region R is stored at a LS in R such that the LS is the member of subset of LSs to which the MH is mapped.

The model is depicted in Fig. 10.10. The regions in the figure are demarcated by heavy lines. Each cell is represented by a hexagonal area. There are two LSs per region, each belonging to a different subset as indicated by filled blue and red circles respectively. Each LS serves roughly for the volume of users in 2–3 cells. The LSs belonging to same subset are fully interconnected. Though the figure does not indicate, each MSC is connected to all the LSs in the same region. In other words, LSs are part of GSM's network subsystem.

10.8.1 The Call Setup Protocol

An MSC initiating a call setup on behalf of a caller sends a request for lookup to the local LS for the required (callee) mobile host (MH). The identity of the local LS can be determined by a simple hash function applied to the callee's ID. The local LS looks in its own registers. If the entry is found then LS returns the cell location of the callee. The requesting MSC can then carry out the call switching between the caller and the callee using the GSM call set up procedures as explained in Chap. 3. If the entry is not found, then the local LS multicasts a request message for the callee to the other LSs belonging to the same subset. If the callee is registered (it should be on) then one of LSs should reply. Following which the call switching is carried as in the previous case.

10.8.2 Update

When a MH moves from one location to the other its location information should be updated. It works as follows. The MH reports for registration to an BS under an MSC in the region where it moves. The MSC applies a hash function to determine the subset of LSs that maintain the location for MH. The process of update depends on the type of the move made by the MH. The moves are of the following types.

- Move within the region.
- Move between the regions.

If a MH moves from one cell to another cell under a same MSC then no update is required. However, if the MH moves from a cell to a cell under a different MSC in the same region, then an entry will be found in the local LS of the subset. The LS will update the information and send a *de-registration* to old MSC.

If the MH did not belong to the current region, i.e., it moved from a different region, the local LS multicast the information to the other LSs of its own set in the neighborhood. The new LS would know the possible regions from which the MH may have come. These regions are those which have common border with the current region. It depends on the location of the current region and its shape. One of the LSs of the neighbouring region must have an entry corresponding to MH. The LS having the entry then delete the same, and sends a delete entry message to the MSC which was serving the MH in the region. In case the registration message from the mobile device itself includes the ID of the previous LS or the region, the current LS can send unicast message to the previous LS.

10.8.3   Data Structures and System Specification

The important data structures for implementation of the lookup and update protocols are:

- location[MH_id]. This is the set of data registers available at an LS. The entry in each register is the Cell_id of the MSC which has the MH with MH_id. Additionally it may contain entries for all MHs whose hash function map to LS. This information would help in call setup between the mobiles belonging to the same LS set.
- LSforRegion[Region]. This is a table to lookup the LSs (other members of the same subset) which are associated with the LS holding the table. Each MH must be associated with one LS in each region which would contain the location of the MH.
- neighborRegion[MSC]. This is an array of neighboring regions for a particular MSC. If the coverage area of an MSC is completely within the interior of a region, the array will be empty. On the other hand, the border MSC (whose coverage area forms a part of the region's border) will have a number of neighboring regions depending on the shape of the regions.

As shown in Algorithm 6 a simple hash function can be used to determine the index of the subset of LSs. Hence, the specific LS in the current region associated with a MH can be found by applying the hash to ID of the MH. The variable numLSperRegion defines the number of LSs in a region. This helps in determining the load on each LS.

Algorithm 6: Method get_LSId(MH_id)

begin
   | **return** *MH_id mod numLSperRegion;* // Apply hash to get LS ID.
end

A MH is expected to send updates about its locations from time to time. The frequency of update depends on the update protocol. On receiving a location update, at first a local update is attempted by the current MSC. If the conditions for a local update are not met, then a remote update is attempted by the MSC. Suppose an MH moves from a cell under MSC_{old} and joins a cell under another MSC, say, MSC_{new}, where both MSC_{old} and MSC_{new} belong to the same region, then a local update is needed. Algorithm 7 specifies local update method. However, no update is needed for the movements of an MH between cells under the same MSC, because GSM underlay takes care of updating VLR.

The update method in Algorithm 8 is executed by a LS when it is informed about the movement of mobile host to the current region. As the update method indicates, in case an MH has moved from a region outside the current region then

---

Algorithm 7: Method localUpdate(MH_id, MSC_{old}, MSC_{new})

begin
> // Executed by the MSC on behalf of a MH.
> LS_id = get_LSId(MH_id);
> LS[LS_id].localUpdate(MH_id, MSC_{old}, MSC_{new});

end

---

remoteDelete method should be executed by the new LS storing location update from the roaming MH. Algorithm 9 gets invoked to delete entry for MH from the LS in the neighborhood. Only one of the LSs in the neighborhood may have a entry for the MH.

Algorithm 8: Method update(MSC, MH_id)

begin
> // Executed by LS of the region.
> **if** *(exists(location[MH_id])* **then**
> > **if** *(location[MH_id] != MSC)* **then**
> > > // MH moved within same region but from one MSC to
> > >   another.
> > > replaceEntry(MH_id, MSC);
> >
> > **end**
> > // Do nothing if location is unchanged
> > **return;**
>
> **end**
> // MH was not in region under the LS of the current region,
>   it must have arrived to the current region from a
>   neighboring region.
> **for** *(i ∈ neighborRegions[MSC])* **do**
> > // Issues a remoteDelete to delete MH entry from LSs of
> >   the neighborhood region. Only one LS have such an
> >   entry.
> > remoteDelete(i, MH_id); // See the Algorithm 9.
>
> **end**
> insertEntry(MH_id, MSC); // Update needed in current region.

end

Algorithm 9: Method remoteDelete(region_Id, MH_id)

on receiving *(remoteDelete)* **begin**
> **if** *(exists(location[MH_id]) in LS[region_Id])* **then**
> | deleteEntry(MH_id);
> **end**

end

The method `remoteDelete` is called by an LS when it determines that a MH has moved from a region outside its own region. It sends remote delete request to LSs of its own set in the neighboring regions. It is assumed that the methods for inserting, deleting, or replacing an entry have obvious implementations and the details of these specifications are not provided here.

A lookup is necessary for paging during call set up. A local lookup is executed by the MSC of the caller to determine if the callee belong to the same region. A region based calling mechanism can be useful for modeling tariffs by a GSM service provider. Algorithm 10 illustrates local lookup method.

Algorithm 10: Method lookup(MH_id, MSC)

> **begin**
> | LS_id = get_LSId(MH_id);
> | **return** *LSforRegion[LS_id].localLookup(MSC, MH_id);*
> **end**

A local lookup fails in the case the local associated LS does not have an entry for the callee. In this case, a remote lookup initiated by local LS by sending a multicast message to the other LSs belonging to the same subset as the local LS in the caller's region. Algorithm 11 combines both local and remote lookup into a single method. One final part of the lookup method is provided by Algorithm 12. It allows a LS to check the location entries when LS receives a lookup message. If an entry is found then it returns the entry. Otherwise, it returns NULL indicating a failure.

Algorithm 11: Method localLookup(MSC, MH_Id)

> **begin**
> | **if** *(exists(location[MH_id])* **then**
> | | // Local lookup successful.
> | | **return** *location[MH_id]*;
> | **end**
> | **else**
> | | // Perform remote Lookup for MH.
> | | **for each** *(region i)*
> | | remoteLoc = LSforRegion[i].remoteLookup(MH_id);
> | | **if** *(remoteLoc != NULL)* **then**
> | | | **return** *remoteLoc;*
> | | **end**
> | | // All remote lookups fail. MH must be in power off
> | | | mode.
> | | **return** *NULL;*
> | **end**
> **end**

Algorithm 12: Method remoteLookup(MH_id)

---

on receiving *(a lookup message)* **begin**
   if *(exists(location[MH_id])* **then**
   | **return** *location[MH_id];*
   end
   else
   | **return** *NULL;*
   end
end

10.8.4   The Cost Model

The cost of each operation required to update the LS entries as MH moves and the find an MH can be modeled using a set of simple assumptions as listed in Table 10.8.

Local Update Cost.

Using the above cost model, the cost of a local update can be computed by analyzing the involved steps.

- First, new MSC must find out its associated location server LS. This requires a simple application hash function. The cost of this step is H.
- New MSC send a message to its local LS for update. This cost is t.
- The LS, on receiving the message, performs a search or register lookup for update which is RL.
- The new LS must send information of this update to the old LS. This enable old LS to purge the entry. The cost of sending this message is t.
- After receiving the information the old LS deletes its register entry. The cost for deletion is MD.

Adding all the cost together, the total update cost: $2t + H + RL + MD$

Table 10.8 Notations used for cost analysis

Notation	Description
t	Time unit for delivery of local network message
X	A multiple of cost of the delivery of remote network message as compared to the delivery of a local network message
RL	Register lookup time at an LS
H	Time to perform hash
MD	Time to perform delete MSC
LN	Lookup time in the neighbouring regions for the new MSC

Remote Update Cost.

The break-up for the cost computation of a remote update is as follows.

- New MSC hashes to determine LS subset which holds the entry. The cost of performing hash is H.
- After identifying the LS subset, New MSC must sends a message to LS belong to subset which is available in local region. The cost of sending this message is t.
- The LS of the local region then determines probable neighbouring regions for the new MSC. This cost is LN.
- The LS then sends delete MSC message to the all the neighbouring regions incurring a cost of Xt
- The next step is to search remote LS for MH entry which takes time RL
- The remote LS sends message to old MSC for deletion incurring a cost of t.
- Old MSC then deletes the MH entry with a cost of MD.
- Local LS now performs a register lookup for creating a new entry for MH. For this it incurs a cost of RL.

The overall cost is obtained by adding all the cost mentioned above. It, therefore, works out as $2t + Xt + H + 2RL + MD + LN$.

Similarly, the cost for local lookup time and the remote lookup time can also be found. These costs are:

1. Local lookup time $= 2t + H + RL$.
2. Remote lookup time $= 2t + Xt + H + 2RL$.

References

1. I.F. Akyildiz, J.S.M. Ho, On location management for personal communications networks. IEEE Commun. Magaz. **34**(9), 138–145 (1996)
2. I.F. Akyildiz, J. McNair, J. Ho, H. Uzunalioglu, W. Wang, Mobility management in current and future communications networks. IEEE Netw. **12**(4), 39–49 (1998)
3. A. Bhattacharya, S.K. Das, Lezi-update: an information-theoretic framework for personal mobility tracking in pcs networks. Wireless Netw. **8**, 121–135 (2002)
4. T.M. Cover, J.A. Thomas, *Elements of Information Theory* (Wiley, New York, 1991)
5. J.S.M. Ho, I.F. Akyildiz, Dynamic hierarchical database architecture for location management in pcs networks. IEEE/ACM Trans. Netw. **5**(5), 646–660 (1997)
6. R. Jain, Y.-B. Lin, An auxiliary user location strategy employing forwarding pointers to reduce network impacts of pcs. Wireless Netw. **1**(2), 197–210 (1995)
7. J. Jannink, D. Lam, N. Shivakumar, J. Widom, D.C. Cox, Efficient and Flexible Location Management Techniques for Wireless Communication Systems, *Mobicom '96* (1996), pp. 38–49
8. E. Pitoura, G. Samaras, Locating objects in mobile computing. IEEE Trans. Knowl. Data Eng. **13**(4), 571–592 (2001)
9. K. Ratnam, I. Matta, S. Rangarajan, Analysis of Caching-Based Location Management in Personal Communication Networks, *The Seventh Annual International Conference on Network Protocols (ICNP '99)*, Washington, DC, USA, 1999 (IEEE Computer Society, 1999), pp. 293–300

10. C.E. Shannon, The mathematical theory of communication. Bell Syst. Techn. J. **27**, 379–423 (1948)
11. N. Shivakumar, J. Jannink, J. Widom, Per-user profile replication in mobile environments: algorithms, analysis, and simulation results. Mobile Netw. Appl. **2**(2), 129–140 (1997)
12. C. Song, Q. Zehui, N. Blumm, A.-L. Barabási, Limits of predictability in human mobility. Science **327**(5968), 1018–1021 (2010)
13. J.I. Yu, Overview of EIA/TIA IS-41, *Third IEEE International Symposium on Personal, Indoor and Mobile Radio Communications (PIMRC '92)* (1992), pp. 220–224
14. J. Ziv, A. Lempel, Compression of individual sequences via variable-rate coding. IEEE Trans. Inform. Theory **24**(5), 530–536 (1978)

Chapter 11
Distributed Algorithms for Mobile Environment

11.1 Introduction

From the prospectives of the application developers, a mobile computing system is a distributed systems consisting of thousands of mobile computers and a set of static computers connected by wireless networks [1]. A major part of the research in mobile computing system is directed towards establishing and maintaining connectivity between two types of computers through bridges between wireless with wired networks [2]. Over the years, however, mobile computing has emerged as a distinct paradigm for problem solving which is characteristically different from conventional distributed computing.

From an abstract point of view, a mobile computing system can be seen as a graph that consists of a fixed core of static nodes and a dynamic set of mobile leaf nodes [3]. Structurally, the organization is similar to a cellular mobile telephone network. The mobile leaf nodes can be viewed as a set of persistent messages moving through graph. With this underlying graph model, traditional distributed algorithms can be implemented directly on mobile system. Unfortunately, a direct mapping of distributed algorithms to mobile environment is not practical due to limited bandwidth, fragility of wireless links and many other resource specific constraints associated with mobile nodes.

A commonsense driven approach to design a distributed algorithm for mobile system will be to assign computing tasks to the fixed part of the system as much as possible. It intrinsically formulates a logical two-tier approach for computing in a mobile distributed environment. By offloading compute intensive tasks to the static computers [4, 5], mobile devices can save critical resources including batteries. Before we expand on the idea of two-tier approach, let us examine the differences between a traditional distributed system and a mobile computing system a bit more in details.

The mobility of a computing node brings up two important new issues in data delivery [6]:

© Springer Nature Singapore Pte Ltd. 2017
R.K. Ghosh, *Wireless Networking and Mobile Data Management*,
DOI 10.1007/978-981-10-3941-6_11

1. Locating a node for delivery of message, and
2. Transparent semantic routing of the message to the node.

Consequently, any attempt to map existing distributed algorithms for execution in mobile computing environment in a simple way is unlikely to meet much success. Nevertheless, observing the differences between mobile computing and distributed systems will help in recognizing the issues that may arise in design of distributed algorithms or restructuring existing distributed algorithms for execution on mobile computing systems.

11.2   Distributed Systems and Algorithms

A distributed system consists of a set of autonomous computers (nodes) which communicate through a wired network. A program which runs on distributed system is typically organized as a collection of processes distributed over different nodes. A distributed computation consists of four iterative steps:

1. Broadcasting,
2. Gathering information,
3. Executing joint computation, and
4. Agreeing on coordinated actions.

The last three steps are closely related. Information gathering in a distributed setup requires the participants to share local information amongst themselves. Similarly, the progress of a joint computation requires exchange of partial results amongst the participants. In fact, any coordinated action requires information sharing. Since the processes are distributed over a set of autonomous computers, all such synchronization requirements can be met either through a shared memory or through exchange of messages over the network among the nodes. A shared memory in a distributed system is implemented at the software level either transparently by extending the underlying virtual memory architecture, or explicitly through a set of library functions. In other words, message passing is the basic interface for sharing and exchanging of information between computers in a distributed system.

All distributed algorithms are designed with following basic assumptions about the capabilities of the participating nodes:

1. The nodes are static and their locations (IP/MAC addresses) are known in advance. No cost is incurred for locating a host.
2. The participating nodes are resource rich, having enough computation power, memory.
3. The nodes are powered by continuous supply of power, and remain active during the execution of programs.
4. The inability to receive a message by a node, due to a power failure, is treated as a failure of the algorithm.

5. The message setup cost is fixed, and same for all the messages. The latency due to message transmission dominates communication cost.
6. The size of a message is limited by size of MTU supported by network, and the transmission cost of a message between two fixed nodes is fixed.
7. Sufficient bandwidth is available for transfer of messages.
8. Transmission of a large amount of data between two nodes is accomplished by fragmenting it into several messages, and transmitting each of these messages separately.

11.3 Mobile Systems and Algorithms

Before dealing with the design of distributed algorithms for mobile environment, there is need to understand how the efficiencies of such algorithms can be evaluated. The evaluation criteria influence the design of efficient algorithms. The efficiency requirements of a distributed algorithm for mobile distributed environment should focus on:

- Minimization of communication cost,
- Minimization of bandwidth requirement,
- Meeting all the synchronization requirements, and
- Overcoming the resource constraints of mobile hosts.

Bandwidth is usually treated as a resource. Therefore, the impact of poor bandwidth can be examined along with the other resource constraints.

Synchronization is a key issue for the correct execution of any distributed algorithm. Unlike static clients, mobile clients can appear and disappear in any cell of a service area at any time. The synchronization techniques have to be adjusted to handle dynamically changing locations of the peers. Thus, there is a need to evolve of a new model for evaluating the cost of distributed algorithms in mobile environments. Some of the easily identifiable cost criteria are:

- Computation on a mobile node versus that on a static node,
- Relocating computation to static host, and
- Communication on wireless channels,

There is also a number of other characteristics of a mobile distributed system which influence the cost computation. In particular, network *disconnection* and *reconnection* introduce complications in evaluation of the cost. Furthermore, the cost model applicable to mobile infrastructured network cannot directly be extended to infrastructureless mobile ad hoc networks. Therefore, separate cost models have to be evolved for different mobile distributed environments.

Finally, the cost model is of little help unless, algorithm designer adopt appropriate strategies in design of algorithms. In this connection, two major issues which an algorithm designer must appropriately address are:

- How a computation in a mobile environment can be modeled?
- How synchronization and contention problems arising thereof can be resolved?

11.3.1 Placing Computation

Whenever an operation is executed on a remote object, at first a message is sent to the node that hosts the object. The desired operation is then performed by the remote node on behalf of the initiating host. It is convenient to assume that the mobile host *logically* executes the required set of operations directly on a remote node by sending a message. Sending a message to a mobile host is a two-step process:

1. The first step is to locate the mobile host.
2. The next step is to actually send the message.

If destination of the message is a fixed host, the above two steps can be carried out by the base station (BS) of the source mobile node within the fixed network. The BS being a part of fixed network would be able to forward the message to the destination node by using the IP forwarding protocol. It does not involve location search. This implies the first step is unnecessary for a destination which is a static node. Thus, sending a message to a fixed host is a lot cheaper than sending a message to a mobile host. Therefore, it is preferable to avoid sending messages to mobile hosts except for the case when both sender and the receiver are under the same BS. Since a mobile host should try to avoid sending messages to another mobile host, executing operations on objects resident in another mobile host should be avoided. So, the first design principle is:

Principle 1 *[7] To the extent possible, all remotely accessed objects should be resident on the fixed hosts.*

In other words, a node which hosts an object, requires both computing power and bandwidth. Therefore, frequently accessed objects should not be stored in mobile hosts. The role of a mobile host in a thread of execution is normally restricted to initiating operations on a remote object by sending message to the fixed node holding the object.

11.3.2 Synchronization and Contention

Whenever a particular resource is concurrently accessed from a number of remote agents, the competing agents should follow a well defined contention resolution protocol. We can treat each resource as an object. A sequence of operations being initiated from a specific place (a mobile host) can be called a *thread* of execution. Thus, an execution scenario is represented by many concurrently running threads trying to operate on an object. For the moment, let us not make any assumptions about where this object is located (at the risk of violating Principle 1). It may be either be resident on a fixed host or on a mobile host. The concurrent threads compete to gain access to the object.

Concurrent operations on an object by the competing threads should not leave the object in an inconsistent state. In other words, any attempt to access a shared object should be synchronized by mutual exclusion of competing threads. Let us examine the issue of object consistency a bit more to understand why mutual exclusion is an important issue for synchronization in a distributed settings. The execution of distributed algorithms can be visualised as a repeated pattern of *communication* followed by *computation*. The computation is limited to the individual hosts and during the execution of a computation, a host may need to communicate with its neighbors or other nodes for exchanging the results of partial computations. So the progress of a computation also needs synchronization. The synchronization requirements, among other things, may involve initialization of parameters for the next phase of computation. Thus a distributed system of hosts exhibit repeated bursts of communication in between the periods of local computations.

When hosts become mobile, one additional cost parameter, namely, *cost of location lookup* is introduced. Furthermore, due to resource poorness in mobile hosts, the cost assignment criteria for computational resources become drastically different from that used for fixed host. The communication cost also needs to distinguish between messaging over the wired and the wireless links. A simple technique, to avoid the high resource cost at mobile hosts is to relocate compute intensive parts of an algorithm to the fixed hosts as much as possible. Badrinath, Acharya and Imielinski [7] proposed three different strategies, namely, the *search*, *inform* and *proxy* to handle the issue of location search cost in the context of restructuring distributed mutual exclusion algorithm on a logical ring network. The techniques proposed by them are generic in nature and, therefore, can be used in synchronization requirements of distributed algorithms such as executing critical section of a code. We examine these strategies in this section.

11.3.3 Messaging Cost

The most important complexity measures of any distributed algorithm is the communication cost. It is dependent on the number of messages exchanged during one execution of the algorithm. But when hosts are mobile, the communication complexity should also include the cost of location search. Location search includes the messages exchanged to locate a mobile host in the coverage area. We know that mobile hosts have severe power constraints. They can transmit messages only on wireless links which require substantial amount of power. Furthermore, wireless links offer low bandwidth. Therefore, the cost of communication over a wireless link is more expensive than the cost of communication over a wired link. Badrinath, Acharya and Imielinski [7] proposed three different measures of cost for counting the number of messages exchanged during the execution of a distributed algorithms

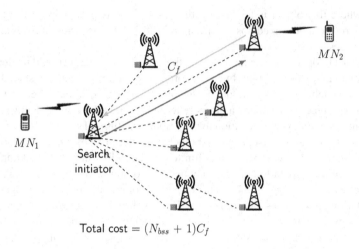

Total cost $= (N_{bss} + 1)C_f$

Fig. 11.1 Search cost

in a mobile computing environment. The cost model is specified by defining the units of cost as follows:

- C_w: cost of sending a message from MH to BS over wireless channel (and also identical to the cost in the reverse direction)
- C_f: cost of sending a message from a static node to another another static by the wired N/W.
- C_s: cost of searching/locating the current base station BS_{cur} of an MH and forwarding a message from a source base station BS_{src} to BS_{cur}.

C_w is assumed to represent a higher multiplicative cost compared to C_f. We may, therefore, assume C_w to be equivalent to k. C_f, where $k > 1$ is an appropriately chosen constant.

The simplest strategy to locate a mobile host is to let the searching base station query all the other base stations in the coverage area. The base station which responds to the query is the one which services the mobile host in the cell under it. The querying base station can then forward the message meant for the mobile host to the responding base station. So, the messages exchanged for a location search as illustrated by Fig. 11.1 are:

1. In the first round, all the base stations, except one, receive message from the querying base station. It requires exchange of $(N_{BS} - 1) \times C_f$ messages.
2. The base station, servicing the searched mobile host, responds. It incurs a cost of C_f.
3. Finally the querying base station forwards a message (data packet) to the responding base station. This incurs a cost of C_f.

Adding all the three costs, the worst case cost for a search:

$$C_s = (N_{BS} + 1) \times C_f.$$

The cost of transmitting a message from a mobile host (MH) to another mobile host (MH′) is determined by overhead of search, and the cost of actual message transfer. The break down of the cost is given below.

1. The source MH sends the message to its own base station BS. The cost incurred for the same is: C_w
2. BS then initiates a search for the destination MH′ to locate its base station BS′ under whose cell area MH′ is currently active. BS delivers the message to BS′. The cost of the locating MH′ and delivering message to BS′, as explained, is C_s.
3. After receiving the message from BS, BS′ delivers it to MH′. This action incurs a cost of C_w.

Now adding all the costs together, the worst case cost of transmitting a message from a mobile host MH to another mobile host MH′ in the worst case is:

$$2C_w + C_s.$$

Figure 11.2 explains how a message from a source mobile can be delivered to a destination mobile.

The analysis of the cost structure which Badrinath, Acharya and Imielinski [7] have proposed, is captured by Fig. 11.3. It succinctly explains two aspects, namely,

Fig. 11.2 Mobile to mobile communication

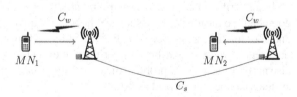

Fig. 11.3 Summary of cost model

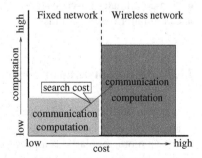

- The major component of the cost in a mobile distributed environment is due to communication.
- However, the computation is also slow in mobile hosts. So, in the cost due to computation is relatively high compared to the cost in conventional distributed system.

Relocating computation on the fixed host makes sense. But, relocation may mean communication between a fixed host and a mobile host. After computation is over, the fixed host needs to report the result back to the mobile host. This would need a search for locating the mobile host.

11.4   Structuring Distributed Algorithms

Attempts to execute distributed algorithms directly without any restructuring for mobile environment may lead to design of inefficient algorithms. Inefficiencies, in design of algorithms for mobile distributed environment, as observed in the previous section arise out of synchronization, the asymmetry in model of the computation, and the imbalance in communication cost between wired and wireless interfaces. From the point of view of algorithm design, the problems are dependent on the abstract notions of coordination and control in distributed algorithms. As an analogy, consider the issue of quality in software design process. The efficiency of algorithms addresses the quality in the problem domain. But when algorithms are converted to software processes, the issue of quality goes beyond the problem domain. It becomes linked to the choice of technologies for the implementation such as computers and their capabilities, underlying network, storage, programming tools and languages, etc.

In a distributed computing environment, the control is not exercised by a single computer. So the efficiency issue, i.e., the issue of quality must consider how control and coordination are exercised in the execution of distributed algorithms. Therefore, in order to structure distributed algorithm for execution in a mobile environment we also need to consider the problem of coordination and control. The class of distributed systems can be categorized as follows.

- Non-coordinator based systems:
- Coordinator based systems.

11.5   Non-coordinator Systems

In a non-coordinator based system, all the machines are equivalent. Therefor, no machine can exercise any control on another machine. A non-coordinator system is known more popularly as a peer-to-peer system. There are two different types of non-coordinator based systems. In the first type of non-coordinator based system, each peer execute the same code. In the second type, a few of the machines execute some specialized code, while the rest execute the same code.

11.5.1 All Machines are Equivalent

In such a system, each machine roughly shares the same amount of computational and communication load. Such systems can easily be modified to work in a mobile computing environment. We illustrate this with Lamport's Bakery algorithm [8] for mutual exclusion. In the Bakery algorithm, a process waiting to enter the critical section chooses a number. It allows all processes which have chosen smaller numbers to enter into the critical section before itself. The ties are resolved by process IDs, allowing the process with the lower ID to enter the critical section. Lamport's original algorithm makes use of two shared arrays, each consisting of n elements. One element is assigned for each process in each shared array. The values in a shared array can be examined by any process. In a peer to peer settings, no shared arrays can be used. So, local variables `choose` and `value` are maintained by each process. A process uses message passing mechanism when it needs to examine the values of local variables of another process. The pseudo code of the algorithm appears in Algorithm 13.

Algorithm 13: Lamport's bakery algorithm

boolean choosing$_i$ = **false**;
int number$_i$ = 0;
while *(1)* **do**
    choosing$_i$ = **true**;
    set value$_i$ = max {value$_j$|$j \neq i, j = 0 \ldots N_{MH} - 1$} + 1;
    choosing$_i$ = **false**;
    for $(j = 0; j < N_{MH}, j\, != i; j + +)$ **do**
        while *(choosing$_j$)* **do**
        | {busy wait ...}
        end
        while *(number$_j$!= 0) && ((number$_j$, j) < (number$_i$, i))* **do**
        end
    end
    ⋮
    { Critical section code}
    ⋮
    number$_i$ = 0;
end

Lamport's Bakery algorithm requires very little computation, and can be easily performed on a mobile device. So, ignoring computation we may just focus on the communication aspects. The execution of the algorithm in a mobile host MH can be analyzed in three distinct parts.

1. Choose own number.
2. Wait for the mobile hosts with lower numbers to avail their turns.
3. Execute the critical section.

In the first part of the execution, an MH fetches the numbers chosen by other $N_{MH} - 1$ mobile hosts in order to set its own number. So, an MH sends a query to all other mobile hosts for fetching their respective local numbers. As the end hosts are mobile, fetching each number involves location search for the other end host. It is assumed that the requester does not move when it is waiting for the replies to arrive. So, location search is not required for the delivery of the replies. Therefore, the message cost incurred for fetching the number chosen by another mobile host $(2C_w + C_s)$. The overall the message cost incurred by MH for choosing its own number is, therefore, equal to

$$(N_{MH} - 1) \times (2C_w + C_s).$$

In the second part of the execution, a requesting mobile host MH waits for all mobile hosts to choose their numbers. Then subsequently, allow those hosts to execute the critical section if their chosen numbers are smaller than the number chosen by MH. The waiting part consists of two steps. It requires communication with other mobile hosts to allow them choose their respective numbers and then allow the mobile host having a smaller number to execute critical section. At the worst, a MH has to wait till all other mobile hosts have finished choosing their respective numbers, and availed their respective turns to enter the critical section assuming each one of them has chosen a number smaller than the MH. The message cost involved in waiting for one mobile host is $2(2C_w + C_s)$. In the worst case, an MH may have to wait for $N_{MH} - 1$ other mobile hosts to take their respective turns before the MH can enter the critical section. This leads to an overall message cost of:

$$2(N_{MH} - 1) \times (2C_w + C_s).$$

The execution of code for critical section may perhaps involve some common resources and possibly subsequent updates of those resources. It does not involve any communication with other mobile hosts. Adding the message cost of three parts, the overall communication cost for execution of Bakery algorithm only on mobile hosts is

$$3(N_{MH} - 1) \times (2C_w + C_s).$$

Therefore, a straightforward way of mapping Lamport's Bakery algorithm to mobile peer to peer distributed system leads to a message cost of the order $6N_{MH} \times C_w$.

The correctness of the algorithm is heavily dependent on the fact that the messages are delivered in FIFO order. However, maintaining a logical FIFO channel between every pair of mobile hosts has to be supported by the underlay network.

11.5.2 With Exception Machines

This system similar to the previous category, where most of the machines execute the same code, except only a few of them, which execute a different code. The machines which execute a different code are known as *exception* machines. An example of this category is Dijkstra's self stabilizing algorithm [9]. It is a system consisting of a set of n finite state machines connected in the form of a ring, with a *token* or privilege circulate around the ring. The possession of the token enables a machine to change its state. Typically, for each machine, the privilege state is defined if the value of a predicate is true. The predicate is a boolean function of a machine's own state and the states of its neighbors.

The change of current state of a machine is viewed as a *move*. The system is defined to be *self-stabilizing* if and only if, regardless of the initial state and token selected each time, at least one token (privilege) is present and the system converges to a legal configuration after a finite number of steps. In the presence of multiple tokens in the system, the machine entitled to make the move can be decided arbitrarily. A legal state of the system has the following properties:

- *No deadlock*: There must be at least one token in the system.
- *Closure*: Every move from a legal state must place the system into a legal state. It means, once the system enters a legal state no future state can be illegal.
- *No starvation*: During an infinite execution, each machine should possess a token for an infinite number of times
- *Reachability*: Given any two legal states, there is a series of moves that change one legal state to the other.

Let us now look at Dijkstra's algorithm involving K states where $K > n$, and system consists of $n + 1$ machines. Machine 0 is called the bottom machine, and the machine n is called the top machine. All the machines together form a logical ring, where the machine i has the machine $i + 1 \mod (n + 1)$ as its right hand neighbor, $i = 0, 1, \ldots, n$. The legitimate states are those in which exactly one privilege is present.

For any machine, let the symbols S, L, R respectively denote the machine's own state, the state of left neighbor, and the state of the right neighbor. The rules for change of states for this system are as follows.

- **Bottom machine**
  if $L = S$ then $S = (S + 1) \mod K$.
- **Other machines**
  if $L \neq S$ then $S = L$.

An initial configuration C_0 may consists of at most $n + 1$ different states. At least $K - (n + 1)$ states do not occur in C_0. Machine 0 increments its state only after $n + 1$ steps. Therefore, it reaches a state not in the initial configuration after at most $n + 1$ steps. All other machines $i \neq 0$, copy states of their respective left neighbors. Hence, the first time Machine 0 computes its state, such a state becomes unique in the ring. Machine 0 does not get a chance to compute its state until the configuration reaches $S_1 = S_2, \ldots, S_n = S_0$.

The details of how the self-stabilization works is not important for structuring distributed algorithms to mobile environment. Let us look at the communication that occurs between two machines. In self-stabilization algorithms, the essential communication perspective is to access the registers for the left and right neighbors. Thus, clearly these class of algorithms are very similar to the previous class of algorithms and the presence of one or more exception machines does not make much of a difference to the communication costs involved. However, only the neighbor's values are needed for the change of state. As most of the neighboring hosts are expected to be under the same BS except for two at the edges, the overhead of wireless communication is expected to be low.

In Dijkstra's exception machine model, a single token or privilege circulates around the logical ring. In such a ring organization of mobile hosts, the communication is restricted between a host and its left or right neighbors. If we structure distributed mutual exclusion algorithm using a logical ring of cohorts, then it should be possible to reduce the communication cost. The algorithm becomes very simple, we just let the privileged mobile to access mutual exclusion. If the privileged machine is not interested, it just passes the privilege to the successor in the logical ring. This way every mobile host gets one chance to use a critical resource in a mutually exclusive manner during one full circulation of the token around the ring of mobile hosts.

The analysis of the message cost of the token ring algorithm outlined above (referred to as TR-MH) is provided below.

> Both the sender and the recipient are mobile hosts. The message is sent first from the sender to its local base station then from there to the base station under which the recipient is found. So the cost of messages exchanged on wireless links is $2C_w$. The cost of locating a mobile host and subsequently sending a message to its current base station is C_s.

Therefore the cost of token exchange between two successive MHs in the logical ring is $2C_w + C_s$. Assuming that the ring consists of N_{MH} mobile hosts, the cost of one full circulation token on the ring is $N_{MH}(2C_w + C_s)$. This cost does not include the cost for mutual exclusion requests met during the circulation of the token. Let K be the number of mutual exclusion requests satisfied during one complete circulation of token around the ring. The maximum number of mutual exclusion that can be met in one circulation of token is $\max\{K\} = N_{MH}$.

Each exchange of a message requires power both at the recipient and at the sender. Every MH accesses wireless twice (once for acquiring and once for releasing) during one circulation of the token through it. So, the energy requirement for executing this algorithm is proportional to:

$$2N_{MH}C_w.$$

11.5.3 Coordinator Based Systems

Many distributed algorithms involve a coordinator. The coordinator bears substantially higher communication overhead compared to other participating nodes. It is basically responsible for resolving the coordination issues related to synchronization. A coordinator may or may not be fixed. In a fixed coordinator based system, one node is assigned the role of the coordinator for the entire duration of execution of the algorithm. However, in a moving coordinator based system the role of coordinator can be performed by different hosts at different times. Thus the coordinator is a function of time.

11.5.3.1 Fixed Coordinator Based System

Apart from the normal optimization for the mobile hosts, the communication pattern involving the coordinator has to be specifically optimized. Such a strategy yields better dividends in terms of reducing the communication cost, because most of the communication load in a coordinator based system is centered around the coordinator. Apart from increased communication load, it increases the probability of a failure, as the coordinator is a single point of failure.

An example of the fixed coordinator system is encountered in the case of total ordered atomic broadcast algorithms. The system consists of N hosts, each wishes to broadcast messages to the other hosts. After a broadcast message is received, a host time stamps the message and sends the same to a sequencer. On receiving the relayed broadcast message from all the nodes, the sequencer sets the time stamp of the message to the maximum of the received time stamps and then broadcast the same back to all the hosts. In this way, the coordinator ensures a total ordering of the broadcast messages. Figure 11.4 illustrates this process in a sequence diagram. Host 3 in Fig. 11.4 is the sequencer or the coordinator. The execution of the above atomic broadcast algorithm is mainly dependent on the coordinator. Therefore, in order to structure the algorithms for execution in a mobile environment, we must first turn our attention to the role of coordinator in a mobile environment. Obviously, if the coordinator is mobile then execution of any coordinated action will be expensive. It is, therefore, recommended that a static host should perform the coordinator's job. Since, the other hosts are mobile, search, inform or proxy strategies can be applied depending on the mobility characteristics of entities in the system.

In the case where the algorithm is directly executed on the mobile hosts without any change, the total cost incurred for each broadcast will be,

1. The cost of initial broadcast: $(N_{MH} - 1) \times (C_s + 2C_w)$,
2. The cost of unicasting received message from the participating nodes to the coordinator: $(N_{MH} - 1) \times (C_s + 2C_w)$,
3. The cost of sending time stamped messages back to participants: $(N_{MH} - 1) \times (C_s + 2C_w)$

Therefore, the overall messaging cost is

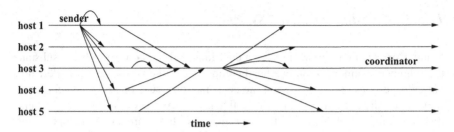

Fig. 11.4 Atomic broadcast using fixed/moving coordinator

$$3(N_{MH} - 1) \times (C_s + 2C_w).$$

This can be improved marginally if the location of the coordinator cached by each base station. The cost in that case would be

$$(2(N_{MH} - 1) \times (C_s + 2C_w) + (N_{MH} - 1) \times (C_f + 2C_w)$$

However, if the coordinator is placed on a BS, the cost is revised as follows:

1. Cost of initial broadcast: $C_w + (N_{BS} - 1) \times C_f$,
2. Cost of informing receipt timestamps to the coordinator: $(N_{BS} - 1) \times C_f + N_{MH} \times C_w$,
3. Cost of broadcasting coordinator's final timestamp to participants: $(N_{BS} - 1) \times C_f + N_{MH} \times C_w$.

This leads to a overall message cost of

$$(2N_{MH} + 1) \times C_w + 3(N_{BS} - 1) \times C_f$$

Thus simple structuring of the atomic broadcast algorithm done by placing the coordinator on a base station leads to substantial savings in the cost of messaging.

11.5.3.2 Moving Coordinator Based System

As shown in Fig. 11.5 the coordinator of the algorithm changes over time. The sender, the coordinator and the receiver sets are the identical, but shown separately for the sake of clarity.

In this case normal algorithm execution at mobile hosts again has the same complexity as in the previous case. However, we can modify the system as follows:

1. One of the three strategies, search, inform and proxy, can be used for all the hosts in the system.
2. As soon as a mobile host becomes a coordinator, the communication load on it rises drastically in a short space of time. Hence the MH should inform its BS

Fig. 11.5 Conceptual model
of a moving coordinator
system

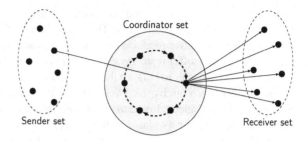

about change of status to coordinator, which is then broadcast to all base stations. Also the MH during its tenure as the coordinator uses the inform strategy, while other hosts use the search strategy.

Using these modifications, each step of the algorithm now requires

1. Cost of broadcast: $C_w + (N_{BS} - 1) \times C_f$,
2. Cost of sending to coordinator: $(N_{BS} - 1) \times C_f + N_{MH} \times C_w$,
3. Cost of broadcasting back the time stamped message: $(N_{BS} - 1) \times C_f + N_{MH} \times C_w$, and
4. Additional overhead associated with change of coordinator: $(N_{BS} - 1) \times C_f + N_{MH} \times C_w$.

Thus the total cost works out as:

$$(2N_{MH} + 1) \times C_w + 3(N_{BS} - 1)C_f + \alpha(N_{MH} \times C_w + (N_{BS} - 1) \times C_f),$$

where a change of the coordinator occurs every α broadcasts. The cost of executing the non-structured version of algorithm is: $3(N_{MH} - 1) \times (C_s + 2C_w)$. So, the saving in cost is significant by simple structuring.

11.6 Exploiting Asymmetry of Two-Tier Model

Most distributed algorithms can be structured suitably for execution on mobile environment by reducing communication costs. Still, if we consider the token ring algorithm described in Sect. 11.5.1, two of the key issues are not addressed, viz.,

1. Every mobile in logical ring has to maintain active network connectivity during the execution of the algorithm.
2. Relocation of computation to balance inherent asymmetry in mobile computing environment is not possible.

For example, none of the mobile hosts in the token ring algorithm can operate either in disconnected or in doze mode during the execution. This is because the token cannot be sent to a disconnected successor node, and also if the mobile, holding the token decides to operate in disconnected mode then other mobiles may have to wait indefinitely to get their turns. The organization of distributed mobile system point towards a two-tier model with inherent asymmetry in node capabilities. The fixed nodes do not suffer from any of the resource related problem which the mobile nodes have. So, in order to balance the inherent asymmetry in the system, if the token circulation is carried out by fixed hosts, then it may be possible for the mobile hosts to operate in disconnected or doze mode. Furthermore, it may also be possible to relocate compute intensive tasks to the fixed hosts. This strategy not only removes the burden on resources of mobile nodes, but also enhances the performance of algorithms.

Using the above two-tier approach, Badrinath, Acharya and Imielinski [7] proposed three different variations for structuring of token ring algorithm. Their main strategy was based on exploiting the inherent asymmetry in computation model as indicated design Principle 1 of Sect. 11.3.1. The token is assumed to circulate on a ring in a previously determined sequence among the fixed hosts in infrastructured part of the network supporting the mobile computation. A mobile host MH wishing to access the token submits the request to its current BS. When the token becomes available, it is sent to MH at its current base station, BS'. After using the token MH returns it to BS' which in turn returns the same back to BS. The cost of servicing token depends on the way location of a MH is maintained.

11.6.1   Search Strategy

Pure search strategy scans the entire area under coverage of service to find a MH. The algorithm consists of set of actions performed by the two component devices, namely, base stations and mobile hosts. Each base station assumed to maintain two separate queues: (i) a request queue Q_{req}, and (ii) a grant queue Q_{grant}. The token access requests by mobile hosts at a base station are queued up in Q_{req}. When the token is received by a BS from its predecessor in the logical ring, all pending requests are moved into Q_{grant}. Then all the requests are serviced from Q_{grant}, while new requests get added to Q_{req}. This implies all the requests made before the time token arrives are serviced and the requests which arrive subsequently are kept pending for the next round of servicing. After all requests are serviced, the token is passed on to the successor base station in the ring. So, the actions of BS are as provided in Algorithm 14 [7]: As far as a mobile MH is concerned, it can request for token servicing at any point of time to its base station. Once token is received from the base station, it uses the critical resource and returns the token after the use. So, the actions performed by a MH are as indicated in Algorithm 15. The correctness of algorithm relies on several implicit assumptions.

1. Firstly, all the message channels are assumed to be reliable and received in FIFO order. FIFO order means that the messages actually arrive and in the order they are sent. So, a mobile sends only one request at a time.

Algorithm 14: Search strategy: actions of BS

---

begin
    on receipt of (an ME request from *MH*) **begin**
    | add *MH*'s request to the rear of Q_{req};
    end
    on receipt of (the token from the predecessor in the ring) **begin**
        move all pending requests from Q_{grant};
        repeat
            remove request from the head of Q_{grant};
            if *MH which made the request is local to BS* **then**
            | deliver the token to *MH* over wireless link;
            end
            else
            | search and deliver token to *MH* at its current cell;
            end
            await return of token from the *MH*;
        until *(Q_{grant} == empty)*;
        forward token to BS's successor in the logical ring;
    end
end

Algorithm 15: Search strategy: actions of MH

---

on requirement for (an access of the token) **begin**
| submit request to current local BS;
end
on receipt of (token from local BS) **begin**
    hold the token and use the critical resource;
    return the token to local BS;
end

---

2. Secondly, a mobile cannot make a fresh request at a base station where its previous request is pending.
3. Thirdly, the algorithm does not handle the case of missing or captured token.
4. Fourthly, a mobile can hold token only for short finite duration of time.

With the above assumptions, it is clear that at any time only one MH holds the token. Therefore, mutual exclusion is trivially guaranteed. The token is returned to the same base station from which it was received. So, after the token is returned back, a base station can continue to use it until all the pending requests before the arrival of token have been satisfied. The maximum number of requests that can be serviced at any base station is bounded by the size of the Q_{grant} at that base station when the token arrives. No fresh request can go into Q_{grant}, as they are added only to Q_{req}. So, a token acquired by a base station will be returned after a finite time by servicing at most all the requests which were received before the arrival of the token. This number cannot exceed N_{MH}, the total number of mobile hosts in the system. It implies that the token will eventually reach each base station in the ring and, therefore, all the requests are eventually satisfied in finite time.

It is possible, however, for a mobile to get serviced multiple number of times during one circulation of token over the ring. It can happen in the following way. A mobile submits a request at one base station BS and after being serviced by the token, moves quickly to the successor of BS in the logical ring and submits a fresh request for the token at the successor. Though it does not lead to starving, a stationary or slow moving mobile may have to wait for a long time to get its turn. We will look into a solution to this problem in Sect. 11.6.3.1.

The communication cost of the above algorithm can be analyzed as follows:

1. Cost for one complete traversal of the logical ring is equal to $N_{BS} \times C_f$, where N_{BS} is the number of base stations.
2. Cost for submission of a request from a MH to a base station is C_w.
3. If the requesting MH is local to a BS receiving the token then the cost of servicing a request is C_w. But if the requesting MH has migrated to different base station BS' before the token reaches BS where the request was initially made, then a location search will be required. So the worstcase cost of delivering token to the requesting MH will be $C_s + C_w$.
4. The worstcase cost of returning the token to BS delivering the token to MH is $C_w + C_f$. C_f component in cost comes from the fact that MH may have subsequently migrated from BS where it made request to the cell under a different base station BS'.

Adding all the cost components, the worstcase cost of submitting a single request and satisfying is equal to $3C_w + C_f + C_s$. If K requests are met in a single traversal of the ring then the cost will be

$$K \times (3C_w + C_s + C_f) + N_{BS} \times C_f$$

Since, the number of mobile host requesting a service is much less than the total number of mobiles in the system, $K \ll N_{MH}$.

In order to evaluate the benefit of relocating computation to fixed network we have to compare it with token ring algorithm TR-MH described earlier in this section where the token circulates among mobile hosts.

- *Energy consumption.* The energy consumption in the present algorithm is proportional to $3K$ as only $3K$ messages are exchanged over wireless links. In TR-MH algorithm, it was $2N_{MH}$. As $K \ll N_{MH}$, it is expected that $\frac{3K}{2N_{MH}} < 1$
- *Search cost.* For the present algorithm it is $K \times C_s$, whereas in the previous algorithm the cost is $N_{MH} \times C_s$ which is considerably more.

11.6.2 Inform Strategy

Inform strategy reduces the search cost. It is based on simple idea that the search becomes faster if enough footprints of the search object is available before search begins. In other words, a search is less expensive if more information is available about the possible locations of the mobile host being searched for. Essentially, the cost of search increases with the degree of imprecision in locations information. For example, if a MH reports about every change of its location to the BS, where it initially submitted a token request, then search is not needed. The difference between a pure search based algorithm to an inform based algorithm is that Q_{req} maintains the location area information along with the request made by a mobile host, and every mobile host with a pending request informs the change in location to the base station where the request is made. Algorithm 16 specifies the actions of a BS [7]. The actions to be performed by a mobile host *MH* are provided in Algorithm 17.

Algorithm 16: Inform strategy: actions of BS

```
begin
    on receipt of (a request from a local MH) begin
    |   add the request < MH, BS > to the rear of Q_req;
    end
    on receipt of (inform(MH, BS') message) begin
    |   replace < MH, BS > in Q_req by < MH, BS' >;
    end
    on receipt of (token from the predecessor of BS in ring) begin
        move Q_req entries to the Q_grant;
        repeat
        |   remove the request < MH, BS' > at the head of Q_grant;
        |   if (BS' == BS) then
        |   |   deliver the token to MH over the local wireless link;
        |   end
        |   else
        |   |   forward token to BS' for delivery to MH;
        |   end
        |   await return of the token from MH;
        until (Q_grant == empty);
        forward token to BS's successor in the ring;
    end
end
```

To compare the search and inform strategies, we observe the following facts about the search strategy:

- An MH makes *MOB* number of moves in the period between the submission of request and the receipt of token.
- After each of these moves, a *inform()* message is sent to BS, i.e. the cost of inform is $MOB \times C_f$.
- Since the location of MH is known after each move it makes, there is no need to search for its location.
- When token becomes available at BS and it is MH's turn to use the token, then it is directly despatched to BS' where MH is currently found.

Algorithm 17: Inform strategy: actions of MH

---

on requirement of (token access) **begin**
  | submit request to its current local BS;
  | store the current local BS in the local variable *req_locn*;
end
on receipt of (token from BS *req_locn*) **begin**
  | access the critical resource or region
  | return token to BS (*req_locn*);
  | set *req_locn* to $\perp$; // $\perp$ indicates null
end
on a move by *MH* **begin**
  | send *join(MH, req_locn)* message to local BS
end
on entering (cell under a new BS) **begin**
  if *(req_locn $\neq \perp$)* **then**
    | send a *inform(MH, BS')* to BS (*req_locn*)
  end
end

On the other hand, in the algorithm employing simple search, BS must search for the current location of MH, incurring a cost C_s. Therefore, the inform strategy is more cost effective compared to the search strategy provided $MOB \times C_f < C_s$. In other words if after submitting a request, the frequency of movement of a MH becomes low then MH should inform BS about every change of location rather than BS searching for it.

11.6.3 Proxy Strategy

Proxy strategy incorporates the ideas from both search and inform strategies. It exploits the imbalance between the frequencies of the local and the global moves made by a mobile host. Usually, a mobile host moves more frequently between cells that are adjacent and clustered around a local area. Using this knowledge, the entire coverage area consisting of all base stations is partitioned into contiguous *regions*, where each region consists of a cluster of neighboring BSes. BSes within a region are associated with a common proxy. A proxy is a static host, not necessarily a base station. The token now circulates in a logical ring comprising of these proxies. Each proxy, on receiving the token, becomes responsible for servicing the requests pending in its request queue. So, the proxy strategy is just a minor variation of inform strategy that can capture locality of moves made by mobile hosts. Only, implicit assumption is that a mobile host must be aware of the the proxy assigned for handling token requests originating from its current cell. Since the movements of a mobile host MH at times can be unpredictable, it may not be possible for MH to pre-store the identity of its proxy. So, each BS may send out periodic beacons that include the identity of its associated proxy. The actions executed by a proxy P are provided by Algorithm 18. Similarly, the actions executed by mobile host MH are provided in Algorithm 19 For convenience in analysis of proxy strategy, we use following notations [7]:

Algorithm 18: Proxy strategy: actions of proxy

begin
  on receipt of (an ME request from MH) **begin**
    `// Request is forwarded by a BS within P's local area`
    add request $< MH, P >$ to the rear of Q_{req};
  end
  on receipt of (a *inform*(MH, P') message) **begin**
    replace request (MH, P) in Q_{req} by (MH, P');
  end
  on receipt of (token from the predecessor in ring) **begin**
    move requests from Q_{req} to Q_{grant};
    repeat
      delete request $< MH, P') >$ from head of Q_{req};
      if $(P' == P)$ **then**
        `// MH located within P's area`
        deliver the token to MH after local search;
      end
      else
        `// MH is in a different proxy area`
        forward the token to P' which delivers it to MH;
      end
      await return of the token from MH;
    until $(Q_{grant} ==$ *empty*$)$;
    forward token to P's successor in ring;
  end
end

---

1. N_{proxy}: denotes the total number of proxies forming the ring.
2. N_{BS}: denotes the number of BSes in the coverage area, which means there are N_{BS}/N_{proxy} base stations under a region.
3. MOB_{wide}: denotes the number of inter regional moves made by a MH in the period between submitting a token request and receiving the token.
4. MOB_{local}: denotes the total number of intra regional moves in the same period.

So, the total number of moves MOB is equal to $MOB_{wide} + MOB_{local}$. Before delivering the token to a MH, a proxy needs to locate a MH amongst the BSes within its region. This search is referred to as local search with an associated cost C_{ls}. With the above notations and assumptions, according to Badrinath, Acharya and Imielinsk [7] the communication costs can be analyzed as follows:

1. The cost of one token circulation in the ring: $N_{proxy} \times C_f$
2. The cost of submitting a token request from a MH to its proxy: $C_w + C_f$

Algorithm 19: Proxy strategy: actions of *MH*

---

on requirement (for access of token) **begin**
   | submit request $< MH, P >$ to local BS;
   | store the identity of local proxy in *init_proxy*;
end
on the receipt of (token from *init_proxy*) **begin**
   | use the token;
   | return the token to *init_proxy*;
   | set *init_proxy* to $\perp$;
end
on a inter regional move begin
   | send a *join(MH, init_proxy)* message to new BS;
   | **if** *(init_proxy $\notin \{P, \perp\}$)* **then**
   | | // P' is the proxy of new BS
   | | new BS sends a *inform(MH, P')* to *init_proxy*;
   | **end**
end

---

3. The cost of delivering the token to the MH: $C_f + C_{ls} + C_w$
   C_f term can be dropped from the cost expression above, if MH receives the token in the same region where it submitted its request.
4. The cost of returning the token from the MH to the proxy: $C_w + C_f$

The above costs together add up to: $3C_w + 3C_f + C_{ls}$

If an inter regional move is made, then the current local BS of MH sends the identity of new proxy to the proxy where MH submitted the request initially. The cost for inform is, therefore, C_f. The worst overall cost for satisfying a request from a MH, including the inform cost, is then

$$(3C_w + 3C_f + C_{ls}) + (MOB_{wide} \times C_f)$$

If the token gets circulated on the set of proxies instead of the set of BSes, then the cost of circulation is reduced by a factor of N_{proxy}/N_{BS}. However, the workload is comparatively higher on each proxy than the workload on a BS. Assuming all three schemes service identical number of mutual exclusion requests in one full circulation of ring,

- N_{BS} static hosts share the load in the search strategy,
- N_{proxy} static hosts share the load under the proxy method.

The efficiency in handling mobility by each strategy can be compared by estimating the communication cost in satisfying one token request.

search strategy: $3C_w + C_f + C_s$
inform strategy: $3C_w + C_f + (MOB \times C_f)$
proxy strategy: $3C_w + (3 + MOB_{wide}) \times C_f + C_{ls}$

The above expressions should be compared against one another in order to determine which strategy performs better than the other. For instance, proxy strategy performs better than search strategy, if

$$
\begin{aligned}
(3 + MOB_{wide}) \times C_f + C_{ls} &< C_f + C_s \\
\equiv MOB_{wide} + 2 &< (C_s - C_{ls})/C_f
\end{aligned}
\tag{11.1}
$$

Search strategy requires a BS to query all the other BSes within a search region to determine if a MH is active in a cell. The BS which currently hosts the MH responds. Then the BS where MH originally submitted the request forwards the token to the responding BS. The search cost is then equal to $(N_{region} + 1) \times C_f$, where N_{region} denotes the number of BSes within a search area. Replacing C_{ls} in Eq. 11.1 by above expression for search, we find:

$$
MOB_{wide} < N_{BS} - (N_{BS}/N_{proxy}) - 2
$$

From the above expression, we may conclude that the proxy scheme performs better than the pure search scheme if the number of inter regional moves is two less than the total number of BSes outside a given region.

Now let us compare proxy with inform strategy. Proxy strategy is expected to incur a lower cost provided:

$$
\begin{aligned}
(3 + MOB_{wide}) \times C_f + C_{ls} &< (MOB + 1) \times C_f \\
\equiv C_{ls} &< (MOB - MOB_{wide} - 2) \times C_f \\
\equiv C_{ls} &< (MOB_{local} - 2) \times C_f
\end{aligned}
\tag{11.2}
$$

The cost of a local search equals $(N_{BS}/N_{proxy} + 1) \times C_f$, since all base stations have to be queried by the proxy in its region and only the local base station of MH will reply. So, the formula 11.2 above reduces to:

$$
N_{BS}/N_{proxy} + 2 < MOB_{local}
$$

From the above expression, we conclude that if the number of local area moves performed by a mobile host exceeds the average number of BSes under each proxy by just 2, then the proxy strategy outperforms the inform strategy.

11.6.3.1 Fairness in Access of the Token

There are two entities whose locations vary with time, namely, the token and the mobile hosts. So we may have a situation represented by the following sequence of events:

1. A mobile host MH submits a request to its current local base station BS.
2. It gets the token from the same BS and uses it,

3. It then moves to the base station BS′ which is the next recipient of the token,
4. The same MH submits a request for the token access at BS′.

The situation leads a fast moving mobile host to gain multiple accesses to the token during one circulation of the token through the fixed hosts. It violates the *fairness* property of the token access among the mobile hosts. So, we need to put additional synchronization mechanisms in place to make the algorithms fair. Interestingly, the problem of fairness does not arise in the algorithm TR-MH, which maintains the logical ring amongst MHs. Therefore, we need to evolve ways to preserve the functionality of fairness of TR-MH algorithm in the token algorithms which maintain logical ring within the fixed network regardless of the mobility of hosts.

Of course, none of the algorithms, search, inform or proxy may cause starvation. Because a stationary mobile host is guaranteed to get its request granted when the token arrives in its local base station. We have already observed that the length of the pending requests in request queue at a fixed host is always bounded. This means after a finite delay each fixed host will release the token. Therefore, each requesting mobile host at a base station will eventually gain an access to the token. In the worst case, a stationary MH may gain access to the token after every other mobile host has accessed the token once from every base station, i.e., after $(N_{MH} - 1) \times N_{BS}$ requests have been satisfied. A simple fix to the problem of fairness is as follows:

1. The token's state is represented by loop count (`token_val`). It represents the number of complete circulations performed by token around the logical ring.
2. A local count `access_count` is attached to each MH. It stores the number of successful token accesses made by the MH.
3. When making an access request each MH provides the current value of access count.
4. When a BS (or the proxy) receives the token, only requests with `access_count` less than the `token_val` are moved from the request queue to the grant queue.
5. MH after using the token, copies the value of `token_val` to its local `access_count`.

A MH reset its `access_count` to `token_val` after each access of the token. Therefore, a MH may access token only once in one full circulation of the token around the logical ring, even if the MH has a lower `access_count`. With the modified algorithm, the number of token accesses, K, satisfied in one traversal of the ring is limited to N_{MH} (when the ring comprises of all BSes), while the value of K could be at most $N_{BS} \times N_{MH}$ otherwise. So the difference between the above modification and the original scheme essentially represents a trade-off between "fairness" of token access among the contending MHs and satisfying as many token requests as possible in full circular traversal of the token.

Of course one can devise an alternative definition of "fairness" as in Definition 11.1.

Definition 11.1 (*Fairness* [7]) A mobile host, MH, having a low access count may be allowed multiple accesses to the token during one traversal of the ring, with the limitation that the total number of accesses made by the MH does not exceed the current `token_val`.

The above definition of fairness implies that if a mobile host MH has not availed its share of token access for a number of token circulations, then MH can access token multiple number of times bounded above by `token_val - access_count`. The above fairness criterion can be easily implemented by simply incrementing `access_count` of a MH on every access.

11.7 Termination Detection

There is a clear evidence that the generic design principle of exploiting asymmetry in two-tier model would be very effective in structuring distributed algorithms for mobile environment. However, the scope of discussion in the previous section was restricted. It is just centered around design of mutual exclusion algorithm. Therefore, we need to examine further how the design principle built around the asymmetry approach could be useful for other problems as well. In this section we focus on termination detection.

Termination of a distributed computation represents one of the global states of the computation. Recording a global state of a distributed systems is known to be difficult [10]. Therefore, it is difficult to record the termination state of a distributed computation. However, the termination, being one of the stable properties of a distributed computation, can be observed. When a computation terminates, there can be no messages in transit. Therefore, it is possible to design an algorithm which does not interfere with the main computation but is able to detect termination of the computation. More precisely, the termination detection algorithm determines whether a distributed computation has entered a state of *silence*. In a silent state no process is active and all the communication channels are empty, taking into account unpredictable delays in message delivery.

An implicit assumption made by most termination detection algorithms is that the main computation never enters an incorrect state. In the case of a mobile distributed system, termination detection is more complex. The complexity is due to the fact that the detection algorithm should also handle the issues arising out of many mobile hosts operating in disconnected mode. Mobile hosts in disconnected mode should not be disturbed. Of course, voluntary disconnection can be planned so termination algorithm can handle them. But, in the cases of involuntary disconnections, mobile hosts may not regain connectivity due to failure. In other words, an incorrect state at times is indistinguishable from a correct state of the computation in mobile distributed systems.

11.7.1   Two Known Approaches

In a termination state the channels are empty. Therefore, no message can reach any of the process and consequently, no processes can become active ever again under this state. There are two fundamentally different approaches to detect termination:

- Diffusion.
- Weight throwing.

A convenient model to visualize a distributed computation is a directed graph that grows and shrinks as the computation progresses [11]. If such a graph contains an edge from a node $n1$ to another node $n2$, then $n2$ is known as a successor of $n1$, and $n1$ a predecessor of $n2$. Every node in a distributed computation starts with a a *neutral state*. Dijkstra and Scholten [11] define that a diffusion based distributed computation is initiated in a neutral state when the environment on its own generates a message and sends it to its successor. After the first message has been sent, an internal node is free to send messages to its successor. So, a diffusion computation grows as a directed graph. After an internal node has performed its node specific computation, it signals completion to its predecessors. In practice, though a two-way communication is possible, the flow of computation messages is only in the direction from a predecessor to a successor. The completion event can be viewed as an acknowledgement for some computation message received earlier by the node. So when completion event is eventually signaled back to environment, the distributed computation is assumed to have terminated.

In weight throwing scheme [12–14], environment or starting process in neutral state has a weight credit of 1 with it. Every message sent by any node is associated with a weight. The sending node partitions the weight available with it into two parts. One of the part is attached to the message before sending it while the other part is retained by the sending node. The computation is started by the environment generating a message of its own and sending it to its successor. Thereafter the internal nodes send messages to their successors as in a diffusion computation. When the node specific computations at a node is over, it signals completion of computation by a weight reportage message to its predecessor besides setting its local weight to 0. The weight reportage message carries the total weight left at a node at the time of completion of the local node specific computation.

11.7.2   Approach for Mobile Distributed Systems

Termination detection in mobile distributed system follows a a hybrid approach [15]. It consists of running a simplified diffusion based termination detection algorithm for the mobile part and a weight throwing based algorithm for the fixed part. The base stations act as bridges between the two parts.

Let us first introduce a few notations which will be convenient to understand the above protocol. A mobile distributed computation can be described by:

1. A special process P_c called weight collector.
2. A set of base station processes denoted by P_i, for $i = 1, 2, \ldots$.
3. A set of mobile processes, P_i^m, for $i = 1, 2, \ldots$.
4. A set of messages.

The computation is started by the weight collector process. However, this does not necessarily represent a limitation of the model. A computation may also be triggered by a mobile process. In that case the weight collection will be performed by the static process representing the current base station for the initiating mobile process. In effect, the starting base station process becomes the environment node.

A mobile process can roam and execute handoff from one base station to another. When a mobile process moves, the distributed computation on that process is suspended. If a mobile process moves away from its current base station and unable to find a new base station to which it can connect, then the mobile process is said to be temporarily disconnected. Further, it is assumed that mobile process cannot carry out any basic computation as long as it remains disconnected.

11.7.3 Message Types

Six different types of messages are needed for the algorithm. These are:

1. M_b: a basic message. If M_b is tagged with a weight w, then it is denoted by $M_b(w)$.
2. $M_{wr}(w)$: a reporting message with a weight w.
3. $M_{ack}(k)$: an acknowledgement for k basic messages.
4. M_{HF}: handoff message. It contains four subtypes: $M_{HF.req}$, $M_{HF.ind}$, $M_{HF.rep}$ and $M_{HF.ack}$.
5. M_{DIS}: message for temporary disconnection. It contains two subtypes: $M_{DIS.req}$, $M_{DIS.ind}$
6. M_{JOIN}: messages connected with rejoining of a disconnected mobile node. It consist of two subtypes: $M_{JOIN.ind}$ and $M_{JOIN.rep}$

Termination detection in a mobile distributed system is of two types:

(i) Strong termination, and
(ii) Weak termination.

A strong termination state is reached when all processes have turned idle, there are no disconnected mobile process or any basic message in transit. In a weak termination state all processes except disconnected mobile processes have reached the state as in strong termination.

The protocol for termination detection in mobile systems should allow for a disconnected process to rejoin the computation at a later point of time. It is possible that a mobile may be disconnected due to failure. In that case the mobile may not join back. If the termination detection protocol does not have a provision to handle such a situation, and then it will not work. Weak termination is an important indication of anticipated system failure due to disconnected mobile processes. So, roll back and recovery protocols can be planned around conditions involving weak termination.

The termination detection algorithm proposed by Tseng and Tan [15] divides the protocol into several parts and specifies it in form of the actions by a mobile process, a base station process and the weight collector process. Before we discuss these algorithms it is necessary to understand how the mobile processes communicate with static processes and while mobile hosts roams.

A mobile process always receives a message from a base station. But it can send a message either to its local base station or to another mobile process. The message, however, is always routed through the base station to which the mobile is connected.

When a mobile moves to another base station while being active then it requires a handoff. A handoff is initiated by sending a $M_{HF.req}$ message. The responsibility for carrying out the rest of the handoff process lies with the static part. Apart of sending handoff, a disconnected mobile node may send a rejoin message on finding a suitable base station to connect with. The rejoin message, denoted by $M_{JOIN.req}$, is sent to the base station with which mobile node attempts to connect. The only other message that a mobile node could send is a signal for completion of local computation. This message is sent to base station. After sending this the mobile turns idle. So the relevant message types handled by a mobile host (MH) are:

- M_b: a basic message which one MH sends to another. M_b is always routed through the base station of the sender MH. A base station after receiving a message M_b from a mobile host (MH), appends a weight w to M_b and sends $M_b(w)$ to the base station of the receiving MH.
- $M_{HF.req}$: This message is sent by an MH to its local base station for a handoff request.
- $M_{JOIN.req}$: This message is sent by a disconnected MH when it is able to hear radio beacons from a base station of the network.

A base station can send a basic message either to a mobile node or to another base station on behalf of a connected mobile. The base stations are also involved in handoffs to facilitate roaming of mobiles. A disconnected mobile may rejoin when it hears beacons from a base station over its radio interface. In order to perform its tasks, a base station has to process and send different types of messages. These message and intended use of these messages can be understood in the context of the protocol discussed later.

11.7.4 Entities and Overview of Their Actions

The termination detection protocol is carried out by actions of following three entities:

- Mobile nodes,
- Base stations, and
- Weight collector.

The termination detection protocol requires support at protocol level for roaming and disconnected mobile processes. A roaming of mobile process is managed by handoff protocol. Handoff protocol handles the transfer of weights associated with basic computation messages to appropriate base station. Similarly, the concerned base stations transfers associated weights of disconnected mobile processes to the weight collector. The transfer of weights as indicated above ensures that every base station can correctly transfer the weights to the weight collector when completion of basic computation is signalled.

The protocol distinguishes between two sets of mobile processes:

- MP_i: set of active mobile processes under base station BS_i.
- DP: set of disconnected mobile processes in the system.

Each active mobile processes is associated with an active mobile node while each disconnected process is associated with one disconnected mobile nodes. The set of mobile processes involved in the computation is given by the union $DP \cup \{\cup_i MP_i\}$.

11.7.5 Mobile Process

A mobile process (which runs on a mobile host) can either receive a basic message from a base station or send a basic message to another mobile process. All messages either originating or terminating at a mobile host (MH) are routed through the current base station of MH. When a mobile process receives a basic message it keeps a count of the number of unacknowledged message received from the concerned base station. So, mobile process knows the number of acknowledgements to be sent to the base station when it has finished computation.

A mobile process P_j^m always routes a basic message M_b through its current base station process P_i to another mobile process P_k^m. The process P_i attaches a weight $w_i/2$ to M_b and sends $M_b(w_i/2)$ to the base station hosting P_k^m. P_i also keeps track of the acknowledgements it has received from all mobile processes. So no additional protocol level support is required at P_j^m for sending a basic message to any other process P_k^m.

P_j^m increments the number of unacknowledged messages by 1 when it receives a basic message from P_i. A local counter in is used by a mobile process to update the count of unacknowledged messages. So, P_j^m knows that it has to send acknowledgements for in messages. Therefore, before turning idle, P_j^m signals the completion of basic computation by sending an acknowledgement for *in* number of messages to P_i. After the acknowledgement has been sent, *in* is set to 0. The summary of the actions executed by a mobile node in the termination detection protocol is specified in Algorithm 20.

Algorithm 20: Actions of a mobile process P_j^m

```
begin
    // For sending a basic message to another process no
        additional operation is needed.
    on receipt of (a basic message from BS) begin
        // Increment number of messages with pending acks.
        in = in + 1;
    end
    on turning (idle from active) begin
        // Send all the pending acks.
        send Mack(in) to current base station;
        in = 0;
    end
end
```

11.7.6   Base Stations

Every message to and from a mobile process P_j^m is routed always through P_i, its current base station process. P_i attaches a weight x from its available weights to every message M_b from P_j^m before sending to the base station process P_l for the destination. P_l receives $M_b(x) = M_b + \{x\}$. It extracts the weight x from $M_b(x)$ and adds x to its the current weight. After this, the message $M_b = M_b(x) - \{x\}$ is forwarded to P_k^m. This way any base station process can control the weight throwing part of the protocol on behalf of all the mobile processes it interacts with.

In order to control the diffusion part, a mobile process P_i keeps track of the messages it has sent to every mobile process P_j^m under it. P_i expects P_j^m to send acknowledgement for each and every message it has received. The completion of computation is signaled by sending the acknowledgements for all the messages of P_i. When all the mobile processes P_j^ms involved in a computation have sent their final acknowledgements to P_i, the termination in diffusion part is detected.

The rules for termination detection executed by a base station process P_i are as specified by Algorithm 21.

Before we consider handoff and rejoin protocols, let us examine two important properties of the protocol specified by actions of three entities we have described so far.

Algorithm 21: Actions of a BS process P_i

---

begin
    on receipt of $(M_b(x)$ for P_j^m from fixed N/W$)$ **begin**
        $w_i = w_i + x;$ // Update local weight
        $M_b = M_b(x) - \{x\};$ // Remove weight from $M_b(x)$
        $out_i[j] = out_i[j] + 1;$ // Record number of messages sent to P_j^m.
        forward M_b (without appending x) to P_j^m;
    end
    on receipt of $(M_b$ from P_j^m for $P_k^m)$ **begin**
        if $(P_k^m \in MP_i)$ **then**
            // P_k^m is local mobile process under P_i
            $out_i[k] = out_i[k] + 1;$
            forward M_b to P_k^m;
        end
        else
            // Destination P_k^m is non local
            $M_b(w_i/2) = M_b + w_i/2;$ // Attach weight to M_b.
            $w_i^b = w_i^b/2;$ // Reduce current weight held.
            locate MH_k's base station BS_ℓ; // BS process P_ℓ
            send $M_b(w_i/2)$ to P_ℓ;
        end
    end
    on receipt of $(M_{ack}(k)$ from $P_j^m \in MP_i)$ **begin**
        $out_i[j] = out_i[j] - k;$ // Decrease number of pending acks by k
        if $(out_i[k] == 0$ for all $P_k^m \in MP_i)$ **then**
            sends $M_{wr}(w_i)$ to P_c;
            $w_i = 0;$
        end
    end
end

Property 1 *If $out_i[j] = 0$ then P_j^m is idle and there is no in-transit basic messages between P_i and P_j^m.*

Proof When $out_i[j] = 0$, all basic messages sent by P_i to P_j^m have been acknowledged. So P_j^m must be idle. As every channel is assumed to be FIFO, if message M is sent before M' over a channel, then M must be received before M' at the other end. When P_j^m turns idle it sends acknowledgement for all the messages it has received from P_i. So when this acknowledgement (which the last among the sequence of messages between P_i and P_j^m) is received by P_i there can be no message in-transit message on the channel because the acknowledgement would flush all other messages before it.

Property 2 *If $w_i = 0$ then all mobile processes $P_j^m \in MP_i$ are idle and there is no in-transit basic message within P_i*

Proof If $w_i = 0$, then the weights held by P_i on behalf of all mobile process $P_j^m \in MP_i$ have been sent back to P_c. This can happen only if $out_i[j] = 0$, for all $P_j^m \in MP_i$. By

Property 1, it implies P_j^m is idle and there is no in-transit basic message between P_i and P_j^m. Hence the property holds.

11.7.7   Handoff

When a mobile process P_j^m moves from its current cell under a base station BS_i to a new cell under another base station BS_k then handoff should be executed. As a part of the handoff process, the relevant data structure and the procedure for managing termination detection protocol concerning P_j^m should be passed on to BS_k.

P_j^m makes a request for handoff to BS_k and waits for the acknowledgement from BS_k. If the acknowledgement is received then P_j^m starts interacting with BS_k for initiating transfer of the data structure related P_j^m from BS_i to BS_k. If handoff acknowledgement is not received within a timeout period, P_j^m retries handoff. The handoff procedure is a slight variation from layer-2 handoff. In a cellular based wireless network, when a handoff is initiated, old base station BS_{old} sends handoff request to mobile switching center (MSC). MSC then forwards the request to the new base station BS_{new} (determined through signal measurements). BS_{old} then accepts the request and handoff command is executed through BS_{old}. So, for the protocol level support for handoff execution, the mobile process should send $M_{HF.req}$ to BS_i identifying BS_k. BS_i accepts the request and also sends $M_{HF.ack}$ to P_j^m. After this P_j^m starts communicating with BS_k. BS_i, before sending $M_{HF.ack}$ to P_j^m, also transfers the needed data structure to BS_k. The negotiation for transfer of link between BS_i and BS_k may involve messages like $M_{HF.ind}$ and $M_{HF.rep}$ between BS_i and BS_k. The handoff process has been illustrated in Fig. 11.6. To keep the protocol simple, P_j^m has been shown to directly approach BS_k for executing handoff. In response to handoff indication message from BS_k, process at BS_i sends a message to BS_k that includes:

- Count of the number of unacknowledged messages in respect of mobile process P_j^m. These are the basic messages for which BS_i was expecting acknowledgements at the time P_j^m sought a handoff.
- A weight $w = w_i/2$.

Fig. 11.6 Illustration of handoff process

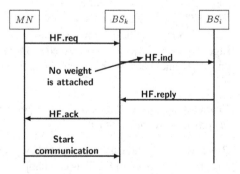

The base station process P_i at BS_i should check if P_k^m is the last mobile process under it. In that case P_i should itself turn idle. But before turning idle, it should send its existing weight credit to the weight collector process.

Once $M(w_i/2)$ has been received at BS_k, it should update its own data structure for keeping track of mobile processes. Thus the summary of the protocol rules for handoff execution are as mentioned in Algorithm 22.

Algorithm 22: Handoff protocol

begin
    // Actions of P_j^m
    on detection of *(Handofff conditions)* **begin**
        // BS_k is the new BS for P_j^m
        // Assume P_k in BS_k handles the request
        send $M_{HF.req}$ message to P_k and wait for $M_{HF.ack}$;
        if *(M.HF.ack received from P_k)* **then**
        | start communicating with P_k; // process P_k in BS_k
        end
        else
        | after time out retry handoff;
        end
    end
    // Actions of P_i of BS_i
    on receipt of *($M_{HF.ind}(P_j^m)$ from P_k)* **begin**
        send a $M_{HF.rep}(P_j^m, out_i[j], w_i/2)$ to P_k;
        $MP_i = MP_i - \{P_j^m\}$; // P_j^m no longer under P_i.
        $w_i = w_i/2$;
        if *($out_i[l] = 0$ for all $l \in MP_i$)* **then**
            // P_j^m is the last mobile process under P_i
            send $M_{wr}(w_i)$ to P_c;
            $w_i = 0$;
        end
    end
    // Actions of P_k of BS_k
    on receipt of *($M_{HF.req}$ from P_j^m)* **begin**
    | sends a $M_{HF.ind}(P_j^m)$ to P_i; // No weight attached.
    end
    on receipt of *($M_{HF.rep}(P_j^m, out_i[j], w_i/2)$ from P_i)* **begin**
        $MP_k = MP_k \cup \{P_j^m\}$;
        $out_k[j] = out_i[j]$;
        $w_k = w_k + w_i/2$;
        send a $M_{HF.ack}$ to P_j^m;
    end
end

11.7.8 Disconnection and Rejoining

It is assumed that all the disconnections are planned. However, this is not a limitation of the protocol. Unplanned disconnection can be detected by timeouts and hello beacons. When a mobile process P_j^i is planning a disconnection it sends $M_{DISC.req}$ message to its current base station BS_i. Then BS_i suspends all communication with P_j^m and sends $M_{DISC.ind}(P_j^m, out_i[j], w_i/2)$ to P_c. It will allow P_c to detect a weak termination condition if one arises.

The rules for handling disconnection are, thus, summarized in Algorithm 23.

Algorithm 23: Disconnection protocol

begin
    // Actions of P_j^m
    before entering *(disconnected mode)* **begin**
        send $M_{DISC.req}$ message to P_i;
        suspend all basic computation;
    end
    // Actions of P^i of BS_i
    on receipt of *($M_{DISC.req}$ from P_j^m)* **begin**
        suspend all communication with P_j^m;
        send a $M_{DISC.ind}(P_j^m, out_i[j], w_i/2)$ to P_c;
        $MP_i = MP_i - \{P_j^m\}$;
        $w_i = w_i/2$;
        if *($out_i[k] == 0$ for all $P_k^m \in MP_i$)* **then**
            send $M_{wr}(w_i)$ to P_c;
            $w_i = 0$;
        end
    end
    // Actions of weight collector P_c
    on receipt of *($M_{DISC.ind}(P_j^m, out_i[j], w_i/2)$ from P_i)* **begin**
        $DP = DP \cup \{P_j^m\}$;
        $out_c[j] = out_i[j]$;
        $w_{DIS} = w_{DIS} + w_i/2$;
    end
end

Final part of the protocol is for handling rejoining. If a mobile process can hear the radio of signals from a base station it can rejoin that base station. For performing a rejoin P_j^m has to execute Algorithm 24.

11.7.9 Dangling Messages

There may be messages in system which cannot be delivered due to disconnection or handoff. Such dangling messages should be delivered if the mobile process recon-

---

Algorithm 24: Rejoining protocol

---

begin

    // Actions of P_j^m

    on rejoining (*a cell in BS_i*) **begin**

        send $M_{JOIN.req}$ message to P_i and wait for reply;

        if (*$M_{JOIN.ack}$ is received from P_i*) **then**

          | starts basic computation;

        end

        else

          | after timeout retry JOIN;

        end

    end

    // Actions of P_i in BS_i

    on receipt of (*$M_{JOIN.req}$ from P_j^m*) **begin**

        | send a $M_{JOIN.ind}(P_j^m)$ to P_c; // No weight attached.

    end

    on receipt of (*$M_{JOIN.rep}(P_j^m, out_c[j], w_{DIS}/2)$ from P_c*) **begin**

        $MP_i^b = MP_i^b + \{P_j^m\}$;

        $out_i[j] = out_c[j]$;

        send a $M_{JOIN.ack}$ to P_j^m;

        restart communication with P_j^m;

    end

    // Actions of weight collector P_c

    on receipt of (*$M_{JOIN.ind}(P_j^m)$ from P_i*) **begin**

        if (*$P_j^m \in DP$*) **then**

          sends a $M_{JOIN.rep}(P_j^m, out_c[j], w_{DIS}/2)$ to P_i;

          $DP = DP - \{P_j^m\}$;

          if (*$DP = \Phi$*) **then**

            | $w_c = w_c + w_{DIS}$;

          end

        end

    end

end

---

nects at a later point of time. So, care must be taken to handle these messages. When a mobile process is involved in a handoff it cannot deliver any message to static host or base station. So, the mobile process hold such undelivered messages with it until handoff is complete. This way message exchange history is correctly recorded. Dangling messages at base stations are those destined for mobile processes involved in handoff or disconnection. These messages are associated with weights which is ensured by weight throwing part of the algorithm. So, handling dangling messages becomes easy. All dangling messages from base station processes are sent to weight collector. The weight collector process holds the messages for future processing. This protocol is specified by Algorithm 25

Algorithm 25: Handling dangling messages

---

begin
    // Actions of weight collector P_c
    on receipt of *(Dangling message with weight x)* **begin**
    | $w_{DIS} = w_{DIS} + x$;
    end
    on completion of *(Reconnection of P_j^m)* **begin**
        // Let M_b be a dangling message for P_j^m
        $M_b(w_{DIS}/2) = M_b + w_{DIS}/2$;
        $w_{DIS} = w_{DIS}/2$;
        // Assume P_j^m reconects under BS_i
        send $M_b(w_{DIS}/2)$ to P_i;
        if *(dangling message list == Φ)* **then**
        | // No disconnected mobile exists
        | $w_c = w_c + w_{DIS}$; // Reclaim residual weight
        | $w_{DIS} = 0$;
        end
    end
end

11.7.10   Announcing Termination

The termination is detected by P_c when it finds $w_c + w_{DIS} = 1$. If $w_c = 1$ then it is a case of strong termination, otherwise it is case of weak termination. In the case of weak termination $w_{DIS} > 0$.

References

1. M.H. Dunham, A. Helal, Mobile computing and databases: anything new? SIGMOD Rec. **24**(4), 5–9 (1995). December
2. G. Liu, G. Maguire Jr., A class of mobile motion prediction algorithms for wireless mobile computing and communication. Mob. Networks Appl. **1**(2), 113–121 (1996)
3. A.L. Murphy, G.C. Roman, G. Varghese, An algorithm for message delivery to mobile units, in *The 16th ACM Symposium on Principles of Distributed Computing (PODC'97)*, pp. 292–292, 1997
4. K. Kumar, Lu Yung-Hsiang, Cloud computing for mobile users: can offloading computation save energy? Computer **43**(4), 51–56 (2010)
5. K. Yang, S. Ou, H.H. Chen, On effective offloading services for resource-constrained mobile devices running heavier mobile internet applications. IEEE Commun. Mag. **46**(1), 56–63 (2008)
6. S. Acharya, M. Franklin, S. Zdonik, Dissemination-based data delivery using broadcast disks. IEEE Pers. Commun. **2**(6), 50–60 (2001)
7. B.R. Badrinath, A. Acharya, T. Imielinski, Designing distributed algorithms for mobile computing networks. Comput. Commun. **19**(4), 309–320 (1996)
8. L. Lamport, A new solution of dijkstra's concurrent programming problem. Commun. ACM **17**, 453–455 (1974)
9. E.W. Dijkstra, Self-stabilizing systems in spite of distributed control. Commun. ACM **17**, 643–644 (1974)

10. K.M. Chandy, L. Lamport, Distributed snapshots: determining global states of distributed systems. ACM Trans. Comput. Syst. (TOCS), **3**(1), 63–75 (1985)
11. E.W. Dijkstra, C.S. Scholten, Termination detection for diffusing computations. Inf. Process. Lett. **11**, 1–4 (1980)
12. S. Huang, Detecting termination of distributed computations by external agents, in *The IEEE Nineth International Conference on Distributed Computer Systems*, pp. 79–84, 1989
13. F. Mattern, Golbal quiescence detection based on credit distribution and recovery. Inf. Proc. Lett. **30**, 95–200 (1989)
14. Y.C. Tseng, Detecting termination by weight-throwing in a faulty distributed system. J. Parallel Distrib. Comput. **25**, 7–15 (1995)
15. Y.C. Tseng, C.C. Tan, Termination detection protocols for mobile distributed systems. IEEE Trans. Parallel Distrib. Syst. **12**(6), 558–566 (2001)

Chapter 12
Data Dissemination and Broadcast Disks

12.1 Introduction

Data management is one of the important challenges in mobile applications. Due to resource constraints, mobile devices are not equipped to run any interesting, nontrivial stand-alone applications. On the other hand, the enabling technologies such as cellular communication, wireless LAN, wireless data network and satellite services have equipped mobile terminals with capabilities to access data/information anywhere at any time. Researchers saw immense potentials in combining two forementioned aspects in complementary roles, for developing a powerful framework for innovative person centric services. The key idea is to organize a mobile application as a set of synchronized activities that requires very little computation at a mobile end host, but capitalizes on globally available resources accessible through networks. This would allow a mobile user to transact both official business, and financial transactions. The possibilities of creating innovative commercial and financial models for anytime, anywhere access of person centric services excited research in mobile data management.

The core problem of data delivery over mobile wireless network became a major challenge to the database community since the adaptation of the concept of object oriented databases. In a wireless network, connectivity is not only flaky, but bandwidth is also low. Furthermore, there is no control on the number of mobile users which may appear in an area of cellular coverage. The scale is simply overwhelming. The conventional data delivery model based on request and response (like HTTP) cannot just match up to the challenge of scale.

The push based data delivery is considered as the most attractive option that may allow a server to avoid being flooded by large number of client requests. Some early work in the area of data dissemination inspired the research for data dissemination in mobile distributed system. In 1734, broadcast emerged as a dominant theme for high volume information dissemination by utilizing print media. Around 1898, radio transmission was introduced, and in 1924 video streaming became a possible with

© Springer Nature Singapore Pte Ltd. 2017
R.K. Ghosh, *Wireless Networking and Mobile Data Management*,
DOI 10.1007/978-981-10-3941-6_12

invention of Television. Electronic transmission media not only served as entertainment channels but also revolutionized dissemination of public information.

Around mid eighties two systems were implemented using broadcast delivery. The first one is known as BCIS (Boston Community Information System) [8]. It was a pilot project for dissemination of news and information over FM channel to about 200 clients having personal computers equipped with wireless interfaces. The system used both push and pull based data delivery methods [3]. The second one called Datacycle [10], was a high throughput oriented transaction system implemented over public telephone system. It exploited transmission bandwidth of optical systems to leverage database as a storage pump, and broadcast records repeatedly on a broadcast channel. A transaction on a host could request an operation on database using a well defined interface provided with the associated access manager. The operation was decomposed into a specification to process records as they appear on the broadcast channel. To complete a transaction, a host submits update/commit requests to the access manager. Using a network uplink, the access manager sends the update request to the update manager, which executes non conflicting updates on the database.

Theoretical results concerning performance of broadcast delivery models were provided in [14]. Wong's result, in particular, states that the lower bound of the bandwidth requirement for the best possible mean response time of a broadcast page is proportional to square root of its access frequency.

In this chapter our focus is primarily restricted to push based data delivery. However, it deals with classification of various options for data delivery in a client server system along with the factors influencing these options. The major part of the chapter is devoted to the idea behind treating an inherently sequential medium such as a wireless communication channel organized in the form of logical disks on the air. Furthermore, it shows that by treating the medium of air as part of a logical memory hierarchy, data delivery mechanism can be organized extending from an individual mobile client's memory to a server's disk.

12.2   Data Access Issues in Mobile Environment

At an end user's level, the major concerns are:

1. Energy efficient accesses of requisite data,
2. Management of range of disconnections, and
3. Efficient processing of queries.

Therefore, indexing, caching and replications are as much relevant in mobile environment as they are over the wired network with stationary hosts. However, due to the unique physical characteristics of mobile terminals and wireless communication medium these issues needed a revisit. In summary, the techniques for data management in mobile distributed environment should be able to handle following four main issues.

1. Mobility
2. Scaling
3. Disconnection
4. Access/delivery modes.

Data related to mobility may far exceed the complexity of any conventional large database. It comprises of locating a mobile object, addressing, routing queries and delivering responses. Some of these issues have been discussed under location management in the previous chapter. The issues arising out of scaling and disconnection are mainly handled through replication and caching strategies. Replication and caching are discussed in Chap. 14. Access and delivery mechanisms are intertwined. The role of delivery mechanism does not mean just putting loads of bits over communication channels, but organizing these bits through a structure that can be effectively exploited to access data. But two most important constraints which come on the way are:

• Availability of limited bandwidth, and
• Availability of limited battery power.

These constraints severely restrict transfer of large volume data. In a cellular based network, the number of active mobile users cannot be controlled. If every mobile uses a back channel to pull data for its own application from a fixed nodes, then the channel saturates quickly and suffers from congestion too often. Availability of limited energy in a mobile device is also a possible cause of planned disconnections, as the user may wish to prolong battery life. So there is a need for energy efficient access methods.

12.3 Pull and Push Based Data Delivery

A client application is the consumer of data and the server is the producer. In other words, data and information are generated at the servers. So, the servers are repositories of data/information that the client applications would require from time to time. A server has to deliver appropriate data which the clients require for the applications to run. There are broadly two data delivery models as shown in Fig. 12.1. A client initiated data delivery is essentially *pull based*. The client sends an explicit request to a server. The responsibility of fetching data rests exclusively on the client. On the other hand, when a server takes the responsibility of transferring data, then transfer takes place in anticipation of a future access. No explicit request are made from any client. The server estimates the data requirements of the client population in a global context. A client must be alert during the time when the required data for its application flows into a broadcast channel from a server. The data delivery model adhering to this protocol referred to as push-based delivery. The delivery model is analogous to TV transmission where the viewers tune to specific channel if they wish to view a TV program. The channel caters to an expected general viewing

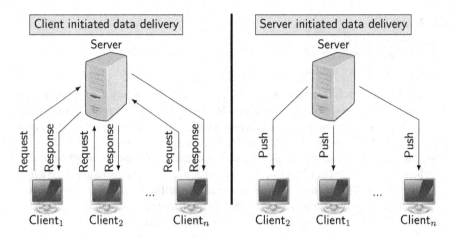

Fig. 12.1 Client and server initiated data delivery mechanisms

pattern on the basis of monthly ratings of the different TV shows. TV transmission, thus, may not necessarily cater to specific individual choices. A similar situation is witnessed in push-based data transfer. The information is not explicitly sought for, but broadcast by a server to all or a group of clients. This method of data transfer is referred to as *data dissemination*.

Figure 12.2 illustrates an implementation oriented view of data transfer mechanism as applicable to the two data delivery models. In the pull-based data transfer occurs in a *request-response cycle*. data transfer. In a push based transfer, data transfer occurs on a *broadcast channel*. The server must have an idea of data that should be pushed. Therefore, there may be a back channel through which profile informa-

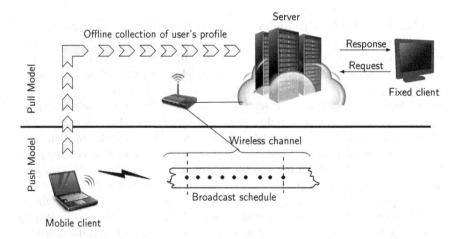

Fig. 12.2 Data delivery models

tion of clients can be collected as indicated in the Fig. 12.2. Otherwise, the data dissemination on broadcast channel can only be organized purely on the basis of a knowledgeable assessment of the data requirements of the clients.

12.4   Dissemination in Mobile Environment

In mobile environment, there is a built-in asymmetry as mobile devices are resource poor. Compute-intensive tasks are executed on the servers. Databases and other storage repositories are also located on the servers. So, data dissemination techniques in mobile environment are built around push based delivery mechanism, and rely on broadcast or point to multipoint transmissions.

Pure push and pure pull represent two extreme data delivery methods. Between the two extremities many delivery methods have been used. These methods were determined by the varying requirements of data from the applications. On the basis of design issues faced by applications, data delivery methods can be broadly classified into four categories.

1. Data oriented,
2. Mechanism oriented,
3. Organization oriented,
4. Bandwidth oriented.

In the data oriented design, a client's requirement of data can be of three types, namely,

1. Publish only,
2. Demand driven,
3. Hybrid.

Certain data objects generated by a server assist a client learn about the occurrences of events. The client does not require to process such data, but needs to know as and when such data objects get generated. A server's obligation is limited to publish such data objects on downlink channel as and when these get generated. A client accesses the desired data by passive listening and local filtering. Some applications may require the clients to explicitly fetch certain data from a server and process them. This requires a pull based delivery, wherein a clients places a demand for its data requirement explicitly in form of queries over its uplink channel. The server sends responses that resolve the queries. A hybrid delivery mechanism represents a combination mechanism, where some data requirements are met by data objects belonging to publish group and others are met by demand driven group of objects. Normally, in a hybrid model there will be only a few objects belonging to demand driven group.

Franklin and Zodnik [6, 7] observed application design spaces can be partitioned according to mechanisms of data delivery, namely,

1. Delivery initiation,
2. Scheduling strategy,
3. Communication type.

Delivery of data can either be initiated by a client or by a server. When initiated by a client it represents essentially a pull model. On the other hand, when delivery is initiated by a server, it represents push model. Scheduling basically deals with the temporal mechanism of data delivery. The data is delivered on some pre-determined schedule. Communication type can be: (i) unicast or point to point, (ii) multicast or point to many points, i.e., one-to-many (iii) broadcast or one-to-all. There is a difference between multicast and broadcast though both represent the communication type that transmits data from one source to many destinations. In multicast the number of recipients are known, whereas in broadcast the recipient can be any one. For multicast, communication, a list of recipients should be maintained.

The organization of data delivery refers to the way data organized for delivery to client. Two possible ways data can be organized, namely,

1. Broadcast program,
2. Selective tuning.

Broadcast program requires a server to anticipate the data requirements of its clients. On the basis of the requirements, the server organizes a push schedule for data on downlink channel. The data objects may be organized on a push schedule based on client access priorities or bandwidth minimization or combination of both. We plan to discuss more about broadcast program subsequently in this chapter as it represents an important and interesting data dissemination technique specially in the context of mobile distributed environments. Selective tuning requires a client to create its own filtering and caching strategies for accessing data from the downlink channel. The server embeds meta data and/or index along with information when pushing data on downlink channel. Air indexing schemes are discussed in the next chapter.

Bandwidth oriented data delivery mechanism is concerned with apportioning of bandwidth for pull and push. Normally, in a mobile environment much of the server data is pushed on a downlink channel. Only a small fraction of bandwidth is allocated for uplink communication. The uplink serves as a back channel for the demand driven data delivery. However, in theory, bandwidth partitioning can be done either (i) statically, or (ii) dynamically. In static allocation, the bandwidth is split in advance between downlink and uplink. But this type of allocation may lead to under utilization when access pattern is dynamic. Dynamic allocation is complex. It requires additional runtime information about the changes in access patterns.

12.5 Comparison of Pull and Push Models

In a wired network, all the computers share the same physical medium (wire) for data transfer. Therefore, data transmission capacities in both uplink and downlink directions are the same. In wireless network, there is an asymmetry in capacity of

Table 12.1 Asymmetry in link capacities of wireless networks

Network type	Technology	Downlink	Uplink
Satellite	DirecPC	400 kbps	56.6 kbps (thru Tel.)
Cable TV	Cable modem	10–30 Mbps	128 kbps (Shared)
Telephone	ADSL, VDSL Modem	2 Mbps	9.6–640 kbps
Wireless	802.11	1–10 Mbps	9.6–19.2 kbps

links in two directions. The asymmetry in link capacities in the case of a few recent examples N/W technologies have been provided in Table 12.1. Even, otherwise, the asymmetry can occur even in a symmetric client-server setup. The anomalies in bandwidths occur due to the fact that:

- Either physically different media are used for the uplink and the downlink connections, or
- The same medium is split asymmetrically for uplink and downlink connections.

As the table indicates, depending on the N/W technology, the variations between the downlink and the uplink capacities can range from 1:8 to 1:500. The asymmetry can arise not only due to the limitation of N/W technology, but also due to *load asymmetry* or *data volume asymmetry*. The load asymmetry is introduced when a few machines in the N/W handle most of the messages. In particular, the service load asymmetry may happen due to following reasons:

- The client-to-server ratio is high, so, the average load on a server is high.
- The updates are too frequent, so, the clients continually poll the servers for new data.

In some application environments, the asymmetry in volume of data arises due to mismatch in the volumes of data transmitted in each direction. For example, in information retrieval type application, a few URLs (a mouse key click) may result in a huge document to be downloaded. So, the requirements for uplink capacity is much smaller than downlink. Typically wireless connectivity may offer only unidirectional connections. So, the clients may be unable to connect by design rather than just due to technical problems.

In a pull-based system, the clients must have a priori knowledge about what to ask for. Pull-based data retrieval is typically similar to the RPC protocol. Each data transfer from the server is initiated explicitly by a request from a client. In response to the request form a client, the server transfers the requested data. The biggest drawback to implement a pull-based data transfer system is that a back channel should be made available to the clients for fetching desired data. The back channel eats away bandwidth available for data transfer. In a typical environment, where the clients are mobile, the congestion in back channel can be real bottleneck for fetching data.

The availability, as well as the use of the back channel for clients is restricted either because of the security reasons or due to the power problem at the clients, or both. The saturation of a server due to huge number of client requests may be another severe problem. Indeed, if the *request rate* is higher than the *service rate*, the server will eventually saturate. However, in traditional applications, it can be controlled.

In summary the scale of mobile computing environment seems to be the most important factor contributing to the drawbacks of pull based data delivery model [2, 11, 12].

The major advantages of a push-based data delivery model can be summarized as follows:

- *Efficiency*: The transfer of data is needed only when the updates arrive at a server, or when the new data gets created. Obviously, a client is not expected to know when the new data gets generated at the server.
- *Scalability*: The push-based data delivery model translates into greater scalability. A client need not poll the server in periodic intervals to check for the delivery of data items it may need.
- *Low bandwidth requirement*: There is no need for deploying a back channel. The transfer of data is initiated by the server when some updates are made or some new data get created. So the utilization of entire bandwidth can be made possible only via downstream link, and more data can flow on the channel. Furthermore, the utilization of available bandwidth can be done optimally as it is coordinated at the server end.

12.6   Classification of Data Delivery Models

In the context client-server paradigm the basic difference between data delivery models lies in the fact whether the data transfer is initiated by a client or by the server. Both pull and push based data delivery can be either periodic or aperiodic.

Aperiodic pull is found in traditional systems or request/response kind of data delivery model. Periodic pull arises when a client uses polling to obtain the data it is interested in. It uses a regular schedule to request for the data. Polling is useful in applications such as remote sensing where a client can wait while sending repeated probes, in periodic intervals, for the arrival of the data. The data by itself, is not critical for immediate running of application. In summary, if the transfer is initiated by the client then it can be one of the following types:

(i) *Request/response*: This is found in the traditional schemes such as RPC. A client uses aperiodic pull over point-to-point physical link between the server. Of course, the server may choose to use an one-to-many link for transfer of data. For the client requesting the data, it appears as point-to-point, while the other clients can snoop on the link and get data they have not explicitly requested.

(ii) *Polling*: In some applications such as remote sensing or control applications, a system may periodically send request to a number of sites to obtain changed values. If the information is sent over a point-to-point link, it is a pull based approach and known as *polling*. But if the data transfer is over an one-to-many physical link then other clients can snoop.

The periodic push can be for the transmission of a set of data updates or newly created data in a regular interval, such as updates in Stock prices. This data delivery model is useful in situations where clients may not always be available. Since the delivery is for unidentified clients, availability of some specific client or a set of specific clients does not matter. The push based model is preferable for various reasons such as:

- High request processing load or the load asymmetry generated by the clients, or
- A large number of clients are interested for the data being pushed, i.e., high client to server ratio.

Aperiodic push is viewed as publish and subscribe type of data dissemination. There is no periodic interval for sending out the data. The biggest problem in aperiodic push is the assumption that the clients are always listening. In a mobile computing environment the clients may like to remain disconnected till the exact time of arrival of the required data for the reason of extending battery life. The clients may also move to the cells different from where they initially wanted to get the data. The push-based model is exposed to snooping, and a client may also miss out the required data, if it is not listening at the opportune time when the data flows on the downlink channel. So, a mechanism is needed to be in place for a client to be able estimate the time for tuning to the downstream channel for the required data. Therefore, such a data delivery model could considered as more appropriate to the situation where what is sent out is not critical to immediate running of the application. On the positive side, the push based transfer uses downstream channel more effectively. In summary, push based data delivery can categorized as follows.

(i) *Publish/Subscribe* [13]: In this model of data delivery, the flow of data is initiated by a server and is aperiodic. Typically, one-to-many link is used to transfer data.
(ii) *Broadcast disks* [1]: Basically, it is a periodic push mechanism. The clients wait until the data item appears on broadcast. In a sense, it is like accessing of a storage device whose average latency is half the interval at which the requested item is repeated on broadcast. The periodic push can use either point-to-point or one-to-many link; though, one-to-many is more likely.

Figure 12.3 provides a broad classification of data transfer mechanisms based on the pull and push based delivery models and physical link characteristics as discussed above.

The characteristics of a link have a role in deciding how the data delivery model can scale up when there is no control in population of clients. In a point-to-point communication, data sent from a source to a single client. Clearly, p-to-p (point-to-point) transfers cannot scale up easily when the number of clients becomes large. In one-to-many communication data is sent to a number of clients. One-to-many communication can be either multicast or broadcast. Usually, multicasting is implemented by sending data to a router which maintains the list of the recipients and

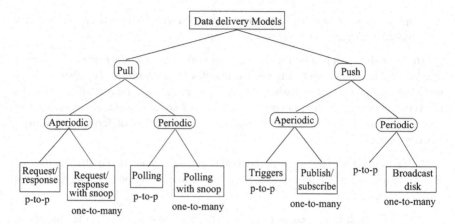

Fig. 12.3 Taxonomy of data transfer

forwards the data to those recipients. So the interests of clients should be known a priori as opposed to broadcast where clients are unidentified. In one-to-many broadcast clients receive data for which they may not be interested at all.

12.7 Broadcast Disk

From the client's perspective, periodic push is similar to accessing a secondary storage. Therefore, the data delivery should be organized to give the best performance to the clients as a local disk would. Suppose in a broadcast schedule, every item appears only once. Then in the worst case, a client may have to wait for one broadcast period for fetching the data item it requires. In the best case, the access can be immediate, and it happens if the client tunes in to listen exactly at time when its item appears in the broadcast channel. It is rarely, the case that all items are accessed equally frequently. Generally, the access pattern tends to be skewed to a few *hot spots*. So it makes sense to capture the pattern of accesses in a broadcast program. *Broadcast disk* is a paradigm for organizing the structure of a periodic broadcast program.

12.7.1 Flat Periodic Broadcast Model

A generic broadcast disk model should be able to capture various access patterns. A flat program is a degenerate case of the generic broadcast disk model. A flat broadcast program shown in Fig. 12.4, can be considered as a logical disk spinning at a speed of one spin in a broadcast period.

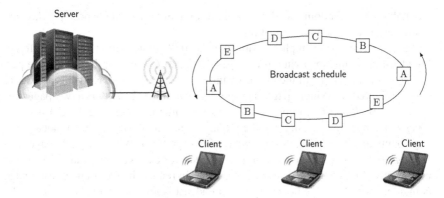

Fig. 12.4 A flat broadcast disk

12.7.2 Skewed Periodic Broadcast

Consider the case when the broadcast data is organized into a multiple number of disks, and each disk spinning with a different speed. The data items are placed into the fastest to the slowest spinning disks in descending order of frequencies of accesses. That is most frequently accessed data is placed on the fastest disk. The least frequently accessed data is placed on the slowest disk.

Depending on whether the broadcast data get updated or not, a periodic broadcast can be considered *static* or *dynamic*. If the sequence of broadcast data remains the same for every broadcast period, then the broadcast is static, otherwise it is dynamic. In the case of dynamic periodic broadcast, the period of broadcast may also vary.

Another way to classify periodic broadcasts would be on the basis of the inter arrival times of two consecutive instances of the same data item. The broadcast is called *regular*, if the inter arrival time of two consecutive instances of the same data item is fixed. The broadcast is *irregular*, if there is a variance in inter arrival times.

12.7.3 Properties of Broadcast Programs

From an abstract point of view, a broadcast programs visualized as an attempt to generate a bandwidth allocation scheme. Given the access probabilities of each client, the job of a broadcast program is to find the optimal fraction of the bandwidth which may be allocated for an item. Assuming no caching at the clients, it is known that the optimal bandwidth that can be allocated for an item is proportional to square root of its access probability [4]. The simplest possible idea would be to generate a random broadcast schedule according to the square root allocation formula; and then hope that this broadcast schedule matches the average inter arrival time between any two instances of same item as expected by the clients. However, the probability is almost

negligible that a random broadcast program may minimize the expected delay due
to the variance in the inter arrival times.

Let us consider an example mentioned in [1]. It illustrates following three different
broadcast programs involving three pages A, B, and C shown in Fig. 12.5. The performance characteristic of the last program (Fig. 12.5c) is identical to the case where
item A is stored on a single-page disk spinning two times faster than a two-page disk
storing items B and C. In this case, the waiting time for accessing page A is either
0 page or 1 pages, assuming that the requirement coincides with the broadcast of a
page boundary. Therefore, average wait is 0.5 page for A. Whereas the average wait
for page B or C is 1.5 pages. Assuming accesses for each page is equally likely, the
total wait $(1/3)(0.5 + 1.5 + 1.5) = 7/6$ page. In reality the requirement for a page
coinciding with the page boundary of a broadcast is low. So adding 1/2 page to the
total wait, we have the delay as $5/3 = 1.67$ pages.

Let us derive the exact expression for the expected delay for an item I from the
point when the request is made. Suppose, a request for the value of I arises at some
point of time t falling in the interval j as shown in Fig. 12.6. If I is scheduled to arrive
during an interval in future, then the maximum waiting time is the interval of time
from the beginning of interval j to the starting of the transmission of I as indicated
in the figure. The time of t may appear any where within interval j. Assuming each
interval to be of unit time, $t \in [0, 1)$, the expected delay is given by

$$\sum_{1}^{N} \int_{0}^{1} \left(t_{max}^{j}(I) - t \right) dt = \sum_{1}^{N} \left(t_{max}^{j}(I) - \frac{1}{2} \right),$$

where N is the number of intervals. Each interval is the time required to transmit one
data item. Using the above formula, the expected delays for the arrival of different
items on the broadcast channel can be computed as illustrated by the Table 12.2.

Fig. 12.5 Broadcast
programs [1]

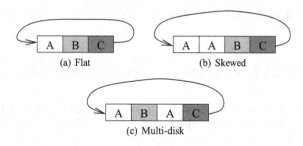

(a) Flat   (b) Skewed

(c) Multi-disk

Fig. 12.6 Formulation of
maximum waiting time

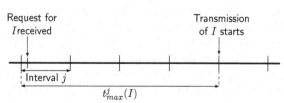

Table 12.2 Expected delays for arrival of items on channel

Arrival of requests	Expected delay					
	$t^j_{max}(A) - (1/2)$		$t^j_{max}(B) - (1/2)$		$t^j_{max}(C) - (1/2)$	
	Skewed	Multidisk	Skewed	Multidisk	Skewed	Multidisk
Interval 1	0.5	1.5	1.5	0.5	2.5	2.5
Interval 2	2.5	0.5	0.5	3.5	1.5	1.5
Interval 3	1.5	1.5	3.5	2.5	0.5	0.5
Interval 4	0.5	0.5	2.5	1.5	3.5	3.5
Average	1.25	1	2	2	2	2

Table 12.3 Expected delays for arrival of items on channel

Access probability			Expected delay		
A	B	C	Flat	Skewed	Multi-disk
0.333	0.333	0.333	1.50	1.75	1.67
0.5	0.25	0.25	1.50	1.63	1.50
0.75	0.125	0.125	1.50	1.44	1.25
0.9	0.05	0.05	1.50	1.33	1.10
1.0	0.0	0.0	1.50	1.25	1.00

The expected delays for the arrival of items A, B and C respectively are 1.25, 2, 2, in the case of clustered skewed broadcast, and 1, 2, 2 for the case of multi-disk broadcast. If the probability of access for each item is equally likely, then the expected delays for an item in two broadcast methods are:

$$\text{Skewed broadcast} : \tfrac{1}{3}(1.25 + 2 + 2) = 1.75$$
$$\text{Multi-disk broadcast} : \tfrac{1}{3}(1 + 2 + 2) = 1.67$$

Table 12.3 gives the computed delays (in terms of page broadcast period) for page requests corresponding to distribution of access probabilities of the clients. In the case of uniform page access probabilities, flat disk is the best. Non-flat programs are better for skewed access probabilities. Obviously, higher the access probability more is the bandwidth requirement. When page A is accessed with probability 0.5, according to square root formula [4] the optimal bandwidth allocation works out to be $\sqrt{0.5}/(\sqrt{0.5} + \sqrt{0.25} + \sqrt{0.25})$ which is 41%. The flat program allocates only 33% (8% less in) bandwidth. Whereas the multi-disk program (in which page A appears twice in the schedule) allocates 50% (9% excess in) bandwidth.

12.7.4 Advantages of Multi-Disk Program

A multi-disk program performs better (results in less delay) than the corresponding skewed program. This problem can be explained by what is known as *"bus stop paradox"*. The paradox is explained as follows. Suppose there are buses plying to different destinations D_1 and D_2, D_3, etc., from a station S. The number of buses to destination D_1 is more than the available other destinations. But all the buses for destination D_1 are clustered in a small window of time t_w in a day, whereas buses to other destination are staggered in more or less in equal intervals throughout the day. Under this scenario, if a person is unable to be reach S within the interval t_w, cannot get to the destination D_1 for the entire day, although the probability of getting a bus to destinations D_1 is higher than the probabilities for other destinations. This happens due the fact that the buses to other destinations are not clustered.

The probability of arrival of a request during a time interval is directly proportional to the length of the interval. This implies that if the variance in broadcast rate (inter arrival rate) of a page is high, then the expected delay increases. If the inter arrival rate of a page is fixed then the expected delay to satisfy any requests for that page at any random time is half of the interval between two successive broadcasts of the same page. The randomness in inter arrival rate can also reduce the effectiveness of a pre-fetching techniques. The client also cannot go into *doze* mode to reduce the power consumption, because the time of arrival of the requested page cannot be estimated. On the other hand, if interval of arrival is fixed, the update dissemination can be planned by the server. This predictability helps in understanding of the update semantics at the client. Therefore, the desirable features of a broadcast program are:

- The inter arrival time of the consecutive copies of a data item should be fixed.
- The length of a broadcast schedule should be pre-defined, after which it should repeat. Equivalently, the periodicity of a broadcast should be fixed.
- It should use as much bandwidth as possible subject to the above two constraints.

12.7.5 Algorithm for Broadcast Program

Algorithm 26 generates a bandwidth allocation for a periodic push based broadcast when information related to page usage is available. This algorithm was originally proposed in [1].

Example
Consider a three disk program in which pages of D_1 to be broadcast 2 times as frequently as D_2 and 3 times as frequently as D_3. That is, the frequencies are: $f_1 = 6, f_2 = 3$ and $f_3 = 2$ and $T_{max} = LCM(f_1, f_2, f_3) = 6$. This implies splitting disks results in following chunks:

Algorithm 26: Generation of broadcast program

---

begin

    order the pages to be broadcast from *hottest* to *coldest*;

    group the pages into multiple ranges;

    `// Each range represents a logical broadcast disk.`

    `// Assume` N_{disks} `disks denoted by` $D_1, \ldots, D_{N_{disk}}$.

    foreach *(disk D_i)* **do**

        `//` f_i`, must be an integral value.`

        choose relative frequency f_i;

    end

    split each disk into smaller units called *chunks*;

    $T_{max} = \mathrm{LCM}\{f_i | 1 \leq i \leq N_{disk}\}$;

    foreach *(disk D_i)* **do**

        split D_i into equal sized chunk $C_{ij}, j = 1, \ldots, T_{max}/f_i$;

    end

    `// Create broadcast program interleaving disk chunks.`

    for *(i = 1; i ≤ T_{max}, i + +)* **do**

        for *(j = 1; j ≤ N_{disks}, j + +)* **do**

            broadcast chunk $C_{j,((i-1) \bmod T_j+1)}$;

        end

    end

end

Fig. 12.7 Bandwidth allocation by broadcast algorithm

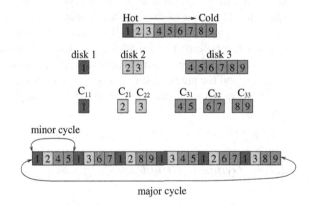

1. Disk D_1: splitting results in one chunk C_{11}.
2. Disk D_2: splitting results in two chunks C_{21}, C_{22}, and
3. Disk D_3: splitting results in three chunks C_{31}, C_{32}, C_{33}.

Though chunk size of a disk fixed, across the disks the size may be variable. Figure 12.7 illustrates the broadcast program generated by the applying the above algorithm. As shown in the Fig. 12.7, disk D_1 consists of a single page and only one chunk. Disk D_2 consists of two pages and each chunk has one page. Disk D_3 has six pages divided into three chunks, where each chunk has two pages. A minor broadcast cycle consists of three chunks, one from each disks D_1, D_2, D_3. Therefore, each minor cycle consists of four pages, one page each from D_1 and D_2 and two pages from D_3. One major broadcast cycle consist of $T_{max} = 6$ minor cycles. So, one major cycle consists of 24 pages. The allocation schedule produces three logical levels of memory hierarchy.

- The first being the smallest and the fastest disk D_1.
- The second being the disk D_2 which is slower than D_1.
- The last being the disk D_3 which is slower but larger than both D_1 and D_2.

12.7.6 Parameters for Tuning Disk Model

Three main parameters to be tuned to particular access probability distribution are:

- *The number of disks*. It determines the *different* frequency ranges with which set of all pages should be broadcast.
- *The number of pages per disk*. It determines set of pages of identical frequency range on broadcast.
- *The relative frequency of broadcast*. It determines the size of disks, and hence the arrival time.

The thumb rule is to configure the fastest disk to have only few pages. This because, adding an extra page to the fastest disk adds significantly to the delay of arrival time for the pages in the slower disks. The constraint requiring frequencies to be positive integers leads to a broadcast schedule with fixed inter-arrival time for the pages. A regularity in inter-arrival time substantially eases the maintenance of update semantics, and the predictability helps the client side caching strategy. All pages in the same disk get same amount of bandwidth as they are broadcast with the same frequency.

12.7.7 Dynamic Broadcast Program

The algorithm discussed above generates a static broadcast program. It means there is no change in the broadcast period, the amount of broadcast data or the values of data. In other words, there is no dynamicity in broadcast data. But it is possible to introduce dynamicity as follows.

- *Item placement*: Data may be moved around in between disks. It means items of data traverse the levels of disk hierarchy. In other words, some item may lose importance while other items may gain importance. The movement of items influences the client side caching strategy for pre-fetching (hoarding).
- *Disk structure*: The hierarchy of disks itself may be changed. For example, the ratios of the disk speeds can be modified. An entire disk can be removed or a new disk may be added.

- *Disk contents*: The contents of disk may change. Extra pages may be added to a disk or some pages may be removed from a disk.
- *Disk values*: Some pages on the broadcast may change in value.

Read-only and update type of broadcasts get affected by the dynamicity involving *Item placement*, *Disk structure* and *Disk contents*. However, *Disk value* introduces dynamicity that is applicable to the update scenario only. The modifications involving *Item placement* or *Disk structure* influences the relative frequencies as well as the order of the appearances of data items already on broadcast. Whereas the update of the value of a data item does not alter the relative frequencies. So, in absence of the updates, the first two types of modifications primarily affect the performance. The performance of client side caching is affected as caching algorithms need information about the latency of data items. This results in client side storage to be sub-optimally used. However, an advance notification may mitigate the problem.

Dynamicity introduced due to *Disk Contents* does not influence the items that appear on the broadcast. However, some items which appeared previously may disappear and some new items may appear. It can be viewed an extreme case of the *Item Placement*, i.e., the items removed may be assumed have infinite latencies and appear in another disk. The clients can cache an item before it disappears if an advance warning is provided. Or even a client can evict the item from the cache to make room for a new item. *Data Value* updates introduces the problem of data consistency. To take care of this situation cached copies at client should be updated or invalidated.

12.7.8 Unused or Empty Slots in Broadcast Disk

The broadcast schedule may consists of many unused slots or pages [5]. It happens specially when the number of pages in a disk is not an exact multiple of the number chunks into which the disk is partitioned. These unused slots may be used opportunistically to enhance the quality of broadcast by including indexes, updates, invalidations, or even the information pertaining to dynamically emerging situation. The guiding principle of broadcast based dissemination is that the number of disks should as small as possible. Normally, in the order of 2–5. However, the number of pages to be broadcast is often substantially large. Therefore, the number of unused slots, if any, is expected to be quite small in number. In other words, it may be possible to tweak the relative frequencies slightly to reduce the number of unused slots.

If unused slots are not used sensibly, it may lead to substantial wastage of bandwidth. To understand how it may occur, let us modify the previous example as follows. Suppose a list of 12 pages are to be placed on the broadcast channel. We divide these pages into 3 disks:

D_1: has 1 page,
D_2: has 2 pages, and
D_3: has now 9 instead of 6 pages.

Fig. 12.8 Many unused slots may be generated by broadcast program

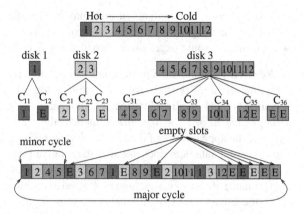

D_1 is smallest and fastest, D_3 is largest and slowest. Let the frequencies of D_1, D_2 and D_3 be 3, 2, and 1 respectively. Since, $T_{max} = LCM(3, 2, 1) = 6$, the chunking algorithm divides pages of D_1 into $6/3 = 2$ chunks, the pages of D_2 into $6/2 = 3$ chunks and the pages of D_3 into $6/1 = 6$ chunks. The number of pages per chunk in disk D_1, D_2 and D_3 are $\lceil 1/2 \rceil = 1$, $\lceil 2/3 \rceil = 1$ and $\lceil 9/6 \rceil = 2$ respectively. So, the chunking requires one empty page each to be padded to each chunk of disks D_1 and D_2. In the case of D_3, a padding of 3 empty pages is needed. So, at total of 5 empty pages are inserted as padding to generate integer number of pages for the chunking of broadcast data. Figure 12.8 illustrates the process of chunking and depicts that 8 empty pages appear in broadcast cycle on a single major cycle consisting of 24 pages. It leads to a wastage of 33% of the broadcast bandwidth.

12.7.9 Eliminating Unused Slot

Unused slots in the chunks in a broadcast schedule are like holes in disk fragmentation. A broadcast schedule consists of three types of chunks:

1. Fully used chunks: every slots in such a chunk have useful data.
2. Partially wasted chunks: some slots in such chunks have data and the other slots are free.
3. Fully wasted chunks: all slots in such a chunk are free.

The simple strategy to eliminate unused slots is to compact the holes in the broadcast schedule. However, the compacting technique applies only under some stringent assumptions [5]. These assumptions are:

1. The client population do not change,
2. No update is allowed,
3. The clients do not employ pre-fetching or caching,
4. The clients do not use the uplink channel,

5. When a client switches to a public channel, it can retrieve data pages without wait,
6. Each query result is represented by one page, and the length of each page is the same.
7. A server uses only one channel for broadcast, and broadcast is reliable.

These assumptions essentially imply that access patterns of the mobile clients remain unchanged over time.

The compaction algorithm first needs to compute the indices of unused slots in each wasted chunk of a disk. The computation of the indices turns out to be simple due to the assumptions presented above. But to concretize the computation formula a few notations become handy.

NP_i : number of pages in disk D_i.
NC_i : number of chunks in disk D_i.
NS_i : number of slots in a chunk in disk D_i.

The basic idea behind the algorithm is to first determine the schedule by Algorithm 26 of Sect. 12.7.5. According to this algorithm, the number of slots are:

$$NS_i = \left\lceil \frac{NP_i}{NC_i} \right\rceil = \left\lceil \frac{NP_i}{T_{max}/f_i} \right\rceil = \left\lceil \frac{NP_i \times f_i}{T_{max}} \right\rceil,$$

where T_{max} is LCM of the chosen frequencies for the disks.

Consider the example shown in Fig. 12.8. The number of slots in a chunk in three different disks as determined by the algorithm are:

$$NS_1 = \left\lceil \frac{1 \times 3}{6} \right\rceil = 1, NS_2 = \left\lceil \frac{2 \times 2}{6} \right\rceil = 1, \text{ and } NS_3 = \left\lceil \frac{9 \times 1}{6} \right\rceil = 2.$$

The execution of the original algorithm organizes the broadcast schedule (major cycle) into chunks consisting of 24 slots. Out of these 8 slots are empty, which implies only $24 - 8 = 16$ slots have useful data. Modified algorithm places a logical cut line at the end of the slot 16. To the right of this cut line there are 8 slots, out of which only 3 have useful data. Furthermore, there are exactly 3 wasted (empty) slots to the left the cut line. The modified algorithm moves the data from the right to the left of the cut line to empty slots preserving their relative order of occurrences. The movement of data is illustrated by Fig. 12.9. So the strategy of the algorithm is compact the holes present in partially wasted chunks by moving data appearing to the right of the cut-line. This action pushes all empty slots to the right of the cut-line

Before formally presenting the modified algorithm, we observe that empty slots are located either in a fully wasted chunk (all free slots) or a partially wasted chunk (with some free slots). The indices of fully wasted chunks in D_i is given by

$$FW_i = NC_i - \left\lceil \frac{NP_i}{NS_i} \right\rceil$$

Fig. 12.9 Eliminating
unused slots

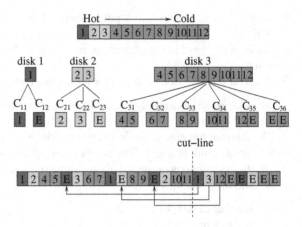

Therefore, fully wasted chunks in disk D_i are C_{ij} where, $NC_i - FW_i + 1 \leq j \leq NC_i$.
So, the number of fully wasted chunks in D_3 of our running example is:

$$FW_1 = NC_1 - \left\lceil \frac{NP_1}{NS_1} \right\rceil = 2 - \left\lceil \frac{1}{1} \right\rceil = 1$$
$$FW_2 = NC_2 - \left\lceil \frac{NP_2}{NS_2} \right\rceil = 3 - \left\lceil \frac{1}{1} \right\rceil = 2$$
$$FW_3 = NC_3 - \left\lceil \frac{NP_3}{NS_3} \right\rceil = 6 - \left\lceil \frac{9}{2} \right\rceil = 1,$$

Let w be the number of wasted slots in a partially wasted chunk in D_i. The value
of w can vary between 1 and $NS_i - 1$, i.e., $1 \leq w \leq NS_i - 1$. There can be only
one partially wasted chunk and it occurs only when $NP_i \neq NC_i \times NS_i$, where all
the quantities have integral values. Therefore, the condition for checking partially
wasted chunk is simply:

$$\left\lceil \frac{NP_i}{NS_i} \right\rceil - \left\lfloor \frac{NP_i}{NS_i} \right\rfloor = 1.$$

The index of the partially wasted chunk C_{ij} is $j = NC_i - FW_i$. The total number of
wasted slots is $NS_i - NP_i$, and the number of fully wasted chunks is FW_i. Therefore,
the number of wasted slots in a partially wasted chunk is given by

$$w = NS_i \times (NC_i - NP_i) - FW_i \times NS_i.$$

So, in chunk C_{ij}, the empty slots are E_{ijk}, where $NS_i - w \leq k \leq NS_i$.

Once we have identified the indices of empty slots, the compaction algorithm
becomes straightforward. The algorithm creates an array Broadcast[.] which
records the pages to be selected in sequence to appear on the broadcast channel. The
modified algorithm [5] consists of two phases.

1. In the first phase, the required number of empty pages are added to the disk chunks as needed for the allocation of same integral number of slots in a minor cycle. So this phase is identical to Algorithm 26.
2. In the second phase, the cut-line is determined and the contents of the occupied slots after the cut-line are swapped with the corresponding empty slots before the cut-line. So, the basic compaction step is to find the corresponding sequence numbers of slots which need to be swapped.

Phase 2 of the algorithm is essentially a compaction step. It does not really make any additional contribution to the original algorithm for creating a broadcast cycle. Algorithm 27 gives the details of this phase and included here for the sake of completeness.

Algorithm 27: Using empty slots.

---
begin
    // Broadcast cycle created by Algorithm 26
    calculate total slots TS in a major cycle;
    calculated total wasted slots TWS in a major cycle;
    determine cut-line $CL = TS - TWS$;
    find the nonempty slots after the CL;
    record these slots in the array *Moved*.
    // Use a sequence number SN to sequence of empty slots in a
        major cycle as $1, 2, ..., TS$
    find out SN of an E_{ijk} before the cut-line and replace it with a record in *Moved* array in sequence.
    // Broadcast the contents of the Broadcast array in
        sequence.
    for $(i = 1; i \leq CL; i + +)$ **do**
    | broadcast *Broadcast*[i];
    end
end

The first step of algorithm computes total number of slots (TS) which is equal to

$$TS = T_{max} \times \sum_{i=1}^{S} NS_i = T_{max} \times \sum_{i=1}^{S} \left\lceil \frac{NP_i \times f_i}{T_{max}} \right\rceil$$

The next step determines the total number of wasted slots (TWS) in one major cycle. Then the cut-line is identified. The computation performed is as follows.

$$TWS = \sum_{i=1}^{S} ((NS_i \times NC_i - NP_i) \times f_i)$$

$$= \sum_{i=1}^{S} \left(\left(NS_i \times \frac{T_{max}}{f_i} - NP_i \right) \times f_i \right)$$

$$= \sum_{i=1}^{S} (NS_i \times T_{max} - NP_i \times f_i)$$

The core of the compaction of data which is performed next. The data slots to right of cut-line are moved into a separate array *Moved*. The slots from which data have been placed in *Moved* array can now be declared as empty. Then data is moved from *Moved* array to the empty slots just before the cut-line. Although compaction algorithm does not disturb chunk orders from disks in minor cycle, it re-orders the pages that make up a chunk. Hence, using compaction requires the client to change the order of servicing queries.

12.8   Probabilistic Model of Broadcast

Wong [14] proposed a probabilistic approach for generating cyclic broadcast schedule. The approach appears impractical though it improves the performance of skewed data access by selecting data items according to their relative access frequencies. Wong's result tells that for fixed-sized data objects, access time is minimized if $\frac{p_i}{p_j} = \frac{\sqrt{q_i}}{\sqrt{q_j}}$ for all i, j. We can simplify the result by summing the denominator over all j, and get $p_i = \frac{q_i}{\sum_j \sqrt{q_j}}$.

The difficulty with the method is that it generates an acyclic broadcast schedule. The access time of a data item could also be arbitrarily large. It performs poorly compared to other skewed broadcast methods discussed later in the text. But Wong [14] proposed a heuristic to work around. The heuristic assumes that items are of equal size. The underlying idea is to convert acyclic broadcast to cyclic one which can give near optimal results. This method is further refined for variable sized data items and presented in a neat understandable format in [9, 15]. A few important parameters of the algorithm are:

1. N items to be broadcast.
2. The length of item i is l_i.
3. Page access probabilities are q_i, for $i = 1, 2, \ldots, N$.

The algorithm states that optimal latency is achieved when following two conditions are met.

C1: Copies of each data item are equally spaced, i.e., inter appearance gap between two copies of same item is constant.

C2: The spacing s_i of two successive copies of same item is proportional to square root of its length l_i, i.e., satisfying Eq. 12.1.

$$s_i \propto \sqrt{\frac{l_i}{q_i}}, \text{ or } s_i^2 \frac{q_i}{l_i} = c, \text{ where } c \text{ is a constant} \tag{12.1}$$

Both conditions cannot be met simultaneously. So, the heuristic only approximates the optimal results obtained from theoretical analysis. Hameed and Vaidya [9] introduced a pair of additional variables B_i and C_i for each item i:

1. B_i: is the earliest time when next instance of item i should be transmitted, and
2. $C_i = B_i + s_i$.

This essentially means C_i is the worst case completion time of the next instance of item i. Using the above idea, Hameed and Viadya proposed a technique for generating cyclic broadcast as provided by Algorithm 28 [9]. The simulation results presented in [9] shows that this method of broadcast performs close to the analytically obtained optimal result. For more details on this algorithm the reader can refer to the original paper.

Algorithm 28: Generating broadcast program.

---

begin
    // Initializations begin.
    $T = 0$; // Represents time parameter.
    foreach $(i \in N)$ **do**
        $B_i = 0$; // Earliest time for next instance of item i
        $C_i = s_i$. // Spacing between two successive copies of i
    end
    // Initialiations end.
    for $(i = 1, i < N, i = i + 1)$ **do**
        compute the optimal spacing s_i using Eq. 12.1;
    end
    repeat
        determine a set of items $S = \{i | B_i \le T, 1 \le i \le N\}$;
        choose i_{min} such that $C_{i_{min}} = \min\{C_i | 1 \le i \le N\}$.
        set $B_{i_{min}} = C_{i_{min}}$;
        $C_{i_{min}} = B_{i_{min}} + s_{i_{min}}$;
        wait for transmission of item i_{min} to complete;
        $T = T + l_{i_{min}}$; // l_i is length of item i
    until $(system\ is\ live)$;
end

12.9 Memory Hierarchy

In a typical client server model, the memory hierarchy consists of

- Client side cache and disk
- Server side cache and disk.

In a push based dissemination system, broadcast introduces an intermediate level of memory hierarchy between the client and the server [1]. If the client's cache or disk does not have an item then broadcast is used to satisfy the request. Otherwise, if a back-channel is provided then the client puts an explicit request for the item. In such a case, the client waits for the item and tunes in at the exact time to access it.

Multilevel broadcast disk places a sub-hierarchy within the broadcast.

- The fastest disk is at the top level and the slowest disk is at the bottom level.
- We can view this combination hierarchy in broadcast system as shown in the Fig. 12.10.

As opposed to traditional memory hierarchy, the sub-hierarchy introduced by broadcast disks has some distinctive features, namely:

- *Tunable access latency*: By choosing number of disks it is possible to control access latency of data items. In fact, it is possible to create arbitrary fine-grained

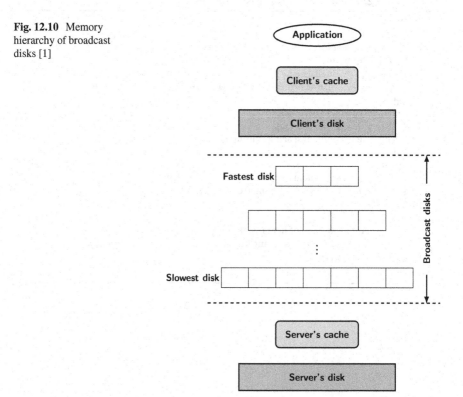

Fig. 12.10 Memory hierarchy of broadcast disks [1]

memory hierarchy with more number of disks. The biggest advantage is that the increasing the number of *disks in air* does not involve any extra h/w cost.

- *Cost variation*: Normally the access cost is proportional to the level of the memory hierarchy. In broadcast system this is true only for the average cost. The instantaneous cost can vary from zero to the broadcast period. It may be cheaper to use a back-channel for fetching the required data than to wait.

12.10 Client Cache Management

In a push based data dissemination, the server uses its best knowledge and the requirements of the clients. However, in a mobile environment, the number of clients which a server may have to serve is very large. So, it is difficult for a server either to gather knowledge or collate the data requirements of all the clients. Many clients may even be unidentified. Furthermore, back channels may not available to the clients to upload their profiles. Thus, the server can possibly determine an expected requirement pattern of an average client which serves a large cross section of clients. Consequently, many clients may have to wait long time for some data which they want quickly, while a few others may observer data flowing into the broadcast channel much before they may actually need it.

In the extreme cases, the average requirement pattern may completely mismatch the requirements of some clients while it may perfectly match the requirements of the other clients. In order to optimize an application's performance, it is important to filter out mismatches of a client's profile from that of the average client. The technique is to employ a client side cache management and use a pre-fetching strategy to store anticipated requirements of data in the client's cache.

In general there are two cache management techniques.

1. Demand-driven.
2. Pre-fetching.

In demand driven caching, a cache miss occurs when the data is accessed for the first time. The data is brought into cache when it is accessed for the first time. On the other hand, pre-fetching represents an opportunistic use of cache resources. The data is stored in the cache in anticipation of future use. Therefore, there is no delay even when the data accessed for the first time. But pre-fetching leads to the wastage of cache resources if the data is not eventually accessed.

The major issue that needs to be addressed before employing any caching strategy is *victim selection*. Replacing a cached page by a new page is the primary concern in a caching strategy. It is critical to performance. For example, sometimes an immediate references to the victim page may occur after it has been replaced, while there is a possibility that no reference is made to a new page which has just been brought into the cache. This situation may occur due to the locality associated with address references. So, the replacement policy should be such that a page having the lowest utility at that moment gets evicted.

In case of a dissemination based information system, the burden of data transfer rests on the server. It introduces certain differences that change the trade-offs associated with traditional caching. So for the sake of completeness, and for a better appraisal of the issues involved, a close examination of the problems associated with of client side caching with relative to push based system is needed.

In a pull-based system, when client faults on a page it can explicitly issue a request for the required page. In contrast, the absence of back channel in a push-based system forces a client experiencing a page fault to keep listening until the required page arrives on the broadcast channel. It essentially represents the fact that the nature of the communication medium (air) in a wireless communication system is sequential. Therefore, no random access is possible. Consequently, a client must wait to access the data in the order it is sent by the server. The access cost, therefore, is non-uniform. The data is not equidistant from the client's cache. It happens due to the multi-disk framework. This is in contrast with a traditional system where the cost is uniform.

12.10.1   Role of Client Side Caching

The role of any caching strategy is to choose an appropriate cache size that gives the best response to a client's applications. A large cache size can provide the best performance, as it is possible to cache most of the data requirements of the applications running at the client by liberally caching data from the broadcast channel. But normally the size of a client's cache is significantly smaller than the size of database at the server. The reasons are two-fold: (i) the cost of installing a large cache is very high, and (ii) a large cache makes the client heavy and thus non-portable. The smallness of cache size puts constraint on the decision as to what should be cached and what data should be evicted from the cache.

In a pull-based system, the performance of caching is optimal if it based on access probabilities. The access time remains uniform for pulling out different items from a server's database. It implies that all the cache misses have same performance penalty. However, this not true in a broadcast system. The server generates a schedule for the broadcast taking into account the access needs of all clients. This way unlimited scalability can be achieved by broadcast for data services. However, the attempt to improve performance for one of the access probability distributions lead to degradation of performance for another access probability distribution.

12.10.2   An Abstract Formulation

Let us consider an abstract formulation of the problem of client side caching. Suppose, a server S disseminating D pages for n clients $C_1, C_2, \ldots, C_n$. Let A_i be the access profile (data requirement for applications) of C_i. The first step is to generate a global access profile by aggregation of the access requirements of the clients. Let $A_s = \sigma(A_1, \ldots, A_n)$, where σ is an appropriately chosen aggregation function. Assume that the server has the ability to generate an optimal broadcast schedule for a given access profile. Let $\beta(A_s)$ be the generated broadcast program. Note that $\beta(A_s)$ is optimal iff $A_s \equiv A_1$. The factors causing broadcast to be sub-optimal are:

- The server averages the broadcast over a large population of clients.
- The access distributions that the clients provide are wrong.
- The access distributions of the clients change over time.
- The server gives higher priority (biased) to the needs of clients with different access distributions.

From the point of view of an individual client the cache acts as a filter as depicted in the picture of Fig. 12.11. The client side cache filters accesses by storing certain pages (not necessarily hot pages) such that filtered access distribution, namely $F_i = A_i - c_i$ matches A_s, where $c_i \subseteq D$ is the set of cached pages. If $c_i = \phi$ then $F_i = A_i$. If the server pattern A_s is different from client's access pattern $\beta(A_s)$ will be different from $\beta(A_i)$. In other words, for the cache-less clients the performance is sensitive to how close is the access pattern to the *average* client's access profile. In general, client cache should filter accesses to close the gap between A_s and F_i.

Fig. 12.11 A view of client side cache

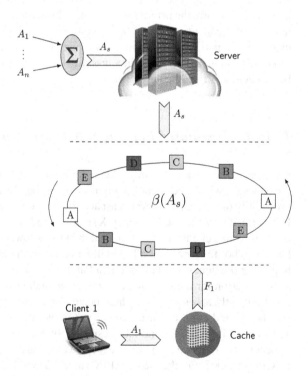

Fig. 12.12 Cost of
prefetching

	Hot	Cold
Hot	2	1
Cold	3	2

Client

Server

12.10.3   Consideration for Caching Cost

The traditional probability based caching at the client is not suitable due to the sequential nature of the retrieval from the broadcast channel. The cache should act as a filter selectively permitting those requirements for which the local access probability and the global access probability are the same. The server allocates bandwidth to each page based on its global likelihood of access. A client should cache only those pages which have significantly higher local probability of access. It is possible that either these probabilities match or they mismatch. So the cost consideration should take into account the *hot* and *cold* categorization of the pages both with respect to the server and the with respect to the client. What is cold at server may be hot at client and vice versa. Therefore, from prospective of a client caching those pages for which the cost of acquisition is significantly higher is an automatic choice. The table in Fig. 12.12 shows the priority for caching. However, in general, it is not possible to have a binary categorization of the priorities as suggested in the figure. In a broadcast disk environment, a client faulting on a page has to wait for the data to appear on broadcast channel. Therefore, in a broadcast disk environment, an appropriate cost based caching should be developed.

12.10.4   Cost-Based Caching Scheme: PIX and LIX

The idea of a cost-based caching scheme for broadcast disk is to increase cache hits of the pages for which the client has high access probabilities. Suppose p_i is the access probability of a page that is broadcast at a frequency x_i. Then the ratio p_i/x_i known as PIX (Probability Inverse frequency X) can be used for selecting victim for eviction of items from a client's cache. If p_i is high but x_i is low, then the item is hot for client but not so hot for server, then PIX will be high. On the other hand if p_i is low but x_i high, then the item is not hot for client but it is hot for server. So, by using least PIX as the criterion for the selection of victim (for cache eviction), we can ensure that a less frequently accessed page which occurs more frequently in broadcast schedule will be evicted from client cache. For example, consider two page a and b with access probabilities 0.01 and 0.05 respectively. Suppose the respective frequencies of occurrence of a and b on broadcast cycle are 2 and 100. Then PIX(a) = 0.005 and PIX(b) = 0.0005. On the basis of PIX values, b will be the victim page. Although the probability of access for b at the client is more than that of a, from the server prospective *b* is hotter than *a*. The server broadcasts page *b* more frequently than it does the page *a*. Therefore, *a* is preferred over *b* for caching. Unfortunately PIX is not an implementable policy, as it requires advance knowledge of access probabilities. So, we need to invent a policy which is an implementable approximation to PIX.

Though access probabilities of a page cannot be measured or known beforehand, we may find an approximate measure of the same. The idea is to find a running average of the number of times each page is accessed. The running average assigns importance to the client's recent access pattern. LIX, as it is known, is an adaptation of LRU and PIX.

It maintains the cache as a singly linked list. For each broadcast disk a separate linked list is maintained at the client. When a page is accessed it is moved to the top of the list. This ensure that the pages accessed recently are not the candidates for eviction. When a new page enters the cache, LIX evaluates the *lix* value for the bottom of each chain. The page with smallest *lix* value is evicted to allow the new page to be stored. Although page is evicted with lowest *lix* value the new page joins the linked list corresponding to broadcast disk it belongs. The *lix* value is evaluated by the ratio of the estimated running average of the access probability and the frequency of broadcast for the page. For estimating of the running probability of access p_i each page *i*, client maintains 2 data items, namely, p_i value and the time t_i of the recent most access of the pages. It re-estimates p_i, when the page *i* is accessed again. The probability estimate is carried out according to the following rules.

1. Initialize $p_i = 0$ when page *i* enters the cache.
2. The new probability estimate of p_i is done when page is accessed next using the following formula

$$p_i^{new} = \frac{\lambda}{currTime - t_i} + (1 - \lambda)p_i,$$

   where λ, $0 < \lambda < 1$, is an adjustable parameter.
3. Set $t_i = currTime$ and $p_i = p_i^{new}$.

As p_i is known for each page and so are their frequencies, *lix* values can be calculated easily. Essentially LIX is a simple approximation of PIX, but it was found to work well [1].

12.10.5 Pre-fetching Cost

The goal of pre-fetching is to improve the response time for a client application. Pre-fetching is an optimistic caching strategy, where the pages are brought in anticipation of future use. The dissemination oriented nature of broadcast system is ideal for pre-fetching, but it is slightly different in approach compared to a traditional pre-fetching scheme. In a traditional system, the client makes an explicit request for pre-fetching. Therefore, it is anadditional burden on resources. But in a broadcast environment

Fig. 12.13 Illustrating
pre-fetch cost

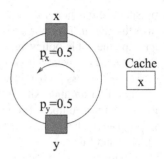

the pages anyway flow past. Therefore, the client can pre-cache the selected pages if these are important. On the flop side, an eager pre-caching results in wastage of cache slots in respect of pages cached *too early*. In a traditional system, an improvement response time at a client can be achieved by

- minimizing the cache miss rate, and
- reducing the cost of a cache miss.

Though the improvement in broadcast environment also depend on the same parameters, here the considerable gains can be achieved by reducing the latency when a cache miss occurs.

Example
Suppose a client is interested in two pages x, y. The server broadcast them on a flat disk with 180° apart. There is a single cache slot at the client. Figure 12.13, illustrates the scenario. Under a demand-driven strategy, the client caches a page, say x, as a result of the requirement for the page. In this case, all the subsequent requests for x can be satisfied without delay, but if there is a requirement for y, then it has to wait till the page comes by on the broadcast. Then x is replaced y, and it remains resident till a request for x results in a cache miss when x again is brought into the cache. In this strategy the expected delay on a cache miss could be one half of the disk rotation. The cost for accessing a page is given by

$$C_i = p_i * m_i * d_i$$

where p_i is probability of access, m_i expected probability of a cache miss, d_i is the expected delay before the page i arrives on broadcast. The total expected cost for access over all pages in demand-driven strategy is:

$$\sum_{i \in \{x,y\}} C_i = 0.5 * 0.5 * 0.5 + 0.5 * 0.5 * 0.5 = 0.25$$

one quarter of a disk spin time.

Suppose we cache the page x when it arrives on broadcast and replace it with y when the latter arrives, the strategy is called *tag team*. The cost will be

$$\sum_{i\in\{x,y\}} C_i = 0.5 * 0.5 * 0.25 + 0.5 * 0.5 * 0.25 = 0.125$$

Therefore, tag team caching can double the performance over demand-driven caching. The improvement comes from the fact that a miss in tag team strategy can only be due to some requirement in half the broadcast cycle. In contrast the cache miss in demand-driven strategy can occur at any time.

12.11 Update Dissemination

In a client-server system update dissemination is a key issue concerning the performance versus the correctness tradeoff. A client accesses from its local cache, whereas the updates are collected at the server. Therefore, keeping the consistency of client's cache with the updates is a big problem. Any consistency preserving—by notification or invalidation—mechanism must be initiated by the server. However, it is possible that different applications require varying degree of consistency in data. Some can tolerate some degree of inconsistency. In general, the environment must guarantee consistency requirement that is *no weaker* than an application's requirement. Obviously, the stronger is the consistency guarantee the better it is for the application. However, the requirement for a stronger consistency hurts the performance as the communication and the processing overheads are more.

12.11.1 Advantages of Broadcast Updates

Specially, if there is no back channel, maintaining the consistency client's cache becomes entirely the responsibility of the server. On the other hand, there are some added advantages of a broadcast system, namely,

- The communication overheads are significantly cut-down as the notification of the updates are initiated by the server. However, in absence of any notification the client has to poll. Polling is not possible unless there is a back channel.
- A single notification will do, as it is available on broadcast to all the clients.
- The client's cache is automatically refreshed at least once in each broadcast period.

12.11.2 Data Consistency Models

The notion of data consistency depends on applications. For example, in a database application, the consistency of data normally tied with transaction serializability. But many applications may not require full serializability. So we need to arrive at some weaker forms of the correctness. In a dissemination based system the notion of consistency is not fully understood till date. Therefore, the focus of our discussion is on a broadcast disk environment where all updates are performed at the server. The type access is allowed to the clients is read-only. The examples of such applications could be stock notification, weather report, etc. The models of data consistency normally employed are:

- *Latest value*: The client is interested for accessing the recent most value. The clients perform no caching and the server always broadcast the updated value. There is no serializability, i.e., mutual consistency among data items is not important.
- *Quasi-caching*: Defined per-client basis using a constraint specifying the tolerance of slackness with respect to the *Latest value*. A client can use cached data items and the server may disseminate updates more lazily.
- *Periodic*: Data values change only at some pre-specified intervals. In a broadcast environment, such intervals can be either be a minor or a major cycle of a broadcast. If a client caches the values of the broadcast data, then the validity of this data is guaranteed for the remainder of the period in which the data is read.
- *Serializability*: The notion serialiability is important for the context of transaction processing. But serializability can be implemented in the broadcast dissemination model, using optimistic concurrency control at the clients and having the server broadcast the update logs.
- *Opportunistic*: For some applications, it may be acceptable to use any version of data. Such a notion of consistency allows a client to use any cached value. It is also quite advantageous for long disconnection.

In *Latest value* model a client has to monitor broadcast continually to either invalidate or update the cached data. In contrast *Periodic* model fits well with the behaviour of a broadcast disk model. It does not require the client to monitor broadcast, since data changes only in certain intervals. *Quasi-caching* and *Opportunistic* models depend heavily on data access semantics of specific applications. *Serializability* model is applicable in transaction scenarios.

References

1. S. Acharya, M. Franklin, S. Zdonik, Dissemination-based data delivery using broadcast disks. IEEE Pers. Commun. **2**(6), 50–60 (2001)
2. S. Acharya, R. Alonso, M. Franklin, S. Zdonik, Broadcast disks: data management for asymmetric communication environments. ACM SIGMOD Rec. **24**(2), 199–210 (1995)
3. D. Aksoy, M.S.F. Leung, Pull versus push: a quantitative comparison for data broadcast, *Global Telecommunications Conference, 2004. GLOBECOM '04. IEEE*, vol. 3 (2004), pp. 1464–1468
4. M. Ammar, J. Wong, The design of teletext broadcast cycles. Perform. Eval. **5**(4), 235–242 (1985)
5. Y.I. Chang, C.N. Yang, A complementary approach to data broadcasting in mobile information systems. Data Knowl. Eng. **40**(2), 181–194 (2002)

6. M. Franklin, S. Zdonik, Dissemination-based information systems. Data Eng. **19**(3), 19–28 (1996)
7. M. Franklin, S. Zdonik, Data in your face: Push technology in perspective. ACM SIGMOD Rec. **27**(2), 516–519 (1998)
8. D.K. Gifford, R.W. Baldwin, S.T. Berlin, J.M. Lucassen, An architecture for large scale information systems. SIGOPS Oper. Syst. Rev. **19**(5), 161–170 (1985)
9. S. Hameed, N.H. Vaidya, Efficient algorithms for scheduling broadcast. ACM/Baltzer J. Wireless Netw. **5**(3), 183–193 (1999)
10. G. Herman, K.C. Lee, A. Weinrib, The datacycle architecture for very high throughput database systems. SIGMOD Rec. **16**(3), 97–103 (1987)
11. C.-L. Hu, M.-S. Chen, Adaptive balanced hybrid data delivery for multi-channel data broadcast, *IEEE International Conference on Communications, 2002. ICC 2002*, vol. 2 (IEEE, 2002), pp. 960–964
12. Q. Hu, D.L. Lee, W.-C. Lee, Performance evaluation of a wireless hierarchical data dissemination system, *Proceedings of the 5th Annual ACM/IEEE International Conference on Mobile Computing and Networking* (ACM, 1999), pp. 163–173
13. Y. Huang, H. Garcia-Molina, Publish/subscribe tree construction in wireless ad-hoc networks, *Mobile Data Management (MDM'03)* (2003), pp. 122–140
14. J.W. Wong, Broadcast delivery. Proc. IEEE **76**(12), 1566–1577 (1988)
15. J. Xu, J. Liu, Broadcast Scheduling Algorithms for Wireless Data Dissemination, ed. by Y. Pan, Y. Xiao. *Design and Analysis of Wireless Networks: Wireless Network and Mobile Computing*, vol. 1 (Nova Science Publisher, 2005)

Chapter 13
Indexing in Air

13.1 Introduction

Push based data delivery [1, 12, 14, 15] addresses the problem of data dissemination on inherently asymmetric low bandwidth wireless channel. The role of uplink channel is restricted to gathering users' profiles in order to determine the composition of broadcast data according to the requirements of mobile users. With simple adaptations of conventional caching mechanisms at the client end, it is possible to improve response times when a client's applications need data. However, the issue of energy efficiency in accessing data over broadcast channel is not addressed. Since a mobile end host operates with a limited power of a small battery, energy efficiency [13] is critical. In this chapter, our aim is to study some of the well known indexing schemes which have been successfully adopted for energy efficient access of data from broadcast channels by portable mobile clients.

At the hardware level, a number of energy efficient chips have been designed specially for mobile devices. Two such examples are, Transmeta group's Crusoe and AT & T's Hobbit chips. For example, Crusoe [9] implementers claim that the processor can prolong the life of battery for mobile devices up to four fold. Typically, AT & T's Hobbit in full active mode requires about 250 mW of power, but in doze mode it consumes about 50 μW of power [2]. So, the ratio of power consumptions between active and doze modes of a mobile device could be as high as 5000:1. Another important point is that if a battery drains out too often it will also require frequent recharging. Although, the new generation of mobile batteries do not care how frequently they are recharged, a battery depending on its type, can last between 500–800 charge cycles [11]. So, an important reason for prolonging the life of a battery is that disposal of used batteries is environmentally hazardous [3, 10].

The requirements for energy efficient operations comes from following two fundamental limitations of mobile end hosts.

1. Need to conserve battery.
2. Need to utilize bandwidth.

© Springer Nature Singapore Pte Ltd. 2017   409
R.K. Ghosh, *Wireless Networking and Mobile Data Management*,
DOI 10.1007/978-981-10-3941-6_13

By conserving battery, a mobile computer can prolong its battery life. By evolving clever techniques for utilization of bandwidth, it should be possible to serve thousands of mobile clients running different applications. However, in order to server the data requirements of diverse applications we need clever indexing techniques.

In wired network, an indexing mechanism primarily reduces the access time of disk based files [5]. The client is always online with an active network connection and waits until the relevant data is retrieved from a local or a network storage. If the data available in the local disk, then the cost of retrieval is significantly low. A wired connection provides high bandwidth, low latency link between the server and the clients. So, even if data is on a server disk, the distance of data from the client's memory is not significantly high.

In a wireless communication environment, indexing schemes have multi-fold requirements, important among these are:

1. Energy efficiency,
2. Scalability, and
3. Fast response.

As explained in the previous chapter, in a wireless environment, broadcast based communication is far more effective than unicast communication. Broadcast allows the communication to scale up gracefully. So, push based data delivery primarily addresses the scalability issues in a mobile distributed system. However, a trade-off exists between energy efficiency and fast response. All mobile devices can tune to a broadcast channel and retrieve the data as per their requirements. In contrast, unicast communication requires a separate channel of communication to be available each time when the need arises. Simultaneous use of many separate channels in the same cell partitions the bandwidth. Therefore, it considerably reduces the utilization of bandwidth. In a broadcast oriented communication, the distance of data from a mobile client's memory is determined by the broadcast schedule of the relevant server. For example, if a client's request coincides with the appearance of a data item in the broadcast channel, then the data is available instantaneously. However, if the request is made after the data has flown past on the broadcast channel, then the client will be forced to wait for the data until a full broadcast cycle has elapsed.

Obviously, a mobile client cannot remain in the active mode for a long time as it depends on the limited power of a battery. Therefore, push based data delivery should incorporate methods to organize the data that would enable a mobile client to anticipate the exact time when its data requirements can be met by the broadcast channel. Unfortunately, the broadcast channel is a strictly sequential medium. It forces a mobile client to turn into active mode from time to time to check and retrieve the requested data from the broadcast disks.

Listening to the downlink channel in order to check whether the required data has arrived or not is referred to as a probe. Tuning time refers to the time that a mobile host spends in probing the downlink channel until it is able to download data from a server. Therefore, an efficient indexing scheme should minimize both the probe and the access times. The access time refers to the difference between the time the request is made to the time when the data gets fully downloaded. So, the access time includes the probes and the download time.

13.2 Address Matching and the Directory

A mobile device operates in two modes, namely, active and sleep. The sleep mode allows a mobile device to shut down its power hungry components including CPU, display, and communication interface. Fortunately, the power requirement of the paging hardware is very little and it remains on. So, a mobile in sleep mode can switch into active mode when needed. Ideally, a mobile client should switch on into *active* mode only when the required data appears on the broadcast channel. So, the broadcast should be organized in such a way that the pager can apply an address matching scheme to determine whether the data arriving on the downlink channel is relevant to the application running on the mobile terminal or not.

The other way to switch from sleep to active mode of operation is on the detection of event triggers. Events triggers typically require tight synchronization, and are handled by system clocks. A system clock is a low energy circuit. It wakes up the CPU and turns a mobile terminal into active mode at pre-determined timings. Thus a mobile terminal can turn into active mode and download the desired data when it becomes available on the downlink channel.

The technique of temporal address matching requires perfect or near perfect synchronization. The client probes the downlink channel from time to time and determines the exact time when the relevant data is published on the broadcast channel. It switches itself to sleep mode for the estimate duration until the required data arrives on broadcast channel.

However, the basic problem in using any of the above methods is that a client must have the advanced knowledge about mappings between the data keys (primary/secondary) with addresses (multicast group/temporal). The mapping, known as a directory, must be either pre-cached by the clients or published by the server mulitplexing it along with the actual data on broadcast channel. The second approach is more appropriate to a broadcast environment, because it is oblivious to the dynamicity of data and the churn rate of clients in a mobile system. So, our goal in this chapter is to study this second approach for energy efficient indexing in mobile environment.

13.3   Preliminary Notions

We introduce some preliminary notions required for the analysis of directory organization of broadcast or published data.

Definition 13.1 (Bucket) A bucket, also known as a page, is the smallest logical unit of the broadcast. For the simplicity, we assume that exactly one packet fits into a bucket.

The data in each bucket is identified by an attribute value or the search key. A client can retrieve the required data identified by search key by simple pattern matching.

Definition 13.2 (Bcast) The broadcast data is divided into local segments called Bcast. Each Bcast consists of data interleaved with directory information or index.

The directory information may include some replications. Replication makes the search efficient when the directory information intermixed with data is pushed into broadcast channel. Each Bcast consists of only one instance of data.

13.4   Temporal Address Matching Technique

The temporal address matching scheme requires that the directory of data files to be published along with the data. Alternatively, directory information can be cached by the clients. However, caching directory at the clients is impractical due to the following reasons.

- Firstly, the directory information across cells may not match. Therefore, cached directory information for one cell is unusable when a client moves to a new cell.
- Secondly, a client entering into system for the first time will not have any directory information for the data broadcast in its home cell.
- Thirdly the data and the associated directory information may change over time. It will require every client to recharge the cache with new directory information.
- Lastly, storing directory at a client may require substantial local storage. So, pre-caching can only be applied to relatively less portable mobile clients.

Therefore, a simpler approach is to have the directory information published along with data on the broadcast channel.

13.5   Tuning Time and Access Latency

The parameters used for the measurement of energy efficiency and the access latency of the of the broadcast data [8] are:

Fig. 13.1 Illustrating timing parameters

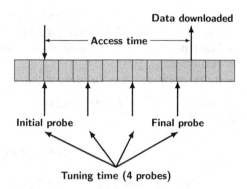

Tuning time (4 probes)

- **Tuning time**: The time spent by a client listening to the broadcast channel, in order to retrieve the required data. It provides a measure of the energy consumption at the client, because the energy spent will be proportional to the time client operates in active mode.
- **Access latency**: The time elapsed (on an average) from the moment a client requests for data to the point when the data actually downloaded by the client. Access latency affects the response time of the application running at the client. The request is deemed to have been issued when the client makes the initial probe.

Both the timing parameters are measured in units of bucket numbers. The tuning time is proportional to access latency. The access latency depends not only on the index but on how the data is organized in the schedule. The number of probes depends on the depth of the index tree to the appropriate leaf where data is located. A mobile client may have to probe a number times to climb down the index tree and determine the exact position of the requested data in broadcast schedule. Figure 13.1 illustrates dependency between the tuning time and the access latency.

13.6   Indexing in Air

The key idea is to come up with an allocation method that multiplexes index with data in an efficient manner [8], such that

- It enables the clients to conserving energy, and
- It enables the server to utilize the broadcast bandwidth efficiently.

First of all, buckets should be self identifying, i.e., whether a bucket represents an index or a data bucket. By inclusion of certain header information, a bucket can provide the identification and allow the clients to determine the position of the bucket in the broadcast schedule. The relevant header information stored in a bucket are described below:

- **bucket_id**: stores offset of the bucket from beginning of the current `Bcast`.
- **bucket_type**: provides the type of the bucket, i.e., whether it stores index or data.
- **bcast_pointer**: stores the offset of the current bucket from the beginning of the next `Bcast`.
- **index_pointer**: stores the offset to the beginning of the next index segment.

A pointer to a bucket can be found by *bucket_id B*. The offset to B from the current bucket B_{curr} is the difference

$$diff\_offset = bucket\_id(B) - bucket\_id(B_{curr}).$$

Therefore, the time to get B from B_{curr} is equal to $(diff\_offset-1) \times t_B$, where t_B is the time to broadcast a single bucket. An index bucket consists of pairs of values (*attribute_value, offset*), where *offset* gives the *bucket_id* of the bucket that contains the data identified by the *attribute_value*. In general an index tree may have multiple levels.

13.6.1 (1, m) Indexing Scheme

A simple minded approach is to uniformly mix index several times within broadcast data. This method is called $(1, m)$ indexing, where every $1/m$ fraction of data buckets is preceded by one full index. The degenerate case of $(1, m)$ indexing occurs when $m = 1$, index broadcast exactly once with data. So, the length of a `Bcast` is equals length of *Data* plus the length of *Index*, i.e., `Bcast` = *Data* + *Index*. The access algorithm using this $(1, 1)$ indexing scheme is as follows.

Algorithm 29: Access algorithm for $(1, 1)$ indexing

// B_{curr} ID of current bucket
// B_{idx} ID of next index bucket
tunes to B_{curr}, and set offset = $B_{idx} - B_{curr}$;
set wakeup_time = offset $\times t_B$, and enter into doze mode;
wakes up after doze mode expires;
// B_{data} is ID of data bucket
obtain the pointer to B_{data};
// B_{curr} now refers to current bucket in the index part
set wakeup_time = $B_{data} - B_{curr}$
wake up again after doze mode expires;
download the relevant data;

13.6.1.1 Analysis of (1, 1) Indexing

A Bcast consists of *Data* interleaved with directory information. The access time has two parts: (i) *probe wait*, and (ii) *Bcast wait*.

Definition 13.3 (*Probe wait*) It refers to the average delay to get to the next nearest index from the time of initial probe for accessing index is made.

Definition 13.4 (*Bcast wait*) It refers to the average delay to download the actual data from the time the index to the required data is known.

In (1, 1) indexing, the index is broadcast once. Thus, the expected delay due to *probe wait* is equal to half the Bcast time. Also the expected delay for downloading data or the *Bcast wait* is half the Bcast time. It means the access time = (*Data+Index*).

13.6.1.2 Tuning Time for (1, 1) Indexing

Tuning time, the time spent on listening, depends on number of probes. It consists of (i) an initial probe, (ii) a number of probes to get the correct index pointer for the required data, and (iii) a final probe to download the data.

The size of a fully balanced index tree T_{idx} is $Index = \sum_{i=0}^{k-1} n^i$, where T_{idx} has k levels. Suppose, each bucket has the space to accommodate n pairs of (search_key, data_ptr). Then, $k = \lceil \log_n Data \rceil$. Therefore, the tuning time $= 2 + \lceil \log_n Data \rceil$.

13.6.1.3 Analysis of (1, m) Indexing

The distance between two consecutive occurrences of index segments in a broadcast schedule is

$$\frac{Data}{m} + Index.$$

Therefore, the probe wait is:

$$\frac{1}{2} \left(\frac{Data}{m} + Index \right).$$

The Bcast wait is

$$\frac{1}{2} \left(Data + m * Index \right).$$

Therefore, the access time is equal to:

$$\frac{m+1}{2m} \left(Data + m * Index \right)$$

As explained earlier, the tuning time is dependent on the number of probes. Thus the total tuning time is equal to

$$2 + \lceil \log_n Data \rceil.$$

However, optimization of the access time depends on the number of times index is replicated in a broadcast cycle. The optimal value of m is determined by differentiating the expression for the access time. It gives the value of m as:

$$m = \sqrt{\frac{Data}{Index}}.$$

13.7   Distributed Indexing Scheme

Distributed indexing improves both access time and tuning time compared to $(1, m)$ indexing by cutting down the replications on indexes. In $(1, m)$ indexing, every $1/m$th fraction of data is preceded by a copy of the index. In distributed index, replication of the index is restricted. We describe three distributed index methods which differ in degree of replications.

- Non replicated distributed indexing.
- Fully replicated distributed indexing.
- Partially replicated distributed indexing.

In non-replicated distribution, one copy of index is distributed over one copy of the data. Basically the index is interspersed with the data. Different index segments are disjoint. Each index segment is followed by the corresponding data segment. Figure 13.2a illustrates an example for this scheme. The first level index refers to a classification based on disciplines such as literature, science and engineering. The second level indexes precede a data segment, only the index relevant to the data segment appears before it. For example, the index segment associated with Engineering data segment appears before it. The top level indexes associated with either literature or science are not replicated.

In a fully-replicated distribution, the entire path starting from the root to a data segment is replicated just before the occurrence of the data bucket. For example, as Fig. 13.2b shows, the full index tree path from the root down to the subtree of Computer Science (CS) is replicated just before the occurrence of CS data segment. It helps to quickly fetch the pointer to the required data. However, as the index is replicated several times, the access time becomes longer.

In the case of partial replication, the upper part of the index tree gets replicated. Suppose B and B' represent two adjacent buckets belonging to the non replicated index at the lowest level. Then index buckets representing the Least Common Ancestor (LCA) of B and B' is placed before the occurrence of the index bucket B'. This is illustrated by Fig. 13.2c. The replicated part of the index prior to the occurrence

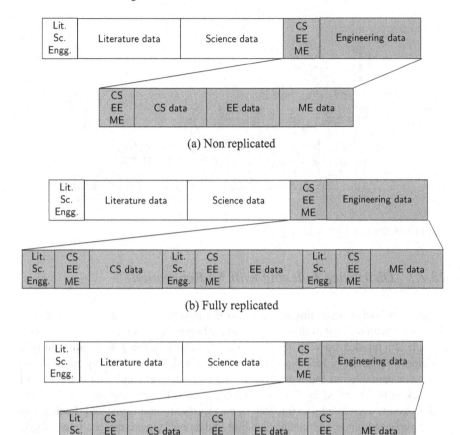

(a) Non replicated

(b) Fully replicated

(c) Partially replicated

Fig. 13.2 Distributed indexing

of CS data segment refers only to the root of the index subtree containing CS data segment. Incidentally, the root also the LCA of the index tree path from the root to the CS data segments. On the other hand, only the index segment (CS, EE, ME) appears before Electrical Engineering (EE) data segment. This is because, the LCA of:

1. Tree path from the root to EE data segment, and
2. Tree path from the root to CS data segment.

is represented by the index segment CS, EE, ME. In other words, partial replication of index is restricted to the upper part of the index tree. The idea behind this kind of replication is to ensure that pointer to non replicated part of index relevant to data can be found quickly. Therefore, it helps to reduce the tuning time.

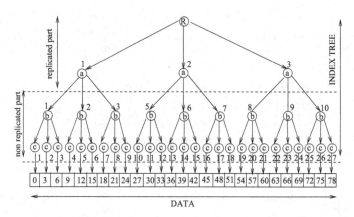

Fig. 13.3 A three level index tree [1]

13.7.1 Distributed Indexing with No Replication

Every data bucket maintains a pointer to the next nearest Bcast. The index is distributed with the root of the index tree at the beginning of a Bcast, and the index buckets are interleaved with the data buckets. The index segments are mutually disjoint. So, the index information is non replicated. The data is organized level-wise. For example, an index tree consisting of four levels and data consisting of 81 buckets is illustrated by Fig. 13.3 [1]. It indicates that the top two levels of the index tree are replicated and the bottom two levels are non-replicated. Each group of the three bottom level branches leading to data buckets are merged into a single link. A general multi-level index tree having $k + 1$ levels can now be described by a straightforward extension of the four level index tree in the following manner. The tree can be viewed as logically partitioned at a level r from the top, where $0 \le r \le k$. The top part of the tree including the root and up to level r constitutes the *replicated* part. The bottom part of the tree from level $r + 1$ up to and including level k defines non replicated part. It consists of a collection of subtrees each rooted at an index node belonging to the level $r + 1$.

The non replicated part of the index appears only once in a Bcast, whereas every node of the replicated part of the index appears as many number of times as the number of children it has in the index tree. For example, consider the tree T_{idx} in Fig. 13.3. T_{idx} is a complete 3-ary tree, in which every node including the root R has exactly three children. The replicated part of T_{idx} defined by the top two levels. It consists of four nodes R, a_1, a_2 and a_3. Each of these four nodes are replicated number of times equal to the number of children they have. So, each of the nodes R, a_1, a_2, a_3 are replicated three times in a Bcast in distributed indexing with replication. The two extreme cases of distributed indexing (i) non replicated indexing, and (ii) fully replicated indexing, occur respectively when $r = 0$ and $r = k$.

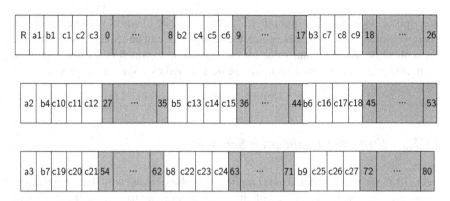

Fig. 13.4 Distributed indexing with no replication

Let us examine the organization of the four-level T_{idx}, shown in Fig. 13.3, a bit more closely. Suppose, nine data buckets reachable from an index node at level 2 from the top are merged together in a single data segment on a broadcast schedule. When using distributed indexing with no replication a Bcast for dissemination of 81 data buckets appears as the one shown by Fig. 13.4 [1]. There is no replication of the index path in any part of the index segment. An index segments consists of either 4 or 6 buckets. Suppose, a mobile host MH wants to access the data bucket 58, and MH makes its initial probe at bucket 2. Then after a sequence for probes, downloads data bucket 58, as follows.

- From bucket 2, MH gets the offset to the beginning of the next nearest Bcast. The root R of T_{idx} is located there.
- From R, the search is successively guided by through index stored at buckets a_3, b_7, c_{19}.
- MH then obtains pointer to data bucket 58 from index stored in c_{19}, and downloads the data.

This means that, starting from R, MH requires four probes to determine the position of the data bucket 58. So, including the initial probe, five probes are needed to download data of bucket 58.

13.7.2 Replication Based Distributed Indexing

The other two distributed indexing based on replications increase the size of the Bcast. But the amount of replication is not as much as $(1, m)$ indexing scheme. Therefore, the access time which is dependent on the size of Bcast, is less compared to that of $(1, m)$ indexing scheme. But compared to the indexing with no replication, the bandwidth utilization is poor. This is due to the fact that the replicated indexes eat away some amount of bandwidth. However, if the index tree is not very big and the replication is not very high, then it helps a mobile client to retrieve data in an energy efficient manner. Furthermore, the tuning time can be reduced by optimizing the replication. An optimum value for r, the level up to which index tree should be replicated to minimize tuning time can be determined by a simple analysis provided later in the next section.

13.7.3 Full Path Replication Scheme

Let us examine the distributed index replication policies along with data organization for broadcast. For the sake of simplicity in discussion, let us assume the index tree T_{idx} has four levels as shown by the picture in the earlier figure. The full index path replication scheme is illustrated in Fig. 13.5. Each index segment represents the entire tree path for the data segment that occurs after it. Suppose a MH wishes to access data bucket with key 73, and the initial probe is made at any data bucket B_x. MH can retrieve the pointer to the next nearest occurrence of the root of T_{idx} from B_x. MH then begins search on T_{idx} along the path from R to the required leaf storing a pointer to the record with the primary key 73. For the sake of concreteness, let us assume that $x = 15$. Then the index path traversed to reach the record with $key = 73$ is given by the sequence of index buckets:

$$\{R, first\_a_3, b_9, c_{25}\},$$

where $first\_a_3$ denotes the first copy of a_3 in the replicated part of T_{idx}. Since, R has the information about the child through which the search can be guided, the search takes us directly to $first\_a3$. Then from there to b_9, and c_{25} along the index tree path.

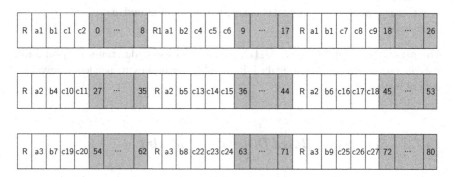

Fig. 13.5 Distributed indexing with full path replication

13.7.4 Partial Path Replication

The partial path replication improves on the full path replication by restricting amount of replications. The basic idea, as explained earlier, is to partition the index tree into two parts, namely,

- Replicated part, and
- Non replicated part.

In our discussion, we assume without loss of generality that the index buckets for Non Replicated Roots (NRRs) are ordered from left to right in consistent with the order they appear in the tree at level $r + 1$. The data buckets or the index buckets which are descendants of NRRs appear only once on each broadcast cycle. Before, we examine the organization further, it is convenient to introduce some notations.

1. R: the root of index tree.
2. NRR: denotes the set of index buckets at $r + 1$ level. These are the roots of the index subtrees in non-replicated part of the index tree.
3. B_i: B_i, for $1 \leq i \leq |NRR|$, is the ith index bucket in NRR.
4. $Path(C, B_i)$: Represents the sequence of buckets on the path in index tree from bucket C to B_i including C but excluding B_i.
5. $Data(B_i)$: The set of data buckets indexed by B_i.
6. $Ind(B_i)$: The part of index tree below B_i including B_i.
7. $LCA(B_i, B_k)$: The least common ancestor of B_i and B_k in the index tree.
8. $Rep(B_i)$: For a $B_i \in NRR$, $Rep(B_i)$ represents a path in replicated part of index tree as defined below:

$$Rep(B_i) = \begin{cases} Path(R, B_i) \text{ for } i = 1, \\ Path(LCA(B_{i-1}, B_i), B_i) \text{ for } i = 2, \ldots, |NRR| \end{cases}$$

9. $Ind(B_i)$: Denotes the non-replicated part of the path from R to B_i.

For the running example, $NRR = \{b1, b2, b3, b4, b5, b6, b7, b8, b9\}$.

Each broadcast schedule is made up of a sequence of $|NRR|$ tuples the form:

$$< Rep(B), Ind(B), Data(B) >, \ \forall B \in NRR.$$

Table 13.1 provides the tuple sequence corresponding to three non replicated roots $b1$, $b2$ and $b3$. Figure 13.6 illustrates the organization of the same 81 data buckets for the running example on a Bcast using partial path replication. Notice that there are exactly nine broadcast segments in the schedule one corresponding to each non replicated root.

Suppose the client wants to retrieve data bucket 66 and it makes the first probe at data bucket 3. The probe directs the client to *second_a1* (second replica of a_1). But as the entire tree is not replicated, the root cannot be accessed. Although the

Table 13.1 Tuples corresponding to non-replicated roots

	b1	b2	b3
Rep(B)	{R, a1}	{a1}	{a1}
Ind(b)	{b1, c1, c2, c3}	{b2, c4, c5, c6}	{b3, c7, c8, c9}
Data(B)	{0, . . . , 8}	{9, . . . , 17}	{18, . . . , 26}

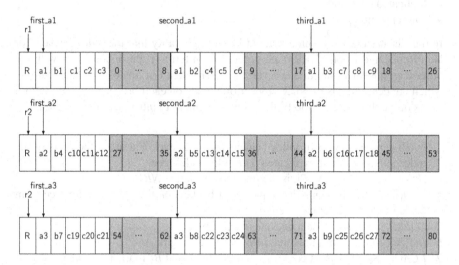

Fig. 13.6 Partial path replication

data bucket is yet appear in the broadcast schedule, the local index does not have a
pointer to access the data bucket 66. It necessitates that there should be some special
provision to climb up index tree in order to guide the client to data bucket 66.

The simple trick that provides the client enough information about climbing up
the index tree is to have each replicated node store a small set of local control indexes.
For example, the local *control index* at *second_a1* should be able to direct the client
to *r2* where the next replica of the root in the index tree can be found. Once root is
located, the client makes the sequence of probes: *first_a3*, *b8*, *c23* and retrieves the
data bucket 66. However, if instead of 66 the client want to find bucket 11, then the
index *second_a2* should direct the client to probe *b2*, *c4* and then 11. Thus, having
a copy of the root before *second_a2* in the index tree would have been a waste of
space.

The role of the control index is two-fold, namely,

1. Climbing up the tree path to the occurrence of the first replica of the root in the
   next broadcast cycle if the data bucket corresponding to the search key has flowed
   past on the current Bcast.

Fig. 13.7 Control index

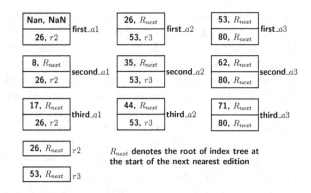

2. Climbing up the tree to appropriate higher level index bucket if the data has not flowed past in the current broadcast, but not accessible from the current index bucket.

So, the correctness of control indexes at each index bucket is critical to search. The control indexes for the example under discussion is provided in Fig. 13.7.

Every index bucket should have provision to store control index, which is essentially a part of replicated portion of the index tree. For understanding how control indexes are formulated, let us consider a path $Path(R, B) = \{BK_1, BK_2, \ldots, BK_s\}$ where $B \in NRR$. By definition, each bucket BK_i in the above path belongs to the replicated part of the index tree. Let $Last(BK_i)$ represent the primary key value in the last record indexed by index bucket BK_i, and $Next_{BK}(i)$ denote the offset to the next-nearest occurrence of BK_i. The control index of a bucket BK_i consist of i tuples of the form:

$$[v, \text{begin}]$$
$$[Last(BK_2), Next_{BK}(1)]$$
$$\vdots$$
$$[Last(BK_i), Next_{BK}(i-1)]$$

where v is the primary key value of the last record in the broadcast segment prior to BK_1. It implies that the records associated with key values less or equal to v have flown past in the current broadcast cycle. The symbol *begin* is a pointer to the beginning of index segment of these record keys reachable in the next broadcast cycle. $Next_{BK}(1)$ points to the next nearest occurrence of BK_1. For example, if $BK_1 = R$, then the next nearest occurrence of R is the beginning of next broadcast cycle.

The number of control tuples in a replicated index bucket x depends on the level of x in the index tree. If the level of x is l, then x should have exactly $l + 1$ control tuples. This is because, x must have a control index entry for each higher level (ancestor) index node (including itself) in the index tree. For instance, the level of a_2 in the index tree is 1. So $a2$ must have 2 control tuples for itscontrol index. As an illustrative example, let us consider the replicated index path $Rep(b4)=\{R, a2\}$. In order to avoid the confusion about which instances of R and a being considered, let the replicated instances be referred to as $r2$ and $first\_a2$ respectively. The value of the primary key in the last data record broadcast prior to $b4$ is same as the last data record accessible from $b3$, which is 26. So, the tuple defining control index in $r2$ should have $v = 26$. It indicates that any record having a key value between 0 and 26 can no longer be accessed in the present broadcast. In order to retrieve the pointer to a record having key value in the range [0, 26], we must to wait until the next broadcast cycle. The next nearest occurrence of R is the beginning of a new broadcast, which is denoted here as R_{next}. So, putting the components of the tuple together, the control index of $r2$ is [26, R_{next}].

Next, let us see how the control tuples for $first\_a2$ are determined. Since $level(a2) = 1$, it must have two tuples. The first tuple should be [26, R_{next}] because the last record accessible before $r2$ is 26. The second control tuple can be found by obtaining the key of the last record accessible from the current index (which is $first\_a2$) is $Last(a2) = 53$. The next nearest occurrence of $a2$ can be found only in the next instance of the index bucket R, which is $r3$ in Fig. 13.6. This implies that the second control tuple of $first\_a2$ is [53, $r3$]. Thus, the control tuples in the replicated bucket $first\_a2$ are: ([26, $begin$], [53, $r3$]) as indicated by Fig. 13.7. In fact, during the current broadcast cycle starting from $first\_a2$, it is possible to get any record whose key belongs to the range (26, 53].

As one more example, let us find the control index for $second\_a2$. The value of the last primary key broadcast before $b5$ is the last key accessible from $b4$ is 35. So, the record with the primary key 35 cannot be retrieved during the current broadcast. Consequently, the first tuple for the control index in $second\_a2$ should be [35, R_{next}]. The primary key of the last record reachable from $second\_a2$ is 53 and if any data with primary key value greater than 53 is to be retrieved then the search must be made again from R. Since, the next instance of occurrence of R is $r3$, the second tuple in $second\_a2$ must be [53, $r3$]. Hence, the pair of tuples ([35, $begin$], [53, $r3$]) constitute the control index for $second\_a2$. From this control index, we conclude that any data bucket with primary key value in the range (35, 53] can be found in the current broadcast.

The case of $first\_a1$ is bit different because none of data buckets has appeared yet in the current broadcast. All records have key in range [0, 26] are accessible from $a1$. So the first control tuple should be [NaN, NaN] where NaN indicate both values (key and offset) are meaningless or invalid. Whereas the offsets in the control tuples for any replica of $a3$ can only lead to the beginning of next broadcast cycle. Possibly, the second control tuples in each may be replaced by NaN to indicate that there is no record having a key greater than 80.

13.7.5   Access Protocol

The access protocol given in Algorithm 30 summarizes the process for downloads record with the primary key K. The actual downloading of the desired record is accomplished by executing Algorithm 31.

Algorithm 30: Access protocol for fetching record with key K

begin
    read the current bucket to retrieve the offset to an index bucket;
    sleep to doze mode waiting for the designated bucket;
    read the bucket and retrieve the first control the index I_{ctrl};
    if $(K \leq I_{ctrl})$ **then**
        `// Record key has flown past in the current broadcast`
        get offset for the next new `Bcast`;
        sleep to doze mode until arrival of next new `Bcast`;
        wakeup and execute Algorithm 31;
    end
    else
        get the offset to appropriate higher level index bucket;
        sleep to doze mode until arrival of designated bucket;
        wakeup and execute Algorithm 31;
    end
end

Algorithm 31: Downloading data

begin
    repeat
        read the designated index bucket;
        retrieve offset to next index;
        sleeping into doze mode waiting for next index;
    until *(index to record with key K is found)*;
    get offset to data bucket having record with key K;
    sleep to doze mode waiting for data bucket;
    read the bucket and download the record with key K;
end

13.7.5.1   Access Latency

The access latency depends on *probe* wait and *Bcast* wait. Let r top levels of the index tree represent the replicated part andthe tree is fully balance consisting of k

levels. The replicated index buckets occur before $Ind(B)$ for each $B \in NRR$. The
set of data buckets $Data(B)$ indexed by each $B \in NRR$ appear immediately after
$Ind(B)$. Therefore, the maximum distance separating two consecutive occurrences
of the replicated index buckets is $Ind(B) + Data(B)$.

Since the control index is present in each replicated index bucket, the probe wait
is determined by the average number of buckets in the segment consisting of $Ind(B)$
and $Data(B)$. The size of $Ind(B)$ is same as the number of nodes in a fully balanced
tree of height $k - r - 1$. This follows from the fact that $Ind(B)$ for a $B \in NRR$,
represents a subtree of the index tree rooted at B. Therefore, the number of nodes in
$Ind(B)$ is given by the expression

$$1 + n + \ldots + n^{k-r-1} = \frac{n^{k-r} - 1}{n - 1}$$

The average size of $Data(B)$ is $\frac{Data}{n^r}$ as $|NRR| = n^r$, and $Data$ is the size of entire
data. Hence, the probe wait is

$$\frac{1}{2} \left(\frac{n^{k-r} - 1}{n - 1} + \frac{Data}{n^r} \right).$$

The Bcast wait is the half of the total length of a `Bcast`. This is equal to $Index +$
$Data + Overhead$. The $Overhead$ is introduced due to replication of the nodes in the
top r levels of the index tree. We know that each bucket is replicated as many times
as it has children. As illustrated in Fig. 13.8, all the replications put together can be
viewed as a fully balanced tree of height $r + 1$ having a single dummy node serving
as the root. Excluding the dummy root, the total number of nodes in the tree shown
above is

$$\sum_{0}^{r} n^i = \frac{n^{r+1} - 1}{n - 1} - 1.$$

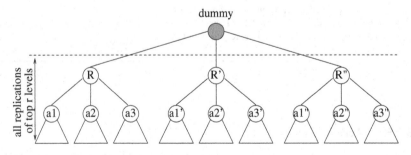

Fig. 13.8 Number of index nodes for the replicated part

The above expression gives the total number of replication of each node in the replicated part of the index tree. However, the total number of index buckets in top r levels without replication is equal to

$$\sum_{0}^{r-1} n^i = \frac{n^r - 1}{n - 1}.$$

So, the index overhead due to replication is

$$\frac{n^{r+1} - 1}{n - 1} - \frac{n^r - 1}{n - 1} - 1 = n^r - 1$$

Adding probe wait and bcast wait, we get the access time as

$$\frac{1}{2}\left(\frac{n^{k-r} - 1}{n - 1} + \frac{Data}{n^r} + (n^r - 1) + Index + Data\right)$$

13.7.5.2 Tuning Time

The initial probe is for determining the occurrence of a control index. The second probe is for accessing the control index. The control index may direct the client to the required higher level index bucket. In the worst case, the client may make up to k = number of levels in index tree. Finally, the client downloads the data. Therefore, tuning time is $\lceil \log_n Data \rceil + 3$.

13.7.5.3 Optimizing Number of Replicated Levels

The probe wait is a monotonically decreasing function which reaches the maximum value at $r = 0$ and the minimum value at $r = k$. The Bcast wait is a monotonically increasing function reaching the minimum at $r = 0$ and the maximum at $r = k$. When r increases from 0 to 1, probe wait decreases by $\frac{1}{2}\left(\frac{Data*(n-1)}{n} + n^{k-1}\right)$ and the Bcast wait increases by $\frac{n^0*(n-1)}{2}$. In general as r increase to $r + 1$

1. Probe wait decreases by $\frac{1}{2}\left(\frac{Data*(n-1)}{n^{r+1}} + n^{k-r-1}\right)$.
2. Bcast wait increases by $\frac{n^r*(n-1)}{2}$.

So increase r as long as

$$\frac{1}{2}\left(\frac{Data*(n-1)}{n^{r+1}} + n^{k-r-1}\right) > \frac{n^r*(n-1)}{2}, \text{ or}$$
$$Data * (n - 1) + n^k > n^{2r+1} * (n - 1), \text{ or}$$
$$\frac{1}{2}\left(\log_n\left(\frac{Data*(n-1)+n^k}{n-1}\right) - 1\right) > r$$

Therefore the optimum value of r is

$$\left\lfloor \frac{1}{2}\left(\log_n\left(\frac{Data*(n-1)+n^k}{n-1}\right)-1\right)\right\rfloor+1$$

13.8   Exponential Indexing

Exponential indexing [14] is a non-tree based parameterized indexing scheme. Every index link stores the maximum primary key value of the buckets within a distance range from the current index bucket. It employs the idea of exponential increase in the range of distances addressable by the consecutive index pointers.

We begin with a description of the basic scheme. The data is assumed to have been sorted beforehand, then placed on broadcast channel. Each bucket in the broadcast channel consists of two parts, namely, (i) data, and (ii) index table. The index table entries are tuples of the form {$distInt$, $maxKey$}, where

- $distInt$: the distance interval or the range from the current bucket within which other buckets are reachable.
- $maxKey$: the maximum value of the primary key of the buckets within the specified distance range.

Assuming $r = 2$, the distance interval $distInt$ takes values 1, 2, 4, ... If N is total number of buckets then ith entry, $0 \le i \le \log N$, of an index table describes the buckets within distance interval of $[2^{i-1}, 2^i - 1]$ from the current bucket. There is no need to explicitly use $distInt$, as it can be inferred from the order of occurrence of the entry in the index table.

Figure 13.9 provides an example to illustrate how it works. Suppose a client is interested to query from a data item with primary key 12 before the first bucket is broadcast. From the index table of bucket 0, it finds that 12 falls between $maxKey$ values of third and fourth entries. This implies the required bucket must be found at a distance between $2^{4-1} = 8$ and to $2^4 - 1 = 15$ buckets away from the bucket 0. So, the client goes into doze mode until bucket No. 8 appears on broadcast cycle. Probing the index table of 8th bucket, the client determines that the bucket required to resolve

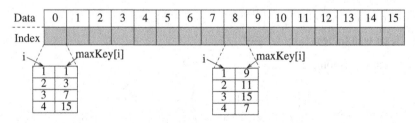

Fig. 13.9 Exponential indexing

query lies between *maxKey* values of second and third entries. So, the bucket having data to resolve the query must 4–7 buckets away from bucket No. 8. The client turns into doze mode yet again, until bucket No. 12 appears on the broadcast cycle. Since, key of this bucket matches the search, the data part is downloaded by the client. In general, the worst case tunning time is $\lceil \log(N - 1) + 1 \rceil$ assuming the broadcast to be error free. For $N = 16$, the client can download data by 5 probes.

Since, wireless channel is unreliable, some buckets may be corrupted during transmission. Errors can be handled easily in exponential indexing. Whenever a probe determines that the bucket being probed is corrupted, a fresh probe can be initiated from the next bucket. For example, if bucket 0 is found to be corrupted in the search instance stated above, then search starts from bucket 1. Assuming both 0 and 1 are corrupted search begins from bucket 2. In other words, every error results only in a small performance penalty.

Some of interesting properties of exponential indexing scheme are:

1. It embeds distributiveness within a linear structure, enabling search to proceed directly from the sequentially next bucket. Therefore, it saves on access latency.
2. Although each search traverses a different logical index tree all searches share index links. So it naturally defines a replicated indexing scheme.
3. The worst case running time for search is logarithm of bcast length when broadcast is error free.
4. Index search can recover quickly from the errors due to distributiveness of the index structure.

13.8.1 Generalized Exponential Indexing

The exponential indexing need not only be based on doubling of distance intervals for index segments. The distance intervals can grow by a factor of any other exponent $r \geq 1$. For example, ith entry in an index table refer to index segment between buckets $[a, b]$, where

$$a = \left\lfloor \sum_{j=1}^{i-2} r^j + 1 \right\rfloor = \left\lfloor \frac{r^{i-1}-1}{r-1} + 1 \right\rfloor$$

$$b = \left\lfloor \sum_{j=1}^{i-1} r^j \right\rfloor = \left\lfloor \frac{r^{i-1}}{r-1} \right\rfloor$$

In exponential indexing, the additional overhead due to presence of index table is substantial. It reduces a bucket's capacity to hold data. The cumulative effect of additional space for index in each bucket increases the length of the broadcast cycle and also affects the access latency. Indexing overhead can be reduced by grouping several buckets together, and associating only one index table for each group. Grouping, however, has a trade-off as it increases search time. For example, if I buckets are grouped together, then in an average $\frac{I-1}{2}$ buckets should be searched within a group to extract the right bucket. It is possible to reduce intra-group probe wait by making a provision for a intra-group index table. This means every index bucket has two types of indexes, viz., *local index*, and *global index*. Having a local index, helps to reduce the tuning time within a group of buckets to 1 or 2 probes:

- 1 probe if the searched data item happens to be among data items stored in the index bucket of the group, or
- 2 probes, if searched bucket occurs in one of the data buckets belonging the group.

It puts an extra overhead in index bucket in terms of having a local index table with $I - 1$ entries. I is an adjustable parameter. However, if I is too small, the purpose of grouping is defeated. On the other hand, if I is too large then the overhead due to local index table dominates overhead of global indexing without grouping.

The access protocol [14] described below has three distinct phases:

1. **Initial probe**: Initially, the client tunes to the broadcast channel and receives an error free bucket b to estimate the time for broadcast for the next index bucket. It then goes into doze mode for the estimated time, and tunes in again.
2. **Index search**: The client tunes into the broadcast channel just before the first index bucket flows into the channel. It then accesses the index buckets which are progressively closer to the desired data bucket. The distance is reduced by the factor of chosen exponent after each access of an index bucket. The client intermittently slips into doze mode every time while waiting between two successive arrivals of error free index buckets.
3. **Data retrieval**: When desired data bucket arrives, the client downloads the data.

The client executes Algorithm 32 to perform initial probe phase and retrieve the first error free index bucket. After this step is over, Algorithm 33 is executed. It performs index search. In case the local index search becomes successful, the data is retrieved. Otherwise global index search is performed by executing Algorithm 34. After index to desired data has been successfully retrieved, the next job is to download the data, which is accomplished by executing Algorithm 35.

Algorithm 32: Initial probe

begin
    repeat
      | read a bucket;
    until (*!corrupted(bucket)*);
    // First error free bucket found
    if (*data(bucket)*) **then**
      retrieve offset to index bucket;
      slip into doze mode waiting for first index bucket;
      read first index Bucket;
      while (*corrupted(bucket)*) **do**
        | slip into doze for $I - 1$ buckets to pass by;
        | read new index bucket;
      end
    end
end

Algorithm 33: Index search

begin
  foreach *(data item* ∈ *index bucket)* **do**
    if *(key(data) == K))* **then**
      | **return** *(data)*;
    end
  end
  // Search for local index in index table.
  if *(data item in range of ith local entry)* **then**
    sleep into doze mode for $i - 1$ buckets to passby;
    execute Algorithm 35;
  end
  // Search for global index in index table.
  execute Algorithm 34
end

Algorithm 34: Global index search

begin
  if *(key(data) in range of ith global entry)* **then**
    slip into doze mode for $\lfloor \frac{r^i-1}{r-1} + 1 \rfloor . I - 1)$ buckets to passby;
    read the index bucket;
    while *(corrupt(bucket))* **do**
      sleep into doze mode for $(I - 1)$ buckets;
      read the new index bucket;
    end
    execute Algoritm 33;
  end
end

Algorithm 35: Retrieval of data

begin
  while *(corrupt(bucket))* **do**
    sleep into doze mode for $(IC - 1)$ buckets to passby;
    read same bucket in the next broadcast cycle;
  end
  retrieve data;
  return *(data)*;
end

To understand how the protocol works, let us consider an example. Let the broadcast cycle be as shown in Fig. 13.10. It uses the exponent 2, and the data grouping consisting of two buckets. Each bucket has the space for six items. We assume that a data item and an index entry are of the same size. An index bucket uses three slots for the index entries, and the remaining three slots are used for storing the indexes. A

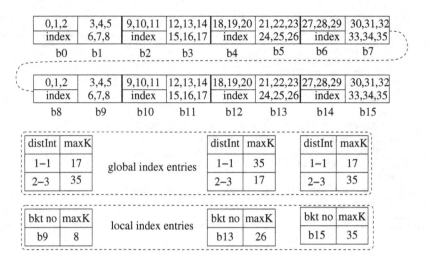

0,1,2	3,4,5	9,10,11	12,13,14	18,19,20	21,22,23	27,28,29	30,31,32
index	6,7,8	index	15,16,17	index	24,25,26	index	33,34,35
b0	b1	b2	b3	b4	b5	b6	b7

0,1,2	3,4,5	9,10,11	12,13,14	18,19,20	21,22,23	27,28,29	30,31,32
index	6,7,8	index	15,16,17	index	24,25,26	index	33,34,35
b8	b9	b10	b11	b12	b13	b14	b15

distInt	maxK		distInt	maxK		distInt	maxK
1–1	17	global index entries	1–1	35		1–1	17
2–3	35		2–3	17		2–3	35

bkt no	maxK		bkt no	maxK		bkt no	maxK
b9	8	local index entries	b13	26		b15	35

Fig. 13.10 Exponential indexing using data segment grouping

data bucket uses all six slots for storing data items. There are four data segments. So, the global index table requires two entries to find the buckets one group away and 2–3 groups away. The local index for a group requires just one entry for accessing the second data bucket of its own group. Suppose, a search initiated by a client for the data item with the primary key 23 in group four at bucket $b7$. Then the client is directed to first index bucket $b8$. Since, the data item with key 23 does not appear either in local data stored at the index bucket or in the local index, global index is checked which directs the client to bucket $b12$. From $b12$'s local index, bucket number $b13$ is obtained which has the item with primary key value 23.

13.8.2 Analysis

The index buckets should have sufficient space for the index entries. Therefore, a data bucket stores more data items compared to the data items stored in an index bucket. Before, presenting the performance analysis, certain notations are introduced in Table 13.2 for our convenience [14]. Using these notations let us understand relationships involving n_{gi}, n_{li} and n_i. These relationships can be derived directly from the organization of the indexing scheme described above. Each group of I buckets has one associated index bucket. This implies that the local index table should have $n_{li} = I - 1$ entries. The total number of index entries is

$$n_i \leq \frac{(B - B').s_d}{s_i}.$$

Table 13.2 Notations for analysis of exponential indexing

Notation	Meaning
N	Total number of data items
B	Data capacity of a data bucket
B'	Data capacity of an index bucket
s_d	Size of a data item
s_i	Size of an index entry
n_i	Total number of entries in an index table
n_{gi}	Number of global index entries in an index table
n_{li}	Number of local index entries in an index table
I	Number buckets in a data segment
D	Number of data segments

Since, $n_i = n_{gi} + n_{li}$, we also have

$$n_{gi} = n_i - n_{li} \leq \frac{(B - B').s_d}{s_i} - (I - 1).$$

In a group of I of buckets there is one index bucket, so each group has a capacity to hold up to $B \times (I - 1) + B'$ data items. It implies that the total number D of data segments in a broadcast cycle is:

$$D = \left\lceil \frac{N}{B(I - 1) + B'} \right\rceil.$$

Any group of data segment should be reachable from a global index table of any group. In addition, the distance range for groups increases by a multiple of exponent r between two successive index entries. Hence, an alternative expression for D is as follows.

$$\sum_1^{n_{gi}} r^{i-1} = \frac{r^{n_{gi}} - 1}{r - 1} \geq D - 1. \tag{13.1}$$

Furthermore, given B' and I, we may also find the minimum value of r as follows:

1. Obtain the first order differentiation of the expression in RHS of Eq. 13.1, and
2. Numerically solve the following inequality.

$$r^{n_g} + (1 - D)r + D - 2 \geq 0.$$

The average latency and the tuning time depend on B' and I. In order to access the bucket b where the required data item is located, at first we need to determine the group of buckets to which b belongs. In absence errors, the average number of buckets that would be accessed before accessing this desired group is:

$$\frac{I}{2} + \frac{I.(D-1)}{2} + 1 = \frac{I.D}{2} + 1.$$

But if the index bucket of target group is corrupted, it accessing data is delayed until next `bcast`. This implies that $I.D$ number of more buckets have to be skipped over. Let the probability of this error be p. This implies the probability of repeating the error k times is $p^k.(1-p)$. When k repeated errors occur, the accessing target group (having data item) could be delayed additionally by $k.I.D$. Hence, the average access latency from initial probe to index search is given by:

$$T_a(is) = \frac{I.D}{2} + 1 + \sum_0^\infty p^k(1-p).k.I.D = \frac{I.D}{2} + 1 + \frac{I.D.p}{1-p}$$

In data retrieval phase, if the search key is found in the first index bucket itself, then data can be retrieved immediately. The probability for this is: $\frac{B'}{B'+(I-1)B}$. Otherwise, the searched item is located in a separate data bucket. The probability of this event is $\frac{B(I-1)}{B'+B(I-1)}$. The average latency for data retrieval is $I/2$ when there is no error. Assuming error in data bucket occurs k times, there will also be an additional delay of $k.I.D$. Therefore, the average latency in data retrieval phase is:

$$T_a(d) = 0.\frac{B'}{B'+B(I-1)} + \left(\frac{I}{2} + \sum_{i=0}^\infty p^k(1-p).k.I.D\right)\frac{B.(I-1)}{B'+B(I-1)}$$

$$= \left(\frac{I}{2} + \frac{I.D.p}{1-p}\right).\frac{B(I-1)}{B(I-1)+B'}$$

Adding index search time to data retrieval time we get overall access latency T_a as:

$$T_a = T_a(is) + T_a(d).$$

Total tuning time will be the sum of three tuning times, i.e.,

1. Tuning time for initial probe to become successful.
2. Tuning time for index search to become successful.
3. Tuning time for data retrieval to become successful.

Tuning for the initial probe depends on an error free index bucket being accessed. The client tunes into a bucket belonging to a group. Let this happen just before jth $(1 \le j \le I)$ bucket in a group. The average time before an error-free bucket appears on broadcast channel is:

$$\sum_{i=0}^\infty p^k(1-p)x_{kj},$$

where x_{kj} is the tuning time if all k buckets are corrupted. If $k + 1$st bucket is an index bucket initial tuning becomes successful. Otherwise, if $k + 1$ is a data bucket then the client must wait until the beginning of the next group to get the next index bucket. This requires an average tuning time of $\frac{1}{1-p}$. Thus we have

$$x_{ij} = \begin{cases} k + 1, \text{ if } k = 1 - j, I + 1 - j, 2I + 1 - j, \ldots \\ k + 1 + \frac{1}{1-p}, \text{ otherwise} \end{cases}$$

Averaging over all the possible values of j, the average tunning time for the initial probe phase is:

$$T_t(ip) = \sum_{i=0}^{\infty} p^k (1 - p).(k + 1) + \frac{I - 1}{I} \sum_{i=0}^{\infty} p^i (1 - p) \frac{1}{1 - p} = \frac{2I - 1}{I(1 - p)}$$

Now let us analyze the average tuning time for the index search. Consider the case when no bucket is in error. Since, the total number of data segment groups is $(r^{n_{gi}} - 1)/(r - 1)$, the size of the search space is also the same. On each step search space is reduced by $r/(r - 1)$. This implies, the worst case tuning time is $\lceil \log_{r/(r-1)}(D - 1) \rceil + 1$. If $I > 1$, one more probe will be necessary if the data is not available in a data bucket. Thus worst case tuning time in absence of errors is

$$T_t = \begin{cases} \lceil \log_{r/(r-1)}(D - 1) \rceil + 1, \text{ if data available in the index bucket} \\ \lceil \log_{r/(r-1)}(D - 1) \rceil + 2, \text{ otherwise} \end{cases}$$

Now let us analyze the tuning time when broadcast is not error free. Let $t(l)$ be tuning time when target index bucket that is l groups away is received. In order to compute $t(l)$ we observe that there are two possibilities:

1. An error free target index bucket is received before l index segments fly past on broadcast. The probability of an error free bucket being received is $(1 - p)$. So for this event tuning time should be $t(l - x).(1 - p)$.
2. The error free target index bucket is found exactly in lth index segment. This implies that the target index buckets received in $l - 1$ groups were found to be corrupted. The error free target index bucket obtained when l group is received on broadcast. So, the tuning time spent when this event occurs is $t(l - 1).p + 1$.

Adding the above two expression gives $t(l)$. Therefore,

$$t(l) = \begin{cases} 0, \text{ if } l = 0 \\ t(l - x).(1 - p) + t(l - 1).p + 1, \text{ if } l > 0, \end{cases}$$

where the maximum value of x is less than or equal to l in the set of $\{1, 2, \lfloor r + 2 \rfloor, \lfloor \frac{r^{n_g} - 1}{r - 1} \rfloor + 1\}$.

If $l > 0$, it is possible that a new round of search may have to be started with $D - 1$ groups away from the next target index bucket. The target index bucket may be repeatedly found to be corrupted for i times. This means overall tuning time is

$$t(l) + \sum_{i=1}^{\infty} p^i(1 - p).i.t(D - 1) = t(l) + \frac{t(D - 1).p}{1 - p}$$

Therefore, the average tuning time for an index search is

$$T_t(is) = \frac{1}{D}\left(t(0) + t(l) + \frac{t(D - 1).p}{1 - p}\right)$$

Now we only need to find the tuning time for the data retrieval phase. If the data item is inside an index bucket, no extra probe is necessary. However, if the data item is in a separate data bucket then 1 more unit of tuning time is necessary. It possible that the data bucket is found to be repeatedly corrupted for k times, then $k + 1$ additional tuning time is needed.

$$T_t(d) = 0.\frac{B'}{B(I - 1) + B'} + \left(\sum_{i=0}^{\infty} p^k(1 - p)(k + 1)\right)\frac{B(I - 1)}{B' + B(I - 1)}$$

$$= \frac{B(I - 1)}{(B' + B(I - 1))(1 - p)}$$

Total average tuning time T_t is, therefore,

$$T_t = T_t(ip) + T_t(is) + T_t(d).$$

13.9 Hash A

Hashing scheme [6] is a direct adaptation of hashing with chaining [4]. It does not require broadcast of directory information with data as the information is embedded with data (contents). Each bucket has two parts, viz., *control part*, and *data part*. The search for data bucket is guided by the information available in control part. The control part of every bucket has following four pieces of information

1. *bucket_ID*: offset to the bucket from the beginning of the current `Bcast`.
2. *Offset*: offset of the bucket from the beginning of the next `Bcast`.
3. *Hash function*: h.
4. *Shift value*: The pointer to a bucket B that contains the keys K such that $h(K) =$ *address*(B).

A client wishing to retrieve a record corresponding to a key K, starts listening until it is able to read a full bucket b. From the control part of b, the client retrieves the hash function h. Then it computes $h(K)$ to determine if its initial probe has missed the index or not. Next it tunes into the physical bucket which matches with the hash value $h(K)$. From the physical bucket it retrieves the shift value. The shift value handles the overflow. If there is no overflow then data record with primary key K should be in physical bucket $h(K)$ provided the record exists in the file. The shift value s is the offset to the logical bucket that should have hash value $h(K)$. This bucket will be $s \times t_b$ units away from the current time, where t_b is the duration of a bucket. So, the client goes into doze mode for $s \times t_b$ time. After the expiry of doze mode, the client starts listening to the broadcast channel to download the data or retrieves another shift value. The search should be done for all the overflow buckets of $h(K)$ before concluding that the record is absent. So, either the search is successful in fetching required data is with key K from the broadcast or it encounters a record with key L such that $h(K) \neq h(L)$. In the latter case, a failure is reported to the client's application.

Algorithm 36 summarizes the process of search described above.

Algorithm 36: Access protocol using hashing

begin
    Probe the current bucket and read the control data;
    Compute hash h;
    if *(bucket_ID < h(K))* **then**
        | slip into doze mode for the time to pass $h(K) - bucket\_ID$ buckets;
    end
    else
        | slip into doze mode till the next `Bcast`;
        | repeat the protocol;
    end
    read slot $h(K)$ and retrieve shift value s;
    slip doze mode for the time to pass s buckets;
    while *(exist(overflow buckets))* **do**
        | read the record;
        | **if** *(record.key == K)* **then**
            | **return** *(found record with key K)*;
        | **end**
        | **if** *(record.key ≠ K)* **then**
            | **return** *(record not found)*;
        | **end**
    end
end

Figure 13.11 provides an example illustrating how the access protocol works. The physical bucket IDs which represent overflow buckets do not carry any logical ID. Suppose we are interested in retrieving record with key $K = 15$, and the initial probe is made at physical bucket 2. From bucket 2, the hash function is retrieved and $h(15) = 4$ is computed. Let the hash function be

$$h(x) = x \mod 4 + 1$$

Fig. 13.11 Retrieving data
bucket with record key 15

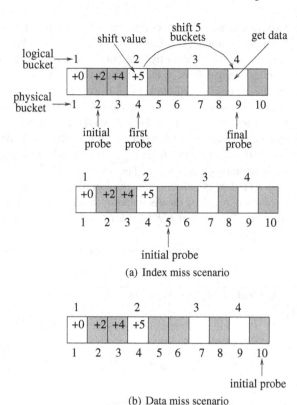

Fig. 13.12 Scenarios
depicting data miss and
index miss

(a) Index miss scenario

(b) Data miss scenario

Since hash value does not match physical bucket $b = 2$, it gets offset $h(K) - b$ and
sets expiry time for arrival of physical bucket 4. From physical bucket 4, shift value
$s = 5$ is retrieved. Since this is an overflow (data with some other key is found here) a
shift value here tells us where the logical bucket 4 can be found. Again the client goes
into doze mode till 5 physical buckets pass by. The client wakes up and starts listening
for data sequentially from there onwards. Assuming logical bucket 4 has the data, the
record with key K gets downloaded.   There are two scenarios [6] where the client
has to wait till next broadcast cycle to retrieve data. The first scenario is illustrated by
Fig. 13.12a. Here the initial probe is made only after the physical bucket containing
the record has passed by in the current broadcast cycle. So, the initial probe missed
the index. The second scenario is illustrated in Fig. 13.12b. In this case, the initial
probe is made at bucket 10. Whereas, the data record with primary key 15 occurs in
bucket 9. Therefore, data miss occurs here.

When a perfect hashing function is employed, the access time is minimized for
conventional disk based files. In a broadcast based dissemination, access latency
depends directly on the total number of buckets in the broadcast cycle. Therefore,
there is need to understand the advantages or the disadvantages.

- Perfect hash function cannot minimize the number of physical buckets required for a file.
- In contrast, if more overflow buckets are used then it reduces the number of half empty buckets and the bucket is better utilized. With less number of half empty buckets, the broadcast cycle becomes shorter. Since the broadcast medium is sequential, a shorter broadcast cycle reduces the waiting time for the next version of the file.
- However, with perfect hashing, the overflow area is smaller. So the tuning time becomes minimum with perfect hash function.

In summary, hashing based broadcast files exhibits

1. Random access behavior for tuning time (hash values and shifts act as control parameters), and
2. Sequential behavior for the access time (the number of buckets matters).

13.10 Hash B

The initial hash function can be improved by modifying the hash function [6]. It works provided an estimate of minimum overflow chain d can be made. The revised hash function is defined as follows:

$$h'(K) = \begin{cases} h(K), & \text{if } h(K) = 1 \\ (h(K) - 1)(1 + \text{minimum-overflow}) + 1 & \text{if } h(K) > 1 \end{cases}$$

The access protocol itself remains unchanged. The suggested change in hash reduces the number of overflows. In fact, if the overflow chain for each bucket is of the same size, say d, then the hash becomes a perfect hash wherein bucket size increased by $(1+d)$ times. For example, if $d = 1$, then $1, 3, 5, 7$, etc., are the physical buckets to which the records are hashed for transmission of useful data. The space of one bucket is left out for overflow. So, the shift values should be computed for the physical buckets $1, 3, 5, 7$, etc. All the shift values incidently is one for all these buckets.

To calculate the access time, a displacement value $DISP(h, K)$ is introduced. It refers to the displacement needed to reach the physical bucket $b(K)$ containing the record with key K from the bucket at $h'(K)$, i.e., $b(K) - h'(K)$. The expected access time can be computed by finding the per key access time and then averaging it out. The worst case per key expected access time computation becomes different depending on whether an index miss occurs or not during the initial probe.

Figure 13.13 depicts the two possible scenarios depending on whether initial probe occurs either inside or outside the interval between $[h'(k), b(k)]$. In the figure $h'(K)$ denotes the physical bucket $h'(K)$ and $b(K)$ represents is the physical bucket where the record corresponding key K is found.

The first case is illustrated by Fig. 13.13a. In this case the waiting time covers between the two consecutive occurrences of the physical bucket $b(K)$ that constitute a full broadcast cycle. Since, the initial probe may occur any where between $h'(K)$ to $b(K)$, it adds in an average $DISP(h, K)/2$ before search can begin. So, the total waiting time is:

$$\left(Data(h) + \frac{DISP(h, K)}{2}\right),$$

where $Data(h)$ denotes the size of the `bcast`. The probability of initial probe itself to be located inside the interval $[h'(K), b(K)]$ is $\frac{DISP(h,K)}{Data(h)}$. Hence, the average per key access time in this case is given by:

$$\frac{DISP(h, K)}{Data(h)} \times \left(Data(h) + \frac{DISP(h, K)}{2}\right),$$

The scenario depicting the second case is analyzed under two sub-cases:

 (i) When the initial probe is made before the physical bucket $h'(K)$, and
(ii) When the initial probe is made after the physical bucket $b(K)$.

These two sub-cases have been illustrated in Fig. 13.13b. Examining both the sub-cases in conjunction, we find that the initial probe can be made any where between the physical buckets in ranges $[1, h'(K) - 1]$ and $[b(K) + 1, end]$. Thus, the waiting time in an average is $(Data(h) + DISP(h, K))/2$. The probability that the initial probe satisfies this second case is $1 - \frac{DISP(h,K)}{Data(h)}$. Hence, the average per key access time in this case is given by:

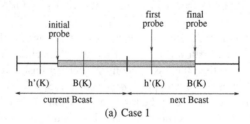

(a) Case 1

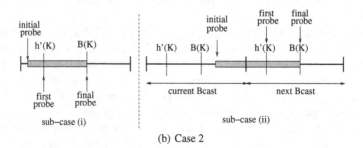

(b) Case 2

Fig. 13.13 Access time using modified hashing function

Fig. 13.14 Comparison of
displacements [6]

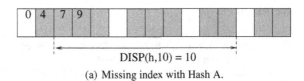

DISP(h,10) = 10

(a) Missing index with Hash A.

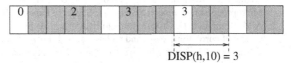

DISP(h,10) = 3

(b) Missing index with Hash B.

$$\left(1 - \frac{DISP(K)}{Data(h)}\right) \times \left(\frac{Data(h) + DISP(h,k)}{2}\right)$$

Once the per key access time is known, the average access time can be determined by summing it over all the keys and dividing by the number of records in the broadcast channel. A good hash function is expected to keep the overflow under a finite small bound.

Figure 13.14 illustrates the waiting time for key $K = 10$ when hash A and hash B are used. The hash function for hash A is $h(K) = K \mod 4 + 1$, i.e., $h(10) = 3$. In the first case, hash A is used and in the second case hash B is used. The overflow bucket (shaded blocks) corresponding to each bucket (unshaded block) is shown next to it.

In the first case (with hash A) physical buckets 1, 2, 3, 4 should have shift values. These are values are 0, 4, 7 and 9 respectively. This implies that any key value mapping to bucket 1 can be found in the bucket interval [1, 5] if it exists in the broadcast file. Likewise, the bucket interval [6, 9] contains all the records with key values hashing into the value 2, and so on. The shift values should be computed for buckets 1, 2, 3, and 4, because these are the physical bucket where the respective hash values map. Note that the shift values are 0, 4, 7, and 9 respectively. The displacement value for searching record with $K = 10$ is 10 as depicted in Fig. 13.14a.

In the second case (with hash B), the length of minimum overflow chain is 2. Therefore, the shift values are computed for buckets 4, 7, 10, 13. For key $K = 10$, $h'(K) = 7$. However, bucket 7 is an overflow bucket. So the shift value 3 from this bucket is extracted and the search restarts from bucket 10. Since, bucket 10 also an overflow bucket, its shift value is obtained. This shift value then leads to logical bucket 4 which contains this key, if it exists in the file. Notice that the displacement for this case is only 3 as shown in Fig. 13.14b.

References

1. S. Acharya, M. Franklin, S. Zdonik, Dissemination-based data delivery using broadcast disks. IEEE Pers. Commun. **2**(6), 50–60 (2001)
2. P.V. Argade, S. Aymeloglu, A.D. Berenbaum, M.V. dePaolis, R.T. Franzo, R.D. Freeman, D.A. Inglis, G. Komoriya, H. Lee, T.R. Little, G.A. MacDonald, H.R. McLellan, E.C. Morgan, H.Q. Pham, G.D. Ronkin, R.J. Scavuzzo, T.J. Woch, Hobbit: A High-Performance, Low-Power Microprocessor, *Compcon Spring '93, Digest of Papers* (1993), pp. 88–95
3. A.M. Bernardes, D. Crocce Romano Espinosa, J.A. Soares Tenório, Recycling of batteries: a review of current processes and technologies. J. Power Sour. **130**(12), 291–298 (2004)
4. T. Corman, C. Leiserson, R. Rivest, C. Stein, *Introduction to Algorithms* (MIT Press, Cambridge MA, USA, 2001)
5. H. Gracia-Molina, J.D. Ullman, J. Widom, *Database Systems: The Complete Book*, 2 edn. (Pearson-Prentice Hall, Upper Saddle River, NJ, USA, 2009)
6. T. Imielinski, S. Viswanathan, B. Badrinath, Power efficient filtering of data on air, *The 4th International Conference on Extended Database Technology, (EDBT '94)*, vol. LNCS 779 (1994), pp. 245–258
7. T. Imielinski, S. Viswanthan, Wireless Publishing: Issues and Solutions, ed. by T. Imielinski, H.F. Korth. *Mobile Computing*, Chap. 11 (Kluwer Academic Publishers, Norwell, MA, USA, 1996), pp. 300–329
8. T. Imielinski, S. Viswanathan, B.R. Badrinath, Energy efficient indexing on air. SIGMOD Rec. **23**(2), 25–36 (1994)
9. A. Klaiber, The Technology Behind Crusoe Processors, *Transmeta Technical Brief* (2000)
10. R.A. Powers, Batteries for low power electronics. Proc. IEEE **83**(4), 687–693 (1995)
11. P. Ramadass, B. Haran, R. White, B.N. Popov, Capacity fade of sony 18650 cells cycled at elevated temperatures: Part i. Cycling performance. J. Power Sour. **112**(2), 606–613 (2002)
12. N.H. Vaidya, S. Hameed, Scheduling data broadcast in asymmetric communication environments. Wireless Netw. **5**(3), 171–182 (1999)
13. K.-L. Wu, P.S. Yu, M.-S. Chen, Energy-Efficient Caching for Wireless Mobile Computing, *Proceedings of the Twelfth International Conference on Data Engineering, 1996* (IEEE, 1996), pp. 336–343
14. J. Xu, W.C. Lee, X. Tang, Q. Gao, S. Li, An error-resilient and tunable distributed indexing scheme for wireless data broadcast. IEEE Trans. Knowled. Data Eng. **18**(3), 392–404 (2006)
15. Y. Yao, X. Tang, E.-P. Lim, A. Sun, An energy-efficient and access latency optimized indexing scheme for wireless data broadcast. IEEE Trans. Knowled. Data Eng. **18**(8), 1111–1124 (2006)

Chapter 14
Caching and Data Replication in Mobile Environment

14.1 Introduction

The combined implication of poor link quality, low bandwidth, network higher latency forces a mobile client to operate in disconnected mode either voluntarily or involuntarily. In the disconnected mode of operation, a mobile user relies on locally cached copy of data. The classical techniques like caching and replications have been extensively exploited to address the issues arising out of information processing and retrieval in mobile environments. In summary, caching and replication ensure that most of the data requests are met from one of the following sources:

- Data available in the memory, or
- Data stored in the local storage, or
- Data available from a remote replica available close by.

By using clever caching and replication strategies, it may be possible to avoid retrieval of data from a distant replica.

Caching in traditional system is employed for fast access of frequently used data items. In mobile environment caching serves following three purposes, namely,

1. Reducing the access latency of frequently used data items,
2. Supporting disconnected mode of operation of mobile devices, and
3. Reducing the network traffic as mobile devices work with cached data.

However, in order to support disconnected mode of operation for longer periods, the granularity of caching should be large. In other words, in anticipation of future use [18], a mobile client needs to cache a large amount of data before turning into disconnected mode. Caching large amount of data known as hoarding. It requires new set of techniques, and also changes the cost model.

The existing replication techniques are designed for fixed networks. In a mobile environment, the last mile connectivity is provided by wireless channels. The network connectivity of an end device is transient in nature. The infrastructure supporting the last mile connectivity consist of stationary nodes and wired networks. Mobile data

© Springer Nature Singapore Pte Ltd. 2017
R.K. Ghosh, *Wireless Networking and Mobile Data Management*,
DOI 10.1007/978-981-10-3941-6_14

services are organized over the stationary nodes. This implies that the replicas may be placed at the stationary nodes. Therefore, the locations of the replica cohorts are mostly known a priori. The handling scalability is a major challenge in replication [9], as the convergence over wide area network is difficult achieve.

The aim of this chapter is to study techniques of both replication and caching. It identifies components in replication algorithms that may either require re-engineering or re-designing for the mobile environment.

14.2 Caching, Prefetching and Hoarding

A cache is a low latency computer memory. Due to high cost, normally, a small cache is installed on a computer. For portability reasons, a mobile computer has a smaller cache compared to a stationary computer. The aim of caching is to store a few frequently accessed temporary data objects for fast execution of programs. A cache memory essentially functions as a filter. It eliminates the repeated accesses to disk or remote computer for data objects. It helps to reduce both latency and network traffic. There are three distinct form of populating cache, namely,

- On demand caching,
- Prefetching, and
- Hoarding.

In demand driven caching, a data object is cached only after it has been accessed once. On the other hand, prefetching is the process of caching data in anticipated future use. Prefetching is done during execution of programs, and generally used in conjunction with caching in order to hide access latencies. Both caching and pre-fetching have been used in file systems to enhance performance [6].

Hoarding means to pre-load copies of data objects so that a mobile computer can work in disconnected mode. In abstraction, hoarding is not different from prefetching. However, it is more appropriate to view hoarding as over-fetching. Hoarding is usually assisted by user defined hoarding scripts which gets executed periodically. The execution of hoarding script is referred to as a hoard walk. A cache miss in the prefetched data is not catastrophic, because during prefetching, a computer operates in connected mode. However, when a mobile computer relies on hoarded data then it operates in disconnected mode. Therefore, a cache miss during disconnected mode of operation leads to a failure.

The advantages of caching in mobile computing environment are as follows:

1. It reduces access latency specially over low bandwidth wireless links.
2. It helps to conserve power in a mobile computer, as it can switch off the network interfaces.
3. It allows mobile applications to execute even when a mobile device operates in disconnected mode.
4. It also helps to conserve back channel bandwidth.

Maintaining cache consistency in a mobile environment is a challenge. Wireless connection is fragile, connectivity is not only intermittent, but bandwidth is also low. It forces mobile computers to operate in disconnected mode from time to time. Resource constraints adds further complication, as only limited number of cache slots are available on a mobile device. So, classical solutions to caching cannot be ported directly to mobile computers. Apart from the known issues concerning cache constraints, a number of other issues also arise which are primarily related to the mobility of end hosts. Some of the challenges, encountered in design of an efficient caching scheme for mobile environments are listed below:

- Predicting the data access pattern and estimating the update rate.
- Minimizing the cost of communication and access.
- Knowing the mobility patterns of the mobile clients.
- Finding the connectivity characteristics.
- Knowing the location dependent information.
- Deciding about the data currency requirement.
- Sending cache invalidation notifications.
- Determining the cache size.
- Computing the latency in resolving the queries.

Let us understand the implications of these challenges. Guessing the data access pattern of a mobile client is hazardous. Many users may have drastically different access patterns. Though in an average, the update rate is expected to be low, the updates may occur in bursts. The cost of data access on a mobile computer depends primarily on two factors, namely, tariff and bandwidth. Bandwidth is usually low, and the tariff is inversely proportional to the bandwidth. Knowing mobility patterns of a mobile client could help in estimating, the time and the duration of disconnection, and consequently, the data access requirements. Prior to disconnection, by caching data according to its predicted access pattern a mobile client can operate in disconnected mode. However, it is difficult to get a reasonable estimate the frequency as well as the duration of time for which a mobile user may operate in disconnected mode. Depending on location, certain data may or may not be available during periodic hoard walk (the process of executing hoarding). So, the decision about what to cache and what to leave sometimes becomes difficult unless the user of a mobile host has specified a profile.

If the latest updated value of a data object important for an application, then caching is not advantageous. On the other hand, if the application can tolerate certain amount of staleness in data, then caching data make sense. So knowing currency requirement (periodicity of update) is an important parameter for caching decision. When data become invalid, invalidation of data must be known to application running on a mobile client. The invalid notifications is usually sent by stationary computers hosting the data objects. But a stationary computer must keep track of the mobile clients which may be using the modified data objects.

Cache size is small, so it becomes a challenge to determine which data items need to be cached when there is a requirement for caching many items. The design of a cache eviction policy is challenging, as it is related to the cost consideration. For example, eviction of data objects from cache may adversely affect latencies in resolutions of queries. Therefore, finding an optimal policy for caching in mobile computing environment is highly involved and more challenging compared to caching in a conventional stationary distributed system. Circumventing asymmetry in resources and unpredictability in connectivity are the two major challenges in designing caching policies in mobile computing scenarios.

14.3   Invalidating and Refreshing Cache

In a mobile environment, each mobile client is connected to network through a base station (BS). The queries from a mobile client is always routed through its current BS to a server. Data is assumed to be replicated on a set of servers. Each server of the set is responsible for resolving queries originating from a set of cells. From the point of view of a mobile client, the base station acts as proxy for a cell area. If a mobile client has cached some data objects, the main concern will be to refresh these objects whenever they get updated. Caching becomes meaningless, if the clients were to check for the freshness of a data object each time an access to the object is made. A mobile computer operating in disconnected mode may not be able to check freshness of cached data for a long time. So, there should be strategy to invalidate cached data when updates are made. The invalidation is viewed as a violation of a server's obligations towards its clients [3]. The server's obligations are known in advance to the clients. Therefore, the clients have some degree of flexibility in handling their respective caches. The extent of a server's obligations determines how the clients evolve their policies for the cache management. Two common types of obligations are [3]:

1. The server sends invalidation messages to the clients who have cached a data item x immediately after an update for x is accepted.
2. Another approach is to let the client verify the validity of their caches. NFS [13] use this approach. It generates a lot of network traffic.

In the first approach, each client is required to register its presence in a cell and also to let the server know each and very data item it has cached. Coda [18] and Andrew [1] files systems use a protocol based on this approach. However, disconnected clients miss the invalid notifications. These clients need to refresh their caches as soon as they get reconnected. A client gets a notification message even if it is not interested to use a cached data item any more. The server is stateful because it has full knowledge of the objects the clients have cached and the states of the cached objects. The second approach defeats the purpose of caching in the mobile clients. As every time a client requires to use cached data it has to verify the validity of the cached objects. In mobile environment none of the above two approaches is suitable for framing the server obligations.

Can there be a third approach? Is it possible to use stateless servers? Stateless servers need not seek any information from clients about the cached data objects.

These servers include a sufficient information in the invalidation messages itself about the updates to data. There are many possibilities for composing invalidation reports (IRs). But, we can identify a few basic characteristics of these reports, namely,

- An IR includes all updates and timestamps when these updates were received.
- An IR is broadcast over downlink (server to clients) channel.
- An IR may either be sent out in fixed periodic intervals (synchronous) or as and when any of the data is updated (asynchronous).

An asynchronous Invalidation Report (IR) enables the clients in connect mode to invalidate the cached objects included in the IR. However, the clients operating in disconnected mode lose their cached data. Since, IRs includes timestamps and recent changes in data items, the disconnected clients after reconnecting back may have to wait for the next broadcast of invalidation reports and verify the validity of their respective caches. However, there is no guarantee about the time of sending IR. Therefore, in theory, IR which a client is waiting for may never be sent.

Synchronous invalidation reports are sent on periodic intervals. A client should listen to IR notifications to find the validity of its cached data. If the cached data item is invalid, the client should refresh the cached data before processing a query. The problem is that if the difference in timestamp of the current IR and the timestamp of a cached item is larger than a threshold, the client cannot be sure about the freshness of the cached item, even if, the current IR does not include the data item. So, the client waits for refreshing cached data. This waiting time gets added to any query processing time concerning the cached data item. There are other implications of using synchronous invalidation reports in use of the cached data, namely,

- If two queries are received during an IR interval, both are processed at the same time in the next interval.
- The answer to a query reflects any updates to the item during the interval in which the query was made. This will still be the case even if the query predates the updates to the data item.

14.4 Strategies for Caching with Stateless Servers

To understand the general concept on which stateless servers for cache management works, let us delve a bit deeper into some of the known strategies [3]. The readers who are interested about more details may refer to the original work by Barbara and Imielinski [3].

14.4.1 TS Strategy

The first strategy known as Time Stamp (TS) strategy [3]. The server is assumed to broadcast invalidation report periodically, say, after every L time units. The server's obligation is to include all the data items that have changed in the last w time units. L and w are unrelated except that $w \geq L$. The invalidation report consists of data objects from a database D with timestamps of their respective latest update times. The server keeps a list U_i, where

$$U_i = \{[d, t_d] | d \in D\}$$

where t_d is the timestamp of the last update to d such that $T_i - w \leq t_d \leq T_i$.

On receiving an IR, a client checks the validity of its each cached items $[d, t_d^c]$, where t_d^c is the timestamp of the cached object d. The client also keeps a list Q_i for all the queries on the cached data items that has been received in the interval (T_{i-1}, T_i). Besides this, the client also has T_{lu}, the last update interval it has received. On the basis of these timestamps, it can determine validity as follows:

- If $T_i - T_{lu} > w$ then, the client has missed an invalidation report which may have carried an update to a cached data. So the entire cache is now useless.
- If $t_d^c < t_d$, then the cached value of d is invalid. So, it should be thrown out.
- If $t_d^c \geq t_d$, then the current value of d held in the cache is valid. So, the client should renew the timestamp of d to time of the invalidation report.

After the cache entries has been updated as above, all the queries received in interval (T_{i-1}, T_i) can be processed. However, if the list Q_i involved some data items not in cache, the client should send those queries over the uplink to the server. The outlines of the algorithm [3] provided in Algorithm 37.

14.4.2 AT Strategy

The next alternative model for cache management is referred to as Amnesic Terminal (AT). In the AT model, a server's obligation is to report the identities of items that have changed after the last IR interval. Timestamps representing the update times are not included with the data items which appear in the invalidation report. The client is also not required to maintain timestamp of the cached items. Therefore, not only the invalidation report is shorter but the pressure on a client's cache memory is also less. The algorithm for this model is also simpler than TS model as timestamp comparisons are not needed. The rest of the cache validation algorithm at the client is similar to TS [3] and provide by Algorithm 38.

14.4.3 Signature Strategy

The third model is quite different from the two previous models. It is based on signature comparisons [4, 12, 14]. A signature is essentially a checksum of the values

---

Algorithm 37: TS strategy for caching

---

begin
  if *(T_i − T_{lu} > L)* **then**
    // Entire cache is outdated.
    drop the entire *Cache*;
  end
  else
    // Check for validity of each item in cache.
    foreach *(d ∈ Cache)* **do**
      if *([d, t_d] ∈ IR)* **then**
        if *(t_d^c < t_d)* **then**
          // Item d in cache is obsolete.
          throw *d* out of *Cache*;
        end
        else
          // Item d in cache is still valid.
          // Update caching timestamp to current time
          $t_d^c = T_i$;
        end
      end
    end
  end
  foreach *(d ∈ Q_i)* **do**
    if *(d ∈ Cache)* **then**
      // Query is on a item d ∈ Cache.
      use cached value of *d* to answer the query;
    end
    else
      // Query is on item d ∉ Cache.
      send query to server over the uplink;
    end
    // Refresh latest update time.
    $T_{lu} = T_i$;
  end
end

---

stored in items. The server periodically broadcasts a set of combined signatures of all the data items of interest. The composition of subset of the signatures in each *combined signature* is known before hand to all the clients. The clients cache not only the data items but all the combined signatures of the subsets that includes its cached data items.

The signature creation process is as follows. For each item i, a signature $sig(i)$ of b bits is computed using the value stored in i. So we have,

---

Algorithm 38: AT strategy for caching

---

begin
   if *(T_i − T_l > L)* **then**
      // Entire cache is outdated
      drop the entire *Cache*;
   end
   else
      // Check for validity of each item in cache.
      foreach *(d ∈ Cache)* **do**
         if *(d ∈ IR)* **then**
            // *d* is obsolete.
            throw *d* out of *Cache*;
         end
      end
   end
   foreach *(d ∈ Q_i)* **do**
      if *(d ∈ Cache)* **then**
         // Current cached value of *d* is valid.
         use cache's value of *d* to answer the query;
      end
      else
         send query to server over the uplink;
      end
      T_l = T_i;
   end
end

$$Pr[sig(i_1) = sig(i_2)] = \frac{1}{2^b}.$$

The signatures of a set of items $i_1, i_2, \ldots, i_k$ is given by

$$sig(i_1) \oplus sig(i_2) \oplus \ldots \oplus sig(i_k),$$

where $\oplus$ denotes exclusive OR. Each individual signature has b bits. Therefore, the combined a signature also has b bits. It has been proved in [8] that if one or more of the items involved in a signature has changed, then the probability of two combined signatures being identical is approximately 2^{-b}. In other words, for a subset of items $\{i_1, i_2, \ldots i_j\}, j \leq k$,

$$Pr[sig_{prev}(i_1, i_2, \ldots, i_j) = sig_{curr}(i_1, i_2, \ldots, i_j)] \approx \frac{1}{2^b},$$

where

1. sig_{prev} denotes the combined signature before the updates, and
2. sig_{curr} denotes the combined signature after the updates were received for one or more items $i_1, i_2, \ldots, i_j$.

Though the probability of the combined signatures before an update for the same set of items being identical is low, it is still non zero. So, the server tries to fulfill the obligation by aggregating the items into sets. This may cause clients to falsely conclude some caches are invalid when they may still be valid.

A mobile client is assumed to have cached n^* items of which a fraction f^* may be invalidated. Let f to be the total items which need to be invalidated for all mobile clients. Then only a fraction of the total updates may belong to any chosen mobile client. This implies,

$$f^* = \rho f, \ 0 < \rho < 1.$$

The server chooses m sets of items $S_1, S_2, \ldots, S_m$ randomly. Each set is chosen so that the probability that an item i appears in S_j is $\frac{1}{f+1}$. The server then creates m combined signatures $sig_1, sig_2, \ldots sig_m$, and broadcasts them. Apart from the k items a mobile client MH has cached, MH also has cached signatures $sig'_1, sig'_2, \ldots, sig'_k$ of k respective cached items. MH compares its signature sets with the corresponding signatures broadcast by the server and sets:

$$\alpha_j = \begin{cases} 1, \text{if } j = i, 1 \leq i \leq k \text{ and } sig_j \neq sig'_i \\ 0, \text{otherwise} \end{cases}$$

It means a MH sets α_j to 1 when it notices that a signature sig_j from the server's broadcast is different from the corresponding cached signature sig'_i.

After having computed α_js, a mobile client is ready to execute invalidation algorithm. It uses a threshold

$$\delta_f = \frac{1}{f+1} \times \left(1 - \frac{1}{e}\right),$$

in order to reduce false alarms about cache being invalid. The details of analysis on how the value threshold has been arrived can be found in [3].

The mobile clients execute Algorithm 39 to invalidate its cache entries. The main idea behind the algorithm is that if an item belongs to too many unmatched signatures, then it is most likely invalid. Hence, such an item needs to be evicted from cache. The problem with the algorithm is that mobile clients must be connected to network to listen to signature updates.

Algorithm 39: Cache invalidation

```
begin
    // Initially all cached items are valid.
    T = Φ;
    for (j = 1; j ≤ m; j++) do
        if (αⱼ == 1) then
            for (i = 1; i ≤ n; i++) do
                if (i ∈ Sⱼ) then
                    | count[i]++;
                end
            end
        end
    end
    for (i = 1; i ≤ n; i++) do
        if (count[i] ≥ mδ_f) then
            // Threshold > δ_f implies invalid cached items.
            T = T ∪ {i};
        end
    end
end
```

14.5   Requirements for Replication

To assess the special requirements of replication for mobile environment, following specific issues related to mobility [2] should be addressed:

1. Does mobility of the end devices introduce new dimensions to the existing data replication methodology?
2. Is it possible to adapt existing data replication algorithms to mobile environment?

As the updates keep coming, the original copy and its other replicas would diverge. The task of replication algorithm is to synch the two types of copies, so that the amount of divergence between the original and any of its replica is tolerable. The threshold of tolerance is dictated by the semantics of the applications running on the replicas. By appropriate characterizations of the types of mobile applications, it may be possible to cope up with varying degrees of staleness in the replicas. However, as far as the replication algorithms are concerned, the requirement is to ensure that the copies do not diverge too much from the original. In other words, the replication algorithms should be *divergence aware*. So, there is a need to revisit conventional algorithms in the context of mobile environment.

Achieving one copy serialization is the ultimate goal of any replication algorithm [5]. This gives an illusion to the applications that there is just a single copy, which is highly available, and contains the latest value of every object in the database [9]. However, a mutual trade-off exists between:

1. A replica containing the latest updates of all objects, and
2. The accessibility of that replica.

For the purpose of one copy serialization, the access to a replica is prohibited till it is made up-to-date. One of the replica is considered as the original or the primary, and all updates typically go through two phase commits for reconciliation. Two phase commit locks all the copies and updates them atomically. Obviously, the synchronization requirement is a bottleneck for the scalability. This algorithm can work well on a LAN based environment. The replication strategy as stated above is known as the pessimistic strategy.

Any approach to enhance the performances of replication algorithms inevitably leads to relaxation of the requirements for having a primary copy. In turn, it allows the replicas to be accessible even if the updates are being made to other copies. Such a strategy decouples the update reconciliation from the replica accessibility. The reconciliation is carried out in the background as the copies being read or written to. In a sense, this approach tacitly assumes that the conflicts occur but with appropriate choice of sharing policies, these conflicts can be managed. In other words, when the conflicts actually arise, these can be resolved by minimal manual interventions. The above strategy of replication is known as optimistic replication policy. CODA file system [17] employs optimistic replication policy.

There are many advantages of optimistic replication [16], namely,

- *Availability of replicas*: Accessibility to data is not blocked. Access latency is reduced, as a client can access data from the nearest available replica.
- *Disconnected operation*: A mobile device can hoard data prior to disconnection. The running of the applications on the disconnected device is not affected, since all the data requirements are met from the hoarded (pre-cached) data.
- *Scalability*: Since replica integration does not demand strong coordination among the replica holders, a large number of replicas can be used to scale up the system.
- *Quick visibility of updates*. The updates applied initially to a client's local copy are marked tentative. They become visible almost immediately.

The update operations are replayed at the replica holders after the final application order is determined by timestamps. Reordering of operations with a number of optimizations is possible on the basis of commutative, associative and inverse properties of operations. Such reordering of operations also leads to increase in concurrency in some cases. Even when a mobile computer is disconnected, reintegration of its cached data can be performed on reconnection. Similarly, when the network gets partitioned, and a replica is located in a partition gets isolated from the rest, its accessibility not affected. After merging, the update logs can be exchanged between the partitions. This update procedures suits well for a mobile distributed environment.

Mobile storage system such as IBM Notes [7], CODA [18], Roam [15] and Bayou [20] all use optimistic replication. The high level goals of an optimistic replication algorithm are as follows:

1. Provides access to data all the times,
2. Guarantees that the fetched value provides "*sufficiently fresh data*", and
3. Minimizes the divergence of values fetched from different replicas.

The extent to which these three goals can be achieved depends on various levels of data consistency guarantees supported by the application environment.

Optimistic replication strategy essentially guarantees the most loose form of consistency known as eventual consistency [20, 21]. Eventual consistency provides the guarantee that all the replicas eventually converge regardless of when and where the updates are applied to them. However, such a consistency guarantee is meaningless unless the reconciliation process is reasonably quick. In other words, the amount of divergence is not much. Typically, eventual consistency is associated with a consistency service that makes the best effort to disseminate updates quickly among the replica holders. This constraint demands for a specification of a well defined process of update reconciliation. The reconciliation process involves following four steps [16]:

1. Update propagation,
2. Update sequence ordering,
3. Conflict detection and resolution, and
4. Update commitment.

The propagation of update is concerned with the accumulation of the updates that were made when a site is isolated from the others. During this step, a site finds the earliest time when it can communicate with another site in order to exchange their updates. An exchange session is known as an anti-entropy session. This protocol of exchanging the updates leads to eventual convergences of replicas.

The sequencing of the updates determines a schedule in which the updates received by different sites should be applied on the replicas. The goals of this step are [16]:

1. The updates should be applied quickly to reduce the latency and to increase the concurrency.
2. The updates should be applied in a way that the users' intent in those updates is preserved.

These two goals can be realized by determining a serialization order for the updates that increases both concurrency and accessibility of the replicas. Among several feasible serialization orders, one should be a chosen. The question is which one to choose. Typically, the easiest way to preserve the intent of updates is to use timestamp ordering. However, this may affect concurrency. Possibly, certain pairs of operations may be mutually commutative, while certain other pairs of operations may be inverse of each other. So, the dependency rules can be exploited for opportunistic reordering of the updates and to increase concurrency.

In a distributed scenario, the users are aware of the conflicts. If the feedback on conflicts get disseminated early enough, the users voluntarily offer to resolve them. In most cases, hardly ever any attempt is made to write files concurrently [18]. Also sharing can be regulated to reduce the scope of conflicts [18]. For example, the UNIX semantics of file sharing seldom leads to update conflicts. However, conflicts in updates occur as the users do not know about the preferences of one another while accessing replicas in isolation. For instance, the application involving calendar reservation for a meeting slot may often lead to conflicts when several users put reservations for the same slot by accessing different replicas. In the booking of meeting slots, the users may be satisfied with a timestamp based automated resolution of conflicts. In fact, in many use-case scenarios, automated resolution of conflicts may improve the experience of the users if the system uniformly accepts one update and ignores the rest. In any case, non-conflicting updates should be accepted. To resolve conflicting updates, sometimes all older updates are discarded in favor of the latest update. The idea behind retaining the latest updates is that the older updates could be temporary modifications. However, a more acceptable reconciliation policy could be a semantic union of the older updates and the latest update. For instance, if two users create the same file with different names, then creation of both may be allowed. By attaching a version number all the updates may be retained. Conflict resolution in any way is a complex procedure, so many approaches are possible.

Committing the updates is a procedure for replica holding sites to agree on the sequence of updates that can be replayed at the sites. Once the commitment process is over the auxiliary data structure related to the execution of conflict resolution can be purged.

14.5.1 Pitfalls of Replication

Gray et al. [9] has pointed out that scaling up contributes to multi-fold increase in the complication of maintaining the consistency of replicas. There may be long waits and deadlocks. The reconciliation of updates poses a difficult problem specially when they are applied at any time, any where, and any way.

A replication algorithm that can manage a large number of copies is preferable in a mobile distributed environment. However, the possibilities of disconnected operation in such an environment lead to frequent execution of reconciliation process. As explained in Sect. 14.5 one copy serializability, i.e., globally consistent replication does not scale well [10].

There are two ways for synchronizing replicas, namely, (i) Eager, and (ii) Lazy. In an eager scheme, updates are applied at every replica as a part of the transactional process while in a lazy scheme updates are applied to one replica and then propagated to other asynchronously.

Apart from method of synchronization, regulating the updates also has an important bearing on the stability of replicas. There are also two ways in which updates can be regulated. One way is to designate only a single node (server) as the owner of the replicas and the copy held by it is the primary copy where the updates are applied. All other servers hold their respective replicas in read-only mode. If a server requires the updates it has to request them from the holder of the primary copy. Another way is, where the updates can come from any of the group of servers which hold the replica of database. In this mode of update, the probability of having conflicting updates is high. A summary of replica update strategies is provided in Table 14.1 [9].

The problem of replication is that every transaction carried out by a node as a part of its execution requires a transactional update at every remote node hosting a

Table 14.1 Summary of replica update strategies

Strategies for replication and propagation of updates		
Ownership	Propagation	
	Eager	Lazy
Master	N transaction One owner	One transaction One owner
Group	N transactions N owners	One transaction N owners
Two tier	$N + 1$ transaction, one owner tentative local updates, eager base updates	

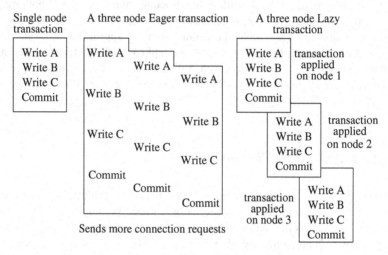

Fig. 14.1 A transaction performs N times as much job with N replicas [9]

replica. So if there are N replicas, a transaction performs its job N times over. Eager replication method requests more connections per transaction, as each update has to be transmitted immediately to all the nodes hosting the replica.

Lazy replication method performs the same amount of job as eager replication, but it performs transaction as a whole on a remote node during an anti-entropy session. Figure 14.1 sourced from Gray et al. [9] neatly illustrates the difference. Lazy replication method leads to large delays in reconciliation process, and defeats the very purpose of replication. A detailed analysis is available in [9]. It concludes some important scaling laws for both eager and lazy replication methods.

Rule 1 (Group deadlocks rate) *In eager group replication, the deadlocks grow at the rate of cubic power of number of replicas and fifth power of the number number of operations per transaction.*

Rule 2 (Group reconciliation rate) *In lazy group replication, the reconciliation grows at the rate cubic powers of the number of replicas and the number of operations per transaction.*

Rule 3 (Master deadlock rate) *In lazy group replication, the deadlocks grow at the rate square of the number of replicas and fifth power of the number of operations per transaction.*

The analysis made by Gray et al. [9] paints a very pessimistic picture about the effectiveness of replication. If system is kept small, *"the curse of scaling"* does not show up. But then in a small system, replication is not be needed at all. All requests for data can be met by a single server which hosts and owns the data. However, without replication no useful work can be done in a mobile environment. Disconnected mode of operation becomes impossible and mobility becomes too restrictive.

Ideally, following four properties are needed for replication to be effective.

- Scalability and Availability,
- Mobility,
- One copy serializability, and
- Convergence or stability.

Scalability and availability are inter-related. But the problem that needs to be addressed is the stability of replicas. With increase in scalability the replicas tend to diverge quickly. The problem gets aggravated with distribution of the replicas as the network latency starts to affect the reconciliation, and the deadlock rates also increase. So, avoiding instability is a major concern.

14.6 Replication Techniques

Replication techniques were developed for enhancing the performance of operations on databases. These techniques do not apply directly to mobile distributed computing scenarios. A few of these techniques are discussed in some details here in this section.

Replication techniques are used for increasing availability, fault-tolerance and enhanced performance in a distributed system. Several copies provide redundancy. If a copy is not available or corrupted, then the information can be extracted from any of the several other copies maintained by the system. Computation can resume by switching over to an available updated replica. Additionally, redundancy gives protections against data corruption and failures. When replicas are distributed, it provides enhanced performance and scalability. Though the replication techniques have a lot of merits, there are problems too. The primary issue is that of maintaining data consistency. Specially, in a distributed system, different copies are modified asynchronously. So, the replicas quickly diverge in unpredictable manner if client applications are allowed to update the copies indiscriminately. The responsibility of preserving consistency can either be handled by an applications or by the middleware (a replica management system). The consistency is maintained through well-defined software contracts between the processes that update/access the data and the storage where the replicas are physically stored. If the processes obey certain specified rules (contract) then consistency model guarantees that data store works correctly.

There are two extremities to approaches for the resolution of update conflicts in replicas. One extreme is a strictly rule based approach, wherein the conflicts automatically get resolved by the application of the rules. A rule based approach may either be application independent or application dependent. In first case, the conflicts are resolved always in favor of the update which bear the latest timestamp. In the second case, a set of conflict resolution rules are defined whereby depending on applications, the incoming updates from a certain set of processes/users have priority over others. The priority rules can be modeled in a way to create a level of hierarchy among the users/processes and the update tagged with a highest priority wins. The other extreme is to allow manual intervention wherein the conflicting updates are not directly updated, but logged separately for a human expert to examine them and resolve. CODA system [18] uses this approach.

There is a set of rule based approaches which depends neither on timestamp nor on process/user priorities. These approaches are based on the notion of relaxed data consistencies. The conflicts are resolved by application of the rules defined on contracts between the application and the data store. Bayou [20] uses this approach. The idea is that from one application to another an users may have a different view of resolving update conflicts. For example, if a user has updated a personal web-page accessing one replica, then these updates must be available when the same user accesses another replica at different point of time. From the point of view of an individual client and the nature of application the conflicts should be resolvable in a specific way.

14.7   Rule Based Reconciliation Approach

In a rule based replication techniques, since reconciliation is rule based, performance primarily depends on the implementation of synchronization according to the rules. One of the most natural approach to replication is two-tier replication where primary copy is held by only one computer which may either be a mobile or a stationary computer.

14.7.1   Two-Tier Replication

There are two types of computers: (i) mobile computers, and (ii) stationary computers. A mobile computer may be disconnected, it may store a replica of database, and may initiate a tentative transaction on some data item. Some mobile computers may perform the role of masters for a few data items. Stationary computers are always connected and they perform the role of masters for the most of the data items.

The replicated data items have two versions:

1. *Master version*: It is the most recent value of the data item received from the master node. It may be stale.
2. *Tentative version*: Local data items may be updated by a tentative transaction. Tentative value is defined as the recent most value due to a local update.

Two types of transactions are possible on a replica:

1. *Base transaction*: Applied only on the master. It produces new master data. At least one connected mobile computer and several stationary computer may be involved in a base transaction.
2. *Tentative transaction*: A tentative transaction is applied on local data available at a mobile computer. It produces a base transaction which should be executed at a time in future on a stationary computer.

Tentative transaction must involve the data items mastered either

- At the mobile computer originating the transaction, or
- At a stationary computer.

Tentative transactions should not be confused with *local transaction*. Local transactions cannot read or write tentative data which corresponds to shared data. Local transaction may be designed only to read/write local data. In other words, tentative transaction must satisfy the following *scope rule*:

Rule 4 (Scope rule) *A tentative transaction must either involve stationary computers, or a mobile computer which originated the tentative transaction.*

The base transactions generated by tentative transactions must pass an acceptance test as indicated below:

Rule 5 (Acceptance test) *The output must pass for a slightly different base transaction results.*

The rule for the acceptance test needs a little elaboration. Consider, for example, the booking of a slot in a meeting room needs to be finalized when booking requests are made from many mobile computers without explicit synchronization. The requests for the meeting slots remain tentative until base transactions generated by the tentative transactions have been performed. In this application, multiple bookings for the same time slot cannot be accepted. This implies only one of the tentative transactions requesting for the same time slot can commit is based on the acceptance test. Usually, the tentative transaction which reaches first gets committed.

In the two tier model, a transaction updating an object must lock the master. Once the master transaction has committed, the updates are disseminated to the replica holders. Usually, the updates are timestamped by the master to avoid stale updates. Thus, the key properties of two-tier replication system are:

- Mobile computers can perform tentative transactions.
- Base transactions are executed with one copy serializability.

- A transaction becomes persistence when the base transaction commits.
- Replicas at all the computers converge to the system state of the stationary computers.
- No reconciliation necessary, if all transactions commute.

14.7.2   Performance Analysis

The performance issue related to the cost in a mobile environment is the number of connection requests made by the mobile devices to the servers holding the replicas. So, the number of connection requests issued by a mobile computer is the key parameter for determining the cost of data accesses. If a data item x is accessed frequently but modified infrequently, placing a copy of x at the mobile computer becomes cost effective. On the other hand, if x is modified frequently but accessed infrequently, then keeping a copy locally at a mobile computer is expensive as local copy of x is most likely be stale. In order to keep the access cost down, the basic problem that needs to be addressed is to minimize the number of requests for connection by a mobile computer.

Possible allocation schemes for a copy of data item could be one copy or two copies. The allocation of a copy just to a mobile computer is impractical. If the mobile device is lost, stolen or damaged, the copy can never be recovered. So, in one copy allocation scheme, only copy of data item is allocated to a stationary computer. In the second scheme, both mobile and the stationary computers hold a copy each of the data item. In both the static allocation schemes, allocation method is unchanged over time. Whereas, in a dynamic allocation scheme, the allocation method changes with time. The three distinct methods of copy allocations [11] are:

1. One copy static allocation,
2. Two copy static allocation, and
3. A family of dynamic copy allocations based on sliding window.

One copy static allocation scheme is referred to as ST-1. Only copy of data item is allocated to a stationary computer. Whenever data is required to be accessed by a mobile computer then a connection request is made. Actual writes can only be executed at the stationary computer which holds the needed copy. Since the stationary computer holds the copy of a data item, no connection request is needed when the operation is a write. Assume that read and write requests are distributed according to Poisson distribution with mean λ_r and λ_w respectively. This means in each time unit, the expected number of read requests is λ_r. Similarly, the expected number of writes per time unit is λ_w. Let θ represent the value $\frac{\lambda_w}{\lambda_w + \lambda_r}$.

In ST-1 algorithm, in order to perform a read, a mobile computer has to request for connection. The number of connections per request is $1 - \theta$. But no connection is needed for performing a write, because a stationary computer holds data.

Two copy static allocation algorithm is referred to as ST-2. It allocates a copy at a mobile computer and another copy at a stationary computer. When operation is read, no connection request is necessary, as the mobile computer holds a copy. But when the mobile computer issues a write operation, the stationary computer should request a connection to the mobile computer in order to update the copy it holds. So, the expected number of connections per request is θ. The average expected cost (in terms of connection requests) of ST-1 and ST-2 algorithms are given in following expressions.

$$\text{AVG}_{ST-1} = \int_0^1 (1 - \theta)d\theta = \tfrac{1}{2}, \text{and}$$
$$\text{AVG}_{ST-2} = \int_0^1 \theta d\theta \quad = \tfrac{1}{2}$$

Sliding window based allocation algorithm is referred to as SW-k. It operates as follows. A bit vector V of size $k = 2n + 1$ is maintained for the current sequence of k read and write operations, where

$$V[i] = \begin{cases} 1, \text{ if the } i\text{th operation is a write,} \\ 0, \text{ otherwise.} \end{cases}$$

One of the computers, either the stationary or the mobile is in charge of maintaining V at any point of time. When the next operation is issued, the leftmost bit of V is dropped off. The vector is shifted by one position to the left, and a bit corresponding to the latest operation is appended to the right. We still have to answer the question: how is it decided which computer should be in charge for maintaining V? The responsibility switches between the mobile and the stationary computers depending on the difference in the number of reads and the number writes. If the reads have the majority over the writes then the responsibility of maintaining the bit vector V rests on the mobile computer. On the other hand, if the writes acquire majority over the reads, then the responsibility switches to the stationary computer. The switching of responsibility occurs when the majority is established. The rules governing this switching are summarized as follows.

1. If the number of reads is higher than the number of writes, and the mobile computer holds a copy then it just waits for the next operation.
2. If the number of reads is higher than the number of writes, and the mobile computer does not have the copy, then a copy is allocated to it.
3. If the number of writes is higher than the number of reads, and the stationary computer holds a copy then it just waits for the next operation.
4. If the number of writes is higher than the number of reads, and the stationary computer does not have the copy, then a copy is allocated to it.

Cases 1 and 3 are straightforward and need no explanation. So let us examine the two other cases.

In case 2, the last operation must be a read. This can be explained as follows. Until the last operation, stationary computer was holding the copy. This means that the shares of the reads and the writes operations before the last operation were equal. Due the to the last operation the majority tilts in favor of the number of reads. The stationary computer then responds to this read, and piggy backs a request to the mobile computer to save a local copy. This also serves as an indication for the delegation of the responsibility of maintaining V to the mobile computer. From this point onwards, the stationary computer propagates the write requests to mobile computer. Likewise, in case 4, the last operation must be a write. So, the mobile computer when responding to the request also piggy backs a request to the stationary computer to save a copy. This request then also serves as shifting of responsibility for maintaining V at the stationary computer.

Assuming α_k as the probability that the majority of k consecutive requests are reads, the number of connection per requests is given by:

$$\theta \alpha_k + (1 - \theta)(1 - \alpha_k)$$

The above expression, for any fixed k, has a value which is greater than $\min\{\theta, 1 - \theta\}$. Since $k = 2n + 1$, the value of α_k is equal to the number of writes in the sequence of k operations, and is less than or equal to n. Hence,

$$\alpha_k = \sum_{j=0}^{n} \binom{k}{j} \theta^j (1 - \theta)^{k-j}$$

Plugging-in value of α_k in the previous expression for the connection requests, and integrating it over all values of θ between [0, 1], we get the average expected value as $\frac{1}{4} + \frac{1}{4(k+2)}$. In summary, Huang et al. [11] concluded the following results concerning the average expected access cost comparisons of three algorithms:

1. The average expected cost of SW-k algorithm is lower than both the static algorithms ST-1 and ST-2.
2. The average expected cost of SW-k decreases as k increase and increases as k decreases.

14.7.3 Caching and Replication in CODA

CODA file system presents a practical example of rule based replica reconciliation method in file sharing. It has similarities with sharing of files over NFS. When a mobile user opens a file, a copy of whole file is cached locally in the client machine. If a mobile client's application has opened the file in write mode, then the server does not allow another mobile client to open the same file in write mode. However, if the first client opened the file in read mode then the second client's request can be honored irrespective of the fact whether the file open request is for read or write mode. This protocol reduces the chance for conflicts. The details of replication strategy have been discussed in Chap. 15. The discussion in this section is limited to the rules used in replica reconciliation process based on versioning.

If one of the clients, who holds the file in write mode, updates the file and then closes it. The file is subsequently transmitted back to the server. Since, CODA treats each session as a transaction, the other clients, each of which have the old copy of the file, continue with the stale copy. A client can specifically request for update notifications by registering a callback break promise with the server. The server transmits invalid notifications to those clients when updates are applied.

The sharing works fine when no partitioning in network occurs. It works even if some user u_1 has opened a file f in read mode ahead of another user u_2 who opened f in write mode. Since u_1's session is scheduled before u_2's session, there is no violation in transactional order. However, network partitions introduce a bit of complication in transactional semantics. Suppose two processes P_1 and P_2 before partitioning hold identical replicas of certain data objects. The file sharing following transactional semantics should implement one copy serializability. In other words, the result of independent executions of processes P_1 and P_2 should be same as that of their joint serial executions on the shared non-replicated data.

Let us first understand how CODA ensures serializability in a single partition. It associates different sessions to each file system call. A typical session is started with an open system call. Read and writes follow there after, and a session is terminated by a close system call. Certain meta data, namely, fid, access right, last modification time, file size, etc., are associated with each file. These meta data can be typically extracted from I-node of file and the data blocks. CODA explicitly identifies which meta data can be read or modified in each session type. There is a client side cache manager called Venus which fetches the data from an available server and acquires necessary locks at the start of a session. So, effectively, the sharing semantics follows the two phase locking protocol in fetching data. In other words the resulting schedule for read and writes in concurrent session in a single network partition becomes serializable.

When network partitions occur, CODA has to resolve conflicts across partitions. The conflict resolution is based on the version number. Each file is associated with a version number that indicates how many times the file has been updated since its creation. Along with relevant data, version number is also supplied to Venus when it fetches a file. When a file is transmitted back to a server by a client, it is tentatively accepted if no other process has the same file when the client and the server were disconnected. This type of conflict can determined by comparing the version number of the client and the server as follows. Let V_c denote the version numbers of file at the time it was fetched by the client. Let current version held by the server is V_s. Let N_u be number of updates made by the client. Then next update of the file from client can be accept if and only if

$$V_s + 1 = V_c + N_u.$$

The above equation implies that update from a client can be accepted if the updates lead to the next version of the file. Only a single client will be able achieve this.

Client side caching

Client side caching enables a mobile client to operate in disconnected mode. Cache coherency is maintained by the clients recording *callback promise* with the server. When a client updates its local cache and transmits to the server for the first time, then all the connected clients who have registered *callback promise* get an invalidation message *callback break*. As long as a connected client has an outstanding callback promise, then it can safely access locally cached file. Once callback break message for a file is received by a client, it can fetch updated copy of the file.

However, disconnected clients do not get this invalidation message. The situation arising out of lost callback can be handled by Venus probing the members of Available Volume Server Group (AVSG) periodically. However, there is still a problem if the preferred server (where Venus registered callback promise) itself is partitioned or unavailable. So, while probing AVSG members, the client also seeks CVV (CODA Version Vector). From CVV, the lost callbacks can be retrieved.

Server side replication

Replication is allowed on the server side. A unit of replication is called a volume. The servers which have copy of a volume called volume server group (VSG). Failures may lead to certain servers being unavailable. Furthermore, a client may not have access to all the servers. The Available Volume Server Group (AVSG) consists of those servers which a client can contact. For a disconnected client AVSG should be empty.

To maintain consistency, an update from a client is transmitted to all the members of AVSG through multiRPC. However, for reading a file, a client contacts only one server in AVSG. The protocol is essentially a variant of ROWA (Read One Write All). However this strategy based on ROWA may create problem when network partitions occur. This problem is handle using the version vector of a file. For example, if a file f is replicated on n servers, then each server S_i stores

$$CVV_i(f) = [v_1, v_2, \ldots, v_n],$$

where v_j denotes that server S_j is aware of version v_j. CVV can be viewed as a kind of a logical vector clock for the updates applied to a file. In the case when a partition occurs, AVSG for the clients become different. But, the version vectors provide information about which updates have been missed by which server. Therefore, the missed updates can be applied. Though comparison of CVVs can reveal conflicts, it cannot resolve conflicts in updates. This can happen when multiple clients update to the same file having acquired write locks from different partitions around the same time. It may happen only in the case, two or more clients simultaneously hold write access to a single file. CODA's policy of allowing conflicting updates relies on the fact that as file sharing uses UNIX like semantics. Therefore, update conflicts rarely occur in CODA. However, if conflicts in updates do occur then the would need manual intervention.

14.8 Relaxed Data Consistency Models

Many applications may not demand strict data consistency. Different data consistency models have been proposed and evaluated in the context of distributed systems. These models differ on the way the latest `write` is defined or determined. Consistency models can be classified into two broad classes, namely,

1. Data centric, and
2. Client centric.

Data centric models preserve system wide consistency guarantees. Every entity ensured of uniform data consistency across the system. In contrast, the focus of the client centric consistency model is to give consistent view of data to a specific client. It is appropriate for the mobile clients accessing data items over the network. For example, if a `read` issued by a mobile user fetches some value v at time t for a data item d, then any subsequent `read` issued for d by the same user must fetch v or a more recent value for d.

Figure 14.2 illustrates that the client centric consistency model focuses on preserving data access semantics for each individual client process. In other words, a client centric data consistency model ensures that the user of a client device get a consistent view from data store though the replicas may have some degree of inconsistencies. Since a mobile client may access different replicas of same data items as it moves, a client centric consistency model is most appropriate for a mobile environment. The origin of client centric consistency models can be traced to Bayou [20]. Bayou is a weakly consistent storage system designed and built at Xerox-PARC. It was intended for development of collaborative applications on a mobile distributed environment.

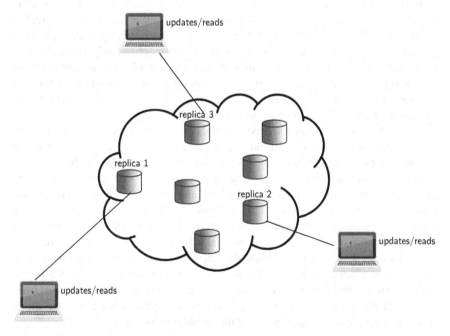

Fig. 14.2 Client centric consistency models

The Bayou designers came up client centric weakly consistent data model being motivated by two particular collaborative applications in mobile distributed environment. The first application is a simple meeting scheduler. It allows only one user to reserve a meeting room for a time slot on behalf of a group of people. The scheduler is not expected to allow the group to decided about a mutually agreeable meeting time as a full-fledged meeting scheduler would do. But like a calender manager, it only displays whether the room is free or reserved in some time slots of a day. It re-reads room schedule and refreshes the user's display in periodic intervals. Suppose the user, who have taken responsibilities of reserving the meeting room, is using a laptop that is partitioned from network. Then the replica R being used by the user cannot be synchronized with other replicas at the moment. If a reservation is confirmed based on the information available in replica R, then there is a chance that the schedule of the meeting may conflict with other reservation requests using different replicas. To account for the situation arising out possibility of using network partitioned replica, the user is asked to provide preferences from several possible time slots. The user's reservation is deemed tentative until the time network partition problem gets resolved. One of the tentative reservation is eventually confirmed. However, the group members using same replica can see tentative reservations immediately from replica R.

The second application that the Bayou designers considered is operating on a common bibliographic database. The users cooperatively manage the database adding entries to it. The users can access any of the several replicas. The operation performed is mainly appending to the database, though occasionally fixing of mistakes in earlier entries is also permissible. In this application, a user may be access a replica which cannot be synchronized on real-time. Entry keys are assigned tentatively when the entries are added to replicas. Since the users may independently assign different tentative keys to same entry, the system should detect duplicates and merges those content into single entry with a single key. In this application the users can even work in completely disconnected manner, a cached copy of the replica can be merged on reconnection in similar manner as suggested above.

While the above examples motivate collaborative applications in a mobile distributed environment, there is an important book keeping angle when replicas are updated by the mobile users. The mobile users are not expected to be careful to acquire locks when they get disconnected either voluntarily or involuntarily. In the case of involuntary disconnection, the locks cannot even be acquired. Furthermore, over slow and expensive communication links (e.g., GSM), keeping synchronized copies is not only costly but difficult as well. However, under the given scenarios, a mobile user may at least want a guarantee that if at time t_{old}, the value v is returned for a data item d, then at a future time t_{new} the value returned for d should either be equal to v or a newer value v_{new}. It is possible that a mobile user updates d from a replica at time t, and then goes reads it from another replica at a future point of time, say t_{new}. If the servers holding two replicas have not synchronized, then the server which is accessed at time t_{new} may provide an older value for d.

14.8.1 Requirements for Session Guarantees

Terry et al. [19] introduced session guarantees for the type of read and write operations mobile users are expected to perform on a weakly consistent replicated system as discussed above. A session is defined as an abstraction for the sequence of reads/writes issued by a mobile user. Since the session guarantees are to be provided per user basis, the consistency models are referred to as client centric consistency models. From a client's prospective, the needed guarantees are:

- **Read Your Writes**. A read operation on a data item always includes the results of the client's own writes which precede the read.
- **Monotonic Reads**. Successive reads return the results of a temporally non decreasing sequence of writes.
- **Writes Follow Reads**. Writes are propagated after the reads on which they depend. It means if a write depends on some read (e.g., an older value being updated), then the causal ordering of such reads and writes should be maintained. This is needed to preserve the traditional read and write orderings.
- **Monotonic Writes**. Writes should be propagated after propagation of logically preceding writes.

For convenience in description and illustration of consistency models, we use some notations described in Table 14.2.

Using the above notations, let us illustrate the meaning of the four client centric consistency models introduced above. In all illustrative figures below, the top half of a figure depicts a correct consistency preserving scenario, while the bottom half depicts the violation of the same consistency guarantee.

We begin with RYW guarantee. It is illustrated by Fig. 14.3. A mobile client performs a write on x on the replica R1, and then it performs a read on x

Table 14.2 Notations used in description of consistency models

Notation	Description
$x_i[t]$	Denotes the version of data item x at time t at the local replica R_i. Whenever the context is clear, reference to time is omitted.
$W(x_i)$	Denotes writing into x by a client on a replica R_i.
$R(x_i)$	Denotes reading x by a client from a replica R_i.
$WS(x_i)$	Denotes the value of x held at the replica R_i resulting from a sequence of writes performed on x at R_i till the time as indicated on the time axis.
$WS(x_i;x_j)$	Denotes that the operation $WS(x_i)$ was performed at R_i at a time t_1 is also performed on x at another replica R_j at a later point of time t_2.

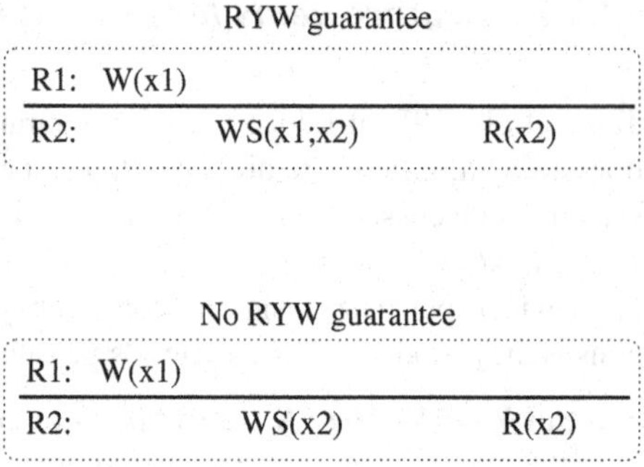

Fig. 14.3 RYW guarantee

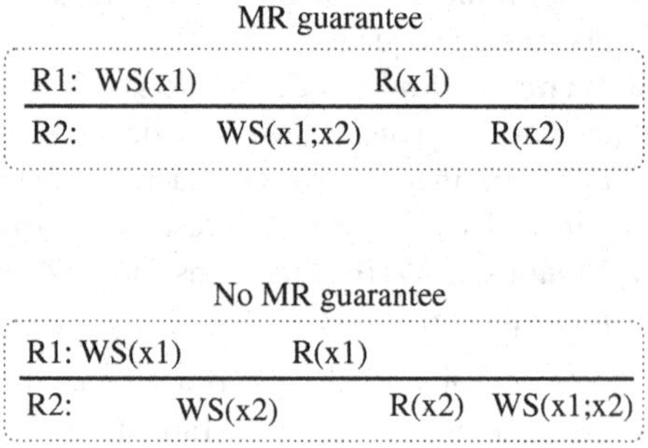

RYW guarantee

R1:	W(x1)		
R2:		WS(x1;x2)	R(x2)

No RYW guarantee

R1:	W(x1)		
R2:		WS(x2)	R(x2)

Fig. 14.4 MR guarantee

MR guarantee

R1:	WS(x1)		R(x1)	
R2:		WS(x1;x2)		R(x2)

No MR guarantee

R1:	WS(x1)		R(x1)	
R2:		WS(x2)		R(x2) WS(x1;x2)

at another replica R2 afterwards. According to RYW guarantee, the effects of the writing at R1 should get propagated to replica R2 by the time the client migrates and reconnects to replica R2. So, when the mobile user performs a read on x the effects of earlier writing at replica R1 is visible, and thus the session guarantee is ensured as indicated in the top half of Fig. 14.3. However, the bottom half of figure shows that write(x) performed at replica R1 is not propagated to R2 even after sometime. Consequently, the version of x stored by replica R2 does not include the effects earlier write to x on the replica R1 by the mobile client. Email is an example where RYW guarantee is useful. A user may read and delete mails from the *Inbox* folder from time to time. Suppose, the user takes a break from reading the mails, and logins to read mails after sometime, then old deleted mails should not reappear in *Inbox*. However, the deleted mails still may be displayed if the display is refreshed from a replica that is not synchronized with the previous replica from where the user accessed the mails earlier.

Monotonic Reads (MR) guarantee is needed for answering queries on databases. It ensures that read operations are performed over the copies that contain all writes whose effects were seen by previous reads within the same session. MR guarantee is illustrated by Fig. 14.4. The top half of the figure shows, a mobile user has performed a write(x) on replica R1, and subsequently performs a read(x) on replica R2. Following write(x), the update gets transmitted to R2. MR guarantee implies that the update made at R1 becomes visible when the user performs read(x) on

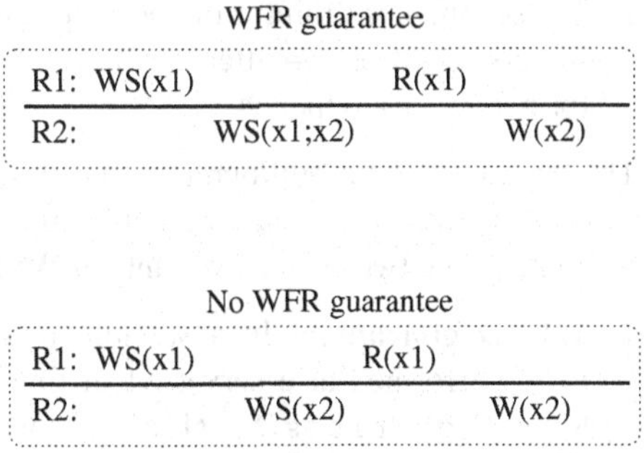

Fig. 14.5 WFR guarantee

WFR guarantee

R1: WS(x1)		R(x1)	
R2:	WS(x1;x2)		W(x2)

No WFR guarantee

R1: WS(x1)		R(x1)	
R2:	WS(x2)		W(x2)

R2. The bottom half of the figure shows that MR guarantee is violated if the earlier updates at R1 are not transmitted to R2 by the time the user performs read(x). The user gets only the local updates made to x. Once again consider the replicated email system. When a mail reader issues command to retrieve all new mails, it display a summary of all new mails. Following this if the user wants to get the contents of one of the mails, then another read command should be issued to retrieve the contents. The content may be held at a different server. With MR guarantee, it ensures that the message contents are retrieved from the server that holds the message contents. Without MR guarantee the read may be issued to a server that does not hold the contents and the user gets an incorrect notification that the mail does not exist.

Writes Follow Reads (WFR) guarantee respects the traditional write and read dependencies. It implies that the writes made during a session on each replica of a database are ordered after any write whose effects have been visible to all previous reads in the session. Figure 14.5 illustrates the meaning of WFR guarantee.

Suppose a mobile client performs a write(x) on a replica R2 after performing read(x) on replica R1. The value written on x will be either on the version of x which the user has read earlier or on a more recent version of x. As we can find in the bottom half of Fig. 14.5 when the mobile user performs a write, the version that gets updated is the local copy of x held on R2. The updates made at R1 has not been transmitted to R2. So the mobile user being earlier connected to R1 does not have WFR guarantee. The mobile user only sees the effect of local writes performed on a replica. WFR guarantee is required for the correct execution is updates on shared bibliographic database. The users contribute entries to build the database. A user may also fix the mistakes in the earlier entries. A natural order fixing of the mistakes is as follows. A user would first issue a read for an entry. If a mistake is discovered in the displayed entry, then the user may perform a write for updating appropriate fields of the entry. WFR guarantee ensures that the update in a replica by a user transmitted to all the replicas having the same entry. It essentially implies that WFR guarantee satisfies two constraints on a write operation, namely,

1. The first constraint ensures that a write properly follows another relevant write in global order.

2. The second constraint is on the propagation of the updates, it ensures that all the servers see a `write` after they have seen all the previous `writes` on which the former `write` depends.

The operations on a bibliographic database requires both the constraints to be satisfied. However, there may be applications which require relaxed forms of WFR guarantee. The two relaxed variants of WFR have been defined [19].

1. **WFRO guarantee**: In a session, if a `read` $r1$ precedes a `write` $w2$ and $r1$ is performed at a server $S1$ at time $t1$ then for a `write` $w1$ belonging to `RelevantWrites`$(S1, t1, r1)$, $w1$ must precede $w2$, where `RelevantWrites` set refers to those `writes` whose effects were seen by performing $r1$.
2. **WFRP guarantee**: If $r1$ precedes $w2$ in a session, and $r1$ be performed at a server $S1$ at time $t1$ then for any server $S2$, if $w2$ has been performed on the replica at $S2$ then for any $w1$ belonging to `RelevantWrites`$(S1, t1, r1)$, the effects of $w1$ will also be in the replica at $S2$.

WFRO guarantee may suffice for update of shared bibliographic database in place of WFR. Suppose, a user finds some fields of a bibliographic entry are incorrect. The user may modify all the incorrect fields of the entry and executes a write for the full entry. Then, it is acceptable for the user to see only the effects of the newest `write`. The `writes` preceding the newest `write` are not important. WFRP guarantee can be used in the case of blog postings and the posting of comments on blogs in a weakly consistent replicated bulletin board. It ensures that the users see the comments on a blog only after the blog post itself has completed. In this case, the relevant `writes` are the blog description. However, if the readers are only interested reading blogs, then WFRP guarantee is not needed.

Monotonic Write guarantee implies that a `write` in a session must follow the previous `writes`. More precisely, if $w1$ precedes $w2$ in a session, then if $w2$ has been already performed on a replica at any server, then $w1$ would also be in the replica and the order of `writes` is $w1 < w2$. Figure 14.6 illustrates the monotonic write guarantee. The figure is self explanatory. MW guarantee is relevant for the operations of a text editor on replica files. It ensures that if a user saves a version of a file and

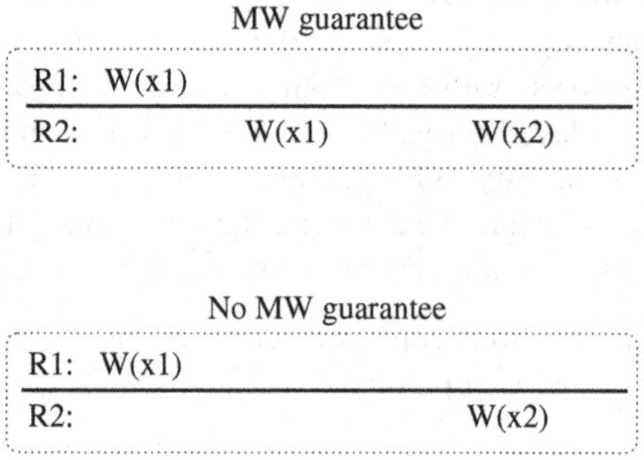

Fig. 14.6 MW guarantee

MW guarantee

R1:	W(x1)		
R2:		W(x1)	W(x2)

No MW guarantee

R1:	W(x1)	
R2:		W(x2)

subsequently save another version of the same file, then the latest version replaces the previous version at all replicas. It ensures that edits related to the previous version is not wrongly applied over the edits of the later version.

14.8.2 Implementation Related Issues

Bayou [19] while implementing weakly consistent replicated storage system identified three major problems for ensuring session guarantees, namely,

1. Bandwidth between the clients and the servers.
2. Storage space available at the clients and the servers.
3. The cost of computation.

From the server side, the implementation requires that every `write` is assigned a write identifier WID by the server. The server must be willing to share

- WID of a new `write`,
- WIDs of relevant `writes` for a `read`, as well as
- WIDs of all `writes` performed on its replica.

Ensuring session guarantees is the responsibility of the session manager which is a part of the client stub communicating with the servers. The session manager serializes the `reads` and `writes` in the appropriate order, and provides the required guarantees. It keeps track of two different set of WIDs.

1. **ReadSet**: WIDs for the `writes` that are relevant to the session `reads`.
2. **WriteSet**: WIDs for the `writes` performed in a session.

Following steps are performed in order to provide RYW guarantee.

- Whenever a `write` is accepted at the server replica, the WID assigned to the `write` is added to WriteSet.
- Before performing a `read` at the server, the session manager checks if its WriteSet is a subset of all updates made to the replica until that time.

The check stated above can be performed either at the client or at the server. In case the check is performed at the client, the server should be pass on the WIDs for all the `writes`. Conversely, the session manager can pass on the WriteSet to the server for carrying out the check.

For Monotonic Read (MR) guarantee, the client's session manager checks that ReadSet is a subset of the replica held at the server being contacted for performing the `read`. Furthermore, after performing a `read` r at the server S at time t, WIDs of each `write` belonging to RelevantWrites(S, t, r) are added to the session's ReadSet. That apart, whatever updates the client has seen earlier, the current `read` r may get the latest updates of the replica maintained at S. These latest updates are results of some `writes` not known to the client. So, including

`RelevantWrites` to the client ReadSet is necessary to maintaining MR guarantee in subsequent time domain. However, the client has to rely on the server for the computation of `RelevantWrites` set.

The implementation of Writes Follow Reads and Monotonic Writes session guarantees require additional support from the server side. It requires servers to obey the following two additional constraints [19].

1. When server accepts a new `write` $w2$ at time t, it should ensure that the write order $w1 < w2$ is true for any `write` $w1$ whose effects are already stored before time t.
2. Anti-entropy or synchronization of replicas is performed with the constraint that if $w2$ is propagated from a server $S1$ to another server $S2$, then for any $w1$ already in replica of $S1$ with write order $w1 < w2$ is also propagated to $S2$.

The above constraints are restrictive, but implementable. By enforcing the above constraints at the server side, the responsibility of maintaining session guarantee could be easily transferred to the client side session manager. Without these constraints, providing session guarantee would require the servers to keep track of each client's ReadSet and WriteSet. This goes against the principle of scaling which is extremely important in a mobile environment. In practice, to respect the write order constraint, it suffices either to simply transfer the whole replica from one server to other, or to compute write order by comparing the timestamps of the `writes`.

With the underlying assumptions of server support for respecting write orders, the WFR guarantee is provided as follows. As with monotonic read guarantee, the ReadSet is expanded by including the `RelevantWrites` each time a `read` is performed by a mobile client. Then before a `write` on the server S at time t, the session manager at the client checks if the ReadSet is a subset of S's replica at time t.

Two additional steps are needed for providing Monotonic Writes (MW) guarantee, namely,

1. For accepting any `write` at time t, the server must include session's WriteSet.
2. Whenever a `write` is accepted by the server, its assigned WID is added to session's WriteSet.

The summary of fundamental operations required in order to provide the four guarantees is provided in Table 14.3.

Table 14.3 Summary of operations for consistency guarantees

Guarantees	Session state updated on	Session state checked on
Read your writes	Write	Read
Monotonic reads	Read	Read
Writes follow reads	Read	Write
Monotonic writes	Write	Write

The servers holding the replicas can synchronize via anti-entropy process for writes pairwise. However, no guarantee on the time bound for the update propagation delay can be given, since network connectivity and latency dominate the propagation delays. Yet, as the motivating applications indicate, the merge procedures are deterministic and the writes are performed in some well defined order. The ordering of writes maintained by logical clocks of the servers which are more or less synchronized by the real-time clock. However, to preserve causal ordering, a server's clock is advanced when it receives writes during anti-entropy session. So, a server will be able to totally order the writes using <timestamp, server ID> pair. Consequently, the server will always be able to resolve same conflict in the same manner. Although the execution history of individual replica server could vary, their combined execution would be equivalent to some global write order. For example, the variation may happen if it is known that writes are commutative when they are performed in some order.

References

1. R.H. Arpaci-Dusseau, A.C. Arpaci-Dusseau, *The Andrew File System* (Arpaci-Dusseau Books, LLC, 2015)
2. D. Barbara, H. Garcia-Molina, Replicated data management in mobile environment: anything new under sun, *Proceedings of IFIP Conference on Applications in Parallel and Distributed Computing* (Venezuela, April 1994), pp. 237–246
3. D. Barbara, T. Imielinski, Sleepers and workaholics: caching strategies in mobile environments. ACM Sigmod Rec. **23**(2), 1–12 (2000)
4. D. Barbará, R.J. Lipton, A class of randomized strategies for low-cost comparison of file copies. IEEE Trans. Parallel Distrib. Syst. **2**(2), 160–170 (1991)
5. P.A. Bernstein, N. Goodman, Serializability theory for replicated databases. J. Comput. Syst. Sci. **31**(3), 355–374 (1985)
6. P. Cao, E.W. Felten, A.R. Karlin, K. Li, A study of integrated prefetching and caching strategies. SIGMETRICS Perform. Eval. Rev. **23**(1), 188–197 (1995)
7. S. Collin, *A Complete Guide to Lotus Notes 4.5* (Digital Equipment Corporation, Acton, MA, USA, 1997)
8. W. Fuchs, K. Wu, J. Abraham, Low-cost comparison and diagnosis of large remotely located files, *The Fifth Symposium on Reliability of Distributed Systems* (1986), pp. 67–73
9. J. Gray, P. Holland, P. Neil, D. Shasha, The dangers of replication and a solution. ACM SIGMOD Rec. **25**(2) (1996)
10. J. Gray, A. Reuter, *Transaction Processing: Concepts and Techniques* (Morgan Kaufmann, San Francisco, CA, 1993)
11. Y. Huang, P. Sistla, O. Wolfson, Data replication for mobile computers. SIGMOD Rec. **23**(2), 13–24 (1994)
12. T. Madej, An application of group testing to the file comparison problem, *9th International Conference on Distributed Computing Systems* (1989), pp. 237–243
13. B. Pawlowski, D. Noveck, D. Robinson, R. Thurlow, The NFS Version 4 Protocol, *The 2nd International System Administration and Networking Conference (SANE 2000)* (2000)
14. S. Rangarajan, D. Fussell, Rectifying corrupted files in distributed file systems, *11th International Conference on Distributed Computing Systems* (1991), pp. 446–453
15. D. Ratner, P. Reiher, G.J. Popek, Roam: A Scalable Replication System for Mobile Computing, *The Tenth International Workshop on Database and Expert Systems Applications* (September 1999), pp. 96–104

16. Y. Saito, M. Shapiro, Optimistic replication. ACM Comput. Surv. **37**(1), 42–81 (2005)
17. M. Satyanarayan, J.J. Kistler, P. Kumar, E.H.S.M.E. Okasaki, D.C. Steere, Coda: A highly available file system for a distributed workstation environment. IEEE Trans. Comput. **39**(4), 447–459 (1990)
18. M. Satynarayanan, The evolution of CODA. ACM Trans. Comput. Syst. **20**(2), 85–124 (2002)
19. D.B. Terry, A.J. Demers, K. Petersen, M. Spreitzer, M. Theimer, B.W. Welch, Session guarantees for weakly consistent replicated data, *The Third International Conference on Parallel and Distributed Information Systems, PDIS '94* (1994), pp. 140–149
20. D.B. Terry, M.M. Theimer, K. Petersen, A.J. Demers, M.J. Spreitzer, C.H. Hauser, Managing Update Conflicts in Bayou, A Weakly Connected Replicated Storage System, *ACM Symposium on Operating Systems Principles (SOSP)* (1995), pp. 172–182
21. W. Vogels, Eventually consistent. Commun. ACM **52**(1), 40–44 (2009)

Chapter 15
Storage Systems for Mobile Environment

15.1 Introduction

Many mobile distributed applications rely on sharing and accessing information from common data repositories. For example, mobile users may share their appointment calendars, access bibliographic databases, and exchange emails. Mobile grid applications [1, 2] have become reality. Though mobile terminals are mainly interfaces for accessing fixed grid services, possibilities exists where mobile terminals may also actively become a part of a grid system, and provide aggrigated computational resources. MPI implementations for android system have been developed [3]. Cluster computing using smart phone is also a reality [4]. The mobile clients should have ability to read and write shared data for the execution of these applications.

Different mechanisms have been explored to facilitate sharing data in mobile environment, namely,

1. Replicated storage system,
2. Distributed objects,
3. File system, and
4. A stacked up filtering layer on the top of VFS.

Each mechanism is implemented at a different level of software stack, and each has some advantages over the others.

For many of the non-real time collaborative applications, such as calendar, email, program development, etc., strong consistency is not important. Replicated storage systems offering different levels of weak data consistency guarantees have been proposed for building such applications. Bayou [5] built by researchers at Xerox Park provides sharing through a replicated, weakly consistent storage system. Bayou storage system has been discussed in Chap. 14.

Distributed object based sharing of data is realized through a tools known as Rover toolkit [6]. Rover is meant for building mobility aware applications. It relies on two mutually supporting mechanisms, namely, Relocatable Dynamic Objects (RDOs) and Queued Remote Procedure Call (QRPC). Sharing of data is in the form of units

© Springer Nature Singapore Pte Ltd. 2017
R.K. Ghosh, *Wireless Networking and Mobile Data Management*,
DOI 10.1007/978-981-10-3941-6_15

of RDOs. RDOs define a distributed object abstraction. Each RDO has a well-defined interface which can hop from one device to another. On the other other hand, QRPC supports non-blocking RPC, hence, allows disconnected operation.

A file system that can support location-transparent, replication independent operations on remote data is the most desirable solution for providing full range of data services to applications running on mobile devices. However, remote access model based on RPC is not suitable for the applications running on mobile devices. As we have seen in the previous chapter, resource poor, low power devices communicating over wireless networks work best with caching and remote synching model. It requires two basic operations, namely, download and upload. A read would transfer an entire file to a local device. Once read becomes successful, other operations on that file can be supported by the local copy. A store operation would cause the file to be uploaded to its remote location. CODA (COnstant Data Availability) [7] was specifically designed to support disconnected mode of operation where a client can access critical data from a cached copy during intermittent remote failures due to network outages. It is a full-fledged file system based on AFS2 [8–10].

InterMezzo File System (IMFS) [11] is not a full fledged file system. It is designed as a stacked up filtering layer in between Virtual File System [12] and one of the native files system such as ext3 [13], ReiserFS [14], JFS [15], or XFS [16]. InterMezzo simplifies but retains most of the protocols of CODA file system.

15.2   Disconnected Mode of Operation

In a fixed network a disconnection is treated as a failure. However, this assumption is impractical for a Mobile Distributed System (MDS). Because, hosts in an MDS often experience disconnection as well as intermittent weak connections. The problem is compounded further by resource poorness of mobile terminals. So, treating a disconnection as a failure may mean a computation can never progress.

Disconnections can be handled either by avoidance or by accommodation [17]. For example, a client may avoid disconnection if both the hardware and infrastructure are 100% reliable and there is no limitations on the resources. However, these assumptions are not only impractical but also unrealizable. One practical solution for avoidance of disconnection would be to ensure that a client is always "logically connected" [17] to services through one of the many replicated servers. Unfortunately, the solution by server replications introduces data consistency problem. Furthermore, replication also relies on the fundamentally unrealizable assumption that the network connectivity is highly reliable. So, building resilience (accommodation) in the system seems to be the most ideal solution. The technique is to ensure that a client continues even when it loses network connectivity. Replication also helps in raising the level of resilience when a client changes its point of attachment. But, it cannot provide a solution without an extra level of autonomy in operation of a disconnected client. The autonomy is possible if the client is able to pre-store its requirements for data before an anticipated disconnection.

Mostly, disconnections are elective in nature, because it occurs with the movement of either the terminal, or the user or the both. Under these situations, a mobile terminal can be prepared before the disconnection actually takes place. Similarly, when a mobile enters the state of weak connection from a strong connection or vice versa, its transitions can be handled by a weak disconnection protocol.

Preserving data consistency is the major hurdle in the management of disconnection. In disconnected mode, a client application may continue execution in stand-alone mode. The execution is made possible by prefetching (known as hoarding) requisite critical data and pre-storing the same locally before an impending disconnection. But the quality of data consistency that can be maintained with a strong connection progressively deteriorates in disconnected mode as modifications and updates get executed over the cached data. With program control it is possible to exercise control over the divergence of the cached copy (called a quasi copy) from the corresponding master copy. However, the degree of allowable divergence depends on an application's level of tolerance in data consistency. For example, in a portfolio management of stocks, it may be perfectly alright to work with a quasi copy dated by 24 h. The problem of cache consistency and its implications on applications is best understood by case studies. Although the quality requirements for maintaining data consistency varies with applications, the issues typical to maintenance of data consistency are the same across the applications. We, therefore, focus on data consistency issues through operations on the shared objects in a MDS environment. The motivation of our study is two-fold, namely to understand (i) how data consistency is handled in disconnected mode, and (ii) how storage of data is handled in MDS environments.

15.3 Rover Toolkit

Rover toolkit [6] is a collection of software tools for a distributed object development environment. Unlike Bayou or CODA, it cannot be classified as a storage scheme. Rover toolkit provides a distributed object system based computing on a client/server environment for applications. It employs client caching and optimistic concurrency control strategy for supporting roving application on resource poor mobile clients.

It works on the idea of exporting objects (code + data) between a client and a server. The roving capability an application is realized through a combination of two supporting mechanisms: (i) Relocatable Dynamic Objects (RDO), and (ii) Queued Remote Procedure Calls (QRPC). The interface of an RDO can be dynamically loaded into a client from a server or vice versa. The approach is aimed at reducing client-server communication requirements. In a sense RDO is an extreme case of a mobile agent with just one hop self-shifting capability. QRPC, on the other hand, permits applications running on a disconnected client to continue making non-blocking RPC, where the requests and the responses get exchanged upon reconnection.

Clients use Rover library interface to import RDOs and export the log of operations that modify the RDOs. An RDO constitutes a fundamental unit of data and code shipment between a client and a server. A rover application imports an RDO from the server into its address space, invokes methods on the encapsulated data as permitted. Finally, the application exports the log of RDO operations back to a server. An RDO may consist of just a single item of data such as a calender data, or it may be as complex as a module that forms encapsulated part of an application. Therefore, to immune a client from malicious or unintentional server attacks, RDOs must be executed in a controlled environment.

A client application operates directly on the cached RDOs, whereas the server-side application replays the operations on its copy of RDO using the exported log. Therefore, server-side application has the responsibilities to detect and resolve the conflicts. The conflict resolution is notified to the clients by the server. All clients initiated non-blocking RPC requests which cannot be satisfied during disconnected mode of operation are logged into the stable storage at the client. A network scheduler at the client side drains out QRPC log containing the RPC requests which must be performed at the server. The primary task of the network scheduler is to open and close network connection and also interact with OS to initiate and terminate connection-based transport links or to power up/down the wireless transmitters.

Like Bayou, a server can either be a static host or a mobile host. But no update operation can be committed unless accepted by a server. Since the server's copy of an object stores the latest value, a client can get the latest value only by connecting to an appropriate server. It means the servers must reside on well connected hosts or preferably static hosts.

Rover toolkit expects a mobile-aware application to define a set of RDOs for data types to be operated on by it and transported between the server and the client. After defining RDOs, the application must be partitioned into two, one has to run on the client and the other on the server. All tasks including object updates, conflict detection, avoidance, and resolution must have to be specified by the application in its server partition. After the application has been developed as mentioned, it must be composed with Rover toolkit. Then the application acquires following four capabilities:

1. It can interact with the runtime system to import objects into the client,
2. It can invoke methods on the imported objects,
3. It can export the log of method invocations to the server, and
4. It can reconcile the client copies objects with those at the server.

15.3.1 Design of Rover Toolkit

The control flow within Rover Toolkit and basic design components are shown in Fig. 15.1. The Rover design issues discussed here focuses on RDOs, QRPC, communication scheduling and preserving consistency. But other issues like relocation of computation, object caching and maintenance of consistency are also discussed.

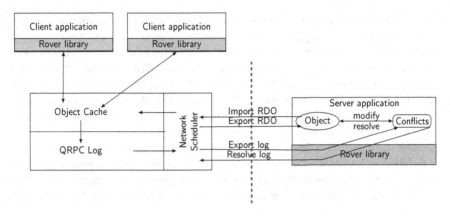

Fig. 15.1 Interaction of application and the components of Rover toolkit

15.3.1.1 RDO and QRPC

A RDO consists of four components

1. Mobile code,
2. Encapsulated data,
3. An interface, and
4. Ability to make outcalls to other RDOs.

A RDO has methods for marshaling and unmarshalling itself. Therefore, it can relocate itself from one machine to another and be stored in the client's cache. A RDO can invoke methods of another RDO.

Every RDO is tied to a home server storing the primary copy of the RDO. A client uses Rover library functions to import secondary copies into its local cache. After a client finished operating with RDOs in a desired way, it again uses Rover library functions to export the operation logs for the mutating methods back to the servers. All data modified by an application are stored within the RDOs. When Rover modifies a locally cached RDO at a client, the corresponding cached copy is marked as *tentative*. Only when the mutating operations are applied to primary copy an RDO is marked as *committed*. Pending commit, the clients can continue to use cached RDOs marked as *tentative*. Optionally, the clients can either poll or register a callback to update locally cached copies of RDOs.

Toolkit allows complex RDOs for creating threads of control when they are imported. For safe execution of RDOs, the toolkit provides authentication and a controlled execution environment. But it does not rule out the possibilities of malicious RDOs compromising the security or integrity of data and execution. In general the security and the safety issues have not been emphasized in the implementation prototype. But it is easy to realize that most of the security and integrity issues are similar in nature as may be found in case of mobile agent implementations.

The idea of RDO is also synonymous to code migration in distributed computing in many ways. It allows application to control the location of the execution of code. In other words, Rover permits applications to move data and/or computation from client to server and vice versa by moving appropriate RDOs on the network. The relocation of computation can be quite useful for shipping code to the source of data, which can filter out huge data to deliver only a small amount of results to the consumer. It reduces the pressure on low bandwidth data transmission link that is typical to wireless communication. But, the success of the approach relys on the fact that the application developers have semantic knowledge which can be useful in tightly coupling data with code and relocate the computation to advantage when network communication is either unreliable or unavailable. For example, RDOs can include situation-specific or application-tailored compression and decompression techniques.

A QRPC may refer to a RDO, a request for a RDO, or any application specific data. QRPC may be used for following tasks:

1. Fetching RDOs in background, and
2. Propagation of updates or resolution between the client and the server.

A QRPC request is logged locally in the persistent storage at the client. The application may register a callback, which will be invoked in case a requested QRPC reports completion. Alternatively, an application can poll the state of the QRPC or block for arrival of critical data. But blocking is not desirable when the client is operation in disconnected mode. QRPC supports split-phase communication model, wherein the uplink and the downlink communication channels may be different. If a client gets disconnected after submitting a QRPC request, the server periodically attempts to contact the mobile host for delivering the reply. The reply may be delivered through a different channel than the channel through which the request was received. Thus, it is possible for the client to close the communication channel after sending the request and tune in at appropriate time to receive the response.

15.3.1.2   Communication Scheduling

The network scheduler is responsible for handling of communication between the client and the server. It allows an application to set priorities in delivery of QRPCs in non-FIFO order. Reordering according to application-specific priorities may be needed for satisfying consistency requirements. The user may choose to send critical update requests superseding certain queued RPCs, specially when the communication is intermittent or expensive. Multiple QRPCs destined for the same server may be batched together to amortise the overheads over a number of RPCs. The network scheduler is responsible for handling the split-phase communication as described earlier.

15.3.1.3 Object Caching

When a mobile client gets connected to the network, Rover prefetches all the useful RDOs to its cache. But the decision to prefetch is left to the application. A CODA like interface for the user specified hoard profiles could have been easily provided for indicating the objects to be prefetched. But Rover implementers shifted the prefetch decision to the applications. The reason behind this decision is explained as follows. By design, a Rover applications is mobile-aware. So, an application, during its execution, can easily handle the preparation of its prioritized prefetch list. The construction of the prefetch list can be guided according to a user's interactions with the application. For example, a Rover email browser can generate prefetch operations for user's inbox for and all recently received messages, as well as some folders which user selects regularly. Rover toolkit lets a client to access the cache and permits certain actions like

1. Flushing RDOs from cache,
2. Verifying whether RDOs are up-to-date or not,
3. Checking consistency information of an RDO.

On the server side following actions are permitted.

1. Automatic validation of RDOs,
2. Checking client cache tags of RDOs for managing consistency of cache.

Cache tags of RDOs at a client are also used for a number of other purposes, such as,

- Verifying an RDO before application uses it,
- Temporary leasing of RDO to another client,
- Registering callbacks for notification of stale RDOs from the server,
- Indicating read-only type of RDOs.

15.3.1.4 Consistency

Application designers are required to enforce consistency scheme suitable to a specific application. But considering our discussion on CODA and Bayou it is clear that only a limited number of schemes are found to be appropriate for mobile applications. In fact, Bayou and CODA both use optimistic concurrency control schemes. Rover also provides substantial support for maintenance of primary copy and tentative update with optimistic concurrency control strategy. As stated earlier, like Bayou and CODA, Rover also supports

- Logging of operations on RDOs
- Replay of logged operation on the server side
- Roll back on the client side in case of conflicts
- Manipulation of log for optimizing QRPC requests, and
- Maintaining RDO consistency vectors.

All Rover applications built so far, use only primary-copy optimistic replica control strategies.

15.4   Mobile Distributed File Systems

A Distributed File System (DFS) allows location-transparent accesses to shared files. However, in a Mobile Distributed System (MDS), apart from location transparent access, the file system must also have capabilities to handle:

- A range of network disconnections,
- Scalability,
- Inconsistency of data, and
- Conflicting updates by clients,

For operations on files at a client, handling disconnection is absolutely essential. There are two known inter-related techniques for disconnected operation on shared data, namely,

1. Replication of data (cloning, copying and caching), and
2. Pre-storing of data (hoarding/pre-fetching) in anticipation of future use.

Caching enhances performance while replication makes the file system highly available. However, downside of uncontrolled replication is difficulty in maintaining consistency in data. Much of the work in implementation of mobile transparent access to shared files, has been in guaranteeing consistencies of the replicas held by the clients and the servers.

In the following two sections, we discuss about two different approaches for design of file systems for mobile distributed environment found in literature [9, 11]. InterMezzo is a lightweight approach that defines a stacked up layer between VFS a native file system. CODA, on the other hand, is a full AFS2 based file system designed to handle a range network outages. The implementation of interMezzo is guided by CODA. It retains most of the file sharing semantics of CODA, but greatly simplifies the involved protocols.

15.5   CODA

CODA project [7, 9, 18–20] was conceived and implemented by M. Satyanarayanan and his group at CMU, and the work began around late 80's. The major motivation in CODA file system was to build a DFS that is resilient to frequent network outages. Network technology around 1980s was not as developed as it is today. An initial prototype was made to carry out experiments in executing reads/writes on a shared file system at disconnected clients then reintegrating the updates on the file copies held at the servers. The idea of putting a client-side cache manager combined with the concept of hoarding turned out to be extremely well-suited for mobile computing environment.

15.5.1 Overview of CODA

CODA provides a common name space for all the files that the clients share. Typically CODA running on a client shows a file system of type `coda` mounted under `/coda`. In contrast NFS file systems are available on per server basis with additional requirement that the file system should be explicitly exported to a client. However, for accessing a file under CODA file system, a client simply need to just know the mount point of `coda`. CODA system running in a client fetches the required files from the appropriate servers and make these available to the client. A full path name for a file in CODA may span over several mount points across many servers. Each mount point would correspond to a partial subtree of the file system in a CODA server. Files are grouped into collections known as volumes at CODA server end. Usually, the files of a volume are associated with a single user. A mount point at a client's end is the place holder where a server volume can be mounted. Figure 15.2 shows that a CODA file system at a client is composed of files from two servers. On the server side, a volume can be viewed as a disk partition in Linux and corresponds to a partial subtree of the file system. So, the CODA name space at a client can be constructed by mounting the volumes on the mount points. A leaf node of a volume may be the root of another volume. Thus, an entire name space may span across different volumes located in one or different servers.

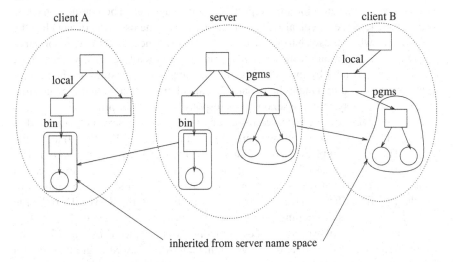

Fig. 15.2 CODA name space in clients

Fig. 15.3 Remote access of
shared files system

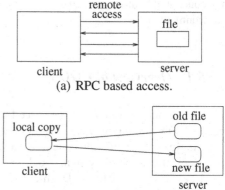

(a) RPC based access.

(b) Upload/download access.

There are two ways to operate on files in shared file system by the contending clients. In the approach followed by NFS, the copy of the file is held at the server. The clients operate on files through RPC as indicated by Fig. 15.3a. Obviously, this approach is not suitable for scaling. The alternative approach, illustrated by Fig. 15.3b, shows that a client downloads a local copy and operates on the local copy. The old copy is held at the server till the time the client commits the updates by uploading the new file.

RPC is basically a request-response based mechanism. The latency of response may depend on several factors including load at the server for processing requests, network latency or failures. So, the first approach does not scale up. CODA uses the second approach. The problem with this approach is that many clients which have copies of the same file may report conflicting updates. The conflicts must be resolved at the server. Typically, in a Unix file system one user (the owner) has the write access while those sharing have read accesses. Since, CODA relies on Unix semantics for operation on files, usually write-write type of conflicts do not arise. If write access is held by many clients, then the applications using the shared files should be designed to handle the updates by any client. When a client updates to a file in CODA file system, the server takes responsibilities to inform its clients.

A file in CODA can be accessed from one of the many file servers which holds a copy. A file handle consists of two parts: Replication Volume ID (RVID) and a file handle. The volume replication database indexed by RVID provides the Volume IDs (VIDs) in which replicas of the required file is available. A query to volume location database with VIDs provides location of file servers which stores the replicas of the file. File IDentifier (FID) is constructed by prepending the Server ID to the file handle. The process of fetching file as described above is illustrated by Fig. 15.4.

The interactions of various CODA components are depicted by Fig. 15.5. The access to the objects in a shared file system in CODA is allowed in granularity of a file. Suppose a user wants to display the contents of a file in /coda directory, e.g., by issuing a cat. The user may or may not be connected to network. The cat command

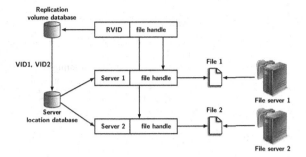

Fig. 15.4 Fetching file in CODA

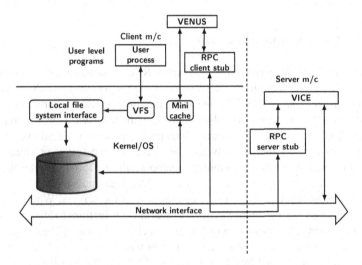

Fig. 15.5 Interaction of CODA components

generates a sequence of system calls like open, read and then write on display, for the required files. All the system calls are executed in *kernel* mode. The kernel at a client requires the services of the Virtual File System (VFS) to open a file before it can service cat. VFS recognizes that the file argument to be a CODA resource and informs the kernel module for handling CODA file system. CODA module works basically as an in-kernel mini-cache. It keeps a cache of recently answered requests for CODA files from VFS. If the file is locally available as a container file under the cache area within the local CODA file system, then VFS can service the call. If the file is not available locally, the mini-cache passes the request for the CODA file to a user level program called *Venus* running at the client. Venus checks the local disk, and in the case of a cache miss, contacts the server to locate the file. When the file has been located it responds to kernel (mini-cache) which in turn services the request of the client program. If the client is operating in disconnected mode, when cache miss occurs then Venus generates an error.

Fig. 15.6 Side effect of
CODA's RPC2

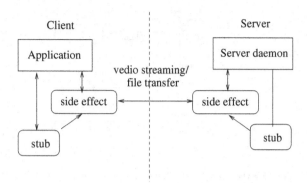

15.5.1.1 Communication in CODA

CODA uses RPC2 which is a reliable variant of RPC with side-effects, and supports multiple RPCs in parallel. Side effects provide hooks for pre and post RPC processing. The hooks are not part of RPC2 but are active parameters. RPC-2 starts a new thread for each request. The server periodically keeps a client informed that its request is being serviced. As side effects, application specific protocols are allowed perform asynchronous transfer of files between the client and the server or streaming of video to the client. RPC2 also has multicast support. Figure 15.6 illustrates the RPC2 mechanism and communication between a CODA server and a client.

RPC2 allows the clients to register callbacks with the servers. When a callback promise is broken, the server multicasts invalidation notifications to all the connected clients. On getting an invalidation notification, a client becomes aware of updates in cached files and may choose to fetch the updates which allow the client to maintain data consistency as needed by the applications. The advantage of RPC2's multicast based notification over RPC's sequential notification protocol is depicted in Fig. 15.7. In multicast based notification the server does not worry if an acknowledgment from a client does not arrive. This is in contrast to the case where each invalidation message is sent in sequence (as in RPC) and the server waits (blocks) for the reply from a client before processing the next invalidation message.

15.5.2 Scalability

A small set of servers serves as a storage repository for all the shared data. A large number of untrusted clients access the shared data. The requirement of scalability in this context is to ensure that the ratio of the clients to the servers should be as large as possible. This necessitates the transfer of most of the functionalities to clients. Therefore, adding more number of clients does not increase the load on the servers. The OS running on each client can filter out all the system calls that do not need interaction with the servers. Only open and close are forwarded to cache

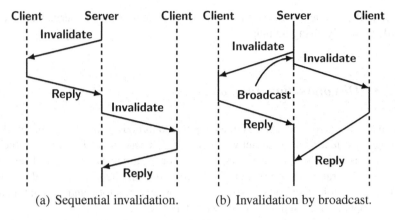

(a) Sequential invalidation. (b) Invalidation by broadcast.

Fig. 15.7 Invalidation notification using RPC and RPC2

manager Venus running on the client. After a file has been opened read, write, seek can bypass Venus. Since the servers are not unduly loaded to support the clients functionalities, and they are trusted, they can bear all the responsibilities for preserving the integrity and the security of data.

The most obvious approach to increase scalability in the use of shared data by large number clients is by employing caching at the clients. But for maintaining the consistency of the replica cache at clients, any update conflict with corresponding server replicas has to be resolved cleverly. The updates are usually generated at the client side. So, the problem is much more complex than just finding a mechanisms to maintain consistency of client-side cache. Specially, since the clients may also use same replicas simultaneously and without each other's knowledge, there is a scope for potential conflicts in client-generated updates.

Another approach of CODA is to disallow any rapid system-wide change. So, the additional update overheads like voting, quorum strategies, etc., which involve interactions of a number of servers and/or clients are eliminated completely. The approach dispenses efficiency in preference to consensus. In summary, the important CODA attributes that attempts maximize scalability and yet preserve the data integrity are as follows:

- The CODA uses the model of untrusted clients and trusted servers.
- The clients cache the data in granularity of entire files.
- Cache coherence is maintained by callback.

Once a file is opened successfully by a client, it is assured to be available in the local cache. The subsequent operations on the cached files at the client are protected from network failures. The idea of caching file in whole also compatible with disconnected mode of operation by the clients. A client is required to register a callback with the server in order to get notifications of about the updates on the cached files. This approach prevents system-wide propagation of changes. Another advantage of callback based cache coherence protocol is that files can be easily moved between servers, all that clients are required to know is a map of files to servers and cache this dynamically changing map.

15.5.3   Disconnection and Failures

The main idea is to make the client as much autonomous as possible. So, the client becomes resilient to a range network failures. If every client is made completely autonomous then there is no sharing at all. This is a degenerate case of personal computers operating in complete isolation from one another. Therefore, the goal in CODA is two-fold, namely, (i) using shared storage repository, and (ii) continuance of client operation even in case of network failures.

Caching can provide limited autonomy to clients with sharing. CODA stipulates caching in granularities of *whole* files. No partial caching is allowed. This approach simplifies the failure model and makes disconnected operation transparent to the applications running in a client. A cache miss can occur only at open. There will be no cache miss for read, write, seek or close. So, an application running on a client operating in disconnected mode will be unaware of disconnection when the required file replicas are locally cached. CODA uses another additional technique called *hoarding* to pre-cache the application specific files from the server in anticipation of a future disconnection. Hoarding is essentially a large grain prefetching and discussed separately.

Server replication is one more strategy employed by CODA to increase availability of shared data. Copies of same file are stored in multiple servers. It provides greater level of availability of shared storage repository. When a client is connected to at least one server, it depends on the server replication. Since many server replications are permitted the period of disconnection is expected to be minimized. The moment client gets disconnected it can switch to cached copy of shared data. While replication strategy improves the availability of data, it introduces the difficulty in preserving data consistency across network.

As mentioned earlier, CODA is viewed as a single location transparent Unix like file system by a client. A volume forms a partial subtree of the shared name space representing is a set of files and directories located at one server. The volume mappings are cached by Venus at the individual clients. CODA uses replications and callbacks to maintain high availability and data consistencies. The set of sites where replicas of a file system volume are placed called *Volume Storage Group* (VSG). A subset of a VSG accessible to a client, which is referred to the client's *Accessible* VSG (AVSG).

The overhead for maintaining replications at a client is controlled by callback based cache coherence protocol. Basically, CODA distinguishes between the replicas cached at clients as *second class* and those at the server as *first class*. If there is any change in a first class replica then the server sends an invalidation notification to all the connected clients having a cached copy. The notification is referred to as a *callback break*, because it is equivalent to breaking a promise that the file copy held by the client is correct. On receiving the notification the client can re-fetch the updated copy from the server. The updates in CODA are propagated to the servers to the AVSGs and then on to missing VSGs (those which are not accessible to the client).

The client operates in disconnected mode when there is no network connection to any site or server in the fixed network. Equivalently, it implies that the AVSG for the client is a null set. In order to make the file system highly available, the clients should be allowed to operate with the cached copies even when the AVSG is empty. Under this circumstance, Venus services the file system calls by relying solely on its cache. When a client is operating in disconnected mode and the file being accessed is not available in cache, a cache miss occurs. Any cache miss cannot be masked or serviced. They appear as failures to the application program. The updates made by a client on the cached copies are propagated to the server when the client is re-connected. After propagation of the updates, Venus re-charges cache with the server replication.

Figure 15.8 illustrate the transitions between cache and replication at the clients in a typical CODA environment. Figure 15.8a shows that all the clients including the mobile client are connected to network. Therefore, the value of some object, say x, is identical across the copies held by the servers and the clients when all are connected. The same holds in a network partition though it does not hold across the partitions. Figure 15.8b indicates that a client operating in disconnected mode can update the value of the object in its cache, but this update will not be visible to server or to other clients even inside the same network partition. But when the disconnected client reconnects, the value of the object in it or at other nodes becomes same.

The high level design goals of CODA file system are:

• To design a highly available and scalable file system,
• To tackle a range of failures from disconnection to weak connection,
• To provide a location-transparent Unix-like single shared name space for the files.

15.5.4   Replica Control Strategy

As stated earlier clients are portable and untrusted. A client has a small storage, data can be willfully tampered or corrupted. It is unrealistic to assume a user will backup the data. Thus, the integrity of data in the replication held by a client cannot be trusted. In contrast the server have big capacities, more secure and carefully monitored by professional administrative staff. This naturally provides the guarantee of quality of data at the servers. Therefore, it is appropriate to distinguish between two types of replications. The replicas at servers represent the *first class* replication. The client replicas represent the *second class* replication. The first class replicas are of higher quality compared to that of the second class replicas. The utility of second class replicas is limited to the clients where they are located. Since the correctness of the execution of a client application depend second class replicas, these replicas must

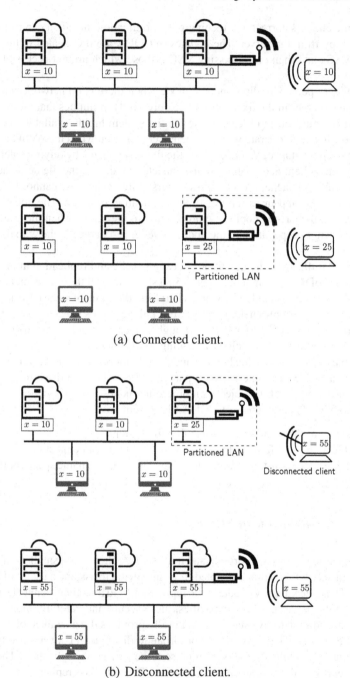

(a) Connected client.

(b) Disconnected client.

Fig. 15.8 Transition between cache and replication at client

be periodically synchronized with their corresponding first class replicas. The basic purpose of the second class replicas is to make the shared data highly available to the clients in presence of frequent, and prolonged network failures.

Figure 15.8b shows that when a client operates in disconnected mode there is actually a network partition between the second class replication held by the client and the all the corresponding first class replications.

The replica control strategy may be either

- *pessimistic*, or
- *optimistic*.

In pessimistic control strategy update is allowed only by one node of a unique partition. So, prior to switching into disconnected mode, a client acquires exclusive lock on the cached object and relinquishes the lock only after reconnection. Acquiring exclusive lock disallows read or write at any other replica. Such an approach is not only too restrictive, but also infeasible in context of mobile clients. The reasons can be summarized as follows.

- A client can negotiate for exclusive lock only in case of a planned disconnection.
- Duration of disconnection is unpredictable.
- Reconnection of a client holding an exclusive lock can not be forced.

In case of a involuntary disconnection there is no opportunity for a client negotiate an exclusive lock for any shared object. Of course, one possible approach may be to play safe and allow lock to a client. However, several clients sharing the same set of files may want to acquire locks and many of these get disconnected at the same time. In a situation like this the system has to come up with sophisticated arbitration mechanism for allowing exclusive lock to one of the contending clients. The client which finally gets the lock will not even know that as it could be disconnected by the time arbitration process completes. Possibly exclusive lock on some objects only for a brief period of disconnection is acceptable. But if the period of disconnection is long then the retention of exclusive lock is detrimental to the availability of shared of data. It is also not possible to force a re-connection of the client holding the exclusive lock. Whereabouts of the client may not be known, and quite likely the client may not even be present in the cell. The whole set of client population may potentially be under the mercy of single lock holder operating in disconnection mode. A timeout associated with exclusive lock can partly solve the problem of availability. The lock expires after a timeout. So other client can take turns to have lock access to the objects. But once the *lease lock* expires the disconnected client loses the control of the lock. Any other pending request lock can be granted. However, the concept of *lease lock* contrary to the purpose of exclusive lock and making file system highly available due to following reasons.

- Disconnected client is in midst of update when it loses the lease of the lock.
- Other client may not interested for the object when lease on lock expires.

If a disconnected client loses lock control, all updates made by it have to be discarded. One simple idea that may alleviate the problem is the lazy release locks. A client continues to hold the locks even after the expiry of the lease unless some other client explicitly places a request at the server. But then the exact timing of the lock release can never be synchronized to avoid overlap with the update activity at the client.

Optimistic replica control mechanism does not allows any exclusive lock. The clients update their cached objects with the hope its update will not conflict with the updates by other clients. It means several clients operating with same set of cached objects in disconnected mode can report conflicting updates on reconnection. Therefore, it requires the system to be sophisticated enough to detect and resolve the update conflicts. But making the conflict resolution fully automatic is extremely difficult. However, it is possible to localize the conflicts and preserve evidences for a manual repair in extreme cases.

The objective of choosing an optimistic strategy is to provide a uniform model for every client when it operates in disconnected mode. It allows concurrency as a number of clients can use a replica of the same object simultaneously. The argument in favour of optimistic replica control also comes from the fact that CODA's cached objects are in granularity of files. In an Unix like shared file system, usually the write access is controlled by only one user while other users typically provided with read accesses. So, a client having write access can update the cached file without creating any update conflicts. Only the clients having read access may possibly get slightly outdated values. But then applications can be tuned to handle such eventualities. In the case of many applications it will not even matter if the data is bit outdated.

Another approach may be to employ optimistic control strategy for disconnected mode and pessimistic strategy in connected mode. While such an approach is possible, it will require the user to be adaptive to the two anomalous situations depending on whether operating in disconnected or connected mode. While a user would be able to do updates in disconnected mode s/he would be unable to do so in connected state as some other client has obtained an exclusive/shared lock prior to the request of this user. Therefore, a uniform model of replica control is preferred.

15.5.5   Visibility of Updates

The design of CODA was initially geared to provide user a fail-safe, highly available shared file system like Unix. Under Unix semantics any modification to a file becomes immediately visible to all users who have access to it. Obviously, preserving this semantics is not only incompatible for scalability but also impractical when users are allowed to operate in disconnected mode. So, CODA implementers settled for a diluted form of the visibility requirement under Unix file operation semantics. The difference between a cached copy of file available at a disconnected client from its latest copy depends on the difference of time of the last update of cached copy and the current time. Hence, a time stamp (`store id`) on replica may be taken as parameter for the distance function that measures the difference between cached replica and its server state. Since CODA allows data sharing at the granularity of file revalidating cached file at the time of opening, and propagating updates at the time closing file should be adequate for most applications. A successful `open` means the contents of the file being accessed is the latest replication available at the server from where the client fetched it. It is possible that the server itself may have a stale copy. Therefore, the revalidation of cached copy of the client at the time of opening a file actually means it is synchronized with the latest replica available at the server site. It may be possible to increase the currency guarantee by querying the replica custodians on the fixed network when the file opening is attempted at a client. The query can be initiated by the server on which Venus dockets the open call.

15.5.6   Venus and Its Operations

The main focus of CODA is on the ability of the clients to work in disconnected mode or in the face of various network failures. So, we first discuss the client side support needed for CODA. Then we describe the server side support.

Figure 15.5 gives a high-level decomposition of CODA components support at a client. Venus is implemented as a user-level program. This the approach made it portable, and easy to debug. The CODA mini-cache which is a part of client's kernel supports only for servicing system calls for the file objects in CODA file system if it is already cached and open has been successful. Kernel uniformly forwards file system calls – whether it is for a CODA resource or a local resource—to VFS. The process of servicing file system calls is as follows.

1. If the call is for a CODA file, VFS forwards that call to mini-cache control.
2. Which in turn determines if the file is already cached, and services the request.
3. In case it is not in cache then the call is forwarded to Venus.
4. Venus actions are as follows:

   a. Contacts the servers, fetches the required object from one of them.
   b. Caches the file in local disk and returns to kernel via mini-cache.
   c. Mini-cache can remember some recently serviced calls and caches these.

The state of mini-cache changes after Venus reports successful fetching and caching of objects from the custodian server, occurrences of callback breaks, and revalidation of client cache afterwards. Since Venus is a user-level program, mini-cache is critical to good performance.

The major task of Venus is fetching objects from accessible servers holding the replicas of the requested file objects. But it has to perform another complicated task, namely, propagating updates to the servers. It operates in three states

1. Emulation
2. Hoarding
3. Reintegration

Fig. 15.9 Venus state
transitions

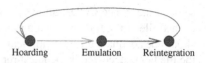

Hoarding   Emulation   Reintegration

The states and transitions between Venus states have been depicted in Fig. 15.9. The states are represented by labeled circles. The transitions from emulation to reintegration represents transition from disconnected to connected state, and transition from hoarding to emulation represents the reverse. So, hoarding and reintegration both are connected states while emulation is the disconnected state.

15.5.6.1 Hoarding

Hoarding is merely a pre-fetching in large granularity. The success of pre-fetching depends on the ability to capture locality with respect to the immediate future. In a mobile client a session of disconnected operation can continue for few minutes to hours or even for days. Therefore, it impossible to implement a hoarding strategy which will allow a client to operate in disconnected mode without failures. It has to take into account following factors:

- Mobile user's file reference behaviour in near to distant future.
- Involuntary disconnection.
- The cost of cache miss during disconnection.
- The physical limitation of cache.

The decision on hoarding becomes easy if a user specifies a profile of references. Disconnection and reconnection are purely random in time. Therefore, involuntary disconnections are hard to handle. However, as a preparatory to voluntary disconnection, it may be possible to hoard the data needed for disconnected operation. Still it is hard to estimate the cost of a cache miss. So, the decision to cache certain objects and not cache certain other objects becomes hard. The combined decision should have twin objectives:

1. Minimize the cost of not caching certain objects.
2. Maximize the benefit in cost of caching certain objects.

Since, the caching decision depends on the criticality of applications running on the client, the cost model should be defined appropriately. Based on the cost model, an object's importance for caching can be represented by a priority factor. Then a hoarding algorithm can perform a hoard walk according to the priority of the object. It is also convenient to define hoarding based on the cache equilibrium. The cache equilibrium signifies that the mobile user's data requirements are mostly met from the cached objects. The cache size limitation disturbs the equilibrium as a result of normal activities. Some cache objects may have to make way for other objects, also some objects may be used more often than others at different instances of time. Therefore,

Venus needs to periodically perform a hoard walk for restoring cache equilibrium. CODA's implementation fixes the interval of hoard walk as ten minutes. However, CODA also allows users to specify the inclusion of a provision for triggering hoard walk at the time of voluntary disconnection in the hoard profile.

15.5.6.2 Emulation

In emulation state Venus assumes the role of the proxy for a server at the client. It performs following important functions.

- Checks the access control.
- Generates temporary file identifiers (*tfids*) for newly created objects.
- Evaluates priorities of mutating objects and applies these to cache these objects.
- Reports or blocks a failures when a cache miss occurs.
- Logs information to let the update activities during disconnected operation to be *replayed* on reintegration.

The tfid of newly created object is replaced by a permanent file identifiers (pfid) at the time of reintegration. The removal of a mutated object incurs more cost compared to that of a non-mutated object. Therefore, the hoarding priorities of updated objects should be very high. None of the deleted objects need be cached. So the lowest priority is assigned to these objects. A cache miss cannot be masked unless the user has explicitly requested for masking it until reconnection. However, the default behavior of Venus, on a cache miss, is to report a failure.

The log is kept as a per volume log. A log entry consist of a copy of the corresponding system call, its arguments as well as the version state of the all objects referenced by the system call.

15.5.6.3 Replay Log and Its Optimization

All the operations during emulation state are logged. The objective of logging is that the operations can be replayed at the server during the reintegration. Only updates are logged. Therefore, it is also alternatively referred to as Change Modify Log (CML).

Optimizing CML is critical for mobile environment as transfer of log requires both bandwidth and time. Considering the criticality of cache during emulation state, on the client end too optimization of CML is important. Some simple optimization techniques are:

- Any operation which is followed by its inverse can be purged from CML.
- If a sequence of operations can mean a single logical operation then just record the one equivalent logical operation in the log in place of sequence of a number of operations.
- Record only the latest `store`.

To understand the techniques mentioned above we provide an example of each. If a mkdir operation is followed by a rmdir with same argument then both operations need not be logged. Because the second operation is inverse of the first and nullifies the effect of the first operation. A close following an open installs a completely new file. So, instead of individually logging an open, the sequence of intervening writes, and finally, a close, all these can be effectively represented by logging just a single store operation for a file. Logically store does not mean entire contents of the file is logged. It merely points to the cached copy of the file. Therefore, a store invalidates preceding stores if any. It means we can just record the last store operation.

15.5.6.4   Recoverable Virtual Memory

In emulation state Venus must provide persistence guarantees for the following:

- A disconnected client to restart after a shutdown and continue from where it left off.
- In the event of a crash during disconnected state, the amount of data loss should not be more than the data loss incurred when an identical crash occurs in a connected state.

To ensure persistence of the kind mentioned above, Venus keeps the cache and other important data structures in non-volatile storage at the client.

The important data structures or the *meta-data* used by Venus consists of

- Cached directories and symbolic link contents,
- Status blocks of cached objects of all types,
- Replay logs, and
- Hoard database (*hoard profile*) for the client.

All the meta data are mapped into the address space of Venus as the *Recoverable Virtual Memory* (RVM). But the contents of the cached files are stored as ordinary Unix files on client's local disk. Only transactional access is allowed to meta data. The transactional access ensures that the meta data is always makes a transition from one consistent state to another. RVM hides the recovery associated complications from Venus. RVM supports only local non-nested transactions. An application may choose to reduce commit latency by labelling *commits* as *noflush*. But the commits still have to be flushed periodically for providing *bounded persistence* guarantee. Venus can exploit the capabilities of RVM to provide good performance with an assured level of persistence. For example, during hoarding state (non emulating state), the log flushes are done infrequently, as a copy is available on the server. However, during emulation the server is not accessible. Therefore, Venus can resort to frequent flushes to ensure minimum amount of data loss.

15.5.6.5 Resource Exhaustion

Since non-volatile storage has a physical limit, Venus may encounter storage problem during emulation state. Two possible scenarios where the resource exhaustion may have an impact on performance are:

1. Disk space allocated for file cache is full.
2. Disk space allocated for RVM full.

When Venus encounters file cache overflow problem, possibly storage can be reclaimed by either truncating or deleting some of the cached files. However, if Venus runs out of space for RVM nothing much can be done. The only way to alleviate this problem will be to block all mutating operations until reintegration takes place. Non mututaing operations can still be allowed. One uniform alternative to tackle the problem of space could be to apply compressions on file caches and RVM contents. A second alternative could be to allow the user to undo updates selectively and release storage. The third viable approach could be free storage by backing up the parts of file cache and RVM on a removable disks.

15.5.7 Reintegration

Reintegration is an intermediate state of Venus between the time it switches form the role of *proxy server* to *cache manager* at the client. All the updates made by clients are propagated to the server during this state. After that, the cache at a client is synchronized with the server's state. Reintegration is performed on one volume at a time in a transactional step. All update activities in the volume remain suspended until the completion of reintegration. The actual task of reintegration is performed by replaying the update log stored by Venus.

15.5.7.1 Replay Algorithm

The CODA implementation views the reintegration activity as execution of replay algorithm at a volume server. The updates made during emulation state is propagated to the server. Reintegration is done per volume by replaying the logged operations directly on the server. The execution of replay algorithm consist of four phases:

1. Log parsing, and acquiring locks
2. Validity check and execution,
3. Back-fetching, and
4. Lock release.

In phase 1, the log is parsed and the operations with the required arguments are identified. Locks are acquired for all the objects referenced in the log. Phase 2 consists of various types of checks and validations. These include integrity, protection and disk space checks. After these checks are over, the conflict detection is carried out. All the operations in the replay log are performed at the server in a single transaction. The conflict detection is a bit of complicated process. In order to determine update conflicts, the store IDs of objects in replay log are compared with store IDs of the corresponding objects at the server. If store IDs do not match then the actions depend on the operations being validated. In the case of a file, the transaction for reintegration is aborted. However, in case of a directory object, conflicts occur

- If the name of newly created object matches with an existing name,
- If the object is updated at the client, but has been deleted at the server or vice versa,
- If directory attributes at the client and the server has been modified.

After determining the conflicts, all operations except store are executed at the server. For store operation an empty shadow file is created for the actual file, and meta data is updated to it. However, the actual data transfer is deferred until phase 3. Then in phase 3 backfetching is executed. Backfetching step transfers the updated files from the client to the server and the fetched files replace the corresponding shadow files created in phase 2. Finally phase 4 commits the transaction and releases all the locks.

15.6   InterMezzo

InterMezzo [11] was conceived as a filtering file system layer between VFS and native file system such as ext3, ReiserFS, JFS or XFS. Therefore, InterMezzo is not to be viewed as a full scale file system, but as a stacked up file system layer over a native file system. The implementers of InterMezzo set the design goals with following ground assumptions [11]:

1. The server side storage of file would depend on a native file system such as ext3, ReiserFS, JFS or XFS.
2. The kernel level file system at a client should be able to exploit the existing file system, and also would require services of a persistent cache.
3. File system objects should have meta data that can support disconnected operation at the clients.
4. Scalability and recovery of distributed state can be implemented by leveraging the existing mechanisms provided by local file system.
5. The system should perform kernel level write back caching.
6. The system should use TCP and exploit existing rsync for synchronization, and ssh/ssl for security.
7. The management of the client cache and the server file system may differ in policy but should use a uniform mechanism.

However, the design simplicity and flexibilities should not affect the ease in operating with files. The operational framework of InterMezzo file system is specified by following characteristics:

1. The objects (files and directories) can be identified by either file identifiers, path names or the triplets of the form <server, device, Inode>.
2. There is a single name space for all files. This means clients see all files exported by a cluster of InterMezzo servers in the form of one large tree. The name space is typically larger than a directory but much smaller than a disk partition.
3. Different file sets can be exported explicitly. It allows flexibility of using a smaller name space as per the requirements. In other words, a user may choose a set of files as the root for a mounted instance of an InterMezzo file system.
4. There is a root directory for each file set, it may also contain the mount points of other file sets.
5. An InterMezzo mount point is conceptually similar, though distinct from a Unix mount point. If the root of file system does not belong to a file set by default, then all the ancestors of a file belonging to that file set will not be visible.

A file set is a fundamental component for operating on files. File Set Location Database (FSLD) is the basic meta-data for file sets. A FSLD is shared by an Inter-Mezzo cluster of file servers. FSLD is implemented as a sparse tree of directories and handled as special object in the file system. Each time file set tree gets modified, an update occurs in FSLD database. A version number is also associated with each such update. So, FSLD can be updated without downloading the latest version.

15.6.1 Filtering Access to Files

The implementation of InterMezzo is in the form an single filtering layer, though the roles of the clients and the servers are kept distinct. This is in contrast to CODA system, where a client is different from a server, and the codes for the two parts are distinct. InterMezzo mechanism for the implementation of two parts remains the same, but the servers have following important responsibilities which is distinct from clients.

1. Maintaining on-disk files as the authoritative states of files,
2. Coordinating the maintenance of state coherence across clients.

A file set mount point on a server is not necessarily a directory. it could be a symbolic link with the target that is a directory on the server holding the data.

The filtering layer of InterMezzo system is named as Presto for Linux and Vivace for Windows. The filter accomplishes the following two tasks:

1. Accesses to validate the freshness of the data held in the local file system.
2. Logs the updates made to the file system.

Fig. 15.10 InterMezzo
system [11]

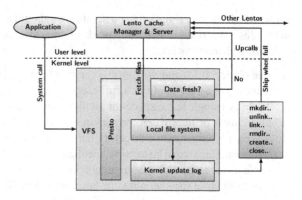

Presto requests are handled by Lento. Lento performs the dual job of a file server and a cache manager in a client. Figure 15.10 illustrates how InterMezzo system works [11]. Presto should have knowledge about the native file system type wrapped over by InterMezzo system. This enable Presto to use all VFS methods of the native file system. Presto performs the two main tasks, namely,

1. Filtering all accesses, and
2. Storing log of all updates.

Lento's modification of cache is independent of filtering and logging. When an accessed file is not available in client's cache, the file is fetched in whole. Directory fetching is implemented by creating sparse files and empty subdirectories for each entries. So, there could be substantial latency in access of directories. However, this latency is amortised by subsequent accesses which become local. A system call for directory operations at clients has to be executed either on the local files or fetched from a server through an upcall to the wrapped file system. The pseudo codes for open and mkdir are provided in Algorithm 40 as examples.

Before an update can be executed on an object, a permission needs to be acquired. On the client side, the updates are made to cache and the operation are logged into a Client Modification Log (CML). During the reintegration process, CML is drained to the server much like it is done in CODA. The server holding the data replays the CML, and forwards the same to other clients who may have also registered for the replica. The forwarding CML to other clients doubles up as update notifications. Therefore, reintegration and update notification are combined into a single processes. The modification log includes the details concerning modifications made to the directory and file attributes, and also the close operation. In the case of a close operation, the modified file has to be back-fetched by server.

A file updated at a server also needs to undergo an almost similar process. The updates are logged or journaled and propagated only to the clients who may have registered callbacks at the server. The clients who do not register callbacks, invalidate the data when they come to know about the updates. These clients have to re-fetch

---

Algorithm 40: Creating and opening a directory

```
int directoryOpen(INODE *inode, FILE *file)
begin
    if (!Data(inode) && !Lento) then
    |   upcall(inode, "get data");
    end
    return bottom->directoryOpen(inode, file);
end
int mkdir(INODE *inode, char *dirName)
begin
    if (!Permit(inode) && !Lento) then
    |   lentoGetPermit(inode);
    end
    rc = bottom->mkdir(inode, dirName);
    if (!rc && !Lento) then
    |   journal("mkdir", inode, dirName); // Log the operation
    end
end
```

---

the data if they still want to work on the data. There is a symmetry in operation of both clients and servers. Lento's task in this context are two fold [11]:

1. File service: on behalf of client it fetches files directories from the servers, while working for the servers it back-fetches files when close calls are executed on those objects at the clients.
2. Reintegration service: reintegration is applied on receiving modification logs (CML) at the servers. For clients invalidation report (update notification) are sent.

An important distinction of a server from a client is that the server implements security. A client, on the other hand, trusts an authenticated server and accepts changes without checking each object. A client can only modify its cache for the purpose of freeing space. Such changes are not propagated to the servers.

15.6.2 Protocols

InterMezzo mostly preserves the protocols used in CODA and AFS. The main protocols are for

- Fetching directory, and files,
- Validating freshness of data,
- Acquiring permission to modify data,
- Breaking callbacks, and
- Reintegration.

Each cached object (directory or file) contains attribute flags HAS_DATA and HAS_ATTR. If these flags are set then it implies that the data and attributes are valid, and callback is enabled in the client. When callback is enabled, the client uses cached data without placing an upcall to the server. Before storing modified objects, the server notifies the clients who hold callbacks on those objects. Independently, BreakCallback request can be initiated by a server to notify clients about modification of data. This request is handled as a multi-RPC to all the clients like in CODA. It avoids handling of multiple timeouts while waiting for replies. When a client seeks to modify data it acquires permission through GetPermit call. A successful acquisition of permission sets HAS_PERMIT flag in status field.

Every object has an identifier and version number. Two objects with same identifier and same version number are identical. The volumes also have a volume version number. Volume version number allows rapid revalidation of entire volume, if none of the objects in that volume has changed. Cached objects are validated with Validate request which can be issued at the level of individual objects or a volume.

Reintegrate request is for propagation of updates. It uses modification log like in CODA. The client modification log (CML) is transferred to the server. The server replays the log and changes the directory tree and then backfetches the files from the client for which client has executed close calls.

Inclusion of version number with the RPCs of the affected files indirectly helps InterMezzo to avoid race conditions in updates. For example, the version number of the parent directory present in the client is included while creating a new directory. It allows the server to ensure that the version held by the client is being modified. If version numbers are not equal then reintegration causes conflicts which need to be handled differently.

15.6.3 Functions of Lento

Lento doubles up as a file server and a cache manager by combining the functions of both Venus and Vice as in CODA. It is implemented as a single threaded event driven program. A new session is instantiated to handle every request. A session basically represents a data structure containing state and event handlers. I/O is performed asynchronously. The kernel signals completion of I/O by raising an appropriate event. Lento is responsible for activating all event handlers and also responsible for garbage collecting sessions when no event can reach them. Figure 15.11a and b illustrate request handling due to an upcall and a network request.

The implementation of Lento is done through Perl Object Environment (POE). Two extra wheels were added to POE, namely, PacketWheel and UpcallWheel. PacketWheel is responsible for network requests from connection. A connection provides the destination session for a request. A request can either be for an existing session or can originate from the request dispatcher. In the latter case, it is either a new session or a specially created session for handling the request. UpcallWheel unpacks requests originating from the kernel that reached Lento via a character device /dev/presto.

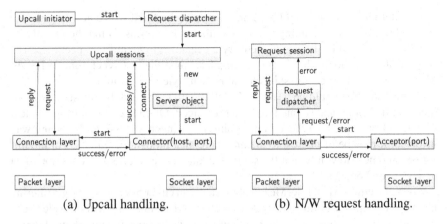

(a) Upcall handling.   (b) N/W request handling.

Fig. 15.11 Upcall and network request handling by Lento [11]

The two wheels are combined with an AcceptorWheel which creates accepted TCP connections.

15.6.4 Recovery and Cache Validation

The simplest process of recovery is to evict all cached entries. Such a wholesale eviction process can be avoided by establishing currency or freshness of cached data. Version stamp is used for the same. The version stamp of equal objects should be equal, and version change is always monotonically ordered. Let us consider what happens when a crash occurs while data is being fetched into cache. If the data is not fully fetched, the system should consider the cached object as fresh. So, the stamping of version number is deferred until the data is fully fetched. In implementation, this is achieved by waiting for 30 s before flushing File System Database (FSDB) buffers. On reconnection to a server, all objects having out of date version stamps should be evicted from cache. If recovery is followed by disconnection, then partially fetched object may be used for availability. Note that incompletely fetched objects can be identified by their creation time, i.e., `ctime` less than 30 s from last flush of FSDB. However, incompletely fetched objects which are modified should not be reintegrated. These objects should be handled as creating conflicts.

A problem arises when a client crashes while modifying existing data. Recovering from crash, the client will find an old version stamp and also old modification time, i.e., `mtime` in `Inode`. If the object has just been fetched, its version stamp may be older than that on the server. However, the data on the client's disk can be newer than that on the server. So, this creates problem of overwriting the latest update on the server. One way to handle this is to accept that some data modification for a short duration may be lost.

An alternative to this would be, Inode may be modified with a new mtime and synched to the disk. Assuming that no modification happens within the granularity of a mtime tick, this allows the recovery mechanism to identify suspect files. The suspect files are those which have mtime later than the last synch time in FSDB. These suspected files can be subjected to rsynch style reintegration.

A third solution could be write the FSDB record to the disk before starting modification. It then indicates that Inode has changed. Of course, it requires a context switch to Lento. The overhead is not going to be much, as disk traffic is any way involved. It may be of interest to mention here, that though the initiation of modification becomes slow in two of the suggested alternative solutions, it does not affect newly created objects.

Overall framework of InterMezzo file system can either be considered as a filtering layer on the top of existing file systems, or viewed as attaching a client side cache for NFS functionalities. This allows client to work even when network goes down. On regaining connectivity, server reintegration happens for modifications made by a client in disconnected mode.

15.7   File System for Connected Clients

Client side caching and replication are the basic design paradigms that ensure availability of data in both CODA and InterMezzo file systems. The fundamental assumption is that adequate storage space is available at a client to hoard data which it will ever need in order to operate in disconnected mode. This assumption disregards one of the major constraints in a mobile system, namely, resource scarcity. How does one design a file system primarily for mobile clients which cannot cache all the needed data? Even otherwise, due to unreliable network services, a file server may become unreachable though mobile client remains connected to the network. The client will not get the data unless the server reconnects back. Therefore, there is a need to serve connected clients by an approach that can ensure availability of data even when the servers get disconnected. The technique obviously calls for a server side caching mechanism.

Instead of a client side view, we turn around and focus on a server side view of file operations. A server's operations can be separated into three phases namely, connected, disconnected or rejoining. Initially when the servers (where data resides) are available, the file services are provided by these servers to the respective clients. This phase is defined as connected phase, the servers answer all file service requests of the clients via RPC mechanism. If any of the file servers fails to answer a file service request within a stipulated time, the part of the file system is disconnected. In this case, the system switches to disconnected phase of operation. During the disconnected phase the file service requests are handled through server side caching. The client, however, continues to probe for the disconnected server(s) on a regular basis. Finally, when the servers and communication channels are back, the file system switches rejoining phase. In this phase, communication link between file system and previously disconnected server is restablished. So, file updates done by the client have to be reintegrated to the file system.

The role of cache is limited to disconnected and reintegration phases. In phase 1, the client sees a single directory hierarchy for the file system. The server side caching takes place as the files are accessed via system calls such as read, write, create, etc. This task is handled by FAM (File Alteration Monitor) library [21]. FAM essentially sends a signal to caching module about file accesses as it monitors these. Before, doing the actual copying the cach server checks contents to see if any older copy of the file is cached earlier. The purpose of this checking is to avoid unnecessary copying of exactly identical copies of the file. It is also possible that files have similar names but different contents. So, if a name matching is found then a MD5 check sum is determined for the new file which is compared with one that is already resident in cache. Identical MD5 checksums means files are identical, and no caching is required. If the MD5 checksums are different then conflict is resolved by moving old files to backup partition by attaching a version number. The backup cache is maintained as a repository which is exported to the users. So, the users can view the repository and may choose to move files from this area to actual file system. Furthermore, if a cache miss occurs, the system automatically examines backup cache area to find if an older version exists. The user is notified accordingly.

15.7.1   Concurrency Control

This file system model uses optimistic concurrency control [22]. As explained already, it avoids locking of files till the time data is to be updated or deleted. This way availability of data is maximized and concurrent non-conflicting accesses are speeded up. Collision can happen when a transaction updates or deletes file between the time it is read by the concurrent transaction and is updated and deleted. When a file is to updated or deleted, it first reads to see if there is change in version number from the time it was read last. MD5sum is used to compare the versions.

15.7.2   Conflict Detection and Resolution

Conflict may occur due to disconnected operation on a cached version of a file. Before disconnection, the cache server may have cached the current version of the file. Immediately after the cached copy is stored, the versions of the file at both the file server and the cache server are equal. Suppose after the file server gets disconnected, many updates were received at the file server. These updates causes file version to change at the file server. The cached copy of the file may have also received many updates and its version also may have changed. Now suppose the file servers reconnects back, the cache server then tries to synchronize the version of files stored in its cache with that of the same file at the files server. In this situation, conflict may

arise as versions of the file becomes different. The system should be able to detect
such conflicts. We need to first arrive at a definition of conflicts to work out strategies
for resolution of conflicts. The definition is as follows:

Definition 15.1 Let t be the last modified time of a file f fetched from a file server
FS when it was stored in cache server CS before disconnection phase. At the end of
disconnection period, a conflict is detected if the mtime of the file at the file server
is not t.

Since mtime is stored in the inode, the system can use this to detect conflicts
by checking that in quality of mtimes of two objects, one stored at the file server
and the other stored at the cache server. Conflict detection and resolution process is
explained in Algorithm 41.

Algorithm 41: Conflict detection & resolution

---

begin
    for each $f_{FS} \in FS$
    // Subscripts fs and ch denote corresponding objects from
        File System and Cache server respectively.
    if mtime(f_{ch}) > mtime(f_{fs}) **then**
        // Conflict is detected
        Make a new version of f_{ch} and copy to backup Cache;
        Copy f_{fs} to Cache;
    end
    else
        if mtime(f_{fs}) < mtime(f_{ch}) **then**
            // Conflict is detected
            Make a new version of f_{fs} and copy to backup Cache;
            Copy f_{ch} to FS
        end
        else
            Do nothing // No conflict detected
        end
    end
end

The scheme is pretty simple and elegant. Note that the implicit assumption in this
conflict resolution strategy is that files are completely partitioned among file servers.
There is no replication of file system. Replication introduces consistency problem
among replicas [23]. As explained earlier in conflict resolution scheme in CODA,
this creates excessive network traffic to restore consistency of replicas. Fortunately,
the caching is centralized at cache server. So, traffic due to consistency maintenance
is minimized. There is just one place of versioning, i.e., Cache Server. It implies only
one system request is needed to check the version of replica and update it if needed.

15.7.3 Cache Replacement

The additional problem which a Cache Server introduces, however, is to deal with problem cache replacement. Eventually backup cache may become full, so there is a need to evict old cached files. The solution is to use Frequency Based Replacement (FBR) algorithm [24]. It is a hybrid of LRU and LFU [25]. FBR divides cache into three segments, namely, (i) new segment, (ii) middle segment, and (iii) old segment. The sizes of these segments are pre-determined by two parameters,

1. F-new: a percentage that sets a bound for total number of cache files contained in new segment. It essentially is a measure for most recently used files.
2. F-old: a percentage that sets a bound for the cache files contained in old segment. This is a measure for least recently used files.

The middle segment consist of those files that are neither new nor old. When a cache hit occurs in new segment, its reference count is not incremented. The idea is new segment of files define a temporal locality. Reference count is incremented when cache hit occurs for a file contained either in middle or in old segments. When it is required to reclaim cache, the file with least reference count in old segment is selected. The files in old segment are ordered in a LRU ordered stack. Ties for cache files with same reference count is resolved by choosing the least recently used one.

References

1. S.M. Park, Y.B. Ko, and J.H. Kim, Disconnected operation service in mobile grid computing. In *International Conference on Service-Oriented Computing* (Springer, 2003) pp. 499–513
2. A. Litke, D. Skoutas, and T. Varvarigou. Mobile grid computing: changes and challenges of resource management in a mobile grid environment. In *5th International Conference on Practical Aspects of Knowledge Management (PAKM 2004)* (2004)
3. Korsgaard P, Buildroot, Making embedded linux easy. *Fecha de consulta: 16 de Mayo de 2014.* http://buildroot.uclibc.org (2015)
4. F. Bsching, S. Schildt, and L. Wolf. Droidcluster, Towards smartphone cluster computing– the streets are paved with potential computer clusters. In *32nd International Conference on Distributed Computing Systems Workshops* (2012) pp. 114–117
5. D.B. Terry, M.M. Theimer, K.Petersen, A.J. Demers, M.J. Spreitzer, and C.H. Hauser. Managing update conflicts in bayou, a weakly connected replicated storage system. In *ACM Symposium on Operating Systems Principles (SOSP)* (1995) pp. 172–182
6. A.D. Joseph, J.A. Tauber, M.F. Kaashoek, Mobile computing with rover toolkit. IEEE Trans. Comput. **46**(3), 337–352 (1997)
7. J.J. Kistler, M. Satyanarayan, Disconnected operation in CODA file system. ACM Trans. Comput. Syst. **10**(1), 3–25 (1992)
8. J.H. Morris, M. Satyanarayanan, M.H. Conner, J.H. Howard, D.S.H. Rosenthal, F.D. Smith, Andrew: A distributed personal computing environment. Commun. ACM **29**(3), 184–201 (1986)
9. M. Satyanarayanan, Scalable, secure, and highly available distributed file access. Computer **23**(5), 9–18 (1990)

10. M. Satyanarayanan, J.H. Howard, D.A. Nichols, R.N. Sidebotham, A.Z. Spector, and M.J. West. The ITC distributed file system: principles and design. In *Tenth Symposium on Operating System Principles*, (ACM, December 1985) pp. 35–50

11. P. Braam, M. Callahan, and P. Schwan, The intermezzo file system. In *O'Reilly Perl Conference* (1999)

12. J.E. Bobbitt, S.A. Doll, M.T. Friedman, P.L.S. Wing, and J.P. Mullally, Virtual file system, US Patent 7,024,427, April 2006

13. S. Tweedie, Ext3, journaling filesystem. In *Ottawa Linux Symposium* (2000) pp. 24–29

14. Hans Reiser. Reiserfs (2004)

15. Albert Chang, Mark F. Mergen, Robert K. Rader, Jeffrey A. Roberts, Scott L. Porter, Evolution of storage facilities in AIX version 3 for RISC system/6000 processors. IBM J. Res. Dev. **34**(1), 105–110 (1990)

16. A. Sweeney, D. Doucette, W. Hu, C. Anderson, M. Nishimoto, G. Peck, Scalability in the xfs file system. In *USENIX Annual Technical Conference* **15** (1996)

17. J.J. Kistler. *Disconnected Operation in a Distributed File System*. PhD thesis, Computer Science, Pittsburg, PA, USA (1993)

18. P. Braam, The coda distributed file system. Linux J. **50**, 46–51 (1998)

19. L. Mummert, M. Ebling, and M. Satyanarayan. Exploiting weak connectivity for mobile access. In *The 15th ACM Symposium on Operating Systems* (1995) pp. 143–155

20. M. Satyanarayan, J.J. Kistler, P. Kumar, E.H.S.M.E. Okasaki, D.C. Steere, Coda: A highly available file system for a distributed workstation environment. IEEE Transact. Comput. **39**(4), 447–459 (1990)

21. Sillicon Graphics, FAM 2.7.0 release. http://oss.sgi.com/projects/fam/ (2003)

22. M. Satynarayanan, The evolution of CODA. ACM Transact. Comput. Syst. **20**(2), 85–124 (2002)

23. J. Gray, P. Holland, P. Neil, D. Shasha, The dangers of replication and a solution. In *ACM SIGMOD Rec.* **25**(2) (1996)

24. J.T. Robinson, M.V. Devarakonda, Data cache management using frequency-based replacement. SIGMETRICS Perform. Eval. Rev. **18**(1), 134–142 (1990)

25. A. Silberschatz, P.B. Galvin, and G. Gagne. *Operating Systems Concepts*, 7th edn. (Wiley, 2005)

Chapter 16
Context-aware Infrastructures for Smart Environment

16.1 Introduction

Let us begin by articulating the attributes and the functions of an environment that can make it smart. Loosely speaking, the smartness of any system lies in its ability to adapt autonomously and intelligently to its environmental changes. An environment consists of surroundings or conditions in which inhabitants live. So, by referring to an environment, we are implicitly interested on adaptations that affect the lives of the inhabitants. Therefore, in the context of our discussion here, a smart environment is the one that adapts itself to the changes in environmental conditions in order to offer qualitative improvements in experiences of its inhabitants. There is an amount of subjectivity in definition of "improved experience". Ignoring the subjectivity for the time being, "improved experience" may be viewed as something that brings comforts to the inhabitants. However, it should be emphasized that the types of experiences which bring comfort vary with the inhabitant's level of expectations or their respective frame of references. Some inhabitants may draw comfort with the reduction in cost of a preferred service. For a another set of inhabitants, the ease of availing the preferred services may bring comfort. For a third set of inhabitants the flexibility in choice of services be a measure of comfortness. In summary, comfortness has multiple dimensions defined by how well the devices and/or the objects create ambients and capture the contexts to respond to the desires of the inhabitants. Obviously, the environment should have ability not only to acquire knowledge about the inhabitants but also to intelligently apply the acquired knowledge to make environmental conditions suitable for the inhabitants. So, we can identify three major challenges in building a smart environment:

1. Understanding of the ambients through fusion of data gathered from various sources in the environment.
2. Understanding the context of each inhabitant and adapting to it.
3. Understanding the communication requirements among various entities of the environment and staging these seamlessly.

© Springer Nature Singapore Pte Ltd. 2017
R.K. Ghosh, *Wireless Networking and Mobile Data Management*,
DOI 10.1007/978-981-10-3941-6_16

Most notably, smart environments are custom built for the purpose they serve. For example, smart homes, smart hospitals or smart healthcare, etc. Each have a different set of goals and autonomously adapt to the requirements of their respective inhabitants. For example, the comfortness is qualitatively different for an in-patient at a hospital from that of a normal person at home. The healthcare needs of a person having history of heart ailments or diabetes is different from an in-patient at a hospital or a normal person at home. Therefore, the exact nature of challenges will depend on the environment type and the inhabitant types. However, the base line challenge pertains to the extraction of context, and the decisions based on correct interpretations of the contexts. In other words, context based infrastructure is fundamental to building of smart environments. Therefore, capturing contexts is critical in enhancing the experience of the users in the environment. The sensors and the controllers measure ambient parameters which provide the inputs for creation of a context. However, the raw data needs to be processed appropriately by reasoning engines to arrive at a context. Apart from the ambient measurement (which give physical properties), a context depends on a number of other factors such as location, emotional states of the users, preferences and historical data about the choices made by the users and so on. Therefore, the creation of a context involves sophisticated reasoning, inferencing and machine learning algorithms. On successful creation of context, context-aware services trigger events which alters users' experience of physical environment. To give an analogy, a correct context would provide an insect's eye view rather than a bird's eye view of the user's ambience [27]. In summary, two distinct set of challenges can be identified [1].

- *Inhabitant centered*: It deals with the interfaces for interactions of the inhabitants within a smart environment.
- *Technology centered*: It deals with the requirements of a smart environment from technological prospectives such as hardware, networking infrastructure, programming and system development. More specifically, there is a paradigm shift in development of systems.

In this chapter, we introduce these challenges from a research prospective. A comprehensive final report on the outcomes of an inter-agency workshop on smart environments sponsored by DARPA, NSF and NIST was summarized succinctly in a paper by Abowd and Sterbenz [1]. Smart applications and services are domain dependent, and too vast an area to be dealt in any comprehensive manner in a single chapter. Therefore, we provide a synopsis of certain research challenges, and focus mainly on the context management systems.

16.2 Terminology and Historical Prospectives

Before going further into the subject matter of smart environments, it may of interest to know a bit of terminology of smart environment and the historical prospective around them. As indicated in Chap. 1, there is a proliferation in terminlogy concerning smart environment. The definition of ubiquitous computing is hardware centric, it does not include a reference to "intelligence part" of the system. The intelligence factor is included in the definition of smart environment proposed in [39]. However, "improved experience" used in the aforesaid definition is unspecified. Secondly, and most importantly, it completely ignores the "hardware sophistication part" of the smart environment. Ambient intelligence is another term which have been used to refer to smart environment from time to time. It refers to the same "human centric" aspect of improved experience in an instrumented world. Around 2010 the term Cyber Physical System (CPS) became more common place. The definition of CPS appears below:

Definition 16.1 (*CPS* [22]) Cyber-Physical Systems (CPS) are integrations of computation with physical processes. Embedded computers an networks monitor and control the physical processes, usally with feedback loops where physical processes affect computations and vice versa.

There are three aspects in definition of CPS:

1. Integration of physical process and computation,
2. Controlled by embedded computers and network, and
3. Feedback loop (adaptation).

CPS appeared close to expressing the both defining aspects of a smart environment, namely "intelligence" and "hardware instrumentation". But as hardware sophistication became mature, CPS definition also became inadequate, and qualifier like "smart adaptive" CPS started appearing. To sum up the term "smart environment" should be seen in the current frame of reference with respect to sophistication in integrating hardware instrumentation with computational intelligence. In that sense, the adequacy of terminology is limited to classical problem of capturing contexts through computational intelligence.

16.3 Designing Context-aware Applications

While the enabling technologies are critical to context-aware smart systems, applications occupy dominant space. In this section we first define the important components in planning smart applications.

16.3.1 Representation of Contextual Data

A context in an environment typically pertains to the inhabitants or the objects within that environment. When we talk about extraction a context, first we need to know how a context is defined. According to Merriam Webster Dictionary [8]

Definition 16.2 (*Context*) A set of, possibly, interrelated conditions in which an entity or thing exists.

It means context is non-existent without an entity or a thing. Furthermore, "possibly interrelated" conditions mean that the context includes constituent pieces of residence information of the entity. This implies in an environment, a context of an inhabitant is represented by:

- The location and proximity
- The state of activities, and
- The sate of emotional conditions of the inhabitant.

The location is geolocation such as latitude, longitude, altitude. Location information is sometimes desired with relative to the locations other objects or things. So, proximity information such as close to a building, close to a lake or a river or near the sea are also included as location information. The change in location or proximity is noticeable when walking, running, traveling in cars, trains or airplane. Location information may also include weather conditions such as humidity, temperature pressure, rainfall, etc.

The state of activity include people, other animate objects and their states of activities at different times. Individuals may be watching movie, attending a telephone call, on a skype meeting, etc. The people in a group may be in conversation or assembled in a hall attending power point presentation or a music concert, etc.

Emotional state of an individual is difficult to obtain. Certain cues may be found from the ambient around the person and also from his/her phone sensors. Facial expressions play a distinctive role in communicating emotions to the outside world. If an environment is sufficiently sensorized with cameras, or visual sensors then it can capture the facial expressions. The background noise can provide information whether a person is weeping or in a happy mood. Gyro sensors found in smart phone can measure acoustic signal in the vicinity of a phone [25]. By using signal processing and machine learning techique, it is possible even a determine or identify individuals apart from the background noise.

16.3.2   Extraction of Contextual Data

The extraction of contextual data means knowing or being able to measure such information. For example, in a smart healthcare system, the vital parameters of a patient would constitute a part of the patient's context. Only when the contextual data for the patient is correctly extracted, a regimen of treatment can be evolved. In general, expectations of inhabitants of a smart environment cannot be met in unobtrusive manner unless the surroundings of the inhabitants can be correctly extracted.

Ambient information is one of the critical input for determining the context. So, the development of sensor network technology and its integration with other existing networks are important for the context extractions. Without going into the details of a system it is difficult to appreciate how the contextual data can be extracted. However, the process involved can be described as shown in Fig. 16.1 [2]. Sensors

Fig. 16.1 Processing of
sensory data to contextual
information [2]

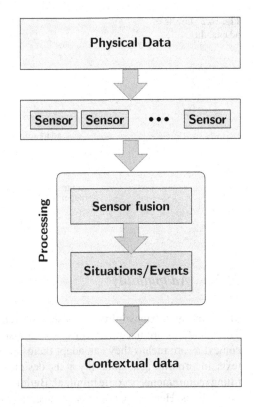

play a distinctive role in gathering data which can be combined using fusion techniques discussed earlier in Chap. 9. After fusion, aggregators may apply inferencing techniques to determine situations or events to which contextual data refer to.

Apart from the environmental data, the two other aspects of data related to the insect eye view of a situation or the events are location data and positioning data. The location data refers to geographical reference data whereas the positioning data refers to the exact the positions of the actors (inhabitants, objects, devices).

Being able to capture contextual data, we could gather information about the context of a person or a system. However, the system should able to interrelate the contextual data to the conditions in which a thing or an entity lives as it represents the current state-of-affairs. So, a concept called situation has been introduced [9]:

Definition 16.3 (*Situation* [9]) A situation is a composite concept whose constituents may be (a combination of) entities and their context conditions.

Situations are thus derived from elementary context conditions. For example, a situation could be that a person in sitting on the far corner of the room and reading a book. A situation has temporal properties such as the time interval during which it holds. The context awareness of a system largely dependent on the ability to correctly derive a situation.

Fig. 16.2 Levels of
adaptability

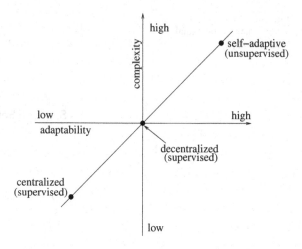

16.3.3   Adaptability

Flexibility and extensibility are basic requirements of a context aware application. These features are necessary for accommodating new services. Applications being context aware means they can adapt themselves to the dynamic nature of their contexts. Incorporating adaptability at the design stages ensures re-engineering or retro-fitting requirements become minimal. Building smart applications has almost infinite possibilities. Hence, adaptability is a necessity in a context aware system. If a system is made fully adaptable, then it is possible to provide a situation or a context as an input and produce control actions or behavior specific to that context. It not only reduces the development cycle of an application but allows new component services to be introduced on demand. Apart from control and management of normal execution, adaptability should include two other aspects, namely, (i) self-healing and (ii) resilience against failures. Self-healing refers to situation where a system diagnoses its failures, localizes the failures and recovers from them. Quite clearly adaptability depends on the ability of the designers to think of the emerging and unseen future workflows of the system.

Adaptability ordinarily captured by installing a feedback loop in context management. Adaptation can be either unsupervised or supervised [10]. Figure 16.2 depicts the levels of adaptability. Complexity of system increases with increase in the level of adapatability. If all control actions are performed under a central control, then everything about system should be known a priori and supervised. In the event of an unknown situation, the system cannot adapt itself or respond properly. However, the complexity of such a system is relatively low. On the other hand, if the control actions are performed in a distributed supervised manner, then the unpredictability increases, but the system may be made more adaptable to unknown situations. The complexity of the system also increases considerably. For example, if a user is mobile and requires a minimum QoS for a multimedia streaming application, then the

Fig. 16.3 Global
characteristics of adaptable
applications

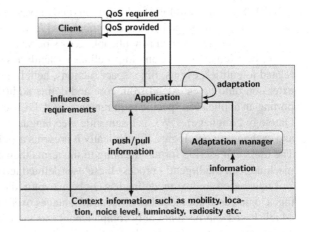

system needs to adjust (high/low) buffering for a minimum playout guarantee. Unsupervised distributed control mostly depend on inferencing mechanism and machine
learning. So, an adaptable application must adhere to a global schema as illustrated
by Fig. 16.3.

16.4 Formal Modeling of Contexts

The notion of context has been in existence since early 90s [18]. Efforts were also
made in developing formalization of contexts [24]. The advantage of a formal model
is that it allows us to formulate various rules, prove theorems and evaluate queries.

The simplest modeling of a context is a key-value pair. However, complex interconnected systems require more sophisticated modeling. Some known modeling
approaches (in decreasing order of popularity) are:

1. Ontology based techniques [7, 30, 38].
2. Unified Modeling Language (UML) based [3, 14].
3. Object Role Modeling (ORM) [20]
4. Logic based modeling [31, 33]

Ontologies are for explicit formal specification of terms in a specific domain
and relationship among these [16]. Ontologies are found to be ideal for a variety of
reasons including the following:

- Sharing common understanding of the structure of information,
- Reusing the domain knowledge,
- Making the domain assumptions explicit,
- Treating the domain knowledge separately from the operational knowledge,
- Analyzing the domain knowledge.

SOUPA (Standard Ontology for Ubiquitous and Pervasive Application) has been proposed for ubiquitous and pervasive applications [7]. It defines two sets of ontologies: one for common set which is applicable across pervasive applications, the other set is for extensions. The core ontology defines vocabularies for expressing the concepts related to entities, events, time, space, actions, belief-and-desire, and policies. The extension ontologies extend from core and define additional vocabularies for supporting an application specific requirements. SOUPA is expressed using OWL (Web Ontology Language). OWL is a semantic web language and standard for encoding and exchanging ontologies. Syntactically it presents a well formed XML document. The users can ascribe formal meaning to the terms they create in OWL. Therefore, machines can intelligently process these user defined terms.

Logic based context modeling has not been explored much. But in formal modeling, a logic based approach has obvious advantages over the other approaches. Using a logic based approach not only completeness and soundness can be established but any complex context can also be created out of a few basic contexts using Boolean operators and quatifiers. It also possible to prove theorems and formulate all the rules in a logical manner.

ORM is primarily for modelling and querying information at a conceptual level. It can express information requirements of any domain or any universe of discourse and is ideal for validating conceptual data models with domain experts. UML, on the other hand, is a unified modeling language used in object oriented software engineering. UML is suitable for object oriented code design, but not ideal for development and validation of conceptual data models. Furthermore, ORM models can also be used for developing UML class diagrams [19]. So ORM provides advantages of both. In context modeling conceptual data validation is important. Therefore, ORM is more popular compared to UML [9].

Chandy and Misra [5] introduced UNITY as model for expressing distributed computation. The idea is to provide a minimal set of notations derived from a restricted form of temporal logic which lends itself well for entire range of development of distributed programs from design to coding and to verification. The program properties are expressed using a small set of predicate relations whose validity can be derived either directly from the program or from the properties obtained through inferencing rules. Roman et al. [33] proposed Context UNITY in order to formalize context-aware design. In their model, a context-aware program belong to a universe which populated by a bounded set of interacting agents. The behavior of each agent is described by a finite set of program types. At an abstract level, each agent is viewed as a state transition system. A context change induces a spontaneous change in agent's state outside its control. But, the operational environment affects agent's state explicitly as per the program definition. The applications are encapsulated as mobile agents. An agent may migrate among connected hosts. Each agent provides its context information to other reachable agents which may influence actions of the receiving agents. The readers interested in learning more details about Context UNITY may refer to [33, 34]. Context UNITY is more about disciplines in organization and development of context aware programming in mobile distributed environment. A reasonable understanding of this framework cannot be met under the scope of this chapter as it would require some background on UNITY [5] and Mobile UNITY [34].

16.4.1 ConChat Model

A simple tuple-oriented representation of contexts was proposed in [31]. The power of the model is demonstrated through implementation of a context based chatting. The model is based on first order predicate calculus and Boolean algebra. Any complex contexts can be built from base level contexts by conjunct and disjunct operators. In this model a basic context is defined by

$$Context(< t, s, r, o >),$$

where,

- t: Denotes type of a context which the predicate expression represents. It could be, e.g., location, temperature, stock price, football score, etc.
- s: Denotes the subject to which the context refers to. For example, if the context is location then subject can be a person, or thing.
- r: Relater may represent either social relationship or comparison operators ($<$, $>$, $\leq$, $\geq$), verb, or preposition.
- o: Object is the value associated with the subject. For example, if t is of type temperature, then its value could be in Farenheit or Celsius.

Examples of some of the basic contexts could be as follows:

```
Context(<Temperature, Outside, Is, 38 C>)
Context(<Stock Price, Reliance, >, 1000>)
Context(<Time, Mumbai, Is, 10:00 01/01/2017>)
Context(<Relationship, Steffi Graf, wife of, Andre Agassi>)
Context(<Train Ticket Status, Mumbai-Delhi, Is, Waiting>)
Context(<Location, Prime Minister, Entering, Parliament>)
```

The values of <Subject>, <Relater>, <Object> will depend on <contextType>. The value of <Relater> can be:

1. Comparison operator: $>$, $<$, $\leq$, $\geq$, etc.
2. Relations such as "brother", "sister", "husband", "wife", etc.
3. Verbs such "Is", "has", or
4. Preposition such as "about", "after", "besides", "entering", "leaving", etc.

16.4.1.1   Operators and Quantifiers

As indicated the model is based on first order predicates, so it has a richer ontology. It allows objects, their properties (unary predicates on objects), relations (n-ary predicates on objects) and functions (mapping of objects to other objects). In other words, it is possible to perform Boolean operations and quantification on these predicates. For example, consider the following expression:

$$Context(< \texttt{Location, Chairman, Entering, Room 344} >)$$
$$\land Context(< \texttt{Activity, Meeting, In, Room 344} >).$$

The above expression means that Chairman is entering room number 344 where a meeting is taking place. Here the conjunct operator $\land$ is being used to create a complex context. Consider a different example given below:

$$Context(< \texttt{EnvironmentalTemperature, Room 344, Is, Low} >)$$
$$\lor Context(< \texttt{Airconditioner, Room 344, Is, On} >).$$

We can also use complement operator $\neg$ to state absence of a context. For example,

$$\neg Context(< \texttt{Location, Chairman, Is in, Room 344} >),$$

says Chairman is not present in room no. 344.

To create richer contexts, we may have one or more arguments of a context predicate to become variable, and quantification operators can be defined over these. Both existential and universal quantifiers can be defined. However, we need to attach a scope with these quantifiers. So, the operator is denoted as $\exists_S$ or $\forall_S$. Essentially, scope S is a set over which the quantifier would make sense. For example,

$$\exists_{loc} X \, Context(< \texttt{Location, Chairman, Is in, X} >),$$

expresses the fact that the Chairman can be found in one of the locations belonging to set loc. Similarly, universal quantifier $\forall$ can be used if a context $\forall_S X \, Context$ $(< t, s, r, o >)$ is true all values of X in the scope S. For example, if want to refer to all persons in a house the expression could be:

$$\forall_{person} X \, Context(< \texttt{Location, X, In, White House} >).$$

One may create context expression for application by using the context expression and quantifiers. For example, a class room controller can provide attendance in a lecture by using the following context expression.

$$\exists_{person} X \, Context(< \texttt{Location, X, Entering, Class room} >).$$

The model uses many sorted logic. It consists of many universes ("sorts") $U_1, U_2,$ $\ldots, U_n$, For example,

- `Persons` refers to all names of person in the system,
- `Location` refers to valid locations, and so on.

Quantification is performed on only over the specific set of values.

16.4.1.2 ConChat Application

ConChat [31] is a chat application which lets users to know about contextual information. For example, it can transfer the following information:

1. Party location
2. Number of other persons (excluding the person engaged in chat) present in the room
3. The identities of other persons.
4. Room temperature, light, and sound.
5. User's mood (happy, sad, or excited).
6. User's status (on phone or out for lunch).
7. Activity in the room (meeting, lecture in progress).

Some of the rules that ConChat uses are:

- If there are more than 3 persons in a room and power-point application is running, then it implies a presentation is in progress.
- If there are more than 3 persons in a room and power-point application is not running, then it implies a meeting is taking place.
- If there is just a one person is a room and MATLAB application is running, then it implies that the person is doing some program development.
- If there are more than five persons in the room, sound level is high and an entertainment application is running, then it implies that some party is on.

Corresponding to each of the above contextual information, an appropriate logical expression can be evolved. For example, in the first case the context information is represented by

$$Context(< \#\texttt{persons}, \texttt{Room}344, \geq 3 >)\wedge$$
$$Context(< \texttt{Application}, \texttt{Powerpoint}, \texttt{Is}, \texttt{Running} >) \implies$$
$$Context(< \texttt{Room}, \texttt{Activity}, \texttt{Room}344, \texttt{Is}, \texttt{Presentation} >).$$

The system level view of the ConChat application is shown in Fig. 16.4. Information about context providers is available with the context engine. Chat application finds the context providers by interacting with the context engine. Context information are gathered by the context providers are made available to the main application. Therefore, one end may query the context of the other end and accordingly adapt to

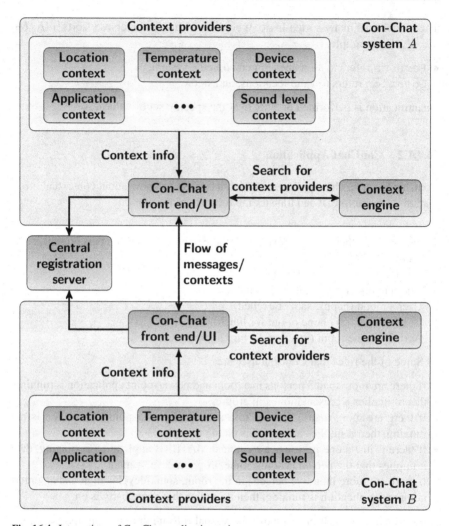

Fig. 16.4 Interactions of ConChat application units

the conversation. For example, if ConChat-A's user is in a meeting then ConChat-B can end the conversation. Suppose ConChat-A would like to stop conversation if some person enters the room. For this to be possible A sends a context query of the form:

$$\exists_{person} XContext(< \texttt{Location}, X, \texttt{Entering}, \texttt{Room}\, 344 >).$$

to ConChat-B. Whenever ConChat-B evaluates the expression to be true it sends a notification to ConChat-A. Then ConChat-A's user becomes aware of person X's presence in the room. As we can see contextual chatting has following advantages:

- It offers more privacy. For example, in an on going conversation a user can place a request for notification when change in situations occurs at the other user's end. When notification appears the first user's end then he/she can stop the conversation or adapt it according to changed situation.
- The users can proactively specify which context can be notified to other users. In fact, an access control regime can be placed by specifying who can see which context.
- Having knowledge of a user's context automatically resolves ambiguities in conversation. For example, context can be sent before the beginning of the conversation in related topic.
- It allows some of the semantic ambiguities to be resolved by the system. For example, when humans engage in conversation every one has the notion of a local context such as time, location, currency units, data format, various units of measurements, etc. Using context most of these can be resolved automatically.

Our focus is here not in implementation of ConChat, but more on capturing context through a formal logic based framework. The interested reader can read the paper [31] for more information and implementation aspect of ConChat system.

16.5 System Requirements

In software engineering, it is a practice to list out user's expectations from a new or modified system. The requirements guides an implementor's execution plan. We follow the same practice here. The requirements of a smart environment originate from two different prospectives, namely,

1. From users/inhabitants.
2. From technology.

We discuss these two sets of requirements separately.

16.5.1 Inhabitants Centered Requirements

All requirements centered on inhabitants of an environment can be seen to have roots at the ways and means in which inhabitants may wish to interact with computing devices, the objects that make up the environment. Considering this, Abowd and Sterbenz [1] listed these requirements from the point of view of developing intelligent HCI. A synopsis of important requirements is as follows:

1. Interfaces for consumption of information consisting of two important aspects, namely

    a. Preserving privacy and security.
    b. Efficiency in response.

2. Scheduling or executing right task at right time.
3. Context awareness and adaptability.
4. Interruption and resumption.
5. Activity and control of interaction.

The efficacy of information consumption depends entirely on the way the interfaces present the information to the inhabitants. The inhabitants may change their locations, the objects in the environment may change location, or the state of the environment may change due to space or the objects getting modified. Some of the agents of change may external, many others could be internal to an environment, while still others may have intangible existence such as emotions, feelings, etc., associated with the individuals. There are two sets of goals for designing Human Computer Interface (HCI) [1] for a smart environment:

1. *Individual goals*: Each human inhabitant in an environment has its own set of priorities. These priorities set goals for person centric services that is expected from a smart environment. We can view these goals broadly as of three types: (i) privacy, (ii) efficiency, and (iii) dynamicity.
2. *Common goals*: Common goals refer to commonality in interactions of the inhabitants with the environment. The goals of each individual may differ considerably due, each person's role, personal preferences, emotions and psychological demeanor. Still there are considerable commonality among the requirements of a group of individuals. When the inhabitants share an environment, there is a natural understanding that the group has a set of common goals. Three things are important here: (i) task scheduling, (ii) task management and (iii) awareness.

A smart environment will require personal biometrics and the ID related information of an inhabitant in order to access person centric preferences and adapt itself to bring comfort to the interacting person. These personal preferences may even include emotional states, and other confidential details. Since, most environment work over Internet in connected spaces, preserving privacy and security of an inhabitant is an important requirement for building smart environment. Efficiency in gathering of inputs and dissemination of outputs are very important goals in design of intelligent HCI. It allows the inhabitants to interact at the right time in the right manner requiring less or no attention. One of the aim of ubiquitous computing is that technology should disappear in background. Any interface which requires attention makes its presence dominate may sometimes intimidate the users. The interfaces should be dynamic, i.e., automatically discoverable, and follow a user as he/she moves about.

The issues related to scheduling refer to determining when a task may begin, when it may end and when it may be interrupted. How would the environment handle interruptions? Whether resumption will happen automatically or require interaction from inhabitants? The task management allows the inhabitants to exercise control over their executions. The flexibility in level of control and the range of control that can be exercised on tasks are important determining factors governing smartness of an environment. Group centric control of tasks can come in direct conflicts with person centric control. The question may arise as to how such conflicts can be resolved. This implies generics should be separable, and designed to complement person centric control.

The next aspect is awareness. Smart spaces must be unobtrusive, and also allow the inhabitants to perform tasks which were otherwise not possible in a normal environment. Awareness of both environment and its inhabitants may evolve with time. Awareness, therefore, is a learning process that smart environment should possess. It allows more and more tasks to be performed not only successfully but satisfactorily as well.

Interruption is particularly to annoying. But there may be situations where interruptions are necessary, but before that two questions need to be settled: (i) how and when notifications related interruption should be communicated?, and (ii) how the interrupted task could be resumed? If inhabitants need to be reminded for resumption, then the reminder should be as unobtrusive as possible.

Finally, the ease in carrying out normal activities is an important issue within a smart environment. It should not be the case the smart environment would force the inhabitants to behave in an expected manner or create disruption in their normal activities, rather it should provide some value added capabilities.

Clearly, the design characteristics an HCI as explained above can be created without a framework of interdisciplinary research. Inputs from cognitive scientists and social psychologists may be key design consideration. Apart from individual preferences, convenience, etc., group centric goals and requirements must co-exist without conflicts in a smart environment.

16.5.2 Technology Related Issues

Network, nodes (computers) and spaces (logical or physical) make up infrastructural framework of a smart environment as illustrated in Fig. 16.5 [1]. We describe technological challenges in each.

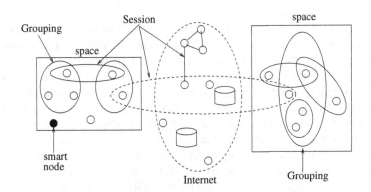

Fig. 16.5 Infrastructural framework of smart environment [1]

Network:

Network creates a physical space in which nodes reside and communicate. Smart spaces are built on the top of network layer. The scale is important because even a single inhabitant may require tens of thousands nodes in the surrounding smart space. A smart space may consist of huge number of embedded bio-sensors, image sensors, ambient measurement sensors (pressure, temperatures, luminosity), motion sensor (presence, vibration, acceleration), chemical activity sensor. Apart from embedded sensors, smart appliances such as toasters, refrigerators, air conditioners, cars, washing machines, cooking ranges, ovens, water sprinklers, etc., may have many on board sensors and computers.

Interconnecting these with implicit and explicit HCIs leads to complex networks. On the top of this, the networked objects should be remotely accessible by smart gears (watches, smart jacket, goggles, etc.) worn by individuals or their phone. The framework of such a physical space with smart objects connected over internet is known as (Internet of Things) IoT. Density of nodes in an IoT could pose serious challenges in protocol design. The priority setting for each object must be carefully done, so that task interruption does not create unpleasant feelings for the users.

Most IoTs rely on wireless channels for network connectivity. Low bandwidth connectivity, promiscuity and interferences makes make these networks vulnerable to attacks of various type. So, security and privacy related issues should be adequately addressed before wireless channels can used. Some of the new research issues that has emerged in this space are related to software defined radios [26]. One of the important technical problem in this respect is interoperability of different communication technologies. The problem of interoperability is not easy to handle, as frame structures used by different communication technologies are different, and the network protocols also vary significantly. It creates problems that cost overheads in terms of assembly and disassembly of frames. Devising single optimized unified network stack is becomes challenging, if not impossible [37]. Nodes with multiple network stacks are complex, expensive and have inherent performance handicaps. Thus following is a summary of important research challenges in network space:

Nodes:

Computations in smart environment are distributive in nature, each node performs a role according to a context. The challenge comes from the nodes embedded to wearable devices. Micro-kernels have to be developed for the nodes so that they can handle specific computation according to a context. For example, bio-sensors attached to patient wearables may monitor vital parameters of a patient, or a personal assistant (PDA) could remotely control a variety of IoTs. Such specialized nodes are referred to as smart nodes. Some smart nodes may perform multiple roles such as controlling inputs from a number of peripherals such as flat touch panels, wireless keyboards, cameras, etc. Handling of faults should be an integral part of the node functionality. For example, connectivity could be lost due to some personal node acting as the only access point for smart objects or internet. All these functionalities for reaching from one point of network to another point and to internet should be possible as many alternative ways as possible. Also some amount of QoS threshold needed for every path in the network. A wide spectrum of nodes over network complying to different standards need a wide variety of transport protocols which should interoperate seamlessly.

Softwares:

Perhaps the most difficult challenge comes from software. Any smart environment will consists some wiring of devices deep inside structures like bridges, or rooms in buildings such as hospitals, business conventions centers, etc. Similarly, devices may be embedded in parts of a rail road car, or a cruise boat. Therefore, embedded devices could become obsolete soon with hardware and software advancements. This means lot of legacy softwares will have to be maintained or re-engineered from time to time. As far as functionalities are concerned a software is not just a piece of code, but it could be a view of the entire workflow that captures many complex engineering and design processes. For example, civil constructions are not always well designed so various amenities that provide building blocks of a smart environment have to be adaptable, and maintainable. A simple instance could be waste water management of a building or the heating/air conditioner system. This may require software to incorporate almost complete understanding of building plan, capabilities of various masonry and plumbing ducts, electrical power supply limitations, etc. Apart from this the software should try to optimize the solutions according to goals set by the inhabitants of the building. The challenges are far too many. We may just list out a few of these.

1. Resource discovery: location and characteristics of nearby resources.
2. Interoperability: devices handling various parts of the workflow to handle connected tasks must interoperate.
3. Location awareness: location of users or devices should be discoverable within centimeters or according to requirements.
4. Mobility awareness: if devices are shifted, or the user has moved, the software should adapt itself to provide optimized solution for the new arrangement of environment.
5. Event management: software should be able to react to emergent situations.
6. Legacy support: already discussed above.
7. Addressing: identity of persons and objects are fundamental to execution of a solution.
8. Security and privacy: specially in public places, it is important to preserve security and privacy of interacting individuals.
9. Fault tolerance: any smart system should implement robust fault tolerance, specially for critical devices. For example, internet connectivity for critical functions should be available through alternative routes when main router is down.

Clearly, the list brings out the inherent complexities that software has to counter in implementation of a smart environment.

16.6   Middleware Architectures

Data fusion carried by sensor nodes is mostly elementary. Aggregators perform tasks of combining and generating higher level context abstractions. Aggregators are generally colocated at context storage so that they may perform some additional tasks such as converting other meaningful contextual referencing of data. For example, GPS location (latitude, longitude) can be converted to a reference point with respect to a room, a building or a football field.

A context management system consists of context storage and centered around the general model of a producer consumer system. Besides producers and consumers, it may additionally consists of aggregators. A producer tells availability of context information to context storage. The job of a producer is to collect raw data from sources such as sensors, configuration files, other static/dynamic sources. These raw data are processed into contextual elements by the producers. Context storage send notifications of events or situations to the consumers who have registered with it. A number of solutions have been proposed for context management, we review only a few of them to give a overview of different approaches found in literature. A recent review of literature in context-aware systems can be found in [9]. A taxonomy of these architectures is provided in Fig. 16.6 with some examples. There are four basic types of architectures: layered, service-oriented, agent-oriented, object-oriented.

Fig. 16.6 Architecture for context management

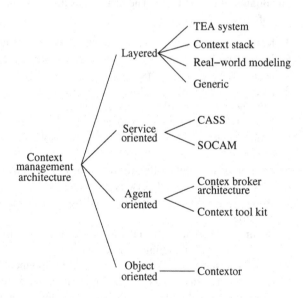

16.6.1 Layered Middleware Architecture

Layered architecture is most common. The lowest layer in any layered architecture is provided by sensors, actuators and other hardware related accessories such as RFID, camera, GPS, etc. TEA system [35] uses a three layer architecture. Sensor layer is responsible for gathering sensory data. An abstraction layer sits on the top of sensor layer. The role of the abstraction layer is to provide cues to the context layer. In that sense, the abstraction layer is kind of tied to the sensor layer for providing abstractions to access sensor hardware and software. The abstraction layer may not, therefore, be considered as a separate layer. The context layer builds contexts using the cues. A scripting layer provides mechanisms to harnessing the context by the applications.

Context stack [40] is another layered architecture. It has five layers: acquisition, representation, aggregation, interpretation and utilization. It uses a context database for storing knowledge and history. The acquistion layer is the lowest layer and deals with gathering of raw data from sensor. The representation layer is responsible for understanding relevance of data such as temperature, pressure, luminosity, location, etc., and their reporting threshold. In some sense it provides the abstractions of sensory data. Then third layer aggregates sensor data using aggregation or fusion and applying virtual context knowledge base. Layer 2 from top interprets the context using machine learning and inferencing mechanisms. The top layer caters to context requirement of applications.

Real world modeling [21] is also a layered architecture. Gathering real world data is performed in phase one from RFID tags, GPS, camera and sensors. In phase two, a real world model is built by associating the data retrieved after phase one from sensors, and other data gathering hardware. Phase two achieves this by performing a sequence of four steps: (i) processing IDs of sensors, (ii) obtaining attributes of objects to which hardware IDs are associated, (iii) recoginition of situations from object's point of view, and (iv) recoginition of semantic and history. Phase three is for service determination. It has two steps: (i) service detetction and (ii) service coordination. The final phase is for provisioning service.

A generic layered architecture [36] is defined on the basis of steps that all layered middleware context-aware architectures perform. Figure 16.7 illustrates the interactions of various components of the proposed architecture. The lowest layer is referred to as lexical level which abstracts sensor signals into the various events of contexts. Syntactical level is the next higher layer which is responsible for translating the context events to elementary context information. The elementary context information are reasoned refined and organized for more processing at a higher level called reasoning level and stored in the context repository. The context repository can be accessed through APIs in the planning level, which is the next higher layer. It applies rules and performs inferencing to build contexts from the context information. Systems then react to changes in the context reaction level.

Fig. 16.7 Generic architecture for context management [36]

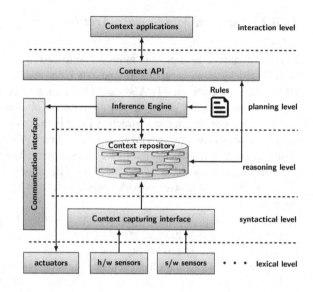

16.6.2 Service Oriented Middleware

CASS (Context-aware Substructure System) [13] is a centralized server based context middleware architecture. It consists of a Sensor Listener, a Rule Engine, a Context Retriever and an Interpreter. Sensor Listener has a communication subclass called Change Listener. It listens to the updates from the sensors and hands over to the Sensor Listener for storing them. The Context Retriever retrieves stored contexts. It requires services of the Change Listener. It provides the context change notifications to applications. The Rule Engine is the central piece of the CASS. It refers to the context repository to retrieve context changes and then applies the rules stored in the knowledge base to determine the actions corresponding to the current context.

SOCAM (Service Oriented Context Middleware) proposed by Gu et al. [17] is an ontology based context interpreter system that provides the following basic services:

1. Reasoning services.
2. Managing consistency of the contexts, e.g., controls smart appliances and reasoning about the activities of the environment inhabitants.
3. Fusing of multiple low level contexts.

As Fig. 16.8 shows, it consists of

- Context providers
- Context interpreters
- Context database
- Service location service
- Context aware mobile service

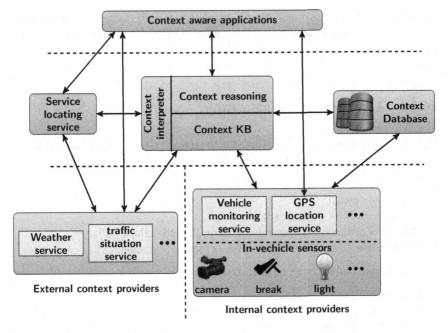

Fig. 16.8 Architecture of SOCAM [17]

Each context provider is registered with service locating service, which enable it to be discovered by others. External context providers get contexts from external sources such as weather information server, or traffic information server, etc. Internal context provider acquire contexts from directly from internal sensors such as in-vehicle camera, head light, break pedal, GPS receiver, etc. Context interpreter creates high level contexts by interpreting low level contexts. It has a inference engine and a knowledge base. Knowledge base provides APIs for other components to query, add, delete, or update context knowledge.

Unified Context-aware Application Model (UCAM) has been proposed in [29]. UCAM consists of UCAM sensors and UCAM services. Internal components of two components interface in a layered manner. Externally, contexts are provided by different UCAM services. In that sense, it can be classified as a service oriented middleware. A UCAM sensor defined by an abstraction over a physical sensor. A UCAM service is a context processing unit. Raw signals collected from physical sensor are subjected to a signal processing step. UCAM sensor can support all basic signal processing such as peak extraction and filtering functions. A preliminary context is created by UCAM sensor's context generation module. This module uses an XML file where sensory profile information is available. The preliminary contexts collected from UCAM sensor is processed further by a communicator which configures communities and manages heterogeneous entities. Context manager and interpreter perform behavior of a context-aware service by using unified contex representation model. Service provider manages a service profile to support applications. Figure 16.9 [29] illustrates the workflow related to context creation and its use for providing context-aware services in UCAM architecture.

16.6.3 Agent Oriented Middleware

Dey et al. [12] proposed an agent based architecture called Context Toolkit. It provides a number of services which includes the following:

1. Encapsulation of sensor.
2. Storage of context.
3. Access control for privacy protection.
4. Sharing of context data over network through well defined APIs.
4. Composition of context to build richer context information.

Context Toolkit defines three main abstractions:

1. Context widgets
2. Context aggregators
3. Context interpreters

The flow of data between these entities are shown in Fig. 16.10. Widgets are mediators between a user and the environment. A widget encapsulate information about one context element such as location or activity. Widgets can be accessed by applications or other components (interpreter, server) through a uniform interface. Aggregators are meta widgets which have abilities to compose contexts information about real world entities like objects, users, devices and places. They provide a gateway service between application and elementary widgets hiding details of sensing mechanism. Server is responsible for aggregation of contexts. Interpreters abstract high-level context from low level context by using inferencing logic. For example, identity, location, noise level can be interpreted as airport ambience. An interpreter can be accessed by widgets, server, other interpreters.

Context Broker Architecture (CoBrA) [6] in reality a centralized layered architecture, it employs agents as mediators for resource poor mobile devices to communicate with the context service middleware. CoBra employs OWL for modeling ontology for context reasoning. It has four components: context knowledge base, context reasoning engine, context acquisition, and policy management which interact among themselves in a layered manner. Knowledge base is a persistent storage for storing context knowledge. It also provides APIs to access stored knowledge. Reasoning module is essentially a reactive inference engine that employs ontologies to determine context knowledge. It may use heuristics to detect and resolve inconsistencies in context knowledge. The role of context acquisition module is similar to that of widgets in Context Tookit [12]. Policy management module consists of inference rules that determines the instructions for enforcing user's policies for dissemination of context change notifications.

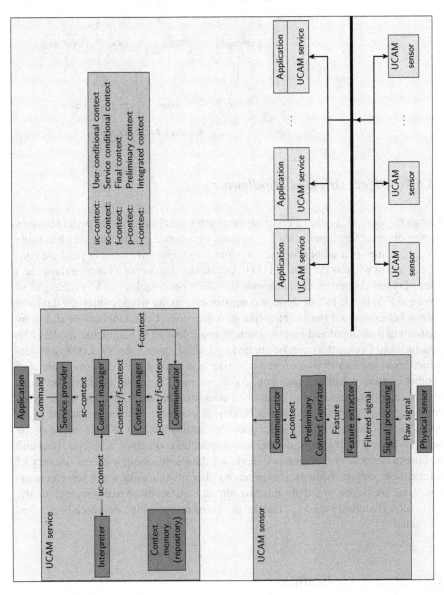

Fig. 16.9 Processing sensor data to context [29]

Fig. 16.10 Data flow in
context toolkit [12]

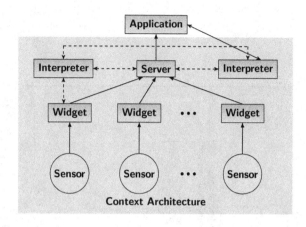

16.6.4   Object Oriented Middleware

Rey and Coutaz [32] defined contextor as a software abstraction to model relations
among observables. It performs aggregation by returning values for an observable
from the values of a set of observables. Contextor appear to extend beyond the concept of sensor widgets proposed in [11]. A contextor consists of a functional core and
a set of typed communication channels on which observables can be exchanged as
shown in Fig. 16.11. In that sense, a contextor essentially wraps contextual data and
control behaviors into single entity like an object does. Contextors can be linked by
connecting their input and output channels much like an I/O autmaton model [23].
Federations of contextors can be created by linking them together. Linking is permitted provided data-in channel of a contextor is compliant with data-out channel of
another contextor. Linking may not be commutative. A colony of interlinked contextors can be encapsulated as compound contextor. So, one can define an arbitrary
composition of contexts so long as linking is possible. A contextor stored as an
XML file (for interoperability) on a node. It contains location of node, name of the
network to which it belongs, control and inspection commands it accepts, data and
meta-data types of output channel, mode for data acquisition, mode of delivery of
information, output channels, maximum number of data sinks it can serve concurrently, etc. A contextor supply information on request, or on query-change mode,
or on subscribe-notify mode. It may be delivered periodically or on each time when
computed.

16.7   Smart Applications

Smart environment, in general, consists of devices and objects that are static or
mobile. A few of these devices can be ultramobile. Mostly smart appliances are static

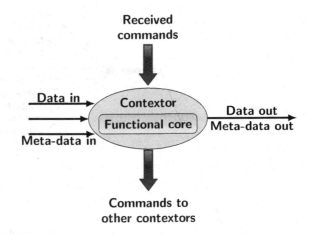

Fig. 16.11 Schematic representation of a contextor [32]

by nature if they are not portable. Though portable appliances may move when carried in person or autonomously, the movement is slow and discrete. For such objects, the environment or surrounding space experience only slight or occasional changes. Creating smart space out of these largely static and infrastructure supported objects or things is simpler compared to when space consists of ultra mobile devices. Ultra mobile devices are mostly carried in person. Not only the surroundings these ultra mobile devices change rapidly and durations of their interactions with applications are short. For example, consider the environments encountered by a smart phone carried by a person. It undergoes changes as the person travels in car, walks from a parking lot to office, or home, or enters airport, etc. Making such ultra mobile devices to be adaptive is an effective step for creation of smart environments. The smartness of an environment depends how effectively the smart applications can make use contextual data from sensors in ultra mobile devices and combine these with the data/measurements obtained from the other sensors in appliances and things in the environments.

The requirements of adaptivity is different from one user to another. Typically, background noise level, intensity of light, presence of other persons in the neighborhood are some of the factors that influence adaptivity. Generally, a mid-range smart phone comes with 10 or more different embedded sensors. Figure 16.12 illustrates the embedded sensors in a smart phone. Since a smart phone is almost always carried in person, the embedded sensors in a phone can provide contextual data related to the carrier and most importantly the immediate neighborhood of the carrier. For example, measurements received from phone sensors not only tell whether the person is in motion but also which mode of transport the person is possibly using. Even the direction of motion can be found in 3D by combining magnetometer, gyroscope and acelerometer measurements. Using these data, the application designers can develop applications that are context aware.

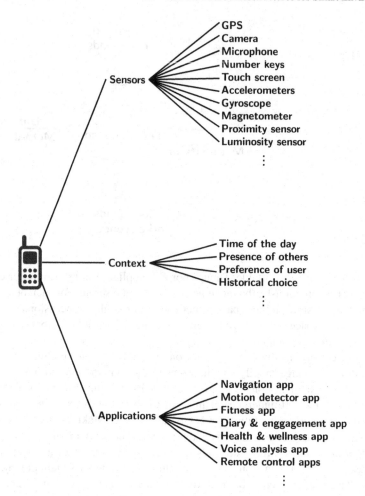

Fig. 16.12 Adaptivity scenario using smart phone sensors

16.7.1   Context-aware Applications Using Smart Phones

Some of the interesting context aware applications that have been developed by using smart phones as communication gateways are:

- GPS assisted transportation and navigation applications.
- Smart phone assisted indoor navigation of visually impaired persons.
- Application for monitoring health and well being.
- Transient social networking using sensing of presence.

Fig. 16.13 Flow of displacement data from wheel to smart phone

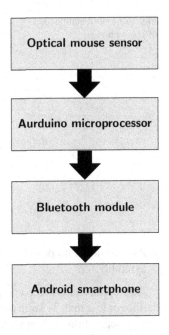

16.7.1.1 GPS Assisted Transportation and Navigation

In GPS assisted transportation and navigation systems are largely developed around GPS data from phones of the users. Simple navigation application like finding route from a source to a destination leverages city route maps to guide the user to destination from the current location. This application are adaptive to the transport modes that a user may be use. The context related transport mode can be derived from accelerometer, magnetometer, and magnetometer sensors. The application can be integrated with bus schedule and the arrivals of buses at a stop or terminus. There are applications such as cab service which enables the commuters to hail cab service through GPS assisted apps. Overall traffic situations of a road network are crowd sourced from phone data and navigation data can be made adaptive to congestion in route, and dynamically reroute path to a destination.

16.7.1.2 Smart Walking Stick

An indoor navigation application and a prototype design for a smart walking stick (for visually impaired persons) have been presented in [15]. It uses two types of embedded sensors: (i) on phone sensors, and (ii) sensors to capture actual displacement through walking stick. The hardware assembly for this prototype consists of:

- A walking stick is modified by putting a trolley like assembly at the end which touches the ground.
- An optical sensor of type ADNS-2610 (used in PS/2 computer mice) is placed about 2–3 mm away from the surface of the trolley wheels.

Fig. 16.14 Orientation axes
of smart phone

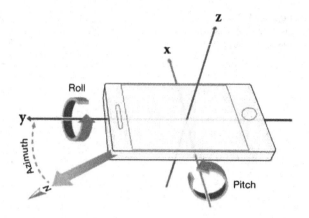

- An Arduino Uno processor board with Bluetooth interface is fitted to the trolley assembly.

The optical sensor record can displacement provided it is either in contact with surface or less than 2–3 mm away from the surface. Therefore, the sensors are placed with a separation of 2 mm from the wheels of trolley. The optical sensor records angular displacements as the wheels roll. The angular displacement is passed on to the smart phone of the user through the sensor board via Bluetooth interface. Figure 16.13 illustrates the flow of displacement data. The smart phone then combines the displacement data with inbuilt magnetometer's rotation data and updates user's position as the user moves on, by dragging the modified walking stick. The orientation axes of an Android smartphone is depicted in Fig. 16.14. The phone uses the route map of the building and guides the user by voice communication over a Bluetooth receiver. The route map can be obtained at the entrance of the building using NFC or RFID tags. For a detailed description of the prototype the reader may refer to [15]. There is enough scope for improving the prototype, and creating a smart walking stick without extensive instrumentation of the indoor environment.

16.7.1.3   MHealthcare

A general framework of mHealthcare was described earlier in Chap. 1. The major thrust in smart personal health care has been to cut down visits to the doctors. The approach is to rely largely on self-monitored report surveys on the status of personal health. Wearable wireless body area network (WWBAN) consists of inexpensive sensors which can be used for long term ambulatory monitoring of the health parameters. The smart phone carried by a person acts as a gateway to communicate data gathered by WWBAN to update the medical data to cloud. The phone can also send priority messages through specially installed context aware Apps for urgent assistances. Figure 16.15 illustrates the architecture of an integrated system for health monitoring. WWBAN connects through smart phone held in person by the user to various health related services over internet. It has options to route data through different network

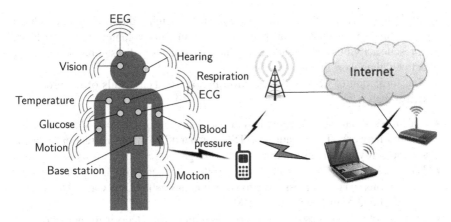

Fig. 16.15 Integrated health monitoring system

connection protocols as indicated by the figure. For example, priority messages in form of SMSes can be sent over 3G/4G network to emergency/ambulance service, to relatives or friends and the specialist physicians. While this is being done the medical report can be sent patient's laptop over WLAN or Bluetooth. Then the report is sent from there to a central medical server using Internet broadband connection.

16.7.1.4 Emergency Alert and Response System

Sometimes organizing immediate professional help in a disaster situation becomes a problem due to several reasons including the strict protocols under which the formal organizations function. For example, a relief train may take several hours before it reaches a rail accident site at a remote location. Under such situations, immediate help is rushed to victims usually by the community volunteers of the neighborhood of the disaster location. The volunteers largely operate in isolation and much of the efforts are, therefore, uncoordinated.

Transient Social Networking (TSN) is a spontaneous social networking based on presence of persons in an geographical region at a specific time or at occurrences of specific events. Following are important features of TSN

- A TSN supports on-demand encounter based formation unlike traditional internet based social networks (Facebook, Google circles, Foursquare, etc.).
- In a TSN, people may or may not know each other but willing to collaborate (people's interests are aligned) for limited time when they happen to encounter one another.
- TSN formation is dependent on both spatial and temporal locality.
- Furthermore, TSN can support latency sensitive communication by exploiting local wireless communication infrastructure, and reduced traffic on internet.

An emergency alert and response service system based on TSN framework has been proposed in [4]. This system dynamically organizes a peer to peer network of smart phones carried by the volunteers present in the neighborhood of a geographhical region. Through a TSN of smart phones, the community volunteers can coordinate their rescue activities and provide emergency assistances to disaster hit victims more effectively than working in isolation.

The formation of TSN is illustrated in Fig. 16.16. The details of the process is described below:

- A distress situation is triggered by a user injecting a Distress Message (DM) into the network. The creation of TSN for handling distress situation happens automatically in response to this initial message.
- The spreading of a DM occurs in controlled manner through a central tracker over internet via cloud messaging to special nodes called Data Carts (DCs) in the neighborhood of the originator of DM.
- DC then spreads the message to a set of community volunteers in the neighborhood forming the TSN.
- Once TSN is formed the volunteers coordinate their activities via cloud messaging for which a special ontology oriented emoji based messaging framework is used. The ontology depends on the disaster type. Alternatively formal logic based modeling can also be used for each disaster type.
- Using a formal modeling framework, complex contexts are determined for a clear understanding of the disaster situation. This will help the untrained community based rescue volunteers not only to find out specific requirements (resources) for handling the disaster but also to coordinate more effectively.
- A volunteer can be part of multiple TSNs depending on the role he/she plays. The privacy requirements are met by access control mechanism based on message flow labeling [28].

The suggested framework is not only realizable [4], but can also be used as a distributed message dissemination service for a variety of interesting purposes. For example, the advertisers can use mobile phone based TSN for targeted promotion of products in a specific area. In a shopping arcade a retailer may promote a new

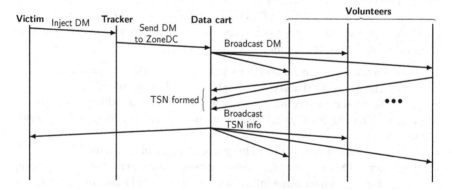

Fig. 16.16 Formation of a TSN for handling a distress situation

product by announcing special discounts to patrons. The patrons may view hot deals and see instant reviews from other patrons about the product.

References

1. G.D. Abowd, J.P.G. Sterbenz, Final report on the inter-agency workshop on research issues for smart environment. IEEE Personal Commun. Mag. **7**(5), 36–45 (2000)
2. S. Bartolini, *Smart Sensor for Interoperable Smart Environment*. PhD thesis, Dept of Computer Science, 2009
3. J. Bauer, Identification and modeling of contexts for different information scenarios in air traffic. Technical report, Technische Universität Berlin, Diplomarbeit, March 2003
4. A. Bhatnagar, A. Kumar, R.K. Ghosh, R.K. Shyamasundar, A framework of community inspired distributed message dissemination and emergency alert response system over smart phones, in *Eigth International Conference on Communication Systems and Networks (COMSNETS)* (IEEE Press, 2016), pp. 1–8
5. K.M. Chandy, J. Misra, *Parallel Program Design: A Foundation* (Addison-Wesley, 1988)
6. H. Chen, T. Finin, A. Joshi, Semantic web in the context broker architecture, in *The Second IEEE Annual Conference on Pervasive Computing and Communications (PerCom 2004)* (March 2004), pp. 277–286
7. H. Chen, T. Finin, A. Joshi, The SOUPA ontology for pervasive computing, in *Ontologies for Agents: Theory and Experiences*, ed. by V. Tamma, S. Cranefield, T.W. Finin, S. Willmott (Springer, 2005), pp. 233–258
8. Context (n.d.), *Merriam-Websters collegiate dictionary*. Merriam Webster
9. P.D. Costa, in *Architectural Support for Context-Aware Applications: From Context Models to Service Platforms*. PhD thesis, Center for Telematics and Information Technology, Enschede, The Netherlands, 2007
10. M. Dalmau, P. Roose, S. Laplace, Context aware adaptable applications: a global approach. Int. J. Comput. Sci. Issues **1**, 13–25 (2009)
11. A.K. Dey, G.D. Abowd, A conceptual framework and a toolkit for supporting rapid prototyping of context-aware applications. Human-Comput. Interact. J. **16**(2–4), 97–166 (2001)
12. A.K. Dey, G.D. Abowd, D. Salber, *Designing and building context-aware applications* Technical report (Gorgia Institute of Technology, 2001)
13. P. Fahy, S. Clarke, CASS—middleware for mobile context-aware applications, in *Workshop on Context Awareness* (MobiSys, 2004)
14. F. Fuchs, I. Hochstatter, M. Krause, M. Berger, A meta model approach to context information, in *The Second IEEE PerCom Workshop on Context Modeling and Reasoning (CoMoRea)* (Hawaii, USA, March 2005)
15. R.K. Ghosh, V. Kataria, V. Mishra, Indoor navigation using optical mouse sensor and smart phone, in *2014 International Conference on Indoor Positioning and Indoor Navigation (IPIN 2014)*, 27–30th October 2014
16. T.R. Gruber, A translation approach to portable ontology specification. Knowl. Acquisition **5**, 199–220 (1993)
17. T. Gu, H.K. Pung, D. Zhang, A service-oriented middleware for building context-aware services. J. Netw. Comput. Appl. **28**(1), 1–18 (2005)
18. R. Guha, Contexts: a formalization and some applications. Technical report, Stanford University, 1992
19. T. Halpin, A. Bloesch, Data modeling in UML and ORM: a comparison. J. Database Manage. **10**(4), 4–13 (1999)
20. K. Henricksen, J. Indulska, A software engineering framework for context-aware pervasive computing, in *The 2nd IEEE Conference on Pervasive Computing and Communications (Percom 2004)*, 2004

21. G. Kunito, K. Sakamoto, N. Yamada, T. Takakashi, S. Tanaka, Architecture for providing services in the ubiquitous computing environment, in *The 26th IEEE International Conference on Distributed Computing Systems Workshops (ICDCSW'06)*, July 2006, pp. 60–60
22. E.A. Lee, Cyber physical systems: design challenges (invited paper), in *International Symposium on Object/Component/Service Oriented Real-Time Distributed Computing (ISORC)* (FL, USA, May 6 2008)
23. N. Lynch, M. Tuttle, An introduction to input/output automate. CWI Quart. **2**(3), 219–246 (1989)
24. J. McCarthy, Notes on formalizing context, in *The Thirteenth International Joint Conference on Artificial Intelligence (IJCAI-93)* (Mountain View, CA, 1993). Morgan Kaufmann. http://www-formal.stanford.edu/jmc/home.html
25. Y.D.B. Michalevsky, N. Gabi, Gyrophone: recognizing speech from gyroscope signals, in *23rd USENIX Security Symposium (USENIX Security 14)*, 2014
26. J. Mitola, *Cognitive Radio: An Integrated Agent Architecture for Software Defined Radio*. PhD thesis, Royal Institute of Technology (KTH), Sweden, 2000
27. H. Nakashima, H. Aghajan, J.C. Augusto, *Handbook of Ambient Intelligence and Smart Environments* (Springer, 2009)
28. N.V. Narendra, R.K. Shyamasundar, Realizing purpose-based privacy policies succinctly via information-flow labels. BDCloud 753–760 (2014)
29. Y. Oh, J. Han, W. Woo, A context management architecture for large-scale smart environment. IEEE Commun. Mag. 118–126, (2010)
30. D. Preuveneers et al., Towards an extensible context ontology for ambient intelligence, in *Second European Symposium on Ambient Intelligence (EUSAI 2004)* (Eindhoven, The Netherlands, 2004)
31. A. Ranganathan, R.H. Campbell, A. Ravi, A. Mahajan, Conchat: a context-aware chat program. IEEE Pervasive Comput. **1**(3), 51–57 (2002)
32. G. Rey, J. Coutaz, The contextor infrastructure for context-aware computing. in *Component-Oriented Approaches to Context-Aware Computing, Held in Conjunction with ECOOP'04* (Oslo, Norway, 2004)
33. G.C. Roman, C. Julien, J. Payton, Modeling adaptive behaviors in contex unity. Theor. Comput. Sci. **376**(3), 185–204 (2007)
34. G.C. Roman, P.J. McCann, *An Introduction to Mobile UNITY* (Springer, Berlin, Heidelberg, 1998), pp. 871–880
35. A. Schmidt, There is more to context than location. Comput. Graph. J. **33**(6), 893–902 (1999)
36. R. Schmohl, U. Baumgarten, Context-aware computing: a survey preparing a generalized approach, in *The International Multi-Conference of Engineers and Computer Scientists, IMECS 2008, Hong Kong*, vol. 1 (March 2008), pp. 19–21
37. A. Singh, G. Ormazábal, H. Schulzrinne, Heterogeneous networking. Datenschutz Datensicherheit **38**(1), 25–30 (2014)
38. T. Strang, C. Linnhoff-Popien, A context modeling survey, in *Workshop Proceedings*, 2004
39. G.M. Youngblood, D.J. Cook, L.B. Holder, E.O. Heierman, Automation intelligence for the smart environment, in *The International Joint Conference on Artificial Intelligence*, 2005, pp. 1513–1514
40. D. Zhang, T. Gu, X. Wang, Enabling context-aware smart home with semantic web technologies. Int. J. Human-friendly Welfare Robot. Syst. 12–20 (2005)

Index

C

Caching & replication
  caching
    AT strategy, 448
    invalidation, 446
    invalidation report, 447
    server's obligations, 446
    signature strategy, 448
    stateless server, 447
    TS strategy, 447
  caching types, 444
    hoarding, 444
    on demand, prefetching, 444
  CODA, 462
    client side caching, 463
  optimistic replication, 453
  relaxed consistency models, 464
    client centric, 465
    MR, 468
    MW, 470
    RYW, 467
    session guarantees, 467
    WFR, 469
    WFRO, 470
    WFRP, 470
    WID, 471
  replication
    performance, 460
    pitfalls, 455
    reconciliation, 458
    techniques, 457
  replication requirements, 452
CODA, 482
  accessing objects, 484
  callback, 486
  callback break, 488
  coherence protocol, 488
  disconnection, 488
  name space, 483

  optimistic replica control, 491, 492
  overview, 483
  pessimistic replica control, 491
  reintegration, 497
  replay algorithm, 497
    back fetching, 497
    parsing, 497
    validity check, 497
  replica control, 489
  RPC based file access, 484
  RPC2, 486
    side effects, 486
  scalability, 486
  system components, 484
  update visibility, 492
  venus, 493
    emulation, 495
    hoarding, 494
    replay log, 495
    replay log optimization, 495
    resource problem, 497
    RVM, 496
    state transitions, 493
Context
  adaptability, 514
  ConChat, 517
    operators, quantifiers, 518
  modeling, 515
Context aware applications, 511
Context middlewares, 526
  agent oriented architecture, 530
  layered architecture, 527
    context stack, 527
    generic, 527
    RWM, 527
    TEA, 527
  object oriented architecture, 532
  service oriented architecture
    CASS, 528

© Springer Nature Singapore Pte Ltd. 2017
R.K. Ghosh, *Wireless Networking and Mobile Data Management*,
DOI 10.1007/978-981-10-3941-6

SOCAM, 528
UCAM, 529
Contextual data, 511
Contextual data extraction, 512

D

Data dissemination, 376
  advantages of push model, 382
  algorithm for broadcast program, 388
    example, 388
  broadcast disk, 384
    flat disk model, 384
    skewed disk model, 385
  broadcast program, 380
  cache management, 399
  caching techniques, 399
  client side caching, 400
    cost , 402
    data consistency models, 405
    LIX, 403
    PIX, 402
    pre-fetching cost, 403
    problem formulation, 400
  comparison of pull and push, 380
  data access in mobile environment, 376
  data delivery models, 377
  delivery methods, 379
  dynamic broadcast program, 390
  elimination of unused slots, 392
  memory hierarchy, 398
  multi-disk program, 388
  probabilistic broadcast, 396
  properties of broadcast program, 385
  selective tuning, 380
  transfer models, 383
  tuning parameters, 390
  types of client requirement, 379
  unused slots in broadcast schedule, 391
  victim selection, 399
Distributed algorithms, 338
Distributed file System, 482

F

File system
  cache server, 505
  connected clients, 504
    cache servers, 507
    concurrency control, 505
    conflict resolution, 505

G

GSM architecture, 56
  base station subsystem, 58
    BSC, 58
    BTS, 58
    TRAU, 58
  control channels, 61
  FDMA, 60
  frame strucure, 63
  logical channels, 60
  mobile originated call, 70
  mobile terminated call, 67
  mobility management, 70
  network subsystem, 59
    GMSC, 59
    home location register, 59
    visitors location register, 59
  signaling protocols, 64
  subscriber identity module (SIM), 57
  TDMA, 60

I

Indexing schemes, 409
  address matching, directory, 411
  analysis of $(1, m)$ indexing, 415
  distributed indexing, 416
    access latency, 425
    access protocol, 425
    control index, 422
    full replication, 420
    no replication, 418
    optimizing replication, 427
    partial replication, 421
    tuning time, 427
    with replication, 419
  exponential indexing, 428
    access protocol, 430
    analysis, 432
    average tuning time, 436
  hash B, 439
    analysis, 439
  hashing A, 436
    access protocol, 437
    control part of a bucket, 436
  indexing in air, 413
  notations, 412
  $(1, m)$ indexing, 414
  temporal address matching, 412
  tuning time, access latency, 412
InterMezzo, 498
  filtering layer, 499
  FSDB, 503

lento, 500
   functions, 502
   protocols, 501

L

Location management
   distributed location management, 327
      call setup, 329
      cost model, 333
      data structures, 330
      update, 329
   global call to mobility ratio, 303
   hierarchical scheme, 302
   incremental parsing
      trie, 323
   Lempel-Ziv text compression, 320
      decoding, 322
      encoding, 320
   LeZi update
      incremental parsing, 323
      probability assignment, 326
   local call to mobility ratio, 303
   paging, 301
   personal mobility, 301, 311
      entropy, unpredictability, 311
      IID model, 318
      LeZi update, 320
      location update, 315
      markov model, 318
      mobility pattern, 315
      modeling movement history, 317
      movement history, 316
      randomness, 311
      surprisal, 311
   registration, 301
   search, 304
   terminal mobility, 301
   update, 303

M

Metropolitan area network, 95
Mobile ad hoc network
   AODV, 196
      control messages, 196
      design decisions, 196
      link error, 202
      multicast routes, 203
      route maintenance, 202
      routing tables, 197
      RREQ, 198
   DSDV, 183

      example, 188
      forwarding table, 187
      link break, 185
      loop free paths, 186
      route advertisement, 184
   DSR, 190
      creation of loops, 194
      overview, 191
      piggybacking RREP, 193
      promiscuous mode, 195
      route discovery, 191
      route maintenance, 192
      route replies, 194
   routing protocols, 181
      count to infinity, 183
      DSDV, 183
   ZRP, 208
      bordercast tree, 211
      interzone routing, 209
      query processing, 213
      route caching, 214
      routing zones, 208
Mobile applications, 10
   logistic & transport management, 12
   mhealthcare, 11
Mobile cloud computing, 7
   architecture, 9
Mobile distributed algorithms, 339
   coordinator based systems, 349
      fixed coordinator, 349
      moving coordinator, 350
   cost model, 341
   locating remote mobile host, 340
   mutual exclusion, 341
      comparison, 358
      fairness, 360
      inform strategy, 354
      proxy strategy, 356
      search strategy, 352
   non-coordinator systems, 344
      equivalent machines, 345
      exception machines, 347
   restructuring distributed algorithms, 344
   synchronization, 340
   termination detection, 361
      dangling messages, 370
      diffusion, 362
      disconnection, 370
      handoff, 368
      hybrid approach, 362
      message types, 363
      rejoining, 370
      termination types, 363

weight throwing, 362
two-tier model, 351
Mobile distributed system, 4
    architectural taxonomy, 5
Mobile IP, 236
    agent discovery, 239
    care-of address, 239
    DHCP, 236
    foreign agent, 238
    home agent, 239
    IP-in-IP, 242, 244
    overview, 238
    registration, 240
    reverse tunneling, 243
    tunneling, 242
Mobile OS, 10, 219
    android, 230
        memory killers, 231
    comparisons, 234
    cross platform tools, 235
    features, 222
    iOS, 232
    J2ME, 225
        configuration, 226
        midlet, 228
        profiles, 227
    platforms, 224
    smartphone, 219
        usage diversity, 221
        usage statistics, 219
    SoC, 220
    symbian, 228
    XIP, 223
Mobile pervasive computing, 4
Moblie ad hoc network, 179
    AODV
        RREP, 200
Mosh, 244
    evaluation, 250
    overview, 245
    speculative local echo, 249
    SSH protocol, 246
    SSP protocol, 247

P
Personal area network
    bluetooth, 126
        maximum bandwidth, 130
        packet format, 130
        physical links, 129
        piconet, 128
        protocol, 132

scatternet, 128
        topology, 128
    infrared, 137
        protocol, 138
        topology, 140
        transport protocol, 142
    summary, 143

S
Smart applications, 532
    E-Alert and response, 537
    mhealthcare, 536
    navigation, 535
    smart walking stick, 536
    TSN, 537
Smart environment, 13, 509
    context aware computing, 15
    driverless cars, 15
        vehicle to vehicle communication,
        16
    system requirements, 521
    technological issues, 523
    terminology, 510
Storage system, 475
    disconnected operation, 476
    QRPC
        scheduling, 480
    RDO
        caching, 481
        consistency, 481
    rover, 477
        design, 478
        QRPC, 477, 479
        RDO, 477, 479

U
Ubiquitous computing, 4

W
WAP, 251
    components, 253
    protocol stack, 254
    WDP, 259
    WML, 255
    WMLScript, 256
    WSP, 258
    WTLS, 259
    WTP, 258
Wireless cellular communication
    cellular architecture
        cell geometry, 24

cell sectoring, 31
cell splitting, 31
Erlang, 34
Erlang B formula, 37
frequency planning, 23
frequency reuse, 21
grade of service, 34
signal to interference ratio, 28
spatial multiplexing, 32
traffic intensity, 34
channel assignment, 39
ACO matrix, 46
distributed channel assignment, 46
dynamic channel assignment, 45
fixed channel assignment, 41
co-channel interference, 27
bel, decibel, 27
handoff, 48
hystersis, 49
mobile assist handoff, 52
mobile controlled handoff, 52
network controlled handoff, 52
policies, 50
received signal strength, 52
Wireless LAN
ALOHA, 113
CSMA/CA, 115
distributed coordination function, 116
DIFS, 118
RTS/CTS, 118
SIFS, 118
MAC and PHY standards, 104
MAC sublayer, 111
mobility support, 96
multiple access protocols, 112
network topology, 102
point coordination function, 122
CAP, 122
CF-ACK frame, 123
CF-poll frame, 123
CFP, 122
PIFS, 122
protocol, 110
radio access technologies, 111
spread spectrum, 105
DSSS, 106
FHSS, 106
standards, 98
summary of standards, 101
technologies, 98
Wireless sensor network
6LoWPAN, 161
header compression, 165

IP over IEEE 802.15.4, 164
IPv6, 162
protocol stack, 165
routing, 170
architecture, 268
characteristics, 266
data aggregation, 287
data fusion, 287
abstract sensor, 294
algorithms, 291
Bayesian, 292
challenges, 291
definitions, 288
Dempsted-Shafer, 292
DSC, 295
inference based, 292
interest dissemination, 290
key design issues, 289
purpose, 292
IEEE 802.15.4
CFP, CAP, 153
CSMA-CA, 154
FFD, 149
MAC frames, 152
RFD, 149
IP integration
downstream routing, 286
non IP solution, 285
proxy gateway, 285
location based routing, 276
energy consumption, 277
multipath based routing, 280
negotiation based routing, 280
QoS, 282
SAR, 283
network organization, 270
operating systems
contiki, 269
RETOS, 267
tiny OS, 269
query based routing, 280
routing, 271
flat network, 273
hierarchical network, 275
LEACH, 275
multipath based routing, 281
negotiation based routing, 282
protocol classification, 272
query based routing, 282
RPL
DODAG, 174
technologies, 148
WSN versus MANET, 267

ZigBee
    coordinator, 158
    device object, 158
    FFD, 150
    IEEE 802.15.4, 149
    protocol, 149

    RFD, 150
    router, 158
ZigBee IP, 175
    CoAP, 172
    REST, 172
    RPL,RoLL, 173

Printed in the United States
By Bookmasters